Publications
of
The Colonial Society of Massachusetts
VOLUME LXXX

Henry Hulton
and the
American Revolution

An Outsider's Inside View

Henry Hulton
and the
American Revolution

An Outsider's Inside View

Neil Longley York

Boston: The Colonial Society of Massachusetts, 2010

Distributed by the University Press of Virginia

DEDICATION

To Frank W. Fox
the master teacher
who changed my life

Contents

Acknowledgments

IFIRST ENCOUNTERED A REFERENCE to Henry Hulton's manuscript history of the American rebellion when perusing the notes to Hiller Zobel's classic study of the Boston "massacre." After reading a microfilm copy of Hulton's account from the Princeton University Library, where it is part of the Andre De Coppet Collection, I decided, with Princeton's permission, to pursue publication. I had just finished my volume on Josiah Quincy Junior for the Colonial Society of Massachusetts and, hoping that the Society would think this a worthy project as well, made my pitch to John Tyler, editor of publications. John shepherded the Quincy volume through to print, as he has this, and I thank him and the other editorial committee members for their support. John also arranged for Jane Ward to copy edit my transcriptions, as she did for the Quincy book, and she once again caught many errors that I let slip by. My debt to her is now doubled. Jeanne Abboud is responsible for the handsome design of this book, and Kate Mertes compiled the index. That this book is about a "loyalist" and the other a "patriot" is not part of some conscious desire to have my own set of Revolutionary American bookends, a yin and yang for their age. Rather, I wanted readers to have yet another man's take on the great events of his life, events that he shaped, events that also shaped him.

Even if it seems hackneyed—apologies to Tennesee Williams here—for authors to say that they have depended on the kindness of strangers, I did on this book even more than on others. I had the added pleasure of meeting some of those strangers, who are now friends. First among these stand a cluster in Andover, England, where Henry Hulton lived out his final days: June Harris, secretary to the parochial council of St. Mary's Church; Peter Hull, St. Mary's Churchwarden; and John Isherwood, a retired solicitor and local historian, who along with his wife, Anne, proved wonderful hosts to my wife Carole and me on our visits there.

John and his contacts in and around Andover helped me piece together possible scenarios for Hulton's years in the neighborhood. I am afraid I put them all—John especially—to a great deal of trouble, and their generosity humbles. Sir Philip Preston, descendant of Henry Hulton and historian in his own right, was most encouraging. He even crossed the channel from his home in France with his wife, Kirsi, and son Tom to become part of our little group at St. Mary's and gather round the vault that holds Henry Hulton's remains. It was a sublime moment. But for engagements that took her elsewhere, we might have been joined by Lady Jennie Bland, who graciously opened to us her home, nearby Blissamore Hall, where Hulton lived during part of his retirement.

My trips to England for research on Hulton, as earlier trips there for previous books, were funded by my department and college at Brigham Young University. I am much beholden to history department secretary Julie Radle, past department chair Arnie Green, and college dean David Magleby for sending me abroad, and trusting that I would return with something to show for it. I must note too the funds made available to me as a Mary Lou Fulton Professor within my college; the Fultons are generous benefactors indeed. Generous, too, was Wallace Brown, professor emeritus at the University of New Brunswick, who allowed me to barge in on his retirement. A distinguished historian of the loyalists, he edited some of Hulton's letters nearly forty years ago and in a sense I picked up where he left off. I am also obliged to genealogist Gregory Preston, who proved most helpful with leads on the Hulton and Preston families.

Hulton's letters and other papers were scattered hither and yon over the centuries. I am grateful to the librarians and archivists who saw to it that I had photocopies or microfilms of whatever landed in their collections, starting with the Princeton University Library and Hulton's history of the rebellion. Added to that were two letter books in the Houghton Library at Harvard University; more or less duplicate copies of another of Hulton's letter books at Harris Manchester College, Oxford University, and the John Rylands University Library at the University of Manchester; Hulton's journal at the John Carter Brown Library at Brown University; a collection of Hulton's essays in the William L. Clements Library at the University of Michigan; autobiographical essays at Boston University; a journal and letters in the Beinecke Library at Yale University; and Hulton's guide to training youth, now at the Norfolk County Record Office in Norwich, England. In addition, I was sent copies of John Temple's letters in the collections at the Henry E. Huntington Library. Finally, it is always rewarding to return to the British Library and the Public Record Office, with their wonderful collections and excellent staffs. To all those who assisted me at one library or another and granted permission to transcribe the texts housed there and included here, I offer heartfelt thanks.

Serendipitous encounters became as much a part of my search for vestiges of Henry Hulton as they have been in all of my historical research over the past three decades. To give one example: I sent a query to Professor Jeremy Black at the University of Exeter, and Jeremy suggested that I contact Dr. Alan Guy at the National Army Museum. Dr. Guy in turn suggested that I check a dissertation he knew of, which I did, and that led to a Hulton source I most likely would never have come across otherwise. This particular source was not listed in any manuscript catalog or research guide I had seen, in hard copy or online. With more and more reference sources available online through the Internet—indeed, with printed and manuscript texts online that can be downloaded and even sent as email attachments—will the serendipitous discovery become more common, or less? And will research in general become more exacting, more precise, or sloppier because seemingly so simple? We should know soon enough.

And to Carole? Words fail. I must think of something else...

PROLOGUE:

In Time, Forgotten

It is pleasing to see the works of Nature, and of Art, in other Countries; and to notice the manners of People in different parts of the world. The mind becomes enlarged by such observations, and acquires many new ideas. But after having passed over all these objects, the mind remains unsatisfied; there is still a void, and a craving. The ostentatious display of wealth and magnificence; the courtly civilities of the Great, and the hackneyed expressions of the gay, and the vain, do not fill the heart. It sighs for the pleasures of social friendship and domestic comforts, under an humble roof; after seeing all the parade, and glory of life.

– Henry Hulton[1]

ONCE CLOSE AS PUBLIC MEN, John Adams and Thomas Jefferson eventually split and were reconciled only after they retired. In the free-ranging correspondence that marked their renewed friendship they discussed the history of their generation as it was already being written. Adams was usually the one to prompt such musings, but not always. In 1813 Jefferson lamented that, so far, both of them had been misunderstood and misrepresented, even in histories that supposedly told the story from the perspective of their own side—the winning side. That prompted Adams to ask when the other side of the Revolutionary tale, the loser's side, would be told. "I have wondered for more than thirty Years so few have appeared: and have constantly expected that a Tory History of the Rise and progress of the Revolution would appear. And wished it," he emphasized. Anticipating Jefferson's asking him why, he added: "I should expect more Truth" in one of those accounts.[2]

1   Henry Hulton, "Observations. In the course of sundry Tours, and voyages", 80 [hereafter "Observations"], from the Mark and Llora Bortman Collection in the Howard Gotlieb Archival and Research Center, Boston University, with some changes to the punctuation. Hulton repeated these sentiments (with but slight variation) in his "Sketches," 49-50, ca. 1780, William L. Clements Library Mss., University of Michigan.
2   Adams to Jefferson, [3] July 1813, apparently in response to Jefferson on June 27th, in Lester J. Cappon, ed., *The Adams-Jefferson Letters* (Chapel Hill: University of North Carolina Press, 1959), 349 and 336, resp. ("apparently," because getting a letter from Monticello to Quincy in just eight days verged on the miraculous). For Jefferson and his concern over Revolutionary era historiography, and his place in it, see Francis D. Cogliano, *Thomas Jefferson: Reputation and Legacy* (Charlottesville: University of Virginia Press, 2006), 44-73.

If in that "Tory" view he expected to be treated more evenhandedly, or at least more consistently, he probably would have been disappointed. After all, because there was no single Patriot view—as he and Jefferson learned through the criticism they thought had been aimed at them by ingrates—logic says that there could be no single or simple "Tory" view either. Each account had its own perspective, each brought out new themes or variations on older ones; no two could be expected to be exactly alike.

Adams did not know it but at the very moment he responded to Jefferson there sat, unpublished, a history of the Revolution written by someone who had indeed been on the other side.[3] It belonged to Thomas Hulton Preston of Beeston Hall, a manor in Norfolk, England. The author of that history was the soon-to-be baronet's father, Henry Hulton. The elder Hulton had died over twenty years before. Although he never met Jefferson, he and Adams crossed paths time and again for the better part of a decade—and crossed figurative swords as well.

Adams does not seem to have remembered Hulton clearly, if at all.[4] But then Hulton probably did not expect to be remembered anyway. He did not write his history of the rebellion for public consumption. In part he wrote it for himself; even more, he wrote it for his five sons, as a guide to their learning the lessons of the imperial past and the larger lessons of life for their own futures. The sons may have gained something from their father's reflections but later generations apparently did not.[5] Hulton's papers, the history of the rebellion included, were eventually sold off and scattered. Some remained in England while others crossed the Atlantic, only to gather dust in various American libraries.

Didactic intent—and in a sense, then, ulterior motive—notwithstanding, Hulton's history has much to offer as one man's view of momentous events, events in which Hulton himself

---

3   "American loyalists have suffered the fate of those who lose the contest–history has relegated them to brief paragraphs at best, or to footnotes at worst," commented Lawrence Leder in his *The Colonial Legacy: Loyalist Historians* (New York: Harper & Row, 1971), 1. Hulton proved the point all too well; even Leder does not mention him. For the continued status of loyalists as "marginal figures" see Keith Mason, "The American Loyalist Diaspora and the Reconfiguration of the British Atlantic World," in Eliga H. Gould and Peter S. Onuf, eds., *Empire and Nation* (Baltimore: Johns Hopkins University Press, 2005), 240-259; and also Maya Jasanoff, "The Other Side of the Revolution: Loyalists in the British Empire" *William and Mary Quarterly*, 3rd series 65 (2008):205-232, who contended (on 209) that "Loyalist émigrés demand a larger, more significant narrative of their own that extends, as the refugees did, across the globe." For a fine case study, set in historiographical context, see Colin Nicolson, "'McIntosh, Otis & Adams are our demagogues': Nathaniel Coffin and the Loyalist Interpretation of the Origins of the American Revolution," *Massachusetts Historical Society. Proceedings* 108 (1996):72-114.

4   In writing to Jedediah Morse on 1 January 1816, where he repeated now famous lines about the Revolution being in the "minds of the people" even before Lexington and Concord, he mentioned the dispatch of troops to Boston in 1768 to protect the American Board of Customs commissioners. He forgot to include Hulton in his list of Board members. Charles Francis Adams, ed., *The Works of John Adams*, 10 vols. (Boston: Little, Brown and Co., 1850-1856), 10:197-199.

5   Although at least one descendant, Sir Philip Charles Henry Hulton Preston, has a copy of the advice that Henry Hulton prepared for his sons and knows the basic outlines of Henry Hulton's life quite well.

participated. Hulton spent over eight years in Massachusetts. He stepped ashore at Boston in November 1767 with hopes of success before him, only to sail away, despondent, in March 1776. He had come as an agent of empire, part of a new five-man commission formed in London to help crack down on smuggling in the colonies. He failed from the beginning to do as his superiors expected. He and the other commissioners were harassed and harried, seemingly from the minute they landed.[6] Three times they scrambled to the safety of Castle William in Boston harbor, convinced that their very lives were in danger.

Often made miserable when he attempted to do his job, Hulton nonetheless enjoyed interludes when life was pleasant and peaceful. He sank roots at his farm in Brookline, close enough to Boston to perform his duties and far enough away to be a haven from the hurly-burly of town politics. He had a growing family, a beautiful country house, and an apple orchard that gave him cider by the barrel. There were even moments when he thought he might make Massachusetts his home. Hulton was both an Englishman who lived apart from most of the colonists around him *and* an American Tory like those few of his neighbors who stood with the crown when forced to choose sides. That he did not mix with everyone in Brookline was as much a function of class as politics. As part of the local landed gentry his social circle would be shaped by his station as well as his imperial office. Although his friendships and enmities reflected and reinforced his position as a king's man, the political did not always determine the personal. He is proof enough that identity could be fluid in the Atlantic world—that the lines separating Briton from American, and Patriot from Loyalist, were not always neatly drawn.

Seven months after arriving Hulton had been joined by his wife, Elizabeth, and their infant son, Thomas, the future baronet. Three more sons would be born before Hulton departed—his American boys, as he referred to them in letters to family and friends back in England. Tellingly, the fifth son and final child would be born in Old England rather than New, where the Hultons returned to start over. When they fled Massachusetts they left most of what they owned behind, the most valuable articles of which—land, house, and furniture—were confiscated and sold at public auction.

The Hultons had been caught up in a diaspora of sorts, a "Britannic exodus" that "changed the world," as Niall Ferguson put it.[7] Some twenty million people emigrated from the British Isles over a three-century span that started in the early 1600s. The vast majority never returned; Hulton was part of the tiny minority that did. He went out as a servant as

---

6   With the exception, that is, of John Temple, already in Boston and alienated from the other four commissioners, whose positions and presence he resented.

7   Niall Ferguson, *Empire* (London: Allen Lane, 2002), 60. Also see James Horn, "British Diaspora: Emigration from Britain, 1680-1815," in P. J. Marshall, ed., *The Eighteenth Century* (Oxford: Oxford University Press, 1998), 28-53, the second of five volumes in *The Oxford History of the British Empire*. For an even broader context of this outmigration and how it helped transform the world–though not always for the better, see Alfred W. Crosby, *Ecological Imperialism* (Cambridge: Cambridge University Press, 1986).

well as an agent of empire, a bureaucrat before we normally think that such persons existed, a precursor to what would become the stock characters of Kipling and Forster. Though he did not stand out among the locals as he would have had he been in India later as part of the raj, he was still in a class apart—despite being a white man among white men.

Hulton had ventured forth believing in a reciprocal empire where mother country and colonies could benefit from and strengthen each other. True, he was a supervisor of tax collectors, customs agents whose job it was to catch smugglers and see to their prosecution and conviction. But he believed, as Richard Hakluyt had preached when Elizabethan England first ventured into the Atlantic, that free trade was not necessary in their expansive empire. "The Revenewes and Customes of her Majestie bothe outwarde and inwarde shall mightely be inlarged by the Toll excises," Hakluyt wrote excitedly in 1584, "and other dueties which withoute oppression may be raised."[8] Hulton would learn firsthand that Hakluyt's words rang hollow to disgruntled colonists. They resented the taxes and often, as a result, the men expected to collect them.

That Hulton defended the Navigation Acts—those laws of Parliament designed to keep trade within the empire—did not mean he was a mindless apologist for the mercantilistic arrangement that had emerged over the years. He is a perfect reminder of the need to avoid oversimplification in discussing strains within the empire, as if the crisis that led to revolution was the simple and inevitable result of imperialists versus anti-imperialists, free traders versus protectionists, or reformers versus defenders of the status quo. At the same time, his reaction to policies with which he disagreed shows the difficulty confronting those who objected to what had been done but had no precise plan for what should be done instead—thus, interestingly, Hulton's view that the foolishness of passing the Stamp Act in 1765 was surpassed only by its repeal.

Hulton would be haunted by the empire that never was but might have been. Hence his history is laced with what ifs: what if this individual had acted differently; what if that policy had been tried? For Hulton, as for other contemplative contemporaries, solutions to problems on an imperial scale required a recognition and restoration of the natural order of things, a return to a harmony of objects within a grand design.[9] The empire as family, a rhetorical device common to Hulton's generation, humanized the hierarchical structure.[10] Hulton joined a long list of people on both sides of the Atlantic who believed

---

8 David B. Quinn & Alison M. Quinn, eds., *Discourse of Western Planting* (London: Hakluyt Society, 1993), p. 64.

9 A view of the world discussed in Arthur O. Lovejoy, *The Great Chain of Being* (Cambridge, Mass.: Harvard University Press, 1936), though with no particular reference to the problems of empire.

10 Peter N. Miller, *Defining the Common Good* (Cambridge: Cambridge University Press, 1994); Gerald Newman, *The Rise of English Nationalism, 1740-1830* (New York: St. Martin's Press, 1997); David Armitage, *The Ideological Origins of the British Empire* (Cambridge: Cambridge University Press, 2000); and Eliga Gould, *Persistence of Empire* (Chapel Hill: University of North Carolina Press, 2000)offer observations about identity in the empire that ought to be contrasted with Benedict Anderson's more general arguments in *Imagined*

that no real improvement in imperial relations would come unless the colonies better understood their proper relationship with the mother country. Like other would-be imperial reformers he decided that the colonies had for too long been allowed to drift away from Britain. Not only had colonists forgotten that Britain was sovereign and that they were subordinate, they failed to see that Parliament had to be supreme within that relationship. Therefore, as he saw it—and as he subsequently wrote about it—the great political dispute that marked his years in Boston had a deep underlying social cause. He was convinced the town had been taken over by "demagogues" and with that a sense of proportion and propriety had been lost. Deference and the order it brought with it had been displaced by the disorder of egalitarianism.

Not surprisingly he tended to equate democracy with anarchy. That put him out of step with Boston's town leaders, but only because he thought their brand of popular politics threatened to bring about the very devolution to chaos that Aristotle had warned might come in any society. Most thoughtful men in his world—future Revolutionaries and future Loyalists alike, as good Aristotelians—feared that possibility. If Hulton and John Adams had ever compared notes they probably would have been surprised at how close they were in their view of human nature and their desire to balance liberty and authority. Both men worried over what they saw as the rise of crass materialism and the decline of civilization ushered in by a new commercial age. Likewise, both seemed to believe that humans made history—that men choose their own destiny, and yet they also verged on a determinism that concluded just the opposite—that vast, impersonal forces had been set loose that no individual could control.

When Adams and his revolutionary colleagues condemned George III in the Declaration of Independence for erecting "a Multitude of new Offices" and sending "hither Swarms of Officers to harrass our People, and eat out their Substance," they had men like Hulton in mind.[11] Hulton's political enemies in Boston condemned him as a political hack, a placeman, a seeker of spoils. Even so they did not wage all-out war against him, despite what he might have thought when he felt most threatened by them. He was relieved that they were able to distinguish between his office, which they found objectionable, and his person, who many found otherwise inoffensive. Sure enough he was not criticized as sharply as some of his colleagues nor did he fear for his personal safety as often as a few of them did. At one point he did flee Massachusetts altogether for a few weeks until tempers cooled and yet he left his family behind in Brookline, confident that those in the protesting crowds who could not distinguish between his person and his post could still distinguish between him and his wife and children. That such distinctions were drawn is

---

Communities, revised ed. (London: Verso, 1991).

11   The Declaration echoed the *Boston Gazette and Country Journal*, 16 November 1767, which complained of the "swarm of various officers"—members of the customs board included—that had descended upon the town, all of them part of a larger scheme to deprive the colonists of their rights.

yet another reminder of the danger of oversimplifying, of painting the imperial dispute in black and white rather than in varying shades of gray.

Hulton had repeatedly sought office but he would never have viewed himself as a mere office seeker. He was determined to raise himself in society but, having no particular interest in or aptitude for business, he hoped to secure a comfortable and, yes, lucrative government post. It was a fairly typical and hardly dishonorable ambition in Georgian England. A sensitive, bookish man, he was not well-suited to the perpetual hobnobbing of the socially ambitious. Resent as he might the system of patronage and preferment that determined careers, he could not easily withdraw from the court scene—unless he was willing to abandon his campaign for a well-paying post.[12] Only after having his ambition soured by life in Massachusetts did he put ambition aside and retreat to the countryside, when still in his early forties.

But the world-weary Hulton of the 1770s had been preceded by a more energetic alter ego in the 1750s and 1760s, a younger man who felt trapped by circumstance. Perhaps not fully recognizing how well his father, a successful Chester glover, had provided for him to have a good start in life, he seemed to be blind to what constituted true poverty. Like so many younger sons whose oldest brother inherited the bulk of the family estate, Hulton could have slipped down in society had he not resolved to work his way up. Even so he was never truly penniless or ever close to it. His brother, who became successful in his own right as a Liverpool merchant, had stepped in for a father who died before Hulton was a year old. Hulton lived most of his life served by others, and he had the good fortune to marry a rich man's daughter. And yet he ventured far afield, to parts of the world where he would not have otherwise gone because he felt driven abroad by financial insecurity—twice to Germany and once to Antigua before his longest sojourn in Massachusetts. One would have thought that each move kept him but a step away from debtor's prison, so distraught did he become when misfortune struck.

Hulton found some solace as a man of letters. He polished his schoolboy Latin to translate poems and found time to compose verses of his own. A piece he wrote in later years about a wistful return to Chester showed his romantic streak, a longing to find a true home. He wanted to be part of the landed gentry, to retire from public life, read for pleasure, dabble in poetry, putter about in a garden, walk through his own crops in his own fields,

---

12   In going to Massachusetts he did not necessarily enter a socially different world, however, despite what he might have thought; personal connections mattered there too—for which see Gordon S. Wood, *The Radicalism of the American Revolution* (New York: Alfred A. Knopf, 1992), 3-92. Nevertheless, any characterization of this as a "deferential" society ought to be made carefully, as the scholars who contributed to the discussion in "Deference in Early America: The Life and/or Death of an Historiographical Concept," *Early American Studies* 3 (2005):227-401 emphasized. That discussion returned to issues addressed in "Deference or Defiance in Eighteenth-Century America?," a roundtable in the *Journal of American History* 85 (1998):13-97. Any notion that eighteenth-century England can serve as the model of a deferential society should be qualified as well.

and wander over hill and dale.[13] Consciously or not he followed the rules for fearing God and comporting himself among men as laid out in *The Compleat Gentleman*, a handbook for genteel living that drew as readily from the classics as holy scripture.[14]

Hulton never aspired to high office or great wealth, and with age he yearned for freedom from daily care, where he could watch his sons grow to manhood and pass on to them what he had learned. Perhaps as a result of losing his father before he even knew him, Hulton was determined to guide his own sons through life's thickets. He doted on them, reveling in being (by eighteenth-century standards) an involved father well before such behavior came into vogue.[15] Religiously devout, he also considered himself a man of reason. Simultaneously adventurous and cautious, he could wax philosophical about fate, taking on the persona of a detached observer of events at one moment, and in the next wallow in self-pity over the blows life dealt him. Defying easy description he was, in short, quite human. He may not have really understood the empire that he saw crumble before his very eyes. In that he was not alone. He may not have understood the wider world either. He would be in good company there, too.

---

13 He seemed to have in view the lifestyle of the "modest gentleman" described in G. E. Mingay, *English Landed Society* (London: Routledge and Kegan Paul, 1962) who owned perhaps 1000 acres and had income from a variety of sources, not just farm produce or land rents, to lead a "genteel but restricted life" (22), with an annual income of £300 or so. For the "gentlemanly ideal" as empire-wide phenomenon see H. V. Bowen, *Elites, Enterprise and the Making of the British Overseas Empire, 1688-1775* (Houndmills, England: Macmillan Press, Ltd., 1996). See too Martin J. Wiener, *English Culture and the Decline of the Industrial Spirit* (Cambridge: Cambridge University Press, 1981) for the economic downside of the country gentleman ideal. Hulton's poetic tribute to Chester is transcribed infra, on 427-429.

14 Henry Peacham, *The Compleat Gentleman* (London: Francis Constable, 1622).

15 See Jay Fliegelman, *Prodigals and Pilgrims* (Cambridge: Cambridge University Press, 1982) for the new notions of patriarchy and paternal authority that were gaining ground in parts of the western world at just this moment.

INTRODUCTION:
Imperial Odyssey

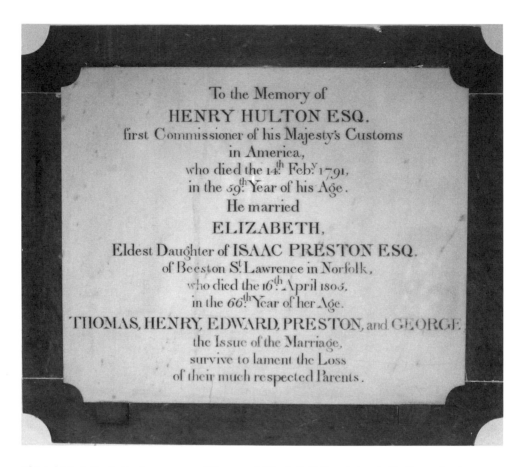

To the Memory of
HENRY HULTON ESQ.
first Commissioner of his Majesty's Customs
in America,
who died the 14th Feby 1791,
in the 59th Year of his Age.
He married
ELIZABETH,
Eldest Daughter of ISAAC PRESTON ESQ.
of Beeston St Lawrence in Norfolk,
who died the 16th April 1805,
in the 66th Year of her Age.
THOMAS, HENRY, EDWARD, PRESTON, and GEORGE
the Issue of the Marriage,
survive to lament the Loss
of their much respected Parents.

This tablet, dedicated to the memory of Henry and Elizabeth Hulton, is located in the west entrance lobby of St. Mary's Church in Andover, Hampshire. The Hultons' five sons intended it as a tribute to their loving parents. Originally placed in the old Norman era St. Mary's Church built on this site, it was hung in the new St. Mary's that replaced it in the 1840s. The dates for Henry are off. He actually died in his 60th year, on 12 February 1790. Photo by the author.

No other Odysseus will ever return to you.

That man and I are one, the man you see...

here after many hardships,

endless wanderings, after twenty years

I have come home to native ground at last.[1]

"I WAS NO SOONER ARRIVED at those years, when it becomes expedient for every prudent person to think of his future establishment," Henry Hulton wrote in one of his memoirs, "than I found I had to enter life without the support of friends, and under the disadvantages of a narrow fortune."[2] If those words held the attention of five readers and no one else, that would have been enough for Hulton; he penned them privately for his sons, not the general public. He did not pretend to have any insights that ought to be shared with the world beyond his family. He claimed no wisdom that should guide the founders of nations or builders of empire. He would have been content if his boys, the oldest of whom was still in his teens, found something in his life worth emulating, something in the "trials and difficulties, which he hath surmounted" that would "urge them to persevere with patience and fortitude, in the course of their duty"—an effort that he wished more parents would make for their children.[3]

Hulton did not set the opening scene of his autobiographical tale as pithily as Charles Dickens might have, but the point came through: he had not been born into a life of ease; he earned what he had. He wanted his sons to appreciate that they had been blessed with more advantages than he, so they ought to pay heed. He overcame adversity that they had been spared, but they would face challenges of their own and they must be able to rise to the occasion. He intended to show them how with vignettes from his own career.

It was advice that his own father, Edward, who died in April 1731, did not live long enough to offer. Henry had been born the preceding June, the youngest of five children, four boys and one girl. John, the firstborn, in 1720, had been followed by Samuel in 1722 and Edward

---

1 Odysseus to his son Telemachus, in Homer, *The Odyssey*, trans. by Robert Fagles (New York: Viking, 1996), 345 (Book 16, 232-236).

2 Hulton, "Account of Travels," 7 [hereafter "Travels"], John Carter Brown Library, Brown University Mss.

3 Ibid., 2-3.

in 1724. Ann was three-and-a-half years older than Henry.[4] Their father died young. So did his middle child and namesake, who preceded him in death. The son of a glove maker to whom he had been apprenticed as a boy,[5] the elder Edward Hulton had, at the time of his death, amassed a considerable estate for a tradesman. He owned buildings and land in and around Chester and, as was the custom, bequeathed the bulk of his property to his oldest son, John, after stipulating that his wife, Mary, be cared for out of the estate until her death. He left Samuel, the second oldest, some investment properties but nowhere near as much as he passed on to John. In addition to some personal effects, both Ann and Henry were given £400, ideally to be held in trust and earn interest until they each turned twenty-one. When necessary that money would "be Imploy'd for his & her Yearly Maintenance[,] Cloth[e]s[,] Education & Preferment in the World."[6]

Innocent Abroad

What little we know about Hulton's early life we learn only from Hulton himself. Of his childhood he said simply that his widowed mother—"pious," "sensible" *and,* notably, "indulgent"—raised him to be virtuous and kind, presumably as a Presbyterian, though at some point he later became an Anglican. Having passed through what he called a "common course of education," which most likely meant being taught by a private tutor with other boys of his age and station, he did not enter into an apprenticeship to learn a trade. Instead, as befitted his family's improved status, he went to live with his older brother John, who had done well as a Liverpool merchant. There the boy was supposed to learn how to make his way in the world of men.

---

4   All five are entered in the Crook Street Presbyterian Church, Chester, baptismal register, The National Archives [hereafter TNA], Public Record Office [hereafter PRO] 400, Record Group 4/161 (from the Family History Library, Salt Lake City, Utah, film no. 20046): John (born 6 August 1720, baptized on 19 August); Samuel (born 1 March 1722, baptized 20 March); Edward (born 29 August 1724, baptized 6 September); Ann (born 26 December 1726, baptized 18 January 1727); and Henry (born 14 June 1730, baptized on 1 July). There is a genealogical table for the Hultons that begins with Henry's great-grandfather Edward, located in volume 22 of the manuscript History of the Bennetts of the District of Chester, 49 vols., begun by J[ohn] H[enry] E[lliott] Bennett, Cheshire Record Office (Family History Library film no. 375325). It omits Henry's brothers Samuel and Edward, inserts a sister named Mary, and puts Ann's birth as 10 July 1730. See too the apparently more reliable source cited at 90 n. 216 infra.
5   The indenture of Edward Hulton (Henry's father) to John Hulton (Henry's grandfather), for 25 March/6 April 1705, from the Chester and Cheshire Archives ZM/F-ZM/AI, is listed on the National Archives website. According to a number of pedigree charts, John Hulton descended through a family line that had been in Chester for several generations at least and could be traced back further still to Hultons in Lancashire, with lands and titles dating from as early as the reign of John I.
6   Hulton wrote his will on 10 July 1730. It was proved in the archdeaconry court of Chester on 24 April 1731. Archdeaconry of Chester, Wills and Probate Records, Cheshire County Council Archives and Local Studies (Family History Library film no. 2145589).

Henry did learn the basics of business but the counting house held limited appeal. His heart lay elsewhere. At age twenty-one, when he should have been ready to go out on his own, he was still undecided on his course in life. He "thirsted for enterprize, and adventure, and glowed with a desire" of doing something for his "own honor, and the service" of his country.[7] Perhaps in seeking a middle point between pressing his youngest brother to be practical and not quashing his ambition, John Hulton devised a plan. Henry, backed by his brother, would set up an import/export firm in Hamburg with another young man from Liverpool, the son of Richard Gildart, past mayor and one of the town's M.P.s.[8] The young man's older brother and John Hulton were friends; the Gildarts already had business connections in Hamburg.[9]

All seemed to be arranged when Henry sailed across the channel in June 1751 and awaited the arrival of his new partner, a passing acquaintance at best. Gildart never arrived. He decided not to go but it was February of the following year before Henry received a letter telling him that the deal had fallen through. By then Henry had lost whatever excitement he carried with him to the Continent. The French that he studied before leaving proved not to be quite the lingua franca he had expected and, under the circumstances, learning German came slowly. The British expatriates Henry lived among formed an ethnic enclave in Hamburg, diplomatically protected by extraterritoriality and exempt from local taxes or laws regulating religious services. Socially they kept to themselves.[10] Hulton wanted to mix more freely among the locals so he moved farther inland, zigzagging from Zelle to Hanover to Brunswick, with his prospects no brighter.

His luck finally changed when he was befriended by a "little deformed Gentleman" named de Ruling, who struck up a conversation with him in English after observing him reading London newspapers in a coffeehouse.[11] De Ruling, as it turned out, was very well connected, a native of Hanover with a post at the ducal court in Brunswick—a "dull town," in Hulton's view, no longer the thriving community it had once been under the Hanse.[12] He and Hulton would remain friends until de Ruling died twenty years later. Hulton's new contact opened doors that otherwise would have remained closed. Most importantly, de Ruling introduced Hulton to Johan Ludwig von Walmoden, at that time still a fifteen-year-old just beginning

---

7 Hulton, "Travels," 10 for education, 9 for thirst.

8 Ibid., 12. There is a brief sketch of Richard Gildart in Romney Sedgwick, *The House of Commons, 1715-1754*, 2 vols. (London: Her Majesty's Stationery Office, 1970), 2:63. Gildart's commercial interests involved the transatlantic slave trade as well as the Baltic.

9 John Hulton's associate, James Gildart, is included among the merchants listed in George T. Shaw, ed., *Liverpool's First Directory* (Liverpool: Henry Young & Sons, 1907), 35, which was taken from the 1766 list compiled by John Gore. Adam Lightbody and Robert Nicholson are on the list as well (at 41 and 43, resp.). All three would be included in Gore's subsequent directories of 1767, 1769, and 1773.

10 Hulton, "Observations," 21.

11 Hulton, "Travels," 18.

12 Hulton, "Observations," 44.

his studies at the University of Göttingen. Hulton now breathed rarified air: Walmoden was thought to be the illegitimate son of George II. Though the king never acknowledged him as such, neither was he expected to keep out of the public eye. His mother was the king's longtime consort. Her grandmother may well have been the first mistress to George I.

Johan von Walmoden spent almost all of his time in Germany. His mother, by contrast, passed many of her days in London, with apartments at both Kensington Palace and St. James. She had met George II in Hanover in 1735 and Johan was born just a year later. All assumed that the king, not Walmoden's husband, was the father. Walmoden knew of the liaison, accepted favors to look the other way and did not seek a divorce until 1740. By then George II's queen, Caroline, had died, so Amelia Maria von Walmoden, nee von Wendt, was reborn as a naturalized subject of the British crown and elevated to the peerage as Countess of Yarmouth. She stayed with the king until his death in 1760. He supposedly forswore his other mistresses for her and the Countess became a fixture in the court, both in London and in Hanover. She was astute enough not to overplay her hand and even members of the cabinet, from the early period with Walpole to later years with Pitt and Newcastle, understood that she could be a useful ally and dangerous enemy.[13]

Hulton made a conscious choice about how he would try to get ahead when he importuned Walmoden for aid. Whatever air of naiveté he had about him that he wanted to preserve, it would have to be balanced with the skills of realpolitik and he would have to be a fast learner to have any chance of preferment. He could play, even be, the innocent at court, but that innocence could turn disingenuous with time—and Hulton was determined not to be a mere poseur. In his mind, at least, he succeeded.

When the king and Walmoden's mother came to Hanover for a summer stay in the palace at Herrenhausen, Hulton moved to Hanover from Brunswick to be close by in case the opportunity arose where he could be introduced to the right person—which for him, Walmoden determined, was the Duke of Newcastle. Cabinet minister and master of political maneuver, Newcastle had become accustomed to being at the center of power. He and Hulton met; the Duke appeared approachable enough. Hulton "had frequent occasions of paying" his "respects to his Grace, who was always in a hurry, and put me off with general assurances."[14] Just turned twenty-two and still without solid prospects, Hulton understood that he had little to offer the Duke and that he was but one of countless supplicants trying to catch the great man's attention. "I cannot urge any motives that may influence Your Grace's regard," he wrote in a necessarily obsequious note, "any further than by granting my request You will lay an infinite obligation on a gratefull heart."[15] But earnestness was

---

13 Charles Chenevix Trench, *George II* (London: Allen Lane, 1973) has a fair amount on the king and his mistresses, including Walmoden. See too Jeremy Black's more expansive *George II: Puppet of the Politicians?* (Exeter: University of Exeter Press, 2007), and Black's *America or Europe? British Foreign Policy, 1739-1763* (London: University College of London, 1998) for Hanover's place in the empire at this time.

14 Hulton, "Travels," 24.

15 Hulton to Newcastle, 22 July 1752, with the apostrophe inserted, Add. Ms. 32728, fo. 254 (Newcastle Papers), British Library [hereafter BL].

not enough. The young Walmoden did not have much political stock and he was not going to risk it for Hulton when Newcastle became evasive. He advised Hulton to relocate to London and position himself for another run at the Duke when the court returned there in the fall, just before the opening of Parliament.

So October 1752 found Hulton in London. Newcastle promised nothing and did not appear inclined to give anything. He was cordial and yet artfully aloof, moving too quickly during this levee or that fete to grant Hulton a formal interview. Hulton went home to Liverpool the following spring, empty-handed, still with no clear future. For the next several years his life would revolve around the comings and goings of the royal court, which could move to Hanover in the summer and back to London in the Fall. In the reminiscences written for his sons he chose this as the lesson they ought to learn from his repeated frustrations:

> In the course of my private life I have strug[g]led through many dif
> ficulties; and had occasion for a great deal of management and oecon
> omy, before I entered upon office. In publick business, I have had a life of
> combat, of labour, and lost; and through the whole have found very little of
> favor, protection, and support. Others, with my opportunities, might have
> improved them more to their worldly advantage; but I have the consola-
> tion to reflect, that I have passed thus far through the storm and have not
> made shipwreck of faith, and a good conscience, and I have a pleasure in
> a relation of these difficulties I have passed through, as the perusal of my
> story may be of benefit to my children, and animate them to persevere with
> fortitude, in their Christian course.[16]

There is suffering and then there is suffering. Hulton, after a year in Liverpool where he may have been content to live off his trust and his brother's generosity, eased the pain of his disappointment by taking a shorter, cheaper version of the grand tour.[17] After a quick trip to the Isle of Wight, then back to Liverpool, he and a friend set out on a more adventurous journey. They visited Blenheim Palace and passed through Oxford on their way to Paris and some extended sightseeing in France. Again Hulton's preference for things English showed through. If the stiffness of upper-class Germans had bothered him, the smugness of lower-class French— their self-assuredness that it was good to be alive and even better to be French—galled more. Still, he could not help but be impressed by the "stout" French women who rowed him and his companion to shore from the ship that carried them across the channel, then hefted them onto their shoulders so that they would not get their feet wet when they landed.[18]

Hulton must have begun to wonder if he was jinxed: his traveling companion died from a fever brought on by a severe case of gout. Hulton buried his friend in Lyons—after bribing

---

16 Hulton, "Travels," 26-27.
17 For which see Jeremy Black, *The British Abroad: The Grand Tour in the Eighteenth Century* (Phoenix Mill, England: Alan Sutton, 1992).
18 Hulton, "Observations," 24-26 for Germans, 83 for the French, 77 for being carried ashore.

Catholic priests to inter a Protestant in their churchyard—and went back to London, hoping again to become part of the fall court.[19] Once more he failed to win an appointment. He stayed on in London and tried yet again in the fall of 1755—doing what else, besides polishing his French and dusting off his Latin, it is hard to say.

At long last he succeeded, but only after "being kept in expectation for several months."[20] In January 1756 he learned that he had been appointed comptroller of customs at St. John's, Antigua. It was not what he had hoped for but at least it was something. It did come with a catch: unlike some largely honorary posts, he would not be able to treat it as a sinecure, sharing the salary with someone else on site. He would have to go himself. He fell ill while preparing to leave, recovered, and made his way to Portsmouth to join a convoy sailing for the West Indies. His brother John accompanied him on the journey down from London "and this proved a final separation."[21]

So after four-and-a-half years of delay Hulton had at last begun to quench his "thirst" for "enterprize and adventure." Back at the beginning he had considered going to the West Indies and then decided against the journey—too far away, in a tropical clime that took many an Englishman to his grave. In the interim he had learned the importance of making the right connections and choosing the right moments to try to get ahead in a world where the few who were privileged over the many proceeded at their own pace, almost oblivious to those beneath them. He was never reduced to dire straits, never had to face the blunt truth expressed in aphorisms about beggars being choosers—because he never had to beg and he always had options from which to choose. But, having set his course on public service by court appointment, he could not afford to say no to anything reasonable just yet.

For someone who lectured his sons on the need for a good work ethic he did remarkably little work over these years. The men and women who took care of his daily needs may well have envied his, to their eyes, relaxed lifestyle. He no doubt saw it differently. It was easier to watch his social betters to see what they had that he still lacked, instead of glancing toward his social inferiors to see how little they had—an obliviousness to the plight of the poor that would not be cured by four years in the slave culture of Antigua. Like so many of his contemporaries in the master class he seemed to worry more about what slavery did to whites than to blacks. Hence his sympathy for the long-suffering wives

---

19 Hulton, "Travels," 32-35.
20 Ibid., 38.
21 Ibid., 40. Apparently Hulton did not go to Liverpool between returning to England in October 1760 and departing for Germany the following April. His brother died that August, intestate. It also appears that Samuel Hulton had died sometime before, since Ann and Henry are the only siblings mentioned in the documents arranging the payment of fees for and management of John Hulton's worldly goods. Ann Hulton was named as administrator; she and family friends Robert Nicholson and Edward Cropper agreed to cover the costs of taking the estate out of probate. See Diocese of Chester, Wills and Administrations Proved at Chester, 1761, Cheshire Record Office (Family History Library film no. 88781).

of planters whose husbands fathered children among their slaves and yet pretended that nothing of the sort went on among them.[22]

Antigua, first settled by the English in 1632, is one of the Leeward Islands. Partly volcanic, partly coral in form, the island's highest point is just over thirteen hundred feet above sea level. Virtually all of the trees had been cleared away long before Hulton arrived. There were no natural springs on the island: no tropical rain, no fresh water. Just over fifty miles in circumference, with only sixty or seventy thousand acres of arable land, Antigua could never surpass a Jamaica in commercial importance but it did come to rival a similarly-sized Barbados in generating wealth. With well over half its land devoted to sugar production it turned a profit for the planters and therefore, again in theory, the empire. There were perhaps 35,000 people on the island, one in ten white, the other nine black, with some of mixed blood. Basically all of the blacks were slaves employed in the sugar industry—the raising and cutting of cane, refining of sugar, and processing of molasses and rum. There was a small but thriving merchant community and the island had its own legislative assembly. The compact town of St. John's acted as the capital and the governor of all the Leewards—Nevis, Montserrat, St. Kitt's, and other islands close by—resided there as well. At any given time there could be a couple of regiments of regulars stationed on the island and the Royal Navy used it as a port of call.[23]

It is very difficult to get a sense of Hulton as agent of empire on Antigua. As comptroller he was expected to work with the collector. Both were in turn expected to coordinate the activities of inspectors who worked the docks at St. John's and Parham, the two ports for legitimate trade on the island. Having the comptroller and collector be one in the same, as was the case before Hulton's arrival, increased the likelihood that corruption—never completely eliminated—could become too problematical. Smuggling was endemic in the sugar islands and potentially threatening to the British as the French began to exceed them in production. The French sugar makers could also sell at a lower price and for a variety of reasons, from more fertile soil to smaller, more efficiently-run plantations, to having greater diversification so that they were less dependent on imports of foodstuffs.[24] Islanders, regardless of their imperial associations—Dutch, Spanish, French, British—routinely traded with each other.

Hulton had crossed over by convoy because the undeclared war that erupted between France and Britain in the forests of western Pennsylvania was about to become official.

---

22 Hulton, "Observations," 109-110.

23 A close to contemporaneous picture was sketched by Bryan Edwards in *The History, Civil and Commercial, of the British Colonies in the West Indies*, 5th ed., 5 vols. (London: W. B. Whitaker, 1819; orig. ed. 1793), 1:453-517 for the Leeward Islands in general, and 472-495 for Antigua in particular.

24 Andrew Jackson O'Shaughnessy, *An Empire Divided: The American Revolution and the British Caribbean* (Philadelphia: University of Pennsylvania Press, 2000) is incisive on such matters. See in particular 60-62 and the endnotes to the observations offered there.

They feared they were going to be overtaken by French warships when they set out; they did not stop after making a landfall at Barbados for the same reason.[25] France as enemy had suddenly become very real to Hulton. What might have been winked at in peacetime would no longer be tolerated during war. Hulton's predecessor had spent more time lining his own pockets than in intercepting illicit goods. Even though Antigua's assembly—*after* Hulton left—would condemn the practice of importing sugar and molasses from, say, French Dominica or St. Domingue, and labeling it as a product of Antigua for export to Britain and sale there or re-export to the continent, individual merchants might not comply unless watched. Illicit goods from the mainland North American colonies most likely became part of the island economy too, bringing Hulton into contact with New England merchants and giving him a foretaste of his later career in Boston. Those merchants preferred to be paid in cash for the flour and lumber they brought in so that they could spend it elsewhere. They did engage in legitimate trade and carried away large quantities of molasses that would be turned into rum back home, but they also filled their ships' holds with cargoes obtained surreptitiously on Dutch- and French-owned islands.[26]

What, exactly, Hulton did to crack down on smuggling is not very clear. How many hours he spent performing his duties is not clear either. On such a small island with such a small population, it might appear to have been a simple enough task. After all, St. John's and Parham, with just five miles separating them, were a short horse ride or long walk apart. But then again a clever smuggler and conniving merchant could find ways to evade detection and an underground economy most certainly existed—but on how large a scale and at what expense to the mercantilistic empire cannot be known.[27] London could not afford, either financially or politically, to be too obsessive about enforcement. Hulton may have been brought in from the outside as comptroller but the new collector was a local merchant; so much for guarding against a potential conflict of interests. Sending a full complement of officials to Antigua would have been cost prohibitive—again, politically as well as financially. Sometimes the enforcers of imperial rule turned a blind eye; sometimes they saw and punished. It was a dynamic that never changed.

The official correspondence for these years is sketchy; so is the personal. Hulton's earliest surviving letter from Antigua was written very late in his four years on the island. It talked not of his duties but of his boredom, his feeling that he was wasting away in exile. "I would not wish any one who feels as I do, to experience what I have done," he complained

---

25 Hulton, "Observations," 100-105.

26 For background see Richard Pares, *Yankees and Creoles* (London: Longmans, Green, & Co., 1956), and Hulton, "Observations," 134-135, for the Yankee preference for foreign sugar and molasses.

27 "Perhaps what human ingenuity could devise, human ingenuity could find a way to circumvent," observed Lawrence Harper in his seminal work, *The English Navigation Laws* (New York: Columbia University Press, 1939), 97.

to a friend back in Liverpool. "I look back on past scenes wherein I was happy, but they will no more return; before me the prospect is dreary."[28]

What he recorded later for his sons was for their character formation, not his retrospective view of the empire, so the focus was on individuals and their behaviors as object lessons. Some people were examples of what not to be, others were examples to be emulated. The dissipated and corrupt collector served as Hulton's first bad example and he was followed by others. The good examples were those who lived in moderation—literally necessary for survival in the island's climate, figuratively necessary for his sons in any social environment.

Hulton arrived with a cold from the voyage and developed a low-grade fever upon landing which lingered for months, but other than that he remained healthy. He developed his own regimen, up early in the morning and to bed early in the evening; exercise, including a morning ride, and frequent bathing; a large meal at midday with only a light supper at night, washed down with water more often than wine. He did not exhaust himself in too many social rounds with Antigua's tiny circle of elites, fearing that those who danced and drank into the wee hours, exhausted and perspiring when they finally went to sleep, were inviting fever and then death. He kept up his reading—James Robertson's history of Scotland and Edward Montagu's survey of ancient republics were two recently published books that he mentioned—so that he could be a good conversationalist as well as intellectually engaged. Equally important, he learned to be a good listener, thereby ingratiating himself with the few men of letters on the island. "The attention of a young Disciple flatters their understandings," he advised his sons, "and the conversation of such men, is the most easy and agreeable way that a young man can receive instruction."[29] He even composed a poem that he, with a close friend on the island, had published to help a widow in distress. The proceeds went toward supporting her household.[30] Her story and that of the others fit into his overall didactic scheme.

---

28 Hulton to Robert Nicholson, 10 February 1760, one of Hulton's twenty-one letters to Nicholson from 1760-1776, in Ms. William Shepherd, vol. XVIII, Harris Manchester College, Oxford University [hereafter "Nicholson Letters"], on 3, transcribed at infra 207-208. Wallace Brown edited all but the first five letters for "An Englishman Views the American Revolution: The Letters of Henry Hulton, 1769-1776" *Huntington Library Quarterly* 36 (November 1972):1-26 and (February 1973):139-151.

29 Hulton, "Travels," 67.

30 [Henry Hulton] *A Poem Addressed to a Young Lady* (St. John's, n.p., 1757), which he reworked and expanded into three parts when he was living in Massachusetts, but had it printed under the same title by John Green and Joseph Russell of Boston in 1773. The friend was Major (soon to be Colonel) Melville of the 38th regiment. They met on the voyage out and shared lodging on the island for a time. Writing the poem became an exercise that Hulton ended up putting in the "no good deed goes unpunished" category: "She cleared about twenty pounds by it. However our readiness to assist the poor woman, was imputed to a cause that did us no great honor, for it was generally insinuated that we took that method of paying her for all favors." Hulton, "Travels," 51. Following printer/historian Isaiah Thomas's original view, Wilberforce Eames, "The Antigua Press and Benjamin Mecom, 1748-1765," *American Antiquarian Society. Proceedings* 38 (1928):303-348 concluded that Mecom, apparently the first printer on the island, had not been the publisher of Hulton's book because he

You must not think my dear Children, that I mention any characters as a record of their crimes or misfortunes, but as a lesson to you: let your minds be ever impressed with a sacred regard to truth, in words, and actions, be assured, that without the practise of integrity, you cannot obtain the divine favour: that industry, prudence, and oeconomy, are necessary to worldly success, and to the enabling You to put your benevolent dispositions into practise. Vanity and ostentation will urge people to actions that have the semblance of virtue. They may be profuse without being generous; and hospitable, without benevolent affections. Such characters will be applauded by the vain, the dissipated, and luxurious; but the sensible and worthy part of mankind, who examine into the motives of actions, will bestow their approbation on the character, only as it appears to act conformably to truth in the circumstances in which it is placed, and the relation in which it stands to those around it.[31]

Hulton emphasized the need for a man to choose his friends and associates wisely, to keep his own counsel, to speak in confidence only to those of proven trust. He was astute enough to realize that by diagraming a formula for success he needed to show how it had worked in his own life if he were to have any credibility with his sons as they grew older. And so he did, writing his life story in fine luck and pluck fashion, using an autobiographical style later made famous by Benjamin Franklin.

The moral of Hulton's Antigua tale unfolds chronologically: soon after arriving he made friends with a well-placed islander who would eventually smooth his way when he returned to London. The islander in question was Samuel Martin, wealthy planter and powerful politician. Speaker of the House in the Assembly, he stood at the center of Antigua's social life. "He was a Gentleman of universal knowledge, of great politeness, and good manners," Hulton informed his sons approvingly, "easy to live with, very communicative, and agreeably instructive, of strict morals, and a religious Man."[32] Martin too preferred water to wine

---

returned to his native Boston the year before. Given Hulton's later antipathy to Benjamin Franklin, it would have been a nice irony if Mecom—Franklin's nephew and onetime apprentice—had indeed done the book.

31 Hulton, "Travels," 60-61.

32 Ibid., 52-53. There are sketches of Samuel Martin and his two most famous sons (Samuel Jr. and Josiah) in Evangeline Walker Andrews, ed., *Journal of a Lady of Quality* (New Haven: Yale University Press, 1921), Appendix, 259-273. There is an entry for the elder Martin in H. C. G. Matthew and Brian Harrison, eds., *Oxford Dictionary of National Biography*, 60 vols. (Oxford: Oxford University Press, 2004), 36:976-977. Richard Sheridan, *Sugar and Slavery* (Baltimore: Johns Hopkins University Press, 1973) also has good material on Martin, and Sheridan refers readers there to two of his journal articles that have even more information. Martin was by all accounts a progressive farmer and kind master to his slaves, which Hulton no doubt noticed. But kind masters were not necessarily abolitionists in the making and for all too many slavery was part of the natural order of things in an unequal world. For Martin's brand of paternalism and Antigua's slave culture in general see David Barry Gaspar, *Bondmen and Rebels* (Baltimore: Johns Hopkins University Press, 1985).

and a good book to pointless conversation. He could be prickly and impatient but with Hulton he found a young man with the right values, the right comportment—with perhaps, on Hulton's part, a dose of imitation serving as the sincerest form of flattery. Hulton spent many hours in the older man's company. When he decided that he could stand it no more, that he had to get off an island that he apparently had left only for short jaunts to other spots in the Leewards, Hulton sailed for London armed with a letter of introduction from "Colonel" Martin to his son.

Knowing that the younger Martin was leery of officer seekers, the older Martin made his attachment to Hulton emphatic. Reading between the lines, he was cautioning his son not to make a virtue into a vice by becoming too fastidious, turning away all who sought his favor. Hulton "is indeed a truly good man," Martin stressed, a devoted friend who had eased his aging and a dedicated public servant as comptroller. He wished Hulton had opportunities in the Indies more worthy of his talents. So highly did he think of him, he told his son, that if Britain took any nearby island from the French in the war then winding down he would do what he could to set him up with a prestigious office and a plantation of his own.[33]

The younger Martin had not lived on the island for any length of time since he was a boy. He had passed on to the Inner Temple after Cambridge and he sat in Parliament for Camelford, a borough in Cornwall. Connected to the Earl of Bute politically, he did not stand out in Commons; rather, he threw his energy into his post as secretary to the lords of the Treasury. Called by two later historians a "joyless man, solitary and self-centred," he never married.[34] Luckily for Hulton he was on good terms with his father and not apt to ignore his wishes, especially when Hulton's appearance seemed so propitious. On his desk when Hulton called were stacks of paper dealing with logistical problems that the British Army had encountered while fighting on the Continent, including letters written mostly in German from suppliers there. "These are Packets of Papers and Letters," sighed Martin, "that I have not been able to read."[35] Hulton offered to translate them and the next thing he

---

33 Samuel Martin to his son, Samuel Martin, 18 July 1760, in the Martin Papers, vol. II, fos. 45-46. Add. Ms. 41,347, BL.

34 There is an essay on Martin in Sir Lewis Namier and John Brooke, *The House of Commons, 1754-1790*, 3 vols. (London: Her Majesty's Stationery Office, 1964), 3:114-117. The younger Martin is most remembered, if at all now, for his 1763 duel with John Wilkes. Wilkes had ridiculed Martin as "base, selfish, mean, abject, low-lived, and dirty" in *The North Briton*, 3 vols. (Dublin: J. Potts, 1763), 2:174-175 in the 5 March 1763 issue (no. 40). Martin and Wilkes both sat in Commons. Martin wounded Wilkes with a pistol shot in their duel. They reconciled later in Paris. See George Nobbe, *The North Briton* (New York: Columbia University Press, 1939), 245-250; and Peter D. G. Thomas, *John Wilkes* (Oxford: Clarendon Press, 1996), 42, who does not pursue the suggestion made by Horace Walpole and picked up by George Rudé, *Wilkes and Liberty* (Oxford: Oxford University Press, 1960), 34 n.4, that Martin had been target-shooting beforehand, with plans to kill Wilkes, not simply wound him. Also see Arthur H. Cash, *John Wilkes* (New Haven: Yale University Press, 2006). For the connection to army provisioning in Germany see 37 n. 43 infra. Ann Hulton commented briefly on Wilkes, Martin, and their duel in a letter to Elizabeth Lightbody of 10 December 1763, at 212-213 infra.

35 Hulton, "Travels," 82.

knew he was back in Germany as part of a special commission to investigate fraud and corruption in the commissary—all of this without yet being released from his post on Antigua.

Fortune had just smiled on Hulton because he returned to London in October 1760 at an otherwise inopportune moment. George II died as Hulton arrived and consequently the Countess of Yarmouth and her son could have done little for him, even if they had been inclined to help. Hulton went to Newcastle first and received the usual noncommital response. His West Indian connection made all the difference. He was given another chance to prove himself, another shot at a better post and a new beginning.

He nonetheless trekked to Germany with some trepidation, fearing that failure there was very likely, which would end his hopes of rising any higher in government service. But then again, if he turned down the new post he would be expected to return to Antigua—a "dreary prospect"—and if he refused to do that, he might never be offered anything consequential again. "The heart grows callous and suspicious from frequent disappointments," he lamented to a friend as he contemplated the choices before him, "and is unwilling to expose itself to fresh pain by connections that may only prove the disingenuity and ingratitude of human nature."[36]

Hulton had been reluctant to recross the channel with good reason. He was about to spend two and a half very trying years on the Continent, arriving in April 1761 and not leaving until September 1763. He made sure that his sons knew how demanding the work was, but how important it had been that he stuck to it.[37] "The business of my department was to examine, audit, and certify, all Accounts whatsoever of moneys due for forage, bread, Waggons, Trains, Hospitals &c." It proved as draining on Hulton emotionally as it was on the commissariat materially. "Vain is the effort of the few, to withstand the torrent, or suppress the powerful iniquity" of the greedy and dishonest, he later lamented.[38] His first day there a provisioner attempted to bribe him, gold in exchange for an army contract, as would others along the way.[39] At least he enjoyed a friendly reunion with Walmoden, the onetime student now an officer in the Hanoverian army, and he was not expected to act alone in his investigations. He had clerks to assist in his duties and former excise official David Cuthbert joined him as a fellow commissioner, as did Sir James Cockburn for a time. Given the resentment of military men at having their actions reviewed by civilians in the field, two army offi-

---

36 Hulton to Nicholson, 24 January 1761, in Hulton, "Nicholson Letters," 15, transcribed at 208-210 infra.

37 "My health was much impaired," he wrote in his "Observations," 182. For context see Richard Harding, "British maritime strategy and Hanover, 1714-1763," in Brendan Simms and Torsten Riotte, eds., *The Hanoverian Dimension in British History, 1714-1837* (Cambridge: Cambridge University Press, 2007), 252-274.

38 From Hulton's "Matters, relative to the Conduct of the Commissariat which attended the Allied Army in Germany, 1760, 61, 62," on 2 and 3, resp., Franklin Papers, Beinecke Rare Book and Manuscript Library, Yale University. This is Hulton's most detailed surviving account of his time in Germany. Hulton reported to the Treasury through Martin.

39 From comments made under "Germany 1763," which may have been in the form of a memorandum rather than from a letter to Nicholson; in Hulton, "Nicholson Letters," 20-21, transcribed at 210-211 infra.

cers, plus a cavalry escort, became part of the entourage—a valuable addition, decided Hulton. Cuthbert and Hulton trusted each other and worked closely together, trying to sort through past accounts while keeping an eye on new contracts. "These accounts were very voluminous, and it was as easy to build the Tower of Babel, as to settle them," as Hulton put it.[40] Their pay rate was a generous £3 per day, enough to live on quite comfortably, in good lodgings, with hearty food and servants to attend them. Even then they had money to spare. Their task could be quite tedious as they reviewed requests and receipts. It could also veer off into detective work, as they sent out clerks to check vouchers for stocks supposedly delivered with stocks actually received. They made few friends and many enemies among the local suppliers.[41] They also had to be careful when dealing with army supply officers, urging them to be diligent without accusing them of corruption. "Oh! The curse of war," sighed Hulton. Some men gained glory from it, others profited from it, "but the Nations are exhausted" and "the Subjects ruined" while "the Youth perish in the field" and "the aged and infirm are afflicted with "famine and disease."[42]

Hulton became one of those who profited from the war, though in a different way. He and Cuthbert impressed men in government, including Newcastle, who was kept informed of what they were encountering in Germany. They continued until they were recalled in the summer of 1763. Investigations would drag on for years.[43] Having reviewed accounts

---

40 Hulton, "Conduct of the Commissariat," 5-6.

41 Hamish Macdonald Little, "The Treasury, the Commissariat and the Supply of the Combined Army in Germany during the Seven Years War (1756-1763)," Ph.D. thesis, University of London, 1981). Little utilized Hulton's "Conduct of the Commissariat" and concluded that Hulton and Cuthbert were able commissioners, though they were perhaps too strident in their zeal to uncover corruption, presuming that those they investigated were guilty unless they could prove their innocence (see 204-208). Cuthbert joined Thomas Pownall and Charles Wolfran Cornwall as commissioners in September 1763 to investigate the claims. Hulton declined the post, offered to him before Cuthbert because his name had been first on their original commission. In *The King's Three Faces* (Chapel Hill: University of North Carolina Press, 2006), 220, Brendan McConville suggested that Pownall exemplified "a new type of man" that appeared in the expanded empire, "the bureaucratic adventurer." Perhaps so—and if so, it is a characterization that could be applied to Hulton too.

42 Hulton, "Observations," 149.

43 An excellent case in point is that of John Jacob Uckermann, who spent five years seeking £20,000 in compensation for forage that he claimed he had provided the British Army between 1761-1762, and for which he had not been paid. With allegations of fraud being leveled on both sides the government finally ruled against Uckermann in 1766, three years after Hulton had gone on to other things. Uckermann's case can be traced in Hulton's "Conduct of the Commissariat," passim (see in particular Hulton's accusation that Uckermann bilked the British, at 103-104), and Treasury papers at the TNA, PRO/T1/431 through PRO/T1/455, passim. See too Hulton and Cuthbert's instructions on accounts dating from 1760 (including Uckermann's) to Thomas Higgins, 1 May 1762 and 5 April 1763, in the Halsey Family Papers, DE/HL/15246 and 15291, resp., Hertfordshire Archives (Frederick and Thomas Halsey had been part of the commissary in Germany during the war). Hulton suspected that he had been moved aside, even though thanked and rewarded, for political reasons. There was much money to be made by those charged, ironically, with ferreting out graft and corruption—profiting from the attempts to control profiteering. Wilkes had alleged in his *North Briton* no. 40 that John Ghest (whose duties were similar to those of Hulton) had

totaling roughly £1 million during his time in Germany, perhaps just a twentieth of the total spent, Hulton estimated that nearly one quarter—£245,000—had been disbursed to dishonest provisioners.[44] Given the politics of the moment, marked by the difficulty of dealing with German contractors whose complaints in Hanover could prove troublesome in London, only a halfhearted attempt was ever made at restitution. Hulton and Cuthbert did not recover much money for the public account—just over £55,000—but they did put a check to fraudulent claims connected to past contracts and they may have made new frauds less likely.[45] And, without really knowing it, Hulton had positioned himself perfectly for a much more attractive post, much closer to home.

Harried Servant

Anew office of plantations clerk had been created under the customs board, a branch of the Treasury;[46] Hulton seized the opportunity to fill it. Given the option of taking this post or returning to Germany, where he would work with Thomas Pownall, a rival when he had been a commissioner there, he opted to stay in London. "I did not chuse to be in any wise connected with Mr. Pownall," he wrote when looking back.[47] At long last he finally seemed to have the job he had dreamed of landing. His post was part of a new wave of imperial reform, not as ambitious as that attempted with the Dominion of New England in the 1680s but ambitious enough to cause a transatlantic disturbance.[48]

---

essentially been blocked in his 1761 efforts to expose corruption in the sale of oats to the army; Wilkes mentioned Uckermann in passing. See 35 n. 34 supra. Gordon E. Bannerman's *Merchants and the Military in Eighteenth-Century Britain* (London: Chatto & Pickering, 2008) examined domestic contracts rather than those on the Continent and found little price-gouging or profiteering among British suppliers.

44 Hulton's figures, as recorded in "Conduct of the Commissariat," 173.

45 See Hulton and Cuthbert's petition to Newcastle of 16 May 1766, Add. Ms. 32,975 (Newcastle Papers), fo. 197 BL. Ever in search of recognition and compensation, they reminded Newcastle of their service and "humbly hope for your Grace[']s favorable opinion of our conduct, and that by your Grace[']s accommodation we may reap some benefit from our Services to the Publick." Also see Hulton's memorial to the Duke of Grafton of 19 November 1766 in the "Conduct of the Commissariat," 187-193.

46 For administrative structure see Charles McLean Andrews's classic work, "England's Commercial and Colonial Policy," the final volume of *The Colonial Period of American History*, 4 vols. (New Haven: Yale University Press, 1934-1938); and these more specialized studies: Dora Mae Clark, *The Rise of the British Treasury* (New Haven: Yale University Press, 1960); Elizabeth Evelynola Hoon, *The Organization of the English Customs System, 1696-1786* (New York: Appleton-Century, 1938); Arthur Herbert Basye, *The Lords Commissioners of Trade and Plantations* (New Haven: Yale University Press, 1925); and Franklin B. Wickwire, *British Subministers and Colonial America, 1763-1783* (Princeton: Princeton University Press, 1966).

47 Hulton, "Conduct of the Commissariat," 170. He made no attempt to hide his disdain for Pownall in this private reminiscence (see 89-95); publicly it is doubtful if he ever said anything critical—far too risky politically to do so. Pownall, he felt, who had also been sent over to review accounts, tried to undercut his authority once he failed to bring him within his own personal orbit. For Pownall see infra 211 n. 2.

48 Proof that London did not see colonial charters as sacrosanct, the Dominion combined all of the colonies north and east of the Delaware River into one between 1686 and 1688. Plans to do the same for the remaining

The chief financial officers of the kingdom, the lords of the Treasury, had started the imperial reform movement by complaining to the privy council, which in turn reported their complaints to the crown. With the king's endorsement and with Parliament preparing to enact legislation for the king's approval, all officials charged with enforcing the Navigation Acts were called to their posts, in anticipation of new laws and tighter enforcement, applicable to the entire empire but aimed at the mainland colonies of North America in particular. "We find, that the Revenue arising therefrom is very small and inconsiderable having in no degree increased with the Commerce of those Countries," the Treasury lords reported to the Council, "and is not yet sufficient to defray a fourth Part of the Expence necessary for collecting it." Moreover, they were convinced "that through Neglect, Connivance and Fraud" the revenue from those colonies "is impaired" and commerce "is diverted from its natural course," making the "wise laws" behind the navigation system useless.[49] In other words, smuggling ran so rampant that it mocked the mercantilistic notion that most trade ought to be confined within the empire.

Samuel Martin had left the Treasury but he continued to watch out for Hulton and helped him avoid being ordered back to Antigua. Technically speaking Hulton had been on an extended leave from his duties as comptroller there. He must have been flattered that the customs commissioners, upon nominating him, expressed "especial Trust & Confidence" in his "Ability[,] Care and Fidelity." He secured his new post, which he would hold "at the king's pleasure,"[50] only after being interviewed by George Grenville, first lord of the Treasury, head of the ministry and enthusiastic champion of imperial reform. Word of

---

colonies to the south were never formalized. The Dominion was brought down in a quasi-revolutionary coup in 1689. New Englanders of the Revolutionary era drew analogies between their situation and that of their forefathers under the Dominion, making Edward Randolph, a customs official, the arch-villain of their past. See Michael G. Hall, *Edward Randolph and the American Colonies, 1676-1703* (Chapel Hill: University of North Carolina Press, 1960); Richard R. Johnson, *Adjustment to Empire* (Leicester: Leicester University Press, 1981); and Robert M. Bliss, *Revolution and Empire* (Manchester: Manchester University Press, 1990).

49 As cited in a privy council report of 5 October 1763, printed in James Munro and Almeric C. Fitzroy, eds., *Acts of the Privy Council of England. Colonial Series*, 6 vols. (London: His Majesty's Stationery Office, 1908-1912), 4:569. The customs board had registered complaints with the Board of Trade about problems within the navigation system in 1758, in the midst of war. See the Board of Trade minutes for 9 November and 5 December 1758 in the *Journal of the Commissioners for Trade and Plantations*, 14 vols. (London: His Majesty's Printing Office, 1920-1938), 10:424 and 433, resp. Also see the "Hints respecting the Settlement of our American Provinces," dated 25 February 1763 and signed "G.," with sweeping recommendations for reform, including fixing the problem of "the Independency of the Revenue Officers on the Governors; for as the Governors have no power over them, they are very little attentive to their Conduct, and the Officers knowing themselves to be accountable only to one another in America, and to the Lords of the Treasury here, they agree among themselves what liberties they shall take, without any regard to the Duties of their Offices." Governors ought to control them more directly, with their salaries increased and paid by the crown, and fees and other perquisites being eliminated. See Add. Ms. 38335 (Liverpool Papers CXLVI), fo. 18 BL.

50 Hulton's commission was (backdated) to take effect on 10 October 1763, the lords commissioners of the customs who issued it referring to their own report of September 28th, which no doubt helped to trigger the Treasury recommendation to the privy council a week later. Dated 19 October 1763, in TNA, PRO/T11/27, fo. 359.

Hulton's efforts in Germany had reached Grenville's ear. Grenville was for many years the bogeyman of American revolutionary history, as if he singlehandedly pushed through the program that caused an imperial crisis. He did not; something very much like it would have come anyway, with or without him. There was little opposition to the legislation that he shepherded through, the Stamp Act included, and there was no thought of using American revenue to pay off the national debt.[51] Rather, Grenville, his king, and his parliamentary colleagues wanted to keep the debt from growing any larger and they expected Americans to help pay annual expenses on their side of the Atlantic that, from London's perspective, benefited them as much as anyone else in the empire. The problem was that what appeared reasonable and fair in their eyes would be seen rather differently by colonists who understood that there were political as well as financial implications to Grenville's program.

Grenville did not contrive a new theory of empire. The commercial regulations that marked his ministry were an extension of older laws going back a century, to 1663 and even earlier, when trade in the empire was legislatively channeled from one destination to another, in ships owned and sailed by subjects of the crown and citizens of the empire—just as Hakluyt had envisioned. Customs inspectors were patrolling colonial American docks as agents of the Treasury by the 1670s; vice-admiralty judges began hearing smuggling cases at nearly the same moment. But there had been very little that was systematic in these earlier manifestations of the navigation system. Grenville wanted new laws and stricter enforcement to bring practice more into line with theory. His timing was poor and his choice of taxes unwise. He miscalculated the economic and political fallout that his program would produce, but his brand of mercantilism was not malicious by intent.

Hulton, on the fringe of imperial regulation in Antigua, was now at the center. He worked out of the custom house on the north bank of the Thames, to the east of London bridge and west of the Tower, caught in the din of fishmongers, commercial agents, and river traffic. Seeking escape for his after-hours, he took up residence several miles away on George Street in Westminster. There, on the western edge of urban sprawl, his sister,

---

51 Expertly put into context by John Brewer in *The Sinews of Power* (New York: Alfred A. Knopf, 1989). Alvin Rabushka's detailed study of *Taxation in Colonial America* (Princeton: Princeton University Press, 2008), does not, oddly enough, draw on Brewer, but Rabushka does examine taxation in all its forms and in all of the colonies that eventually rebelled, and he attempted to do so without getting caught up in the historiographical disputes over a reciprocal empire. Even so, he concluded (on 757) that, allowing for exceptions in certain areas, the navigation system "may have been a net positive for the colonies." For Grenville's program in particular see John L. Bullion, *A Great and Necessary Measure* (Columbia: University of Missouri Press, 1982); with the reaction by Thomas Slaughter, "The Empire Strikes Back: George Grenville and the Stamp Act," *Reviews in American History* 12 (1984):204-210; and P. D. G. Thomas, *British Politics and the Stamp Act Crisis* (Oxford: Clarendon Press, 1975). Also see Eliga Gould's "Fears of War, Fantasies of Peace: British Politics and the Coming of the American Revolution," in Gould and Onuf, eds., *Empire and Nation*, 19-34; and the overview in Jacob M. Price, "The Imperial Economy, 1700-1776," in Marshall, ed., *The Eighteenth Century*, 78-104.

Ann, came down from Chester to keep house for him. Unmarried and increasingly devoted to her younger brother, she was concerned that he had not recovered from the stress he endured on the continent and that he would soon be drained by new demands. "The task they have set him seems to be," she wrote a friend back home, "after combating ye knaves in G[ermany], to find em in America and ye West Indies."[52]

After spending a Christmas holiday with Ann in Bath, Henry set to the task before him, prodigious as it was. He was expected to coordinate communication between London and customs officials in North America and the West Indies, and was authorized "to lay his observations thereupon" before the customs commissioners, who could in turn pass them to the Treasury. It was a short step from the Treasury to other officials at White-hall and parliamentary leaders at Westminster. But then the administrative apparatus was in such disarray that establishing a regular correspondence—and, in effect, instituting a bureaucratic chain of command—proved a formidable task, with letters passing back and forth over the breadth of the Atlantic sometimes taking six months to complete a circuit. Hulton did his best to routinize communications that were haphazard and reporting that was irregular.[53] Historian Charles Andrews's reflections on the navigation "system"—which was hardly systematic in nature—are worth remembering here:

> England's commercial policy was slow in the making; it never reached the stage of exact definition, even in the days of its greatest influence; and it can be understood only by a study of its principles in operation over a period of one hundred and fifty years. In its relation to the colonies in America, it was never an exact system, except in a few fundamental particulars. Rather it was a *modus operandi* for the purpose of meeting the needs of a growing and expanding state. It followed rather than directed commercial enterprise, and as the nation grew in stature it adapted itself to that nation's changing needs.[54]

---

52 Letter of 10 December 1763, edited by E. Rhys Jones and printed as "An Eighteenth-Century Lady and Her Impressions," *Gentleman's Magazine* 297 (July-December 1904):195-202; quotation from 196, transcribed infra on 212-213.

53 See, for example, his report on ships caught smuggling between the end of the war in September 1763 and the following March. "No certain Account of Seizures in N. America can be prepared in this Office unless the Collectors of the Customs in the several provinces be duly Authorized to Receive the King[']s share of Fines & Forfeitures," he informed the customs board. What he learned, if he did not already know from his days on Antigua, was that customs officials did not always work well with each other, much less with provincial authorities, and even officers in the Royal Navy. Report of 22 March 1764, signed by Hulton, in Add. Ms. 38,337, fo. 245 (Liverpool Papers) BL.

54 Andrews, "England's Commercial and Colonial Policy," vol. 4 of *The Colonial Period of American History*, on 2, though, on 425n-428n, Andrews does make a distinction between the "old colonial system" and the policies pursued after 1763.

The challenges Hulton faced were compounded by other irritations: the job was not exactly what he thought it would be, the salary was reduced by a tax that he thought he should not have to pay, and the ministry pursued policies with which he disagreed. Hulton was miffed that he ended up as the plantations "clerk" rather than the plantations "secretary," a change in designation that took place after he accepted the post. The customs commissioners decided to have only one secretary in their office, although Hulton as head "clerk" would have a staff of other clerks to assist him. Perhaps the commissioners did so at the urging of the existing secretary so that he, not Hulton, could continue to receive whatever legal fees were charged in connection with the office. Fees, as Hulton knew from his years on Antigua, were as crucial—and as controversial—to the navigation system as tax rates. Many of those who held their appointments through the customs commission subsisted on those fees, which, for the lowest paid—men far lower on the scale than Hulton—could bring in considerably more than their salaries, if they were paid any salary at all. Understandably, fees were yet another source of friction between the agents of empire and those they policed.

Worse, as Hulton discovered, his salary would be subject to the land tax even though it was paid through the customs commission. He had received £300 per year as comptroller on Antigua, a salary, boosted somewhat by fees, that had been treated as exempt from the land tax in England and local taxes on the island. Normally those in the customs service posted abroad did not pay domestic taxes because their offices were tied to revenue generated outside the kingdom. As Hulton saw it he fell into the same category, residence in England notwithstanding. His new annual salary of £500 would be reduced by £90 to cover the land tax. Since he would be working much harder at his new post than the old, in his view that meant he was actually working for less even though technically being paid more. Hulton protested to the Treasury for an exemption from the land tax. Despite securing a finding in his favor by the attorney general, it appears that the dispute lingered and the Treasury lords did not decide one way or the other before the post was eliminated.[55]

Nor was Hulton necessarily comfortable with the policies he was expected to help enforce. He did not disagree with Grenville's desire to reform the system; just the opposite. He knew from firsthand experience that some Navigation Acts on the books were

---

55 See Hulton's memorandum "Germany 1763," among the "Nicholson Letters," 20-26; and his letter to Nicholson of 17 December 1763 in ibid., 26-32, transcribed at infra 210-211 and 214-215, resp. Also see his petition to the Treasury of 27 June 1766—with attorney general Fletcher Norton's supportive finding of 8 December 1764 attached—in TNA, PRO/T1/445, fos. 217-221. The petition was read before the lords of the Treasury on 2 April 1766, with consideration postponed—indefinitely, by all indications. Along the way Hulton had appealed to the Duke of Newcastle in January 1766 (see Add. Ms. 32,973, fo. 326, Newcastle Papers, BL) and through Newcastle, to the Marquess of Rockingham then, and again in July (Add. Ms. 32,972, fos. 759-761 and Add. Ms. 32,976, fos. 15-17, Newcastle Papers, BL, resp.). Since the appeal to Rockingham is still among Newcastle's papers, it would appear that the Duke chose not to send it along.

inadequate and should be replaced: thus he could see the need for the 1764 American Revenue Act, commonly called the Sugar Act, to replace the Molasses Act that had stood since 1733. In Hulton's opinion that earlier act had been the unfortunate result of lobbying by West India planters. "Instead of operating as a fund of Revenue" it had become a "source of Smug[g]ling and corruption." Those who were supposed to enforce the law actually acted in collusion with those who broke it, which "introduced a depravity of Morals, and alienated the Subjects from their duty to Government."[56] To the extent that the new law checked lawless behavior, it worked. But if Hulton ever had any enthusiasm for the Stamp Act as it wound its way through Parliament he lost it soon enough. His view of that act, as he looked back on it twenty years later, anticipated that of some later historians.

> The Officers for the receipt of this Revenue were appointed, and the Ministry were pleased with the prospect of a considerable aid, by means of this new duty. But the first object of establishing authority, and respect to government had been neglected. Ignorant of the State of the Colonies, they rushed into a measure which from the Constitutions of the several Governments, they could not support against the clamours, and opposition of the people. The consequence is well known. From this time a spirit of resistance was adopted in America against all Revenue Laws; and the authority of Parliament, which at first was questioned, became to be in general denied; and any means to avoid, or prevent the execution of those Laws, was deemed right.[57]

However skeptical Hulton may have been about the Stamp Act at the moment it became law, he did not make his doubts public. He went about his job, sending out dispatches from his superiors and gathering responses from the colonies as they trickled back to London. If he offered advice on policy to the ministers at Treasury or subministers in customs, he did so guardedly, veteran as he had become of court politics. Knowing when to speak and when to hold his tongue was by now second nature.

Natural as his circumspection was then about imperial politics, it is somewhat odd that Hulton wrote so little later for his sons about the most important personal decision he made during these years, stating simply: "In the month of Sept. 1766 I was married to your Mother, at which time I was confident my Establishment would continue in London."[58]

---

56 Henry Hulton, "Some Account of the Proceedings of the People in New England from the Establishment of a Board of Customs in America, to the breaking out of the Rebellion in 1775," 2, unpublished manuscript, Andre De Coppet Collection, Princeton University Library. Transcribed infra, beginning at 107.

57 Hulton, "Travels," 96-97, with some changes to capitalization.

58 Ibid., 101. Material was appended on 160-167, noting the marriage at St. Anne's in London, the birth dates and places for all five boys, the death dates for Henry and Elizabeth, and their being interred at a church (St. Mary's) in Andover. The official marriage record, for 20 September 1766, is in St. Anne's Church (Soho, Westminster), Church of England parish registers, 1686-1931 (Family History Library, film no. 918609).

Perhaps he considered it unseemly to talk of how such matches are made; perhaps he thought the boys would know what it meant to marry well if they followed his advice in other areas; perhaps he thought it too obvious to require explanation, since she as much as he raised them. In any event it had been a most fortunate day for Henry Hulton when he met Elizabeth Preston, his future wife and the boys' future mother. She proved to be a true partner in life, sharing his ideals, standing by him in his trials, raising five sons in circumstances quite different from those of her own more sedate childhood. Eight years younger than Henry, she was the daughter of Isaac Preston, a country gentleman in Norfolk. Preston also owned a townhouse in London; presumably Henry and Elizabeth met when she was in the city, at one social gathering or another. It is not too difficult to imagine an occasion where their paths might have crossed. They would have seemed a likely match: he a decent godfearing fellow with a well-paying government job, she the daughter of a wealthy man who could bring some money as well as a good name with her. They moved to Gerrard Street in Soho, closer to the city center but still in Westminster, not far from Covent Garden.

Elizabeth, like her new husband, probably expected to live a comfortable life in greater London. That was not to be. In just over a year Henry would end one job and begin another—over three thousand miles away. Hulton recognized he was asking much of her when he reluctantly accepted another post, a post requiring them to traverse the Atlantic for North America. "It was very severe to me to be compelled to remove to a remote part of the World," he reminisced, "and to occasion her to withdraw herself from all her friends," and, he might have added, to be informed of this when she was pregnant with their first child.[59]

Hulton may have felt that he had no choice. His position as plantations clerk was about to be eliminated after four years, in yet another wave of imperial reform. The prime mover this time around was Charles Townshend, Chancellor of the Exchequer in a ministry headed nominally by William Pitt, now Earl of Chatham. Though a crown appointee rather than a true civil servant and therefore serving at the king's pleasure, Hulton, like other bureaucrats, could expect to keep his job if he did it well and did not offend the wrong people. He had held onto his clerkship through Grenville's ministry, then Rockingham's, and was continuing on as Pitt's got underway. But with Pitt incapacitated, Townshend became the dominant force in the ministry, and he was determined to bring his own brand of reform. That included terminating Hulton's old job, though not because of anything that Hulton himself had done or failed to do. Townshend had met Hulton; he talked with him about reforms that he and like-minded parliamentary colleagues had mulled over. As Hulton recalled it, Townshend

---

59 Hulton, "Travels," 101. Thomas was born in London on 29 August 1767.

sent for me, and told me of their intention and desired I would consider what goods it might be proper to lay a duty on in America. I answered him, Sir, before you lay any fresh duties in America, it might be best to see those well collected that are already laid. Why, are they not says he[?] No Sir, the Duties on Sugar, Wines, and Molasses, are not. Well, says he, we shall appoint a Board of Commissioners, and more Officers to see to the better management of the Revenue in that Country.[60]

The next thing Hulton knew the office of plantations clerk had been closed, a new American Board of Customs had been formed in its place, and he was one of five men named to it. He did not seek or even want the post. It would be at the same salary as the one eliminated and he would have to relocate his new family across the ocean in a strange land, an expensive proposition taking him into a potential minefield. His new post would be paired with a spate of new taxes that could be counted upon to irritate the very people he was being sent to live among.[61] None of this boded well. Hulton would have preferred to stay in London but, once again, he was confronted with the reality of his career choice: even after all these years he could not afford, financially or politically, to say no if he had no better prospects—and he did not have them.

The new American-based board had actually been suggested by the customs commission itself, perhaps at Townshend's instigation, even though that meant surrendering some of its own power.[62] The new board would answer directly to the lords of the Treasury. The London-based commissioners were willing to give up some of their power because they decided that the colonies were too far away for them to manage effectively, particularly since there was so much resistance to the Navigation Acts and so many problems within the customs service itself. The new board, acting on site, would, they thought, be

---

60 Ibid., 99. Hulton's concerns were shared widely, though not necessarily always expressed publicly. According to William Knox the Earl of Bute told him, when contemplating imperial policy after the French and Indian War, that "we ought to set about reforming our old Colonies before we settled new ones." See Knox's recollections in Historical Manuscripts Commission, *Report on Manuscripts in Various Collections*, 8 vols. (London: His Majesty's Stationery Office, 1901-1914), 6:282. For Knox as imperial reformer see Leland J. Bellot, *William Knox: The Life & Thought of an Eighteenth-Century Imperialist* (Austin: University of Texas Press, 1977), at 42-70 for Bute and Knox's report that prompted the comment.

61 The three key elements in Townshend's program are in Danby Pickering, ed., *The Statutes at Large*, 46 vols. (Cambridge: Joseph Bentham, et al., 1762-1807), 27:447-449, 7 George III c. 41 (customs commissioners) and 27:505-512, c. 46 (new duties); and 28:70-71, 8 George III c. 22 (reconfigured vice-admiralty courts), with details for the latter laid out in Munro and Fitzroy, eds., *Privy Council*, 5:151-153.

62 Dora Mae Clark, "The American Board of Customs," *American Historical Review* 45 (1940):777-806; and idem, *Rise of the Treasury*, 174-184, discuss the Board's genesis, pointing out that most contemporaries thought Townshend was the man who pushed it and that some thought Charles Paxton played some sort of behind the scenes role too.

able to keep a closer eye on both trade and trade enforcement, weeding out the corrupt from within their own ranks and bolstering those who tried to be diligent in performing their duties.[63] After virtually no debate Parliament passed a bill in June 1767 enabling the king to form the new board and appoint men to it. A badly fragmented opposition saw no opportunity to rouse the public or stop Townshend—as would be the case with virtually everything Townshend hoped to carry into law.[64]

The original report did not designate a place for the commissioners to take up residence. By the time that the American board was formally created—on 14 September 1767—Boston had been decided upon. That in itself was a signal that great change was intended, that Whitehall had effectively thrown down the gauntlet and taken up the challenge for a contest between imperial authority and provincial autonomy at the very heart of resistance to the navigation system.[65] Hulton was named first in the commission, which perhaps in some informal, purely honorary sense made him senior to the others, but he was not designated the commission's chair. The chair would end up as a rotating position; all five members took turns occupying it. Whoever acted as chair did so for procedural purposes only. There were no special powers, no heavier voting weight assigned to the office. "We do hereby give unto you or any three of you," the Treasury lords informed the new commissioners, "full Power and Authority to manage, direct and cause to be levied and collected" all of the duties on any goods carried to or from the mainland colonies of North America, plus Bermuda and the Bahamas.[66] The West Indies remained under the London board's jurisdiction. All other officers holding king's commissions in the colonies, both civil and military, were instructed to cooperate with the board. Although board members were not expected to do actual inspections themselves, they had a general warrant to search any vessel within their jurisdiction, day or night, and all dock facilities during daylight hours. More importantly, they also had authority to hire and fire other customs

---

63 See the customs commissioners report to the lords of the Treasury of 30 April 1767, recommending the American board's creation, in TNA, PRO/T1/459, fos. 84-85.

64 Grey Cooper, who was friendly to Townshend as well as to members of the opposition in Rockingham's camp, introduced the bill in the Commons on June 3, which passed its third reading twelve days later and went from there to the Lords. R. C. Simmons and P. D. G. Thomas, eds., *Proceedings and Debates of the British Parliament Respecting North America*, 6 vols. (White Plains, N. Y.: Kraus International, 1982-), 2:510 and 512, resp.

65 P. D. G. Thomas, *The Townshend Duties Crisis, 1767-1773* (Oxford: Clarendon Press, 1987) noted (on 33) that Philadelphia had been considered at one point and that the choice of Boston "proved a political blunder." See too John Phillip Reid, *In a Rebellious Spirit* (University Park, Pa.: Pennsylvania State University Press, 1979), 6-10, on how the choice of Boston fed local fears that Whitehall and Westminster acted provocatively, in a dangerous attempt at law enforcement—a danger that Hulton understood, perhaps better than those who sent him there.

66 Published to show the public precisely what was intended, as *George the Third, by the Grace of God, of Great-Britain, France and Ireland, King, Defender of the Faith, &c. To our trusty and well-beloved Henry Hulton, John Temple, William Burch, Charles Paxton and John Robinson, Esqs. Greeting* (Boston, 1767), 2.

officials based in the colonies, and to use revenue generated by the Navigation Acts to pay salaries and other expenses.

Heretofore the men of the customs service had been unable to keep revenue ahead of costs. Annual overhead, mostly in the form of salaries, accounted for more than monies collected. The vast majority of men on the payroll were from the colonies, not the mother country. They virtually monopolized the lower paid posts. The full panoply of officials in Boston before the commission's creation—comptroller and collector, surveyor and searchers, weighers and gaugers, landwaiters and tidesmen—had accounted for roughly £1000 annually in salaries. Creation of the new board better than trebled those costs. The commissioners alone added £2500 to the total for the Boston area, and close to another £1000 was allocated for a secretary, a cashier, clerks for both of them, and two inspectors general. Then there was the solicitor and his clerks, who accounted for another £200 or so.[67] New Englanders already resentful of the imperial tax collectors in their midst bristled at the seeming profusion of new costs and new posts. The expectation that duties would be paid in pounds sterling rather than paper money or by some other means proved just one of many irritants to merchants throughout the colonies.[68] It was not the amount in fees that mattered most—a mere pittance, compared with the hundreds of thousands spent annually to maintain troops in the colonies and pay the salaries of other royal appointees, the hundreds of thousands in lost revenue due to smuggling, and the millions generated in trade overall.[69] The disgruntled would complain that the primary motive in enforcing the laws was to fill the pockets of bureaucrats while reminding colonists that what they considered rights were, in London's eyes,

---

67 The 1772 salary schedule is included in Great Britain Commissioners of Customs in America. Customs Papers, 1764-1774, Ms. N-2091, Massachusetts Historical Society library [hereafter MHS]. A 1768 report done at the request of the new American board, signed by Joseph Harrison (collector) and Benjamin Hallowell (comptroller), laid out the structure for Boston as it had evolved to that point. It is in TNA, PRO/T1/465, fos. 179-193. George Wolkins edited it as "The Boston Customs District in 1768," *Massachusetts Historical Society. Proceedings* 58 (1925):418-445.

68 Commenting on affairs in Boston that led to the dispatch of troops to the town, Moses Franks wrote to the Marquess of Rockingham on 3 October 1768: "'Tis very certain, my Lord, that the new Board of commissioners at Boston (at best discordant) brought many of the troubles on themselves, by a conduct the reverse of conciliating in times so imbittered. But as if they studied to aggravate the ill humour of that misguided unfortunate Country, to drive them to some outrage, in order to justify measures of violence against them. They have required of the Merchants (thro the provinces) to do, what absolutely is not in their power. They have ordered that all duties shall be paid in Silver only, Gold is rejected, & paper too. Tis repeating the Severity of the Egyptian Task Masters, make Bricks without Straw. And must operate fataly, to unite the whole in the Boston Spirit, which was generaly disaprov'd; but it will not rest there; for it will inevitably occasion a Universal system of illicit Trade, when all will Be set at deffiance." Wentworth Woodhouse Muniments [WMM]/R1/1101, Sheffield Archives.

69 Although the *Boston-Evening Post*, 9 April 1770, misreported the commissioners's salaries by adding an extra zero to each amount, boosting them to £5000 each, for a total of £25,000—an honest mistake or an attempt to fix more public attention on the customs service?

privileges. That John Robinson, the collector for Rhode Island, was named one of the five commissioners only added to the resentment. It seemed that London had deliberately chosen someone who was alienated from the local population.[70]

Robinson was already in Boston when the board was formed; so was John Temple, one of the other board members. Robinson hailed from England and Temple, though Boston-born, had spent years in the mother country trying to position himself in society through family ties to the Grenvilles. Hulton made the voyage across with the remaining two appointees, William Burch, a fellow Englishman, and Charles Paxton, a Massachusetts man then in London.[71] As plantations clerk Hulton had had dealings with all but Burch, either in person or by mail, because all three were already involved in the navigation system.[72] Those dealings should have warned him that trouble lay ahead. Paxton, an ambitious customs officer based in Boston, had become close to Francis Bernard, the royal governor. Zealous in his quest to catch smugglers, to many merchants his actions were anathema. They felt that his primary motive was to become wealthy at their expense. That he had lived for so long in Boston added insult to injury.[73] Temple, who had been surveyor general of the customs in the northern colonies since 1761, loathed both Paxton and Bernard. Not only that; he thought the new board a mistake, despite his being appointed to it. He preferred things as they had been before and saw no logic to the elimination of his old post.

---

70 For Robinson as symbol of imperial policy gone awry, see Edmund S. Morgan, *The Stamp Act Crisis* (Chapel Hill: University of North Carolina Press, 1953).

71 "Arrived Capt. Watt from London, in whom came a most unwelcome Cargo, Vizt. Henry Hulton, Wm. Burch and Charles Paxton, three of the Commissioners appointed to receive the Duties by the late Act of Parliament imposed on the Colonies." Entry for 6 November 1767 in "John Boyle's Journal of Occurrences in Boston, 1759-1778," *New England Historical and Genealogical Register* 84 (1930):142-171, 248-272; quotation from 252. Boyle noted that they were accompanied by Samuel Venner (their secretary), John Porter (comptroller general), John Williams (inspector general), and a "number of Clerks;" and that Robinson and Temple were already in Boston.

72 For an example of these earlier contacts see Joseph Harrison's letters from London to John Temple of 12 July and 9 August 1765 in the Bowdoin-Temple Papers, Winthrop Papers (reel 46), MHS; also printed in the *Collections of the Massachusetts Historical Society* 6th series 9 (1897):65-66, 67-69. Harrison, collector for the port of Boston, had gone to see Hulton about the arrears in his pay, stretching back all the way to 1761. Hulton was kind and patient, Harrison assured Temple, and he was looking into Temple's complaints about another matter that involved John Robinson as well as Governor Bernard.

73 Acting on a rumor that the Massachusetts council would be appointed by the crown rather than by the lower house of the assembly, Paxton importuned Viscount Townshend, Charles Townshend's older brother, to ask the king to name him to it. See Paxton to Townshend, 22 December 1764, Ms. S-691, MHS. He was ten years premature. That change would not come until the Massachusetts Government Act of 1774—but Paxton's request shows how widespread the talk was of making changes to tighten imperial authority. Looking back on the underlying causes of revolt, John Adams would point to Paxton as a customs officer in Boston—and James Cockle in Salem—because they were using writs of assistance as early as 1759, which in turn helped precipitate the debate over them two years later. See Adams to William Tudor, 29 March and 15 April 1817 in Adams, ed., *Works*, 10:244-247 and 274-277, resp.; and the discussion in M. H. Smith, *The Writs of Assistance Case* (Berkeley: University of California Press, 1978). For Paxton and the "local demonology" that developed in Boston, see Smith's "Charles Paxton: Founding Stepfather," *Massachusetts Historical Society. Proceedings* 94 (1982):15-36.

Therefore he took an almost perverse joy in the board's many failures. Looking back, "I little thought at that time that Mr. Temple was the fomenter of resistance to the authority of Government, and persecution of its Officers, which he afterwards proved to be," Hulton lamented to his sons.[74]

Hulton's complaints about Temple were proof enough that problems came as much from within the customs service as from without, from the board itself as well as subordinate customs officials unhappy with new rules and new faces. "'Tis said, these Commissioners, are resolved to make all the Officers do their Duty Strictly" because "New Brooms sweep clean" complained a New Yorker not looking forward to change.[75] But he need not have worried. The new board did not bring with it a new way of doing the king's business and it is not very helpful to dismiss the board as an egregious instance of "customs rackateering"—the charge leveled by a later American historian, Oliver Dickerson. Perhaps without his realizing it, American protestors had posthumously converted him to their cause. In Dickerson's depiction the empire, as exemplified by Townshend's program, had become the captive of a spoils system, with emphasis shifting from the regulation of commerce to the generation of revenue, revenue intended to enrich corrupt individuals rather than benefit the larger community. The navigation system, once the "cement of empire," Dickerson concluded, had been shattered by men who replaced a benign mercantilism with a poisonous form of imperialism—foolishly and shortsightedly by some, with malice aforethought by others. Ironically, they pursued commercial policies that were anti-commercial at their core.[76]

But malice is difficult to find among the men at Whitehall and Westminster who formulated American policy in the 1760s. Foolishness is easier to spot, but it was foolishness in trying to better manage something old rather than in attempting to try something new. There was never a clear dividing line between the desire to regulate trade and the desire to raise revenue. Both impulses were present from the beginning.[77] And those elements

---

74 Hulton. "Travels," 107.

75 James Parker to Benjamin Franklin, 21 January 1768, in Leonard Labaree, et al., eds., *The Papers of Benjamin Franklin*, 39 vols. (New Haven: Yale University Press, 1959–), 15:27.

76 Oliver M. Dickerson, *The Navigation Acts and the American Revolution* (Philadelphia: University of Pennsylvania Press, 1951); with observations made more briefly in idem, "England's Most Fateful Decision," *New England Quarterly* 22 (1949):388-394. Not only was Dickerson overly influenced by the complaints of protesting Americans in the 18th century, he was reacting to post-World War II protectionism that he thought was a throwback to that era and a danger to the free trade ideas that had taken hold of the Atlantic world in the 19th century. Dickerson's assertion that "had it not been for the unfortunate personalities of Robinson, Paxton, and Hulton there might have been no Revolution" (*Navigation Acts*, 210) is good drama, but not especially good history. Variations on Dickerson's view seeped into many works, from Wickwire's *British Subministers*, pp. 121-131 to Lawrence Henry Gipson's magnum opus, *The British Empire before the American Revolution*, 15 vols. (New York: Alfred A. Knopf, 1936-1970), 10:119-120, 241-242.

77 A point made persuasively in Thomas C. Barrow, *Trade & Empire: The British Customs Service in Colonial America, 1660-1775* (Cambridge, Mass.: Harvard University Press, 1967); underscored in Thomas M. Truxes, *Defying Empire: Trading with the Enemy in Colonial New York* (New Haven: Yale University Press, 2008).

of Townshend's program considered dangerously innovative—restructuring the vice-admiralty court system, new duties on items such as tea, or creating a civil list of imperial officials to free them from provincial control—were intended to fix problems in the old apparatus, not erect a new one. Protesting Americans often claimed that they simply wanted to return to the days before Grenville and Townshend, to the empire they had known and loved.[78] But that was because the old rules had not been enforced. If enforced they would have been deemed as unacceptable as the new ones.

And yet modern scholarship has shown that the idea of a reciprocal empire, where mother country and colonies would each benefit from the relationship, was not so skewed after all. The colonial economy had grown at an even faster pace than that of England. For some sectors of the economy that growth was despite membership in the empire; for others it was only because of it.[79] At the same time, it is equally true that the colonists responded to reality as they perceived it at the moment, not reality as a later generation of historians might construct it.[80] To a growing number of them, especially those in and around Boston when Henry Hulton arrived on the scene, the navigation system seemed to be oppressive and Parliament appeared increasingly tyrannical. Hulton's presence as a member of the new American Board of Customs only reinforced those impressions, as criticism escalated and political opponents were demonized.[81]

---

78 The views of Thomas Cushing, speaker of the Massachusetts House, expressed in a letter to Stephen Sayre of 6 November 1770, can be taken as fairly representative of this position. In response to the charge that complete repeal of the Townshend program would bring a "rise in our Demands," that the colonists would "insist upon the Repeal of the Navigation Acts & be contented with little short, if any thing, of a state of Independency," Cushing responded "I can assure You that is so far from the Truth; that in case the Revenue Acts were Repealed, the Board of Commissioners removed, and the Troops withdrawn & we were put in the same state we were in before the stamp act was passed that People in general would be satisfied & so far from being desirous of being Independent of Great Britain that they would dread the very thought of it." Misc. Bound Documents, 1770-1773, MHS. Cushing was not being disingenuous, but events to come could make it appear that he was—unless, again, the fluid state of social identity and political aspiration within the empire are taken into consideration.

79 John J. McCusker and Russell R. Menard, *The Economy of Colonial America, 1607-1789* (Chapel Hill: University of North Carolina Press, 1985), 46-50. "The dispute between Britain and the colonies was not over Parliament's right to regulate this or that trade, or to tax a particular activity, or to pursue a specific policy," McCusker and Menard concluded. "The conflict centered on the issue of power over the long haul, on the shape of things to come, on who would determine the future of the British Empire in the Americas." (357)

80 For which see Bernard Bailyn, *The Ideological Origins of the American Revolution* (Cambridge, Mass.: The Belknap Press of the Harvard University Press, 1967).

81 Even John Adams, who prided himself on his use of logic and law, wrote a harangue for a Braintree town meeting in March 1772: "What is the Tendency of the late Innovations? The Severity, the Cruelty of the late Revenue Laws and the Terrors of the formidable Engine, contrived to execute them, the Court of Admiralty? Is not the natural and necessary Tendency of these Innovations, to introduce dark Intrigues, Insincerity, Simulation, Bribery and Perjury, among Custom house officers, Merchants, Masters, Mariners and their Servants?" L. H. Butterfield, et al., eds., *Diary and Autobiography of John Adams*, 4 vols. (Cambridge, Mass.: Belknap Press of Harvard University Press, 1961), 2:58.

Even Hulton's high salary grated on some nerves, as did other perquisites to the job. As a case in point, Hulton was made "principal deputy receiver" for the Greenwich hospital tax in June 1768. With that he became a multiple officeholder and therefore susceptible to the sort of criticism directed repeatedly at lieutenant governor cum chief justice Thomas Hutchinson. The tax was used to support a hospital in Greenwich, England, for sick or injured seamen. Part of the funding came from a six pence per month tax on seamen's salaries, a rate set by Parliament in 1696 and applied to the colonies since 1729. Hulton did not go out to collect the tax himself; rather, he paid others in the customs service to do it for him at fifty-two colonial ports, from Georgia to New Hampshire, from Quebec to Nova Scotia. He was allowed a 10% commission on all funds collected, which in a good year could bring him over £200—a tidy sum.[82] The receiver, Thomas Hicks, who lived in London, took his cut as well.

Not surprisingly, seamen in the colonies did not like paying the tax or dealing with those officials who collected it. Wages routinely went underreported or were not reported at all. Some fishermen—notably in Marblehead and Salem—refused to pay altogether, contending that they were not sailors in the sense intended by Parliament. When the board replaced the collector for the port of Salem, in part because he was not collecting the tax, the press cried foul, complaining that it was a tax on a hospital local sailors would never use and it was being pushed by a man who profited directly from its collection.[83]

For aggrieved colonists the hospital tax was yet another example of imperial reaching into provincial pockets. Navigation acts—the sole focus of most historical studies—came and went; fees were a constant. They were split among various officials, commonly the collector, comptroller, and lesser officials, by task. They added a profit incentive to enforcement only slightly less irritating to local merchants than similar practices—and for considerably more money—used in the vice-admiralty system.[84] Vessels were charged to

---

82 Hulton's letter of appointment, dated 29 June 1768, is in the TNA, PRO/Admiralty [hereafter ADM] 80/131. Hulton was still deriving income from this fund long after he had left Massachusetts and was living in relative comfort in the English countryside. The last payment to his account was on 9 October 1783, for £16:17:11 (in TNA, PRO/ADM80/132). See too Joseph Freese's essays, "Some Observations on the American Board of Customs Commissioners," *Massachusetts Historical Society. Proceedings* 81 (1969):3-30; and "Henry Hulton and the Greenwich Hospital Tax," *American Neptune* 31 (1972):192-216. John Phillip Reid, *Constitutional History of the American Revolution*, 4 vols. (Madison: University of Wisconsin Press, 1986-1993), 2:170-171, placed the hospital tax in the context of disputes over Parliament's authority to tax the colonies.

83 From the "Journal of the Times" for 24 October 1768; see also 16 December 1768. Items for the "Journal" were composed in Boston, sent to papers in other colonies where they were printed, and then turned around and reprinted in sympathetic Boston newspapers; gathered and edited by Oliver Morton Dickerson (and hence his eventual bias?) as Boston *under* Military Rule (Boston: Chapman & Grimes, 1936), on 10 and 36, resp. The allegation in the "Journal" for 22 May 1769 (on 102), condemning the "anti-commercial principles" behind the Townshend program and the "haughty[,] imperious and indelicate behaviour" of the American board would be echoed by Dickerson.

84 See Carl Ubbelohde, *Vice-Admiralty Courts and the American Revolution* (Chapel Hill: University of North Carolina Press, 1961), and how military officers as well as civilian officials got caught up in enforcement in Neil R. Stout, *The Royal Navy in America, 1760-1775* (Annapolis, Md.: Naval Institute Press, 1973).

clear ports on arrival and departure. Taken individually these charges did not amount to much money, often less than a shilling, perhaps just a few pence.[85] But not only did fees have to be paid; bills of lading had to be presented, bonds posted, and certificates issued, all of it a bother to those wanting to set sail or drop anchor and unload. Rates were not fixed by Parliament, the Treasury, the customs commission in London or even necessarily the American board; local collectors routinely set their own. Not only did local merchants and shipowners complain; so did royal officials who felt that their own authority was being circumvented. A furious Governor Guy Carleton of Quebec informed the board that he would have none of such practices. When the collector there changed the fee schedule without consulting him, he exploded, "I only comply with the will of the King, our master." He would not "suffer Acts of Parliament to be confounded with the Mercinary Iniquity of Men in Office."[86]

Disputes within the imperial ranks could cut even closer than royal governors versus customs officials. Hulton had had glimpses of divisions within the customs service when he was plantations clerk. Yet another of the ironies of what followed once he arrived in Boston is that he and John Temple, their many disagreements notwithstanding, could agree on one thing: when possible, it is better to soothe than to offend. All the same it was impossible to please everyone, although Hulton apparently tried to do just that. Thomas Hutchinson, for one, thought him just the man for a difficult job. Upon meeting Hulton after his arrival in Boston, Hutchinson described him as "sensible" and prudent" and as "well calculated for the post at the present times as can be."[87]

Perhaps Hulton's attempts to placate all parties made it impossible for him to get along with a strong-willed, unforgiving man like Temple, who was determined to clear opponents from his path. Hulton would not—could not, really—take Temple's side in his long-running dispute with Governor Bernard. The customs commissioners and Treasury lords,

---

85 See, for example, the fees paid to the custom house in Piscataqua, New Hampshire—a busy port, just upriver from Portsmouth—in 1765, in TNA, PRO/T1/483, fo. 239, and the case study offered by Alfred S. Martin in "The King's Customs: Philadelphia, 1763-1774," *William and Mary Quarterly*, 3rd series 5 (1948):201-216.

86 Typescript of Carleton's letter to the American Board of Customs, 4 July 1770, Great Britain Commissioners of Customs in America, Ms. N-1511, MHS. As a contrast, see the appeal from the collectors of Boston, Portsmouth, and Falmouth that they continue to be allowed to set their own fee schedules, undated but circa 1770, preserved in Add Ms. 38,391, fos. 155-156 (Liverpool Papers) BL.

87 Hutchinson to Richard Jackson, 9 December 1767, Thomas Hutchinson Letterbooks, Massachusetts Archives XXV:230, from the MHS typescript, 225. He had earlier described the newly arrived board members as "sensible and discreet men" to Israel Mauduit, Mass. Archives XXV:223-224, from the MHS typescript, 209. Bernard Bailyn, *The Ordeal of Thomas Hutchinson* (Cambridge, Mass.: The Belknap Press of Harvard University Press, 1974), 141-147, noted that Hutchinson's name had come up when the board was being formed. It was not a post Hutchinson wanted. "There is no Office under greater discouragement than that of the Commissioners. Some of my friends recommended me to the Ministry. I think myself very happy I am not one." Hutchinson to ____, August 1768, Mass. Archives. XXVI:320, from the MHS typescript, 663. He feared that to take it would be political suicide in the province. He was probably right, but then he ended up committing political suicide anyway.

had they paid attention, would have seen that, if they were going to name Temple to the new board, they ought to send Bernard elsewhere. There was bad blood between them; they would not work together as agents of empire. Temple had been trying to get Bernard removed since 1764, alleging that he was corrupt, that he and a minor customs official were guilty of profiteering and blackmail. Temple succeeded in getting the minor official fired; Bernard was another matter.[88] And all of the talk in London of reform notwithstanding, the commissioners went forth with no clear connection to Bernard and other imperial officials outside of the customs service. Their powers were independent of Bernard's and his of theirs—which weakened both.[89]

Bernard refused to be cowed and held onto the governor's chair, even though he knew that his power was ebbing. He would have been happy to leave the Bay Colony—but not until he had a post equal to his ambition. In private he urged bold imperial reform. In public he was more timid. Hulton found his ideas appealing and was convinced that, had London listened, things might have gone differently. Whether Bernard was on the right reform track is now moot. He was scarcely able to save himself. Having arrived in Massachusetts after serving as governor of New Jersey, initially Bernard, an Englishman, had gotten on well with the various political factions in the province. By the onset of the Stamp Act crisis five years later he had become increasingly marginalized. His own councillors voted consistently against him and sided with the lower house of the assembly when disputes arose pitting executive against legislative power. Those councillors were chosen by the house, not the governor, not the crown. Bernard had the authority to prorogue a legislative ses-

---

88 For the permutations of this affair, which pitted James Cockle, collector for Salem (see 48 n. 73 supra), against Temple as surveyor general see the folder "1764 Mr Cockles Suspension," in Great Britain Commissioners of Customs, Letters [typescripts], 1764-1774, Ms. N 1511, MHS, fair copies in PRO/T1/441, and originals between Temple and Thomas Whately in the John Temple Papers, STG Correspondence, Box 13, folder 6, Henry E. Huntington Library, where Whately discloses that Temple was being considered for the American board back in the earliest planning stages. Temple had complained to Whately of Bernard's "insatiable avarice" even before the Cockle affair broke—see his letter of 10 September 1764, ibid, fo. 10. Neil Stout edited most of the collection at the Huntington as "The Missing Temple-Whately Papers," *Massachusetts Historical Society. Proceedings* 104 (1992):123-147. He noted that Temple has yet to have his biographer, beyond what Stout offered there and the brief essay by Charles Akers, "New Hampshire's 'Honorary' Lieutenant Governor: John Temple and the American Revolution," *Historical New Hampshire* 30 (1975):78-99. Stout would later write the entry for Temple in John A. Garraty and Mark C. Carnes, eds., *American National Biography* [hereafter *ANB*], 24 vols. (New York: Oxford University Press, 1999-2004), 21:433-435. Also see Jordan D. Fiore, "The Temple-Bernard Affair," *Essex Institute Historical Collections* 90 (1954):58-83.

89 Secretary Samuel Venner's report to London on how the commissioners began their tenure at once underscores and understates the problem of separable lines of imperial authority: "Mr. Hulton, Mr. Burch, and Mr. Paxton arrived here on the 5th instant, and on the 16th qualified themselves together with Mr. Temple to enter upon the Execution of their Office as the Law directs, and opened their Commission that day, having previously accommodated themselves with a proper House for carrying on the Business of the Customs, in Obedience to their Lordships Commands signified to them by your Letter of the 4th of September last." Venner to the Treasury Lords, 21 November 1767, TNA, PRO T1/461, fo. 266. Bernard is nowhere mentioned and was apparently in no way involved.

sion. He could even dissolve the assembly and call for an election before reconvening it. But exercising his authority could cost him his power, so he had to proceed carefully.

Town politics compounded his problems.[90] Boston was essentially self-governing, virtually autonomous from provincial or imperial control. Bernard, more than anyone else in the colonies at the time that Hulton crossed the Atlantic, gave credence to the charge that Massachusetts was becoming ungovernable because Boston was a law unto itself. Until Boston was controlled, he warned repeatedly, no imperial official could do the king's bidding or uphold acts of Parliament.[91] The town's sixteen thousand people were crowded onto a narrow peninsula that could be a bustling, jostling place—the east side of which was crammed with docks, wharves, warehouses and shops. The town meeting ran the town, with freemen voting for those who would represent them in the lower house, various town officers, and, most importantly, the selectmen who acted as an executive committee on town business. Many of those who rose to power in the province did so first through the town, Samuel Adams foremost among them. Political caucuses like the Loyal Nine and political action groups like the Sons of Liberty played a role in shaping Revolutionary America, but none rivaled the town meeting in importance. Imperial officials found that fact difficult to accept and yet they made no significant attempt to change it until 1774. By then it was far too late.[92]

Hulton may well have wondered if it was not already too late when he came ashore on the morning of 5 November 1767, his ship having dropped anchor in Boston harbor the night before. He had said his goodbye to Elizabeth just as she was regaining her strength

---

90 The commissioners would have received a chilly reception, even under the best of circumstances. They arrived at a particularly poor time, little more than a week after the town meeting resolved to "promote industry, Oeconomy, & Manufactures among ourselves" to offset the "heavy debt incurred in the course of the late Warr" and the weight of "very burdensome Taxes." *A Report of the Record Commissioners of the City of Boston, containing the Boston Town Records, 1758 to 1769* (Boston: Rockwell and Churchill, 1886), 223, from the town meeting of 28 October 1767, and the report agreed to on December 22nd (226-230) that complained about the impact of the Townshend duties on local trade.

91 Colin Nicolson, *The "Infamas Govener"* (Boston: Northeastern University Press, 2001) sympathetically—though not uncritically—reviews Bernard's stormy career. That town selectmen and governor had nothing but disdain for each other by the time that Bernard returned to London showed through all too clearly in an exchange of notes between them in February 1769. The selectmen implied that Bernard had misrepresented the town to London, that misrepresentation resulting in the dispatch of troops then bivouacked among them. Bernard retorted that whatever difficulties the town had, it had brought upon itself. Printed in *A Report of the Record Commissioners of the City of Boston, containing the Selectmen's Minutes from 1769 through April, 1775* (Boston: Rockwell and Churchill, 1893), 6-9, along with the town's original "address" of 16 February 1769, Bernard's curt response two days later, the town's rejoinder on the 22nd, and Bernard's, even more terse, on the 24th. Bernard had already reached an impasse with the General Court, with the lower house asking for his recall the previous July.

92 G. B. Warden, *Boston, 1689-1776* (Boston: Little, Brown and Company, 1970) is incisive on Boston's peculiar place in the imperial crisis. See too Pauline Maier, *From Resistance to Revolution* (New York: Alfred A. Knopf, 1973); William Pencak, *War, Politics, & Revolution in Massachusetts* (Boston: Northeastern University Press, 1981); and John W. Tyler, *Smugglers and Patriots* (Boston: Northeastern University Press, 1986).

from the birth of Thomas. She would join him the following June, with Thomas, a servant or two, and with Henry's sister, Ann, who lived with them for virtually the entire time they were in Massachusetts. To Ann fell many of the duties of running a household once Henry purchased a farm in Brookline. She had stayed with the family in town for nearly a year before then, in their rented house. If Henry had been able to purchase something in Boston proper he might never have gone into the countryside. He was only able to purchase the farm through a third party. Had he made the offer himself, he might have been rebuffed, as he was in Boston whenever he tried to buy real estate there.[93] Both he and Burch had found that the longer they were in town, the more difficult it was for them to secure lodging, so Burch went out to Dorchester while Hulton settled in Brookline.

For once disappointment in one setting had brought opportunity in another. As in London, Hulton was able to set up a household removed from the hustle and bustle of city life. According to Ann, "My Brother lives on a spot of Earth which he calls his own," one so satisfying to him and Elizabeth "that they would not chus to change it for any other spot in New England."[94] Henry's preferred schedule was to work four days a week in Boston and remain on his farm the other three, where he puttered about, seeing to his orchards and livestock, spending time with Elizabeth, and watching his family grow. It was already a prized property when he bought it, with thirty acres, a two-story house and outbuildings put on the market by Jeremiah Gridley's family when Gridley died. Hulton added a greenhouse, a new barn, and planted saplings so that eventually he had around eight hundred apple trees. "I could not conceive a domestic Situation in this Country where I could be happier than I am at present," he wrote to a friend back in England, in seeming contentment. "We are indeed out of the World of business, of politics, and pleasure, but we have a World of happiness within ourselves."[95]

Henry and Elizabeth brought three more sons into the world during their Massachusetts years: Henry, born in Boston in May 1769, with Edward and Preston following in October 1771 and October 1773, both at the house in Brookline.[96] When Edward was just under a year old he and his brothers were left in the care of their aunt Ann and the household

---

93 As explained by Ann Hulton to Elizabeth Lightbody, 25 August 1772, in *Letters of a Loyalist Lady* [hereafter *Loyalist Lady*] (Cambridge, Mass.: Harvard University Press, 1927), 51-52, transcribed infra on 271-272. The editors, Harold Murdock and Charles Miner Thompson, only identified themselves by their initials, at the end of their introduction (on xii), not on the title page. The title page states "Ann Hulton," the introduction "Anne Hulton," and indeed both spellings turn up in contemporary documents. Even so, Henry used "Ann," her name is recorded as Ann in the Chester baptismal registry (see supra 26, n. 4), and she signed her older brother John's will "Ann Hulton" (supra 30, n. 21). Also see infra, at 340 n. 2.

94 In an earlier letter to Elizabeth Lightbody, 29 May 1770, ibid., 20, transcribed infra at 242.

95 Letter of 5 November 1771 to Robert Nicholson in Hulton, "Nicholson Letters," 26. Hulton mentioned the apple trees and greenhouse in a letter to Nicholson of 21 November 1772, ibid., 66. Both are transcribed infra, at 261-262 and 273-274 resp.

96 According to the entries Hulton made at the end of his "Travels," 160-162, Henry was born on 18 May 1770, Edward on 18 October 1771, and Preston on 2 October 1773.

servants while their parents embarked on an exciting adventure. They traversed nearly fourteen hundred miles of sometimes rugged country in eight weeks, better than eight hundred miles by land, another five hundred plus over water, all the way to Quebec and back. They set out from Brookline on 26 August 1772. Accompanied only by their driver and one other servant, they traveled the breadth of Massachusetts by two-horse coach, through towns that rarely—in some instances, never—saw carriages on their dusty, rutted roads. After crossing into New York and reaching Albany they headed north, crossing and recrossing the Hudson until they reached Fort Edward, just below Lake George. They went on a bateau—crewed by others—the length of Lake George into Lake Champlain, on into the Richelieu River to the St. Lawrence, then to Montreal. They sailed by ship to Quebec. When they left Quebec for the return journey they sometimes traveled by land in a post chaise, by water in a canoe, then back down the lakes, again by bateau, to Fort Edward. Picking up their own horses and carriage, they went by a different route to try to avoid some of the more broken terrain in eastern New York and western Massachusetts. In that they largely failed, but they were back safely in Brookline on October 20th.[97]

Although finding food and shelter suitable to their tastes was a challenge the entire trip, they never went without. The most they roughed it was a four-day period passing back down Lake George, where once they had to put ashore and sleep in a tent made from the bateau's sail, eating cold food, shivering through an even colder rain, not changing their clothes for days on end. They were never in any particular danger except those inherent to such travels—real enough, and Henry was rightly impressed with Elizabeth's fortitude. She "supported all her difficulties with great spirit," he reported proudly.[98]

Much of what he saw pleased him—the land more than the people. "It is amazing how rapidly the back parts of this Country are settling, and with what little means of living people sit down in the inhospitable woods," he marveled.[99] He did not think Canadians took advantage of what nature provided them. Fertile soil was not put to good use because the people, descendants of a French peasant culture, lacked the industriousness

---

97 Hulton left the fullest account in his "Observations," 191-226, a variation of which was printed in the Appendix to *Loyalist Lady*, 100-107. He offered additional details in some of his letters, most notably those of 28 October and 3 December 1772, in "Copies of Letters & Memorials written from Boston commencing Anno 1768," 2 vols. [hereafter "Letterbooks"], 1:52-61, Houghton Library, Harvard University, transcribed on 272-273 and 276-278 infra; and to Robert Nicholson of 21 November 1772 and 10 May 1773 in the "Nicholson Letters," 65-67 and 62-65, resp., and transcribed on 273-274 and 278-279 infra. Also see Hulton, "Sketches," 123-126. In May 1771, when Elizabeth was pregnant with Edward, they had taken a briefer, less arduous trip by carriage through southern Massachusetts and into Connecticut.

98 Hulton to Robert Nicholson, 10 May 1773, in Hulton, "Nicholson Letters," 62, transcribed on 278-279 infra. As he wrote to his brother-in-law, Jacob Preston, "she behaved heroically, and never was daunted, or lost her spirits, under any difficulty. And we were sometimes in circumstances that put our fortitude to the tryal." Letter of 28 October 1772, in "Letterbooks," 1:53, transcription on 272-273 infra.

99 Hulton to Robert Nicholson, 10 May 1773, in Hulton, "Nicholson Letters," 63, with a transcription infra at 278-279.

of British colonists to their south. "The people," he observed with a bit of disdain, were "very lazy and dirty yet very chearful and happy."[100] He seemed to think that they were not yet worthy of the opportunities bestowed on them by incorporation within the British empire. That he was proud to be part of that empire was evident in his choice of places to visit. As a board member he could have gone north purely for imperial affairs, to consult with customs officials stationed in Quebec—and indeed he did stay in the upper town as a guest of the port's collector. But there was much more to the trip than the adventurous or business sides to it. It was a pilgrimage, a trek to an imperial shrine. Twice Hulton stood atop the cliffs where British soldiers had picked their way up in the dead of night, making possible Wolfe's great 1759 victory outside the walls of Quebec. He strolled the Plains of Abraham, site of the decisive battle where Wolfe died leading his men to glory, a place now "remarkable"—sacred ground of empire that caused him to scribble a poem to Wolfe's memory, on the spot.[101]

Hulton's pride as an Englishman, his pride as servant of the crown and agent of empire, would color his view of all things American, whether in Canada or Massachusetts. There were those moments when he could see himself as both English and American, and believe that he had found a new home within the same expansive imperial community. "I Bless God my family have been and are well and enjoy every blessing this can afford," he wrote in one of his more peaceful moments at Brookline.[102] At those private interludes to his public life he expressed no desire to ever leave. "I now have three Boys," he wrote a friend in England, "and from any thing I can yet see it is probable that I, and my family after me, will remain in these parts."[103] But there was something about American attitudes that bothered him, an inappropriate pride in place. The irritation burst through in a letter to Elizabeth's brother, who had just returned from his own grand tour of the Continent.

> You have seen the World in the polished, we, in its rude State. You have gone over the Boasted remains of Antiquity, and observed the Conscious pride of those who demand respect from the lustre of their descent, and glory in what they have been. We have seen the face of nature as it was left at the flood; uncleared, and uncultivated and mankind in a state of equality. But tho' we cannot glory in heroic actions or claim the honours of an illustrious Ancestry, yet do not think that we are without an imaginary superiority, that we do not pride ourselves in the possession of advantages over others.

---

100 Hulton to Jacob Preston, 28 October 1772, in Hulton, "Letterbooks," 1:52. Transcribed at 272-273 infra.

101 See infra 395 for the poem, from Hulton, "Observations;" 226-227; also in *Loyalist Lady*, Appendix, 106-107, with the usual slight differences (and 103 for the "remarkable" comment).

102 Hulton to his brother-in-law, Jacob Preston, 31 August 1771, in Hulton, "Letterbooks,"1:38, transcription on 260-261 infra.

103 Letter of 21 April 1772, addressee unidentified, ibid.," 1:46 and 45, resp., transcribed infra at 266-268.

> Happy delusion! Where are the people, or where is the mortal, that has not a little fund of this self-flattery? That cannot place himself in some point of view, where he can look down upon others? This gratification to pride, is a most comfortable cordial, and makes the wretched support many evils—but what say you, is your boast? Why we boast a glorious Independency. We look on the rest of the World as Slaves, and despise titles, and honour. And as we cannot glory in what we have been we pride ourselves in what we shall be. The little island of Great Britain is a small inconsiderable spot. We shall be the Empire of the World, and give Law to the nations.[104]

When Hulton wrote "we" he really meant "they." He did not share their boosterish self-confidence that they were destined to lead, that even the mother country herself ought to—and someday would—bow before them. Although he could appreciate the raw energy so evident in Massachusetts he was more ambivalent about the lack of polish he saw there: on the one hand, he found the honesty and directness of many people refreshing; on the other, he wished for some happy medium between the artfulness of self-styled sophisticates and the artlessness of the common sort. And it was the common sort, with the complicity of their social betters, who made his life as a customs commissioner so miserable. Inability to do the job he was sent to do gnawed at him, causing anxieties that he had never felt on Antigua. Although those anxieties did not match what he had experienced in Germany,[105] "a sense of duty, inclination, and zeal for the service, will carry men a great way," an exasperated Hulton complained to the Treasury, "but the best kept minds will be damped by a long endurance of persecution from their enemies, and neglect from their friends."[106]

Hulton's short trips around southern New England and long excursion into Canada were also an escape from the cares, even the dangers, of office. All of the commissioners but Temple felt the pressure. John Robinson had had to look over his shoulder even before he was named to the board.[107] Hulton, Burch, and Paxton had been threatened with abuse from the day of their arrival in town—inauspiciously, on the annual Pope's Day

---

104 Letter of 31 August 1771, ibid.,1:40-41, with some changes to capitalization and punctuation. For an even more sarcastic edge when Hulton talked of "foolish notions of Independence," see his letter to Samuel ___ of 24 May 1774 in ibid., 1:88-93. They are transcribed on 260-261 and 300-302 infra, resp.

105 After he retired he wrote of his time in Germany: "When I look back on the scene of severe trial I endured, I almost tremble at the recollection, and wonder I shou'd so have combated, and prevailed. I consider this arduous service performed the most trying and important of my life." Hulton, "Travels," 142.

106 Hulton to Thomas Bradshaw, secretary to the Treasury lords, 29 June 1770, in Hulton, "Conduct of the Commissariat," 239-240, with the full letter transcribed at 245-246 infra.

107 The board in general and Robinson in particular became the target of a biting series by "Candidus"—possibly Samuel Adams—in the *Boston Evening-Post*, 21 November, 12 and 26 December 1768, into 16 January and 13 February 1769. The more famous "Junius Americanus" series would later take swipes at the commission too, notably in ibid., 17 and 24 December 1770, and 28 January 1771.

where Boston was the scene of rowdy merrymaking. Hulton had actually spent his first night ashore under John Temple's roof and shrugged off the taunts as nothing serious. He tried that approach any number of times, hoping that would ease the tension. Sometimes it worked; more often it did not.

Hulton would never be beaten by street toughs, never be tarred and feathered by a mob. Others in the customs service—dozens of others—would not be so lucky. They suffered all of the pain and humiliation that accompanies such physical abuse.[108] Hulton's closest call came in June 1770, which prompted his second flight to Castle William. The first time had been two years before, in the aftermath of the *Liberty* incident. John Hancock owned the *Liberty*, a sloop engaged in the transatlantic trade. In the eyes of customs officials like Joseph Harrison, Boston's collector, and Benjamin Hallowell, Boston's comptroller, Hancock was nothing more than a successful smuggler. They looked for an excuse to go after him and the *Liberty*'s master provided it by unloading his cargo before he received proper clearance. They ordered that the sloop be seized. As it was being towed away from the dock by a British warship a crowd set upon them when they were foolish enough to linger too long at the scene. Bloodied and frightened, they fled to Castle William. Hulton and the board members—all except Temple—followed in short order, after first seeking sanctuary on the HMS *Romney*, then in the harbor.[109] They entreated Governor Bernard to request that troops be dispatched to restore the peace and enable them to perform their duties.[110] Customs officials, including Hulton and his colleagues on the board, again,

---

108 Perhaps the most famous case involved John Malcom, who was tarred and feathered by a Boston mob in January 1774. See Thomas Hutchinson to the earl of Dartmouth, 28 January 1774, in TNA, PRO/CO 5/763, fo. 45 (where Hutchinson spelled the name "Malcolm"). That incident was included in the list of outrages compiled for *The Report of the Lords Committees, Appointed by the House of Lords to Enquire into the several Proceedings in the Colony of Massachuset's Bay* (London: Charle Eyre and William Strahan, 1774), 33-34, and used to justify tougher policies against the colonists. For details on and documents pertaining to this affair, see Frank W. C. Hersey, "Tar and Feathers: The Adventures of Captain John Malcom," *Publications of the Colonial Society of Massachusetts* 34 (1937-1942):429-473.

109 See the note signed by Hulton, Robinson, Burch, and Paxton requesting sanctuary on 11 June 1768, in Add. Ms. 38,340, fo. 259 (Liverpool Papers) BL. They justified their actions in a letter to the Treasury Lords of January 1769, a copy of which is in Hulton, "Conduct of the Commissariat," 197-201. Bernard's vindication of their withdrawing to the Castle, dated 22 December 1768, is in ibid., 202-205 (also signed by Hutchinson, Andrew Oliver, and Robert Auchmuty).

110 Hulton alludes to the *Liberty* affair in his "Account," transcribed at 128 infra. Legal scholar John Phillip Reid uses it to show how local control of the law could be used to negate claims of imperial authority. See his *In a Rebellious Spirit*, 74-130. George Wolkins, "The Seizure of John Hancock's Sloop 'Liberty,'" *Massachusetts Historical Society. Proceedings* 55 (1921-1922):239-284 has stood up well. Thomas Hutchinson recounted the event in his *The History of the Province of Massachusetts-Bay*, 3 vols. (Cambridge, Mass.: The Belknap Press of the Harvard University Press, 1936), 3:136-140. Also see Hutchinson's letters to Richard Jackson of 16 June and 7 July 1768 in the Hutchinson Letterbooks, Mass. Archives XXVI:310-312 and 315-316 (MHS typescripts 644-648 and 656-658, resp.); Francis Bernard to the earl of Hillsborough, 11 and 18 June 1768, in the Francis Bernard Papers, 6:311-314 and 623-624 in the Ms. Sparks 4, Houghton Library; Benjamin Hallowell's affidavit of 11 June 1768 in Add. 38,340, fo. 251 (Liverpool Papers) BL; and Hallowell's testimony before the Treasury lords on 21 July 1768 in TNA, PRO/T1/468, fos. 338-340.

except for Temple, who stood apart from them on this issue—would never be forgiven for that by leaders of the political opposition.[111]

Henry, with Elizabeth and Ann, did not leave Castle William until after the troops finally arrived in October. Hulton and his colleagues did their work there as best they could. Only Temple went back and forth to town with any regularity. He alone among them had left his family in Boston proper. With the troops's coming, anti-board rhetoric intensified. Hulton was relieved to have soldiers about, although they did not act as a police force and "the temper of the people is not changed."[112] He could not yet know that their being in Boston would precipitate his second, even more precipitous, flight to the Castle. The only incident that had reached Henry and Elizabeth's household before they moved to Brookline had occurred in May 1769. The house they were renting caught fire and Elizabeth, nearly nine months pregnant, called outside for help. Her servant and one from the neighbor's put the fire out. No one else came to her aid and one woman passing by called out loudly, "it is only the Commissioner['Js house, let it burn."[113] Once it became common knowledge that Hulton had bought Gridley's estate the windows of the then empty house were broken.[114] It would be many months after the family took possession until anything else happened.

The two regiments that had arrived in October 1768 were reinforced by another two some months later. Because the town seemed peaceful enough those additional regiments left the following fall—but not before Francis Bernard, who did not to wait to be relieved before sailing away. Hutchinson would have to act in Bernard's stead for two years until he had the governor's office formally bestowed on him. Hulton and the other commissioners were disappointed to see Bernard leave; doubly so to see half of the troops depart. Hulton predicted no good would come of it. The Boston "massacre" of 5 March 1770 fulfilled his direst prophecies, when soldiers slew civilians in a burst of violence that had been building for days. Captain Thomas Preston and eight enlisted men were subsequently tried for murder before Massachusetts judges and jurors. All but two of them were acquitted, and those who were convicted were found guilty of manslaughter, not murder. During the many months they were held in the Boston town jail awaiting trial they feared for their lives. "But the injury to the commissioners of the

---

111   The town meeting's assertion (on 13 September 1768) of rights and condemnation of troops being sent to Boston—which also called for a convention of town delegates from throughout the province to meet (see *Report of the Record Commissioners...Boston Town Records, 1758 to 1769*, 261-264)—did not single out the commissioners for attention. Josiah Quincy would in his 1774 pamphlet (see infra 74 n. 161), an indication of how individual grievances were gradually combined into one conspiratorial whole.

112   Hulton to Robert Nicholson, 6 April 1769, Hulton, "Nicholson Letters," 34, transcribed infra at 225-226.

113   Hulton, "Travels," 111.

114   As Hulton reported to Robert Nicholson, 6 April 1769, in Hulton, "Nicholson Letters," 36, transcription infra on 225-226. Perhaps it was this incident, or more likely the earlier incident in town, that a local historian referred to many years later when he stated that "an inhabitant has acknowledged that, in youth, he joined with other thoughtless boys in breaking" Hulton's windows because he was "a tory." John Pierce, *An Address at the Opening of the Town Hall in Brookline on Tuesday, 14 October 1845* (Boston: White & Potter, 1846), 22.

customs was greater," wrote Thomas Hutchinson later, "not merely as it respected their character in England, but as it tended to expose them to the resentment and wrath of the people of the town."[115] In the aftermath, the remaining two regiments were pulled out of the town and bivouacked at Castle William. Anticipating that action, four of the five commissioners—Temple, not surprisingly, the lone exception—decided that the board should postpone meeting for the time being. With that it ceased to conduct business for over four months, despite Temple's vehement protestations.[116]

John Robinson, who had wanted a leave for months, sailed to London at Hulton's urging to report on the deteriorating state of affairs.[117] Paxton took refuge at a friend's house in Cambridge. Leaving their families behind, presumably safe in Hulton's home at Brookline, Hulton and Burch rode off to Piscataqua, New Hampshire. There they fired off a letter to the duke of Grafton, head of the current ministry as well as first lord of the Treasury. They painted a dark picture indeed, contending that it was virtually impossible to reconvene the board. Not only had the troops been pulled out of the town proper; their presence in the Castle meant that there was not enough space for the commissioners to go there with their families, as they had done following the *Liberty* incident in 1768. Equally troubling, they had been indicted by the Suffolk County Superior Court for allegedly writing malicious falsehoods about the people. Moreover, they faced possible indictment for alleged involvement in the "massacre," it being said that shots had been fired at the crowd from the custom house windows on King Street—their meeting place as board members. "The passions of the people of Boston which had been irritated for a length of time by inflammatory publications, and other base arts of their faction['s] leaders" had "burst forth," making "the situation of the servants of the Crown"—*and* "four of the Commissioners" in particular—extremely "critical & alarming," they informed Grafton. They would allow time "for the passions of the multitude to subside" before resuming their posts.[118]

---

115 Hutchinson, *History*, 3:201.

116 For Temple's pleas to his colleagues to reconvene, see the typescript of board minutes from 8 March-1 July 1770, where Temple could not get his colleagues to meet, in Great Britain Commissioners of the Customs in America, Ms. N-1511, 42-64, MHS. His complaint to Lord North, then first lord of the Treasury and head of the ministry, on 2 July 1770, ibid., is in the folder "Mr. Temple's Letters to Superiors in England," 32. The standard account of developments leading up to the "massacre," the event itself, and the aftermath remains Hiller B. Zobel, *The Boston Massacre* (New York: W. W. Norton, 1970). For a contrasting view see my "Rival Truths, Political Accommodaton, and the Boston 'Massacre'," *Massachusetts Historical Review* 11 (2009):57-95. Zobel has a fair amount on the American board. I do not discuss it in my essay.

117 "Mr. Hulton has long been of Opinion that one of us should go home. Mr. Burch has been obstinate against it. Paxton has been rather neuter, but inclining to Mr. Burch's opinion. It is certain that if Government does nothing this Parliament that we cannot stand our Ground, and it will not be a small support that will enable us to make head against the Opposition." Robinson to Thomas Hutchinson, 1 November 1769, in the Hutchinson Letterbooks, Mass. Archives XXV:335a, from the MHS typescript, 340.

118 Commissioners to Grafton, 3 April 1770, TNA, T1/476, fos. 233-237. Another copy is in Hulton, "Conduct of the Commissariat," 209-218. In the press battle that took place between the "massacre" in March and the trials that began in October, the commissioners became a favorite target, their requests for troops and

A·VIEW OF PART OF THE TOWN OF BOSTON IN NE

1ˢᵗ *Beaver*   5 *Mermaid*
2ᵈ *Senegal*   6 *Romney*
3ᵈ *Martin*   7 *Launceston*
4 *Glasgow*   8 *Bonetta*

On fryday Sept.ʳ 30ᵗʰ 1768, the Ships of WAR, armed Schooners, Transp. and Train of Artillery, with two pieces of Cannon, landed on the L. a Spring on their Cables, as for a regular Siege. At noon on Saturday playing, and Colours flying, up KING STREET. Each Soldier having

Paul Revere's engraving of British troops landing at the Long Wharf on 1 October 1768. Christian Remick apparently drew the scene in 1769, which Revere engraved on a copper plate the next year. Given the caption describing the troops marching "with insolent Parade" into town, the seemingly polite inscription to the Earl of Hillsborough was probably a bit of sarcasm. Hancock's dock, complete with buildings and

A VIEW OF PART OF THE TOWN OF BOSTON IN NEW ENGLAND AND BRITTISH SHIPS OF WAR LANDING THEIR TROOPS! 1768

To the Earl of Hillsborough His Majesty's Secry of State for America. This VIEW of the only well Plan'd EXPEDITION, formed for supporting ye dignity of BRITAIN & chastising ye insolence of AMERICA, is humy Inscrib'd

... the Harbour and Anchored round the Town; their Cannon loaded ... the fourteenth & twenty-ninth Regiments, a detachment from the 59th Regt ... re Formed and Marched with insolent Parade, Drums beating, Fifes ... nds of Powder and Ball.

A Long Wharf
B Hancock's Wharf
c North Battery

ENGRAVED, PRINTED, & SOLD by PAUL REVERE. BOSTON.

ships at anchor, is to the right. The town house stands at the end of the long row of buildings leading off the wharf. Faneuil Hall is the second prominent structure to its right. The largest of the British warships, the 50 gun HMS Romney, is to the right of the wharf's end. Critics of imperial policy blamed Hulton and the other commissioners for the troops' presence. Courtesy of The American Antiquarian Society

Town leaders, by contrast, decried the commissioners for their actions, for being the cause of imperial unrest. The confiscation of Hancock's *Liberty*, the arrival of troops, the incident on King's Street, all were offered as proof that conspiracy was afoot and evil abounded. "No period since the perilous times of our venerable Fathers had worn a more gloomy and melancholy aspect," the townsmen lamented, and Britain's CONSTITUTION seems fast tottering into fatal & inevitable ruin."[119] They put the commissioners at the center of all of their troubles—the personification of foolish policies and imperial power run amuck.[120]

Hulton and Burch had returned in May, Burch picking up his family at Hulton's and going back to Dorchester, Hulton resuming life in Brookline. "My family are in good health and our situation would be agreeable enough if these people would suffer us to live in peace," he wrote, "but contention and broil seem necessary to the existence of a Bostonian and indeed our present circumstances are very critical and alarming, as our lives and properties depend on the caprice of our Sovereign Lords the people."[121] Hulton's fears were realized when a mob descended on his house late one night in June. He and his servants scared the men off but, worried they would return, Henry grabbed Elizabeth and they fled to a neighbor's while it was still dark. They hid in his outbuildings until the next morning, then they scurried to a friend's house in Cambridge. Hearing that Burch had taken his family to the Castle, Henry decided to pack Elizabeth, the two boys, and Ann off with him

---

their efforts to control trade helping to precipitate a crisis. See the pointed criticism of them offered in both *A Short Narrative of the Horrid Massacre in Boston* (Boston: Edes and Gill, 1770) and *Additional Observations to a Short Narrative of the Horrid Massacre in Boston* (Boston, 1770). True to form, Oliver Dickerson contended that someone may well have fired shots from the custom house windows, in his "The Commissioners of Customs and the Boston 'Massacre'," *New England Quarterly* 27 (1954):307-325. The commissioners were also caught up in the controversy surrounding provincial secretary Andrew Oliver, who was accused of making public *in camera* proceedings of the council on the "massacre" and, more importantly, of repeating—or misrepresenting?—one councillor's comment that there were plans in place to drive all of the soldiers and the commissioners out of town. See Royal Tyler's supposed statement to that effect in TNA, PRO/CO 5/759, fos. 114-116, and the subsequent hearings on fos. 623-659, which were later printed as *The Proceedings of His Majesty's Council of the Massachusetts-Bay, Relative to the Deposition of Andrew Oliver, Esq.* (Boston: Edes and Gill, 1770), and also included in *Journals of the House of Representatives of Massachusetts*, 55 vols. (Boston: Massachusetts Historical Society, 1919-1990), 47:257-289.

119 From the instructions to the town's representatives to the General Court—one of whom was John Hancock—approved by the town meeting on 15 May 1770, printed in *A Report of the Record Commissioners of the City of Boston, Containing the Boston Town Records, 1770 Through 1777* (Boston: Rockwell and Churchill, 1887), 26-32; quotation on 26.

120 Ibid., 34, minutes of 13 July 1770, and their letter of that same day to Benjamin Franklin, who acted as the lower houses's agent in London, printed in Labaree, et al., eds., *Papers of Franklin*, 17:186-193.

121 Hulton to Robert Nicholson, 11 May 1770, in Hulton, "Nicholson Letters," 47, transcribed infra at 241. Also see Hulton to Lord North, 25 June 1770, and to Hutchinson four days before, in "Conduct of the Commissariat," 229-232 and 233-235, resp., transcribed at infra, 243-245. He had gone briefly to Rhode Island almost immediately after returning home, worried that he was still not safe. Colin Nicolson, "A Plan 'to banish all the Scotchmen'" *Massachusetts Historical Review* 9 (2007):55-102, connects this incident to larger tensions in the colony produced by conflicting notions of "Britishness."

there too, where they remained into November.[122] Servants stayed behind at the house. Paxton fled to the Castle as well. Hulton's critics huffed that there had been no real attack, that Hulton had staged it himself to try to win sympathy in London and get troops back into Boston.[123] Hulton, by contrast, was convinced that Temple was somehow involved.[124] At least there was space at the Castle, because one of the two regiments garrisoned there after the "massacre" had been pulled from the province altogether.

Hulton's suspicions about Temple are a crucial indicator of the board's sorry state.[125] Temple's obstructionism did not block policymaking by the board because only a majority of three—any three—was needed for a vote to carry. But Temple made his dissatisfaction known in both Boston and London, feeding public criticism in the one and private questioning in the other. Paxton was convinced that Temple had been undermining the Board from the beginning. "He seems to have flattered himself that by raising a clamer against the new Board," Paxton confided in one letter, "he should be able to demolish it to Establish himself in his Old place."[126] Temple, for his part, warned a well-connected London friend, "if Government do not ere long find itself quite aground in this Country from the perfidy[,] baseness and Deception of its own Servants, I have entirely lost what little Judgment I may have had and will thenceforth acknowledge myself to be no other than a meer dreaming Idiot."[127] The commissioners, in combination with Bernard, he predicted, would cause "a

---

122 Hulton, "Travels," 116-117. Hulton recorded one incident in particular in their stay at the Castle (which lasted from June into November): "In the month of October we had a violent storm of wind and we were apprehensive that our house (which was situated in the highest part of the Castle) would tumble down about our ears. About the height of the storm, at ten o-clock in the morning, it came into my Sister[']s head, to take up the little child Henry out of his bed lest the chimney shou'd fall that hung over the room he was in. In about a quarter of an hour after he was taken up, the chimney did fall, broke thro' thereof, and filled the bed out of which the child had been take quite over with bricks and rub[b]ish: so that had he not been providentially taken up the child must have been killed." Ibid., 119.

123 The Governor's Council did not accuse Hulton of staging the incident, though it did conclude that whatever happened "would not have been committed at all had he been in Boston." In other words, he brought his troubles on himself. See the note about the Council for October 1770 in the Bowdoin-Temple Papers, Winthrop Papers (reel 47).

124 Ann Hulton repeated the rumor that Temple was involved in an undated letter written sometime in 1771, in Loyalist Lady, 39-40, transcribed infra on 255-259. She considered Temple "as diabolical" a person who ever lived.

125 Sympathetic as Hutchinson was to the board's plight, he also recognized that it had become its own worst enemy. See his unsent letter of 16 February 1769 and an undated letter, apparently to John Pownall, in the Mass. Archives XXVI:345-347 and 417-419, MHS typescript, 725-727 and 912-915, resp.

126 Paxton to Viscount Townshend, the lord lieutenant of Ireland, 6 November 1769, in Misc. Bound Documents, 1766-1769, MHS.

127 Temple to Thomas Whately, 4 November 1768, Temple Papers, fo. 59. Temple did not actually leave for another two years, during which he decided not to discuss the board anymore with Whately, since Whately was being sent letters by Bernard, Hutchinson, and others arguing that he was in fact the problem. See Temple's "Memorandum," ibid., fos. 59-61, and his "memorial" of February 1772, fos. 72-73, protesting his removal and the behavior of the other board members. He found out he had been removed from the board when he arrived in London in late December 1770. Hulton considered Temple so poisonous that he attributed James Bowdoin's turn against Bernard to Temple's influence rather than to any significant policy differences. See Hulton's history, 145-146 infra.

war between these colonies and their mother country." Because he claimed that he acted "upon principle" and his ostensible colleagues did not, within a year of their arrival he had decided he would have as little to do with them as possible.[128]

Ultimately Temple was taken off the board and replaced with Benjamin Hallowell, Boston's comptroller. By then it was late 1770 and Temple had given up completely on the others—and they on him. Their final break had been building since 1769, when a majority of the board voted to remove Samuel Venner as secretary and replace him with Richard Reeve, who had been the board's clerk. Venner had come over from London; Reeve was from Boston. The majority decided that Venner was siding with Temple, whereas they considered Reeve loyal to them. Temple interpreted Venner's removal as the first step toward eliminating him and he was quite likely right. Temple complained that Reeve did not keep him informed of board business and board meetings, and that the other commissioners were behind it. When he did meet with the others, it could involve firing people he had hired and hiring replacements to whom he objected—fruitlessly.[129]

Venner protested to the Treasury that the board exceeded its authority in removing him, since he too had a crown appointment.[130] The board complained to the Treasury about both him and Temple, not just because of their connection to each other, but because Venner seemed to be siding with Jonathan Sewall, yet another royal appointee in Massachusetts. Sewall was the province's attorney general and the board felt that he had botched the *Liberty* case. It wanted David Lisle, their solicitor who had come over from London, to go after Sewall for his lack of vigor in prosecuting Hancock. Lisle was not inclined to pursue the matter. Temple would have nothing to do with any of this.[131]

---

128 Temple to George Grenville, 7 November 1768, Bowdoin-Temple Papers, Winthrop Papers (reel 47). Also printed in William James Smith, ed., *The Grenville Papers*, 4 vols. (London: J. Murray, 1852-1853), 4:396-397. "So long as such men are continued in offices in America," Temple wrote to Admiral Samuel Hood on 7 July 1770, "it may be expected animosities between Britain and the Colonies will continue even if all the late Revenue Laws were repealed." Bowdoin-Temple Papers, Winthrop Papers (reel 47) MHS. Interestingly enough, Temple, whose pen could drip acid, particularly when it came to Paxton and Bernard, did not direct anything personally insulting toward Hulton.

129 See Temple's complaint to the duke of Grafton, 14 May 1769, in "Mr. Temple's letters to Superiors in England," a folder in Great Britain Commissioners of Customs, Letters [typescripts] 1764-1774, 10, MHS; echoed in his letter to Newcastle, 25 October 1769, TNA, PRO/T1/469, fos. 185-189.

130 See Venner's memorial to the Treasury of 29 October 1770, protesting his treatment by the board, in TNA, PRO/T1/476, fo. 429; also his memorial of 14 May 1771 in TNA, PRO/T1/482, fo. 192. Much of the Venner material has been transcribed, in the folder "Memorial of Samuel Venner to the Lords of the Treasury," in Great Britain Commissioners of Customs, Letters [typescripts], 1764-1774, MHS.

131 The board's frustrations with Sewall and Venner (because Venner allegedly informed Sewall of what the board was passing on to London) are evident in the minutes from board meetings held at Castle William, from August 1768 into January 1769, in TNA, PRO/T1/471, fos. 7-15. The board's complaints to Treasury about Temple and Venner are in ibid., fos. 429 and 435-436, resp., dated 20 February 1769. For Sewall, the board, the *Liberty* affair, and divisions among imperial officials see Carol Berkin, *Jonathan Sewall* (New York: Columbia University Press, 1974), 45-77 and passim. This appears to be the same David Lisle who was involved in the controversial case of onetime slave Jonathan Strong, a case that caught the attention of Granville Sharp

Such was the disordered state of affairs for the American board by early 1769. The Treasury lords were at a loss, unsure what to do about such squabbling. They chided the board for removing Venner, which was beyond their authority—so Venner was right. But then, given the circumstances, they did not order that he be reinstated—so he would not receive satisfaction. Although they did not recommend to the king that Temple be removed, they did tell the board that dissenting opinions did not need to be recorded, which would be one way of silencing him. Furthermore, if anyone on the board courted "Popularity by a factious Opposition to the Opinions of their Associates," then the lords would recommend that that person be removed by the king—which of course only reinforced the determination of Hulton and the other three board members to have Temple removed. Criticizing the board for poor reporting and an apparent decline in revenue from the Navigation Acts, the Treasury lords's secretary also tossed out this sop: "My Lords are not insensible to the Difficulties with which You have been surrounded, & the Opposition You have had to encounter since your first landing in America."[132]

They could appreciate that an underfunded and overextended customs service could not be expected to tick on like clockwork. Friction between the component parts was inevitable.[133] They focused instead on the colonists' protests against the board's very presence among them and the questioning of their own authority when creating the board at all. It was that questioning of imperial authority, on this issue and others, that most troubled leaders in Whitehall and Westminster. When the Privy Council heard testimony in June 1770 about the disturbances in Boston culminating in the "massacre," John Robinson who had gone to London with Hulton's blessing—depicted the board's difficulties as symptomatic of the larger dispute. He stressed "that the Establishment of the Board was considered by many" Bostonians "as an unconstitutional Measure, because the last Revenue Laws which the Board was to carry into Execution, were considered in that Light."[134]

and is discussed in F. O. Shyllon, *Black Slaves in Britain* (London: Oxford University Press, 1974), 18-23 and passim. Lisle, a barrister with the Inner Temple, had previously acted as solicitor for the Wine License Office in London. See the affidavit of Williams Adams, dated 8 September 1767, in the TNA, PRO T1/456, fo. 132 attesting to Lisle's qualifications for the customs commission.

132 Grey Cooper, for the Treasury, to the American Board, 29 June 1769, TNA, PRO/T28/1, fos. 338-342.

133 Yet another case brought to their attention eventually would be that of inspector general John Williams. His grievances—from the board's appointment of another man whose assignment impinged on his own, to his allegedly poor treatment by the board (Temple excepted; Temple took his side)—were expressed in a letter to the board of 13 March 1769, in Ms. S-363, Great Britain Customs, MHS, and in a letter to the Treasury of 1 March 1776, in TNA, PRO/T1/522, fos. 309-310. Williams proved he was made of stern stuff a month after the *Liberty* incident, facing down a mob that formed at his Boston house, demanding that he resign his post. He refused; the crowd went away. See Bernard to Hillsborough, 18 July 1768, Bernard Papers 7:7-10; and Hutchinson to ____, 21 July 1768, Mass. Archives XXVI:315-316, MHS transcript, 656-658.

134 Benjamin Hallowell, Temple's eventual replacement, and Francis Bernard joined Robinson in testifying before the Privy Council over a two-day period, 26-27 June 1770. TNA, PRO/Privy Council [hereafter PC] 1/9/48, fo. 5.

After much fact-gathering and venting on the floor of the Lords and the Commons, Parliament had sputtered and fumed but did little more than exchange resolutions with legislators in Massachusetts. Parliament issued its resolution in February 1769; the Massachusetts assembly responded in June; Parliament refused to acknowledge its response. Just as reports from the American board of customs were vital to the case against Bostonians made in Parliament, the presence of the board in Boston was part of the case presented in Boston against Parliament.[135]

Sadly for Hulton, he and the other board members had been caught in the middle of a dispute not of their making and yet they could hardly stand apart from it.[136] Viewed by their critics in the context of larger issues, they took on a symbolic role far beyond anything they were actually called on to do as commissioners.[137] In effect, they became scape-

---

135 *Journals of the House of Commons*, 32:107-108 for the resolution, which was introduced in the Lords in December and made its way through the Commons, to be approved the following February. Letters from the customs board were among the evidence presented—see ibid., 32:75, for 28 November 1768. The resolutions passed by the Massachusetts House on 29 June 1769 are printed in *Speeches of the Governors of Massachusetts, From 1765 to 1775; And the Answers of the House of Representatives to the Same* (Boston: Russell and Gardner, 1818), 176-180. They included: "Resolved, as the opinion of this House, that the constituting a board of commissioners of customs in America, is an unnecessary burthen upon the trade of these colonies, and that the unlimited power of the said commissioners are invested with, of making appointments, and paying the appointees what sums they please, unavoidably tends so enormously to increase the number of placemen and pensioners, as to become justly alarming, and formidable to the liberties of the people." The House here essentially repeated allegations against the customs board first made in its circular letter of 11 February 1768. Printed in *Journals of the Massachusetts House*, 44:236-239 (the resolutions of 29 June 1769 are in ibid., 45:168-172). The House had already complained to Dennys DeBerdt, agent for the colony in London, that it could be argued that trade "may be easily carried on, and the acts of trade duly enforced, without this commission; and, if so, must be a very needless expense, at a time when the nation and her colonies are groaning under debts contracted in the late war, and how far distant another may be, God only knows." Letter of 12 January 1768, printed in *Speeches of Governors*, 130. Also see the "letter" from the Massachusetts House to the Treasury, 17 February 1768, printed in the *Boston Evening-Post*, 4 April 1768, where the Board is ignored in favor of higher concerns. The "Merchants of Boston" would complain about the board in *Observations on Several Acts of Parliament* (Boston: Edes and Gill, 1769).

136 Proof of which can be seen in the October 1769 committee report "appointed to vindicate" the town, in *Report of the Record Commissioners...Boston Town Records, 1758 to 1769*, 303-325, and two pamphlets, all sparked by the *Liberty* affair and the subsequent dispatch of troops. *Letters to the Ministry* (Boston: Edes & Gill, 1769) reproduced letters from the commissioners, Bernard, Gage, and Hood to London, contending that mobocracy was taking hold in Boston because they had insufficient authority to act. *An Appeal* (Boston: Edes and Gill, 1769), published "By Order of the Town," endeavored to counter that view, emphasizing the abuse of power committed by imperial officials—the American board of customs included, whose members were never in real danger. Their flight to the *Romney* and then to Castle William was farcical, staged to justify the stationing of troops among civilians. In this dispute as in the later "massacre" controversy, both sides relied on what legal historian John Phillip Reid called "forensic" evidence, where they argued their side of the case, leaving it to their opponents to argue for themselves, yet they claimed to be telling the whole truth. "Facts were shaded by the people of Boston just as they were by the commissioners of the American customs," observed Reid, *Rebellious Spirit*, 51.

137 With tensions escalating the town meeting issued a statement of grievances and rights in November 1772. The customs commissioners were singled out in two of the twelve "Infringements and Violations" of those rights, printed in *Report of the Record Commissioners...Boston Town Records, 1770 Through 1777*, 94-106.

goats of empire, despised by their critics and an embarrassment to other imperial officials whose lives became more difficult because the board was placed among them.

Francis Bernard's ambivalence about them exemplified the problem. Bernard did not see what he could do to assist the customs service before the board's arrival; the board's presence only made matters worse, though he was careful not to cast any aspersions on its members (except for his longtime rival John Temple). Like John Robinson he testified before the Privy Council. There he lamented that customs officers were unable to perform their duties unless they had troops and fleets at their back. Often, after they seized a suspect cargo, crowds would form and stage a "rescue," whisking off whatever the officials had confiscated, by brute force if necessary, so that there would be no evidence should a prosecution be attempted. "The officers of the Customs grew very indifferent about making Seizures" as a result, Bernard concluded.[138] He himself had more or less given up in the aftermath of the *Liberty* riots. The attorney general could not identify anyone to charge with a crime; his council had turned against him; the town meeting did as it saw fit. Therefore when Hulton asked for protection he had to answer that he had none to offer.[139]

What Bernard did not say was that the commissioners' repeated requests for assistance had further complicated his already complex role as governor. In the wake of the *Liberty* affair they begged him to send for the regulars. He responded that he had to have the Council's approval before doing so—which, by that point, he knew he would never receive. When Hulton asked if the board could go to the Castle for sanctuary, Bernard went along with him, while at the same time making it clear to Hulton—and to his political opponents—that he did not think conditions in the town were all that dangerous.[140] He and Hulton may have both been imperial officials, but their priorities were not necessarily aligned: Hulton's top priority was enforcing the Navigation Acts, Bernard's was maintaining his power base. So Bernard minced words when it suited his purposes, hoping that Hillsborough or Gage would take the hints that he gave them that soldiers were needed, while at the same time he could say that he had not officially asked for them—thereby

---

138 TNA, PRO/PC1/9/48, fo. 17. For examples of complaints from the field by harassed officials, see the board's report to the Treasury of 12 June 1769, TNA, PRO/T1/471, fo. 371; and Arthur Savage to Thomas Hutchinson, 20 February 1770, Hutchinson Letterbooks, Mass. Archives XXV:355-360, from the MHS typescript, 363-365. Bernard had complained to Hillsborough in a letter of 9 July 1768 that "every Seizure made or attempted to be made on land at Boston, for three years past," had been "rescued or prevented." *Letters to the Ministry*, 39.

139 Bernard to Lord Barrington, 4 March 1768, Bernard Papers 6:96-99; also printed in Edward Channing and Archibald Cary Coolidge, eds., *The Barrington-Bernard Correspondence* (Cambridge, Mass.: Harvard University Press, 1912), 147-150.

140 Bernard's noncommittal position was implicit in the customs board minutes for June 1768 that ended up in Add. Ms. 38340, fos. 265-285 (Liverpool Papers) BL. Bernard had made them explicit, even before the *Liberty* incident, in a letter of 9 May 1768, to Barrington, in Channing and Coolidge, eds., *Barrington-Bernard Correspondence*, 157. Also see ibid., Appendix III (264-293), and the fair copy in Bernard Papers 8:182-228, Bernard's recapitulation of the "State of the Disorders" leading from the *Liberty* affair to the arrival of the troops, written probably just as he was preparing his *Select Letters* (see infra 95, n. 231).

reinforcing popular criticism of the board for overreacting. Once the troops arrived Bernard did what he could to hasten the board members' return to town, at the same time letting them know that he was not there to serve them; he had a colony that was spinning out of control.[141]

It was not that Bernard disliked Hulton—he was, after all, a godfather to one of his sons[142]—nor was he insensitive to the board's plight. Himself the target of biting invective, he could empathize with Hulton and his colleagues when the seemingly constant press attacks became personal.[143] But if the rhetorical attacks never ceased, physical assaults did not keep pace. In fact, for Hulton at least, they ended almost as soon as they began. Aside from the midnight assault on his house in June 1770 he had suffered only small indignities and those occurred in Boston, not Brookline. When he and his family returned home after their second flight to the Castle he bought a large dog and put up a loud bell to ring in case of attack—his neighbors promising to come if he rang.[144] He never had to put their promise to the test.

Perhaps that was because he had finally been conditioned to accept rather than attempt to change the people and their ways. In the first months after the commissioners arrived they had complained bitterly to whoever would listen about the incessant smuggling, the general ignoring of the Navigation Acts, and the abuse of customs officials. How, they wondered aloud, could Boston's leading men stand idly by while Paxton was burned in effigy? How could London do nothing when a Connecticut court ruled writs of assistance unconstitutional? Thomas Hutchinson, whose Boston home had been utterly gutted by a mob in the Stamp Act crisis, commented too knowingly that

> The Commissioners of the Customs make great complaints of the insufficiency of the laws in being for preventing illicit trade and I suppose have made the necessary representations. On the other hand the people think the laws already in force to be very grievous and very unwillingly submit to

---

141 See Bernard's series of notes to the commissioners of October 8th, 19th, and 22nd, and November 12th, in the Bernard Papers, 7:211-215. "The State of affairs in Boston is full as bad as the Reports you have received make it," he had written to Lieut. Col. William Dalrymple in Halifax, on 2 July 1768. "All real Power is in the hands of the lowest Class; Civil Authority can do but what they will allow." Bernard Papers, 5:266. He dared not request that Dalrymple come at the head of troops. The commissioners had already written to both Dalrymple and General Thomas Gage in New York, Dalrymple's commander, asking for their aid. They responded that their hands were tied. See Gage to the commissioners, 21 June 1768, and Dalrymple, 23 June 1768, in TNA, PRO/T1/465, fos. 181 and 185, resp. Admiral Samuel Hood, with an independent naval command, did respond, sending two small warships down from Halifax.

142 Hulton's second son, Henry, born in 1769. Burch was the other godfather; Ann Hulton was godmother—as she would be for Edward and Preston too. From Hulton's "Travels," 161-162.

143 For a taste of which see various "Journal of the Times" entries in Dickerson, ed., *Boston under Military Rule*, notably that of 10 October 1768; and the "Candidus" essays in the *Boston Evening-Post*, beginning 21 November 1768 and running intermittently through 13 February 1769. "Peter" was one of the few who came to the commissioners' defense, in the *Boston Gazette*, 29 August 1768.

144 Ann Hulton to Mrs. Lightbody, on 21 December 1770, *Loyalist Lady*, 29, transcribed infra, on 250-251.

the execution of them. It is very disagreeable to be under constant apprehensions of danger and I know of no way of avoiding it but by an unjustifi-
able compliance with the prevailing principles.[145]

Hutchinson lamented having to choose between standing on principle and risking one's
safety or setting principle aside in order to avoid harm. Hulton eventually understood that
he faced that very dilemma, and that he might have to reconcile himself to a situation
that he did not like but could not change. "When I was assaulted in my house 3 years ago
at midnight I got no relief by my complaints," he sighed in the fall of 1773, "and when I was
pelted by the Mob this last summer I took it quietly, and said nothing, and I am told they
now say I am such a patient[,] quiet Gentleman, they will trouble me no more."[146] Indeed,
the next year when he was riding in a post chaise through Cambridge, where people were
still stirred up by the so-called "powder alarm," he was recognized and allowed to pass
through unscathed. Hallowell, traveling behind him, was accosted and had to ride franti-
cally, pistols drawn, for the guard on the neck leading into Boston.[147]

Hulton spoke more truthfully than he knew when he commented in the summer of
1771 that all was quiet and "the people will continue so long as they are allowed to dis-
avow the authority of Great Britain with impunity."[148] The board met, it conducted business, but it did nothing particularly threatening to its critics. Posts were filled and some
duties were collected, but there was no sustained program to stamp out smuggling, in
Massachusetts or anywhere else.[149] With Robinson staying in England on extended leave

---

145 Hutchinson to Richard Jackson, in London, 18 April 1768, Hutchinson Letterbooks, Mass. Archives XXVI:300,
from the MHS typescript, 624. For Hutchinson, disputes did not reach a head until January-March 1773
and his debate with the council and house over imperial authority versus colonial autonomy. The customs
commissioners became part of that debate because of their role in enforcing the Navigation Acts and their
salaries being paid by London. See John Phillip Reid, ed., *The Briefs of the American Revolution* (New York:
New York University Press, 1981).

146 Hulton to the Reverend _____, 8 October 1773, in Hulton, "Letterbooks," 1:66-69, transcribed at 282-283
infra.

147 See Hulton's "Letterbooks," 1:106-107, from a letter of 8 September 1774 (transcription on 308-309 infra), and
his "Account," 182, 213 infra. Hallowell's version of events is in a letter to Grey Cooper of 5 September 1774,
TNA, PRO/CO5/175, fos. 52-55. On September 1st General Thomas Gage, by then governor of Massachusetts as
well as commander-in-chief of the British armed forces in North America, had sent soldiers from Boston to
seize munitions stored in Medford, just outside Cambridge. Local militiamen mustered (too late), believing
that his troops had taken stockpiles belonging to the people of the province rather than, as he contended,
to the crown.

148 Hulton to Robert Nicholson, letter of 3 August 1771, in Hulton, "Nicholson Letters," 52, transcribed on 253-255
infra.

149 Which is not to say that the board ever changed its tune about the need for a more effective show of imperial force—such as in the letter to the Treasury (signed by Hulton, Paxton, and Hallowell) after customs official Charles Dudley experienced difficulties in Rhode Island. "So long as People may go on undisturbed in
the commission of illicit practises Things may remain quiet in this Country, but when an attempt is made to
check and restrain them we shall find the same resistance and opposition as we have allready experienced;
and we are firmly persuaded that our present security, and the peaceable state of this Town, is owing to the

the board remained at four members from 1770 on, Hallowell having replaced Temple by the end of that year.[150] That Robinson had turned what Hulton thought would be a short leave into an indefinite stay proved irritating. With one board member gone, none of the other four could expect to be granted leaves in turn.[151] To their credit they did see through an increase in revenue generated by the Navigation Acts, enough to pay the salaries of virtually all civilian officials of the empire in the colonies. Even so, between 1768-1774 the customs service on the mainland of North America rarely collected more than £40,000 a year.[152] John Temple had no doubt been right: it was better to collect a little money and not offend the many rather than attempt to gather a lot. But then, at London's direction, that small amount was spent in a manner offensive to critics of the empire. The revenue was used to create a "civil list" that freed royal governors and other crown appointees from their dependance on elective assemblies for their salaries. That civil list cost more political capital than it was worth.[153]

As a function of survival—political if not literal—the men of the customs service had learned to live in a legal gray area before the commissioners arrived in 1767. Sometimes they enforced the law; sometimes they did not. That behavior did not change; the commissioners themselves even adopted it. One could contend that a similar dynamic plays itself out in every society, where the legally permissible is ultimately determined by what is socially acceptable. Understanding that truism is necessary before pondering the problems peculiar to empire.

Rendezvous of His Majestys Ships in this harbour, and the apprehension that some further measures would be taken by Government." Letter of 6 May 1771, TNA, PRO/T1/482, fo. 200.

150 Robinsons's additional leave requests of July 1771 and August 1773, which the Treasury lords approved, are in TNA, PRO/T28/1, fo. 359.

151 Hulton to "P____ Esq." in London, 8 December 1773, Hulton, "Letterbooks," 1:77, transcribed infra at 308-309.

152 See Barrow, *Trade & Empire*, 244-245, with Barrow working directly off the records compiled for 1768-1772 by Charles Steuart, the American board's paymaster (in TNA, PRO/AO1/844/1137). "An Account of the Gross Receipt, Payments and Net Produce of the Customs in N America" for the years 1767-1774 ranged from a low of £8235 (in 1767) to a high of £49,113 (in 1772), with a slip back down to £30,156 (in 1774). Those totals included revenue generated by seizures and confiscations as well as the routine collection of duties. Thus, £3119 of the £49,113 brought in during 1772 came from seizures and penalties, with over half of that total resulting from the actions of naval officers rather than customs officials. TNA, PRO T1/461, fos. 243-244.

153 Just as Hulton had had questions about the local tax liability with his salary as plantations clerk, he worried over whether his customs board salary could be taxed by Massachusetts. A legal opinion given to the Treasury said that it could—see the report of John Dunning and William de Grey of 13 February 1770 in TNA, PRO/T1/479, fo. 13, but the privy council determined that it should not be—see the 1771 order from the king-in-council sent to Governor Hutchinson, printed in Leonard Woods Labaree, ed., *Royal Instructions to British Colonial Governors, 1670-1776*, 2 vols. (New York: Appleton-Century-Crofts, 1935), 1:375. The General Court had pressed for collection the year before, which Hulton paid. Hutchinson, following his instructions, argued for the exception; the House refused. See *Speeches of the Governors*, 306 (Hutchinson on 4 July 1771) and 307 (the House the next day). Earlier the House had pressed on collecting the rent it believed it was due when the commissioners took up residence at Castle William. See its resolution of 14 July 1770 in *Journals of the Massachusetts House*, 45:188—yet another flashpoint pitting executive against legislative authority, and imperial against provincial power.

One Massachusetts resident professing to be a friend to government wrote Thomas Hutchinson early in 1770, concerned that "pride and ambition" were driving the colonists down a road to revolution that they did not really want to travel. "I wish the Board of Commissioners were dissolved, coud the dutys be collected without 'em," and "I cant see why they may'nt," he added. "If the revenue Act be repeal'd, I suppose there will be an end of them."[154] The Townshend Revenue Act of 1767 was indeed repealed a few months later, all but the duty on tea. The end of the act did not mean an end to the American board of customs, however, because there still lingered a desire to bring Americans into line. Nonetheless there was no will to match the desire and no real program to do so anyway, even under the so-called Coercive Acts of 1774, Parliament's first truly punitive legislative program in the unfolding crisis.[155] The Tea Act of 1773 that had further modified Townshend's earlier act led directly to the tea party, and the tea party to those acts. Anger and suspicion were revived on the American side of the Atlantic, culminating in the first Continental Congress and the formation of provincial conventions, quasi governments in the colonies that attempted to displace royal authority and parliamentary authority, but without declaring independence.[156]

Hulton had fled to Castle William for the third and final time a couple of weeks before the tea party—in anticipation of being in danger, not because he had come under real attack. Admiral Montagu, naval commander on the scene, assured the Treasury lords that he would assist the commissioners should they ask for his aid.[157] Apparently they did not. As much as Montagu might decry the "mob" that ruled Boston, he also emphasized that there was little that he could do, short of leveling the town, to change the situation.[158] So while he watched events unfold essentially as a bystander, during the day Hulton went about his business at the custom house in Boston or at Castle William in the harbor, and even went home occasionally during daylight hours. He left Elizabeth, the boys, and Ann back in Brookline, and returned there himself shortly before Christmas. Nothing had happened to him or his family. The next time he left it would be for good. His family followed soon after, never to return.

They made that final departure, taking what personal effects they could, in October 1774. Elizabeth, the boys, Ann, and eventually the servants a half dozen or so joined

---

154 Israel Williams of Hatfield to Hutchinson, 23 January 1770, Hutchinson Letterbooks, Mass. Archives XXV:352, from the MHS typescript 360.

155 For British actions in 1774 see P. D. G. Thomas, *Tea Party to Independence* (Oxford: Clarendon Press, 1991); and David Ammerman, *In the Common Cause* (Charlottesville: University of Virginia Press, 1974), for the American reaction.

156 Discussed masterfully in Benjamin Woods Labaree, *The Boston Tea Party* (New York: Oxford University Press, 1964).

157 Montagu to Charles Jenkinson, a vice-treasurer, 8 December 1773, Add. Ms. 38208 (Liverpool Papers), fo. 21, BL.

158 Montagu to Philip Stevens, Treasury secretary, 17 December 1773, in TNA, PRO/CO 5/247, fos. 173-174.

Henry at a rented house in Boston. Hulton, Burch, and Hallowell lived essentially cheek by jowl. They had hoped that the Treasury would supplement their salaries to cover their increased expenses and decreased revenue from the customs. They petitioned the Lords to "give Us such relief in future, as may encourage Us to persevere with chearfulness and zeal in the execution of our duty." [159] Conditions worsened before anything could be done by London. At least it had been easier to find lodgings now, with many of those sympathetic to the resistance movement getting out of town while the decidedly fewer who supported imperial authority hoped to get into it. Eventually the Hultons moved into the spacious house, with attached garden and small pasture, left by Sir William Pepperrell, a friend who had already taken his family to England. [160] Troops were back in town; the connections that critics had made between the commissioners and the unconstitutional placing of standing armies among civilians were made again as they had been in 1768, this time more stridently. [161] Hulton wondered, "If the Colonies are to be reduced to obedience, what is to become of us till order is established?" If he and the other commissioners were located elsewhere in the colonies, "we shall be exposed to the like indignities we have experienced. If we are recalled, there is an end of authority. If we remain at Boston, we must stand the issue of the storm." [162]

With his prospects looking ever bleaker, Henry assumed that the end had come, that he and his family would go elsewhere. "We are anxious for our future destination, as there seems no prospect of peace and comfort, on this Continent for some time to come." [163] Having made enemies in Germany when posted there, he had made even more in the colonies, and in a much more contentious setting. His hope to find a new assignment must have been mixed with a fear that he had become *persona non grata* in London, his career finished. [164] By the time that he managed to talk Ann into returning to England ahead of the rest of the family, the fighting had started and Boston truly was a town under siege. Try as he might he could not get Elizabeth to take the boys and leave without him. [165]

---

159 The customs commissioners to the Treasury Lords, 30 May 1774, from a copy in Hulton, "Conduct of the Commissariat," 259-262; quotation on 260.

160 Hulton to Robert Nicholson, 22 January 1776, in Hulton, "Nicholson Letters," 95, transcription at infra, 341-342. Pepperrell, grandson of the victor at Louisbourg, had inherited the baronetcy and the estate. He was one of the few Council members who had sided with the crown and went into exile, and a godfather (along with Admiral John Montagu) to Henry's son Preston, born in Brookline in October 1773.

161 Josiah Quincy Jun'r, *Observations on the Act of Parliament commonly called the Boston Port-Act Bill; with Thoughts on Civil Society and Standing Armies* (Boston: Edes and Gill, 1774).

162 From a letter of 18 January 1774, apparently to Jacob Preston, in Hulton, "Letterbooks," 1:82, transcribed on 292-293 infra.

163 Letter of 12 June 1775, addressee unknown, ibid., 1:131, transcription infra on 323-324.

164 See his letter of 21 April 1772, addressee unknown, ibid. 1:45, transcribed on 266-268 infra, where even that early he had an inkling that his reputation in London could soon be ruined.

165 Hulton letter of 30 November 1775 (presumably to Elizabeth Lightbody), ibid., 1:169, for Ann; letter of 30 July 1775, to Robert Nicholson, ibid., 1:142, for Elizabeth. Both have been transcribed infra, at 338 and 330-331, resp.

He had developed a siege mentality long before any real siege began. He had begun to detach himself from public affairs months before and only went through the motions of doing his job—like dozens of other imperials officials, no doubt. He thought that the board might be recalled to London; it was not. With the closing of Boston as a port in the summer of 1774 he had shifted the board's meetings to Salem, and then back to Boston again in response to events in the countryside.[166] The board's authority was reaffirmed; Hulton had at least nominal duties to perform throughout the siege with the limited non-military traffic in the harbor, and with the proceeds from duties and reports that trickled in from other colonies.[167] He was convinced that the fighting that erupted on 19 April 1775 actually had a bright side: it thwarted a rebel plot that would have been launched five days later to take over Boston from within. He was wrong but his belief that the rumor could be true was an indication of how far he had removed himself psychologically before he left physically.[168]

After nearly sixteen months of being huddled in Boston, Hulton, his family, and their servants boarded a ship bound for Halifax. From there they would go to England—and soon, they hoped. Some emigrés like the Hultons were leaving their new home to return to their old one. Many more were leaving the only home they had ever known. In the journal Henry had been keeping for some months he made an anguished entry for March 10th, when he thought his ship would set sail. The passion expressed there in his private despair is very different from the dispassionate, ironic tone he had taken for so long in discussing the downward spiral of public events.

---

166 The King wanted the commissioners safely out of Boston as soon as he heard about the tea party—see Dartmouth to the Treasury lords, 1 February 1774, in TNA, PRO/CO 5/250, fos. 145-146. The Treasury lords anticipated that revenues—and supplemental salaries—would be adversely affected as a result, so they directed "the Commissioners to report" to them "how much it may be reasonable to allow such Officers respectively as a compensation for such their losses." Treasury board minutes, 31 March 1774, enclosed with the King's instructions to Governor Gage, 5 April 1774, in TNA, PRO/CO 5/205, fos. 462-463.

167 See the letter of 7 October 1775 signed by Hulton, Paxton and Hallowell, with a legal finding by Daniel Leonard in their support, accepted by General William Howe, stipulating that they still had authority in Boston. TNA, PRO/T1/513, fos. 287-289. By the time that Hulton sailed for home, trade between the rebellious colonies and the mother country had been statutorily cut off, beginning with New England, then all but New York, North Carolina and Georgia (when they still had a semblance of royal government), and finally all the colonies that eventually declared independence. For the sequence see Pickering, ed., *Statutes*, 31:4-11 (25 George III c. 10), 31:37-43 (25 George III c. 18), and 31:135-154 (26 George III c. 5). And with that the navigation "system" essentially came to an end, *but*, the mercantilistic thinking behind it did not necessarily disappear as well, even as formal empire in the Americas became eclipsed by informal empire. See Vincent T. Harlow, *The Foundiing of the Second British Empire*, 2 vols. (London: Longmans, 1952, 1964), 2:1-6, 254-280; and Esmond Wright, "The British Objectives, 1780-1783: 'If Not Dominion Then Trade,'" in Ronald Hoffman and Peter J. Albert, eds., *Peace and the Peacemakers: The Treaty of 1783* (Charlottesville: University of Virginia Press, 1986), 3-29.

168 He repeated the rumors as facts in letters of 7 and 21 May 1775, addressed to Robert Nicholson and "Sam'(possibly Samuel Horne) respectively, in Hulton, "Letterbooks," 1:146-153 and 127-130, resp. (out of chronological order). The letters are transcribed sequentially at infra 320-323.

What accumulation of distress! A severe season! A pressing foe! Hundreds of people to be crammed on board each Vessel, without seamen to navigate them, or provision to support the passengers on the Voyage. Oh! The heart racking pains of every parent; the ruin of fortune; the shipwreck of property not attended to: go we must, and fly from the wrath of Man, unprovided against the rude elements, trusting only in an Almighty protection for our deliverance...taking a last farewell of my dwelling, and shipwrecked substance, which I was obliged to abandon, I cast a look on my old faithful dog Argus; he seemed to know, and sympathize in my distress, and drew tears from my Eyes.[169]

Hulton did not sail out of Boston harbor that day. His leave-taking would be prolonged because nothing seemed to be going quite right—a somehow fitting close to his years in Massachusetts. What little baggage beyond personal effects the family had taken from Brookline had been stowed aboard a schooner and sloop belonging to the customs service. Virtually all of the men who had been part of the service in and around Boston were joining the exodus, or had gone already. Hulton's own ship, built for carrying army supplies, was refitted with berths for the trip up the coast to Halifax. Seamen were at such a premium that the captain had to settle for some marines to have enough hands to get under way. The marines broke into the liquor stock, got hopelessly drunk, and had to be removed and replacements found from among the sailors of other vessels in the convoy being assembled off Nantasket. This must have frayed nerves already worn by dislocation and a long winter under siege. For five days before boarding ship the members of the household had waited anxiously in Boston, with intermittent artillery barrages causing them to fear that an assault would be launched before they could get away, all the negotiations for a peaceful evacuation notwithstanding. Once they were aboard it still took their convoy over two weeks to ready itself, wintry weather turning fair, then wintry again. Fatigued by the events of the preceding months as well as the voyage itself, the Hultons and other evacuees put into Halifax on April 2nd.

It would be another three months before they could secure passage on a ship bound for England—this, even with Hulton's political connections. Hulton, at least, had been able to find a place to stay in town almost as soon as they arrived. Others less fortunate had to remain on the ships that carried them. Though safely ashore the Hultons paid a premium to sleep on a hardwood floor, with no bedding.[170] Hulton found better lodgings to tide them over until they could depart—which they did on July 12th, with a

---

169 From Hulton's "Journal at Boston," begun on 2 December 1775 and kept through 10 April 1776, when the family found accommodations in Halifax, in Hulton, "Letterbooks," 1:189, 190, transcribed infra at 350, with slight changes to some capitalization.

170 Ibid., 1:197-221, note for 3 April 1776, transcribed infra, on 352.

rough but quick crossing, arriving at Dover a month and a day later. Whatever Hulton had thought about making a new start for himself in Massachusetts nearly nine years before must have seemed from another life. He was once again an Englishman, a proud son of Britannia, thrilled and relieved to be home. He would never leave again.

> We feel ourselves very happy in being once more in our native land; of which blessing no one can be sufficiently sensible who has not lived out of it, and I wish all murmurers to make the experiment, especially if they are sons of liberty: that they may enjoy the sweets of it for a while under the Boston Demagogues. I am persuaded that in no Country in no period of time, there was ever a state of society, in which the people were so improved, so generally comfortable and happy, as in the present one of Great Britain.[171]

Country Gentleman

It took the Hultons the better part of a year to get settled. They spent a few days in Kensington at the home of Elizabeth's younger sister Alice, who was married to the Reverend Whitley Heald. They then shifted to Westminster and the Berkeley Square townhouse of Elizabeth's older brother, Jacob, who had inherited the Preston family estate when his father, Isaac, died in May 1768. After that Henry and Elizabeth were back in Kensington, renting a house from the prominent physician Sir George Baker until Henry could find something more permanent—but *not* in London. He was "desirous to get down into the Country," as Ann put it.[172] She had herself moved, from Chester to Stanstay (near Wrexham) for her health, which was beginning to fail. She considered going on to Bath, then went back to Chester.

In the fall, Henry and Elizabeth took a long vacation at Beeston Hall, Jacob Preston's seat in Norfolk. It appears that Henry had not been to Beeston before, when Isaac Preston, Elizabeth's father, was still alive. Jacob Preston was in the midst of renovations, both to his grounds and to the manor house.[173] Henry was at once intrigued and impressed, by the

---

171   Hulton to Robert Nicholson, 22 August 1776, Hulton, "Nicholson Letters," 98, transcribed at 358 infra. James H. Stark, *The Loyalists of Massachusetts* (Boston: James H. Stark, 1910), included (on 133) a list of those men who removed to Halifax from Boston. Hulton is shown as having twelve in his household, which meant that he, Elizabeth, and the four boys were accompanied by a half dozen servants. Which of those servants had first come out from England, whether any had joined the household in Massachusetts, and how many crossed over (or back to) England is not clear.

172   Ann Hulton to Elizabeth Lightbody, 19 August 1776, *Loyalist Lady*, 88-90, transcribed infra at 357. Also see Henry to Robert Nicholson, 22 August 1776, Hulton, "Nicholson Letters," 98, with a transcription infra at 358.

173   He went from renovating the manor house that Hulton visited to building an entirely new one within a decade. See the discussion (and illustrations) of both in Richard Haslam, "Beeston Hall, Norfolk," *Country Life* (February 1983), 270-274, brought to my notice by Sir Philip Preston, who gave me his copy.

undertaking and by his brother-in-law. "He attends to his affairs, repairs the houses and barns on his Estates, has quietly improved the roads in the Neighborhood, and is now busy with the improvements about his house and garden," Henry wrote to Ann approvingly. He "is really a very virtuous good Character and a Christian, which for a Man of taste, fortune and education that has made the grand tour is saying a great deal in this luxurious age."[174]

Seeing what his brother-in-law was doing at Beeston Hall most likely stirred Henry's desire to do something similar, to be a man of good fortune and refined pleasures, living at ease—but productively and responsibly—on the land. He did not have the wherewithal to be a Jacob Preston, but he could make himself an approximation of what had long been an ideal. He had already had glimpses of how it might be when he was on his farm in Brookline. Despite having to leave so much behind in Massachusetts he was hardly impoverished. Still, he had to be careful. Although he continued on as deputy receiver of funds for the Greenwich hospital tax from the colonies, the spread of war and end of royal government from the Maine country to Florida meant that there was less and less collected for him to receive. Likewise, though he kept his post and salary as a member of the American board of customs, he was paid from the proceeds of Navigation Acts and those proceeds dried up with the war. He still had other assets—cash, property—that he had before he and Elizabeth married, and whatever Elizabeth brought with her, but he would have to keep his ambitions modest.

It became clear enough to Hulton that he would not be appointed to any new office. Perhaps knowing that London held no opportunities for him reinforced his desire to spurn society there, and to retire from the government service that had defined his life to that point. The countryside, he decided, "comports more with my temper, and fortune." He had had his fill of the "worthless and vain," of "the arts and intrigues of designing men."[175] He would put aside ambition and worldly care, purifying himself on the land—a bucolic catharsis for himself and his family. "During this time we sought to make a purchase of an improvable estate in the country," Hulton explained to his sons, "and to this end made advertizements in the public papers, and in consequence had many offers of land in different parts of the country." He envisioned himself as a gentleman farmer, engaged in "a pleasing occupation" that supported its own little community. "It employs many industrious people, and what is gained thereby is a real increase to the publick stock; and no reproaches attend the individual, for what he acquires by this mode of improving his substance."[176] He and Elizabeth looked far and wide for just the right place, from Lancashire to Shropshire to

---

174   Letter of November 1776, Hulton "Letterbooks," 2:7-12; quotation from 9, transcription on 359-360 infra.
175   Letter of 25 August 1777 to Ann, ibid., 2:13, transcribed infra on 362.
176   Hulton, "Travels," 126 and 134, resp. The American version of this was the yeoman farmer, which carried with it the same tensions between ideal and real, between farming as noble experiment and commercial enterprise—for which see Drew R. McCoy, *The Elusive Republic* (Chapel Hill: University of North Carolina Press, 1980).

Somersetshire to Dorsetshire. Henry even considered Wales—until a friend warned him off: as an Englishman he might meet a cold reception there.[177] He finally settled on the village of Burcott, just a mile to the west of Wells, in Somerset. There he could rent a house from Peter Taylor, onetime deputy paymaster and old acquaintance from his commission days in Germany, and in the meantime look for something more permanent.

Henry and Elizabeth had enough time and money to make a leisurely trip out to Wells, leave instructions with workmen renovating the house, tour southern Wales, and purchase furniture in Bath and Bristol. The two older boys traveled with them to Burcott; the two younger followed some time later in the care of their maids.[178] The reunited family was not in the house long before Taylor called. Hulton and Taylor had not been all that friendly in Germany, but Hulton had kept relations civil. Taylor lived alone in apparent good health and very comfortable circumstances. He visited with Hulton at the rented house and invited all of the Hultons to his own home, where he greatly enjoyed the four boys. And yet he was soured by life, cynical about there being any meaning to it. For Hulton he became an object lesson: the price that is paid when virtue is sacrificed to vice, when the pursuit of material gain consumes all else.

> He was in perfect health, and good spirits, when we parted, and the next evening he returned from Dinner quite hearty, but suddenly expired at nine o'clock. He was a Man, bold, rude, and uncultured, but of very strong natural parts: had the talent to make himself useful to great Men. To the World he sacrificed, took advantage of extraordinary opportunities, and amassed a prodigious fortune, but with all his affairs wretched. He built a pallace, of which he had no enjoyment, for he lived without domestic consolation, the sure consequence of unprincipled attachment.[179]

Hulton did not particularly lament Taylor's passing. Hearing that his old benefactor on Antigua, Colonel Samuel Martin, had died caused considerably more sorrow. Remembering Martin took him back to another friendship from his earlier years, David Cuthbert, his fellow commissioner in Germany during the Seven Years War. Cuthbert's "spirit and fortitude were unequalled," he recalled fondly, and Martin had "shone with distinguished lustre," standing out "amidst the impurity and profligacy of the West Indies."[180] He suffered an even deeper sense of loss when Ann passed away in January 1779. He had brought her

---

177 Hulton, "Travels," 127.
178 Henry to Ann, 19 September 1777, Hulton, "Letterbooks," 2:16-18, transcription at 362-363 infra.
179 Hulton to Ann Hulton, 10 December 1777, ibid., 2:24-25, transcribed on 365-366 infra.
180 Hulton to Dr. Percival, March 1778, ibid., 2:55, transcription infra on 372-374. Cuthbert died in November 1768, Martin in March 1776. Cuthbert had left Hulton a £150 cash bequest in his will. See TNA, Prerogative Court of Canterbury [hereafter PCC] 11/943, fos. 181-182.

to Burcott to be with him some months before, when illness made it difficult for her to live on her own. "She endured a great deal for many months, but for some weeks past had been gradually declining, and seemed freer from pain than heretofore," he wrote when consoling an old family friend. To her, and to others that he told of Ann's death, he talked of hope through Christ's resurrection for them all.[181] Ann had always been devout; perhaps her faith had strengthened Henry's own. Just past fifty-two years old when she died, Ann was buried in St. Cuthbert's Church at Wells, "next to the great Seat in the Chancil."[182]

For Hulton there was also joy to balance the sorrow. "I am more settled, retired, and at my ease, than I have been for some years past,"[183] Hulton could report from Burcott. But the living situation that he had there, despite its comforts, was still not what he had had in mind. Having finally found the "large tract of improvable land" he had been seeking ever since leaving London, Hulton moved the family in September 1780. The new location that he found to play out his dream was in Hippenscombe, Wiltshire, a one thousand acre farm that he leased from the earl of Ailesbury, who owned a fair amount of property in the neighborhood.[184] After making arrangements for a tenant to reside on site at Hippenscombe, Hulton set up the family just to the east in Hampshire, at Blissmore Hall, which served as a working farm as well as a residence. This country seat in Clanville had had a succession of recent occupants, the owners preferring to rent it to others.[185] The Hultons were among those "others," retaining the Hall for three years before Henry made one last move: to neighboring Andover. He had always felt that the expense was too great at Blissmore; besides, as he grew older it was easier to be in town rather than out in the country, so he rented a house from a Mr. Pollen.[186] There he, Elizabeth, and the boys (if they were not in boarding school) lived until he died seven years later.

---

181 Quotation from a letter to Mrs. F. Hincks, 13 January 1779, Hulton, "Letterbooks," 2:62, transcribed at 382 infra. Also see Hulton's letters on the same date to Mr. Cotgreave, and Elizabeth Lightbody, Ann's longtime friend and correspondent when she lived in Massachusetts, in ibid., 2:60-61 and 64-65, resp., transcribed infra at 381-382, 383. Hulton had commented on her illness, which may have been stomach cancer, in a letter to a Mrs. Tylston, 24 August 1778, ibid., 2:85-86, transcriptions infra at 378-379.

182 Hulton, "Travels," 128. Ann's burial at St. Cuthbert's is recorded in the parish burial register, but the exact spot near the chancel, if ever marked, was lost with renovations done during the Victorian era. My thanks go to Ruth Harris, a volunteer at St. Cuthbert's, and Sheila Jenkins, the verger there, for tracing what they could of this faint trail; thanks also to John Isherwood, for putting them on it.

183 Hulton to Robert Nicholson, 27 September 1777, in Hulton, "Letterbooks," 2:19, transcription infra at 363-364.

184 Hulton to Dr. Percival, 1 September 1780, Hulton, "Letterbooks," 2:101-102, transcribed on 391 infra. Hulton dealt with a fellow named Michell who had a leasehold from the earl, rather than with the earl himself.

185 Hulton dealt with a land agent, Mr. Leversuch, rather than with the actual owner. The current owners of the house and lands, Sir Christopher and Lady Jennie Bland, kindly shared with me an informal history of the Hall. There were a number of different owners in the eighteenth century and an even larger number of occupants who rented or leased the property. At one point the house was later renamed Clanville Lodge. The Blands have chosen to take it back closer to the older name. It is now Blissamore Hall.

186 Hulton, "Travels," 129-131.

Blissamore Hall, as viewed from the edge of the ha-ha separating the house from an adjoining pasture. Known as Blissmore Hall in Hulton's era, the core of the house appears to date from the early 17th century. There have been various additions and renovations since that time, all of which have added to the Hall's charm. Photo by the author. By permission of Lady Jennie Bland.

Money worries meant that Hulton enjoyed something less than an arcadian idyll. The farm he leased at Hippenscombe did not produce enough in cash crops for him not to worry about money; Blissmore may well have cost more in rent than it generated in revenue. In Massachusetts during peak years he had earned well over £700 annually from his commissioner's salary and his cut of the Greenwich hospital tax. The £80 or so it cost him annually just to rent Blissmore Hall[187] took a sizeable bite from his much reduced income, which he feared would drop even lower. The Treasury had ruled at the end of 1776 that the commissioners continue being paid quarterly, just as when they were on duty in the colonies, and from the same source as before: revenue from the Navigation Acts. By June 1779 there was essentially nothing left in that fund and the commissioners themselves had to direct that payments from it be suspended.[188]

Hulton traveled back and forth to London—staying for several months at least, on one occasion, trying to work out something more permanent for himself and his "brother commissioners." That Lord North, head of the government, declined to give him an audience was an indication of what a political and financial liability the board had become, though no one in the ministry would be tactless enough to say so publicly. The commissioners' salaries were paid through April 1780 but "nothing was then determined as to our future provision."[189] It was just as well for Hulton and his former colleagues that the American board of customs was formally disbanded in October 1783.[190] So long as they had at least nominal employment the newly formed commission looking into loyalist claims would not consider their cases. No slight was intended. Even though "as the matter now stands no Allowance ought to be given for the present to Mr. Hulton," the claims commissioners added, as a polite touch, that he "appears to us to have done his Duty extreamly well."[191]

---

187 This figure comes from a "Survey by Farmer Winter with additions 1792, 1794, 1797 & undated survey of Weyhill," Ms. DD Ewelme d. 50, Bodleian Library, which was transcribed and sent to me by local Andover historian John Isherwood. Leversuch, who set the amounts, was apparently not above gouging renters like Hulton who came in from outside and were not familiar with the going rate or lands in the area.

188 The Treasury's ruling on 20 December 1776 is in TNA, PRO/T29/45, fo. 426. The commissioners' warning that the fund was being drained dry is in TNA, PRO/T49/48, fo. 291. Hulton expressed his frustrations about the insufficient produce of his farms, and legal problems too. "During the winter of 1783 I thrashed my Crop at Blissmore Hall, and was happy to get rid of the burden of that farm in the Spring, especially as I had a very troublesome litigious man of a Landlord to deal with, who lay upon the watch to take any advantage; and actually commenced an action against me in the King's Bench in Westminster, of which Court he was an attorney, in order to extort money from me, by dread of a Law suit; which he being an attorney cou'd carry on without expence, and I was glad to pay ten pounds extorted from me by him to get his receipt in full." Hulton, "Travels," 133.

189 No future provision in Hulton, "Travels," 132. Hulton noted North's refusal to see him, but without any bitterness, in his "Travels," 129.

190 The recommendation for formal termination is dated 16 October 1783, in TNA, PRO/T28/2, fo.185.

191 A ruling handed down 21 May 1783, in TNA, PRO/ADM80/132. The claims commissioners put the estimated value of his confiscated Brookline estate at £1294, and his personal estate at £1200.

It was the claims commissioners's understanding that Hulton and the others would be provided for somehow. It was that somehow—and when—that remained aggravatingly vague. North's successors had been more approachable but nothing was done during Rockingham's ministry, nor Shelburne's, nor the one following, a coalition pairing North with Charles James Fox. Not until 1785, under the younger Pitt's ministry, did Hulton and the other board members obtain a promise that they would receive a lifetime pension of £250 a year. "So this was the issue of my life of toil and combat in the Service of the Public," Hulton concluded—none too happily—after his years of petitioning. He ended his career as he had begun it: at the mercy of court politics.[192]

While Hulton sought his pension he also looked to the loyalist claims commission for compensation. His long spells in London, lingering about, seeking audiences, anxious for good news, took him to the commission as often as it did to the Treasury. An old friend from Massachusetts, in London to settle his own accounts, crossed Hulton's path. Though glad to see him Hulton seemed "much dejected & whines & cants like a Methodist Preacher."[193] Even a patient man would have fretted with good reason. The commission took nearly eight years to complete its work, from 1782 to 1790, reviewing claims for losses, making preliminary judgments, paying small amounts as installments until a final decision could be made.[194] Once Hulton got on the list he started receiving £50 each quarter, increased at his request to £60 by 1788.[195] He claimed £1820 all totaled in losses.[196] Initially allowed £1400, that amount was increased to £1550. He died before the final amounts could be paid. The balance went to Elizabeth—but exactly when it is difficult to say.

---

192 Hulton, "Travels," 147-153.

193 Thomas Aston Coffin to Mary Coffin, 16 September 1784. Thomas Aston Coffin Papers, Box 1, Ms. N-1005, MHS. Coffin wrote that "the Whole Board of Commissioners that were at Boston have been much neglected & I believe are most of them very poor." However, "Mr Paxton tho rather older is the same—he bows & scrapes & is the gay Man he ever was—complaining very much of his Poverty—but then those that know him say without Reason & that he has got Money."

194 For the loyalist claims commission in general (with nothing in particular on Hulton) see John Eardley-Wilmot, *Historical View of the Commission for Enquiring into the Losses, Services, and Claims, of the American Loyalists* (London: J. Nichols, 1815); and Hugh Edward Egerton, ed., *The Royal Commission on the Losses and Services of American Loyalists, 1783 to 1785* (Berkeley: University of California Press, 1915). There were over £10 million in claims filed for lost property (real and personal) and unpaid debts. Over 3200 claims were settled, with virtually no one receiving a full amount, but nearly 2300 claimants received something—Hulton among them. The Penn family was awarded just over half of its claim—£500,000, the largest by far (of £944,817 claimed).

195 Laid out in TNA, PRO/T50/31, fo. 10. The final installment was prorated at £25:6:8, because he died during the January-April 1790 quarter. With that the installment payments ended and Elizabeth presumably received the balance at some point.

196 Proceedings of the Commissioners of American Claims, in TNA, PRO/ADM12/109, fo. 164, dated 31 March 1790—after Henry had died. He had been paid £420 by installments, so the balance to his heirs stood at £1130.

The Hultons were like thousands of others who lost virtually everything that they left behind when they fled the colonies.[197] The process of confiscation began before the revolt became a revolution, when Massachusetts was still a colony in the empire with very few people—even among those leading the revolt—committed to creating a new state in an independent nation. Nevertheless, indications of what would come followed hard on the heels of the fighting at Lexington and Concord on 19 April 1775. Less than three weeks later the provincial convention resolved that all those who could not give assurances of their "good intentions and regard to the interests of this country" be disarmed. The provincial convention had already resolved, not even a week before, that the property of those who had fled to Boston or out of the colony altogether—a group that included the Hultons, of course—should have their houses watched over and furniture removed for safeguarding, if necessary.[198] The formal confiscation, condemnation, and sale of loyalist property would not come for another few years, well after the political Rubicon of declaring independence had been crossed. Property no doubt disappeared from supposed safekeeping during these years. It seems to have happened to the Hultons, so it most likely happened to others as well—but, since from the state's perspective the property was no longer theirs, claims would have to be filed by those who purchased the property at public sales.[199] When estates began to be put on the auction block in 1779 men like Henry Hulton and the other

---

197 After Henry's death Elizabeth tried for well over a decade to recover assets in Massachusetts through a lawyer that Henry had hired there, John Lowell of Boston. Before leaving they had entrusted some of their furniture to Mrs. George Inman. She indicated in her will that the furniture was theirs, but on her death it was sold anyway. The Hultons wanted the cash value for the furniture from that estate sale. They had left a bond with yet another party, from which partial payments were made to them in 1789 and 1791. Payment then stopped, even though Lowell had succeeded in getting the bond transferred to his own account. Elizabeth wanted the balance (total value of £888, of which £400 had been paid) in annual installments of £100, the arrangement to which she and Henry had agreed with the original bondholder. She did not receive satisfaction on either issue, despite trying with Lowell's son after the senior Lowell died, and even after pointing out that her son Henry was a barrister at Lincoln's Inn. See Elizabeth's three letters to the Lowells, the first undated (but before January 1792), 14 November 1800, and 20 January 1803, in bMS. Am. 1582, fos. 267-269, Houghton Library.

198 Disarming, on May 8th, safeguarding property, on May 3rd, in *The Journals of the Provincial Congress of Massachusetts in 1774 and 1775* (Boston: Dutton and Wentworth, 1838), 202 and 534, resp. That this eventually turned into a problem is evident from the Massachusetts house of representatives resolution 23 March 1776 to send a committee to Boston to track the "abandoned" property of the customs commissioners and other "*avowed Enemies of the Rights of their Country.*" The committee reported (on April 3rd) that buildings had been occupied without permission, and property had been illicitly seized or even sold by private parties. *Journals of the Massachusetts House*, 51 (part III): 37 and 75, resp.

199 A Mrs. Abigail Newell of Roxbury took furniture out of the Hulton house at Brookline. She refused to return it and does not appear to have been prosecuted for her pilfering. See David Edward Maas, *The Return of the Massachusetts Loyalists* (New York: Garland Publishing, 1989), 281.

customs board members had already been declared enemies of the state, in absentia.[200] Hulton was one of only two Brookline residents to lose his property in this fashion. Hulton's thirty-acre farm, with buildings, was sold in 1781 for $1220 in paper money, local currency.[201]

Hulton had been the political odd man out in Brookline, as were loyalists in general throughout Massachusetts. The overwhelming majority of them were native-born, not immigrants from the mother country.[202] Trying to define who they were beyond that and what they believed on the basis of those who submitted claims can be dangerous.[203] Not all who took flight filed claims; hundreds, perhaps thousands with loyalist sympathies never even left, protected by their own silence or by others who put kinship or friendship over political allegiance. Although those who held crown appointments, and more particularly posts in the customs service, were the most likely of all to "become"—or perhaps it should be "remain"—loyalists, that does not, in and of itself, make them a cohesive group.

Henry Hulton, William Burch, Benjamin Hallowell, and John Robinson all ended up in England—as did well over five thousand others from the rebellious colonies. Other than attempting to make sure that his "brother" commissioners received the pay they were due, Hulton had almost no contact with them. There were no reunions, no regular correspondence. They were not determined to maintain a shared identity based on a failed past. As Englishmen who had never severed ties with home, Hulton, Burch, and Robinson could be more easily absorbed within the culture than those who truly were coming to a strange land, a mother country

---

200 *An Act to prevent the Return to this State of certain Persons therein named, and others, who have left this State, or either of the United States, and joined the Enemies thereof* (Boston: Benjamin Edes, 1778), passed by the Massachusetts state legislature on 16 October 1778. Thomas Hutchinson headed the list, with Francis Bernard next in line. Hulton, Burch, Hallowell, and Paxton were all there too.

201 Purchased at auction by David Cook, on 12 May 1781. See Maas, *Massachusetts Loyalists*, charts on 308 and 309 resp. For the value assigned to Hulton's estate before it was put up for auction see the reports of 14 September 1779 and 26 March 1781 in TNA, PRO/AO/12/82, fos. 93 and 92, resp. Also see John T. Hassam, "Confiscated Estates of Boston Loyalists," *Massachusetts Historical Society. Proceedings* 10 (1895-1896):162-185. There were 159 "estates" sold in that fashion in Suffolk County (Boston and outlying communities, Brookline included). The house and property of William Pepperrell sold for the most (£102,000), with Thomas Hutchinson's a close second (just under £100,000).

202 Wallace Brown, *The King's Friends* (Providence: Brown University Press, 1965), noted that claimants from Boston represented only 1 in 100 of the residents there, and claimants from the rest of the colony only 1 in 1000 of the total population. Roughly 90% of the claimants were native-born. "In the last analysis," Brown concluded, "Loyalism was often a state of mind, an emotional commitment." (40) Also see Brown's less statistical, more discursive *The Good Americans: The Loyalists in the American Revolution* (New York: William Morrow and Company, 1969); and Maas, *Massachusetts Loyalists*. For individual portraits, Stark, *Loyalists of Massachusetts*, is still useful, as are Lorenzo Sabine, *Biographical Sketches of Loyalists of the American Revolution*, 2 vols. (Boston: Little, Brown and Company, 1864); and E. Alfred Jones, *The Loyalists of Massachusetts* (London: The Saint Catherine Press, 1930). All three have information on Burch, Hallowell, and Paxton as well as Hulton.

203 The most thoughtful discussion remains William Nelson, *The American Tory* (Oxford: Oxford University Press, 1961).

in name only. Transplanted loyalists did not comprise, or even seek to form, a distinctive subculture.[204] Most were drawn to London at one point or another. They more or less disappeared into the larger urban scene. Some made an effort to keep their plight in the public eye; others did not, nor were they encouraged to by Whitehall or Westminster.[205]

Hulton did not assiduously trace the progress of the fighting, hoping that a British success here, an American reversal there, would mean that he might be able to go back to Massachusetts or to some other outpost of empire. He put all of that behind him when he left London, in a conscious effort to withdraw from public life. There is in his surviving letters a determination to rise above the pettiness of the world, to develop a broader perspective, looking beyond the expansion of empires and rise of nations.[206]

> We are here in peace and retirement, and know little of what passes in the World, and happy for Us in these distracted times, that We are somewhat removed from the fury of the storm. Alas! The prospect is gloomy, and I fear the issue of these publick calamities. Who would have imagined the progress of this rebellion, and present state of affairs? Rapid are the advances of Commercial nations towards their Summit of glory, but short is the duration of their Splendour. The internal corruption that great commerce produces, would soon urge a Nation to its decline, without the ingratitude of its Colonies. But there is an hand unseen that directs the whole; and it is no wonder that He should make wicked nations the instruments of each other's punishments.[207]

---

204 Thomas Hutchinson did stay in contact with Charles Paxton, "who seemed much affected with the thought of being buried in London...he would give 100 guineas to be laid by his father and mother under the Chapel in Boston." Peter Orlando Hutchinson, ed., *The Diary and Letters of His Excellency Thomas Hutchinson, Esq.*, 2 vols. (London: Sampson, Low, Marston, Searle, & Rivington, 1883, 1886), 2:240-241. He also stayed in touch with Burch, who he had in fact suggested as a successor to his deceased lieutenant governor, Andrew Oliver. He had thought his exile would be temporary; it was not. See Hutchinson to Dartmouth, 29 March and 4 April 1774, in TNA, PRO/CO 5/769, fos 71-73 and 74-75, resp.

205 Mary Beth Norton, *The British-Americans* (Boston: Little, Brown and Company, 1972) tracked 1440 heads of families who left the colonies for England, noting, at least in London, the clustering of some groups in some neighborhoods. Adapting to their new circumstances was taxing—"an intensely disillusioning experience" for all too many (42).

206 Although he did have enough interest in American affairs to be among the subscribers to William Gordon's *The History of the Rise, Progress, and Establishment of the United States of America*, 4 vols. (London: Charles Dilly, 1788), from the list at the beginning of volume 1. Curious about American society and increasingly sympathetic to colonial protests against imperial policy, Gordon had left England for Massachusetts and secured a pulpit at Roxbury in 1772—in a local congregational church, not an Anglican parish. Hulton heard him preach there and was favorably impressed—see Ann Hulton's undated letter, ca. 1771, transcribed infra, at 255-259. Gordon returned to England in 1786, after gathering a cache of documents and interviewing leading Revolutionaries for his history.

207 In a letter from Henry to Ann, March 1778, Hulton, "Letterbooks," 2:30, transcribed on 366-367, infra, with some changes to capitalization, and the apostrophe added. He expressed similar sentiments in other letters: to

Hulton instead immersed himself in household affairs, taking particular pleasure in the upbringing of his sons. There were now five: Elizabeth delivered George in September 1778, when the family lived in Burcott. Young George's Aunt Ann and Uncle Jacob, Elizabeth's brother, were there the next month for the christening.[208] The older boys had been placed as boarding students with their tutor in Wells, close enough for them to go home on frequent visits. "The Boys come over once a fortnight, and it is a great delight to hear their little tales, to see the big Joy sparkling in their Countenances" when they talked about what they were learning.[209] The proximity of that tutor had been one of the primary reasons Hulton chose Burcott for a time. He continued to search for good schools or tutors once they moved to Blissmore Hall, with the boys going out to Bath and Blandford and Andover—wherever their father thought they would be well taught. While in Burcott he compiled "sketches," with copies for each boy made later at Blissmore, that he hoped would act as a guide for them. He offered them aphorisms on truth and virtue, on reason and faith; he posed questions about the purpose of life and the nature of happiness, then offered his own brief views; he even composed prayers that they could use for their personal worship.[210] He wanted them to become accomplished young gentlemen, independent enough to find their way in the world, sociable enough to see that they could not make it on their own. He certainly did not want them to think that he was a self-made man. "I have been comforted and supported by your dear Mother" in all that had been accomplished, he stressed.[211]

Elizabeth was at Henry's side to the end. He died in February 1790, a few months shy of his sixtieth birthday, when their oldest son, Thomas, was in his early twenties and youngest, George, was not yet in his teens. She continued alone what she and Henry had started together, keeping a comfortable home and seeing her boys on to manhood. Henry made

Charles Dudley, 25 March 1778, ibid., 2:39-46; to William Pepperrell, 28 March 1778, ibid., 2:36-38; and to Thomas Cotgreave, 15 April 1778, ibid. 2:57, transcription at 368-372 and 376-377 infra. Also see Hulton's attempts to console Cotgreave upon the death of a loved one, in a letter of 18 March 1780, ibid., 2:97-98, with a transcription infra at 389-390. He emphasized the joy of the separated in life being reunited beyond the grave.

208 Noted in Hulton, "Travels," 162.

209 Hulton to Dr. Percival, March 1778, in Hulton, "Letterbooks," 2:48, transcribed on 372-374 infra.

210 "Sketches. With a view to fix right Principles in the minds of Children, and lead them to Just Sentiments, and a virtuous Conduct." Manuscript copy in the Norfolk Record Office, MC 36/139, 481X1, portions of which are transcribed on 417-427 infra. As Hulton explained to Elizabeth Lightbody, his sister Ann's long-time friend, "I have a desire that my Children should reap some advantage from my having lived; that they should be distinguished by liberal endowments, and virtuous improvements; and would flatter myself that if in future life they find advantages from the benefits of a right cultivation, they may reflect with pleasure that they owed something to the example, and precepts of their father," Letter of 8 September 1778, Hulton, "Letterbooks," 2:91-92, transcribed infra at 380-381.

211 Hulton, "Travels," 151.

St. Mary's Church in Andover, Hampshire, from the southeast corner. It stands as a splendid example of the once-popular Victorian Gothic style and is well-maintained, with an active congregation. When Hulton was interred another St. Mary's stood on the spot. The inscribed stone slab covering Hulton's burial vault then formed part of the chancel floor. When the new St. Mary's was built in the 1840s with a floor at a higher elevation, the old floor was turned into a crypt as part of the foundation, separated from the new floor by a low ceiling. Photo by the author.

her the "sole executrix" of his will.[212] Her brother Jacob also gave her a role to play in the disposition of his estate, which would pass to her son Thomas on the condition that he add the name Preston to Hulton. These terms had been agreed to many years before, when the Hultons were in Massachusetts and Thomas was just a boy. Jacob Preston had no sons and wanted the estate—which he had inherited from his father—to be kept intact, passed down through male heirs in the family.[213] He died in 1787. Thomas did not take on the Preston family name until his mother died in 1805, aged sixty-six. Until then she and her sisters Jane and Alice took responsibility for keeping the estate solvent. Ten years later Thomas was made a baronet and presided over Beeston Hall as Sir Thomas Hulton Preston until he died in 1823.[214]

Thomas had done well for himself, aided by parents and an uncle who combined a concern for his future with a desire to preserve family wealth and station. He and Edward enrolled at Caius College, Cambridge—two university men, whose father had never had such an opportunity. Thomas entered Caius in 1787, in time for his father to enjoy the moment; Edward was admitted just a week after his father's death. Unlike Thomas, who left before

---

212 TNA, PCC 11/1190, fo. 186, dated 4 September 1789, with a codicil added 7 February 1790, just five days before he died. This will is at the TNA, but also available online now through the National Archives website, as are all of the other wills noted below. And Hulton's last message to his sons, as expressed here? "I have only to wish they may continue by their good Conduct to deserve the affection of their surviving parent and the blessings of heaven." Henry left Elizabeth stocks and cash (the amounts not enumerated), £750 in bank drafts, a house in Chester being rented to three doctors, the leasehold at Hippenscombe, furniture, and personal effects—essentially everything. She could dispose of any of it as she saw fit, even should she marry again, so long as "she made provision for their children." Brief notices of Henry's passing appeared in the *Gentleman's Magazine* 60 (February 1790):185, and *The European Magazine, and London Review* (February 1790):160. Mrs. G. M. Turner, of the Hampshire Record Office, kindly ran down the entry in St. Mary's register for Henry's burial (17 February 1790).

213 Jacob Preston's will is in TNA, PCC 11/1207, fos. 193-203, dated 28 May 1774, with a codicil added 8 March 1786. Preston had named Henry Hulton and Whitley Heald, his brothers-in-law, as executors to the original will (despite Hulton's being in Massachusetts), along with his wife, Mary. It was a considerably larger estate than Henry's. Elizabeth Hulton's will is in TNA, PCC 11/1140, fos. 69-73, dated 30 May 1790, with two codicils (in 1799 and 1804). The will was not proved until 28 August 1805, though she had died on April 16th of that year. She was generous to all of her sons and to her servants in her bequests as well.

214 His will is in TNA, PCC 11/1672, fos. 183-187, drawn up 12 February 1823, opening with language that no doubt would have pleased his father: "I commit my Soul to the God of all mankind in the hope of a joyful resurrection through the merits of my blessed Saviour Jesus Christ." The royal license authorizing Thomas Hulton to add the surname Preston was issued 22 May 1805 (from a photocopy of the warrant itself, kindly provided by Sir Philip Preston). There are at the Norfolk Record Office various examples of agreements between the Prestons and tenants on the family estate. I even found (and purchased) one through the online auction house, eBay, dated 11 October 1803, where the sisters rented 117 acres, "more or less," at the Beeston Park Farm to Mary and John Cubitt. The annual rent was paid mostly in kind (117 bushels of wheat, 234 bushels of barley). Alice Preston Heald's will is in TNA, PCC 11/1467, fos. 187-193. Alice died in 1807. Jane Preston's will is in TNA, PCC 11/1756, fos. 60-63. She died in 1829, without marrying. Her grand-nephew (the grandson of Henry Hulton), Henry George Hulton of Lincoln's Inn, was one of the witnesses to the will. The family eventually sold Beeston Hall and the lands around it.

taking a degree—expected behavior of someone destined for the landed gentry—Edward earned a bachelor's and master's before beginning a long and distinguished career as a member of the Anglican clergy.[215] Edward's son Thomas would also matriculate at Caius, and that after having attended Eton. Thomas and Edward's brother Henry, the first of the Hulton boys to be born in Massachusetts, had been sent to Norwich when he was in his mid-teens to learn the law with a local solicitor. He became a barrister, with chambers in Lincoln's Inn. His son, Henry George Hulton, followed his footsteps into the law and Lincoln's Inn. His younger brothers, Preston and George, had become officers in the king's dragoons.[216]

Henry Hulton would have been proud that he had sons who entered honorable professions, that they stayed close to their mother, and that they in turn had children who made their mark in the world. He would have been pleased that Hultons and Prestons formed family ties that would last many years, with Hultons who made their way to Norfolk and Prestons who moved to Hampshire. And he would have been touched to know that when his son Henry lost a child in infancy, Henry chose to have that child buried with his grandparents. The three were placed together in a vault at St. Mary's Church, Andover, where they remain to this day.[217]

Imperial Reformer

Had Henry Hulton not become an agent of empire his thoughts would most likely have never turned to imperial reform. His interests had lain elsewhere—until he left England. His insularity until that point was typical of Britons during his age and not so different from Americans of a later generation who cannot be bothered to know

---

215 See the entries for Thomas and Edward Hulton in J. A. Venn, *Alumni Cantabrigienses*, 10 vols. (Cambridge: Cambridge University Press, 1922-1954), Part II, 3:483 and 484, resp. Edward Hulton's will is in TNA, PCC 11/2010, fo. 146, written on 28 November 1816. Cambridge also awarded him the LL.D., in 1815.

216 Henry Hulton's will, dated 19 May 1820, is in TNA, PCC 11/1629, fos. 295-298. The will of his son, Henry George Hulton, from 9 January 1845, is in TNA, PCC 11/2010, fos. 353-354. Sarah Lawrence, *The Descendants of Philip Henry, M.A.* (London: Simpkin, Marshall, and Co., 1844) includes (on 53-55) genealogical information for Anne Henry, daughter of Philip Henry, who had married Henry Hulton's grandfather, John, information that is carried through Henry and Elizabeth Hulton, and their five sons. According to this source, Preston Hulton, who became a cavalry officer, married but had no children, and George, also a cavalry officer, did not marry. The genealogical chart preserved among the Bennett materials in the Cheshire Record Office (see supra 26 n. 4) lists Preston as a captain in the 21st Light Dragoons and George as a captain in the 1st Royal Dragoons, with George dying in Spain in 1814.

217 For the inscription, transcription on 430 infra. The stone slab that covers the vault was once part of the floor in the nave of St. Mary's. When the church was rebuilt in the 1840s a new floor was built above the old and the vault cover is now part of the floor to the crypt. There is also a plaque to Henry and Elizabeth Hulton's memory in the west entrance to St. Mary's, which is pictured in the guide to *St. Mary's Church Andover* (Andover, England: Hearn & Scott, 2005), 14, and supra, 24. The five sons paid for the plaque, stating on it that they "survive to lament the Loss of their much respected Parents."

much of the wider world. He contemplated the empire's internal workings because he had been caught up in them. That his thoughts grew out of his experience in no sense diminishes their importance. True enough, he expressed no profound ideas, he offered no unique insights. Indeed, he sounded very much like other reform-minded Britons—more prominent then, better remembered now—when he discussed the problems of empire. But appreciating what he had to say does not require any specious claim for originality; rather, the fact that so much of what he said echoed others is a reminder that the empire did not crumble because no one had ever imagined that it could. On the contrary; anticipating that very outcome drove most of the policies whose failures Hulton witnessed firsthand, sometimes as participant, other times as observer.

He knew that he had stepped into a difficult situation when he set forth to Boston. The "Account" that he wrote after returning to England was obviously tinged by hindsight as well as experience. Nonetheless, most of the opinions that he expressed there, after the fact, had already been formed when he was still in Massachusetts. Even before leaving England, as plantations clerk he had well understood the unpopularity of the Stamp Act and the dangerously mixed message sent by its repeal. When taking his post as a customs commissioner he knew that the American board was joined inseparably with the Town shend duties—in real terms, as new tax legislation was tied to stricter enforcement, and in symbolic terms among those colonists looking for proof of a plot hatched in London to subvert their rights. The escalation of antipathy, as demonstrated in the *Liberty* affair, led to soldiers being garrisoned among civilians and dire warnings from George III that the empire teetered on the edge of catastrophe, something the king had not done in the Stamp Act crisis. Opening a new session of Parliament in November 1768 he contrasted imperial affairs at that moment with how they had stood at the close of the previous session. Then the colonies were showing a "just sense of their Duty"; now, by contrast the "Spirit of Faction" had taken hold again. Boston especially appeared "to be in a State of Disobedience to all Law and Government." Town leaders had "proceeded to Measures subversive of the Constitution" that "manifest a Disposition to throw off their Dependence on *Great Britain*."[218]

This was the frightening prospect looming before Henry Hulton of Brookline, Massachusetts, royal commissioner of the customs, because if disaster did happen he would in some sense have to account for it and, rightly or not, possibly even accept responsibility for it. There was a fatalistic side to him that considered a break inevitable, that concluded

---

218 J. Wright, ed., *Sir Henry Cavendish's Debates of the House of Commons, during the Thirteenth Parliament of Great Britain*. 2 vols. (London: Longman & Co., 1841, 1842), 1:31, speech from the throne of 8 November 1768. George III—or, more correctly, the advisers who drafted his speech—missed the mark here. There had been no dramatic shift in attitudes or behavior between June and November 1768. Those wanting to "throw off" dependence were seeking some sort of governmental autonomy within the empire, not complete political independence from it.

there was nothing he or anyone else could do to prevent it. And yet he could not allow himself to slip into historical determinism, to think that social courses are irreversible—that, where one policy failed, no other could succeed. We can see his uneasy juxtaposition of future as fixed and future as malleable in a letter that he wrote in 1772, when, for the moment, crisis had passed.

> The people in this Country I believe are more at their ease than the peasantry in any other. They are the proprietors of the soil they cultivate; they know no subjection to great Lords; and enjoy the benefits of protection from a Government whose authority they are always disputing. Independency was the principle the first settlers set out upon, when they quitted England to cultivate the wilds of America: and the same spirit is continued in their descendants. And from the immense Country that remains to be cleared, and settled, and the mildness of the British Government, it is probable they will be several ages before they are brought into that state of order, and subordination that prevails in European nations.[219]

Hulton seems in this passage to have started as Crèvecoeur on the American character and turned into Tocqueville on the American future before reverting into a Grenvillesque defender of the British empire. He blamed the colonists for being too stubbornly provincial. But then he conceded that the mother country had contributed to their delinquency by being too permissive. The basic problem was not their obstreperous behavior; rather, it was the state of mind behind it. They had been allowed to turn what were intended to be privileges into rights—mistaken notions that needed to be corrected. For Henry Hulton, social psychologist as social engineer, the first priority had to be to change minds and hearts; proper actions could only flow from proper thoughts. Thus his advice to Townshend before being named to the customs board that no new duties be introduced until it was proved that the old duties could be collected. "The authority of Government should be well established, before it is proposed to raise a Revenue from any people."[220] The navigation laws had gone unenforced for so long that colonists resented any attempt to enforce them. Demagogues from among them could easily play on their fears, stirring the disloyal to assert themselves violently while the loyal shrank back in terror. The "common sort," once they became aware of their political power, no longer deferred to their social betters.

---

219 Hulton to de Ruling, May 1772, Hulton, "Letterbooks," 1:49-50, transcription on 268-269 infra, with some changes to punctuation and capitalization..

220 He claimed that he offered this advice to Townshend in 1767, before being named to the commission—not just in his "Account," written when he was safely back in England. See his letter when he was still in the thick of it in Boston: see 21 April 1772, addressee unknown, in Hulton, "Letterbooks," 1:42-48, transcribed infra at 266-268.

Paradoxically, they questioned the elites's every move, even their very motives, and yet they were easily duped by the new leaders they chose to replace them.

Even though Hulton had his doubts about the colonial social compact, he made the political contract his starting point for change. "The form of Government in this Country is too much of the Democratic to allow proper vigor to the executive branch," Hulton declared after having lived in Massachusetts for the better part of a year.[221] "No nation will retain distant Colonies long in subjection, the Government of which is established upon a popular plan."[222] Not only that; the colonies enjoyed too much governmental autonomy, allowing them to act with virtual political impunity. The independent tendencies that their ancestors carried with them in founding the colonies had gotten stronger, not weaker, over time. Obsession with commerce had blinded imperial policymakers to the colonial reality: these were not just simple plantations, mere economic enterprises; they were full-fledged societies. But "the Question has been how shall we extend our commerce," not how shall these societies be shepherded along, Hulton chided. There had not been a clear, consistent policy—a true master plan. "This minister had one plan, the next another, no general Parliamentary and national conduct has been fixed on to be abided by, so that Government has by a change of measures been let down, and the respect to its authority has been very much lessened."[223] Ministries rose and fell and when they fell, so did the policies they championed. So went the troubled course of colonial history, as Henry Hulton interpreted it

The notion of a plan—of *the* plan—was alluring, at least in the abstract. "One steady plan pursued a little while would convince the people that the nation would not give up its authority," claimed Thomas Hutchinson.[224] Hutchinson did not explain what that plan ought to be. Francis Bernard did and Hulton found his explanation convincing. In the aftermath of Lexington and Concord, Hulton lamented that "had the plan laid by Sir Francis Bernard been carried into execution, it is probable all would have been quiet here long ago, but by delay, and expedients, these Colonies are near lost to G[reat] B[ritain]."[225]

In letters back to England, Bernard had started pushing for structural reform soon after taking his post as governor of Massachusetts. He considered all of the existing forms

---

221 Hulton to de Ruling, 23 August 1768, ibid., 1:3, transcription infra on 223-224.

222 Hulton to Edward ____, 5 February 1770, ibid., 1:9, transcribed at 228-231 infra.

223 Letter of 21 April 1772, unknown addressee, Hulton, "Letterbooks," 1:43, transcription on 266-268 infra.

224 Letter of 26 May 1768, apparently never sent, in the Hutchinson Letterbooks, Mass. Archives XXVI:307, from the MHS typescript, 639. Hutchinson found a sympathetic ear with Hulton—as he found a sympathetic reader, Hulton having read the first volume of Hutchinson's *History*. Still, they did not agree on all things. Hulton would have hope for the Massachusetts Government Act in 1774; Hutchinson would not.

225 Hulton to Samuel ____, 21 May 1775, Hulton, "Letterbooks," 1:129, transcribed at 322-323 infra. Dennys De Berdt, when agent for the Massachusetts House, had thought that Bernard was a "Tool" of Hillsborough, whose ideas would only further the earl's "oppressive measures." See De Berdt to House Speaker Thomas Cushing, 1 June 1769, in Albert Matthews, ed., "Letters of Dennys De Berdt, 1757-1770," *Publications of the Colonial Society of Massachusetts* 13 (1912):375.

flawed, whether they be in proprietary colonies like Maryland and Pennsylvania, colonies like Rhode Island and Connecticut that were all but self-governing, or others—the majority, actually—that were in some sense "royal" because governors and other key officials were crown appointees. Massachusetts was the logical starting point; changes made there first could then be extended elsewhere.[226] Bernard became more emphatic with the Stamp Act crisis. "The Question will not be whether there shall be a Stamp Act or not," he warned, "but whether America shall or shall not be Subject to the Legislature of Great Britain."[227] Like Hulton he would contend that fundamental reform should have come before controversial parliamentary legislation: hence the political disaster produced by the Stamp Act. Bernard thought the perfect moment to instruct the colonists on the mother country's sovereignty and parliament's supremacy had been in the 1640s, when parliament ruled England without a king. He was not by that observation advocating a return to the Interregnum; rather, he wanted to underscore how political disputes in the mother country, coupled with inconsistent policies in the colonies, confused matters on the most fundamental level, so that the proper constitutional—constitutional, not simply political—relationship between mother country and colonies had never been fully articulated much less consistently applied. "It is my opinion that all the Political Evils in America arise from the Want of ascertaining the Relation between Great Britain & the American Colonies," he wrote in the midst of the Stamp Act crisis, and "hence it is that Ideas of that Relation are formed in Britain and America, so very repugnant & contradictory to each other."[228] He called on crown and parliament to speak with a single voice and then devise a coherent policy.

In the case of Massachusetts he contended that at the very least the governor's council ought to be appointed by the crown rather than selected by the members of the lower house of the assembly, as stipulated in the 1691 charter. He also contended that local leaders ought to be brought under more effective control.[229] His most visible target was the Boston town meeting; his ultimate target was the democratic excess that he believed had created a social as well as political imbalance in all of the colonies, not just Massachusetts. Henry Hulton was not alone in sharing Bernard's desire to make colonial government less "democratical"; so did many others who ended up alienated from colonial society and living in

---

226 Bernard to Barrington, 15 December 1761, in Channing and Coolidge, eds. *Barrington-Bernard Correspondence*, 43-44. A more complete compilation of Bernard's writings is being edited by Colin Nicolson as *The Papers of Francis Bernard*, 3 vols. (Boston: The Colonial Society of Massachusetts, 2007—). This particular letter is in 1:166-68. Also see Bernard's letter to Charles Townshend of 18 May 1763 (ibid., 1:360), where Bernard commented that Massachusetts "alone affords an ample field for such disquisitions [on imperial reform]; but they are too delicate for any but private letters."

227 Bernard to Barrington, 23 November 1765, ibid., 95-99, quotation from 96; original in the Bernard Papers, 5:47-55; quotation from 50.

228 Ibid.

229 As a case in point see Bernard's letter to Lawrence Monk, 23 December 1768, Bernard Papers, 7:239-249.

England as political refugees.[230] Bernard finally went public with his most essential ideas in 1774, at the same moment that Parliament began debating the legislation that irate colonists would label the "Coercive Acts." Coincidentally or not, elements of the Massachusetts Government Act echoed Bernard.[231]

Lest Bernard be dismissed as a venomous hardliner, it should be pointed out that he coupled a tightening of government with a loosening of the navigation system. Attempts to squeeze foreign trade out altogether were as foolish as they were impossible, he emphasized. Lemons and wine were smuggled in constantly from Portugal, laws to the contrary notwithstanding. Everyone knew it, no one tried to stop it, so change the trade laws that excluded them. He faulted Parliament for listening too long to an over-influential West Indies lobby, in 1733 with the Molasses Act, and again in 1764 with the new Sugar Act. More attention needed to be paid to North America, whose products were increasing at a rapid rate. Parliament would be wiser to encourage American economic enterprise rather than restrict it, passing legislation better attuned to an empire with ever-expanding markets.[232]

Even so, Bernard should not be given too much credit. He was hardly a visionary who saw farther or looked deeper. In a fit of pique during the Stamp Act crisis he wrote confidants that Americans ought to be given some seats in Parliament to silence their protests about taxation without representation. But then he concluded that thirty seats "should be sufficient" for the North American mainland colonies and fifteen for the West Indies— all in the House of Commons, none in the House of Lords. "Take them at their Words let

---

230 George Chalmers, a native Scot who made a career for himself as a lawyer in Maryland and then left in the loyalist exodus, stands as a good example. See his *Political Annals of the Present United Colonies from their Settlement to the Peace of 1763* (London: J. Bowen, 1780), and his more sardonic, embittered *An Introduction to the History of the Revolt of the Colonies*, 2 vols. (London: Baker and Galabin, 1782 for vol. 1; Boston, 1845, for vol. 2), which he recognized had too hard an edge (given his office-seeking), so he withdrew it before the second volume was released. Grace Amelia Cockcroft discusses both books in *The Public Life of George Chalmers* (New York: Columbia University Press, 1939); Lawrence Henry Gipson reviews the first book, John A. Schutz the second, in Leder, ed., *Colonial Legacy*, 13-36 and 36-58, resp. Peter C. Messer, *Stories of Independence* (DeKalb, Il.: Northern Illinois Press, 2005), 45-69, also has insights on Chalmers. John Schutz, along with Douglass Adair, edited *Peter Oliver's Origin & Progress of the American Rebellion* (San Marino, Calif.: The Huntington Library, 1961). Oliver was in places even more biting and bitter than Chalmers. He barely mentioned the customs board and did not talk about Hulton at all, despite their knowing each other in Boston. Janice Potter, *The Liberty We Seek* (Cambridge, Mass.: Harvard University Press, 1983) discusses loyalist fears that a delusive search for equality would only bring anarchy (though with no mention of Chalmers or Hulton).

231 Bernard's *Select Letters on the Trade and Government of America* (London: W. Bowyer and J. Nichols, 1774) were published on 15 February 1774, just as the debates leading to the Massachusetts Government Act were getting underway. See Pickering, ed., *Statutes at Large*, 24 George III c. 40 for the act itself. For Bernard as reformer see Nicolson, "*Infamas Govener,*" 82-108; Aeilt E. Sents, "Francis Bernard and English Imperial Reconstruction" (Ph.D. dissertation, University of Missouri, 1973); and Richard Koebner, *Empire* (Cambridge: Cambridge University Press, 1961), 130-149.

232 See, for example, Bernard to the Earl of __, 25 October 1763, in Bernard's *Select Letters*, 1-4.

them send Representatives for the present Time & for the present Purposes."[233] In effect, what he meant was: call their bluff. Once their pleas for representation were shown to be disingenuous, those seats could be taken away.

Bernard was almost cavalier in his disregard for American arguments; he was utterly unrealistic if he thought his plan could have worked. He would in fact abandon it eventually, *not*, he wrote defensively, because it had been inherently unworkable, but because the moment had passed.[234] That he had once held up Ireland as a successful case of putting to rest disputes over representation and legislative supremacy in the empire proves that he did not have a good grasp of the issues involved. Ireland's place in the empire could be every bit as confused—and politics there every bit as contentious—as in the American colonies.[235]

There would be many desperate plans to stave off military confrontation through political tinkering, whether it be by granting the colonists more autonomy through their own legislatures, giving them seats in Parliament, or creating something in-between. None had much appeal on either side of the Atlantic.[236] If they had little chance of success when transatlantic relations were cool and calm, they had no chance at all when political disputes heated the air. Bernard's ideas did nothing to stave off revolution; nor would have Henry Hulton's, had Hulton made them public. As advocates of imperial reform, perhaps Hulton, Bernard, and the rest were at war with themselves, their preferences locked in combat with their logic. Not surprisingly, there had been Revolutionary Americans who argued that independence was inevitable; so had members of Parliament who objected to punitive policies supposedly designed to keep the empire whole. They were joined by at least one loyalist, Daniel Leonard, who for all his arguments defending the empire, sighed

> After many more centuries shall have rolled away, long after we who are
> now bustling upon the stage of life, shall have been received to the bosom
> of mother earth, and our names are forgotten, the colonies may be so far
> increased as to have the balance of wealth, numbers and power in their

---

233 Bernard to Barrington, 23 November 1765, Bernard Papers, 5:51; printed in Channing and Coolidge, eds., *Barrington-Bernard Correspondence*, 93-102. He thought it prescient enough to include in his *Select Letters*, 29-37.

234 Bernard, *Select Letters*, v. As he put it, "we must admit the Execution of it would probably be attended with great difficulties, if its theory should be approved; and therefore it may be considered only as a pleasing reverie." Bernard attached his "Principles of Law and Polity," a sort of imperial syllogism extended through ninety-seven points to lay out his "plan" for imperial reform (71-85). There is a variation on it in Add. Ms. 38342 (Liverpool Papers, special papers, 1773-1777) BL.

235 For which see my *Neither Kingdom Nor Nation: The Irish Quest for Constitutional Rights, 1698-1800* (Washington, D.C.: Catholic University of America Press, 1994).

236 See my two essays: "Federalism and the Failure of Imperial Reform," *History* 86 (2001):155-179; and "Thomas Crowley and Americans in Parliament, 1765-1775" *Quaker History* 91 (2002):1-19.

favour, the good of the empire make it necessary to fix the seat of government here; and some future GEORGE, equally the friend of mankind with him that now sways the British sceptre, may cross the Atlantic, and rule Great-Britain by an American parliament.[237]

Leonard accepted reluctantly what his revolutionary adversaries embraced enthusiastically. Henry Hulton could not do either. He had looked beyond the constitutional issues and the political disputes, searching for the social core. In finding it—if he did in fact find it—he also found how hard it would be to alter. Americans had, he feared, opened the Pandora's box of democratic politics. For him republicanism could too easily devolve into mindless egalitarianism, where resentment against being kept in one's place might lead inadvertently to a society where no one had a sense of belonging—where people were more alone, more powerless than ever before, all in the name of equality. His ambivalence about such a society unfolding in the future would be shared by Tocqueville in a later generation; it would even be shared by some of his erstwhile opponents among the Revolutionary generation, once they had founded their new nation.[238]

---

237 From Leonard's 5ᵗʰ "Massachusettensis" essay, 9 January 1775, reprinted in Bernard Mason, ed., *The American Colonial Crisis* (New York: Harper & Row, 1972), 37. "All colonies have their date of independence," proclaimed Isaac Barré during debates in the House of Commons on 3 February 1766. "The wisdom or folly of our conduct may make it sooner or later. If we act judiciously, this point may be reached in the life of many of the members of this House." Simmons and Thomas, eds., *Proceedings and Debates*, 2:144.

238 "Men were always only half aware of where their thought was going," wrote Gordon S. Wood in *The Creation of the American Republic, 1776-1787* (Chapel Hill: University of North Carolina Press, 1969), 389, about the Revolutionary generation's experiment with republicanism, a theme he developed more fully in his *Radicalism of the American Revolution*. Also see Edmund S. Morgan, *Inventing the People* (New York: W. W. Norton, 1987); and Terry Bouton, *Taming Democracy* (Oxford: Oxford University Press, 2007).

Henry Hulton's
Writings

H ENRY HULTON WROTE A FAIR AMOUNT—official reports, private letters, journals, reminiscences, personal essays, and poems—but most of what survives is not
in his hand. Many of the reports that he authored when he was a customs commissioner were put into their final form by clerks. When Hulton returned to England and began
collecting his letters and collating them with other writings, he employed scribes, at least
in one case to produce multiple copies.[1] The two letterbooks that he left were prepared, in
part, by copyists from originals that have not been located. Consequently there is no way
of knowing how complete that collection is, nor can we know which letters were copied in
their entirety and which only in segments.[2] Even Hulton's "Account" appears to have been
revised over time, and written by a number of hands.[3]

Short of subjecting all of the documents to the intense methods used to enhance ancient
texts, I cannot be sure that what is still visible on the page is all that was ever there. There
are even questions about what is still visible. Is what appears to be a comma actually a
period? Or is what appears to be a comma simply a point where the pen dragged? Moreover, was an individual letter written in lower case, but larger than others nearby in lower
case, capitalized in the writer's mind—or not? I cannot profess to know. Even so, I have
not presumed to make changes beyond the obvious and ultimately—I think—minor. I have

---

1   This is the case with his letters to Robert Nicholson between 1760-1776, one set of which is the John Rylands
University Library, University of Manchester, the other at Harris Manchester College, Oxford University.
Neither would appear to be in Hulton's hand. Nor are they identical, but, unless the originals are ever found,
it is impossible to know how the copyists altered them. The Norfolk County Record Office has one copy of
the "Principles" (see 418 n. 1 infra) that Hulton composed for his sons and it too does not appear to be from
his pen. It was made from the original in the possession of Hulton descendant Sir Philip Preston. The other
four copies—one having been written for each of the five boys—have yet to turn up.

2   These are the two volumes at the Houghton Library, Harvard University. Hints that the letterbooks were
highly selective, both in the letters they included and, among those they included, which portions, can be
found in Hulton's letters to Thomas Percival of March 1778 and Elizabeth Lightbody of 13 January 1779, at
372-374 and 383 infra, resp.

3   And since it too seems to have been composed as a type of summary, with Hulton consulting letters and
journals as he went, the difficulties of determining when true originals were used only multiply.

filled in words with missing letters, such as expanding "wch" to "which" and "threatned" to "threatened," and other words where Hulton (or his copyists) shortened a suffix, as in writing only the "g" of an "ing." I also inserted apostrophes where called for in the possessive case, which Hulton almost never did. By contrast, Hulton often used an apostrophe as a type of shorthand, such as "cou'd" instead of "could"; likewise for should and would. I produced the words in full, so that readers would not get the mistaken impression that Hulton was unusually informal in his habits and casual in his language. For the same reason I substituted "and" whenever Hulton (or, again, his copyists) used "&," and I put periods after most of his abbreviations (such as with "Mr."), which he did rarely.

I made these and a few other changes—including commas or semicolons or periods, inserted here or deleted there—silently, for fear that long lines of brackets and a parade of footnotes would prove too distracting.[4] I do not want readers stumbling where Hulton assumed they could pass through quickly. The only name whose spelling I changed was "Barnard" to Bernard, which a copyist—or perhaps even Hulton himself, misremembering—might occasionally offer as a phonetic rendering of the onetime governor's last name. Other names, even if misspelled—such as "Guadalupe" for the West Indies island of Guadeloupe—I kept as they were. I left other nouns that appeared to be capitalized in that form, as was the eighteenth-century convention. Hulton dated his correspondence in a variety of ways and not always in the same place. I moved all of the dates to the top, organized chronologically and identified by day, month, and year, when known.

Other than that, and what I have already enumerated, I changed very little. I did not add words (unless so indicated by brackets) or bowdlerize to improve Hulton's prose. The words as well as the ideas are Hulton's, not mine. Hulton's poetry I left untouched, on the assumption that his contractions, ampersands, and punctuation had a more deliberate literary purpose than in his prose.

Included here are Hulton's "Account" of the American rebellion, all of the letters from Hulton's two-volume letterbook, twenty-one letters to Hulton's friend Robert Nicholson that came from a different source, a couple of letters from yet another source, and many of the essays that Hulton wrote later for his sons when he was retired, which he seems to have begun at Burcott, continued at Blissmore Hall, and worked on even after he moved to Andover.[5] I put the page numbers to Hulton's "Account" in brackets; I deleted them from

---

4 I am thinking here of two very fine books, whose purposes differ somewhat from mine: J. A. Leo Lemay and
    P. M. Zall, eds., *The Autobiography of Benjamin Franklin: A Genetic Text* (Knoxville: University of Tennessee
    Press, 1981), with its heavily bracketed material; and Verner W. Crane, ed., *Benjamin Franklin's Letters to the
    Press, 1758-1775* (Chapel Hill: University of North Carolina Press, 1950), with its many footnotes.
5 Not only from the "Principles" (see supra 101 n. 1), but from the "Sketches" at the William L. Clements Library
    mss., University of Michigan.

his other writings. I included too most of Ann Hulton's surviving letters.[6] I made the same changes to Ann's writings that I did to her brother's, all of which were intended solely to make the Hultons more accessible to modern readers. I hope that they would have approved of my choices.

What follows is admittedly one-sided and incomplete. All of the letters are from the Hultons, none are to them; and it is quite possible that the letters I turned up are only a small part of their total correspondence. But a close reading of them can reveal much. They can, for example, show how people separated by thousands of miles used letters to keep alive a sense of kinship and community. The long-distance friendship that joined Henry Hulton and Robert Nicholson, the similar friendship that sustained Ann Hulton and Elizabeth Lightbody, were hardly unique. Transatlantic ties, called on to stretch over years at a time, were formed by countless others in Britain and the Americas as well. They carried on correspondences that survived, even without a postal service as we would know it, with letters that kept personal connections vital. In those letters can also be found information about public affairs that we now know to be wrong—about the fighting at Lexington and Concord, about the casualty rates of Americans there and at Bunker Hill—but that was the result of misinformation, not disinformation, mistakes sometimes corrected with time, sometimes not. It is even interesting to see, in the case of Henry Hulton finding a job in the customs service for the ne'er-do-well John Hincks, a nepotism that even then could extend to public posts as well as to family businesses. Hulton's world was different from ours; it was also very much the same.

---

6 Which is to say, all twenty-four that were published previously in *Letters of a Loyalist Lady* (Cambridge, Mass.: Harvard University Press, 1927), and one from E. Rhys Jones, ed., "An Eighteenth-Century Lady and Her Impressions," *Gentleman's Magazine* 297 (August 1904):195-198. The Reverend Jones apparently obtained these letters through the Lightbody family line. If he owned them outright, there is nothing to indicate that they were part of his estate when he died. See the will for Edward Rhys Jones, probated 3 September 1946, listed in the Principal Probate Registry index, *Wills & Admons H-J*, voume 4 for that particular year.

Some Account of the Proceedings
of the People in New England
from the Establishment of a
Board of Customs in America,
to the breaking out of the Rebellion
in 1775

Chapter 1

Progress of American Revenue from the Act of the 6th George II to the Establishment of a Board of Customs in America.

I N THE YEAR 1733 THE PARLIAMENT passed the Act of the 6 George II Chap. 13 for the encouragement of His Majesty's Sugar Colonies.[7]

By this Act Duties were imposed on the produce of American Plantations [and] foreign West India Islands not under the Dominion of His Majesty of

> 9d[8] a Gallon on Rum & Spirits
> 6d a Gallon on Melasses
> & 5 per Quart on Sugar. [1]

This Act obtained by the influence of the West India Planters, instead of operating as a fund of Revenue, was the source of Smug[g]ling and corruption.

The Ministry, having granted the Planters their desires, took no measures to inforce the Act, but winked at the prostitution of the national authority, at the connivance of the Officers of the Customs, and the illicit Commerce of the People; which introduced a depravity of Morals, and alienated the Subjects from their duty to Government.[9]

---

7   Pickering, ed., *Statutes at Large*, 16:374-379, 6 George II c. 13. It taxed rum at 9 pence per gallon, molasses at 6 pence per gallon, and sugar at 5 shillings per 100 "weight avoirdupois"(100 pounds, at 16 ounces to a pound) it brought into the British American colonies from outside the British empire, with certain exceptions. It did not affect the sugar trade between the British colonies and those of Spain and Portugal—showing that the driving concern was to control, not necessarily to exclude, foreign trade, with France the primary threat and therefore the French West Indies the primary target. Nevertheless, the statute's emphasis on the importance of the West Indies plantations to the empire, coupled with the expressed intent to punish anyone who interfered with enforcement by the customs service, no doubt rubbed some merchants on the mainland colonies the wrong way. Equally galling was the profit incentive for those involved with enforcement, the proceeds from penalties or forfeitures to be divided, "one third part thereof for the use of his Majesty, his heirs and successors, to be applied for the support of the government of the colony or plantation where the same shall be recovered, one third part to the governor or commander in chief of the said colony or plantation, and the other third part to the informer or prosecutor who shall sue for the same."

8   That is, pence per gallon.

9   Michael Kammen's *Empire and Interest* (Philadelphia: J. P. Lippincott Company, 1970) gives the scholar's stamp to the contemporary's observation, with Kammen finding that national policy had become increasingly the creature of interest group politics.

No attention was paid to the conduct of the Revenue [2] Officers, and indeed, from the dispersed state of the Trade, and wide extent of Coast in a new settled Country, under different Governments, where the authority of the Crown was feeble, little could be expected from the most virtuous and vigilant Officers.

On passing this Act several additional Officers of the Customs were appointed to carry it into execution, whose Salaries were to be paid out of the Duties arising from the Act, but many of these soon gave up their Offices, on there being no prospect of their receiving any Salary on those terms. [3]

If the Act was impolitic, or could not be carried into execution, why was it suffered to remain so long unrepealed?

If the conviction of the guilt brought on the Subject and Officer by perjury and connivance was not a sufficient inducement with the Ministry, yet the consideration of alienating the Subjects from the Laws and Authority and making them Enemies to Order and Government should have prevailed with them. No, for many many Years the temptation to illicit practises was open and unrestrained, and the Officers countenanced in giving [4] a sanction to perjury, and sharing in the advantages of connivance.

In their Accounts no returns were made of Duties received on foreign West India Voyages. The Vessels all entered in ballast, hence Smug[g]ling became established and Principle corrupted, by an indulged prostitution of the Law.

This Law, though it did not operate, yet continued unaltered 'till 1763. 'Till which time, America never seems to have been considered in any other than a Commercial light. The objects, of establishing good Government, and supporting the authority of the [5] Mother Country, were lost sight of.

Mr. George Grenville, who was Minister at this time, was intent on Schemes of National Oeconomy. The peace with France was just concluded, and he saw with concern the amazing debt of the Nation, [a] great part of which had been contracted in the defence of America.[10] He therefore thought it just that that Country should bear its proportion of the publick burthen. In this view the Act of the 4th George III Chap. 15 was passed. Establishing new Provisions and Regulations for improving the American Revenue, and [6] defending, securing, and Protecting those Dominions; and then an additional Duty was laid on foreign white

---

10 The national debt had stood at roughly £75 million by the outbreak of the French and Indian War in 1756 and exploded to nearly £140 million by war's end seven years later. Annual interest on the debt was just under £5 million and annual expenses hovered around £8 million, with annual revenues at £10 million—which meant there loomed an annual revenue shortfall of £3 million or so. Grenville wanted to curtail, not end, deficit spending. It was estimated that posting troops on the North American mainland after the war and paying the expenses of an expanded customs service would run roughly £400,000 annually. Grenville knew that his entire program, both the introduction of new navigation acts and better enforcement of old laws, would not have covered even that amount. It would, however—he hoped—get the colonists used to the idea of paying higher taxes *and* impress on them the legitimacy of parliamentary supremacy. He knew that he had taken a calculated risk in raising financial, political, and constitutional issues simultaneously.

Sugar, and duties on several other articles imported into America, and the duty on foreign Melasses was reduced to 3d a Gallon, and provision was made by this Act for the distribution of Seizures to be made by Officers of the Navy, who were intended to be empowered to act as Officers of the Revenue, on board his Majesty's Ships for the support of the Laws of Trade, and Revenue in America.[11]

In July 1763 the Secretary of State wrote to the several American Governors, in very strong [7]

[8 blank]

terms urging them to support the Officers of the Revenue.

Acquainting them that an Act had passed for improving that Revenue, and that the Commanders of His Majesty's Ships would be furnished with Deputations from the Commissioners of the Customs in consequence thereof.

Several small Vessels were accordingly employed in North America and in June 1764 His Majesty's Schooner *St. John*,[12] Lieutenant Hill Commander, made a seizure at Rhode Island.

Some days after the people rose on an Officer and party of Men, who went on shore to take a Deserter, and rescued him; then took the Officer prisoner and wounded most of the Boat's [9] Crew with Stones. They afterwards sent a Sloop, and some Boats full of Men to the Battery, and fired several shot at the Schooner, and did not desist 'till the *Squirrel* Sloop of War, then there, brought her broadside to bear upon the Battery.

Notwithstanding this outrage and insult no notice was taken of it by Government and the Colony of Rhode Island continued to brave the authority of Great Britain, in several acts of provoking insult unchastised.[13]

Mr. Grenville continued his attention to American regulation and Oeconomy, the next Session of [10] Parliament, and upon the Principle adopted in the former Session, he got the sanction of Parliament to the famous American Stamp Act.

The Colonies had been made acquainted the Year before (1764) through their Agents that Parliament expected them to raise a Revenue towards defraying the necessary charges

---

11   Pickering, ed., *Statutes*, 26:33-52, 4 George III c. 15, which stated at the outset that revenues would be raised "*for defraying the expenses of defending, protecting, and securing*" the North American mainland colonies. It included foreign coffee and wine as well as sugar, molasses and rum. Foreign sugar was taxed at 6 pence per 100 weight avoirdupois (see 107 n. 7 supra), foreign molasses at 3 pence per gallon and foreign rum was banned altogether. The "drawbacks"—tax rebates, in effect—allowed on certain wines, calicoes, and muslins are proof enough that the drawbacks granted to the East India Company for its tea in the Townshend duties three years later were a continuation of, not a departure from, established practice. There were also detailed provisions on enforcement, Parliament realizing that the new duties would not bring in the intended revenue if the old lackadaisical mode of collection was not changed. And yet smuggling cases could still be prosecuted in common law courts as well as before vice-admiralty judges, the question of overlapping jurisdiction never being answered to the satisfaction of provincial or imperial authorities. The act regarding Royal Navy involvement, passed separately, is in ibid., 28:70-71, 3 George III c. 22.

12   Hulton (or his scribes) did not underline or italicize such things; I made the change, here and infra.

13   See the discussions in Stout, *Royal Navy*, 65-68; and David S. Lovejoy, *Rhode Island Politics and the American Revolution, 1760-1776* (Providence: Brown University Press, 1958), 36-37.

for their defence, and the Administration of Civil Government that their Assemblies might make the necessary provisions if they would. But the Assemblies neglected doing any thing therein, and the Parliament passed the Stamp Act the next Session.[14]

Though the Principle might have been just and the mode proper, yet the extention of the duty to such a number of Articles, and the Quantum with which many of them were charged, was certainly grievous, and in any view it was highly impolitic to lay a new duty, so burthensome on the Subject in its immediate operation, [11] as the Stamp Act would have proved; and the event shewed how erroneous the measure was, of attempting to raise a Revenue in a remote Country, where the powers of Government were weak, and the Legislators not thoroughly acquainted with the particular local circumstances of the several Provinces. [12]

As soon as it was known in America that it was in agitation to lay a Stamp Duty in the Colonies, a spirit of opposition to the measure was raised throughout the Continent; and several of the Colonies' Assemblies passed resolves, declaratory of their Title to all the rights and priviledges of Englishmen.

No doubt if Mr Grenville had continued in Administration, but the Stamp Act would have been greatly altered, on the inconveniences attending its operation [13] being properly represented, but the People did not wait for such gentle means of seeking redress. The ferment that was raised against the Act was soon followed by violence and outrage, and the People vented their fury on the individuals that were most obnoxious to them.

At Boston they pulled down the houses of Lieutenant Governor Hutchinson, and Mr. Hallowell, the Comptroller of the Customs, assaulted the Secretary of the Province (Mr. Oliver) who was appointed the Stamp Master for that District, and obliged him to [14] resign his Commission.[15]

At Rhode Island they pulled down the houses of Mr. Howard, Dr. Moffatt, and Mr. Johnson, and throughout the Continent obliged the Stamp Masters to renounce the exercise of their Offices.

After having prevented the operation of the Stamp Act, a Plan of resistance to the Authority of Parliament was concerted throughout the Continent.

In October 1765 a Congress was held at New York, of Deputies from the several Provinces, in which they passed sundry declarations [15] of Rights and Liberties, and of the Grievances under which they laboured, amongst which they resolved that they were "entitled to all the Rights and Liberties of the natural born Subjects within the Kingdom of Great Britain."

"That they were not , and from local Circumstances could not be represented in the House of Commons in Great Britain."

---

14 Pickering, ed., *Statutes*, 26:179-204, 5 George III c. 12.
15 See Morgan, *Stamp Act Crisis*, 119-158 for the rioting in Boston and elsewhere in the colonies; and also the documents that Morgan assembled and edited as *Prologue to Revolution* (New York: W. W. Norton & Company, 1959).

"That the Stamp Act and several other Acts had a manifest tendency to subvert the Rights and Liberties of the Colonists, and that it was their duty to endeavour by a loyal and dutiful address to His Majesty, [16] and humble applications to both Houses of Parliament, to procure the repeal of the Stamp Act [and] of all Clauses of any other Acts of Parliament whereby the Jurisdiction of the Admiralty is extended and of the other late Acts for the restriction of American Commerce."[16]

Had Mr. Grenville continued in power, perhaps such measures would have been adopted, as would have convinced the Americans that they should not insult the authority of Parliament with impunity; but at the close of that Session of Parliament, in which the Stamp Act was passed, a Regency bill was brought into the [17] House, and Mr. Grenville differing in opinion with the Members in the Cabinet, as to the Princess Dowager of Wales being nominated as one in the Regency, in case there should be a demise of the Crown during the Minority of the Successor, he was no longer able to maintain himself as Minister and retired from the publick service.

On Mr. Grenville's resignation, the Marquess of Rockingham was appointed first Lord of the Treasury, and as a new Minister frequently comes in, in opposition to his Predecessor, so he generally adopts different measures. [18]

In this State of the Ministry, the advices of the proceedings of the Americans against the operation of the Stamp Act were received and the Ministry, instead of being awakened by the outrages of the Americans to a support of the Power of Parliament, sought to draw a popularity to themselves, by attending to the clamours that were raised against the conduct of the former Administration. The Merchants and Manufacturers were urged to join in Petitions against the Act, and the Ministry resolved to [19] support a repeal of it.

Nevertheless the Court was adverse to the Measure, and on the first moving of this business in the House of Commons, there were a great number of the King's Servants in opposition to Administration, but the Ministry being bent upon the repeal, and the Cabinet considering that rejecting the measures of the Ministers must occasion a change in the Ministry in the middle of a Session, and throw the National affairs into confusion, they yielded to the [20] Ministers in Office, and suffered the Stamp Act to be repealed. Thus the National authority gave way to Commercial views, and the popular cry. The Colonies triumphed, the Stamp Act was repealed, and from that day the Parliament of Great Britain was no longer respected. Their right to make Laws binding on the Colonies was denied. The operation of their Acts was resisted and the principles of Independence in general avowed.[17]

---

16 C. A. Weslager, *Stamp Act Congress* (Newark, Del.: University of Delaware Press, 1976), 200-202, prints the resolutions of 19 October 1765 from which Hulton quoted, along with the memorials to the king, lords, and commons, on 204-214. A contemporary copy of the resolutions can be found in *Proceedings of the Congress at New-York* (Annapolis, Md.: Jonas Green, 1765), 15-16, with the three memorials on 17-24.

17 Hulton blurred what American patriots had kept distinct at this stage in their protests. Those who argued most forcefully for American rights—notably Daniel Dulany in response to Grenville's program and John Dickinson in response to Townshend's—did not advocate "independence." Rather, they argued for some

In the debates on the repeal of the Stamp Act, Lord Chatham made a [21] famous speech, in which he said he rejoiced that America had resisted. This declaration had a great effect on the Americans, and they were animated in their resistance to the authority of Parliament by hearing of the Speeches of several great Personages in their favor.[18]

After repealing the Stamp Act in 1766 the Parliament during the Rockingham Administration made a further alteration in the American Revenue by the 6th George III Chap. 52, whereby some of the Duties laid by the 4th George III Chap. 15 were [22] repealed, and the duty reduced on all Melasses Imported to 1d per Gallon.[19]

In the Summer of 1766 the Rockingham Party went out of Office, when they were succeeded by the Duke of Grafton as first Lord of the Treasury and Mr. Charles Townshend as Chancellor of the Exchequer.

After so much had been done and undone in the affair of American Taxation, one would have thought that the Ministry would have suffered that business to have lain quiet for some time; at least, one would have imagined that measures would have been [23] taken to strengthen the hands of Government, and support its authority, before any new Revenue Laws had been imposed.

To enact, and suffer that act to be denied and trampled upon with impunity, must be very degrading to Government; yet in one instance it might have been thought most prudent

---

sort of legislative autonomy, but without rejecting parliamentary authority altogether. See Dulany's *Considerations on the Propriety of imposing Taxes in the British Colonies, For the Purpose of raising a Revenue, by Act of Parliament* (Annapolis, 1765) and Dickinson's *Letters from a Farmer in Pennsylvania* (Philadelphia: David Hall and William Sellers, 1768), which brought together essays first published individually in newspapers around the colonies, beginning in December 1767. Both Dulany and Dickinson argued for rights within the empire and professed their attachment to crown and country. Even after the shooting started in 1775, Dulany rejected the notion that full independence was either necessary or desirable; Dickinson embraced it only reluctantly. Thomas Whately, adviser to George Grenville and friend to John Temple, figured in the debate with his defense of "virtual representation" in *The Regulations lately Made concerning the Colonies and the Taxes Imposed upon Them considered* (London: J. Wilkie, 1765).

18 Pitt was still in Commons, not yet elevated to the peerage as earl of Chatham. His speech, part of a back-and-forth debate with Grenville in the Commons on 14 January 1766, can be found in Simmons and Thomas, eds., *Proceedings*, 2:88. Also see ibid., 2:135-151, Commons debates of 3 February 1766, where the three basic positions on the question of American taxation were laid out: that Parliament neither could nor should tax Americans directly (Isaac Barré, echoing his mentor, Pitt); that Parliament constitutionally could tax them but, for practical political reasons, should not (Henry Conway, in a position taken by many who followed the Marquess of Rockingham); and that Parliament had both the constitutional authority and the political and financial need to do so (Hans Stanley, in what would be the clear government position only after North formed his ministry in March 1770). Pitt had upheld Britain's sovereignty and parliamentary supremacy in his January 14th speech, even as he denied Parliament's authority to tax the colonists directly. He objected to the stamp act as a perversion of the navigation system, which he fully supported.

19 Pickering, ed., *Statutes*, 27:275-287, 6 George III c. 52 for the 1766 revision to the 1764 sugar act. Under this new act all molasses imported into the colonies was taxed at 1 pence per gallon, the British West Indies included. Here the concern for revenue took priority over the preferences of the West India lobby. Other goods were covered as well, with some being eligible for drawbacks.

to submit to the indignity and not inforce a complyance with the Law; but to repeal the measure, and not guard against the consequences; to plunge the Nation again into [24] circumstances of receiving aggravated insult and indignity, is truly astonishing, and for several years to bear an accumulation of disgrace from its Subjects, without an exertion of power in the support of its honor, and authority, is very surprizing; yet such was the Case.

In April 1767 the Commissioners of the Customs in London presented a Memorial to the Lords of the Treasury on the propriety of Establishing a Board of Customs in America; and amongst other reasons [25] represented that the oppressions the Officers of the Revenue labour under in America have lately grown to such an enormous height, that it is become impossible for them to do their duty, not only from the outrage of Mobs, but for fear also of vexatious Suits, Verdicts, and Judgments in the Provincial Courts, and even of Criminal Prosecutions.

Soon after this Memorial was given in, an Act was passed to put the Customs in America under the management of Commissioners to reside in that County. [26]

Immediately on the passage of the Act for Establishing a Board of Customs in America an Act was passed imposing duties on Paper, Glass, Red and White Lead, Tea, and Painters' Colours, for defraying the charge of Administration of Justice, and the support of Civil Government.[20]

This Act, se[t]ting aside the bad policy of laying duties on British Manufactures, was laid on such Articles, as made the ascertaining the duties on them very fretful, and troublesome; particularly the Paper, of which there were more than sixty sorts expressed on which the duties varied, and these [27] articles being of small bulk, might be easily run and the payment of the duties be evaded. But as the Stamp Act had been repealed the Year before, it was very extraordinary that fresh duties should be imposed and no effectual measures taken to support the authority of Government, or conciliate the minds of the people. Instead of that, the Commissioners were sent out with this new duty act in their hands, which took place in four days after they opened their Commission. [28]

The Stamp Act was imposed on so many articles, and laid so heavy on some of them, as made it severe, and raised the greatest opposition and resistance from the people to its operation. It was repealed without limitation, and the Americans triumphed in their

---

20 Ibid., 27:505-512, 7 George III c. 46. Indicative of the power struggle going on beneath the surface between provincial and imperial authority, the act also provided that anyone taking an imperial official to court in a dispute over enforcement of the navigation acts would have to pay treble the court costs if the suit failed—an attempt to counter the intimidation of customs officials by local mobs. Even more important, the act (as Hulton quoted in part) provided for a civil list to free royally-appointed imperial officials from provincial legislatures by allowing "such monies to be applied, out of the produce of the duties granted by this act, as his Majesty, or his successors, shall think proper or necessary, for defraying the charges of the administration of justice, and the support of civil government, within all or any of the said colonies or plantations."

victory.[21] Had it been continued on some articles of little consequence, the authority would have been supported, and there might have been a better plea for altering the mode of taxation from that to other Articles; but as the people by resistance, and opposition, had [29] compelled Government to repeal the former Act, so, as they equally resented the imposition of the new duties, they resolved on the like measures to get rid of them; and as the Commissioners came out just as they took place, they considered the appointment of a Board of Customs as only a method adopted by Government, to support that Act, so that the bad Policy of joining the new Duties with the Establishment of the Board, increased their resentment to the latter measure. [30]

In the Year 1771 under Lord North's Administration the Duties that had been imposed in 1767 were repealed, except those on Tea, and in 1773 the Duties that had been paid at home on Tea exported to the Colonies were taken off, and the East India Company entered on a Measure of Shipping their Teas to America for Sale on their own account, which produced a further opposition and resistance to the Laws of Parliament.[22] [31]

[32 blank]

21 Ibid., 27:19, 6 George III c. 11 for repeal of the stamp act. Note that Hulton did not call attention to the Declaratory Act (ibid., 27:19-20, 6 George III c. 12), coupled by Parliament with that repeal, which stipulated "That the said colonies and plantations in *America* have been, are, and of right ought to be, subordinate unto, and dependent upon the imperial crown and parliament of *Great Britain*; and that the King's majesty, by and with the advice and consent of the lords spiritual and temporal, and commons of *Great Britain*, in parliament assembled, had, hath, and of right ought to have, full power and authority to make laws and statutes of sufficient force and validity to bind the colonies and people of *America*, subjects of the crown of *Great Britain*, in all cases whatsoever." The controversial word "tax" was deliberately not used in this sly but futile attempt to assert imperial authority and yet not provoke a constitutional dispute. For context see my "William Dowdeswell and the American Crisis, 1763-1775," *History* 90 (2005):507-531.

22 Repeal was actually in 1770, near the beginning of North's ministry. Subsequent revisions to the regulation of the tea trade in the colonies between 1771 and 1773 are in Pickering, ed., *Statutes*, 29:4-8, 160-165, 12 George III c. 7 and c. 60, resp.; and 30:74-77, 14 George III c. 44.

Chapter 2

Obstructions to the Collection of a Revenue in America, from the extent of the Coast, and the Nature of the Trade and Commerce

THE DISTRICTS OF MANY OF THE PORTS in America were very extensive, abounding with numbers of Bays, Creeks and Harbours, convenient for the run[n]ing of Goods and some thousand of Vessels were employed in the Coasting and fishing trade, which neither entered or cleared at any Custom house.

The People had been long accustomed to a great liberty of trade. All along the Coast were scattered [33] settlements. The first object in set[t]ling the Country was to dispose of the Lumber cut down from the Lands that were cleared. They built Vessels to transport it for a market to the West Indies, which returned with Cargoes of Melassas, and other Goods, and they carried on this trade as suited their Convenience, frequently run[n]ing the whole, or great part of their Cargoes, in shore, in some of the Bays or Creeks, in the unset[t]led parts of the Country.

The neglect of the Coasting Vessels of entering [34] and clearing at the Custom House, when going within the same Province, had been overlooked. They were employed in bringing, concealed under their Wood and Lumber, the Goods that had been smug[g]led (into some of the distant Creeks, and Bays, by the larger Vessels) to the great Towns, where those Commodities must be brought for a Market.[23]

These Coasters were decked Vessels, from twenty to ninety tons burthen, and were often used in foreign Voyages.

From the extent of the Harbours, or Districts, where Custom Houses were [35] established, and there being no legal Wharffs or Quays, great frauds were commited even within the Ports of Entry, and of the Casks which were legally imported, not half the Duties were paid for the quantity which such Casks usually contained.

Many Vessels were employed in the transport of Fish to the Southern parts of Europe, and if they came to any Custom House on their return, they reported either with Salt, or in Ballast.

---

23 For the navigation system as it was supposed to work see the fourth and final volume of Andrews, *Colonial Period*; and Barrow, *Trade and Empire*, for how it actually worked.

In the Eastern parts of the Massachusetts Bay, the Lumber Trade was so dispersed, as not to be brought [36] to a central Port.[24]

In Maryland, Virginia and North Carolina, where there are no large towns, the Planters and Merchants being settled all over the Country, had been long indulged in loading and unloading their Vessels, in different parts, on all the great rivers, many of them remote from the Custom Houses, or any Officer.

In South Carolina one hundred and thirty or forty Schooners were employed in bringing the Produce of the [37] Country to Charles Town, and pretending to trade only within the Province with Country produce, they came in and out of Port without Entering, or Clearing, without Permit, or Register. And when the Officers seized any of them, they met with so many difficulties, and embarrassments, in the Provincial Law Courts, that they were deterred from prosecuting such Vessels.

These Schooners frequently made Voyages to the foreign West Indies, [38] smug[g]led Cargoes of goods from thence, and assisted in the clandestine discharge of larger Vessels.

In Rhode Island, Connecticut, Pensilvania and Maryland, there were no Officers appointed by the Crown, but those of the Customs. The State of Government, and the local situation of the Country, through this wide extended Continent, were great bars to any regulations, and the temper of the People, and timidity of the Officers, prevented the carrying into execution the Laws already [39] in being.[25]

Such was the State of the Trade in America, on the Establishment of the Board of Customs. In most of the Colonies there was no drawing the trade to any Center without the greatest inconvenience to the People; and throughout America, the Trade had been so long habituated in indulgences, so well practised in Smug[g]ling, and the Officers so long used to connivance, and neglect, that to establish and inforce regulations for better management, required more authority than the Board possessed, or than Government might chuse to exert. [40]

---

24 Robert G. Albion, *Forests and Sea Power* (Cambridge, Mass.: Harvard University Press, 1926) and Joseph J. Malone, *Pine Trees and Politics* (Seattle: University of Washington Press, 1964) discuss the problems associated with regulating the use of colonial timber for the Royal Navy, with its need for masts and spars, a variation on the larger problem faced by the navigation system. The American Board of Customs was not directly involved in this aspect of trade. A surveyor-general of the woods was supposed to manage the forests.

25 In Rhode Island and Connecticut virtually all provincial posts were elective, as provided by charters approved by Charles II in 1663 and 1662, respectively. These and other colonial charters can be found, arranged alphabetically, in Francis Newton Thorpe, ed., *The Federal and State Constitutions*, 7 vols. (Washington, D.C.: Government Printing Office, 1909). The proprietors of Pennsylvania (the Penn family) and Maryland (the Calverts) appointed the governor and other key officials but, as in "royal" colonies like Massachusetts—where the crown appointed the governor—much power had shifted to the assembly. Leonard Woods Labaree laid out the general structure in *Royal Government in America* (New Haven: Yale University Press, 1930); Jack P. Greene, *The Quest for Power* (Chapel Hill: University of North Carolina Press, 1963) showed how, even in the supposedly more placid Southern colonies, the same divisive issues over liberty and authority, and provincial versus imperial power, arose as in New England. Also see Bernard Bailyn, *The Origins of American Politics* (New York: Alfred A. Knopf, 1968).

Chapter 3

Obstructions to the Revenue from the temper of the People, at the time of the Establishment of the Board of Customs

FROM THE STATE OF THE PROGRESS of Smug[g]ling and corruption, in consequence of the Act of the 6th George II[26] it may well be imagined that the Establishment of a Board of Customs in America, could in no wise be agre[e]able either to the Trader, or the Subordinate officers.

The latter had very small Salaries annexed to their employments, and consequently depended very much on the Fees of [41] of their Offices and to keep well with the Trade was necessary, not only for their support, but for their ease and personal comfort in the Society, so that the new Establishment which awakened the fears of all the Smug[g]ling Traders, likewise allarmed all the Officers of the Customs; who dreaded too nice an inspection into their conduct, and foresaw they must either offend the Traders by an attention to their duty, or draw on themselves the censure of their Superiors, by a neglect of it. [42]

[43 44 blank]

The Act for laying a Duty on Paper, Glass, Tea, and Painters' Colours, being passed about the same time with the Act for Establishing a Board of Customs in America, the People thought the Board was appointed merely in consequence of that Act, which they considered only as a new way of enforcing the raising of Money in the Colonies, without their Consent,[27] the authority of which they had been taught to dispute, and deny; and now resolved as far as they were able, to defeat the operation of these Acts. Therefore, [45] though the appointment of a Board of Customs at another time might have been considered in a favorable light, it was now looked on as a means to rivet the Chains of oppression and the resentment of the People against the measure was vented on the Board and its Officers.

The Newspapers teemed with everything that could inflame the Passions, the grossest abuse was used, and many fals[e]hoods asserted as facts, to rouse the People to resist the authority of Government and ill[-]treat its Officers.

Nor was the persecution of the Servants of the Crown confined to the modes of [46] Slander, and violence on this (American) side the Water, for their Enemies were not less

---

26 Pickering, ed., *Statutes*, 16:374-379, 6 George II c. 13 (the 1733 molasses act).
27 Ibid., 26:33-52, 4 George III c. 15 (the 1764 sugar act).

assiduous in misrepresenting their conduct, and blackening their character at home and every means was used to put the Commissioners in an unfavorable light.[28] Every exertion of their authority was exag[g]erated into Acts of Severity and oppression. But whenever they mitigated the severity of the Law, what ever lenient measure they adopted, or hard Case they relieved, was never told.[47]

[48 blank]

The Popular Governments in most of the Colonies subject every publick measure to the animadversion of the People at large, and they are ready upon every occasion to run into riots and disorder. The opposition to the Stamp Act had been attended with many circumstances of outrage and violence, yet that Act was finally repealed. An Act of oblivion was passed, and no person was punished for any of the enormities that had been commit[t]ed.

The People remained [49] confident that it was owing to their clamour and resistance that the Stamp Act was repealed; and shewing the same Spirit and using the same means they were persuaded would have a like effect, if in future any measures were adopted by Government that should be disagre[e]able to them.

The repeal of the Stamp Act was imputed to fear. This begot a confidence in their own power and an audacity in abusing and ill[-]treating every one who was in the Service of Government or respected its authority. [50]

[51-52 blank]

---

28 Hulton, like Bernard and other imperial officials, was convinced that opposition politics compromised national policy. They all feared that when a Camden or a Pitt (Chatham) criticized acts of Parliament, or questioned Parliament's authority to tax the colonists, the "demagogues" among the colonists were emboldened, causing an overwrought minority to intimidate a loyal but more passive majority into silence.

Chapter 4

Insufficiency of former measures adopted for
Security of the Revenue in America

THE MINISTRY OF LATE YEARS seems to have been aware of the necessity of making further provision for the support of the authority of Government, and securing respect to the Laws.

In several of the late Acts of Parliament relative to the American Revenue, further regulations were made for securing the payment of the duties and preventing illicit Commerce, and in the Act of the 4th George III [53] all forfeitures and Penalties relating to the Trade and Revenue of the Colonies might be prosecuted and sued for in the Court of Admiralty and by the 7th George III, the Superior Court in each Colony was empowered and directed to grant Writts of Assistants[29] to the Officers of the Customs, to enter any place and search for and seize any prohibited goods.[30]

In consequence of this last Act, four judges of Admiralty were appointed, with separate Districts including the whole Continent of North America, at established Salaries of six hundred pounds [54] per Annum and several of the Governors, Judges of the Superior Courts, and Attorneys General, in the different Provinces, had Salaries appointed by the Crown, out of this Revenue.[31]

---

29 writs of assistance.

30 Pickering, ed., *Statutes*, 26:33-52, 4 George III c. 15 (sugar act) and 27:505-512, 7 George III c. 46 (Townshend duties).

31 Ibid., 8 George III c. 22. When Hulton took office as plantations clerk in 1763 there were eleven vice-admiralty courts in the mainland colonies. The judges, almost all of whom were themselves colonists, were not paid salaries. They were expected to subsist off of court fees. A new court based at Halifax was added in 1764, a salaried (£800 per annum) English judge on the bench, with original as well as appellate jurisdiction over trade and revenue cases from anywhere in the colonies. The 1768 reconfiguration added another three courts—in Boston, Philadelphia, and Charleston—to create four distinct districts, with all four courts having both appellate and original jurisdiction. Cases heard in the other vice-admiralty courts could be heard there on appeal, as well as cases on appeal that started in common-law courts. The four judges (largely colonists) were paid £600 a year, but they were still expected to supplement their income from court fees. For the jurisdictional boundaries laid out in 1768, see Fitzroy and Munro, eds., *Privy Council*, 5:151-153. It was 1769 before the new system was fully in place. See Ubbelohde, *Vice-Admiralty Courts*, 128-147. Despite all the changes, vice-admiralty court jurisdiction was concurrent with, not separate from or superior to, that of the provincial common-law courts.

By the Mutiny Act provision was made for the Supply of the Troops in the several Provinces with sundry necessaries enumerated therein.[32]

But these regulations and provisions, were in no wise effectual, towards maintaining the authority of Government, and supporting the Revenue Laws. [55]

There were many causes that prevented the Officers from exerting themselves in their duty, and many grievances they laboured under.

The charges of prosecutions in the Provincial Courts of Admiralty, were very high, so that the expence of Prosecution of Petty Seizures was often greater than the goods would sell for.

There were combinations amongst the People, to prevent the Sale of the Goods seized so that the Smug[g]ler might buy them in again at a low rate.

The Magistracy in general were backward in [56] supporting the Officers, though they were under constant apprehensions of violence from the People, in doing their duty.

The Officers had no probability of obtaining redress for any injuries they received, by a process at Law, before a Jury of the People, who held the very Laws under which the Officer acted, to be Unconstitutional.

In some of the Colonies, the whole powers of Government were in other hands than those of the Crown, so that it was [57] hardly possible to carry the Revenue Laws into execution in those parts.

The Person who was called in such Provinces the King's Attorney was Attorney for the interest of the Province, and not for the Crown. But where such Officer was appointed by the Crown he gave little assistance to the Officers of Revenue[,] especially if he had no Salary from the Crown.[33]

Many of the Superior Courts of Justice in America refused to grant Writts of Assistants to the Officers of the Customs, though repeatedly applied to for that purpose by [58] direction of the Commissioners, and several of the Colonies refused to comply with the Act for providing the necessaries for the King's Troops Stationed therein. And on the refusal of the Province of New York to comply with that Act an Act of Parliament was passed suspending the Legislative Authority of their Assembly, 'till they complied therewith.[34]

---

32 Pickering, ed., *Statutes*, 26:305-318, 5 George III c. 33, the "quartering act" that was part of Grenville's 1765 program.

33 Hulton was most likely thinking of his frustrations with Massachusetts attorney general Jonathan Sewall in the 1768 *Liberty* case.

34 The New York suspending (or "restraining") act is in Pickering, ed., *Statutes*, 27:609-610, 7 George III c. 59. Acting on the complaint of General Thomas Gage, Parliament instructed the New York assembly not to pass any new legislation until it had complied with the quartering act of 1765. The issue, which dragged through 1766 and into 1767, was sidestepped when the legislators eventually granted funds without specifying that they would be used for housing and provisioning the small (but growing) contingent of regulars then in New York. See Merrill Jensen, *The Founding of a Nation* (New York: Oxford University Press, 1968), 211-240, 334-335; and Joseph Tiedemann, *Reluctant Revolutionaries* (Ithaca, N.Y.: Cornell University Press, 1997), 117-124. John Dickinson, as the "Pennsylvania Farmer," thought Parliament's intervention in this dispute every bit as dangerous as the revenue-raising motives behind the Townshend duties.

The appointment of Officers of the Navy, to act as Officers of the Revenue, did not answer the end proposed.

Some of those Gentlemen who exerted themselves in this Service were greatly [59] embarrassed by Prosecutions in the Provincial Law Courts, for Civil Actions, in consequence of their having made Seizures of Vessels, and Goods as Officers of the Customs. And the general dislike which the Gentlemen of the Navy had to being employed in this Service was a great means of preventing them from exerting themselves in this business. Besides, the large Vessels employed in the Navy were of little Service in the prevention of illicit trade, which being generally [60] carried on by small Vessels along a dangerous Coast and in all Weathers, required to be watched by vigilant Cruizers drawing little Water. And on this idea the Commissioners fit[t]ed out a Sloop called the *Liberty* at a considerable expence[,] which soon after was destroyed by the People of Rhode Island, for which insult and injury no reparation was demanded by Government.[35]

If the Officers of the Customs on Shore [61] attempted to do their duty they were assaulted and abused; so that in general they were deterred from exerting themselves at all. For there was scarce a port in America where an Officer had endeavoured to make a Seizure, or refused a complyance with the will of the People, that he had not been Tarred and feathered.

This mode of punishment was a new invention and used generally towards the Officers of the Customs. They Stript him, put him in a Cart, tarred and feathered him, and then led him in the view of the publick through the Town.[36] [62]

|63-64 blank|

The Smug[g]ling had been carried on to a great extent[,] yet few Seizures had been made in the New England Governments for two years prior to the Establishment of the Board of Customs, and only one prosecuted to effect.

In August 1765 the disturbances began at Boston, on account of the Stamp Act.

---

35 See Stout, *Royal Navy*, for the ill-fated *Liberty*, 140 and 193 n. 54, Hancock's sloop that was confiscated and turned to customs service duty in 1768. The rules for naval involvement in the profit-sharing aspects of cargoes and ships condemned for smuggling were laid out in Pickering, ed., *Statutes*, 25:345-351, 3 George III c. 22. (in 1763).

36 For the crowd as mob, and the mob as political weapon, see Gordon S. Wood, "A Note on Mobs in the American Revolution," *William and Mary Quarterly*, 3rd series 23 (1966):635-642; Pauline Maier, "Popular Uprisings and Civil Authority in Eighteenth-Century America," *ibid.*, 3rd series 27 (1970):3-35; Richard Maxwell Brown, "Violence and the American Revolution," in Stephen G. Kurtz, ed., *Essays on the American Revolution* (Chapel Hill: University of North Carolina Press, 1972); Dirk Hoerder, *Crowd Action in Revolutionary America* (New York : Academic Press, 1977); and Jesse Lemisch, *Jack Tar vs. John Bull* (New York: Garland Publishing, 1997).

In 1766 the Officers at Boston were resisted at [65] Noon day in making a Seizure, and being unsupported were obliged to retire without making the Seizure.[37]

Though the several instances of assaults on Officers and resistance to the authority of Parliament had been regularly made matter of information to the proper Offices at home[,] yet no measures had been taken to prosecute and punish the Offenders, or strengthen the hands of Government.

The Smug[g]lers triumphed in their success, and the Officers of the Revenue were deterred from their duty. [66]

[67-68 blank]

---

37 Morgan, *Stamp Act Crisis*, 119-158, examined how Boston set "the pace" in resisting imperial authority by targeting those charged with enforcing the navigation acts, the stamp act first and foremost. Also see Barrow, *Trade and Empire*, 186-212, and (on 202) the September 1766 affair of Daniel Malcom, to which Hulton may have been referring (*may*, because it involved a search for possible seizure rather than a straightforward seizure). Benjamin Hallowell and Charles Paxton, among others, were thwarted in their desire to search Malcom's warehouse. See too TNA, PRO/T1/446, fos. 103-133 and TNA, PRO/T1/452, fos. 205-212. When Paxton sailed to England he would use this incident as proof of the need for reforming the customs service—leading indirectly to the creation of the American board.

Chapter 5

Modes of resistance to the operation of the Revenue Laws in America, 1767-1768

SOON AFTER THE OPENING the Commissioners of the Customs at Boston in November 1767 a series of letters began to be published at Philadelphia called the Farmers letters.

The first letter was on the conduct of Parliament in suspending the Legislation of New York 'till that Colony should comply with the billeting Act. In the next he endeavours to shew that the new Duties on Paper, Glass &c. are Unconstitutional. In the third he says the meaning of these letters is to convince the People of [69] the Colonies that they are in the most imminent dangers, and to persuade them immediately, vigorously, and unanimously to exert themselves in the most firm, but most peaceable manner for obtaining relief; and pursues this Subject through a series of twelve letters.

These letters were written with more temper than any publications that appeared at this time against the measures of Parliament, and had great influence in riveting the new Doctrines in the minds of the people. [70]

The Principles denying the right of Parliament to tax the Colonies, and asserting their independency were propagated with great success;[38] and openly avowed in writings and

---

38 [Dickinson], *Letters from a Farmer*. Bernard characterized Dickinson's *Letters* as an "American creed" and therefore a dangerous sign of what could follow. Bernard to John Pownall, 20 April 1768, Bernard Papers, 6:109. Bernard, like Hulton, did not see the distinction between taxation and legislation made by some members of Parliament as well as by protesting Americans, much less follow Dickinson's argument about legislative intent as the crucial factor in separating the constitutional from the unconstitutional. By contrast, the anonymous editor of *The Report of the Lords Committee, Appointed by the House of Lords to Enquire into the several Proceedings in the Colony of Massachusetts Bay* (London: William Bingley, 1774) saw the distinctions that Hulton, like Bernard, missed. Most American patriots at this point accepted some modicum of parliamentary authority, despite their objections to being taxed directly. Even as late as 1774 and the first Continental Congress, the delegates there were reluctant to squeeze Parliament out of the legislative picture altogether, a reluctance that explains the careful wording of their resolutions—for which see my "The First Continental Congress and Problem of American Rights," *Pennsylvania Magazine of History and Biography* 122 (1998):354-383. For Dickinson's importance see Bailyn, *Ideological Origins*, 160-229; Robert Webking, *The American Revolution and the Politics of Liberty* (Baton Rouge: Louisiana State University Press, 1988, 41-60; Clinton Rossiter, *Seedtime of the Republic* (New York: Harcourt, Brace and Company, 1953), 326-361; and Milton Flower's biography, *John Dickinson: Conservative Revolutionary* (Charlottesville: University of Virginia Press, 1983).

Speeches: and any one who dared to oppose the popular opinions, was exposed to insult and resentment. And the frenzy of the People was raised to such a height, that a forcible opposition to the execution of the new Laws of Revenue was threatened. [71]

At this time the ordinary Newspapers teemed with the most seditious and inflammatory pieces and the most licentious publications against particular Characters.

The heart burnings that were raised against Government, vented themselves on the Servants who were to support the Authority, or execute the Laws.

Governor Bernard became involved in disputes, and contest, with his Assembly; and he, and the Commissioners of the Customs were constant objects of abuse in the Newspapers. [72]

Instead of opposing the New Laws by violence as was threatened, a plan of Oeconomy and industry was set on foot. The apparent design of which was to allarm the trading and manufacturing people in Great Britain rather than to answer the ends and purposes pretended.

The Articles now charged with Duties were to be entirely disused and encouragement was given to manufacture the same among themselves. The Consumption of British [73] Manufactures in general was discountenanced, and a preference given to those of America.[39]

The Town of Boston instructed their Representatives to promote a remonstrance from the General Court against the late Laws, and the Merchants entered into an Association not to import any goods from Great Britain for a limited time[,] and a Committee was appointed to correspond with the Merchants in other Provinces, to excite them to adopt similar measures, and they [74] who refused to subscribe were to be discouraged in the most effectual manner.

Early in 1768, the House of Representatives passed resolves to discourage the Use of foreign Superfluities, and Addressed His Majesty, and wrote to His Secretary of State on the Subject of their present grievances, and transmit[t]ed an Account of their proceedings to the Speaker of every Assembly on the Continent to influence them to Similar measures.

On the 29[th] February a [75] most audacious Libel was published in Edes and Gill's Newspaper on Governor Bernard, which he laid before both Houses of Assembly, and at the

---

39 Arthur Schlesinger, *The Colonial Merchants and the American Revolution* (New York: Columbia University Press, 1918) remains a basic source on merchant associations and the non-importation movement in general. J. E. Crowley, *This Sheba, Self* (Baltimore: Johns Hopkins University Press, 1974) takes a provocatively different approach. Whatever success Americans enjoyed in seeing the stamp act repealed had as much to do with opposition within Parliament and support among London merchants as it did with attempts to unify the colonies through economic warfare: non-importation of British goods, stimulation of home manufactures. They would not receive as much transatlantic support in protesting Townshend's program, and they could not stay unified among themselves either.

General Sessions. The Chief Justice gave a very strong and pointed charge to the Grand Jury in respect to Libels; however, they did not present the publisher of the Libel on the Governor.[40]

The letter from the House of Representatives to the Speaker of the Several Houses of Assembly on the Continent, was to [76] communicate their minds and receive the Sentiments of the other houses of Assembly representing the operation of the Revenue Laws, as infringements of their natural and Constitutional Rights, as they were not represented in Parliament; and from their Local circumstances, they never could be equally represented there and consequently not at all. At the same time they submit[t]ed to consideration as further grievances the granting of Salaries to the Judges of the Land, and others, by [77] the Crown, independent of the People. The Act for providing Enumerated Articles for the King's Troops on their march, and the appointment of a Board of Commissioners of the Customs in America; and the sentiments and complaints in this letter were thrown into their petition to the King.

In June 1768 the Governor, by directions from the Secretary of State, called upon the House to rescind a resolution of a former House, but they passed a Vote that they would not rescind. Upon which according to the [78] directions he had received, he dissolved the Assembly.[41]

---

40 Nicolson, *"Infamas Govener,"* 162-163; Hutchinson, *History,* 3:13. The essay in question, a brief piece by "A True Patriot"—apparently Joseph Warren—actually appeared in the *Boston Gazette* on 7 March 1768, not February 29th. It was in reaction to a letter to Bernard from the earl of Shelburne, secretary of state for the southern department, endorsing Bernard's blocking of some who had been selected for the Council by the House (printed as well). Shelburne emphasized that Bernard had acted properly and chided the Council for not letting Hutchinson take a seat on it, simply because he was already a holder of multiple offices. The "true patriot" condemned the notion of executive power behind Bernard's actions as an "odious doctrine" and implied that Bernard was a "villain" for holding it. Bernard later wrote Hillsborough (on 25 January 1769) that he thought Benjamin Edes and John Gill, owners of the *Boston Gazette,* verged on treason—"mercenary" printers at the beck and call of "Faction." Bernard Papers, 7:126-128.

41 The text of the House's circular letter of 11 February 1768 is in *Journals of the Masssachusetts House,* 44:236-239. In enumerating the "hardships" caused by Parliament's new acts, the House included: "And also the commission of the Gentleman appointed Commissioners of the Customs to reside in America, which authorizes them to make as many appointments as they think fit, and to pay the appointees what sums they please, for whose mal-conduct they are not accountable: from whence it may happen, that officers of the Crown may be multiplied to such a degree, as to become dangerous to the Liberty of the people, by virtue of a commission which doth not appear to this House to derive any such advantages to trade as many have been led to expect." (238) In April the King called on the House to rescind its letter. In June it refused and asked that Bernard be replaced with someone more "worthy to represent the greatest and best Monarch on Earth." (Ibid., 45:96, 30 June 1768) See, in this same appendix (217-235), various letters written by the House in January-February 1768 to Camden, Chatham, Rockingham and others, professing loyalty to crown and parliament, and yet protesting policies championed by both. Logic would say that they would not be happy with anything short of independence. They were trying desperately to avoid pursuing that logic.

As soon as they were apprized of the Orders he had received, they formed a Committee, to prepare a petition to the King to remove the Governor, but for want of proof of the facts alledged in support of divers Articles, it passed off 'till the next year.[42]

In June 1769 the House passed several Articles of Complaint against Governor Bernard, and petitioned His Majesty for his removal from the Government.[43]

The Governor went [79] home in August 1769, but could not obtain a Copy of this Complaint 'till a few days before he sailed from Boston; and when the matter came to an hearing before the King in Council, the Governor fully refuted the Charges as unjust and untrue; and they were in no wise able to support by facts, what they had boldly alledged against him to his Majesty, and the complaint was dismissed to his honor, and their disgrace.[44] [80]

The year 1768 opened with opposition to the Revenue Laws, and combinations not to import Goods from Great Britain.

The Commissioners of the Customs were receiving frequent Accounts, from different Ports, of resistance to their Officers and abuses of them in the execution of their duty. Of Custom House Boats being burnt, and of goods seized being rescued out of the hands of the Officers; yet no satisfaction for these assaults, or effectual [81] support to the Officers, could be obtained.

Many of the abuses of the Officers were attended with very cruel Circumstances, such as Strip[p]ing them naked, tarring and feathering them, beating them with Clubs, decrying them through the streets in ignominy, loaded with blows & reproaches, and exposed to cold, and nakedness.[45]

In the month of March 1768 Mr. Hancock[,] an eminent Merchant at Boston, most audaciously ran in a Cargoe of Wines into Boston; many people were employed in landing them from the Vessel, and carrying them to [82] the Merchant's Cellar, but no one dared to appear and give information of their proceedings and the Master, the next day entered his Vessel in ballast.

Prosecutions were set on foot by the Commissioners against Mr. Hancock, and several others concerned in the fact, which were defeated for want of evidence, though a number of people who were said to have been present at the time, and were sumonsed to give evidence, denied any knowledge of the fact, which they were called upon to support. [83]

---

42 By the summer of 1768, Bernard had become convinced that the moment of truth had arrived. "We are now just entering into that critical Situation which I have so long ago foreseen must come sooner or later; that is, the Time of Trial, whether this Town &c will or will not submit to Great Britain when she is in earnest in requiring Submission." Letter to John Pownall, 11 July 1768, Bernard Papers, 6:131.

43 House resolution of 29 June 1769 and petition to the crown of 27 June 1769 in *Speeches of Governors*, 176-180 and 188-191, resp.

44 Nicolson, "*Infamas Govener*," 198-210.

45 Complaining of Boston's lawlessness, Benjamin Hallowell, then comptroller for the port, warned Lord North "as long as this spirit prevails here, every officer under the Crown who does his duty will be the object of popular resentment." Letter of 17 December 1765, Add. Ms. 61,683, fo. 9 (Blenheim Papers) BL.

From this time there were frequent disturbances, mobs, and allarms to distress the Commissioners.

For several Evenings in the month of March a number of people armed with Clubs assembled about the houses of some of the Commissioners, blowing horns, beating drums and making hideous noises, so that the families quit[t]ed their houses, expecting the mob would proceed to violence and on the 18[th] March, the day of the repeal of the Stamp Act, they paraded through the Streets in the evening, making violent crys and noises at the houses of the Governor and some of the Commissioners. [84]

From the first outrages in the Year 1765 the Governor and Magistrates had been losing their authority over the people.

As the new doctrines gained ground, many of the Council adopted the popular opinions and stood forth as assertions of the rights of America. And such of that Board as had shewed a disposition to support the authority of Parliament had been left out in the next Annual Election of Councillors, and others returned in their room, [85] whom the Governor had negatived.

Most of the people of property were averse to the New Laws of Parliament, and no Magistrate would stand forth to support the Officer whose duty it was to carry them into execution. The Mob were ready to be assembled on any occasion, and every Officer who was obnoxious to them was exposed to their resentment without the least probability of receiving any protection. [86]

There being frequent disturbances in Boston, and the Commissioners of the Customs under continual apprehensions for their safety, as the Governor had often told them he could give them no protection, they wrote to Commodore Hood, Commanding his Majesty's Ships at Halifax, for assistance and he immediately sent a Schooner, and afterwards the *Romney* Man of War, of fifty guns, to Boston. [87]

In May 1768 the Officers of the Customs were resisted in remaining on board a Vessel from London, and at a Town Meeting it was resolved not to let the Governor have the use of Faneuil Hall to entertain his Company on the day of the General Election, if he invited the Commissioners of the Customs to Dinner for that day. And Mr. Hancock, the Major of Cadets, tore off the Seal from his Commission, because the Governor would not promise not to invite the Commissioners to dinner on that day.[46] [88]

---

46 See 150 infra for another election day incident, five years later. The first incident in particular captured the personal element in the battle over imperial authority and local autonomy. Town selectmen—Hancock one of them—would not give permission for Faneuil Hall to be used for the election-day dinner until they were promised that the commissioners would not be invited to attend. Once the Governor's council assured them that no invitation would be forthcoming, they approved, with Hancock underscoring "that the Hall is at their service on said Day with the restriction enjoin'd by the Town." *A Report of the Record Commissioners of the City of Boston, containing the Selectmen's Minutes from 1764 through 1768* (Boston: Rockwell and Churchill, 1889), 292, minutes of 11 May 1768.

On the ninth of June the Sloop *Liberty*, out of which Mr. Hancock had run the Cargoe of Wines before mentioned, was seized by the Officers of the Customs, on which a great riot ensued. The Officers were grosly abused, and the mob burnt a barge belonging to the Collector, and the Commissioners fled from their dwellings that night, apprehensive for their personal safety.

The next day, finding the people still outragious, and that they could not execute the Laws but at the peril of their own, and their Officers' lives, [89] the Commissioners took Shelter on board the *Romney* Man of War, with their families. and three days afterwards returned from thence into Castle William, in Boston Harbour.

The Commissioners fitted out the Sloop that had been seized, and condemned, as a Custom House Cruizer, and called her by her original name the *Liberty*. She continued to cruize awhile, and made some Seizures, but whilst the Master was on Shore at Rhode Island, the people of the town seized him, went on board his Vessel, scut[t]led and burnt her, the Account of which outrage was sent home, but no further enquiry was made into the matter, nor any satisfaction made to Government for the insult.[47] [90]

---

47 See 121 n. 35 supra.

Chapter 6

Exertions of Government in support of its Authority. 1768

UPON THE REPRESENTATIONS made to Government of the opposition to the Laws of Revenue at Boston, two Regiments of foot and a detachment from a third were ordered from Halifax to Boston and two others were sent from Ireland to support the Magistrates in the execution of the laws and protect the Servants of the Crown.

Before the arrival of the Troops the Select Men of Boston sent circular letters to all the Towns in [91] the Province to Summons a Committee of Convention; which assembled at Boston, to consult on the emergency of affairs, in despight of the Governor; and it is not probable they would have seperated on his Orders for that purpose, if the Troops had not been just at hand.

When they had certain advice of their being near the Harbour, they retired home.

The two Regiments from Halifax arrived the latter end of October, but were refused to be billeted or Quartered in the Town and after some time, Quarters were hired for them by [92] direction of the Governor, which occasioned altercations between him and the Council and the Select Men of the Town.[48]

The four Regiments finally were all quartered within the town of Boston, but much difficulty arose in providing accommodations for them and the townspeople[,] dissatisfied with the Military being sent amongst them, used every means to render their situation

---

48 Hulton was right, but only in part. Neither the town nor the army looked for an excuse for a bloodletting; on the contrary, both would compromise—within limits. On September 21st the selectmen had been emphatic: according to their understanding of the quartering act, no troops could lawfully be billeted in the town proper until the barracks at Castle William were filled. Once the troops arrived, however, the selectmen proved more flexible, *after* they were given an indication that they could carry their theoretical point without causing a practical conundrum. Both the 14th and 29th regiments went into town, not to the Castle. Some were sent to encamp on the Common. Note the significance of the word "favor" as recorded in the following, when Colonel William Dalrymple, overall commander of the newly-arrived troops, approached town authorities: "The Collo. afterwards represented to the Selectmen that he had not a sufficient number of Tents for his Troops and entreated of them as a favor the use of Faneuil Hall for one Regiment to lodge in till Monday following, promising upon his honor to quit said Hall at that time—in consequence of said request & taking into consideration the hardship of the Troops must be exposed to while remaining in the open air, the Selectmen consented thereto—"; from *Report of the Record Commissioners...Selectmen's Minutes from 1764 through 1768*, 311. The selectmen pressed Dalrymple to move his men out once that Monday came, and resisted allowing him to use the old factory house in that odd (to an outsider, at least) combination of confrontation and avoidance that had come to typify imperial and local relations.

disagre[e]able and to find cause of quarrel with the Soldiers; and they, and the Country people, enticed many of them to desert. [93]

Commodore Hood with his Majesty's Ships from Halifax came to Boston in the month of November, and about the same time General Gage, Commander in Chief of the Army in America, came from New York and remained a short time at Boston.

Major General Mackay[,] who was to have had the command of the Troops on this expedition, was drove off the Coast to the West Indies and Colonel Pomeroy of the 64th Regiment had the command in Boston 'till his arrival in the Spring.

After the arrival of the Fleet and Army the Commissioners came up from the Castle to Boston the beginning of November. But such was the Spirit of resentment against them that no one would rent me a house in the Town. [94]

About the middle of October 1768 there was published in the Boston News Papers a Copy of the Proceedings of the Council of the Province, on the 27 and 29 July past.

Fifteen Members of that Council presented an Address to General Gage on his arrival at Boston, and Petitions were sent to both Houses of Parliament by some of the Members of the Council independant of the Governor: In all of which they endeavoured to exculpate the town of Boston, and reflected on the Commissioners of the Customs [95] as the causers of the late riots and disorders, and asserting that they had retired to the Castle without sufficient reason, and with a view to bring reproach on the town and to cause Troops to be sent to Boston.

Upon this occasion it was proposed by the Commissioners that the conduct of the Board should be supported in a Memorial to the Lords of the Treasury, when Mr. Temple expressed his disapprobation of their leaving the town and dissented from the rest in opinion as to the propriety of their retiring to the Castle [96] in consequence of the riot of the 10th June, and as the four Commissioners were particularly reflected on by the Council they thought it necessary, in vindication of their own characters, to declare to their Lordships that the representations in the Minutes of the Council and the Address to General Gage, were, as far as they reflected on them, false, and unjust. And they took leave to observe, one reason which influenced those Gentlemen to these proceedings, "The leading Members of the Council, in the opposition to [97] Government are nearly tied to Mr. Temple by marriage and as he takes a part different from Us, it was necessary to cast a reflection on our conduct to justify his behavior."

The Commissioners mentioned some other instances in the conduct of the Select Men and of the People, as being done in order to set their conduct in an unfavourable light, in vindication of which, they referred to the Affidavits of their Officers, and other papers, in relation to the riot of the 10th June, and to the Answers to some Queries proposed [98] to four principal Gentlemen in the Service of Government in the Province, which they presumed, would satisfy their Lordships, of the necessity and propriety of their retiring to the Castle and their remaining there in the execution of their Commission, did not the proceedings of the Town Meetings of the Council and Assembly, and last of all, of the Convention that was held in Boston, in defiance of Government, support them in the Steps they had taken. And they concluded with saying. "We can chearfully go on in the exercise of [99] our Commission, though exposed to the grossest misrepresentations of our Conduct, and continually experiencing the utmost Calumny and abuse, for our adherence to our duty, satisfyed that we shall not suffer in Your Lordships' opinion on slight grounds, and that every allowance will be made for our conduct, in the critical Situation we are in, and the arduous Service in which we are engaged, though we cannot but lament the unhappy Constitution of this Government, where those who should be Councellors for the Crown are dependant on the Voice of the Representatives of the People for their [100] Annual Election. And therefore, it is no wonder, that to secure their approbation, the honor and dignity of Government are often sacrificed, and the most flagrant violations of the Peace and Order of Society passed over with impunity."[49]

In the Answer from the four Gentlemen before mentioned, they gave their opinion, "that from the Spirit which had been excited in the populace against all the Commissioners of the Customs, except Mr. Temple, they could not have remained long in safety in the town of Boston, after the seizure of the Sloop *Liberty*, [101] but would have been in great danger of violence to their persons and properties, from a Mob which at that time it was generally expected would be raised for that purpose."

"That it had been found by experience, that the authority of Government was insufficient, to restrain, suppress, or punish, the several Mobs which had been assembled since the 14th of Aug. 1765, in some of which felonious Acts of violence had been commit[t]ed, and we are of opinion, that at the time You retired to the Castle there was no probability that the same [102] authority could have had any greater force, in restraining, suppressing, or punishing a Mob raised against the four Commissioners of the Customs than another Mob which preceded it, and we are of opinion, that You could not have returned to Town, and executed Your Commission with safety, at any time after Your withdrawing before the arrival of his Majesty's Troops."[50] [103]

[104-106 blank]

In December 1768 both Houses of Parliament passed sundry resolves respecting the Proceedings at Boston, in the months of June and September.

That the Declarations, Resolutions, and Proceedings, in the Town Meetings at Boston on the 14 June and 12 September, were illegal and Unconstitutional, and calculated to excite Sedition and insurrection in his Majesty's Province of the Massachusetts Bay.

That the Town had been in a State of great disorder and confusion, and the peace of the Town had at several times been disturbed by tumults of a dangerous Nature. [107]

---

49 The commissioners's complaints—dismissed as whining by their political opponents—were turned against them by being made public, such as in *Letters to the Ministry* (Boston: Edes & Gill, 1769), 85-86, a memorial of 16 June 1768 from the commissioners to Treasury, printed to embarrass Hulton and his colleagues.

50 From the Treasury's response, written by Grey Cooper, 29 June 1769, TNA, PRO/T28/1, fos. 338-342.

That neither the Council of the said Province, nor the ordinary Civil Magistrates, did exert their Authority, for suppressing the said riots and tumults.

That the preservation of the publick peace and the due execution of the Laws became impracticable, without the aid of a military force, to support and protect the Civil Magistrates and the Officers of his Majesty's Revenue.

That the appointment at the Town Meeting on the 12 September of a Convention to be held in Boston on the 22nd of that Month of Deputies from the several Towns and Districts [108] in the Province, and the issuing a precept, by the Select Men of Boston, to each of the said Towns and Districts, for the Election of such Deputies, were proceedings subversive of His Majesty's Government, and evidently manifesting a design in the Inhabitants of Boston, to set up a new, and Unconstitutional Authority Independant of the Crown of Great Britain.

That the Election by several Towns and Districts of Deputies to sit in the said Convention and the meeting of such Convention in consequence thereof, were daring insults offered to his Majesty's authority, and audacious usurpations of the Powers of Government. [109][51]

The Letters which Governor Bernard and other Servants of the Crown had written to Government in the Summer of 1768 having been laid before the House of Commons, copies of them were sent out to America and they were printed at Boston. Upon which the Town published an Appeal to the World, in vindication of themselves. And passed several violent resolves against the Governor, the Commissioners of the Customs &c, declaring that many of the letters and Memorials were false, scandalous and infamous libels. And directing the Select Men, to complain to proper Authority, that the Authors of them may be proceeded with according to Law, and brought to condign punishment.[52] [110]

---

51 The first steps toward the resolution were taken on 28 November 1768, when North presented sixty letters, memorials, and other documents to the House of Commons as proof of unrest in Massachusetts. The resolution was actually drafted in the House of Lords and revised by Commons before final approval in February 1769. Printed in the *House of Commons Journal*, 32:107-108, but already circulating in the colonies as it worked its way through Parliament—see the *Boston Evening-Post*, 20 March and 17 April 1769.

52 *An Appeal to the World; Or a Vindication of the Town of Boston* (Boston: Edes and Gill, 1769).

Chapter 7

Internal difficulties the Board of Customs
had to combat with on its Establishment

UPON THE ESTABLISHMENT of the Board the Commissioners had much labour in preparing proper Instructions, and forms of business for the Several Officers; and it took a considerable time to receive, and digest, the Accounts of the State of the Trade and Revenue in the several Ports. In all which business, they had little assistance from several of the Subordinate Officers, appointed by the Treasury. [111]

Their Secretary was a poor, mulish, insignificant Creature, their Solicitor a drunken wretch and their two Inspectors General who were to visit, and report the State of the Trade and Revenue in the several Colonies[,] were unacquainted with the business of [the] Office they were to set about. And one of them was much more intent, on possessing the Officers with an opinion that he was of greater consequence than his Superiors, than in attending to the discharge of his duty. Even two of the Clerks of the Office, appointed by the Treasury, were insufficient [112] to their duty and were rather a burden, than of Use in Office, but the most distressing circumstance, to the operations of the Board, on its establishment and for some years after, was the opposition of Mr. Temple, one of its Members, to the conduct of his Brethren and the persecution and abuse they underwent from the Spirit he fomented against them.[53]

Before his appointment as Commissioner, he had been Surveyor General of the Customs of the Northern District of America. Highly lifted up [113] with his consequence as Surveyor General, he thought himself reduced by being appointed a Commissioner.

He could not submit to share his imagined consequence with anyone and it was sufficient that he had an equal in Office to make him hate the Man.

He was vain and superficial, in no wise a Man of education, knowledge, or business. Confident, arrogant, [word scratched out] and ignorant; yet with some address, and a little specious shew he passed upon people at first [114] as a Man of parts, and cleverness. His vanity, and assuming manner might only render him worthy of contempt; but the wickedness of his heart, made him justly the object of detestation and abhorrence.

---

53 Samuel Venner, as secretary; David Lisle, as solicitor; John Williams and John Woolton as inspectors general. Hulton did not make it clear, here or elsewhere, which two clerks he had in mind.

If he was offended with another, he was implacable in his resentment. And whoever shewed countenance to the object of his hatred drew on himself his malignancy and shared in the bitterness of his vengance.

It was equally dangerous to oblige him, for his pride [115] could not brook the sight of the Man who had done him favours.

[Entire paragraph scratched out in the manuscript.]

He bore an inveterate hatred to Governor Bernard and was a great fomentor of the troubles, and disturbances, that were raised against him in his Government. [116]

When it was told to the Governor that Mr. Temple had said he should be content to go to the Gates of Hell[,] if he could plunge him therein, the Governor replyed "I may perhaps be carried to the gates of Heaven by saving him from destruction."

Mr. Temple would not attend his Brethren to the Governor on their arrival nor wait on him to qualify into Office. Nor would he visit Mr. Paxton, a Brother Member, or join at any of those Parties where the Commissioners were invited to Dinner (except once at the Lt. Governor's), but entirely [117] seperated himself in opinion, and conduct from his Brethren, espousing the Popular party. And he drew off their little insignificant Secretary, Mr. Venner, from his duty to the Board, and to act unbecoming his confidential Office.[54] And other subordinate Officers he spirited up against the Commissioners, and the measures of the Board. [118]

---

54 Venner was dismissed from office in 1769—see 66-67 supra for the controversy surrounding his firing.

Chapter 8

Heads of the Faction at Boston on the Establishment of the Board of Customs 1767

THERE HAD ALWAYS BEEN a faction in Boston which had given disturbance to Government: and from the Nature of the Constitution, the People were always under the influence of some artful Demagogues. It was said that Governor [left blank] during his Administration from 17[ ]to 17[ ] gave countenance to many low factious People, and by his conduct cherished that Spirit which [119] disturbed the administration of his Successors.[55]

When the Stamp Act took place, Mr. Otis, whose father had been disap[p]ointed in succeeding the Office of Chief Justice, vehemently opposed the execution of it, and became a declared enemy to Governor Bernard and Government.

Mr. Samuel Adams was then his Coadjutor in the house of Assembly. This latter person insinuated himself into the confidence of the Members by his Speeches in the house, and by writing in the news papers, in opposition to Government. [120]

He watched every opportunity to put the conduct of the Governor in an unfavorable light, and to allarm the People with the danger that threatened their rights, and liberties. Ever zealous and active, he adapted his addresses to the individuals according as he discovered their prevailing temper, and dispositions. With some he prevailed by his affectation of Patriotism, by his cant and hypocrisy. With others by cunning, and plausibility, and where he found his insidious arts ineffectual, he had recourse to allarming [121] their fears, and intimidated them with the dread of popular displeasure: for though he had justly forfeited the good opinion of his fellow Citizens by his peculation and abuse of a publick trust,

---

55 He was no doubt leaving space for Thomas Pownall, governor from 1757-1759. Though an Englishman—and, like Hulton, someone who tried to make his way up in society through government appointments—Pownall had succeeded the thoroughly unpopular William Shirley. His ability to get on well with provincial leaders meant that his time in office would be idealized by Bernard's and Hutchinson's critics, on the assumption that he would have done better. Perhaps so; perhaps not. Hulton had no reason to care for Pownall, who had been a rival in Germany during his investigations of the commissary there.

yet such was his Art, that he now was their Political Dictator, and gave the tone to their opinions and practises.[56]

When the Board arrived at Boston in November 1767 Mr Otis's popularity and influence were on the decline, and Mr. Adams, together with Dr. Cooper, a smooth, artful, civil [122] Jesuitical Priest, with Mr. James Bowdoin, one of the Council, were the Leaders of this Faction.[57]

Mr. Bowdoin was a Man of large property, and had great influence with the People, though he was rather of a severe and gloomy disposition, than possessed of the arts of Popularity.

He had been upon friendly terms with Governor Bernard, but having lately married his Daughter to Mr. John Temple, one of the Commissioners of the Customs, who bore a mortal enmity to the Governor, he from that time [123] became adverse to his Administration, joined the Faction, and supported every measure that tended to distress Government.

Governor Bernard having received some instructions which he communicated in confidence to the Council, they desired he would leave them with the Board to be shewn to the other Members, which he consented to, upon a charge that no Copy should be taken of them. In the next newspapers the whole appeared in print, and when the Governor, with some warmth charged the Board with a [124] breach of the injunctions he had laid them

---

56 John C. Miller's *Samuel Adams: Pioneer in Propaganda* (Boston: Little, Brown, and Co., 1936) gives us a Samuel Adams whose actions—though not his motives—echo Hulton. Pauline Maier's essay in *The Old Revolutionaries* (New York: Alfred A. Knopf, 1980), 3-50, presents a more complex man, noting that just because Adams predicted a war for independence as early as 1768 does not mean that he advocated it at that same moment. Likewise see William Fowler's brief but incisive *Samuel Adams* (New York: Longman, 1997); and John K. Alexander, *Samuel Adams* (Lanham, Md.: Rowman & Littlefield, 2002) .

57 For Otis go first to Williams Pencak's essay in *ANB*, 16:838-840; and Clifford K. Shipton, et al., *Sibley's Harvard Graduates*, 18 vols. (Boston: Harvard University Press, 1933–), 11:247-287 (class of 1743), a continuation of the series begun by John Langdon Sibley in 1873, picked up by Clifford Shipton decades later, long since published by the MHS, and now edited by Conrad Edick Wright. William Tudor's florid *The Life of James Otis* (Boston: Wells and Lilly, 1823) ought to be balanced with John J. Waters Jr., *The Otis Family* (Chapel Hill: University of North Carolina Press, 1968). For more on Mercy, Otis's sister who was married to leading patriot James Warren, see Kate Davis's *Catharine Macaulay & Mercy Otis Warren* (Oxford: Oxford University Press, 2005), and Lester H. Cohen's introductory comments to the reissue of Warren's *History of the Rise, Progress and Termination of the American Revolution*, 2 vols. (Indianapolis, Ind.: Liberty Fund, 1989; original ed., 1805). Warren's history depicts the commissioners in just the way Warren's brother probably saw them. Charles Akers wrote a biography of Samuel Cooper, *The Divine Politician* (Boston: Northeastern University Press, 1982). Cooper, pastor of the Brattle Street congregational church in Boston, was one of the "black regiment" of ministers decried by Peter Oliver—see Schutz and Adair, eds., *Peter Oliver Origins*, 29 and 43-45, with Cooper part of a "sacerdotal Triumvirate," along with Jonathan Mayhew and Charles Chauncy. Hulton slammed the "Independant Ministers" in his "Account," 179 infra. The best starting place for James Bowdoin, as for his son-in-law John Temple, is in the *ANB*, in this case an essay by Gordon C. Kershaw (at 3:272-274), who also wrote a full-length biography, *James Bowdoin II* (Lanham, Md.: University Press of America, 1991). Bowdoin was in the Harvard class of 1745 (see *Sibley's Harvard Graduates*, 11:514-550).

under, Mr. B[owdoin] answered with a smile that no Copies had been taken, for that they had been printed from the original.

There were several Subordinate Characters in the Faction. The most ostensible was Mr. John Hancock, who became possessed of large property from an Uncle. He was a Man without parts, or education, and though ignorant, uncultured, and weak, yet of that benevolence of disposition, that under proper [125] influence, from the weight of his fortune, he might have passed through life with reputation; but falling into the hands of designing bad men, he was made a prey of and became a dupe to the party, who drew him in to give a Sanction to all their wicked measures; made use of his purse to further their Schemes and consumed his Substance upon the adherents of faction and in supporting Sedition, and Treason.[58]

This Mr. Hancock is the same Gentleman who in the Year 1768[,] to brave the [126] Commissioners of the Customs and shew that the Revenue Laws should not be executed, caused a Cargoe of Wines to be boldly run on shore one night. And though the Commissioners failed of evidence on the prosecution, yet the fact was undoubted.

Many persons besides the Master of the Vessel were involved in the guilt of perjury from this violation of the Law. And another Master lost his life, by overstraining himself in unloading the Vessel and died before the next Morning. [127]

[128-130 blank]

Mr. Otis[,] though declining in his popularity, yet was very violent in his invectives against the Commissioners of the Customs, and published some very scurrilous reflections on them; more particularly pointing at Mr. Robinson. Mr. Robinson and he met at the Coffee House where they had a severe combat with Sticks. Mr. Otis was much beaten and afterwards brought an action against Mr. Robinson. The Action was tried, and Mr. Robinson was cast in £2000 damages, but before the trial he went to England. [131]

In a similar Action the Grand Jury would not find a bill when Mr. Temple was the Aggressor, but now when an odious person was in their power, the Jury loaded their verdict with the most enormous damages. A like Action was tried at the same time between two Townsmen, when the Jury gave about twenty pounds damages.

Mr. Robinson did not return to Boston for several years, and in the mean time his friends by publishing a concession on his part, obtained from Mr. Otis a [132] relinquishment of the Verdict of damages given against Mr. Robinson.

Mr. Otis soon after by his intemperance became disordered in his mind, was repeatedly confined and lived neglected. It was said when he first entered into opposition to Government, that he declared he would set the Continent in a flame, though he perished in it. He soon saw his declaration fulfilled, and lived a monument of his own depravity.

---

58 William Fowler, *The Baron of Beacon Hill* (Boston: Houghton Mifflin, 1980) is decidedly more sympathetic, as are virtually all of Hancock's biographers.

He is said to have died in 1783. Suddenly by a flash of Lightning.[59] [133]

[134 blank]

During these times, the publick news papers groaned with abuses on the Governors, and Servants of Government; and no one dared to write or print any thing in opposition to the ruling faction; 'till at length one Mayne, a Scotchman, who was printer of a news paper, and a Stationer, and had a talent for humour, began to expose the Characters of the tyrant Patriots. This they could not bear. Profuse in their invectives upon others, whenever they felt the lash themselves, they swore destruction to the Author [135] and they actually assaulted and wounded Maine in the publick Street, and would have murthered him, had he not kept them off with a pistol, which he drew from his pocket.

This Person towards the close of the non-importation agreement in 1770 took the pains to publish an account of the Goods imported into Boston during the time the Colonies were under engagement not to import such Goods, which account was distributed through the other Colonies, whereby the double [136] dealing of the Bostonians was exposed, and the other Colonies were led to break up that agreement. However, all this ended in the ruin of Maine. The faction wrote to his Creditors in London, and represented him in such a light, that they were induced to send out to Mr. Hancock, a power of Attorney against him. Mr. Hancock immediately seized on his effects, which being chiefly books, were sold to a great loss.

After the assault on his person Meine fled to [137] England, where he thrown into Goal by his Creditors, though at the same time his Stock at Boston was in the hands of their Attorneys.[60] [138]

---

59   Otis was struck down in the doorway of his home, in just the manner Hulton described—and as Otis himself had apparently wished—on 23 May 1783. Hulton was thus working on the "Account" at least as late as 1784, and probably beyond.

60   John Mein. William Pencak wrote a brief piece on him for the *ANB* 15:201-202. Revolutionary-era printer Isaiah Thomas also offered reflections on Mein in his *The History of Printing in America*, 2 vols. (Albany: Joel Munsell, 1874; orig. ed., 1810), 1:152-154.

Chapter 9

Governor Bernard and Governor Hutchinson

WHEN GOVERNOR BERNARD went to England in 1769, Lieut. Gov. Hutchinson succeeded to the Chair.

These two Gentlemen had the misfortune to be in the Seat of Government in very difficult times, when the Authority of the British Parliament was disputed and denied, and the Constitution of the Colony over which they presided did not give them authority sufficient to inforce obedience to the Laws of Great Britain.

In respect to their abilities, and liberal [139] endowments, they had few equals in America, and none exceeded them in their regard to the true interest of the Province, and in their desires, and endeavours, to promote the real happiness of the People. Yet, no two Gentlemen have been more abused.

Designing men, taking advantage of the temper of the times, made use of every art to inflame the minds of the People, and prejudice them against their Governors, and Government. Wrought into consequence as the Leaders of faction, contention became necessary to the support of that consequence. And from the [140] liberty of the press, the most illiberal, malicious, and unjust accusations against the most respectable Characters in Office were propagated, and from the credulity of the People received as truth.

Sir Francis Bernard was bred a Civilian, was an exceeding good Classic Scholar, and had a fine taste in Musick, and Architecture. As a friend, a neighbour, and companion, no one was more easy and agre[e]able, without ostentation or ceremony, he lived with ease with his friends, told a thousand good Stories, and every body [141] was pleased and happy in his Society. He was perhaps too open and communicative. A person of less abilities and merit than himself, with more address, art, and intrigue, might have succeeded better. He perhaps was not sufficiently disguised, and did not practise enough the courtly manner and courtly arts, for one in his Station.

There is often a thin layer of Gold, or Silver, with a high polish, over a base metal; but that which is pure, though less Shining, will last longer. And men, conscious of their own worth and integrity, often despise those little arts [142] which the worthless and vain make use of, to carry their designs.

Governor Bernard's letters on the Trade and Government of America, and the Principles of Law, and Polity, applied to the American Colonies[,] shew his great abilities, his liberal Sentiments, and attachment to the real interest of both Countries.[61]

---

61   *Select Letters* (see supra, 95 n. 231); Nicolson, '*Infamas Govener*' is Bernard's only biographer to date.

Governor Hutchinson was a native of Boston. He was a Gentleman of great natural abil
ities, much cultivated and improved by reading and Study. He had made himself master
of several [143] Languages and had acquired a thorough knowledge of the Laws of his
Country, though he had never practised at the Bar. He had filled several Offices of honor
in the State, and the Province is greatly indebted to his assiduity, and virtuous resolution,
in being rid of a pernicious paper Currency, which laid the foundation of that credit and
opulence it now enjoys.

When he came to the Chair he was Chief Justice of the Province, in which Character he
had acquired the greatest reputation, as a Judicious Lawyer, and an honest Man. [144] And
in the Office of Judge of Probates he proved his great integrity, benevolence, and humanity:
attending with temper and patience to the most laborious business, and giving his Council
and advice freely to the Widow and the Orphan. In his manners he was most gentle, and
amiable. Though his opinion was respected by all, and everyone acknowledged the superiority of his Judgment, yet he always expressed himself with the modesty of a Young Man,
and drew a reverence to the Sentiment, by the manner in which it was delivered. [145]

If we may judge from events, it may be lamented that Mr. Hutchinson succeeded to the
Government; as it is generally imagined that the Ministry delayed taking rigorous measures
with the Americans, from the hopes which he gave them, of his being able to accommodate
matters by lenient means. He certainly had too good an opinion of his Countrymen; and
perhaps too great a confidence in his own arts of persuasion, in his own ability to reduce
their turbulent Spirits, to Order and Government.[62]

Could a prudent, a temperate American, look upon what the Leaders of the People had
then in view, but as the height of folly, and madness? Could any one conceive to what desperate resolutions Republican fanaticism will lead a people, 'till he saw the revolt of the Provinces of New England, and their avowing rebellion, and attempting an independency? [146]

---

62 Nelson's chapter on Hutchinson in *The American Tory*, 21-39, paved the way for Bernard Bailyn's *The Ordeal
of Thomas Hutchinson* (Cambridge, Mass.: The Belknap Press of the Harvard University Press, 1974). John
Phillip Reid took issue with parts of Bailyn's argument in a review eventually reprinted in Hendrik Hartog,
ed., *Law in the American Revolution and the Revolution in the Law* (New York: New York University Press, 1981),
20-45. William Pencak, *America's Burke* (Lanham, Md.: University Press of America, 1982) also questioned
some of Bailyn's characterizations, most notably the notion that Hutchinson was a prudent pragmatist,
"bewildered by revolutionary change" (vi). Pencak saw a passion that drove Hutchinson to develop a mar-
tyr's complex. Close to his extended family but aloof otherwise, it was unlikely that Hutchinson and Hulton
could ever have become confreres. Also see Andrew Stephen Walmsley, *Thomas Hutchinson & the Origins
of the American Revolution* (New York: New York University Press, 1999). Neither Walmsley nor Pencak have
anything on Hulton, and they deal with the customs board only in passing.

Chapter 10

Opposition to the Revenue Laws at Boston, 1769 and 1770

IN THE FALL OF THE YEAR 1769 Governor Bernard went to England, Commodore Hood returned to Halifax with some of the King's Ships that had continued at Boston, and took with him the two Regiments that had been brought from Ireland and General Mackay went back to England, leaving the 14th and 29th Regiments at Boston under the command of Lt. Col. Dalrymple.

Commodore Hood had an attachment to Halifax, and persuading himself that the town of Boston was orderly and would remain quiet with [147] two Regiments only, and being desirous to carry back two Regiments with his Ships to those Quarters, he was induced to represent that there was no necessity for the whole of the Military to remain at Boston.

General Mackay[,] weary of a command where he saw his Soldiers insulted without being able to relieve them, or exercise his power in keeping the Subjects in Order, was glad to have part of the troops removed, so that there could be no occasion for him to remain at Boston.

After the Commodore [148] and General with some of the Ships and two of the Regiments were gone, the people grew more bold and violent in their resistance to the Laws of Revenue.#[63]

#Several Letters and Memorials from the Servants of the Crown in America to Government at home, having been laid before Parliament, Copies thereof were sent back to America, and the Grand Jury at Boston about the close of 1769 found bills of indictment against the Commissioners of the Customs for divers misrepresentations in their Official Correspondence with the Treasury.

Every means was used to compel the inhabitants to subscribe to the Regulations which were set up by the heads of the party in opposition, not to import or use British Goods, Tea, &c. brought from thence. And such of the Merchants and Importers as refused to subscribe to the terms that were thus imposed were marked for resentment, and underwent the persecution of the Mob; and during the [149] latter part of the Year 1769 and to near the close of 1770 the town of Boston was subject to the will of a set of arbitrary Demagogues, who kept every one in Subjection. And he who dared to dispute obedience to their usurped authority

---

63 This is the first of several insertions that Hulton (or his scribe) made, on this page and on others that follow, marked by the "#" where a paragraph would have been inserted, had space allowed. It was instead written off to the side. I moved it into the text proper.

was in danger of having his house pulled down and of being dragged out by the Mob, and abused in the grossest manner. In short[,] in these times such was the temper of the people, as bore down every principle that combated with their views. They would get free from all restraint of Revenue Laws, and in doing this every [150] thing was just and lawful. A general timidity prevailed, and a silent assent to acts of outrage and violence. In vain were the Magistracy applied to in behalf of Sufferers, no one would stand forth; and to be freed from imaginary grievances, the People submit[t]ed to a real tyranny: for the Demagogues having raised the passions of the people, employed them to intimidate, persecute, and bear down, whomsoever they pleased.

But notwithstanding all the associations and Subscriptions not to import British Goods and the persecutions of such as dared to persist in that [151] branch of Commerce, there were many persons who outwardly appeared in support of the Combinations against importing Goods from Great Britain, who secretly brought in quantities of such Goods and a book was published in the Year 1770 which was circulated through the other Provinces, containing the names of the persons, and the Cargoes of Goods imported or brought by them into Boston by which the pretended Patriotism of those Men was exposed, and they brought to disgrace in the Southern Provinces; and the publication had a great effect towards bringing the [152] inhabitants to the Southward, to break off from this combination.[64]

During the non-importation agreement, it was a practise to mark the doors of such persons as dared to import goods from Great Britain, or who would not sign the agreements proposed by the Leaders of the People, by set[t]ing up an hand with the word, Importer. This was done by Boys and Young People, who gathered round the Doors, and insulted any one who should dare to go into the Shop, or Store of the person so marked.

One of these hands or [153] other mark being fixed at the door of an inhabitant, and several persons being gathered round the house, one Ebenezer Richardson passing by reproved the people, and removed the hand that had been set up; upon which the crowd pursued him to his dwelling house, and violently broke the windows, throwing Stones and other things at him, in the room where he had sheltered himself; finding the rage of the people to increase and himself in imminent danger, he at length fired a musket amongst them which killed a boy named Schneider.

Richardson was afterwards taken into custody, and remained [154] in Goal till April 1770[,] when he was tried.

---

64 [John Mein], *A State of Importations from Great-Britain into the Port of Boston* (Boston, 1770). See too the one-page broadside ordered printed *At a Meeting of the Merchants & Traders, at Faneuil-Hall, on the 23d January 1770* (1770) identifying and condemning those who had not complied with the non-importation stipulations, who in so doing "have in the most insolent Manner *too long* affronted this People, and endeavoured to undermine the Liberties of this Country, to which they owe their *little* Importance; and that they deserve to be driven to that Obscurity, from which they originated, and to *the Hole of the Pit from whence they were digged*."

From this time the resentment of the People against the Soldiery, the Commissioners of the Customs, and the Laws of Revenue, continually increased. They sought occasions of quarrelling with the Soldiery, insulted them in their Posts of duty, and otherwise 'till the Storm broke forth on the 5 March 1770 when the people, as by concert, attacked several of the Centries on their Posts, particularly the one placed as a Guard at the Custom house. He was posted within call of the Main Guard [155][,] who hearing him cry out when he was attacked, the Captain sent a party to his relief.

The people still were violent in their abuse, both of the Centry and party. The Captain soon followed. The People rushed up to the ends of the bayonets, throwing brick bats, and striking the Soldiers, daring them to fire. and one of the most desperate attempted to wrest the Musket out of the hands of one of the Soldiers, when he fired and was followed by the rest of the party, who killed and Wounded six or eight of them; and then the rest dispersed.[65]

The Governor and Council assembled that night. The [156] party of Soldiers were delivered up, and the Captain surrendered himself into the hands of the Civil power.

The next day the people assembled in Faneuil Hall. They were urgent in their demands for justice. The Governor and Council were assembled in the town house. The two Regiments were under Arms, the 29th in King Street and the 14th at their Barracks under Fort Hill. The people were very clamorous, and insisted on the two Regiments being withdrawn to Castle William. Lt. Col. Dalrymple[,] the Commander[,] was in Council, as was Capt Cauldwell of the *Rose* Man of War, then in the Harbour.[157]

The Colonel wanted to act under the advice and direction of the Governor and endeavoured to persuade others that the command in town lay in him. The Council adjourned to the afternoon, without coming to any resolution, in the interim the Colonel went to some of the Counsellors, and endeavoured to prevail with them to advise the Governor to recommend it to the Colonel to withdraw the Troops. When the Council met in the afternoon the Colonel asserted that one Regiment, the 29th which had been on guard on the 5[th][,] should go to the Castle. The Committee from the People increased in insolence on this concession, and insisted that both [158] Regiments should go to the Castle, and at length to quiet their minds it was agreed to.#

#What were the whole of the Colonel's views or motives in this business do not appear, but many people blamed him for this conduct, and imputed it to various causes. From an attention to his after behavior I imagined that he wished to keep well with the people and had in view to succeed as Governor of the Province.

---

65 *The Boston Gazette* 12 March 1770 account was soon after coupled with Paul Revere's engraving of the event, which depicted a massacre, pure and simple—innocent American civilians slaughtered by murderous British soldiers. Three from the crowd died that night, one the next morning, and a fifth well over a week later. Another half dozen were wounded. Zobel, *Boston Massacre*, remains unsurpassed on the events leading to the "massacre," the "massacre" itself, and the subsequent trials.

After this advantage gained over the Soldiery, the next device was to get rid of the Commissioners of the Customs. In order to render them still more obnoxious a story was propagated that at the time the people were killed in King Street, there was firing out of the Custom House and that the people had been killed from thence, by persons employed by the Commissioners. [159]

Under this suggestion, one Manwaring , an Officer of the Customs in Boston, was taken into Custody, upon the evidence of a french boy, who was his Servant. Two other Persons (one of them a Porter to the Board of Customs) were committed to Goal, along with Manwaring, upon suspicion of being concerned in firing out of the Custom House on the 5th March.

These accusations, joined to the former odium against the Commissioners and Revenue Laws, threw the people into the greatest ferment, and an Officer of [160] of the Customs scarce dared to shew his head in Boston. The evidence of the French boy, and of about Sixty others, relative to the affair of the 5th March, were industriously taken and circulated through the province, and Mr. Bowdoin wrote letters to many Members of both Houses of Parliament, inclosing Copies of these affidavits, which were printed, so that people's minds were prejudiced and inflamed, before the Parties accused could be heard, or brought upon their trials.[66]

Four of the Commissioners, after the affair of [161] the 5th of March[,] retired from Boston. Mr. Robinson went to England, Mr. Paxton removed to a friend's house at Cambridge, and Mr. Burch with his family sheltered themselves with me at Brooklyn.

From an apprehension that the violent temper of the People would lead them to the utmost outrages, and excesses, against the Persons of the Commissioners, Mr. Burch and myself thought it best for Us to retire for a while out of the Province, and the latter end of March we went to Piscataqua.#

#But though we remained there unmolested, yet the Governor shewed great apprehension for the peace of the town, in case Mr. Paxton should come there, and said it would be out of his power to protect him if he came into the Province, but that Mr. Temple might come and welcome, and he would answer for it no affront should be offered to him.

About this time the Superior Court sat at [162] Boston when Richardson was tried and found guilty, but the Judges did not proceed to his condemnation.

One day, whilst the Court was sit[t]ing, the Demagogues of the People came into Court, after having dined with Mr. Temple, one of the Commissioners, and endeavoured to prevail on the Judges to bring on the trial of the Soldiers. The Court behaved with a proper Spirit on the occasion: adjourned and did not bring on these trials during that Term. The temper of the People at that time was no wise disposed to listen calmly to Law, and evidence and

---

66 The town produced *A Short Narrative*, which was countered by a rival view and different affidavits in *A Fair Account of the Late Unhappy Disturbance At Boston in New England* (London: B. White, 1770), which in turn prompted the town's retort in *Additional Observations*.

the Court gained great [163] reputation with all sensible and temperate people, by their conduct throughout the whole of these troublesome affairs, in these distracted times.

The latter end of April the Commissioners returned from Piscataqua to Brooklyn.

The appearance of things would not suffer them to go to Boston, and in the course of the next month the temper of the People rather increased in violence, than subsided; so that they thought it prudent to remove again from the neighbourhood of Boston, but returned again the begin[n]ing of June.

The Spirit of resentment against the Importers of English Goods, and the Officers of the Customs continued as [164] violent as ever.

One Owen Richards[,] a Tidesman[,] was dragged from on board a Vessel where he was stationed on duty, and put into a Cart, where he was stripped naked, tarred and feathered, and led in this manner in the Cart for several hours, a shocking spectacle through the town. He brought a Civil action against a person who was chief actor on the occasion, and recovered a trifling damage. He then brought a criminal action against him, but having only his own evidence to support it, it fell through, and he himself was brought in to pay [165] damages to the other Party, who cast him into Goal for twelve pounds charges, from which he was released by Order of the Commissioners, to pay the Charges.

On the 19th June one Mr. McMaster, a Scotch Merchant and Importer, was taken out of his room, placed in a Cart and made to expect the same treatment that Richards had experienced; but fainting away from an apprehension of what was to befall him, they spared him this ignimony, and contented themselves with leading him through the town in the Cart [166] to Roxbury, where they turned him out, spitt[l]ing upon him, and otherwise contemptuously and rudely treating him.

That same night of the 19th June 1770, after my family were all in bed in my home at Brooklyn (which was a dwelling in the Country, at some distance from any other) I was waked out of my sleep, with a gentle tapping at the Door of the house. On which I got up, and enquired who was there, a voice answered I have a letter for Mr H, from the Grenades, which came by the Express from New York this Morning. Upon which I desired him to wait a little and I would come down. Having slipt on [167] my breeches and waistcoat, I took my sword in my hand, and being cautious of opening the House door, I went to the parlour Window, and having opened the Shutter, a man stood there. I asked him for the letter, and opened the Window a little. He said I have a letter indeed, and advanced, put[t]ing his hands out, with an intent to lift up the sash, upon which I clapt it down, and he instantly struck two violent blows at me, with a bludgeon which broke the upper part of the Window, frame and all; but resting on the middle part did not touch me. No sooner had he given the first blow, than all the Windows round were broke in the same manner, by people placed at each of them. The family [168] immediately rose in the greatest consternation, and Mrs. H opening the Window shutter in her room had a large stone thrown at her[,] which happily missed her. Imagining the people would break into the house, and seek to murther me[,] I ran to the Servants' room at the head of the back Stairs with my sword in my hand, leaving two

Servant Men at the bottom. The people without kept uttering Oaths and execrations for some time, swearing, "dead or alive, we will have him," but at length they withdrew, and I soon after retired to a Neighbour's house till daylight, and passed the following day [169] at Mr. John Apthorp's at little Cambridge. Mrs. H and myself not thinking it safe to return home, we remained at his house for two nights, and hearing that Mr. Burch with his family was gone to the Castle, we came home the following morning, and carried the Children and part of the family from Brooklyn to the Castle. This was the 21 June, and from that time to the 7th November we remained on Castle Island, the Governor allowing Us to make use of his appartments, which were fully occupied by the Commissioners, and Servants, and Officers of the Board.

I made a representation to the Governor and Council [170] of the attack made upon me, but they took no pains to detect the Perpetrators of this mischief, though it was well known that the people came from Boston and might have been discovered. Some of the Council said I had hired People to come out, and break my own Windows, and from several circumstances there was strong reason to suspect that Mr. T, one of our own Members, had been the means of this assault being made upon me.[67]

The violence of the people continued during great part of the Summer, but towards September it abated. They fell off from their Non [171] importation agreement, and their resentment against the Military and Commissioners in some measure subsided.

About this time Commodore Gambier arrived from England to relieve Commodore Hood and Governor Hutchinson delivered up the Keys of the Fort at Castle Island to Lt. Col. Dalrymple when the Guard from the 14th Regt. marched into the Fort, and the Provincial Garrison withdrew.

Had further measures been pursued at this time for the amendment of the Government, and the plans proposed by Governor Bernard for an alteration in the Charter been adopted, it [172] is probable that the Constitution might have been set[t]led without further disturbances, and peace and order and good Government have been established in the province.

The trial of Captain Preston and the Soldiers, which had been put off 'till the temper of the People was a little cooled, came on about the latter end of October, when they were all acquitted.

Manwaring and the Custom House servant who had been accused by the French Boy were discharged from their bail, and the Boy [173] was convicted of perjury.[68]

---

67 Thus Ann Hulton's snide comments about Temple (see supra 65 n. 124). If Temple was involved, there is no proof of it yet.

68 Preston's trial ran from October 24-30; Preston was acquitted and set free. He soon after returned to England. The trial of the eight soldiers ran longer, from November 27-December 5. Six were acquitted of all charges; two were convicted of manslaughter, allowed to plead benefit of the clergy, and released after being branded on their left hands. Their regiment had been transferred to New Jersey months before. L. Kinvin Wroth and Hiller Zobel brought together various sources in an attempt to reconstruct Preston's and the

Richardson remained in Goal upwards of a Year afterwards, when he was finally discharged on the King's pardon.

The acquittal of the Soldiers and Captain Preston, the breaking up the Non[-] importation agreement, with the arrival of Commodore Gambier, produced a change in the behavior of the people, and Government at home were pleased to think they had come to their Senses, and would now remain quiet, having seen the error of their doings. The plan proposed by Governor Bernard, and approved by [174] Lord Hillsborough, Secretary of State for America, for an alteration of the Charter of the Massachusetts Bay, was therefore laid aside, but more particularly owing, as was supposed, to the representation of Governor Hutchinson after he came to the Chair.[69] He had some attachment to the Old Charter and great confidence in his own address and ability in managing the People and persuaded himself that he should be able to keep things quiet and the Ministry were easily prevailed on to abstain from a business that would be attended with some trouble and difficulty and the success of which was uncertain. [175]

From the 7th November 1770 I remained in quiet at my house at Brooklyn. Mr. Hallowell came out Commissioner in the room of Mr. Temple the latter end of December following, and we continued to do the business of the Board unmolested from that time. [176]

[177-178 blank]

---

soldiers' trials in volume 3 of *Legal Papers of John Adams*, 4 vols. (Cambridge, Mass.: Harvard University Press, 1965). The printed transcript for the soldiers' trial was published from the notes by John Hodgson, *The Trial of William Wemms...* (Boston: J. Fleeming, 1770). The record as constituted there—which John Adams, one of the counsel for the defendants, found objectionable—ought to be contrasted with the version sent by Hutchinson to London, in the PRO/CO 5/759, fos. 382-402. The testimonies for Preston's trial are in fos. 355-368. The four civilians, Manwaring included, were tried in a single day, December 12th, with the jurors not even leaving their seats before pronouncing the men innocent. There is no surviving transcript for that trial, just brief notices in the *Massachusetts Gazette*, 13 December 1770; the *Boston Evening-Post*, 17 December 1770; and the *Boston Gazette*, 17 and 24 December 1770; and ibid., 18 and 25 March 1771, and 1 April 1771, for the fate of Charles Bourgatte, the "French servant." A fragment of what is apparently Bourgatte's testimony is in the Boston Public Library, Ch.M.1.8, 217. Manwaring, who worked for the customs service, later petitioned the Treasury for compensation, 4 August 1771, TNA, PRO/T1/486.

69 Hulton gives the impression that a formal plan had been agreed to at Whitehall to punish Massachusetts, when in fact it had not. See the discussion in Nicolson, *"Infamas Govener,"* 186-191.

Chapter 11

Mr. Temple and Dr. Franklin

MR. TEMPLE[,] THOUGH ONE OF THE Commissioners of the Customs, yet took every measure to embarrass the Service and render his Colleagues odious in the Eyes of the people. There were the strongest suspicions that he published the most unjust aspersions on them and that he secretly countenanced and supported the Leaders of the faction.

The Commissioners had no doubt but that [179] the wicked proceedings respecting the Officers of the Customs on the affair of the 5th March 1770 originated with him.[70]

His father in law was the most active in collecting, publishing, and forwarding, the ex parte evidence of near Sixty people, that was taken on that matter, within a few days after, the main end of which was to load the Commissioners and Officers of the Customs with plan[n]ing the destruction of the People, and being [180] accessaries in the Slaughter of that evening.

He endeavoured to make a dissention between the Commissioners and Mr. Sewal, the Attorney General of the Province; and drew the little Secretary of the Board to be aiding in that dark transaction; the investigation of which brought on the suspension and dismission of the Secretary.

It was very grievous whilst the Commissioners had such a combat without doors, and much labour [181] and difficulty with their own Officers from the weak state of Government in America, to have a constant contest and wrangling on every matter that came before them; and to have their opinions exposed, and conduct misrepresented by one of their own body.

Very frequent at this time were the publications in the News papers reflecting on the conduct of the Board and the Characters of the individuals of it, and [182] there was no doubt

---

70 There is no evidence that Temple went about poisoning people's minds. It is interesting to note, however, that the *Short Narrative* included a half dozen sworn affidavits that muzzle flashes could be seen coming from the Custom House or, more vaguely, that the sound of guns firing could be heard above the heads of the soldiers on King Street. With the acquittal of Manwaring and the other three civilian defendants in the third trial the matter was dropped, although their innocence was separable from the issue of whether or not someone else was in the Custom House and indeed fired down into the street from an upstairs window. Revere's engraving of the scene shows a gun barrel; Henry Pelham's original version, from which Revere borrowed, did not. For more, go to Clarence Brigham, *Paul Revere's Engravings* (New York: Atheneum, 1969), 52-78. As in much else about the "massacre," this question has yet to be answered.

who was the author of them. At length a Pamphlet came out aspersing many Characters. Everyone supposed Mr. Temple to be the Author of it; and he got into some quarrels on the occasion. One Gentleman whom he assaulted and knocked down, made a complaint to the Grand Jury; but they would take no notice of it, though his evidence of the assault was very clear and well supported.[71] At length Mr. Temple went to England and there was a Solemn hearing before the Privy Council respecting [183] his conduct in America. And by the judgment of that august assembly, he was dismissed from his Office of Commissioner of the Customs in America, and Mr. Hallowell was appointed in his room.

Mr. Thomas Whateley, who had been Secretary to Mr. George Grenville when he was first Lord of the Treasury, and had then been a friend to Mr. Temple, was under Secretary of State to Lord Suffolk at the time of Mr. Temple's dismission, and taking compassion of his circumstances he used his influence to serve him, and some time after Mr. [184] Temple was appointed an Inspector of the Customs in London, in which Office he continued 'till after the death of Mr. Whateley.

Some time after Mr Whateley's decease, Mr. Temple made a visit to his Brother, a Banker in the City, and desired to see the Packet of American Correspondence of his late Brother, as there were some letters of his amongst them, which he should be glad to look over. Mr. Whately brought out the bundle of letters, and left Mr. Temple some time in the room by himself, and when he returned he put back the bundle which he [185] had never attentively looked over.

At opening the General Court of the Massachusetts Bay at Boston in May 1773 a number of letters were read in the House said to have been written by the Governor (Mr. Hutchinson) in 1769 when he was Lt. Governor, and by Lt. Gov. Oliver when he was Secretary of the Province and others to Mr. Whateley, late Secretary to the Treasury.

The greatest resentment was raised against the Governor on the report of these letters. They soon after were printed, and indifferent people did not see [186] that matter in them, as could give just cause to the violent proceedings that were grounded on them.[72] For the

---

71 The pamphlet in question was a spoof, *A Dialogue between Sir George Cornwell ... and Mr. Flint* (Boston, 1769), with Cornwell a visiting Englishman and Flint a native New Englander. Flint walked Cornwell about Boston, disparaging various "prerogative" men, including the "lieutenant governor" (Hutchinson), once an "unsuccessful *smuggler*" who was driven by "*ambition* and *avarice*." (5) Temple denied that he was the author. See the discussion in Bailyn, *Thomas Hutchinson*, 128-130.

72 *Copy of Letters* (Boston: Edes and Gill, 1773). Printed there were eighteen letters written between May 1767 and October 1769, all to Thomas Whately, with six from Hutchinson, four each from Andrew Oliver and Thomas Moffat, and one each from Robert Auchmuty, Nathaniel Rogers, G[eorge] Rome, and Charles Paxton (Paxton, a single paragraph, on 20 June 1768, calling for troops). The most infuriating to local patriots was Hutchinson's of 20 January 1769, calling for "an abridgment of what are called English liberties." (16) The *Liberty* incident had prompted Hutchinson to come to the defense of the board, which also irritated his political opponents: "People have absurdly connected the duties and board of commissions, and suppose we should have had no additional duties if there had been no board to have the charge of collecting them." (ibid. 7, letter of August 1768).

Council and Assembly came to several strong resolutions on the matter, and concluded with a Petition to His Majesty, that he would be pleased to remove the Governor and Lt. Governor from their Posts in the Government.[73]

These letters[,] though written four or five years before, from private Gentlemen to their friend not then in publick Office, were used to stir up the minds of the people against them, now they were in high Stations, [187] and to draw on them the censure of their Royal Master for what had been done by them before they were acting in the Government of the Province.

Lt. Governor Oliver wrote to Mr. Whately the Banker, Brother of the Gentleman to whom the Letters had been written, and who was Executor to their deceased friend, and in return Mr. Whately acquainted him that he had shewn the Packets of his late Brother's American Correspondence to no one but Mr. Temple; and the general opinion was that Mr. Temple had taken them out of the Packets when he was permit[t]ed to look them over at Mr. Whatelys. [188]

The resentment against the Governor was very high whilst this matter was before the House, and it was not advisable for the Commissioners to appear in Boston for several days whilst the people's passions were in a ferment. On occasion of the annual Election in May there was a public Dinner given by the General Court, to which the Commissioners had not been invited, since their being at Boston. Govenor Hutchinson thought fit to send them invitations to the publick Dinner, given on this occasion, after he came [189] to the Chair, which they accepted, but on their going out from the Entertainment, a large Mob was assembled at the Door, who cursed the Governor for having invited the Commissioners, and abused and pelted them with Stones, and dirt; even in the face of the Company, and before the Guard of Cadets who were in Arms at the door; nay, some of those Guards were the foremost in the abuse.[74] [190]

When Mr. Whately came to know what use had been made of some letters written to his late Brother, he called upon Mr. Temple as the only person who had seen the letters of his late Brother. Mr T. denied having taken any out of the bundle that had been shewn him. This brought on altercations and publications between them, which ended in a duel, wherein Mr. Temple wounded, and afterwards near killed Mr. Whately, and his conduct

---

73 House resolutions of 16 June 1773 and a letter from the lower house and council to the Earl of Dartmouth, 29 June 1773, printed in *Speeches of the Governors*, 405-409 and 398-400 resp. Hutchinson had aggravated his political opponents with his response that the letters he sent Thomas Whately were essentially none of their business. See his message to the House of 9 June 1773 in the *Journals of the Massachusetts House*, 50:40-41 (the House resolutions of June 16th are on 58-61). The House request that both Hutchinson and Oliver resign passed overwhelmingly on June 23rd, 80-11 (ibid., 50:75).

74 "May 27 [1773]. Two of the Commissioners were very much abused yesterday when they came out from the Publick Dinner at Concert Hall, Mr Hulton and Mr Hallowell. Wm Mollineux, Wm Dennie, Paul Revere & several others were the Principal Actors." Edward Lillie Pierce, ed., *Letters and Diary of John Rowe* (Boston: W. B. Clarke, 1903), 245.

in this matter was greatly censured.[75] After the duel a publication appeared [191] from Dr. Franklyn to exculpate Mr. Temple from taking the letters, and declaring that he himself was the person who sent them over to Boston, but did not say how he obtained them.[76]

During the whole controversy between Great Britain and America[,] Dr Franklyn had been held in great esteem, and confidence by the Ministry. He was Deputy Post Master General in America, and his Son was Governor of the Jersies. At the same time he himself was Agent for Philadelphia, and other Provinces, and the grand Political [192] Adviser and Director of the Colonies. On one hand he fomented disturbances in America, and stir[r]ed up the people to resistance of the Laws of Parliament, and assured them of the timidity of the Ministry, and of their being supported by the Merchants and Manufacturers; and on the other, he endeavoured to impress the Ministry and Nation with the great consequence of the Colonies[,] their power and importance, by which means he supported faction and sedition in the Colonies, influenced the Ministry at home to try lenient measures, and to yield to the [193] temper of the times, thus preventing the exertion of authority on one side, and weakening the bands of respect and obedience on the other, he from step to step prepared the people for an open revolt from Great Britain.[77]

---

75 Most of the dispute leading to the duel and the duel itself, which produced its own set of accusations about Temple's behavior (did Temple stab Whately with his sword when Whately was down and defenseless?), can be found in *A Faithful Account of the Whole of the Transactions relating to a late Affair of Honour between J. Temple, and W. Whately, Esqrs.* (London: R. Snagg, 1774). Both men wisely walked away from the dispute after the resort to pistols and swords. Temple remained emphatic that he stole nothing from Whately—see his letter to Earl Temple, 14 December 1773, Add. Ms. 57,828, fos. 1-7 (Grenville Papers) BL. Temple and Thomas Whately, who had been very friendly through the mid 1760s—Whately having recommended Temple for the customs board when it was being formed—had developed strains in their friendship as the result of Temple's political allegiances in Boston. See, for example, Temple to Whately, 21 January 1771, Temple Papers. Also see Benjamin Hallowell to John Pownall, 29 September 1773, in B. F. Stevens, ed., *Facsimiles of Manuscripts in European Archives relating to American Affairs, 1773-1783*, 25 vols. (London: G. Malby and Sons, 1889-1895), no. 2029, where Hallowell sounds very much like Hulton in his low regard for Temple, in the Whately affair and in general. Also see the Hulton letter of 15 March 1774, transcribed infra at 298-299.

76 Printed in the *Faithful Account*, 21; also in Labaree, et al., eds., *Papers of Benjamin Franklin*, 20:513-516. Also see the "Tract relative to the Affair of Hutchinson's Letters" in ibid., 21:414-435. Bailyn, *Hutchinson*, 244-259 discussed the Temple-Whately affair and the "mystery" surrounding the letters. Bailyn thinks that Thomas Pownall may have given the letters to Franklin, but concedes that his conclusion is "conjectural." (225 n. 7) Hutchinson offered his own view in his *History*, 3:282-298. Also see the discussion by Hutchinson's great-grandson in Hutchinson, ed., *Diary and Letters*, 1:82-93, and Hutchinson's account of a reconciliation between the two in London (ibid., 1:209-211), when Temple called on Hutchinson "alone and unexpectedly." John Doran, editor of *The Last Journals of Horace Walpole During the Reign of George III From 1771-1783*, 2 vols. (London: John Lane, 1910), 1:243n. passed along the claim that Hugh Williamson got the letters for Franklin from the (as yet non-existent?) "British Foreign-Office."

77 Hulton's animus toward Franklin had erupted as early as the Boston siege, when he called him an "arch-traitor! this most atrocious of men," on 22 January 1776, in the "Nicholson Letters," 93, transcribed at 341-342 infra. That Franklin could be capable of duplicity at any point in his career is clear in the tone of Cecil Currey's *Road to Revolution: Benjamin Franklin in England, 1765-1775* (New York: Anchor Books, 1968). David T. Morgan, *The Devious Dr. Franklin* (Macon, Ga.: Mercer University Press, 1996) is not as caustic. Gerald Stourzh provides a sophisticated appraisal of Franklin's changing positions and changing loyalties in

The Non-importation agreement in 1769 and every measure to distress Government, and keep up the spirit of resistance, was furthered and supported by his means.

He was Agent to the Province of Massachusetts at the time when the [194] complaint against the Governor and Lt. Governor came home, for writing the Letters, which the Doctor now avowed himself to have sent back to Boston.

The matter was ordered to be heard before the King and Council. The Doctor was desirous to prevent such a solemn discussion of the business, but it could not be dispenced with and as Agent to the Province he was to support the Charge, of which he had furnished the grounds.

Never was a fuller [195] Assembly of those august Judges, and never was a person more severely handled than the Doctor was by Mr. Wedderburne, the Solicitor General, and Council for the Governors.

The Charge was dismissed, with the severest censure, and the Doctor became an abhorred Character, and he and Mr. Temple were both dismissed from their employments under Government.[78] [196]

[197-198 blank]

Benjamin Franklin and American Foreign Policy (Chicago: University of Chicago Press, 1954), as has, more recently, Gordon S. Wood in an essay on Franklin in *Revolutionary Characters* (New York: Penguin Press, 2006), 65-90, which offers a briefer version of views first expressed in *The Americanization of Benjamin Franklin* (New York: Penguin Press, 2004).

78 Alexander Wedderburn, the solicitor general, took an hour to verbally eviscerate Franklin in the cockpit on 29 January 1774, for which see Labaree, et al., eds., *Papers of Franklin*, 21:37-70. Catherine Drinker Bowen used the cockpit scene as her closing Franklin vignette in *The Most Dangerous Man in America* (Boston: Little, Brown and Company, 1974), 227-243.

Chapter 12

Opposition by the Town of Boston and the Province of Massachusetts Bay in 1772 and 1773 [and 17]74 to the Revenue Laws. [199]

[200 blank]

IN OCTOBER 1772 THE INHABITANTS OF BOSTON at a Town Meeting appointed a Committee of Correspondence to consist of twenty one persons, to state the Rights of the Collonists, and of this Province in particular, as Men, as Christians, and as subjects, to communicate and publish the same to the several Towns in this Province and to the World, as the sense of the Town, with the infringement and violations thereof that have been, or from time may be made; also requesting of each town a free communication of their sentiments on this subject. [201] And on the 20th of November following the Town received the report of this Committee, which was approved and transmitted to the several Towns in a letter of Correspondence from the Committee, all which were printed together with some Messages from the town to the Governour and his Answers, respecting the Salaries said to be granted by the Crown to the Judges of the Superior Court

The Town of Boston had now established a plan of communication and Correspondence, not only with the several towns in the province, but with the several great towns on the Continent, where the like measures were entered into.[79]

In the month of March 1773 the House of Burgesses of the Colony of Virginia entered [202] into several resolutions for supporting the legal and constitutional rights of the Colonies in General; by these, a standing Committee of Correspondence, and Enquiry was to be Established between them and the other Colonies on the Continent, and this mode was adopted by most of the other Colonies, to correspond and communicate to each other all matters wherein the common welfare, and safety of the Colonies were concerned.

Governor Hutchinson in his speech on opening the General Court in January 1773 took notice of these proceedings of the town of Boston, and entered into an argumentative State

---

79 See *The Votes and Proceedings of the Freeholders and other Inhabitants of the Town of Boston, in Town Meeting assembled, According to Law* (Boston: Edes and Gill, 1772), for the proceedings beginning on October 28th and carrying through November 2nd. Richard D. Brown, *Revolutionary Politics in Massachusetts* (Cambridge, Mass.: Harvard University Press, 1970) reviews this stage in Boston's drift toward revolution.

of the question, exposing the [203] principles that they had adopted and endeavouring to support the supreme authority of Parliament over the Plantations.

Both the Council and Assembly in their Address in answer, entered largely into the argument, and did their utmost to support the new doctrine. And the Governor in his speech at the close of the sessions, entered further into the subject, and replyed to them both.[80]

In this Sessions the House addressed the Governor in respect to the Salaries said to be granted to the Judges of the Superior Court by the Crown, and voted a Grant to them for the year ensuing, to which [204] the Governor refused to give his assent.

They then passed some resolves, respecting said Judges, that if any of them should accept of, and depend upon the pleasure of the Crown for his support independant of the Grants, and acts of the General Assembly, he would discover that he had not a due sense of the importance of an impartial administration of Justice; that he is an Enemy to the Constitution, and has it in his heart to promote the Establishment of an Arbitrary Government in the Province.

In this Sessions the Governor by Message applied to the House that the Province House might be repaired, but they declined [205] doing it, as the Governor did not receive his support from the Province.

The House by Message applied to the Governour, for the use of the Province arms, for some new Artillery Corps to be raised, but he declined granting their request.

After this Sessions of the General Court, matters subsided, and the summer went off pretty well, but towards the fall there was a report that the East India Company were going to send out Cargoes of Tea to America on their own account, to be disposed of at publick sale, by Consignees to be appointed for that purpose.

Some duties had been taken off this Article at home, and though it retained the 3d duty in America, yet it was expected [206] that it would be sold so low as to defeat the schemes of the smug[g]lers, who had been long concerned in the Dutch Tea trade, and had supplied great part of the Continent with that article from Holland.

Immediately a fresh ferment rose. The Continent was put in motion, and every mode of resistance to this measure was to be adopted. [207]

[208-210 blank]

---

80 Legal scholar John Phillip Reid edited these January-March 1773 exchanges expertly as *The Briefs of the American Revolution* (New York: New York University Press, 1981). They were also printed, without comment, in *Speeches of the Governors*, 336-396.

1773

November 3

The Mob assembled at Liberty Tree, and sent for the Merchants to whom the Tea expected from the India Company was reported to be consigned, and required them to refuse accepting such Commission. The Gentlemen refused to attend, or to comply with their request. The Mob grew riotous, and commit[t]ed some outrage at the Store of Mr Clark, one of the Consignees, but was dispersed. The Governor could not assemble a sufficient number of Members to make a Council, and the Sherriff was gone out of town to dinner.

November 5

Continuation of the [211] Town Meeting respecting the Tea Consignees, and violent Speeches used against them, and the Commissioners.

November 8

A Mob at night paraded the town with a great noise, but dispersed without doing any mischief.

November 17

A Mob at night committed a violent outrage on the dwelling house of Mr. R[ichar]d Clark, one of the Tea Consignees, broke the Windows and destroyed his furniture.

After the former assault on Mr. Clark at his Store, an association of the Merchants was proposed for their mutual defence, but it fell through.

November 18

A Town Meeting send a Committee to the Tea [212] Consignees requiring them to resign. Violent speeches were made against all Commissioners. The Gentlemen refused to comply with the requisition of the Town. A publication appeared in the Spy to justify the Murder or assassination of the Commissioners &c.

November 19

The Tea Consignees prayed the Governor and Council for protection.

November 23

The Governor and Council met on the Petition of the Tea Consignees, and recommended to the Select Men, to keep the peace of the Town.

The Town of Boston has brought the other towns in the Neighborhood to join [213] in chasing out the Tea Consignees and not to give them any Shelter. The Gentlemen have not slept in Boston for Several Nights past.

November 24. Thanksgiving Day

November 25

Secret Meetings are held at Faneuil Hall of the Committees of Boston and the Neighbouring Towns and most of the fire Arms in town are buying up.

November 26

The Governor and Council met, and sat 'till four O'Clock on the present State of Affairs, but no measures were taken to support the authority of Government.

November 27

Sunday Capt Hall in the Ship *Dartmouth* arrived from London, with the long expected Tea. [214]

Monday 28 November 1773. Town Meeting, violent resolves. November 29th. A meeting of the people from the Town and Country at the old South Meeting. The Governor sent a Proclamation to them to disperse, which they treated with contempt, and passed many violent resolutions respecting the Tea and the Merchants to whom it was consigned, which they caused to be printed.

The people took Captain Hall's ship with the Tea on board into their care, and Custody, and placed 25 Armed men on board her.

The Towns in the neighbourhood of Boston hold meetings—train, and prepare their Arms, and pass resolves similar to those passed in the Town of Boston. [215]

On Monday the 28th in the Evening The Merchants to whom the Tea was consigned took Shelter in Castle William, and the next day the Commissioners of the Customs thought it best to go there, for their own security.

The Meeting of the people was dissolved on Tuesday, after fixing on signals for their assembly by Day or night. The rest of the Week passed off without any assaults or mob[b]ings, but the people's passions were still very violent, and expressed by the most extravagant threats against the Governour, Commissioners, &c. It was resolved the Tea should be sent back at all events.

December 10[th]. Mr. Roach[,] the owner of Capt Hall's Ship[,] declared that he had been compelled by threats to promise to send [216] back his ship with the Teas on board, but that now she should not sail with them, nor did he consider himself obliged to fulfil any promise so extorted from him, and they might do their worst with him.

December 13. A Meeting of the Committees of the several Towns on Mr. Roach's declaration.

December 14. A meeting of the people in general at the old South Meeting, calling themselves the Body, on the same matter. They sent a Committee of ten, along with Mr. Roach, to the Collector, and obliged him to demand a Clearance outward for his Vessel, which he refused to Grant, whilst his Cargo inwards remained undischarged. [217]

December 16. The Body assembled, obliged Mr. Roach to go to the Governour and demand a Let pass for his ship, which the Governour refused to grant. On Mr. Roache's return to the

Body with this answer, after a violent inflam[m]atory speech, the Meeting was dissolved, and they proceeded on board the three Vessels, at the Wharfs, with the Tea on board, when they hoisted up the Tea, broke the Chests, and threw the whole over board into the Water. Many hundreds were employed in this business. Their threats and noise were heard very plain at Castle William. Before nine in the Evening the work was finished, when they dispersed with three huzza's.[81][218]

After the destruction of the Tea the fury of the people subsided, and the Commissioners returned to their families before Christmas from the Castle, and held a Board in Boston on the 30th December.

A few days after the Tea was destroyed, the people having notice that about half a Chest had been saved by a person in Dorchester out of the Quantity that had floated on the water, a number of them went disguised in search of it, but entered a wrong house, terrified the family, and rummaged the house over, then obliged the Man to go with them to his neighbour's dwelling, which they searched in the same manner, and having found the Tea, brought it away and destroyed it. [219]

January 1774. The Dealers in Tea in Boston were notified by the people, that they should not be allowed to sell any Tea after the 20th of January, and they who did not conform thereto, were to be the objects of resentment.

The Town of Plymouth having entered into such like violent resolutions respecting the Tea, and Consignees, as the town of Boston, a number of the respectable inhabitants thought fit to make a protest against the said Resolutions, one of them coming up to Boston soon after, was visited by a party of the True Sons, who compelled him at the risk of tar and feathers, to sign a recantation, drawn up by them, which was published in the papers. [220]

The Governor's second son and one of the Consignees, who had married the daughter of Colonel Watson of Plymouth, having taken Shelter at his father in Law's, with his Lady—the people of the place, having notice, came in the Evening, and threat[e]ned him with their resentment, if he did not remove immediately. It was then a snow storm, he beg[g]ed to have leave to remain there till the morning, the storm still continued the next day, but the people obliged them to turn out, and travel off in the midst of it.

At Lexington a Young Woman going to a Dancing party, took with her a little tea for the Company. No sooner had the people without got notice, [221] than they broke in, took the

---

81 Labaree, *Boston Tea Party*, surveys many of these developments. Francis S. Drake assembled contemporaneous documents for his *Tea Leaves* (Boston: A. O. Crane, 1884). Alfred F. Young's biography of George Robert Twelves Hewes, *The Shoemaker and the Tea Party* (Boston: Beacon Press, 1999) notes the differences that crept into Hewes's supposed recollections of the event offered a half century later, but perhaps Young should have been even more skeptical of Hewes as a reliable source than he already was. Hulton's "many hundreds" may not have numbered even one hundred actual participants on board the *Beaver*, *Eleanor*, and *Dartmouth*.

young Woman in her best attire, payed her with a Coating of Tar and feathers, and in this manner led her in exhibition.

At Marblehead they have lately erected an hospital for inoculation on one of the Islands near the town. Some of the Patients coming off sooner than the people thought they could be free from infection, they administered to them the general recipe and exhibited them to the Town with the Coating of Tar and feathers and were with difficulty restrained from going over, and burning the Hospital.

On the 20th January[,] the day fixed for the venders of Tea to cease from selling that [222] article, a large bonfire was made before the Custom house, and a small Cask of damaged tea was bro[ugh]t up to be consumed in it. The Board was then setting, and a large Mob soon assembled, shouting and huzzaing.

One Mr. Leonard[,] a Corn Merchant in Boston who had been suspected of having assisted in forming the Protest of some of the Inhabitants of Plymouth against the Resolves lately entered into by that Town, had his Store broke open, and his Ledger book of Accounts, and papers taken out. The person strongly suspected was a man who had been a servant, and was then in some share of business with him. Leonard advertized a reward, and described the suspected person. His Ledger was sent [223] back, but the papers were carried to Edes and Gill['s] printing Office, he was threat[e]ned with their being printed, and it was said there was amongst them a Journal of the times, and a letter to some town in the Country, advising them not to adopt the resolve of the Town of Boston.

On the 25th January in the Evening, John Malcolm, an Officer of the Customs, who had been tarred and feathered at Casco Bay for making a seizure, was taken out of his house in Boston, put into a Cart, strip'd naked, tarred, and feathered, punched with a long pole, beaten with Clubs, led to liberty tree, there whipt with Cords, and though a very cold night, led on to the Gallows, then whipt again, calling on him to curse the Governor and Commissioners. [224] There he prayed to have an end put to his misery, and that they would hang him outright, but this favor they would not grant, but led him back in the Cart a mile and a half to the North End, still naked, in the Cold.

January 26. This day in the Evening the Essex smallpox hospital, on an Island near Marblehead, was burnt down by the people. They who perpetrated the act were prepared with Tar tubs &c, and set fire to the house, without awaking the people in it, who were obliged to fly in the cold, with scarce anything to cover them, and were beat and abused by the people without in their flight.

In February two men who were suspected to have had [225] a hand in burning the Essex Hospital were taken from on board a Vessel at Marblehead, and committed to Salem Goal. In the Evening several parties came over from Marblehead, attacked the Goal, and rescued the prisoners.

February 26. The Governor this day opened the General Court and in his speech to the Council and Assembly, he signified His Majesty's disapprobation of the appointment of Committees of Correspondence, in various instances, which sit and act during the recess of the General Court by Prorogation: And both Houses in their Address in answer, entered into an argumentation, and vindication, of the appointment of such mode of correspondence, and did [226] not at all rescind from the measures they had adopted.[82]

The House of Representatives soon after their meeting, entered into an enquiry, respecting the Conduct of Peter Oliver Esq., the Chief Justice of the Province, who had accepted of a salary from His Majesty for that duty, out of the Monies raised in America by the Act of the 7th George III.

Then they came to several resolutions thereon, and made a remonstrance to the Governor and Council, praying that he might not be suffered to sit and act as Chief Justice, but forthwith be removed from the said Court, in answer to which, the Governor declined granting their request.

Then the House of Representatives addressed the [227] Council, and laid a copy of the Governor's answer before them, and prayed that they would advise thereon, and act and determine as they should judge proper. And two days after, the house waited on the Governor with a fresh address, urging him to take their former remonstrance into further consideration, and to take the advice of the Council—thereon, and every step for the removal of the Chief Justice from the Superior Court. To this the Governour gave them an excellent answer, and shewed the impropriety of their request.

The Superior Court met without the Chief Justice, they adjourned for one Week, and afterwards till June.

Notwithstanding the Governor's answers, the House of Representatives proceeded to form [228] articles of Impeachment against the Chief Justice for receiving a Salary from His Majesty and on the 25th of February sent a Committee to the Governour, to acquaint him thereof, and desired that he would be in the Chair, that they might lay the same before the Governor and Council.

The next day he sent them a Message, signifying that the process they had attempted to commence, was unconstitutional and that he could not shew any countenance to it.[83]

Nevertheless, they sent a Committee, with the Impeachment to the Council Board, upon receipt of the Governor's Message. And on the 28th, the Council sent a Message to the Governor, acquaint[ing] him therewith, and desiring to be informed when he would [229] be

---

82 Hulton was off by a month. Hutchinson's speech, where the Governor was "required to signify His Majesty's Disapprobation of Committees of Correspondence," was on January 26th. The House committee appointed to carry on the correspondence went ahead with its business. See the *Journals of the Massachusetts House*, 50:102-103 and 112. The House had created the committee on May 28th, by a vote of 109-4, in response to a plea from the Virginia House of Burgesses, made on March 12th (ibid., 50:11-14).

83 The House resolution for impeachment, which carried 92-8 on February 24th, is in ibid., 50:199-201. Hutchinson's refusal to accept that resolution two days later—because it appeared unconstitutional—is in ibid., 50:205. The House had taken its first move toward this position during the previous session (see proceedings for 25 June 1773, ibid., 50:86-88).

present with the Council to proceed on this business. And the next day the house sent up another Impeachment of the Chief Justice.

On the 3rd of March the Governour sent a Message to the Council, wherein he exposed the absurdity of the request in their Message of the 28th of February.

On the 4th of March, the Council acquainted the Governor by Message that since their Message of the 28th the House had laid upon the Council Table, Articles of Charge and Complaint against the Chief Justice, and as the Governor had had these laid before him, together with the Articles of Impeachment, and had declined acting on the latter, they desired to be informed what his determination was with [230] regard to the articles of charge and complaint.

On the 7th March the Council, and on the 8th the House of Representatives, sent Committees with long Messages to the Governour, entering into argument with him, and justifying their proceedings respecting the Chief Justice.

On the 9th March the Governor sent a Message to both houses wherein he shewed his disapprobation of their late proceedings, and that he could not neglect bearing publick testimony against them, and preventing them from proceeding any further in the same way, and then the General Court was prorogued. [231][84]

On the 5th March Mr. Hancock delivered an Oration to the People, to commemorate the Massacre of the 5th March 1770 in which the greatest reflections were made on the Military, and the passions of the People were inflamed, by the most violent invectives against Government.[85]

About this time one Goddard travelled through the Continent to establish a Provincial Post Office, independant of government.

On the 5th March the Brig *Fortune* arrived from London having 28 ½ Chests of Tea on board, the property of sundry Merchants in Boston.

The next day in the Evening the Mob went on board, forced open the Hatches, hoisted up the Tea, [232] broke the Chests and discharged the Contents into the Water.

A person who had confined another for debt in Cambridge Jail, was taken out of his house one evening, by a body of people, and compelled to walk with them to Cambridge, and there to sign an instrument, and release the Debtor from Confinement.

A number of people assembled, and broke into the house of Capt. Jones of Weston, ransacked every part, and destroyed the furniture. The Mistress of the family who had lately lain in, was left exposed to the inclemency of the weather, having the Windows of her room all broke. [233]

---

84 The House refused to accept Hutchinson's view on March 7th; it had proceeded with formal articles of impeachment against Oliver on March 1st. See ibid., 50:232-236 and 212-217, resp.

85 All of the annual "massacre" orations delivered between 1771-1783 were gathered together and published as *Orations Delivered at the Request of the Inhabitants of the Town of Boston to Commemorate the Evening of the Fifth of March, 1770*, second ed. (Boston: Wm. T. Clap, 1807); Hancock's, of 5 March 1774, the fourth to be given, is on 39-53.

Chapter 13

Proceedings on the Departure of Governor Hutchinson
June 1774

GOVERNOR HUTCHINSON LEFT BOSTON early in June 1774 and before his departure, was addressed by many of the Merchants, and principal inhabitants of the town, to the number of 128 by the Episcopal Clergy, and Gentlemen of the Law, and he went away with a persuasion that the people would be brought to comply with the requisitions in the Boston Port Act,[86] and that they would enable him in a short time, to put their conduct in so favourable a light, as that through his mediation the King's Ministers might be induced to recommend to His Majesty, the opening the Port of Boston again.[87] [235]

However[,] he was scarcely gone, before great murmurs arose against the persons who had signed the Addresses. For some time the Addressors buoyed themselves up, and seemed to make head against the faction of the people. And they once endeavoured in a town meeting to call the Committee of Correspondence to account, and proposed, after having exposed the ill use they had made of the confidence of the people, to have moved for a dissolution of that Committee. But on the first vote they were greatly outnumbered by

---

86 Pickering, ed., *Statutes*, 30:336-341, 24 George III c. 19. See Ammerman, *Common Cause* and Labaree, *Boston Tea Party* for general context, and the discussion of British policy-making in Bernard Donoughue, *British Politics and the American Revolution* (London: Macmillan & Co., 1964); and Thomas, *Tea Party to Independence*. See too the interesting back and forth offered by Ian R. Christie (British perspective) and Labaree (American perspective) in *Empire and Independence, 1760-1776* (New York: W. W. Norton, 1976).

87 The address, dated 30 May 1774, was printed in the *Boston Gazette*, 6 June 1774, and reprinted in Stark, *Loyalists of Massachusetts*, 123-125. "Sundry inhabitants" of Marblehead felt compelled to object to the address, in a meeting of 3 June 1774 that was reported in the *Boston Evening-Post*, 6 June 1774. None of the commissioners signed the May 30th address—because they were not asked to, because they avoided involvement, or for another reason entirely? This address and another from barristers and attorneys offering their "testimonial" to Hutchinson's service were first printed as broadsides, *Addresses &c. to the late Governor Hutchinson* (n.p.), which prompted a two-page response (also n.p.), "*a true List*" of those who had signed the merchants' address, with their places of business identified, so "that every Friend to his Country may know who is Assisting to carry the Execrable Purposes of the British Administration into Execution"—in other words, so that they could be intimidated into silence, the sort of political bullying that prompted Hulton's equation of democracy with anarchy. For Hutchinson's failed efforts as peacemaker in London see Bailyn, *Hutchinson*, 267-330, and Hutchinson's own brief retrospective in his *History*, 3:329-330, where he said that he arrived to find that the Massachusetts government act had been passed—whose consequences he "dreaded." Where Hulton saw the possibility for improvement, Hutchinson foresaw disaster and proved the more astute of the two.

the ruling faction, and from that time no effort was made to withstand the Tyranny of the Committee of Correspondence.[88]

Indeed the Addressors did not act from a principle of [236] obedience to the Laws of Great Britain; some signed from personal respect to the Governor; many, thinking he would endeavour to get the Port opened again, and would be glad to represent their conduct in a favourable light from this Address; but there was no bond of union, or firm principle of opposition to the ruling faction that they acted upon.

The committee immediately marked the Addressors to Governor Hutchinson as objects of their resentment; and upon the report of the new act for regulating the Government of the Province,[89] they spread throughout the Country the most unjust and groundless reports, as to the intentions of Government towards the Province, such as that their Lands were to be lotted out into Lordships, and to [237] be taxed. About this time the heads of the bill for the better Government of Quebec came over, and the indulgence thereby granted to the French inhabitants of that Country, to enjoy their religion, was interpreted as a prelude to changing the Religion of the other Colonies and that it was intended to compel them to become Roman Catholics.[90]

Thus deluded by the Committees in the several towns of the province, and inflamed by the Ministers against Government who took advantage of the latter act to alarm them on the subject of their Religion; The people were wrought up to the highest degree of resentment against Great Britain, and talked of nothing but dying in defence of their religion, and liberties. [238]

---

88 See Brown, *Revolutionary Politics*, 194-199; and the tantalizingly brief minutes for 27-28 June 1774 in *Report of the Record Commissioners...Boston Town Records, 1770 Through 1777*, 177-178.

89 Massachusetts government act, in Pickering, ed., *Statutes*, 30:381-390, 24 George III c. 45 (the new quartering act is in ibid., 30:410-411, 24 George III c. 54). Although, again, it was not as ambitious as the changes brought with the Dominion of New England in the late 1680s, it did attempt to redistribute power in the colony, from the legislative to the executive, and from the elective to the appointive, thereby—from the perspective of its supporters—restoring balance and ending the demagoguery born of anarchy. Not only was the council to be appointed by the crown, sheriffs were to be appointed by the governor, and sheriffs would in turn select jurors. Town meetings were to be called only with the governor's approval and restrict themselves to agendas that he had approved. Thus there were implications for Massachusetts law as well as Massachusetts politics, as long-term reform was mixed with short-term punishment. But North's timing in 1774 had been no better than Grenville's in 1765. The supposed solution to one problem introduced yet another. Recriminations flew across the Atlantic in both directions; suspicions deepened rather than eased.

90 The Quebec Act is in Pickering, ed., *Statutes*, 30:549-554, 24 George III c. 83. Hulton exaggerated when he claimed that critics feared Catholicism would be imposed on them. Rather, they feared that the religious toleration allowed Catholics in Canada, coupled with the lack of a legislature there, would be the first step toward a tightening of imperial administration, leading ultimately to a crackdown on (even if not an elimination of) colonial legislatures, and perhaps some sort of attempt to tighten church government in the colonies through a much-feared Anglican episcopacy. See Carl Bridenbaugh, *Mitre and Sceptre* (New York: Oxford University Press, 1962), 333-334; Alan Heimert, *Religion and the American Mind* (Cambridge, Mass.: Harvard University Press, 1966), 387-395; and Peter M. Doll, *Revolution, Religion, and National Identity* (Madison, N.J.: Fairleigh Dickinson University Press, 2000).

At this time the Boston Committee circulated a letter through the Country, urging the People to unite in a solemn League and Covenant, not to use any British Goods, or have dealings with any who did, till their grievances were addressed. [91] Almost every town entered into some agreement, similar to what was proposed by the Boston Committee: From which time there was an <u>open resistance to the operation of the new Acts</u>, and the Addressors of Governour Hutchinson; and they who complied with, or endeavoured to enforce the Laws of Great Britain, were declared objects of persecution.

Mr. F[rancis] Green[,] a Merchant of Boston, and one of those [239] who signed the Address to Governor Hutchinson, having occasion to travel into Connecticut, on his private affairs, was no sooner arrived at a town called Windham in that Colony, than the people gathered about the Tavern where he lodged, in a tumultuous manner, and compelled him, with many threats, to leave the place. He went on to Norwich, but there the same spirit raged against him, and he was obliged to quit the Colony, without doing his business.

One Colonel Fitch[,] high sheriff at Windham[,] having censured this behavior of the people, a large number of them assembled, and resolved to Tar and feather any person who should do any work for him, so that his Corn, and hay, remained in the fields uncut.[92] [240]
[241-242 blank]

91 Issued as an untitled, two-page broadside, addressed "Gentlemen," dated 8 June 1774 and signed by William Cooper, town clerk, also printed in Boston newspapers, and discussed in Brown, *Revolutionary Politics*, 191-209. The call for a "solemn league" against British importations caused a bigger stir than Hulton allowed for here, as town leaders in Boston found that sympathy for their plight did not guarantee a united response from other towns in the province. There were even dissidents in Boston—as over forty men made clear in a statement on June 29th, printed in the *Boston Evening-Post*, 4 July 1774. Gage had condemned the solemn league in a proclamation of 29 June 1774, printed in the *Massachusetts Gazette*, 30 June 1774.

92 For the June 23rd Windham town meeting that condemned those who signed the addresses to Hutchinson see Peter Force, ed., *American Archives*, 9 vols. (Washington, D.C.: M. St. Clair Clarke and Peter Force, 1837-1853), 4th series, 1:445.

Chapter 14

Proceedings of the People in the Province of Massachusetts Bay after the arrival of General Gage as Governor to the Close of 1774

1774 MAY 13 GENERAL GAGE ARRIVED at Boston as Governor of the Province and Commander in Chief of His Majesty's Troops, and brought with him the Act for blocking up the Port of Boston, which was to take place the 1st June.

Instead of shewing a disposition to comply with the conditions of the Act, the People sent Expresses to the other Provinces, to excite them to join in resisting the authority of Great Britain; and no sooner was the General Court met than the House petitioned the General to appoint a Fast [243] that, according to the trumpet of Sedition, might be sounded from the Pulpit. But instead of complying with their request the General adjourned them to meet him at Salem and he went to reside at Danvers near Salem.[93]

The Port of Boston being now shut up and the Officers of the Customs removed from thence[,] the Commissioners established their Board at Salem.

Early in June two Regiments of foot arrived at Boston from England, and towards the latter end two more. And encamped on the Common, under the command of Lord Percy. And on the 1st July Admiral Graves arrived in his Majesty's Ship *Preston*, to relieve Admiral Montagu. [244]

The other Colonies entered into Subscriptions for relief of the distressed inhabitants of Boston, and Vessels laden with provisions were sent by way of donations, from many parts; and the Assemblies of Virginia, and New Hampshire, were dissolved by their Governors, for adopting measures for support of the Bostonians.

The Council, in their address to General Gage, charged his two predecessors as Authors of their grievances, upon which he stopt them short, and would hear no more, but answered them, that their address was an insult [245] on the King and his Privy Council, and an affront to himself and he would not receive their address.[94]

---

93 Richard Frothingham's intensely whiggish *History of the Siege of Boston*, 6th ed. (Boston: Little, Brown, and Company, 1903; orig. ed., 1849) presents a Gage who was as villainous as he was incompetent. Gage fares much better in John Richard Alden's *General Gage in America* (Baton Rouge: Louisiana State University Press, 1948).

94 The Council's message to Gage of 9 June 1774, with Gage's response five days later, are in *Speeches of the Governors*, 414-415; also in the *Journals of the Massachusetts House*, 50:291.

The Governor finding the Assembly were about appointing Members to a General Congress and other matters than what belonged to the business of the Province, he sent the Secretary to prorogue them. The House suspecting his errand, locked the doors against him. Upon which he returned to the General who sent him back immediately, directing him to dissolve them. which Order he published on the outside the House, the doors being still locked against him.[95] [246]

As the Governor would not consent to appoint a Fast, the Ministers of Boston took upon them to appoint a day of prayer through out the Province for Sunday, July 17.

A form of an agreement was now circulated through the Country which the people were called upon to sign, being a Solemn League and Covenant, whereby they engaged not to hold any intercourse or consume any manufactures of Great Britain. And the Governor issued a Proclamation against the Publishers and Signers of the said Solemn League and Covenant.

At a Town Meeting at Boston it was proposed |247| to dismiss the Committee of Correspondence, which motion was supported by the Addressors to Governor Hutchinson, but after warm debates it was carried against the proposal and the Addressors became more particularly the objects of resentment.

In the month of July the General went from Danvers to Boston, and remained there about ten days. But notwithstanding the presence of the General and so large a military force encamped, and the operation of the Port Act, yet no disposition appeared in the people to comply with the requisitions of it. Nay, they were supported in their resistance by the Donations and promises from the other Colonies. No one stood forth in the cause of Government, the liberty spirit [248] increased in the Country, and the people in the back parts of the Province, inflamed by false reports of taxes to be raised upon them, and the alteration of their Government, adopted every measure that was proposed to them of resistance to the authority of Great Britain. The town meeting of Boston fomented this Spirit and at the latter end of July, sent a General letter to all the Towns in the Province, urging them to advise and act in this dangerous Crisis: in consequence of which, it was resolved that County Meetings should be held.

Early in August the *Scarborough* Man of War arrived from England, with the New Acts of Parliament, for an alteration of the Charter, and regulating the Government of the province which took place the 1st August. [249]

The 59th Regiment from Halifax and the 23rd from New York arrived at Boston. And one Lt. Col. [Charles] Lee, on half pay in his Majesty's Service who had been stirring up Sedition in the Southern Provinces, arrived at Boston from New York and associated himself with the leaders of the Faction.

---

95 Ibid., 416, on 17 June 1774. With Gage having dissolved the legislature, the next time he received a memorial would be in October, from the extra-legal provincial convention then sitting in Concord. Gage's proclamation of June 17th dissolving the General Court was printed in the *Massachusetts Gazette*, 23 June 1774.

August 8

The New Council were sworn in at Danvers. Four Gentlemen named to be Counsellors, took time to consider, only ten qualified this day, and were not enough to act.

The next day a town meeting by adjournment was held at Boston, and on the 10ᵗʰ the Delegates from the Province to the Continental Congress, set out from Boston for Philadelphia.

August 12

The General sent for the Select Men of Boston, [250] and acquainted them, that if they had any business that they thought necessary to call a town meeting upon, if they would propose it to him, he would consider it. They said they had an adjournment of one already to be held. Upon which he said, that by the late act that could not be and that he should take care the Act should be carried into execution. However, not only Town Meetings are about to be held in other places, but Country Meetings are also performed, by Delegates from the several Towns, to advise and act at this alarming Crisis.⁹⁶

August 16

The General met the Council at Salem, when they who qualified this day, with those who had before accepted, made twenty five Members. [251]

Before the meeting of the Council, it was strongly reported that the Country Members would not qualify, they being greatly threatened by the people. However, when they got together they seemed to pluck up their spirits, and when the Board broke up they appeared satisfied with what they had done; and they who had not before seen the Governour, were quite happy and pleased with his spirit, and behaviour.

The next day, the Council met again, and proceeded on business with great harmony, good dispositions, and spirit. But the people in the Country are yet in a state of infatuation, and madness. They have begun to hold their County Meetings, and have resolved not to suffer the Courts of Justice to be held, under the new Acts. [252]

August 23. The Town Meeting was notified to be held at Salem the next day, in defiance of the new Act for regulating the Government of the Province. The next morning early the General came to Salem from Danvers, sent for the Committee, and ordered them to disperse the people that were assembling. They accordingly seperated, but before they had notice in an hurrying manner, below stairs, they named sundry persons to appear at the County Meeting. The Governour published a proclamation against these illegal town meetings, and a few days after, Mr. Fry, a Justice of the peace, issued a Warrant for arresting

---

96 Gage informed the selectmen of the new rules governing town meetings under the Massachusetts government act. The selectmen responded that they "had no need of calling a Town Meeting for we had now two alive by Adjournment." Gage "looked serious and said 'he must think upon that,' adding 'that by thus doing we might keep the Meetings alive for ten years'." That, of course, was precisely the point. *Report of the Record Commissioners ... Selectmen's Minutes from 1769 Through April, 1775*, 225; minutes of 13 August 1774.

the Committee of Correspondence at Salem, two of them entered into Bonds to appear to answer the charge, the rest [253] refused to recognize. And the Justice had not the fortitude to commit them. Immediately, town meetings were held in many places, and they proceeded in all the towns, to chuse Delegates to their County Meetings.[97]

Now followed a general persecution of the new Councellors, and a resistance to the Courts of Justice.

At Barrington, the people prevented the Inferior Court of Justice from proceeding in business, though prior to the new Act taking place; they seized and detained the person of the Judge, and obliged him to adjourn the Court sine die,[98] saying they would have no more Courts.

At Springfield, they compelled the whole Court to [254] appear before the people then assembled, to the number of 3000, and obliged them to sign an engagement, not to take or execute any office, under the new Regulating Act.

At Worcester, the Committees of Correspondence for the County met, and published resolves to urge the Inhabitants to prevent the sittings of the Courts of Justice under the new act and to devise ways to reassume their original mode of Government: and the people assembled, when the Court of Justice was to have sat, and prevented their proceeding to business. Several Gentlemen of that town, having protested against the proceedings of the people on a former occasion, were now compelled to sign a recantation, as were six of the Justices of [255] the County, for having aspersed the people in their Address to General Gage.[99]

At Concord, they prevented the Court from proceeding to business, and at Boston the Jurors all refused to act, denying the legality of the Court.[100]

The people now assembled in many parts of the Country, and visited the dwellings of the several new Counsellors. Some were intimidated, and resigned their seats. Others were compelled to resign by threats of violence, from numbers of people in Arms, and the rest were obliged to fly to Boston for security. So that though twenty six had qualified in August, only fourteen were remaining, and in Boston, early in September.

---

97   See the *Boston Evening-Post*, 29 August 1774, for Salem, and other issues for various county meetings, such as Worcester on August 30th and Middlesex on August 31st (ibid., 12 September 1774) and Suffolk on September 6th (ibid., 19 September 1774). The Salem town meeting of June 19th had included in its message to Gage: "A happy Union with Great-Britain is the Wish of the Colonies., 'Tis unspeakable Grief that it has in any Degree been Interrupted. We earnestly desire to repair the Breach. We ardently pray that Harmony may be restored. And for these Ends every Measure compatible with the Dignity and Safety of British Subjects we shall gladly adopt." The conciliatory sentiments expressed here should not be dismissed as disingenuous—as they were likely to be by a Hulton or a Bernard, even if there was implicit threat combined with explicit plea. Printed in the *Massachusetts Spy*, 23 June 1774.

98   Without setting a date for the next sitting.

99   Developments in Worcester on the eve of war are the focal point of Ray Raphael's *The First American Revolution* (New York: The New Press, 2002).

100 For Concord see Robert A. Gross, *The Minutemen and Their World* (New York: Hill and Wang, 1976).

On the 1st September, the General caused the powder in the Magazine at Medford, near Cambridge, [256] to be removed to Castle William.

The next day the people from many towns to the number of 3 or 4000, assembled at Cambridge, seized the persons of Mr. [Thomas] Oliver, the Lieut. Governor, of Mr. Phips, the high sheriff, of Mr. Lee and Mr. Danforth, Counsellors. The two latter resigned their offices and the high sheriff was compelled to sign a paper that he would not issue the Writs under the new Act.

Mr. Oliver was permitted to go to Boston, to see the Governour, and returned to the people again; he was not apprehensive of all their designs and gave such an Account of the matter to the Governor as made him not suspect any danger to the Lieut. Governor, otherwise, the Governor would [257] have taken measures for his security, and protection.

When Mr. Oliver returned home, the people grew more violent, and outragious, and they finally compelled him to sign a paper, renouncing his seat as Counsellor. Whilst the people were assembled at Cambridge, and were waiting the return of Mr. Oliver from Boston, the Commissioners of the Customs passed through the town, on their return from Salem. The people suffered the first chaise to pass quickly along, but soon pursued Mr. Hallowell and he narrowly escaped being taken. He happened to have a brace of pistols. The cry was "stop him, stop him, he has [258] killed a Man. When the chace grew warm he got out of his chaise, mounted his servant's horse and, with a pistol in each hand, kept the people off, and got safe to the Guard on Boston neck, and that evening all the Commissioners of the Customs went into Boston for safety.

Upon occasion of removing the powder from the Magazine at Medford, and the affair of the following day at Cambridge, a report was spread through the Country, that the troops had fired upon the people, and that several of them were killed; and that the Admiral had fired on the town of Boston, and was laying it in Ashes. Immediately expresses were sent off from place to place with this intelligence, and it was carried in a short time to New York.[101] [259]

The people from several towns of Connecticut marched out with their Arms, towards the relief of Boston, and were with difficulty persuaded to return, when the Account was contradicted. One Justice of the Peace remonstrated with them, and told them it was high treason to take up Arms against the King; upon which he was brought before the Tribunal of the people, and obliged to sign a recantation, of their drawing up.

From this time appearances grew every day more hostile. The people were preparing their fire Arms, and melting all the lead they could get into bullets, and there was not a

---

101 When word reached members of the Continental Congress that Boston had been bombarded by the Royal Navy, there were those—John Adams included—who were almost relieved, thinking that the British had started what many concluded was an inevitable conflict. And yet these same men were also relieved to hear that the rumors were false after all, so confused were feelings at the moment. Fear of war could be coupled uneasily with eagerness for it, not to achieve full political independence and form a new nation, but to better secure rights within the empire—which I addressed in "Our First 'Good' War: Selective Memory, Special Pleading, and the War of American Independence," *Peace and Change* 15 (1990):371-390.

musket to be sold in Boston, but was bought up. Town meetings, and Country meetings were frequently holding [260] and the people were training in Arms, and assembling in bodies in many parts. The Courts of Justice were shut up, and all civil Officers were either silenced, and intimidated, or parties in the forwarding Anarchy, and rebellion.

The General now thought fit to bring some Cannon to the neck, and to throw up an Entrenchment thereon, and he caused the 59th Regiment, that was stationed at Salem, to encamp on the neck, to cover the works that were carrying on. Five Regiments were in the town, and one at the Castle; notwithstanding which, the people expressed themselves in the most insolent manner, and threatened to come down, and destroy the fortifications that [261] were erecting. They secretly removed several Cannon from Boston, and dragged them into the Country beyond Watertown.

The Governor now removed the province papers from Salem, which had been the Established seat of Government, and the Board of Customs, since the Boston Port Act took place; and the Commissioners of the Customs ordered their officers from thence to Boston. Several transports were dispatched to Quebec for two Regiments, and to New York for one from thence.

Whilst things were in this state of confusion, and disorder, and people's minds were in a constant ferment, it is no wonder that their passions were vented in frequent acts of outrage and violence. [262]

The latter end of August, and early in September, County Meetings were held for Middlesex, Suffolk, and Essex, in which they entered into many resolves, denying the authority of the British Parliament, and determining to resist the operation of its acts, and giving their opinion that a provincial Congress was necessary. Refusing obedience to the Courts of Justice under the present Constitution, requiring the Counsellors to resign their seats, forbid[d]ing the Collectors of taxes to pay any Monies to the provincial Treasurer, and urging the people to appear in Arms.

It is said the intention of the people, is to resume their original Charter, that the Representatives now to be chosen, shall appoint a new Governor, and Council, and that the Government is to be established at Worcester. [263]

The Select Men waited on the General, with an Address, expressing the apprehensions of the Town, and Country, from the Fortress erecting at the entrance of the Town, and soon after, the Delegates of the County of Suffolk, presented another, on the same subject, and assured him that nothing less than an immediate removal of the ordnance, and restoring the entrance of the town to its former state, could place the inhabitants in that state of peace, and tranquility they ought to live.[102]

All this time they were arming, removing Cannon, and making every hostile preparation in their power; which the General mentioned to them in his answer.

---

102 The selectmen's complaints and Gage's answer, both on September 6th, are in *Report of the Record Commissioners...Selectmen's Minutes from 1769 through April, 1775*, 227.

Bricks were bought at Medford, for the Barracks [264] which were laden on board two Vessels, but no sooner was it known they were for the use of the Army, than the people rose, and sunk the Vessels and the person who sold them was obliged to fly for shelter to Boston. Straw that was bringing from the Country, for bed[d]ing for the soldiers, was taken, and burnt, by the people at Roxbury.

September 25

The Episcopal Clergy in Connecticut are now the objects of persecution. Those Ministers at a Convention held at New Haven, were drove out of the town; one of them, a Mr. Peters, had his house searched for papers, and at this meeting was very ill used by the people, his gown was striped off his back, and torn to pieces, they crying out, it was the Emblem of the Whore of Babylon; a little Girl, his Daughter, who clung about him whilst they were abusing him, had a sword [265] run into her thigh. He is since come to Boston for safety.

The people are now greatly elated with the news from the Congress, which has approved, and adopted, the resolutions of the County of Suffolk.[103]

The convention of committees for the county of Worcester, have divided the county into seven districts, each of which is to raise a Regiment. The Captains and subalterns are to be chosen by the private men and the field officers by the Captains, and subalterns, and it is recommended to each of them, to provide themselves with one, or more field pieces, and the Civil Officers under the Charter, prior to the first day of June, are desired by them to exercise their respective Offices.

September 26

A number of Carpenters have been employed for [266] several days past, in preparing Barracks for the Troops, but the select men and Committee of Correspondence now order them to desist.

Several Cannon are now mounted on the fortification lately thrown up on the Neck.

A Provincial Congress is to be held the second Tuesday of October, at Concord; the town of Boston has chosen Delegates there, and instructed their Representatives to join them, after they are Dissolved, which they take for granted will follow, as soon as they meet as a General Court, which is to be at Salem the 5th October.

September 29th. The Governour's Proclamation was published for the General Court not to meet as was intended the 5th October.[104]

---

103 The Suffolk resolves were printed in the *Boston Evening-Post*, 19 September 1774 (and in other newspapers around the colonies), and were later included in Worthington Chauncey Ford, ed., *Journals of the Continental Congress*, 34 vols. (Washington, D.C.: Government Printing Office, 1937), 1:31-39.

104 *The Journals of the Provincial Congress of Massachusetts in 1774 and 1775* (Boston: Dutton and Wentworth, 1838) contain the proceedings over three sessions from October 1774 through July 1775, with those of county conventions appended. Gage's September 28th directive is on 3-4. For the emergence of the provincial

The General having purchased some Ordnance Stores of [267] one Mr. Scott, the people having notice, would not suffer them to be carried away, and a guard of soldiers was obliged to be sent to the store to bring them off.

The people afterwards assembled about Mr. Scott's house, threatened him severely, and marked him as an object of their resentment.

The building of the barracks having been suspended by the orders of the Committee of Correspondence to the Workmen, and one Master Carpenter having dared to continue to work for the military notwithstanding, he was this Evening seized by a number of men who put him on board a Boat, and carried him with a halter about his neck to Cambridge, where after much ill usage, they suffered him to go [268] about his business. And he returned the next morning to Boston.

October. Whilst the people were training themselves to Arms, and making every hostile preparation on their parts, they seemed greatly dissatisfied with the general proceedings, for the defence of the town, and the security and accommodation of the troops; and they prevented the bringing in of straw, and materials for the Barracks, and the Carpenters and Labourers from being employed in the service of Government. They even would not suffer a Boat to be built for the use of the Navy in the town, and in their behaviour towards the Military, they shewed the height of insolence, notwithstanding which, the General, the Officers, and Troops, behaved with great temper, forbearance.*[105] *Their acts of outrage were not resented, and many impertinent requisitions of the Committee were acquiesced to, but all was construed into fear, for upon every concession they grew more audacious. And the [269] Committees of Boston, and Worcester, had the presumption to send to the General, that if he did not level the Works he had prepared on the neck, the Country would come in, and demolish them.[106] [270]

---

convention as quasi-legislature and as a crucial part of the transition from province in the empire to state in the nation, see Richard B. Morris, "The Forging of the Union Reconsidered: A Historical Refutation of State Sovereignty Over Seabeds," *Columbia Law Review* 74 (1974):1066-1093, particularly Morris's appendix on 1091-1093. Jackson Turner Main, *The Sovereign States, 1775-1783* (New York: New Viewpoints, 1973), 123-142, saw the formation of provincial conventions as a first step toward revolution, subconscious though it might have been. In the case of Massachusetts the transformation occurred when the provincial convention resolved to continue meeting even though Gage ordered that it not. Also see Agnes Hunt, *The Provincial Committees of Safety* (Cleveland: Winn & Judson, 1904).

105 Inserted from the margin where it had been written by Hulton's scribe, perpendicular to the text.

106 The selectmen had complained to Gage on 9 September 1774 about his "erecting a Fortress" on the neck. He responded on the same day that he did so as a precaution, not as a device to cut Boston off from the mainland. It was his duty, he stated, "to preserve the peace, and to promote the happiness of every Individual; and I earnestly recommend to you, and every Inhabitant, to cultivate the same spirit—and heartily wish they may live quietly and happily in the Town." *Report of the Record Commissioners...Selectmen's Minutes from 1769 through April, 1775,* 228. For context see Warden, *Boston,* 287-306, and, more broadly, Benjamin W. Labaree, *Colonial Massachusetts* (Millwood, N.Y.: KTO Press, 1979), 218-289.

Chapter 15

Proceedings of the Provincial Congress of Massachusetts Bay, and the Continental Congress in Philadelphia. 1774 [271]

[272-274 blank]

September 27th

THE DELEGATES OF THE COUNTY OF PLYMOUTH passed several resolves similar to those in the other Counties, and resolved that they had no connection with or dependance on Great Britain than was stipulated with the King by their Ancestors, and that the interposition of any other power on Earth in their affairs, and more especially in attempts to tax, or even legislate for them, and that of the King himself, in any other manner than is provided by the original Compact, is an infraction of their rights, and that it was the duty of every man, and body of Men, to oppose with all their power, the execution of the late acts of the British Parliament. [275]

And they recommended if any persons should be seized for contending for their liberties to make reprizals, by seizing and keeping in custody every Servant of the present tyrannical Government, and all such as had favoured or abet[t]ed their measures, and detain them till their friends were restored to their families safe and uninjured.[107]

October 10

Though the General had issued a Proclamation discharging the members of the General Court from their attendance at Salem the 7th instant, the day they had been summoned to meet, yet the Representatives assembled there [276] the 7th instant notwithstanding, to the number of ninety, chose a Chairman and Clerk, and published resolves reflecting on the General, and resolved themselves into a provincial Congress to meet with others to be joined to them at Concord the 11th instant.[108]

Many Counties now have had meetings of Delegates from the several towns, where the most extravagant resolutions have been passed, denying the authority, and refusing all obedience to the Acts of Parliament, voting the Counsellors, and all who should accept officer under the Acts, Enemies to their Country, and resolving to arm and die in the defence of their Liberties.[109]

---

107 Printed in *Mass. Provincial Congress*, appendix, 622-625.

108 Ibid., 5-7, for the provincial convention's refusal to comply with Gage's order, on October 5th.

109 Ibid., appendix, 601-660, prints the resolutions from nine different counties, starting with Berkshire (at a meeting in Stockbridge) on 6 July 1774.

October 13

The Delegates from the several Towns in the province, having formed themselves into a provincial Congress at Concord, [277] sent a Committee, with a Message to the General, in which they express their apprehensions from the hostile preparations making on Boston neck, earnestly urge him to demolish the same, in order to quiet the minds of the people; in answer to which he assured them, that the works he had constructed, unless annoyed, would annoy nobody; representing, that their warlike preparations had made it necessary, pointing out their hostile treatment of the troops, and exhorting them to a more decent, and dutiful conduct.

October 14

The Provincial Congress resolved that the Collectors of [278] Taxes throughout the Province be advised not to pay the same to the Provincial Treasurer, and afterwards they adjourned to Cambridge.[110]

About the same time a Committee from the County of Worcester presented an Address to the General, making a similar requisition, with that from the provincial Congress, respecting the dismantling the fortifications on the neck.[111]

About this time appeared some resolves of the Continental Congress at Philadelphia, tending to support the Inhabitants of the Massachusetts Bay in their opposition to the late Acts of Parliament, and resolving that every person who shall accept any Commission [279] in any wise derived from the Act of Parliament for changing the form of Government in the Massachusetts Bay, ought to be held in detestation by all good men.[112]

The provincial Congress at Cambridge on the 21 October passed a resolve respecting the new Counsellors, and others who had accepted, or acted under Commission or authority derived from the Act of Parliament of the last sessions, for changing the form of Government in this Province, requiring them to give satisfaction to this injured Province within ten days, by causing to be published in all the Boston Newspapers acknowledgement of their former misconduct, and renunciations of the Commissions; [280] and authority mentioned, on pain of being considered as infamous betrayers of their Country, and that their names should be published repeatedly, so that being entered on the Records of each town, as Rebels against the state, they may be sent down to posterity with the Infamy they deserve. They further resolved, that as the unnecessary and extravagant consumption of East India teas had much contributed to the political destruction of the Province, to recommend an abhorrence and detestation of all kinds of East India teas, as the baneful vehicle of introducing Despotism and Slavery [281] into this once happy Country, and to recommend that every town, and district, appoint a Committee to post

---

110   Ibid., 19.
111   Printed in the *Boston Gazette*, 17 October 1774, from the meeting of October 14th.
112   Hulton must have had in mind the memorial approved by Congress on October 21st (see infra 175, n. 115).

up the names of all such as should sell or consume so extravagant and unnecessary an article of luxury.

On the 26th October they voted to equip and hold in readiness to march at the earliest notice, one fourth at least of the Militia of the Province, that the private Men of each company should chuse a Captain, and two Lieutenants, and that the Captain and subalterns of each Battalion should chuse the field Officers to command the same; and the select Men of each town were to provide Arms and Ammunition, with [281] out delay, if not already provided, with a full stock. They further resolved that as the Monies assessed by the General Court were resolved not to be paid to the Provincial treasurer for obvious reasons, to appoint a Receiver General for these monies, and appointed one Henry Gardner for that purpose. And all Sheriffs, Collectors, and Constables, were recommended to comply with and execute the direction of this resolve. Then they published a resolve for a General Thanksgiving throughout the Province for Thursday the 15th December.[113] [283]

The Continental Congress had been sit[t]ing at Philadelphia from the beginning of September and on the 20th of October they published an Extract from their Votes, and proceedings, which was signed by the Delegates from twelve several Colonies, containing fourteen articles, as an association binding themselves and their Constituents to abide thereby.

By this association they were not to import any Goods from Great Britain or Ireland, or any East India tea, or any British Molasses, Syrops, Panels, Coffee, or Piemento, or Wines from Madeira, or the W[estern] Islands, or foreign Indigo, [284] or any slaves after the 1st December.

That after the 1st March next they will not purchase or use any East India tea whatever; or any Goods agreed not to be imported, which they shall have cause to suspect were Imported after the 1st December.

This association, with several other articles to continue till the Acts imposing duties on sundry Goods imported into America, together with the clauses in Acts extending the powers of the Courts of Admiralty, sending home persons for trial for offences committed in America, the four acts of the last session respecting Boston, and the Massachusetts Bay, and extending the [285] limits of Quebec &c., are all repealed. And in case they are not repealed by the 10th September 1775, they associate not to export any merchandise or commodity whatsoever to Great Britain, Ireland, or the West Indies, except Rice to Europe.[114]

The Continental Congress that had been held at Philadelphia during the Months of September and October, seperated at the close of the latter month, and then Extracts from their Votes, and proceedings, were published under the heads of a Bill of Rights, a list of Grievances, Occasional Resolves, an association, an Address to the people of Great Britain,

---

113 *Mass. Provincial Congress*, 31-34.
114 The details for the "Association" are printed in Ford, ed., *Journals of Congress*, 1:75-80.

a Memorial to the Inhabitants [286] of the British American colonies, and an Address to the inhabitants of Canada.[115]

Amongst other things they set forth as their Right to participate in their Legislative Council, that they are not represented, and from their local and other circumstances cannot properly be represented in the British Parliament, that they are entitled to a free and exclusive power of legislation in their several Provincial legislatures, where their right of representation can alone be preserved, in all cases of Taxation and internal polity, subject only to the negative of their sovereign. And they Resolve, that sundry Acts of Parliament relative to the Revenue, Admiralty, Massachusetts Bay, and Quebec, are infring[e]ments and [287] violations of the Rights of the Colonists, all which they say are impolitic, unjust, and cruel, as well as unconstitutional.

The Provincial Congress was adjourned to the 23d November, but early in that month the General published a proclamation, pointing out the illegal proceedings of their former meeting, and their dangerous tendency, and warning all persons at their peril from assembling again, under the like pretences.[116] However, they assembled at Cambridge, agreeable to their Adjournment.

Amongst other resolves of the County of York, assembled in Congress November 1774, they published one, respecting W[illia]m Pepperrell, who had large possessions of Lands in that County, [288] but having accepted a seat at the Council Board they resolved that he ought to be detested by all good Men, and recommended it to the people to withdraw all connection and dealings with him, and to take no further lease of his farms, and if any one should become Tenant on such Estates, they were to be treated in like manner.[117]

December 12

The Resolves of the Provincial Congress that had been assembled at Cambridge, for some time past, were published. In these they approve and adopt the Resolves of the Continental Congress that had been assembled at Philadelphia, and they further resolve, that [289] after the 10th October next none of the Goods that had been prohibited by the General Congress from being imported into the Colonies, should be permitted to be sold, or bought; and they recommended the appointment of Committees of Inspection, to see the Resolves

---

115 Printed in ibid., 1:82-90 (address to the people of Britain, approved on October 21st); 1:90-101 (memorial to the inhabitants of the colonies, approved that same day); and 1:105-113 (address to the people of Canada, approved on October 26th, just before Congress adjourned). There was also a petition to George III, on 1:115-121. A declaration of rights had been approved on October 14th—see 1:63-74. Edmund Cody Burnett, *The Continental Congress* (New York: The Macmillan Company, 1941), 33-59, reviews what was done in this first congressional gathering. For Congress and the October 14th declaration see my "The First Continental Congress and the Problem of American Rights," *Pennsylvania Magazine of History and Biography* 122 (1998):353-383.

116 *By the Governor. A Proclamation* (Boston: M. Draper, [1774]), also printed in newspapers, such as the *Boston Evening-Post*, 14 November 1774.

117 The fourth of nine resolutions agreed to on November 16th, printed in the *Boston Gazette*, 5 December 1774.

of the said Congress duly executed and they were to apply to the several merchants, and Traders, at that time, if the Acts complained of were not sooner repealed, to take an Inventory of all such Goods, Wares, and Merchandize, then on hand, requiring them to offer no more for sale; and if they refused, they were to take them into their own possession, to be stored at [290] the risk of the Owners, until the said Acts were repealed, and to publish their names, that they might be treated as Enemies to their Country. And they resolved, that this should extend to all Goods &c., of the Growth, production or manufacture of Europe, Imported from Great Britain, or Ireland. They further address the People by a Publication to all the Freeholders in the Province, pointing out to them their present situation, exhorting them to attend to their military discipline, and to provide those who were not supplyed with arms, and Ammunition, and that each town should pay its own minute men, who were to be kept in constant readiness.[118] [291]

On the 10 December they dissolved themselves, and recommended it to the several towns forthwith to elect, and depute members to a new Congress, to be held at Cambridge the 1st February.

In consequence of the resolves of the General Congress, Committees of Inspection were appointed in several towns, of the different provinces, sixty-three were chosen at Boston, and this Inquisition was to pry into the conduct of each individual, and report as to what he bought or sold, eat, drank, or wore, spoke, or wrote, and many acts of violence, of cruelty and torture were exercised in the course of the proceedings in this new mode of tyranny. Several more Gentlemen now were drove from their dwellings, and obliged [292] to take shelter in Boston, particularly Colonel Chandler of Worcester, Colonel Jones of Westown[,] Colonel Watson of Plymouth, and Colonel Gilbert. The latter returning home one evening was fired at. The ball passed very near him, he made to the place from whence the report came, when a man walked off, saying "ah didn't miss you, you damn'd tory, I meant it for your heart." It was said that the people intended to have branded the Gentlemen, who fled from their persecutions with an R. in the forehead.

About the 10th December His Majesty's Order in Council arrived to prevent the Exportation of Military stores from Great Britain. Immediately after this the Assembly of Rhode Island passed an act [293] to provide a large quantity of powder and Military stores, to raise troops and appoint General Officers.[119] And the Cannon from the fort at Newport was removed to Providence, to fortify that place as a post of defence,

---

118 *Mass. Provincial Congress*, 69-72, a memorial addressed to the "Freeholders and other Inhabitants" of the towns in the province.

119 Order in council of 19 October 1774, with stipulations renewed in April 1775, and again thereafter. In Munro and Fitzroy, eds., *Acts of the Privy Council*, 5:401.

The People at Piscataqua and its neighbourhood assembled in Arms, seized on the Fort in the River, and carryed off the Great Guns of the fort, the fire Arms, and about 100 barrels of Gunpowder, that was there in store.[120]

February 1, 1775

The Provincial Congress assembled again at Cambridge, and soon after passed a resolve, strictly forbid[d]ing the People from furnishing the Army with any Military [294] Stores or supplying them with necessaries to enable them to take the field.

They published Resolves urging the Militia in general to perfect themselves in Military discipline, and the Towns and districts to encourage the Manufactory of fire Arms, and Bayonets, and recommended to them to cause their respective proportions of the Province Tax to be paid into the hands of Henry Gardner of Stow, lately appointed Treasurer of the Province by the former Congress; and after appointing the 16th of March as a day of fasting and prayer they adjourned to meet at Concord on the 22nd of March.[121] [295]

[296-298 blank]

---

120 Reported in the *Boston Gazette*, 26 December 1774.

121 *Mass. Provincial Congress*, 62-65, resolution on December 8th for munitions, and 86-87, 7 February 1775, for public money to Gardner.

Chapter 16

Instances of Persecutions in New England whilst the Country was in a state of Anarchy. 1774 [299]

[300-302 blank]

September 1774

SEVERAL OF THE COUNCIL were obliged to sign resignations of their Offices, in terms dictated to them by the people. The houses of such as were not found at home, were searched in every part, by the rude multitude, and the family compelled to swear that they were not concealed therein.

One Mr. Willard, a Councellor, was taken in Connecticut by the people, and as he would not at first resign his Office, they condemned him to the Mines at Simsbury in that Government, which is a punishment inflicted on Malefactors, and they carried him [303] several miles on the road there before he yielded to their outrage and violence, but at length he submitted to make a resignation of his Office.

Several Sheriffs and their Deputies who had issued Writts under the new Regulating Act, were compelled to renounce acting under its authority, and the persecution of the Addressors to Governour Hutchinson was all the while continued; and many of them were compelled to sign recantations, of the people's drawing up, expressing their sorrow for having so done, against the opinion of the people. All these renouncings of the Councellors and Sheriffs, and recantations of [304] the Addressors, were published in the public Newspapers, and these Counsellors who had taken shelter in Boston were continually threat[e]ned by the people, and every means in their power was used, still to intimidate and compel them to resign.

These several Gentlemen being now reduced; all, who were called Tories, or were any wise suspected to be friendly to government, became objects of persecution, and were compelled to sign such declarations as the body of the people thought fit to impose upon them, and many who delayed to submit to the terms prescribed to them met with very severe and cruel treatment. One person was put in [305] a coffin, and was near buried alive; another, was tyed by a log of wood which was sawed through, and he was near suffering the same fate.

In most of the towns they had now erected very high Liberty poles, to serve as Beacons, or signals, and if any one was refractory, or did not submit to the demands of the People, it was usual to hoist him up on the pole till he complied.

Mr. [Timothy] Ruggles of Hardwick, one of the Council, having sheltered himself in Boston, the people vented some of their resentment against him, on a fine Stallion of his, which was esteemed of great value. This horse they poisoned. [306]

Colonel Gilbert, who was a friend of Governor Hutchinson's, and a reputed Tory, whilst he was in an Inn on a journey, and his horse was at the door, the people took off the saddle, and drove nails through it so that when he mounted, the nails pierced the horse which reared, and threw him off, whereby his Collarbone was broke.

A little boy belonging to the Admiral's Ship, was thrown down by a person who swore he would break his leg, and then he took it up, and wrenched it til it snap[p]ed.

Another little boy, a child of Captain Holland's, the Engineer, was seized at his own door by a man who with both his hands[,] squeezed his throat till [307] he had almost throt[t]led him, saying, he was a tory child and should be served so.

Mrs. Oliver, the wife of the Chief Justice, was not allowed to come to Boston to her husband, nor suffered to write to him.

When the people visited Mr. [Daniel] Leonard's house, one of the Council, several shots were fired into one of the Chambers where he was suspected to be hid.

Dr. Russel of Lincoln, who had given offence, as being a reputed tory, had his chaise fired at one evening, when another person was in it, and the ball passed between the young Gentleman's legs who was in the Chaise.

It were endless to relate all the various modes of persecution, and torture, practised on [308] those who were deemed by the People unfriendly to American liberty.

A poor aged person in Connecticut, who had been severely treated by his breech being pounded on a stone hearth, was in great danger of his life, from the severity of the blows. One Dr. Beiby, who was sent for to attend him, expressing himself with some warmth at the cruelty and inhumanity of the treatment, was seized by the people, strip[p]ed, had hot pitch poured over him, then he was taken into the swine sty, and there rolled in their filth, and had it cram[m]ed into his throat, and Eyes. [309]

One Man was sowed up in the skin of an Ox, just fleed,[122] with the entrails in it. Some were put upon long pieces of sharp wood, and hoisted up and let down again, and tortured for some time in this manner, to the diversion of the people; some were tied by the hair of the head to an horse's tail, and dragged along in this manner. One person was confined for several hours in a chamber with a smoky fire, and the chimney stopt at the top, so that he had near perished with the smoke; some were repeatedly doused out of a boat into the water, till [310] they were near drowned, to make them renounce their opinions, and subscribe to the terms imposed upon them.

The Independant Ministers kept the people's passions ever in a flame, by their prayers and sermons: fast days, and days of prayer, were often held; they roused the people's

---

122 In this context: butchered.

resentment against the King, and Parliament, whom they charged with every thing tyrannical, and unjust; then expostulated with the Almighty, as being his chosen race, that he should not leave them, and urged the people to fight and die for their liberties. One of these pious [311] Ministers concluded a prayer with "and we pray, O Lord, thou wouldst take all the Tories both here and at home, and bind them hand and foot, and cast them into the bottomless Pit, where the smoke of their torments may ascend for ever and ever."

At the close of the month of September and early in October, the Inferior Courts of Common Pleas were to have been held at the Counties of Barnstable and Plymouth. But at the time of the meeting of the Justices, the people assembled at the Court Houses, and voted it inexpedient for the said Courts to sit, and compelled the Justices to sign Declarations expressive of their abhorrence of the late innovations, attempted in the Constitution, by sundry late Acts of [312] Parliament, that they would not aid or countenance the execution of the late Acts, or hold or exercise their Commissions in any other way than what is prescribed by the Charter; and they further compelled such of them as had signed Addresses to General Gage and Governor Hutchinson, to sign a paper, acknowledging their errors, and praying forgiveness.

Many accounts are now received of outrages and violences committed on the Episcopal Clergy, in Connecticut.

On the 6th at 2 in the morning, a dreadful fire broke out in the wood house adjoining to the dwelling house of Mr. Frye at Salem, which consumed 10 or a dozen houses. All his Effects were destroyed, and the family narrowly escaped with their lives. Mr. Frye had been an acting Justice [313] and while the General was at Danvers, he in several instances acted for the Crown, particularly in obliging the Committee to enter into recognizances, on the affairs of the town meeting and from several circumstances, there was strong reason to suspect that the house had been designedly set on fire.

A subscription was entered into at Salem for the relief of the sufferers by the late fire, but after the collection was made, the people voted Mr. Frye, who had been the principal sufferer, and two others, to be Tories, and Enemies to their Country, and therefore that they should have no benefit from the Money that had been raised.

November 5

Advice was received from Baltimore in Maryland that a Vessel with some Tea on board being arrived at that [314] place from London and that the duty had been paid thereon by one Mr. A. Stewart, one of the Owners of the Vessel. They compelled him to go on board the said Vessel and burn the Tea on board, so that both the Tea and ship were destroyed. And this was represented to be done as his own voluntary act.

Captain McGinnis of the 38th Regiment going home one evening, was questioned by the town Watch, and not answering quite to their satisfaction, one of the Watchmen took down a long pole, with a hook at the end of it, from the Watch house, and cut through his face from his ears to his mouth, yet no punishment was inflicted on the Offender for this outragious assault, whilst the soldiers have been severely [315] chastised for the slightest offences against the townspeople.

In December, the Constable of the town of Hardwick, came to Boston, and paid over to the Treasury of the province the monies that had been collected by him for Taxes on the people of his town. On his return, the people compelled him to refund all those moneys out of his private stock, to be paid to the new named Treasurer by the Provincial Congress under the dread of condemning him to imprisonment in the mines at Simsbury in Connecticut. [316]

[317-318 blank]

Chapter 17

Proceedings in the Province of Massachusetts Bay, whilst the Country was in a State of Anarchy and Rebellion. 1775

February 1775

SEVERAL OF THE INHABITANTS of Marshfield, having represented to the General that they were under apprehensions of assaults and violences from the people in the neighbouring Towns, as they had shewed themselves well disposed to Government: the General ordered a party of one hundred Men, under the command of Captain Balfour to be posted at Marshfield, for the protection of the well[-]disposed subjects.[123]

Towards the close of this month, many of the inhabitants, from the interior part of the Province, took shelter from the [319] persecution of the people in the Country, who were assembled in many places in Arms, with intention as it was said to disarm all those called Tories or such as would not join in their measures. A number of Inhabitants in the town of Petersham, who had entered into an association for their mutual defence, finding the spirit of persecution very strong against them, assembled together in an house, resolving to defend themselves to the utmost.

The house was soon surrounded by many hundreds of the people, and they were obliged after some days to capitulate and submit. The people, after [320] disarming them, ordered them to remain each at his own house, not to depart from thence, or any two of them to be seen together upon pain of death. And in most parts of the Country a Watch was set upon such as were reputed Tories, that they should not remove from their dwellings in order, as is supposed, that the people may be able to secure them, whenever any of their own party shall be taken up by Government.

The General having received information of some Ordnance and Military Stores being secreted in a building at Salem, Colonel Leslie was ordered down from Castle W[illia]m, [321] with part of the 64th Regiment. They disembarked from the Transport on Sunday the 26th February at Marblehead, marched into Salem during afternoon service, and after meeting with some detention at a draw Bridge they passed over, and not finding the stores where they were expected, they returned to Marblehead, and reembarked in the

---

123 For divisions in Marshfield, pitting pro-government townsmen against those favoring protest, see Force, ed., *American Archives*, 4th series, 1:1249-1256; and the *Massachusetts Gazette*, 9 March 1775.

Evening. That night many hundred people got under Arms in the neighbouring towns, and marched towards Salem, but the Troops met with no obstruction from the people at Salem, or Marblehead.[124]

March 1775

One of the Inhabitants at Petersham, who [322] had submitted as before mentioned, returned to Boston for security, and afterwards went to visit his friends in the country. But his own relations assisted in laying hold of his person, and inflicting a punishment upon him; he was condemned to hard labour for three weeks, chained at night to the floor and on Sunday was led into the Meeting, and received a spiritual admonition from the Minister for his erronios conduct.

A Ship arrived at New York from London. The Master landed some part of the Cargo in the Jersies, contrary to the resolves of the [323] Continental Congress. And the Merchants being detected, the Goods were taken by the Committee of Elizabeth Town, and the Merchants submitted to an humble confession of their offence, left the Goods to be dealt with as the Committee should see fit, and engaged to give £200 towards building the Hospital, in order to be restored to the favour of their fellow Citizens.

The General Committee of Charles Town, South Carolina, interdicted all Commerce with Georgia, as they had not acceded to the Continental association.

A Country man from Ballerica [Billerica] having tempted a soldier [324] to sell his Arms, was detected and secured at the Guard on the Neck. And the next day the Man was drummed through the town, on a sled, tarred, and feathered. This brought great resentment against the Officer of the Guard, who permitted this kind of punishment to be inflicted on the Culprit, and a Committee from Belerica waited on the General, and delivered to him a most insolent and audacious remonstrance on the subject.[125]

Governour Wentworth of New Hampshire dismissed several Persons from their Civil and Military employments, who had been leaders in the attack and robbing of the King's Fort in December last. [325]

In the first part of this month the Accounts from New York of the proceedings of their Assembly, and of the Merchants and Traders in town, were such as showed a disposition in them to refuse acquiescence to the measures of the General Congress, but the body of the

---

124 *Boston Gazette*, 6 March 1775, supplement, and *Massachusetts Spy*, 9 March 1775, for contemporaneous accounts. Notable later accounts include Charles M. Endicott, "Leslie's Retreat at the North Bridge of Salem," *Essex Institute. Proceedings* 1 (1856):89-135; and Eric W. Barnes, "All the King's Horses ... And All the King's Men," *American Heritage* 6 (October 1960):56-59, 86-88. Hulton erred. The troops did indeed meet with "obstruction," the locals refusing to lower a privately-owned drawbridge that the soldiers needed to cross to get to the north side of town. Leslie had already argued with the locals over whether he was marching on the king's road or the people's thoroughfare. Leslie briefly considered using force, then thought better of it, and a compromise was reached. Hulton missed a perfect illustration of the problems surrounding assertions of imperial authority and local autonomy.

125 The incident, involving Thomas Ditson of Billerica, was reported in the *Massachusetts Gazette*, 17 March 1775.

people soon after voted for chusing Delegates to the Congress, intended to meet in May. And the General Assembly of that Province voted most of the Acts of Parliament that has passed in the present reign relative to America, to be Grievances.[126]

The Provincial Congress of Massachusetts Bay, assembled at Concord, on the 22[nd] March, and entered on business, by publishing [326] a Resolve urging the people to persevere in the measures that had been recommended, for put[t]ing the Colony in a compleat state of defence.

March 20[th]

An Express arrived from a place called Westminster in New York Government, bordering on the extreme part of the province to the northwest, to acquaint the General that the people had obstructed the sit[t]ing of the Court of Justice, that the sheriff had raised the posse to get possession of the sessions house, and before he could drive out the intruders, he had been obliged to fire on them, in which one man was killed, and another wounded. That the people being afterwards joined by others, had drove off the sheriff's party, and taken [327] him and other prisoners, and kept them confined in Jail.

April

Early in this month advice was received that the two houses of Parliament had addressed His Majesty on the subject of the disturbances in America, expressing that the Province of Massachusetts was in a state of actual Rebellion, and praying his Majesty to take effectual measures for the suppression of it.[127]

The Provincial Congress was then sit[t]ing at Concord, and upon these advices, a difference arose in opinion as to the Steps to be taken. A parson Murray, who was a delagate for three or four towns, had already a good deal embarrassed the proceedings of the Congress, during this sit[t]ing, [328] by insisting on satisfaction being made to the East India Company for the loss sustained in the destruction of the Tea, prior to every other business; urging that they never could expect the smiles of Heaven on their resistance, till they had

---

126 See Tiedemann, *Reluctant Revolutionaries*, 216-219.

127 Basing their findings on letters sent by Gage to London between June-December 1774, solicitor general Alexander Wedderburn and attorney general Edward Thurlow ruled on 2 February 1775 that the behavior of the Massachusetts provincial convention "is prima facie Evidence of the Crime of Treason." TNA, PRO/CO5/159, fo. 48. George III denounced the rebellion in a proclamation of 23 August 1775 and asked Parliament at the opening of a new session the following October 26th to support his view that "those who have long too successfully labored to inflame My People in *America*, by gross Misrepresentation, and to infuse into their Minds a System of Opinions repugnant to the true Constitution of the Colonies, and to their subordinate Relation to *Great Britain*, now openly avow their Revolt, Hostility, and Rebellion." Simmons and Thomas, eds., *Proceedings and Debates*, 6:89. The Lords voted their support by a margin of 76-33, with 19 peers soon after writing a dissent (ibid., 6:70-74); Commons approved, 278-108 (ibid., 6:88-90). The King and North had both considered Massachusetts as being in a state of rebellion by the Fall of 1774, and the King endorsed a joint resolution by the Lords and the Commons in February 1775 that a "part" of the province had rebelled against the constitutional authority of crown and parliament.

made compensation for that flagrant act of injustice. This man, by his great volubility of speech, drew many members to his opinions, and was so great a bar to Mr. [Samuel] Adams, who was for precipitating measures, that the latter moved to expel him from the meeting, but could not get such a vote to pass. Deputies attended this congress from Rhode Island and Connecticut. And they, and the other provinces to the Southward, advised the [329] Massachusetts Congress to wait till the meeting of the Continental Congress in May, before they proceeded to extremities; and indeed, the members themselves, when they came to cast about the expence of maintaining an Army, and foresaw the difficulties of raising Money, and providing necessary provision, and stores, were greatly disheartened at the prospect before them.

The Provincial Congress at Concord voted themselves a pay of 5/ a day, during their sitting, to be paid out of the Monies in the hands of H J Gardner, who had been named Treasurer of the Province by a former Congress. But however well disposed the people might [330] be to the cause, yet few had ventured to pay their receipt of Taxes to Mr. Gardner, and all that he had received made but an inconsiderable sum.

Adams and Hancock, thinking it not safe for them to return to Boston, each made a motion for the other to be requested by the Congress to remain with the body. Upon a suggestion that they wanted to go to Boston, upon their own affairs and the Congress voted their presences absolutely necessary, to remain and assist in the business they were upon.

These Leaders, who had nothing else for it, but to precipitate the matters, and [331] keep up the spirit of the people by every means, were urgent to plunge them deeper in rebellion, and terrified them with a thousand fears of their own creating, in case the King's Troops were successful. And they had such influence over the inhabitants of Boston, that soon after the first advices in April, many families dayly left the Town; others sent all their valuable Effects, and furniture into the Country. And all seemed desireous of moving from thence, though without any habitation to fly to, or where they could [332] have a prospect of procuring any of the comforts of life.

They seemed to expect some sudden Judgement or destruction to fall on the Town, or that the Military would destroy the people. Though Boston was certainly the only place of security in the Province to those who were disposed to remain quiet in their dwellings.

April 10th

Colonel Gilbert of Free Town had for a considerable time past been obliged to keep [333] himself with some of his friends in a posture of defence in his dwelling house, being much threatened by the people; as from his principles, and conduct, he was greatly the object of their resentment; being known to be a man of great resolution, they had not dared to make an assault, but lay on the lurch to catch him, if he should dare to go abroad. However, growing weary of delay and watching, at length they assembled the [334] minute men of the County, to the amount of 1500, who went armed and accoutered, to take this single Man; but he escaped on board a Man of War, at Newport. They then divided into parties, and went to the houses of his friends, and took 29 people, whom they called Tories, prisoners, spoiling them of their Arms, and ammunition, and compelled them to make such acknowledgements as they thought fit to impose upon them. Eleven of them being more obstinate than the rest, they condemned them to Simsbury mines in Connecticut, but on [335] their road there, they were brought to submit to sign such articles as the people were pleased to dictate to them.

April 14

The Provincial Congress published an Ordinance for the accommodating such of the Inhabitants of Boston as should at this time remove into the Country. And the next day they issued a proclamation for a fast on the 11th May, and then adjourned to the 10th of May.

On the 18th, at eleven at night, about eight hundred Grenadiers, and Light Infantry under [336] the command of Lt. Col. [Francis] Smith, were ferryed across the Bay to Cambridge, from whence they marched to Concord about twenty miles.

The Congress had been lately assembled at that place, and it was imagined that the General had intelligence of a Magazine being formed there, and that they were sent to destroy it.

It seems upon the Troops embarking, the signal, by a light from one the steeples[,] was given to Charles town across the Water, and this was forwarded through the Country, so that before daybreak the people in general [337] were in Arms, and on their march to Concord. About daybreak a number of them appeared before the Troops near the meeting house at Lexington. They were called to, to disperse, when they fired on the Troops, and ran off; upon which the Light Infantry pursued them, and brought down about 15 of them.

The Troops went on to Concord, and executed the business they were sent on, and on their return, found two or three of their people not yet dead, yet scalped, and their noses and Ears cut off, which exasperated them very much. [338]

A prodigious number of people now occupied the hills, Woods, and stone Walls along the road.

The light troops drove some Parties from the hills, but all the road being inclosed with stone Walls, served for a cover to the people, from whence they fired on the troops, still run[n]ing off whenever they had fired, but still supplied with fresh numbers, who came from many parts of the Country. In this manner were the troops harrassed in their return, for seven or eight miles. They then were almost exhausted, and had expended near [339] the whole of their Ammunition, when to their great joy they were relieved by a Brigade of Troops under the command of Lord Percy, with two pieces of Artillery. The Troops now combatted with fresh ardor, and marched on their return, with the best countenance, receiving sheets of fire all the way for many miles, and yet having no visible Enemy to combat with, for they always skulked, and fired from behind Walls, and trees. They likewise possessed themselves of the houses on the road side, and fired from the Windows on the Troops, [340] but this cost them dear, for the Soldiers entered those dwellings, and put all the men to death.

Lord Percy has gained great honour by his conduct through this day of severe service. He was exposed to the hottest of the fire, and animated the Troops with great coolness, and spirit. Several Officers were wounded, and about 150 of the soldiers were killed and wounded, but many hundreds of the people have fallen.

The Troops returned to Charles town about sunset, after having marched forty, some near fifty miles, and being engaged from daybreak in action, without respite or refreshment. Happily [341] the *Somerset* Man of War of 64 Guns had been stationed between Charlestown and Boston, a few days before, and she awed the people of Charlestown in such a manner, that on the return of the troops, they sent to Lord Percy assurances of their peaceable behaviour. However, he did not march immediately into the Town, for being pressed by fresh numbers of the People arriving from the neighbourhood of Salem, when he got to Charlestown neck, he possessed himself of the heights above the town, and was relieved by a fresh body of six hundred troops from Boston, under the Command of [342] Brigadier General Pigot, and my Lord's party returned about ten in the evening to Boston.[128]

The Troops who occupied the heights above Charlestown early the next morning threw up intrenchments, and prepared to secure the heights with artillery, in order to maintain that Post. But the people from the Country coming down in great numbers on the Boston side, and possessing themselves of the heights and Roxbury meeting house, and all parts round from Cambridge to Dorchester, the General ordered back the party from Charlestown, [343] and evacuated the heights above it, and immediately further dispositions were made, for strengthening the Lines, and fortifying the Town on the side of the Common by raising Batteries on the several eminences and throwing up Intrenchments, where it was judged most proper for defence.

The Troops were much harrassed with all this duty, but went through it with great cheerfulness, but besides guarding against the attempts that might be made from without, they had a more dangerous Enemy within the town.

The communication with the Country had been cut off from [344] the 19th April, and during the early part of that month, many of the inhabitants had been removing themselves into the Country, and there was a general opinion amongst the people that some sudden and great calamity was to befall the town, and several persons who were supposed to be in the secret, were very urgent with their friends in town to remove out of it as soon as possible; and it was pressed upon them in such a manner, as expressed some speedy destruction being to fall on the place.

---

128 David Hackett Fischer, *Paul Revere's Ride* (New York: Oxford University Press, 1994) may well become the equivalent for Lexington and Concord of what Hiller Zobel's book has been for the Boston "massacre." Note that Hulton—and his sister Ann—believed reports stating that the colonists had fired first at Lexington, and that they scalped British soldiers at Concord. See Henry to J. ____ Esqr., April 1775, in the "Letterbooks," 1:123-127, and Ann to Mrs. Lightbody, also in April 1775, in *Loyalist Lady*, 76-80 (the original of which is in the Houghton Library, Murdock Ms. 24), transcribed infra on 318-319 and 316-318, resp.

The Inhabitants of Boston were known to be all provided [345] with fire Arms, and upwards of four thousand men were supposed to be in the town, ready to rise up on any signal of an attack being to be made from without.[129]

After the intercourse with the Country was cut off, and no persons were allowed to go out of the town, the inhabitants grew very urgent and clamorous to be let out to their brethren in the Country: And the select Men had several interviews with the General, to settle the conditions on which they should be allowed to quit the Town.

At length it was agreed, that upon delivering up their Arms, they should be suffered to leave the place, taking with [346] them their necessary furniture and effects. In consequence of this, about fifteen hundred Arms were delivered up, and passes were granted to such people as applied for them, and the inhabitants kept removing into the Country, from day to day, in great numbers.

There was now very strong reasons for judging what the threatened destruction before mentioned was to have been, and which made the affair of the 19th April to be considered as an happy event by the servants of Government, and the people called Tories in Boston.

Many of the Officers of the Army lodged in private [347] houses in the Town. On Monday the 24th April it was intended to have a publick dinner for the servants of the Crown, in honor of St. George, and Lord Percy was to have given a Ball on the Wednesday following.

Now from all circumstances it was generally believed, that there was a plot laid, to have sacrificed the Officers of the Crown, on one of these two nights. That the Military were either to have been taken off in their Lodgings, after their return home on the 24 at night, when they were to be supposed to be in liquor, or that the whole assembly were intended to have [348] been blown up at Lord Percy's ball. And upon the rising of the inhabitants in Town, on one of these occasions the People of the Country who were all ready, were to have rushed down in thousands on the Lines.[130]

The Detachment of Troops that had been stationed at Marshfield for some time past were now called in, and a number of the Inhabitants of that place who had rendered them-

---

129 Hulton passed along to his sons—and whoever else read his account—what had been rumored to be true when he was there. However wrong the supposition was, it did seem plausible to some in town at that moment, given the suspicions in the air and the credence given to tales of conspiracy. Gage only had about 3500 troops at his disposal and on April 19th well over half were engaged in a desperate struggle to get back to safety. When the troops were out, Gage was in a town that still had hostile residents within it and many of them were indeed armed; hence his insistence that weapons be turned into him in the days that followed. Frothingham, *Siege of Boston*, understandably passed over such rumors; so did Allen French's more expansive, more rigorously researched, and better balanced *The First Year of the American Revolution* (Boston: Houghton Mifflin Company, 1934), and 122-124, for Gage's order that civilian arms be turned over to the military.

130 Hulton returns to the rumor that proved untrue. Fischer, *Paul Revere's Ride*, 261-267, discusses the real as opposed to fanciful concerns that followed the fighting at Lexington and Concord.

selves obnoxious to the people in general, by their attachment to Government, came up with them to Boston for refuge.[131] [349]

Transports were sent to Halifax to bring up the remainder of the 59th Regiment from thence to strengthen the Garrison, and whilst the Army within were employed besides their ordinary duty in the works of the Lines, in raising Batterys, and throwing up intrenchments, four Ships of the Line, and several frigates, and Sloops, were stationed in the best manner for the defence of the Town, and Castle, and their Boats employed in watching and Guarding the harbour.

The Rebels[,] who occupied all the Country in the [350] neighbourhood of Boston, did not make any advances towards the Town or preparations for attacking it by throwing up Intrenchments, and raising Batteries. The people from the neighbouring Towns who first formed the Blockade, were said to have been relieved by those from the remote parts of the Country, and the first were said to be returned to their farms, to be ready to join the body when any signal should be made to them for that purpose.

Many families from the neighbourhood of Boston [351] had fled into town on the first alarm, after the begin[n]ing of the action on the 19[th] and had not time to bring any of their effects off with them.

The Rebels made free with the provisions, apparel, and furniture in these dwellings, drank all the liquors that were in Store, and wasted and destroyed such part of the property as they could not consume.

During all this time there was great dread amongst most of the inhabitants of Boston, both friends and foes to Government; lest the town should be destroyed whilst they were in it. And yet to any rational person, [352] after so many of the ill-disposed inhabitants had removed themselves out of it, there was no danger to be apprehended, except from some of the Desperadoes that remained behind, lest they should set it on fire; however, many who were well disposed went by Water to Halifax, Nantucket, London, and other parts, and for those who were otherwise, they either joined themselves to or sought for refuge from the Rebels without.

The Rebels had stoped the Posts and opened the Mails, and prevented all supplies of provision being sent into town, so [353] that most people were soon reduced to salt provisions, and what fish could be caught in the harbour.

The refugees from Boston soon filled the houses & barns in the neighbouring Country, their Goods remained in the open fields, and they without any provision for their support.

A Provincial Congress was now sitting at Watertown, and they thought fit to issue an order for the distribution and reception of the Refugees from Boston, who might be so poor as not to be able to provide for themselves, these they calculated to be about five thousand, and apportioned them to be received into all the towns of the [354] Province that were

---

131 French, *First Year*, 28-30 discusses Marshfield and at least alludes to most of the political and military developments that Hulton included in his account.

upwards of ten or twelve miles from Boston, which part was supposed to be occupied by their troops, or furnishing to their supply.

The expence attending the support of these people, this Congress took upon themselves to say should be made good by some future Congress, or Provincial Assembly, out of the Province Treasury.

Very exaggerated reports of the affair of the 19th April were spread over the Country, and no sooner were they arrived at New York, than the people rose [355] in great ferment, and being urged on by the presence of Mr. Adams and Mr. Hancock of Boston, who were on their Road to Philadelphia to meet the Continental Congress, they proceeded to great licentiousness and disorder, obliging all the inhabitants to swear to abide by the resolves of the Continental Congress, whatever they should be. Many persons fled from the dread they were under from these violent invaders of Government, and embarked immediately for England. The Assembly of the Colony of Connecticut was [356] sit[t]ing when they received an account of the affair of the 19th April, and they immediately dispatched two of their Members, Dr. Johnson and Mr. Wallcot, with a letter from their Governor to General Gage, to be informed of the truth of Facts. As report had been made to them, they had conceived a very disadvantageous impression of the behavior of the King's Troops, but from the General's answer to their Governor's letter, both of which were printed, there should seem great reason for them to be satisfyd with the Conduct of His Majesty's forces [357] on that occasion, and with the means pointed out by the General for a reconcili- ation with Great Britain; and the Gentlemen who were sent on the part of the Colony, appeared satisfied of the truth of the reports they had here heard, and disposed to endea- vour to prevent their Assembly from entering into any violent measures on the occasion; but whatever report they may make, that thwarts with the prejudices of the people, one cannot expect to have much [358] weight with them, as the whole Country seems entirely given up to frantic Enthusiasm, and will accept nothing as truth that combats with their absurd notions.

May

The Provincial Congress at Watertown published two resolves, one for the several towns to elect Members to a new Provincial Congress to meet at Watertown the 31 May, and another declairing General Gage utterly disqualified to serve the Colony as [359] a Governour, and in every other capacity, and that no obedience ought to be paid to his Writts for calling an Assembly, or to his Proclamations, or any other of his acts or doings, but that he ought to be considered, and guarded against, as an unnatural and inveterate Enemy to the Country.[132]

---

132 Resolution of 5 May 1775, *Mass. Provincial Congress*, 192-193, condemning Gage "as an instrument, in the hands of an arbitrary ministry, to enslave the people," whose troops had, without provocation,

In the course of this month, several transports arrived from England, with Marines and Recruits for the Army at Boston, and towards the latter end, three General Officers arrived in the [360] *Cerberus* Frigate, viz. General [William]Howe, General [John]Burgoine, and General [Henry] Clinton.

The assemblies of Rhode Island interdicted the Export of Provision from those Colonies, in order to prevent the supply of His Majesty's troops, and every measure was taken by the people to prevent fresh provision and forage getting into Boston. A detachment of Troops was sent down to an Island in the Harbour, which was near to the Continent, to bring off a quantity of Hay, but a large body of the People assembled on the shore, [361] fired on the party, and obliged them to go off without compleating their business, and afterwards they burnt the hay that was left behind.

Encouraged by this success, a week after they landed from Chelsea on Hog Island, and Noddles Island, near the town, and carried off the stock that was on them. The Schooner *Diana* being sent against them got aground, and was a long time exposed to the fire of a large body of People near Chelsea; at length she was burnt, [362] but Lt. Graves, who commanded her and defended her with great bravery for many hours, withdrew with his people before she was destroyed. The Rebels returned the next day to the Islands, carried off what they could of the remaining Stock, and burnt the houses on Noddles island, and set fire to Hay that was on other Islands in the Harbour.

June

Advices have been received that a body of people [363] from Connecticut have surprized the fort of Ticonderoga, made the Garrison prisoners, and removed them to Hartford Goal, that they afterwards proceeded across Lake Champlain, and coming suddenly to St. Johns they took the King's Sloop and made prisoners a Sergant and 12 men, who were stationed there, but that some Canadians and a part of the Regiment from Montreal had come down upon them and oblige them to retire with loss.

This expedition was concerted by the Boston Delegates [364] to the Continental Congress, along with Mr. Trumball the Governor of Connecticut, at Hartford, and must have been undertaken at the time that Doctor Johnston and Mr. Wallcot were sent with the letter before mentioned to General Gage.

Advices were received from Piscataqua, and the Eastward, of violent proceedings of the people of the Country, who were all in Arms, and frequently entered the town of Portsmouth in large bodies, terrifying the inhabitants, and searching their houses for obnoxious persons under various pretences. [365]

"inhumanly slaughtered" innocent people.

About the middle of June a number of transport Ships arrived from Cork with 3 Regiment [of] foot, and one of Light horse, when General Gage issued a Proclamation, promising his Majesty's pardon to all those who should forthwith lay down their Arms, and return to the duties of peaceable subjects, excepting Samuel Adams and John Hancock, and ordering the use and exercise of the Law Martial, throughout the Province.[133] [366]

---

133 Gage's decree was printed as a broadside, titled simply *A Proclamation*, dated 12 June 1775, "By His Excellency The Hon. *Thomas Gage*, Esq.," and was also printed in newspapers (see the *Essex Gazette*, 12 June 1775), although fewer than usual because of the turmoil in the Boston press caused by Lexington and Concord.

A Summary of the Persecutions and Distresses undergone by the Commissioners of the Customs in America [367]

[368-370][134]

1767

September 24th. The Commissioners of the Customs sailed from Gravesend in the Ship *Thames*, and arrived in Boston Harbour in the Evening of the 4th of November. The next day they landed, and immediately were exhibited in Effegy round the town, along with the Effegies of the Pope, Pretender and Devil, all which were cast into the bonfire at night.

Before the arrival of the Commissioners the heads of the faction in opposition to Government at Boston had a meeting to consult in what manner they should treat the Commissioners on their arrival. At this meeting it was proposed to assassinate them on their first coming on shore, and this proposal was overruled by one voice only.

1768

Early in the Spring there were frequent Mobs in the Evenings, and alarms about the Commissioners' houses, which occasioned a great deal of family dread and distress. The Commissioners represented to Governour Bernard the danger they apprehended to their persons, but he told them he could give them no protection, and his Council affected not to credit the representations made to the Governour by the Commissioners. [371]

The Commissioners[,] finding they could have no protection from the Government of the Province, acquainted Commodore Hood at Halifax of their situation, who sent the Schooner *Hope* immediately to Boston and in the Month of May ordered the *Romney* Man of War of fifty Guns to Boston Harbour.

The People persisted in their practises of Smug[g]ling in Cargos of Goods, in open violation of the Law, threatening vengance to any Officer who should dare to make a seizure.

In the month of June the Collector and Comptroller made Seizure of a Vessell from which a Cargo of Wines had been run on shore, which occasioned a great Riot, and violent persecution of the Revenue Officers. The Collector and some other Officers were bruised, and very ill[-]treated by the Mob. The Commissioners fled from their dwellings, and took shelter in different houses that night, and the ferment continuing the following days, they first took refuge on board the *Romney* Man of War, and some days afterwards retired into Castle William, where they were obliged to remain the whole summer.

---

134 Hulton attached newspaper clippings to these pages.

The latter end of October some Regiments arrived at Boston for the support of the Laws, and protection of the Servants of Government; and early in the next month the Commissioners came up to Boston from the Castle, and resumed the exercise of their Commission in Town. [372]

Some time after the Commissioners had retired to the Castle, General Gage came to Boston from New York, when fifteen Members of the Council presented an Address to him, in which they passed severe and unjust reflections on the conduct of the Commissioners; and they sent petitions to both Houses of Parliament, to the same purport.

But notwithstanding all their pretentions they fomented a Spirit of revolt in the people, from the authority of the British Government, and at the time of the arrival of the troops, there was actually a convention from several Counties assembled at Boston, in defiance of the Governor's authority; and with the declared intention to take upon themselves the powers of Government; but upon the landing of the troops these Deputies immediately dispersed.

Mr Hulton's family arrived from London at Boston, but five days before they were obliged to fly from the Town; and on their return from the Castle no one would rent Mr. H. an house, and he was obliged to pay half a pound a Week for poor illfurnished Lodgings in a house that rented for only 18£ per Annum, and not being able to get proper accommodations in town, he was in a manner under the necessity of purchasing an house in the Country. [373]

1769

The People had now entered into resolutions not to Import any Goods from Great Britain, and violent persecutions were stir[r]ed up against all those who did not comply with the popular resolves. The Revenue Officers were threatened and intimidated; and if they attempted to do their duty, they were tarred and feathered, which punishment, with many aggravating circumstances, was inflicted on many of them in different parts.

The newspapers were filled with scurrilous and inflammatory publications against the servants of the Crown, and the Commissioners were personally abused, and pointed out as objects of the people's resentment.

There had been four Regiments in Boston during the Winter of 1768, under the command of General Mackay: and Commodore Hood came from Hallifax in the fall of that year, and remained at Boston during part of the next. The General found a great deal of difficulty and embarrassment from the insolence of the people towards the troops, and the want of support from the civil Magistrates, or their partiality towards the towns people, in every matter of dispute between them and the soldiery, for the former were forever seeking cause to provoke, and distress the latter.

Commodore Hood was about to return to Halifax, and was desirous to carry back the two Regiments with him that came [374] from thence; and the General, no doubt, was pleased to have the Command divided, so that there needed be no occasion for his remaining at Boston: where he was subject to insult and injustice, and to see the authority of his Country trampled upon, without being able to enforce the execution of its Laws. No doubt these Gentlemen thought that two Regiments would be sufficient to keep the town in awe, so, as that the people would not venture on any outragious acts. General Mackay went to England, and Commodore Hood returned to Halifax, with two Regiments.

The Magistrates had long shrunk from their duty, or had joined in opposing the Laws. Government was now prostrate at the feet of the popular Demagogues. Whatever they asserted in their harangues at the town meetings, or published in the Weekly newspapers, became doctrine and Law to the people. They were intirely at the devotion of these Leaders, of whom every one stood in awe, and it was living in a dreadful state of thraldom, to be forever under the apprehension of being the victim of their vengeance.

1770

The people grew more violent in their insults and abuses of the Servants of Government, and all those who would not adopt the popular resolves were objects of persecution. There were frequent assaults on the soldiery, and even the Centries were attacked upon their Posts in the Streets of Boston [375]

On the 5th March in the Evening (the People being prepared for a general rising) a Mob gathered about the Custom house, and assaulted the Centry, who after suffering much abuse, called to the Main Guard. A party came speedily to his relief, but they were likewise grossly assaulted, and abused; till at length they were compelled to fire in their own defence, and killed and wounded several of the people. This occasioned a most violent ferment in the town; the Commissioners and Officers of the Customs were obliged to flee out of it, and several of them took shelter in Mr. H[ulton']s house at Brooklyn

The next day it was agreed in order to pacify the People, that the two Regiments in Boston should withdraw to Castle William; and they accordingly left the place, leaving the Captain of the Guard, and the Soldiers who fired on the Mob, prisoners in Goal; and all the Servants of Government at the mercy of the People.

Depositions were now taken to prove that a person fired out of the Custom house windows, at the time the soldiers fired on the people; and that the Commissioners were the abettors of the Murders that had been committed; and some of their Officers were accused and committed to goal, as parties therein.

Immediately a violent spirit of resentment appeared against the Commissioners, and they were for a considerable Time in dreadful alarm and apprehension in the Country, not daring to go [376] to Boston.

Copies of the Letters and Memorials which the Commissioners had sent home on the subject of the former riots in Boston had been sent back to the people; and the Grand Jury had found bills of Indictment against them, for the misrepresentations alledged to be therein. They were now accused as Enemies to the Province, and abettors of murder, and it was resolved to prosecute them in the provincial Courts of Justice.

The Superior Court met the latter end of March. Mr. Robinson, one of the Commissioners, went to England; two others (Mr. Burch and Mr. Hulton) thought it most prudent to retire for some time out of the Province, and took shelter in Piscataqua, leaving their families at Brooklyn. They remained in New Hampshire for several Weeks in safety, but were told that if they should attempt to establish their Board there, or if Mr. Paxton (another Member) should come there, that the Governor could not answer for their protection. The latter end of April they returned to Brooklyn, but they soon found that they could not remain there in security, nor venture into Boston; and they continued for some time in constant dread and alarm.

About the middle of May Mr. H. went to Rhode Island, thinking it best to keep out of the way for some time. He returned from thence about the middle June. Three days after at midnight [377] he was assaulted in his house at Brooklyn by a Mob from Boston, who in an instant broke all the lower windows, and with many violent imprecations swore they would have him dead or alive, but they retired without entering the house. As soon as they went off, he took shelter in a neighbouring house till day brake; then he fled to another's about three miles off, where he remained for two days, making a representation to the Governour of the assault upon his house and person. This being laid before the Council, produced no other effect, than the remarks of some of the Members, that he had hired some people to break his own windows, in order to bring a reproach on the Province.

The Commissioners now found there was no security for them in the Country, and retired a second time to Castle William; where they remained till November following.

Commodore Gambier arrived at Boston Harbour in the month of October, and about that time the non[-]importation agreement was broke up, and the passions of the people seemed to have subsided. The Captain and soldiers who had been in confinement since the 5th of March were tried and acquit[t]ed, and there seemed to be a disposition to keep order in the town, so that the Commissioners ventured to return, and carry on business again in Boston. [378]

1773

The Commissioners had continued to carry on for a considerable time their business unmolested, but at the meeting of the General Court the latter end of May, a great ferment arose in Boston, on account of Governour Hutchinson's letters, which had been written by him to some friends in England; and now were returned back, and communicated to the Members of the General Court.

Violent were the threats against the Governor and the Crown Officers on this occasion.

At the meeting of the General Court it was usual to have a public Dinner. To this Entertainment the Commissioners were invited by the Governor, which was the first time that any compliment of the kind had been paid to them. On the Company's going away after dinner, a Mob was assembled at the Door, who assaulted the Commissioners in the grossest manner, throwing stones, dirt, and brickbats at them, all the way through the streets to their houses, and abusing and cursing the Governor for having dared to invite them to dinner. The Cadet Company in their uniforms, were under Arms before the door at the time, and two of that Corps left their Arms, and were the foremost in the abuse of the Commissioners. [379]

In the fall of the year the minds of the people were greatly agitated on the report of some Cargoes of Tea, subject to duty, being expected for sale, on account of the East India Company. On the arrivals of these Vessels, the people assembled for several days, and called in the Country Delegates, to advise with on the alarming occasion. They had several meetings at the Old South Meetinghouse, being too numerous for Faneuil Hall. At the first of these meetings the Governor sent a Message to them, by the high Sheriff, requireing them to disperse immediately. This they treated with the greatest contempt, and threatened the Governor and the Commissioners with their utmost resentment.

The Commissioners foreseeing the storm, had already thought it prudent to retreat, and on the 30th of November retired for the third time to Castle William. The town of Boston was in one continued ferment till the middle of December; when after a general meeting at the Old South, on the evening of the 16th they went on board the several Vessels in which the Tea was laden, and destroyed the whole by throwing it into the water.

After they had gratified their rage on the immediate object of their resentment, the violence of the people's passion subsided by degrees; and the Commissioners ventured to return to Boston during the Christmas holy days. [380]

The Tea Consignees were likewise obliged to take Shelter in Castle William, and were ever after held in so obnoxious a light by the Townsmen that they dared not appear again in Boston till it was in the possession of His Majesty's Troops.

Great was the anxiety and family dread undergone for a course of years; being subjected to continual alarms from an enraged multitude; from whose fury there was no shelter, or protection to be found in the Country; and no relief or redress to be hoped for, or obtained, after having suffered the weight of their vengance.

Many were the inconveniences expressed, many the losses sustained, and distresses endured; and heavy the expences attending these frequent alarms, flights, and removals.

1774

In consequence of the outrage committed by the people of Boston at the close of the last year, the Boston Port Act was passed, and a Bill for altering the Constitution of the Province, the Council of which was now appointed by the Crown.

General Gage arrived as Governor in the spring of the year, and some Regiments of foot to support the authority of the Laws.

The Port of Boston being shut up, the Commissioners and their Officers were removed to Salem, and the General resided in the neighbourhood of that place. [381]

On the first meeting of the new Council, a violent ferment spread through the Country, and every means was used to intimidate the Members, and several of them immediately resigned their appointment, or declined taking their seats at the Board.

County Meetings were now held to prevent the execution of the Laws, and concert measures for resistance to the authority of Great Britain. Every one was busy in providing Arms and Ammunition, and training for action.

The General having notice of a quantity of powder being in the Magazine at Medford, thought proper ro have it secured and removed to Boston. The next day the whole Country in the Neighbourhood assembled at Cambridge, and surprised the Lieut. Governour, and some of the Counsellors, whom they compelled to resign their Offices.

Whilst the People were in the midst of this business, who should pass through Cambridge (in their way from Salem to their Country houses in the neighbourhood of Boston) but the Commissioners of the Customs, in seperate Chaises. The people suffered Mr. Burch and Mr. Hulton to pass on unmolested; but Mr. Hallowell having spoke to some of them, and he being more known, and obnoxious, was pursued by several of them, who cried out "he [382] had killed a man" finding himself pursued, he quitted his Chaise, and mounted his servant's horse, galloping as fast as he could with a pistol in each hand. The pursuers encreasing from every house till he came to Roxbury Street, and he with great difficulty getting to the Guard on the neck before he was overtaken. From the Rage the people were in, it is most probable he would have been instantly murdered, could they have laid hands on him.

The rest of the Commissioners immediately took shelter in Boston#,[135] where they remained till the town was evacuated, except Mr. Burch, who went to England in October 1775.

On occasion of the General's removing the powder from Medford, an alarm was spread through the Country, and it was reported that the Soldiers had killed some of the people, and that the Admiral had fired on the Town of Boston. Immediately the people in many towns of Connecticut took to their Arms, and marched towards the relief of Boston, and were reluctantly sent back, on finding the account prove false. But this shews that the people in the remote parts were now ready to revolt. [383]

1775

The People of the Country had been preparing for action during the fall and Winter; and the Army had been strengthening the Lines on Boston neck; but an intercourse was still open between the town and Country during the Winter. One or other of the Regiments marched some miles into the Country daily; and the market people came every day to town as usual, and few of them went back without a musket or two, which they carried out unmolested by the Guard. But besides the Enemy that were training without there was a formidable body of Rebels within the town, who were all provided with Arms. Every thing was prepared and they only waited for a proper opportunity to give the Signal for a general rising in Arms.

---

[135] Hulton inserted at the bottom of the page: "#September 3rd 1774."

Many of the inhabitants of Boston had withdrawn themselves into the Country in the Spring of the year, and several persons who seemed disposed to remain in town, had private notice from their friends in the plot, that a sudden blow was intended to be struck; and they were urged by all means to get out of the town, as they would wish to escape from that destruction that would fall on those who continued in Boston. [384]

Most of the Officers of the Army had private Lodgings seperate from the Troops in Barracks, and about this time the General gave orders for all Officers to sleep in the Barracks with the Soldiers.

A public Entertainment was to have been given on St. George's Day, and it was afterwards said that the People were to have rose that night, after the Officers were gone to rest, (supposing they would be in private Quarters), and that ten or twelve men were fixed on to watch, and surprise each Officer.

The intimidation that had been given to sundry Persons of the town, and the orders of the General, seem to strengthen the suspicion of some such plot being concerted.

The affair of the 19th April prevented the intended Entertainment, and that night was surely the most alarming that could be imagined. The two bodies of troops that had been sent to Lexington were returning to Charlestown weary and fatigued, with the long march, and severe duty of the day.

A fresh Corps was sent over in the evening to Charles Town, to cover and support them in their return. There was then only six hundred troops left in the town, so that the [385] Guard at the Lines consisting only of one hundred and fifty men could not be strengthened. The men did duty for forty[-]eight hours unrelieved.

At this critical time the whole country had taken Arms, and were coming down towards Boston, and there were between five and six thousand men now in town, prepared with Arms, waiting only the signal to rise. We continued for a day or two in this ticklish situation; the People appeared very insolent and audacious; but the spirit and good conduct of the General on this occasion brought the Select Men to submit to the giving up the Arms of the Townspeople into his Custody, on his permitting them to go out of Town with their effects; and many thousands of the seditious inhabitants soon joined their rebellious friends in the Country.

About a month after this the Generals Howe, Clinton and Burgoine arrived from England. We were now shut up from all communication with the country, and from this time obliged to live on salt provision, fish, or such casual supply of fresh meat as could be procured by sea, from distant parts; which always came very dear, from 1/ to 1/6 the pound. [386]

The Rebels possessed themselves of several eminences between Boston and Cambridge, which they strengthened by Lines and Works; and from their great numbers, and their use of the spade, they could throw up extensive intrenchments in a night's time. This we experienced on the morning of the 17 of June, by their playing on the north part of the Town from a Battery erected the preceding night at Bunker's Hill.

The event of that day, though it proved to the honour of our Arms, and relieved us from immediate anxiety, and dread, yet occasioned great pain and distress to every loyal subject.

We had scarce given vent to our joy on seeing the flight of our Enemies, than we were called to mourn and lament over the Gallant men who were killed and wounded in our defence. The streets were soon filled with these objects of our respect, and compassion; and the cries of the Women and Children over their dead and wounded husbands and parents were truly lamentable.[136]

The smallness of the Garrison at Boston would not allow the General to take all the advantages that might have arisen by the flight of the Rebels from Bunker's Hill. They continued to fly in confusion even from Cambridge, but [387] finding they were not pursued, recovered from their panic, and repossessed themselves of their former Posts, and made a strong work at Roxbury Meeting.

We were long threatened that the Town should be set on fire by the people within, whilst the Rebels under favour of the confusion and the advantage of their numbers, should make a general assault. In the month of June, a great fire broke out at night in the middle of the town, and from the circumstances we were in, we were under great apprehensions till it was reduced.

About the middle of July several Transports arrived with four Regiments of foot from Ireland.

Early in that month the Generals Washington and Lee came to Cambridge, being appointed by the Continental Congress to the command of their Army, which was now to be called the Army of the Confederate Provinces.

The Rebels had now provided themselves with some hundreds of Whale Boats, from the Island of Nantucket. These Boats were very light, and were rowed with prodigious swiftness.

In these they made descents on the Islands in the harbour, in sight of the Men of War, and were very audacious in their attempts, carrying off People from the Islands, and [388] burning houses and barns. Nay, they burnt the Light house, and a few nights after returned and burnt the dwelling house on that Island, killed the Officer of Marines stationed there, and made his party Prisoners.

We were now every day subject to alarms, and threatened with the number of Whale Boats that were assembled at Cambridge; and made to expect that we should be assaulted by great numbers of all sides, so that we never went to bed without apprehension of an attack; and sometimes we were awaked at midnight with furious cannonadings.

The Rebels threw up intrenchments on the side of Roxbury, near our advanced post, and frequently fired on the Lines with some pieces of Cannon; and almost daily attacked,

---

[136] Hulton offered more details in his letter to Robert Nicholson of 20 June 1775, in Hulton, "Nicholson Letters," 78-86, transcribed infra at 327-329. Richard Ketchum's *Decisive Day* (Garden City, N. Y.: Doubleday, 1974) has become the standard account of Bunker Hill.

and fired upon the Centries; which sometimes drew on a Cannonading on our part, but in general the Lines and Centries received their fire, without returning any.

The Rebels prevented all in their power any supplies of Fuel, provision, or Forage coming to us. There was now great sickness in town, both amongst the Army and the People; and it was very lamentable to be witness to so much distress [389] one could not relieve, and to see one's Children and friends languishing for fresh provisions, and the comfortable accommodations they had been accustomed to; but those evils appeared light in comparison of what we apprehended in the course of the Winter, if we were not powerfully supported, relieved.

Most of the Inhabitants of the town, in the interest of the Rebels, had now removed out of it; and indeed many of those who were friends to Government sought to Embark for Great Britain, and other parts, to escape from the impending calamities.

On the 31st of July soon after midnight, we were awaked with a furious cannonade of Great Guns, and an heavy fire from small Arms in several Quarters. We immediately rose, apprehending the Rebels were making a general attack on the town in all parts; but it proved to be a feint from our side.[137]

General Gage went home in the begin[n]ing of October, leaving the command with General Howe. [390]

1776

Most of the Ships that were sent from England with supplies of Provision and Coals for the Garrison at Boston, were either taken, or drove off the Coast, so as not to arrive in Season. And the Troops and Inhabitants were a good deal distressed for want of those articles. During the Winter a number of houses were pulled down in Boston for fuel for the Army.

In the month of February the Rebels advanced their works near the water side, opposite to Barton's point, and threw shott and shells into the Town, whereby some houses were damaged.

A Battery was erected under Mount Whordom against their new works, but played with little effect, and though the Inhabitants were alarmed, and incommoded, both by shot and shells from the new works, and on the Roxbury side; yet there was little apprehension from their present operations, that the Rebels would possess themselves of the town. But on the 5th March at day break we were surprised with a view of many thousands of them at work on the hill upon Dorchester neck, opposite the South end that commands the Town. Upon this it was immediately resolved to dispossess them of those heights; and in the afternoon [391] between two and three thousand troops were Embarked with intention to land on

---

[137]   Hulton wrote about aspects of the siege in letters to Robert Nicholson of 30 July 1775 and 22 January 1776, in Hulton, "Nicholson Letters," 86-95, transcribed at 330-331 and 341-342 infra, resp.

the neck, a back of the hills which were occupied by the Rebels; but the weather proved so stormy that the men could not be landed; and the next morning it was found that the Rebels had so far strengthened themselves in their new post, that it was most adviseable to give over the attack.

The Rebels now played furiously upon the town each night, which was returned from our several Batteries.

On the 7th in the Morning, it was given out in Orders that the Troops were to quit the town. Immediately a general scene of distress and confusion arose. Houses were left, and furniture neglected. Everyone was only intent in providing for his own safety.

As soon as it was publickly declared that the town was to be evacuated, the Commissioners of the Customs applyed to General Howe for a Transport Ship to carry themselves and their Officers. The General referred them to Admiral Shuldham, as he had no Ship under his direction that could accommodate them. [392]

The Admiral told them there were six Victualers under his command, laden with provisions for the fleet, and that they might have any one of those they would chuse. There was no time to be lost; many other persons were applying for passages; and they were obliged to fix on a Vessell immediately.

They took their chance of the Ship *Hellespont*, one of those that was named to them. The Ship was still laden with the greatest part of her Cargo of Victuals, and though the Commissioners expected she would be discharged immediately, yet the suddenness of their departure obliged them to go on board before the Vessell was prepared to receive them.

On the 9th March at midnight, during a furious Cannonading, orders were signified for the Transports to go down to Kingroad the next day at noon.

The Commissioners were obliged to rise, abandon their dwellings, and ship off their families immediately. They walked above a mile through the town, and before day were on the Wharf ready to Embark.

When they got on board, the Ship was in no condition for a Voyage; she was without seamen, and filled with the Provision she brought out; so that they were obliged to leave many packages containing liquor, stores and valuable furniture on the Wharf, [393] for all their cabinet Ware, and bulky furniture was left entirely behind.

Twelve Marines were procured to assist as seamen in getting the ship down to Nantasket. With difficulty they got her away from the Wharf in the afternoon, and in the Evening brought her to Anchor abreast of the Town. During the night, the Marines got drunk with the Liquors of the passengers; here was a fresh scene of trouble and distress—with much difficulty six of them were removed from on board, and four seamen obtained from a Man of War, to carry the Ship down. At this time the Cabbin and Steerage were filled with the families of the Commissioners and their Officers—Thirty[-]six Men, Women and Children had lain in the Cabbin and state rooms, without accommodations; and no births were yet fixed up, other than the few standing ones in the state room and Cabin.

When the ship got down to Nantasket, it was many days before these necessary conveniences were fitted up. And the ship was daily discharging her lading by piecemeal to the Fleet, as each Ship wanted Victuals; so that the passengers were constantly incommoded to the last hour.#[138] The necessary ballast was not begun to be put on board till the day before the fleet sailed; and to the last moment it was taking in. Nor was there sufficient on [394] board when the Vessell sailed; so that the seamen afterwards declared, that had they had a severe passage, the Vessel must have overset for want of ballast. We were to have had six good seamen from the *Lively* Man of War to navigate the ship; nearly at the last hour, six indeed were sent, but they were Yankees; neither were they seamen; nor could be trusted. And one night, through neglect of the Mate, they steered the ship so much to Leeward, that we had great difficulty in recovering the convoy again.

On arrival at Halifax we could scarce obtain the least Shelter. The numbers that had arrived before us had filled every house. Many families were still obliged to remain on board the Ships. Mr. Hulton's family were taken into part of a friend's house, and lay for a considerable time on the floor; but Mr Hallowell's family continued for many days on board the Ship, before they could have a place to put their heads in.

We were here equally distressed for Victuals as at Boston. Very scanty was the supply of fresh meat, and that was poor, and sold at an extravagant price, so that had it not been for Fish, many people must have been in danger of starving—in short for those necessaries of Fuel, lodging and provision, no place could be more scarce, dear & wretched [395]

Some time after their arrival at Halifax, the Commissioners applyed to General Howe, for a Transport ship to carry them home. He answered that he wished to serve them, and soon after made them an offer of a Vessell in no wise capable of accommodating them. But on the arrival of the *Renown* transport ship with donations, the General made a tender of her to the Commissioners, for their accommodation; and it was generally understood that they were to go home in her, but the General afterwards made them acquainted that she neither was at his disposal, nor could any Vessel then in the harbour be allotted for the Commissioners, as they stood in need of every one for the Army; however, this ship remained at Halifax after the Army sailed, and was afterwards engaged to carry the 65th Regiment to England, and the Commissioners hired the ship *Aston Hall* to transport themselves, their Officers &c. to London. The *Renown* being an armed Vessel, and having upwards of one hundred Officers and soldiers on board; the Commissioners engaged the Captain of her to keep company with the *Aston Hall*, and the two ships sailed together from Halifax the 18th July. The next day they had a violent gale of wind, so that with much difficulty they weathered the Isle of Sables. In tacking off this Island, the two ships separated, and did not join Company again; and we were for some time in great apprehension

---

[138] Hulton inserted at the bottom of the page: "#below they were crouded, and choaked with smoke. upon deck, they were exposed to sleet, snow, and cold piercing march winds."

of falling in with the Rebel Privateers, [396] some of which we were told at Halifax were advised to look out for us; but we happily escaped them, and though we had rather a severe passage for the summer season, we arrived off of <u>Dover</u> in twenty[-]five days, and landed there the 13th <u>August</u>. [397]

Letters

[Henry Hulton to Robert Nicholson]

Mr. R. Nicholson   *Antigua   10 February 1760*[1]

Dear Sir

I had lately the pleasure to receive your favour of 15 October by way of Guadalupe. You certainly think I am possessed of a good deal of patience, by letting me continue so long without hearing from you, or you imagine as I have been several Years an Exile from my native Country, that my affections are so far estranged from it, as to leave me indifferent to the affairs of it, and the concerns of my friends. Indeed I find my connections with England lessening, without my attachments strengthening here. I seldom hear from any one except my Brother or Sister. He informs me [of] no News and she has sufficient weight upon her to give little room to other thoughts. How hard is it for a person of benevolent affections, to be separated from his friends! To stand alone in the World! I am alone, unsupported, a Stranger in the World—without a home—my youth is now past—my expectations are damped. Nine years of anxiety and solicitude are a great trial of a man's patience, and almost sufficient to sour his Temper—yet this I have experienced with little outward consolation, advice or sympathy.

If you imagine me possessed of right Sentiments, and generous affections, you cannot think I can reflect on our past friendship without much tender feeling. I would not wish any one who feels as I do, to experience what I have done. I have no one to share in the troubles which oppress me. I look back on past scenes wherein I was happy, but they will no more return; before me the prospect is dreary. This life, though short, has many changes; nothing is certain—may you be happy. I assure you it will be a matter of great pleasure to me to hear that you are so.

Could you inform me of no events amongst our friends? As to the Publick we have heard with great Joy the glorious events of 59.[2] I have lately read two good productions, Robertson's history of Scotland and Montague on the rise and fall of antient Republicks.[3] I could wish to have your Townspaper sent me by Vessels coming to any of these Islands. There is always in it some Townside news which I am glad to see. I have often desired Brother to send it me, but in vain. Will you be so kind? If you will, I'll rummage amongst my scraps of Poetry and send you some in return, though I assure you I'll rhyme no more. Some time since a Gentleman sent me a Latin Poem on the King of Fairies, desiring me to translate it. I neglected it some time till he pressed me much. I send it to you, inclosed with a song on 59[4] that I may be beforehand with you. The latter I could not refuse, as it was designed for our publick dinner, on the taking of Quebec, but no one could find a tune for it—don't think I waste my time in Rhyming. I assure you I find better employment.

Pray make my Compliments to Mr. Hodgson and I wish him happy in his new state. What is J. Dobson about?

I wish my best respects to Mrs. Nicholson, your Brother's, Mr. Cropper's, Mr. Lightbody's[5] familys, and all friends.

Your Most Obedient Servant,

Henry Hulton

---

1 The first of twenty-one letters from Hulton to Liverpool merchant Robert Nicholson between 1760-1776 [hereafter "Nicholson Letters"] in Ms. William Shepherd, vol. XVIII, Harris Manchester College, Oxford University, on 1-6. Nicholson, who died in August 1779, was a friend to the entire family, as indicated in his involvement with the disposition of the estate of Henry Hulton's older brother John (see supra 30 n. 21). There is another copy of Hulton's letters to him in the Shepherd Mss. (MCO) in the John Rylands University Library, University of Manchester, with some slight variations in spelling and punctuation. It appears to be the later transcription of the two but, lacking the original, it is impossible to say which is the most accurate.

2 Referring, no doubt, to the British naval victory at Quiberon Bay off the coast of France and the surrender of Quebec, leading to expectations that all of New France would fall soon.

3 William Robertson, *The History of Scotland*, 2 vols. (London: A. Millar, 1759); Edward Wortley Montagu, *Reflections on the Rise and Fall of the Antient Republicks* (London: A Millar, 1759).

4 Appended to the above letter as pp. 6-8 ("In Orcadam Regem," the Latin original) and 8-12 ("On the King of the Fairies," Hulton's English translation of it).

5 Adam Lightbody, the husband of Ann Hulton's friend and correspondent. Most of Ann's surviving letters to Mrs. Lightbody are transcribed here.

[Henry Hulton to Robert Nicholson]

Mr. R. Nicholson   *24 January 1761[1]*
Merchant in Liverpool

Dear Sir

I own myself indebted to you for the favour of a letter some time past but hope the uncertain situation I have been in, will excuse to you for my not writing.

I expect to hear from the Baron[2] by the next Mails, which perhaps will determine the point of my going to Germany, or not. He is desirous to see me there, but I am less solicitous as to an employment with the Army, as I am afraid I should not gain much reputation in it; there have been loud clamours lately against the management of the Commissaries, and people grow weary of the heavy expences of the War in Germany.

If I do not go to Germany, I cannot expect any effect from my Solicitations till after the Parliament is chose, and then I can hardly hope for advancement at home, for to be sure my Interest is not equal to what it was, had I returned a year sooner I might have got something handsome, events have fallen out a little unlucky for me but it is not becoming a right mind to be disturbed by those disappointments which arise from causes independent of its own prudence and skill.

To spend life in the West Indies is a dreary prospect. I have suffered much in being unriveted from past connections, and I cannot enter into new engagements with that warmth I have formerly done. Indeed it is rare to meet with proper objects on whom to place our confidence and affection. The heart grows callous and suspicious from frequent disappointments and is unwilling to expose itself to fresh pain by connections that may only prove the disingenuity and ingratitude of human nature.

I have met with a few great and good characters in different parts, and it is worthwhile turning over a good deal of rubbish to find a few diamonds.

Interest, vanity and pleasure are the bane of the generous affections, they contract the mortals view into its own little significance and prevent the mind from exerting itself in any thing worthy or good: and yet one or the other of these engages the chief attention of most people in this great World of London. For my own part, I am here alone. I have no Business in the City, no employment elsewhere. I am not fond of Cards, and have no ear for musick. As to the playhouses, they never were in a lower state, nor were ever more crowded. They have few tolerable actors, and they act little but the same trash over again. The Beggar's Opera, Minor, and Jovial Crew have been acted half the nights this Winter.

I go down every Saturday to Waltham's tow, and stay til Tuesday. Mr. Basnett bears his misfortunes with great resignation and is pretty chearful when he has company. We had Miss Friend and Mrs. Cockshutt at different times to spend the Holidays there. Miss Basnett is returned to the Boarding School at Clapton and I believe Mr. Basnett has thoughts when she comes from thence for her to go to Liverpool.

My Brother wrote me since his return from Buxton, that my sister was in a bad State of Health, which gave me much concern. I wrote to her but have not heard from either of them since.

I hear you are likely to have an opposition at Liverpool. If so, I should not choose to be with you till after the Election.

I shall conclude my Letter with an extract from the last I had from my friend Mr. Ruling at Brunswick, as I think the sentiments will please you.

"I hope you received my Letter in which I explained to you my reasons in regard to your circumstances, being very sensible to all that concerns your affairs. The greatest blessing in human life is I think to sympathize in the troubles of our friends and enjoy the satisfaction of a good conscience. I know by experience that Adversity is the school of Wisdom where the Virtues are all cherished, Prosperity that of Folly where the Vices are encouraged. Philosophy and Religion are the best supports in our Life, which, without rules of morality is a wayward uneasy being, with snatches only of Pleasure; but under the regulation of Virtue, a reasonable and uniform habit of enjoyment."

I am with my best respects to Mrs. Nicholson, Mr. Cropper's, your Brother's, Mr. Light-body's families, and all friends.

Dear Sir

      Your Most Obedient
      humble Servant
      Henry Hulton

---

1   Hulton, "Nicholson Letters," 12-19.
2   Johan von Walmoden, illegitimate son of George II, who had befriended Hulton on his trip to Germany in 1751.

Germany 1763[1]

On my arrival at Head Quarters in Germany I was set down to certify accounts to Contractors &c. The Vouchers for these were so irregular and so much confusion and Iniquity were detected that I was very cautious in certifying; and wherever I detected any fraud I prosecuted it to the utmost. To give you a proof of this, the very first day I was at Paderborn, even before I began business, a man came to me, and offered me a Ton and [a] half of Gold to get him a Contract (about £15,000). This person did get a Contract (not through my means) and I kept such an eye on him as to detect his Iniquity and I arrested him at Head Quarters, had him confined and he was brought to ruin.

In the course of business I happened to detect some orders given by Monsr. de Masson (the Duke's prime minister) which I thought gave opening to great frauds. I represented the evil—was not attended to—insisted upon it—was dropped and removed from my department—had a very severe one appointed to me, where I could be of little service. I wrote to the Treasury with a state of my Conduct, and this was the first notice they got of the iniquitous business going forward.

The Commission of Enquiry was appointed some time after in which I was placed and when we were called home it was intended that Mr. Cuthbert and I should have been in the German Commission; but either the contractors by their friends prevented us being kept together or Mr. Pownal through interest got appointed unto it[2]—but I was intended by Mr. Grenville to be Secretary to the Commissioners of the Customs for the plantations. Yet when my constitution was made out, it was only plantation clerk.

The salary was to be £500 per Annum, without being subject to the Land Tax. Not being called Secretary, the Secretary got the fees of my Office, and to do a good turn the Secretary's office gave in my name to the Commissioners of the Land Tax as subject to it, which ought not to have been done. However, I am saddled with £90 per Annum. I gave up my place at Antigua, which was above £300 per Annum, and my present employment is reduced by taxes £125 per Annum.

What I want and expect now is to have the Land tax made up to me, and my employment was never intended to be subjected to it.

Mr. Cuthbert and I were employed a year at Whitehall in the business of our enquiry, that no doubt the Treasury will pay us for, and I expect a handsome Gratuity for my German services; but the countenance and recommendation of some people of consequence with the Ministry is necessary to obtain even our just pretensions. The German Office has closed with great reputation and Mr. Cornwall[3] and Mr. Cuthbert will, I don't doubt, both of them have handsome gratuities and good employments.

It was a more easy matter to liquidate unsatisfied demands at Whitehall than to attack and prosecute a set of Contractors &c. in Germany. To charge these people with frauds in their past accounts—to revise those acts with infinite Labour and lay the proofs before the Treasury—to stop payments of Money to these people and seize many others, by which the iniquity was greatly checked—to recover back considerable sums to Government—to do this not unsupported and unprotected only, but under every discountenance abroad was a bold and arduous task: and I may safely say that there could not have been found in Germany two men besides ourselves to have gone through what we did in the course of that commission.

---

1   Inserted in Hulton, "Nicholson Letters," 20-26. Hulton appears to have extracted these paragraphs from a longer epistle, presumably to Nicholson.

2   Little, "The Treasury, the Commissariat and the Supply of the Combined Army," passim, depicted Pownall as a very effective government agent, doing what he could to reduce fraud. The one full biography, by John A. Schutz, *Thomas Pownall* (Glendale, Calif.: Arthur H. Clark, 1951) has very little on Pownall in Germany (and that is at 197-199).

3   Hulton may well have wished that his career had taken him as far as Charles Wolfran Cornwall's would carry Cornwall. After serving as a commissioner in Germany, Cornwall returned to England, was elected to the House of Commons five years later and eventually rose to become House speaker. But then he had connections that Hulton did not—as a onetime student at the Westminster School, as a barrister trained at Lincoln's Inn, and as a cousin (and then brother-in-law) of Charles Jenkinson, the future earl of Liverpool, who was an undersecretary of state before he became a secretary to the Treasury lords.

[Ann Hulton to Elizabeth Lightbody]   *Westminster   10 December 1763*[1]

I intended writing to you as soon as I knew where our situation in London would be, but we are not yet fixed; my Brother has been looking out some time for more convenient lodgings. We are here three miles from the Custom House. His employment is a new establishment by Mr. Grenville, and the business is to examine and give instructions to the officers of His Majesty's Customs in the plantations, and no one can be appointed without a certificate from my Brother. There are numbers now waiting to receive instructions from him, and he has first to learn by consulting Acts of Parliament, and then he is to form a plan for conducting the Business, which has not before been under any regulations. It is very extensive, being not only appointing new officers, but an inspection over all the officers abroad, in order that they do their duty, and the prevention of frauds. Mr. Grenville appears to have it much at heart, and hopes thereby to find a great increase in the Revenue. My Brother is dependent on none but Him and the Commissioner of ye Customs, both [of] whom he has immediate communication with. The salary fixed is £500 per annum and ye fees supposed to be above £200. The task they had set him seems to be, after combating with ye knaves in G[ermany], to find 'em out in America and ye West Indies. I am concerned it is a place that requires so much attention and care, for the constant application and perplexing difficulties he has been subject to above two years past has I fear injured his health, and relaxation and exercise would be best for him. He intends going to Bath about Xtmas, as he's advised.

It is surprising how he has got through such arduous circumstances. A kind providence had supported and protected him, else he must have been crushed to pieces when contending with a host of wicked malicious and powerfull enemies. Every man in Germany from the Duke to the lowest was his foe. He could lay open such a scene of iniquity as would be amazing. Every art was used to bring him over or ruin him, first by flatteries and allurements, then by embarrassments and traps to ensnare him, then by false oaths and accusations, by reproaches and threats. He was threatened with private revenge if not public satisfaction (the Lords of the Treasury say they wonder he was not assassinated). All this he had to support alone, but after remonstrating to those who had it in their power to stem the torrent of iniquity in vain, he wrote to the Treasury, and their Lordships immediately appointed the Commission of Inquiry, investing the Commissioners with a power greater than the Secretary of State has here. This struck terror and gave a check to the iniquitous practices which, if carried on, and the war continued a few years longer, must have exhausted the Treasure of Britain, and proved its ruin, even though we had still been successful in arms. It is strange there was not a man in Germany that would make a stand against the general corruption. There was some few of honest hearts, but intimidated by power and carried by the stream, not one man to be found in whom skill, honesty, spirit, and ability were united. Nor were there, they say, any men that would have undertaken and gone through what Mr. Cuthbert and my Brother did, nor would they again, I believe, upon any consideration whatever. Mr. Cuthbert is a fine old gentleman, but I doubt his heart is broke by these German affairs. My Brother could have got £50,000 in six months' time after he went over, with much less trouble than it cost him not to do it, though it must have been on terms too hard for him to submit to.

Methinks 'tis a strange world I am got into. I can't stir out but I must either be jolted in a hackney coach, or have a German valet attending me that can scarce speak a word of English. Indeed, I walk in the park sometimes, when the weather is good, and I've company, and yesterday I presumed to venture out by myself to call upon a young lady whom I had been to see oftener than once with my Brother. But it's a shame to say I lost myself, and could neither find the way there nor home again, though at length I arrived safe back, to my great joy.

It is expected the Court will be very gay soon when the Hereditary Prince arrives. They say the Princess Augusta is in very poor spirits on the prospect of her change of circumstances, and that the Hereditary Prince has not a great deal of zeal, having, it's said, another attachment. This alliance can be no great advantage to England, which, however, is very generous in its Dowry to the Princess.[2]

Yesterday Mr. Wilkes' trial with the Secretary of State, at the Court of Common Pleas, was decided in favour of Wilkes, and £1000 damages allowed him. Lord Halifax and Mr. Wilkes both live in the next street to us, that is Georges Street. Wilkes' house was illuminated last night, and the mob went with musick and played before his Door, shouting for Wilkes; then they went to Lord H[alifax]s's, doing the same and cursing Lord H[alifax]. Tomorrow Wilkes is to be brought before the House of Lords to answer ye accusation of writing a libel, and it's expected he must stand in the Pillory. I hope he will recover of the wound he received in the duel for Mr. Martin's sake, a gentleman my Brother is more obliged to than any man in the world.

---

1   E. Rhys Jones, ed., "An Eighteenth-Century Lady and Her Impressions," *Gentleman's Magazine* 297 (August 1904):195-198. Jones chose seven letters from a larger collection in his possession, of which this was the first in chronological order. The last three would be reproduced in the book identified at 217 n. 1 infra. Ann Hulton did not refer to Elizabeth Lightbody by her first name in their surviving correspondence, addressing her always as Mrs. Lightbody. Elizabeth Lightbody's husband, Adam, was a very successful Liverpool merchant who left a sizeable estate upon his death in 1778. See TNA, PCC 11/1043, fos. 106-109.

2   "Hereditary prince" meaning the Duke of Brunswick, husband of Princess Augusta, George III's oldest sister, who had been granted an £80,000 dowry by Parliament.

[Henry Hulton to Robert Nicholson]

Mr. R. Nicholson   *London   17 December 1763*[1]
Merchant Liverpool

Dear Sir

I did not write after the receipt of your favour of the 3rd October, as I was daily expecting to see you in town and have been much disappointed that you could not undertake the Journey, as I flattered myself with great pleasure in the Interview—and was sorry by your last Letter to hear the Occasion that prevented it; but hope your health is now reestablished. Your Brother did us the favour to dine one day with us and another day I was with him, along with Mr. Percival, whose acquaintance I am much pleased with.

I have been much engaged in entering into the detail of my new Office and this before I was well recovered from the fatigues of business abroad. My health was there impaired, and my present attention prevents its reestablishment—but I intend going to Bath next Friday for three weeks and hope that will recover me.

The Ministry have much at heart the improvement of the American Revenue and are taking proper measures towards it. The Treasury thought it necessary to separate this branch from the other service in the customs and to appoint a person to the charge of the plantation Affairs under the Commissioners, who are to be particularly attentive to the conduct of the Revenue Officers in America and to prepare all the correspondence and business from the Board with them—and Mr. Grenville did me the honour to appoint me to this department as an approbation of my past Services and confidence in future ones. I am now engaged in this business, which will be growing every year, and I hope to make mine an office of Utility and thereby advance my own consequence. My Office and business is detached from the Secretary's and is in effect a Secretary for the plantations, as I have an immediate communication with the Board—but they don't chuse to have two Secretaries and I am only called Plantation Clerk, with an appointment as Secretary and two clerks under me.

I was very much concerned at the unfortunate affair of Mr. Martin with Mr. Wilkes.[2] Mr. — [Martin] has been very much my friend and did me great Justice in representing my Conduct to the former as well as present Board of Treasury. He told them there never was in his or any country two men of more distinguished Integrity or that had a greater claim upon Government for their services than Mr. Cuthbert and myself. It is an unhappy thing that this affair of W[ilkes] is still drawn on and both houses have been taken up in enquiring into circumstances that have fallen out in consequence of it. Mr. M[artin] is in Flanders.

You remember Dr. Demainbray at Liverpool. He has now a good place in the Customs. I reminded him the other day of my being his pupil then and he recollected you and several friends. He told me Mr. Grenville had spoken of me to him — Says the Dr., "he is engaged in a very extensive and arduous department" — and says Mr G[renville] "it is nothing new to him: we know him well from his services in Germany" and said many handsome things of me; so you see I stand very well with one of the first great men.

I am &c.,

Henry Hulton

---

1   Hulton, "Nicholson Letters," 26-31.

2   Hulton was alluding to the duel fought between Martin and Wilkes, prompted by Wilkes's insulting comments about Martin. See supra 26 n. 35 and 37 n. 43.

[Ann Hulton to Elizabeth Lightbody]   *Willaston 4 September 1767*[1]

Dear Mrs L. is I imagine in the Country where I hope She enjoys health and pleasure and benefit by her journey to Buxton.

I have many things to tell you, and some very interesting events I must communicate to my Friend.

I received a letter from my Brother date August 29th, that Morning about 5 o'Clock my Sister was happily Delivered of a fine Boy. She had a severe time. The Midwife attended from Thursday till then (Saturday), when my Brother wrote She was better than could be expected, and proposed to suckle it herself.[2] A few hours after this stranger arrived in this world my Brother received a summons from the Treasury to prepare for going to the New World, which is matter of great concern to him, I suppose you have heard of the new commission to be established in America. They have appointed my Brother to be one of the Commissioners even before his Knowledge of it, or acquainting him with it and he says there has been something very extraordinary in the Circumstances of all the employments he has had, as he has been appointed to them all without a particular solicitation for that Office. In the present Affair they have behaved very genteel to him, he took no measures to be appointed but rather avoided it. The offer from his Grace the D[uke] of G[rafton] to be the first in the Commission was a mark of great Confidence—had he declined accepting this offer, he must have remained at home on his bare salary, and should never have been taken notice of again by the treasury.

There are some circumstances (he says) in the alteration that will tend to soften the change of Situation and as Providence orders his Lot he chearfully acquiesces.

But he must go immediately as soon as the Commission has passed the great Seal. It will be a great embarrassment to him. He can not possibly remove his Family and Effects, Therefore he will endeavour to get Leave to stay til Spring, though the Treasury are bent on a speedy Establishment of the Commission.

Now you must Know that my Brother and Sister, it seems, are desirous for me to accompany them. He says I may be sure it would make them very happy, and that he shall be in such a situation as to give me every advantage that the place and society can yeild, and for my comfort we shall not be exposed to such a corruption of manners, as in London, for the Presbyterians have the Majority at Boston. I shall let the Commissioners know that his Sister, if she goes, does not intend to set up for a fine Lady, but for something more uncommon a Merchant—a Character, however, which She thinks She can act with greater propriety and advantage, as well as satisfaction to herself. Some usefull employment as Traffick or cultivating a small Plantation in the Country will be most agreeable to my genius and inclination and best for health. Whatever scheme I pursue I shall submit to his judgement and direction, and shall beware of any partnership; have seen enough of that. I have continued here a great deal longer than I intended, but this house not being set, and my Brother having none in the Country this Summer, and I find riding about and going to Parkgate to Bathe, very conducive to my health, my Brother therefore encouraged me to stay a while longer—besides there has been a great many repairs necessary here, which the Tenant was desirous to have done whilst I was here. The Bearer of this goes to Mr. Carle to get some Deal Balk for repairing our Barn. I hope to leave here the latter end of next week or the week after, and to be in London by the 20th of this month—My Brother's Wedding Day. Perhaps I may take another Dip or two the next Spring, and I don't know but Miss J: will come here and spind a day at Parkgate if I don't go up before, and the Weather be good.

I've gone often to Chester and Parkgate where I met many of my acquaintance, and it has been very agreeable.

I understand Dr. P[ercival] is likely to fix at Manchester. I was at Chester last Saturday, and believe shall go next there, was very glad to find Mr C[ropper?] so much better.

It is a mysterious part of the Providence of God, when he permits his Servants to be incapacitated for usefulness, and to labour under languishing affliction and severe Tryals, when he could ease 'em with a word. But surely it is that they may have the more experience of his Faithfulness, and Goodness, and he of their Obedience, and Love, That they may know the Loving kindness, the care, and Wisdom, of that God, that Pilots their Ship, when it is covered with Storms and Waves, and that they may be encouraged more and more to Trust Him, who can Deliver when all the help of Man is vain. I reflect with pleasing Admiration and Gratitude on the Dealings of Providence, even the Afflictive dispensations, when he hath placed me amongst strangers and in such circumstances that I stood most in need of the kind aids and soothing voice of Friendship. When I seemed destitute and sinking into the Grave, A Gracious God appeared for my relief, and wrought out deliverance for me though unworthy and distrustfull. It is impossible for those who do not feel what a sufferer feels to know, how in circumstances of Distress, even neglect wounds, and how doubly grateful and endearing consolatory, and supporting, at such a season, is the officious kindness of a friend.

I look to the highest cause, acknowledge and adore the Sovereign Hand that hath mingled some bitter ingredients in my portion to quick my relish for the blessings of life, and perhaps prepare me for a more prosperous Scene, or however, no doubt, to teach Me a more entire dependance upon and resignation to him under all Events. O, may I learn duty to improve present mercies, and maintain an habitual, humble, resigned and grateful frame, That I may not be taught the value of my enjoyments by a deprivation of them. Several circumstances have concurred to weaken my attachment to England. Though I have many friends here in whose happiness I must still be interested, and shall take my leave with an heavy heart, if I do not indulge a secret hope of revisiting my native country, But if Providence does not permit us to meet again in this world, I trust in some happier Region we shall, and with Transport and glowing Gratitude, review, and recount, Those Steps, and that Discipline, by which our heavenly Father has led us to, and prepared us for, a State of perfection and happiness. That this may be, though at some distant Period, that you may long enjoy the present Scene and an increasing felicity in your family, is the ardent Wish and Prayer of Dear Yours.

A II

My Compliments to all friends. I've received several Obliging letters from Mrs. W, and am ashamed not to have answered her last so long agoe, but I believe it would be as easy to keep up a correspondence from North America as this Place. Opportunity so rarely happen immediately from hence, besides one does not know always when they go. J[ohn] H[Incks] is not set sail yet. It will be strange if my Brother should go to America before him. I don't know what detains the former. The Bride and Groom, Mr. And Mrs. Wrench, were engaged to Dine ay my Brother's the Day my Sister was taken ill, and so my Brother was obliged to excuse himself from receiving them on that Account. He did not know Mr W. till they called on him, before then he wondered we should be surprized at his geting a Wife when had so much money—let him be what he would, yet if he came up to London with £40,000 he would find 500 ready to have him. In his next Letter he said he did not think above 250 even there, but everyone to their taste.

---

1   H[arold] M[urdock] and C[harles] M[iner] T[hompson], eds., *Letters of a Loyalist Lady* (Cambridge, Mass.: Harvard University Press, 1927), 3-7. This is the first of twenty-four letters written by Ann Hulton included in the book and transcribed here. Henry Hulton's note of 13 January 1779 informing Elizabeth Lightbody of Ann's death is the final letter in the text proper and is transcribed infra on 383. Henry's letter to Robert Nicholson of 20 June 1775, transcribed infra at 327-329, is included as an appendix to the book, along with Henry's notes about the 1772 trek to Canada.

2   She refers here to her sister-in-law, Elizabeth Hulton, who had just given birth to Thomas, the first of the Hultons' five sons.

[Ann Hulton to Elizabeth Lightbody] *London 17 December 1767*[1]

... To Day we have the pleasure to receive two Letters from my Brother of the 5th and 15 November, giving an Account of his Voyage and safe Arrival at Boston, a pretty good Voyage of six weeks. He was sick half the time. As for J[ohn] Hincks[2] he never was ill, but eat and drank all the way. Our next Attention is to what reception the Commissioners met with. Many people think they will meet with difficulties having Turbulent Folks to deal with. My Brother is pretty well known there and in the W. Indies by his late employment, and we hope from what we have heard that they are rather prejudiced in his favour, though his present Commission will not help to recommend.

He says they happened unluckily to arrive on the most riotous day in the year, the 5th November. [He] believes the mob carried twenty Devils, Popes, and Pretenders, through the Streets, with Labels on their breasts, Liberty and Property and no Commissioners. He laughed at 'em with the rest. By the last Letter, all was very quiet.

We had a Note from Mrs. Rogers yesterday. One of her little Boys was recovering of a Fever, Mrs W. was very ill, and almost all the Servants ill too. Mr R. they say died worth 60,000, which he bequeathed to Mr R.

Miss Newton is gone over to Venice with Lady Wright...

Your Affectionate friend   A H

---

1   *Loyalist Lady*, 8.
2   John Hincks, a cousin. Henry would use his influence to place him in a customs post in the West Indies.

[Ann Hulton to Elizabeth Lightbody]   *London 15 February 1768*[1]

The Receipt of Dear Mrs L. favor gave Me great pleasure, and was glad to find your family was well—wish Mr and Mrs R L joy of their Son. My Sister and I are as happy as we can be in our absense from my Brother, and as busy as we can be in preparing to go to him. We shall embark I believe sooner than we thought of, for there is but one Vessel appointed fit for us to Sail in. It's called the *Boscowen*, Captain Jacobson. The Merchants are so obliging to give my Sister the choice of her Company in the Cabbin, there being many persons desirous to go in the same Ship

The company fixed on are the Collector of Bahama, his Lady and young Child, who have made the Voyage before and therefore have experience and will know how to bear the squalling of Brats. My little Nephew was innoculated in the height of the fashion in the Cool way. My Sister I believe would never innoculate one so young again, as it's distressing not to know their complaints when they are so very ill. She had a wet Nurse, though as much averse to it as you are, and her prejudice against them is far from being removed. It was necessity obliged her to it, and great importunity from us all prevailed on her, for the Life of the Infant seemed to depend upon it. The Error was in the month, Nurse not putting it to suck of so long a time, till it could not. It did very well for a week by feeding, then declined till it was just expiring, but soon recruited at the Breast and is now a fine Boy. I hope Mrs A's are got safe through innoculation.

I was much Surprized to hear by yours of the Death of Miss N. Bent. Mrs K. and Miss T. spent the evening with Us not long agoe and we supped with them last night but one.[2]

It was indeed very providential J[ohn] H[inck]s's not going to Florida. Though his Stay here did seem to be the effect of prudence, yet I hope it will prove for the best. The Commissioners have appointed him Clerk of the Minnets, which they say is the best place in the disposal of the Board.

The Commissioners began an Assembly at Boston in order to wear off the prejudice of the people and to cultivate their Acquaintance. There were about 100 at the first Opening of it, and my Brother had the honor of dancing the first Minnuet. J[ohn] H[incks] made no small figure at it, and is very easy and happy with them all, but the Misfortune is there are no fortunes there.

Our Estate at W. is to be sold at L. the 10th of Next Month as you'll see Advertised. Mr E. writes me that my being present is not necessary and I shall willingly be excused Crossing the Water this time of the Year, but intend being at Chester in a fortnight's time.

---

1   *Loyalist Lady*, 9-10.
2   Apparently what follows to finish the sentence was lost—the editors left a blank space here.

[Ann Hulton to Elizabeth Lightbody]

Castle William, Boston Harbor

Dear Madam
June 30, 1768[1]

I presume it will be agreeable to you to hear that my Brother's Family had a good Voyage of 5 Weeks and arrived all well at Boston the 5th Instant. You will be surprized to hear how we were obliged to fly from the Place in six Days after and take Refuge on board the *Romney* Man of War, lying in Boston Harbour. Mrs Burch, at whose house I was, had frequently been alarmed with the Sons of Liberty surrounding her house with most hideous howlings as the Indians, when they attack an Enemy, to many insults and outrages She had been exposed since her arrival, and threatened with greater violences. She had removed her most valuable Effects and held herself in readiness to depart at an hours notice. The Occasion soon happened. When my Sister and I accompanyd her at 10 o'Clock at night to a Neighbour's house, not apprehending much danger, but we soon found that the Mobs here are very different from those in O[ld] England, where a few lights put into the Windows will pacify, or the interposition of a Magistrate restrain them, but here they act from principle and under Countenance, no person daring or willing to suppress their Outrages, or to punish the most notorious Offenders for any Crimes whatever. These Sons of Violence, after attacking Houses, breaking Window[s], beating, Stoning and bruizing several Gentlemen belonging to the Customs, the Collector mortally,[2] and burning his boat, they consulted what was to be done next, and it was agreed to retire for the night. All was ended with a Speech from one of the Leaders, concluded thus, "We will defend our Liberties and property, by the Strength of our Arm and the help of our God, to your Tents O Israel."[3] This is a Specimen of the Sons of Liberty, of whom no doubt you have heard, and will hear more.

The next Day the Commissioners had sufficient notice of their danger and the Plots against them. All their friends Advised 'em to retire to a more secure place, The Governor particularly telling 'em it was not in his power to protect 'em.

That Evening Saturday We set off in a Barge under a Convoy of Man of War Boats, with Marines, their bayonets fixed, to the *Romney*, a fifty Gun Ship of War, lying ready in the Harbour. About fifty of us Refugees were well accommodated and very genteely entertained there for nine Days, the Captain's Lady being on board. On the 21st Instant We removed to this Castle, by the Governor's permission. This was a Scene you will believe quite new to me, and indeed the series of events since leaving Old England appears romantic.

I must own I have been ashamed of the Presbyterians, but have the satisfaction to hear they are very different, these being Oliverian Independants.[4]

From the inherent Republican, and levelling principles, here's no subordination in the Society. Government is extirpated, and it is quite a State of Anarchy. There are some sensible and good people that are greatly alarmed at their impending fate. The infant Colonies have been advancing toward a State of Independency. Many things have concurred to bring on the Crisis sooner than expected. The Sedition has been falsely represented at home as a dying Faction — but the defection is too general; most of the other Provinces are only waiting to see the event of this effort in Boston. The poison of disaffection has been infused and spread by inflammatory writers over the Continent. Lord Camden and Lord Chatham's Speechs on the Repeal of the stamp Act has opened to them a new view of their priviledges, and I dare say they are enrolled in their Records, as sacred as their Charters, from this Authority, the Authority and power of the British Parliament to tax them is openly denied. To this purpose the Assembly here sent a Petition to His Majesty[,] which it was thought proper at home not to present.

The Credulity of the Common people here is imposed on by a number of Lies raised to irritate and inflame them. They believe that the Commissioners have an unlimited power given to tax even their Lands, and that it's in order to raise a Revenue, for supporting a Number of Bishops that are coming over &c. They are inspired with an enthusiastic Rage for defending their Religion and liberties. Every Officer of the Crown that does his duty is become obnoxious, and they must either fly or be sacrificed. The Attacks were always in the dark, several hundreds against one Man, and there's great Reason to believe that the Lives of some in particular was aimed at—As to my Brother and Mr. Burch, we often hear that it[']s generally said They have no personal peak[5] to them. As Gentlemen they would treat 'em with great Civility, but as Commissioners most dreadful threatenings are denounced against all. They are prohibited setting foot on Shore against their peril, and in case any of them does, the Sexton of each Church has orders to give Notice by tolling a Bell, when all the Bells are to ring as for Fire to alarm the Inhabitants and raise the Mob to tear 'em to pieces. They likewise threaten to drive Us hence, saying this Castle belongs to the province and not to the King, But have not yet taken this step to an Open Rebellion, though from good intelligence we know they have been plotting to surprize us in the Night. Should they make this desperate attempt, they might massacre Us[,] but their Escape would be impossible, for the Man of War; this is all our security at present.

However hard the fate of us fugitives may seem, we must acknowledge there are many favorable circumstances attending. It is happy for Us that our flight was in the Summer, for this Island they say would not be habitable for Us in the Winter. Though it now appears delightful and a most Agreeable Summer Retreat. I am Your Affectionate A H

---

1   *Loyalist Lady*, 11-14.
2   Joseph Harrison, the collector, was beaten badly, along with his son and Benjamin Hallowell, the comptroller, but all three men recovered. Harrison's small boat was indeed hauled ashore and burned.
3   These lines from 2 Samuel 20:1, shouted by a dissident rallying those rebelling against King David, would have resonated with a devout Ann. The tribes of Israel, once united tenuously under David, were again dividing; the turmoil brought catastrophe. Whether Ann would have seen George III as causing the contention in his empire as David precipitated the crisis in his kingdom is another matter.
4   This is her characterization of local Congregationalists—ecclesiastical anarchists whose lineage could be traced to the English Civil War. In her mind they had been brought to life by Oliver Cromwell and they would not rest content until the Church of England had been utterly destroyed, with nothing left in its place.
5   pique.

[Ann Hulton to Elizabeth Lightbody]   *Castle William   12 July 1768*[1]

This incloses my letter of the 30th past (intending to be sent by a Ship bound for Liverpool) which informs you of our critical Situation, in which we are likely to remain some time till Government is restored and its Servants supported. The business of the Commission in the mean time carried on here. My Brother has had a vast deal on his hands ever since he came Out. We found him just recovering of a fever caught by Lodging in an unaired Bed in a House he had taken about 4 Miles from Boston[,] in the Country (it's about 2 Miles off Us here besides one mile by Water), of no use to us now, though half of the Furniture is brought there, and there's a Negro Servant employed in the Garden. Mr Burch's and my Brother's Families have Apartments here in the Citade[l], which are rather elegant than Commodious. Two of the Commissioners besides are of our Mess, but don't Lodge here. One of 'em goes every night to the *Romney* and the other Lodges in the Barracks. The Clerks all Lodge in the Barracks, and make separate families. The fifth Commissioner, Mr. T[emple] is connected with the Town in every respect. He does not Associate with us though he Lodge[s] here to save appearances.[2]

This is our Situation, and you are not to imagine us, though, in a state of banishment, secluded from Society or the rest of the World. It is rather like one of the Publick water drinking places in England. We have a great many Visitors come every Day from Boston incog[nito], and are seldom less than twenty at dinner. We live luxuriously though I don't find provisions so cheap as I expected, but I believe We Government people pay dearer. The increase of our Naval Force has added to the gaiety of the place. The task assigned me, steward of the Household and Mistress of the Ceremony of the Tea table Morning and Evening is no little business I assure you. This fine Climate agrees well with us all and every body seems much happier in their exiled state than on the Land of Liberty. Mrs. B[urch] is a well[-]bred, agreeable woman. She says surely there never was a number of persons jumbled together so agreeable to each other, and I hope she will have more rest now we are better guarded, for she seldom went to bed before 3 o'Clock in the Morning for watching the Enemy.

The Sons of Liberty within these ten Days several unexpected strokes of[3]   their   The Dissolution of the General   in consequence of Dr. Hilsbrough   to the Governor on their refusal   Resolutions of the Last House   the Forces from the back Settlements   Towns, leaving open to the Indians—and of Ships and Sloopes of War arrived here from Jamaica. We have now no less than five Stationed round this Island as our Guard. The Commodore has shown great Attention to the Service, and sends word if they are not enough he will come himself, but we are now sufficiently guarded, having each a Ship near our Window, however another Ship . . . Captain Corner has made a discovery that this harbour will admit of many Ships of the Line. This was unknown to Government before. It's reported that a Regiment of Soldiers is on the way from New York to Boston. The seventeen Members that

Voted for Rescinding are now persecuted as much as the Commissioners and worse, being more in their power. Dear Madam, Your Affectionate Friend A H

Governor Bernard has just now drank tea here with Us. His Excellency says, two more such years as the past and the British Empire is at an End.

---

1   *Loyalist Lady*, 14-17.
2   Robinson slept on the *Romney*, Paxton in the barracks. Temple actually spent many nights on shore.
3   The editors of a *Loyalist Lady* inserted a note at this point: "A piece of the letter is here torn away. Other blanks left in the following pages indicate a like mishap." (16n) Readers should imagine the gaps above as if they were aligned at the right edge of the paper of the original letter.

[Henry Hulton to Mr. de Ruling]

Hohentham near Halle, Saxe

Mr. De Ruling

23 August 1768[1]

It is a considerable time since I had the honor to write to You; indeed, the attention I have been obliged to give to the business of the Revenue, in which I am engaged, has not allowed me time for my private correspondence, and my health has suffered by close application. However, I am at present pretty well, and had the satisfaction to be joined by my family here from England, in perfect health, about two months ago.

It would be impossible to give You a State of the affairs in this Country, and of our situation in it, in the compass of a letter. The Americans, having been long indulged by Great Britain, were extreamly averse to the payment of any duties towards defraying the expence which the Mother Country was at in maintaining and defending them; and the Parliament having laid a Stamp duty on America about four Years ago, which they afterwards repealed, upon the clamours and remonstrances of the Americans, and their friends at home. These people imagined that the same measures would produce the like consequences; and upon the establishment of a Board of Customs, and laying some new duties in America in the last Year, the like clamours, and opposition to the measures of Government arose. The most inflammatory publications were spread through the Colonies and every plan was concerted that might counteract the resolutions of Parliament. They cry aloud for liberty, and boast of loyalty to their Sovereign, but their notion of liberty is licentiousness, and their loyalty a spirit of independence, denying the authority of Great Britain.

Such was the temper of the Colonies when we Commissioners arrived here. The Demagogues of the People have been stirring them up to resistance ever since our arrival; whilst the several Assemblies have been remonstrating with the Ministry at home; and complaining of the hardship of their fate in being taxed by the Parliament of Great Britain. We continued to act in our duty at Boston as long as it was safe for our persons to remain there; but the Civil Government being in so relaxed a State as not to be able to give Us any support, and there being no troops there to protect Us, we were obliged to retire into the Castle, on a small Island in the harbour about three miles from Boston; where we shall remain untill Government at home takes measures to support its authority here.

From the account I have given of our situation, You will conceive it to be very disagreable, and our task an arduous one; however, I can reconcile myself to the former, and do not doubt to go through the latter, when we are supported.

The form of Government in this Country is too much of the Democratic to allow proper vigor to the executive branch; and the ease with which landed property is acquired, tends to keep up those independent leveling principles which the first Set[t]lers brought with them. There being new land sufficient for all comers to this Country, and the necessary provisions easily raised, population goes on amazingly. The climate in this part of America is very healthy, though I think the winter colder and the Summer hotter than in England.

If you are desirous to read the history of New England, I would recommend You Hutchinson's lately published. That Gentleman is Lt. Governor of this Province; a native of it and one who is an honor to it and to mankind; however, he has the misfortune, like the best characters in most Countries, not to meet with due honor from his Countrymen. He has been persecuted and vilified for what should have rendered him most respected.

---

1   Henry Hulton, "Copies of Letters & Memorials written from Boston commencing Anno 1768 [hereafter "Letterbooks"]," 2 vols., Houghton Library, Harvard University, 1:1-4.

[Henry Hulton to Mr. de Ruling]

To the Same   6 April 1769[1]

About the middle of November we returned to Boston from the Castle, four Regiments being arrived there by order of Government for our protection, and the support of the Laws. And we have since continued to exercise our Commission quietly in town; but the temper of the people is not altered, and the ferment that has been raised throughout the Country, against the authority of Parliament will not soon subside. There will require an alteration in the Constitutions of these Colony Governments, to maintain this Country in proper subordination to Great Britain: and I do not doubt that measures will be taken this Session of Parliament, to support its authority, and secure the future obedience of the Colonies.

We have had a pretty good Society this Winter, from an addition of a number of Servants of the Crown. I found great difficulty on my return to town to get either a house, or lodging, from the prejudice of the people against the Commissioners; so that I was in a manner obliged to look out in the Country and I have bought a house about five miles from Boston with about thirty Acres of land; and I flatter myself with a great deal of happiness in this retirement. The business of the Commission will require my attendance in Boston four days in the week, and the other part I hope to employ with my family, and little improvement upon the farm.

---

1   Hulton, "Letterbooks," 1:5-6.

[Henry Hulton to Robert Nicholson]

Mr. Robert Nicholson   *Boston 6 April 1769*[1]
Merchant in Liverpool

Dear Sir

I am obliged to your for your kind favour of the 23rd December and much concerned to hear of the Indisposition of your family—but hope your young ones are recovered and that they will be continued as future blessings to you. We have all been very well, both during our exile at the Castle and since our return. The sea air and salt water were of great service to us, and little Tom Thumb has been so well nursed, and tossed about that he is thought a wonderful child by other folks besides his father and Mother, and I shall be very well satisfied if the young American that is coming is but equal at its age to the young Englishman.

We have gone through many perils, and besides all the resistance and resentment that we have found from the people, we have had to combat with many difficulties that have been stirred up by persons near ourselves, and our Secretary is gone home under suspension.[2] We have an arduous task—but the raising a Revenue is only a secondary consideration until the authority of the Laws is restored.

We returned to Boston from the Castle about the middle of November, and have since that time exercised our Commission in quiet, having the protection of his Majesty's troops. But the temper of the people is not changed, and as they cannot attack us publickly, they publish the most gross and illiberal calumnies against us and the other Servants of the Crown, nor could we have the prospect of any redress from a prosecution in their courts and by their juries.

The Servants of Government here are now pretty numerous, and we have a good Society with them and a few families in town. But as to the people in general and their politics, I would wish to avoid saying any thing of them. Let your Republicans, Independents and

Zealots for Liberty come to Boston. They will then learn the value of good Government and the respect they owe to the Laws and Constitution of their Country.

When we returned from the Castle it was with difficulty I procured Lodgings for my family at a high rate in Town; for such was the prejudice of the people against the Commissioners that no one would rent me a house; and I found myself under the necessity of looking out for one in the country, and at last I have been obliged to purchase one to which I shall remove soon. It is about five Miles from town, with 30 Acres of Land; but no sooner was it known to be the property of a Commissioner, than the people broke the windows. However, I flatter myself with a great deal of happiness in that retirement.

The business of the board will call me to town four days in the week, and the other three I hope to spend in quiet with my family. The close application I have had to business since my being in America makes it necessary for me to have some relaxation and exercise.

I return you thanks for the Newspapers you sent me and shall be obliged to you for them by such opportunities as after from your post—I am &c.

Henry Hulton

---

1 Hulton,"Nicholson Letters," 32-37.
2 Samuel Venner.

[Ann Hulton to Elizabeth Lightbody]   *Boston   10 April 1769*[1]

I had the pleasure to receive D[ea]r Mrs L[ightbody']s Kind favor. Was truly concerned for your Affliction, which I had heard of before, doubt not you bore it with your usual patience and resignation, and trust you still experience the care and goodness of God all sufficient. I hope domestick happiness has succeeded to the afflictive Scenes in yours & Mr N[icholson']s families.

We have resided quietly here since November, and I hope we shall be in no more dangers or alarms from lawless Mobs, yet it's uncertain what may be on the first execution of the spirited resolves of Parliament, however salutary the effects will be to the Establishment of Government, and the good of the Colonies. But it is certain that our safety and quiet depends on the Army and Navy being here, and that Opposition will be vain when G[reat] Britain is resolved.

They have no other way now but scurrilous abuse, which constantly employs some wicked Low genius. Government, its Friends and Servants, are the Objects. Indeed, Mr B[urch] and my Brother are most favorably treated of any of the four Commissioners as it's said they came here Strangers to the Country. But against those in Office who are Americans the inveteracy is inconceivable, as acting against their Country they say is an Aggravation. The Gentlemen of the Army share in the Abuse. The Commanding Officer, General Pomeroy, is an amiable worthy Man, and takes great care that his men shall give no real Offense.

This is a very large Town. I have not seen half of it yet. It is joined to the Continent by a small neck of Land, so there's but one way out of the Town by Land. You will suppose our Acquaintance is not very general, nor do we wish it to be, we have enow,² for we have been much engaged ever since we came from the Castle, in receiving and paying Visits to different Persons. Most of the better sort of People that we've conversed with seem sensible of the great want of a reform, or alteration in the Constitution of Government here, for certainly the Tyranny of the Multitude is the most Arbitrary and oppressive. There's no justice to be obtained in any case, and many Persons awed by the people are obliged to court Popularity for their own Security. This is only to be done by opposing Government at home. If the People took a dislike to any One, they would make nothing of pulling down their houses. Several persons were threatened with this for no other reason than Visiting Us at the Castle, and it would certainly have been done, with a deal more mischief, had not the Troops arrived Seasonably for our Protection, as well as that of every person of property. Yet there are very few to be met with that will allow the right of taxation to the British Parliament; therefore we avoid politicks.

We are in Lodgings, for there was never a House to be had for a Commissioner when we returned to Boston, and this occasioned my Brother to purchase one, in order to secure a dwelling Place. It is in the Country, five Miles off in an agreeable Situation; has some Land to it. He intends keeping a Cow, and to reside there all Year if it be practicable, but the Winters are very severe here. It is a more unequal Climate than Old England, the extreams of heat and Cold very great, and the changes from one to the other Sudden, frequently on the change of the Wind, yet the Climate agrees with Us.

Here is a very good Assembly set up since we came, the best there is in all America they say, about sixty couple dance every night, once a fortnight, though another called the Liberty Assembly is set up in Opposition. Besides these there is a Concert every other week. I am limited by my paper. Give me leave to hint that it will be a good Opo³ to enclose a few Lines in the parcel to let me know how you and your family and friends do⁴ It is to come by a Vessel to sail from London in August. My Brother and Sister join in Respects to you, Mr L[ightbody,] and all friends. Yours Affectionately
    A. H.

---

1   *Loyalist Lady*, 17-19.
2   enough.
3   opportunity.
4   The editors left a space here, meaning a break in the text—word(s) missing. They did this in many of the letters that follow as well.

[Henry Hulton to Edward   Esq.]   *5 February 1770*[1]

Dear Sir,

I am obliged to you for your french exercise. It was truly french; for the paper was full, and yet there was little in it— little interesting, I mean; for we were in hopes to have heard much of your good self and family, of which not a word. Excuse me if I content myself with plain English in return. You are au faite[2] in french. I cannot write it without help, and have not time, if I had patience to look into Dictionaries. It must be owned I am not much endowed with that Virtue, though I lived for some time under the instruction of a laborious German commentator. However, I satisfy my conscience in the want of it, by a reflection that your very patient folks are not people of warm passions; that they can sit still, and see cooly the misfortunes of their friends, without stir[r]ing to help 'em, and therefore, if I had more of that Virtue, I might have less of the social ones. Now, if you are persuaded of this, I am sure you must pity me; what a life of discipline and tryal have we not had, for upwards of two years past? Our patience is almost worn out, and if Government does not do something effectual this year, they had better withdraw their servants, and leave these people to themselves. I need not say anything of the weakness of Government, and Tyranny of the people here. The inclosed newspaper shews it sufficiently. The poor Lt. Governour[3] has nobody to stand by him—there is a general Lachete,[4] as Governor Bernard calls it. Such Councellors! Such Magistrates! Such a constitution! A few Demagogues govern the people. They sett the town bells a ringing, gather all the tag-rag together, then harangue the Mob, talk treason; stir up sedition, pass resolves, and every Man that does not say and do as they please, is afraid for his life, property, or reputation. Yet no one dares set himself against them: though there are two Regiments in town, no Counsellor or Magistrate will dare, or perhaps does not chuse, to make use of them.

It is not possible to give you a thorough idea of these people, and of the state of Government in this Country, in words; you must see it to believe things are, as they are.

Government at home set out wrong in their first Establishment in this Country. They were glad to get rid of a troublesome set of people, and gave 'em what charters they desired. They did not look to the remote consequences, nor consider the trouble they should give to their successors in office. No nation will retain distant Colonies long in subjection, the Government of which is established upon a popular plan. Yet the New England Governments are the most popular that can be devised.

In the Massachusetts province the Representatives are chosen once a year, and they, together with the old Council, chuse the New Council, so that the Council who ought to support the honour and dignity of the Crown, depend on the favour of the people for their Annual election.

Any town having forty familys has heretofore been entitled to send a Representative to the General Assembly; and the people are obliged to chuse a person resident in their town.

Two or three people, (generally the Tavern keeper[,] the Justice, and the Minister) lead the town and get themselves returned Members. In such an Assembly there are many low, ignorant, illiberal shoestringed people, who are easily led by a few crafty designing Men; and these ride the people and make disturbances in the province, bellowing out for liberty, and independence, and raising a clamour from the apprehended dread of taxes, troops, Bishops, and Commissioners.

Every township manages its own prudential affairs at a meeting of the people at large; and every political doctrine is there canvassed freely. And thus they become the constant cause of faction, and sedition. Every man has a voice at these meetings and it is generally the strongest lungs that carries the argument. The sensible and moderate part of the people avoid these meetings, as they cannot oppose popular measures without being exposed to insult and resentment.

The Governor, though appointed by the Crown, is dependant on the people for his salary, and for the sake of peace and harmony, he endeavours to be on good terms with the people; indeed, his power is so limited, that in any contest with them he would reap little but uneasiness to himself. He can negative a Counsellor on the day the new Council is proposed to him by the Assembly, but cannot suspend him afterwards. He can only make or suspend a Justice of the peace with the approbation of his Council, and he can scarce do any act of Government without the advice of his Council; and to be sure, if the matter is the least unpopular, they will not advise him to it. At the meeting of the last Mob Governours, mentioned in the inclosed Newspaper, the Lieut. Governour would have issued a Proclamation for them to disperse, but his Council would not assent to it, and the Mob issued their resolves to the terror of the inhabitants, in defyance of his authority. You see the genius and manner of their Cromwelian Progenitors in their answer to the Lt. Governor. Scripture is brought in, to cover Treason, and Murder.

These people have likewise been suffered to adopt the most democratic form in their religious establishment.

They are mostly Independants, or Congregationalists. Every Township, which answers to our parishes, is a separate Congregation, quite independant of every other power in Church affairs; as are their Ministers of each other. The people chuse their own Minister and pay him what they please to raise among themselves; their Clergy thus become dependant on them for support. The Minister must preach what doctrine suits the people, and live and do just as they please; so that having no real power, they are obliged to acquire an artificial one, which they do by trimming with the people and accommodating themselves to their whims, and humours, and they manage them very dexterously. To please the present passion, in their long prayers they expostulate with the almighty, and pray him to remove their grievances, and the dark clouds that are hanging over them; then they warn their people with a glorious enthusiasm and rouse 'em in the cause of liberty and independence.

You will see that our Establishment every way seems to have ben intended for preserving the glorious spirit that reigned about 120 years ago; and indeed it has been as well kept, as if it had been bottled, corked, and waxed. Some allowance must be made for an increase of ferocity, from the settlement of a wild country in a rude state of society.

Though this Government should be altered, yet the prospect of order, subordination, and a civilized state is remote. Everything tends to maintain the levelling spirit; great quantities of land remain to be cleared and settled. Every settler is a freeholder. The Crown has retained no quit rents, or other tenure in these provinces. No one will be a servant, or rent an estate from another. No Estates are entailed, but a Man's property is divided among his children pretty near equally. And there are many people in reduced circumstances, whose parents possessed the greatest fortunes, or held the first Offices in the province. Families soon rise and soon go to decay here; the richest are connected with the poorest, and the lowest are related to some of the highest. Levelling is the principle, and there seems to be no political method yet adopted to secure the continuance of property in a family.

The genius of the people seems to revolt against acknowledging a superior. No pains are taken to instill into Children a respect for Kings, Governours, Magistrates, or superiors. The doctrine, that one Man is as good as another; that we are all born of the same parents; all flesh and blood alike, is early instilled into children's minds. The servant will not call the person he lives with, Master; and they have the utmost aversion to wearing any thing in the shape of a livery, or performing any Office of allegiance on your person, or table. We have, however, a Coachman, who has the fortitude to drive us in spite of the ridicule of his Countrymen, who point and look at him with contempt, as he passes by. The people are very inquisitive, and what we should call impertinent; they never give on a direct answer, but commonly return your question by another, and if you fall in with them on the road, or at a public house, they will directly enquire of you, who and what you are, and what is your business. One day I overtook a Country man on the road; and after saying something to him about the weather, he began, Are you from Boston? What is the news? Are you a Merchant? Mehaps you are going into the Country to get in your debts? Can you lend a body a hundred or two pounds? No. You can if you would.

The nature of these Governments allows every Man to talk and discuss freely upon all Government, and political matters; and they are all politicians. There are five presses that publish weekly newspapers in the town of Boston. The people are litigious, and perfectly versed in all the little chicane of the Law. The Governor and Commissioners have long been the objects of the grossest abuse in the public papers, but they can have no redress. But if a friend of Government offends one of them, he will be made to pay for it. For instance, a licentious printer abused Mein, a brother printer, and friend to Government. Mein hit him a stroke or two with his cane; an action was commenced and and Mein has been fined about £100 for the affair. The Patriot Otis abused all the Commissioners in the public papers; Mr. Robinson thrashed him heartily. Otis is now prosecuting him at Law, the grand Jury have found a bill, and there is no doubt a Jury will give as much as they can against Mr. Robinson. About the same time, Mr. Temple, another Commissioner, (though not one with the other four) knocked down Mr. Fluker, a Gentleman of fortune, and friend to Government. Mr.

Fluker proved the fact by two witnesses, with himself, but the Grand Jury would not find a bill against Mr. Temple.

The weakness of Government, the want of some power to which you can resort for protection, makes every one afraid of his neighbour. The desire of popularity of being well spoken of and not offending the people, is the predominant value and the people knowing their own power, being bred up in sentiments of equality, are presuming and arrogant to the last degree. And it is a great gulp that a person must take on his first coming here, to bear with their manner after being used to that attention and respect which people in a civilised state of society shew to superiors, and each other. They have no sense of that distance and respect due to superior characters, and the most common Mechanic will take to pieces the Governor's conduct, and judge of your merit as a Divine, a Lawyer, or Philosopher, be your abilities ever so eminent.

Provisions are cheap, and land easily acquired; and from the principles of equality and independence that prevail, every Man will work just as he chuses; so that you who employ him, are obliged to solicit as a favour the Man who is to do any labour, or business for you. Every Man conceives himself to be something above the station he is placed in. The large towns abound in shop keepers, who retail English goods; these are all stiled Merchants, though they depend on the credit of the Merchant in London for their continuance in that character. Yet they pretend to give themselves consequence by subscribing not to import British Goods. It is from the great towns that all the sedition and resistance to the authority of Parliament has arisen. The Lawyers raised a hue and cry against the stamp Act, and the traders expecting they should be checked in their clandestine trade, by the regulations that would be established under a Board of Customs, have supported the clamour against the power of Parliament. The duties they pay are trifling, but their being prevented from carrying on a commerce contrary to the regulations of law, it is that is the grievous burthen; and these interested persons set up for Patriots, and poison the minds of the poor country people, telling them they shall be enslaved, and their Estates taken from them.

I have now given you a long detail of affairs here, which I thought would be agreeable at this time, when American matters are (I suppose) much the subject of conversation. I shall excuse you for half the quantity of paper in return and I hope you will write me particularly as to our friends and the public news.

We have passed over the winter very chearfully, and have felt no inconvenience from our situation in the Country, though the weather has been very severe for some weeks past. The children come on very well, and I hope Mrs. H will write to Mrs. H[incks] and give an account of herself, and her family affairs; I beg you will present my best respects to all the family, and I remain with great regard. Dear Sir.

---

1   Hulton, "Letterbooks," 1:7-18.
2   very accomplished.
3   Thomas Hutchinson.
4   cowardice.

[Henry Hulton to Thomas Bradshaw, Esq.]   *12 March 1770*[1]

As I had not the honour of hearing from you, after having wrote a number of letters, in consequence of your desire, I did not intend to have troubled you again, but to go on in the course of my duty in the best manner I could, and to submit to the severity of my fate without complaining; and this I have done, till my three brethren and myself are fairly worn down with this life of trial, combat, and anxiety.

Government will be informed particularly from Lt. Governour Hutchinson of the event that has taken place here, and as it had been thought advisable (to prevent fatal consequences) that his Majesty's two Regiments which were quartered in Boston, should be withdrawn from thence to Castle William, it is become matter of great concern to us, to provide for the carrying on our Commission in any wise free from insult, and violence.

The general report now is that the people having carried their point of compelling the troops to quit the town, will not suffer any violence to be used to the person of the Commissioners, or other servants of the Government, who may remain behind. But what security have we for our safety a single day? The Governour, the Magistracy, have no authority, no power! The Demagogues have the people entirely at their devotion; hundreds of Men are in Arms, and the lives and properties of every one depends on their caprice. The Commissioners are considered as having brought the troops here, are pointed out in the public papers as the Abettors of murder; and every means has been used to inflame the minds of the people, to punish us, as the objects of their vengance.

You cannot conceive the anxiety of our minds from this distracted situation, and the reasons must be obvious to you, why in these circumstances, we cannot hazard a debate at the Board, as to what measures should be taken for the service, and the safety of ourselves and familys.

Mr. Robinson has taken the resolution to go to London, and he will acquaint you particularly as to public matters and the state of the Board, and Revenue business.

Mr. Burch, Mr. Paxton, and myself, at first intended to retire into Castle William with our familys, and the Officers of the Board; but as we might be even there subject to persecutions (on Account of our Mem[oria]ls to their Lordships) in the Superior and General Courts, which meet this Week, we think it will be best to take shelter out of the province, whilst they are siting, and adjourn the Board from time to time, but Mr. Robinson will be able to acquaint you further of the measures we may take.

H. H.

---

1   Hulton, "Conduct of the Commissariat," 206-209. Bradshaw was secretary to the Treasury lords.

[Henry Hulton to Robert Nicholson]   *Near Boston 4 May 1770*[1]

Dear Sir

As the people in America had been so long suffered to resist the constitutional authority of Great Britain uncorrected, you will hardly have been surprized at those events that have taken place at Boston: but I am sure you must have felt for the servants of the Crown and have sympathized with us in the Insults persecutions and distresses under which we have laboured.

The Resolves of the several Assemblies being adopted as principles by the people's combinations were formed to defeat the operation of the Revenue Laws, prevent the Importation and Sale of British Goods, and persecute and distress all those who came not into the agreement proposed to answer those ends. The few who were so hardy as to refuse submission to the terms prescribed were marked for Oppression—their names were published in all the Papers as persons to be avoided and held in Infamy and Abhorrence. The servants of the Crown, particularly the military, were insulted and the grossest abuses and indignities used to some of the lower officers of the Revenue in several ports; but no Magistrate stood forth to stem the torrent to protect the injured or maintain the authority of the Laws. The infection was general, and the fanatic rage of independant Levellers bore down all order and respect to government (Mr Murray at Boston indeed shew'd a firm spirit to the last, but he was alone[2]). I think the disease has been universal through the British dominions. Let me except one part of its subjects—to the honour of Scotland, her sons have kept free from the general contagion they have not joined either at home or abroad in the defection from authority, but proved themselves good subjects and supporters of Government and order.[3] From the unrestrained licence permitted to the mob, it became very unsafe at Boston for anyone who did not adopt the popular measures the mob assembled frequently about the houses and shops of the persons called Importers, to insult and abuse them and their customers, if any should dare to enter these shops. As they were in their acts of outrage at one house, a person named Richardson passed by; the word was given that he was an Informer—they pursued him to his dwelling and proceeded to such violence, that at length he fired on them, and killed a boy. A few nights after, the mob attacked the centry on duty at the Custom House; he was supported by a party from the main guard the insults and abuse of the mob increased, some of the soldiers fired and killed three or four people. The alarm was given, the town arms seized and town and country took to arms. Notwithstanding the Officer and his men were that night committed to jail, nothing would satisfy the people the next day but the two Regiments must withdraw from the Town into the Castle. Some thousands were assembled together. They expected the country to come in and were determined to try the issue. The Lt. Governor in council received such a message from the people that by the unanimous advice of his council he desired Col. Dalrymple to withdraw the two regiments to the Castle, where they are now.

The Demagogues of the People had now carried one main point, and could exercise their power uncontrouled. The getting rid of the military was a necessary step to getting rid of the Commissioners, and the first being done, there was little difficulty in the latter.

They had long loaded their newspapers with the most injurious and bitter invectives against us, holding us out as enemies to their Country. They now charged us as assassins, abetters of murder, and contrivers of a plot to massacre the inhabitants and objects of their immediate vengeance to give these accusations the appearance of truth, and to induce a belief of them in the minds of the people, it was given out that they could prove orders were sent from the Custom House for Richardson to fire, and that several guns were fired out of the Custom house windows the night the people were killed by the Soldiers.

A Committee of the leaders of the people was set up, evidences were sought for to depose to facts that never existed. Bills of indictment were found against three persons belonging to the Custom House for murder by firing out of the windows. They were committed to jail, and after several days confinement bailed out. All this roused the passions of the people in town and country against the Commissioners to a pitch of fury not to be described, and answered the intentions of the Demagogues by making us retire for our own security. Mr. Robinson went for England, Mr. Burch and his family to my house in the Country and Mr. Paxton to a friend's in Cambridge.

The Superior Court sat about the middle of March, and resolved with unanimous consent of the Bar to adjourn to June. When this got abroad the Demagogues came into Court and urged their proceeding to business, and they sat accordingly the 21st of March. Government was then prostrate! Seeing the people had got all the power into their hands, and the Superior Court so far overawed as to depart from their resolution to adjourn, Mr. Burch and myself resolved to retire out of the province for a while, till the passions of the people should subside, and something like order be restored, and we went directly to Piscataqua in the Government of New Hampshire, leaving our families at my house.

On Friday the 2nd of April the tryal of Richardson came on at Boston, and the judges when they summed up the evidence gave it unanimously as their opinion in their charge to the [jury] that the crime could not amount to more than manslaughter, if so much. About nine the next morning the jury brought in their verdict guilty of Murder, to the astonishment and horror of every honest Man, thereby establishing a new doctrine, that from henceforth no man is safe, either in or out of his house. The Court gave no sentence, and it is supposed by some that they will not accept of the verdict. They immediately adjourned to the 29 of May, when the jury brought in their verdict guilty, there was universal clapping of hands, and signs of applause. After the adjournment of the superior [court] at Boston, we returned to my house, but found matters at Boston only more inflamed and further measures of resistance gone into. Several ships are arrived from London loaded with goods, which is thought the Importers will be compelled to reship for London. No partial repeal will satisfy these people; and they are supported in their resistance by the accounts and publications received from home—they hold town meetings almost dayly, and a paper called the

Whisperer, and the remonstrance of the Livery of London have been there publickly read.[4] We see no likelyhood of being able to hold a Board in Boston, nor is there a prospect of finding a place of rest for us in America. The times are violent and distressing, and our situation truly lamentable.

---

1 Hulton, "Nicholson Letters," 38-46.

2 Justice of the peace James Murray took depositions after the "massacre" at Hutchinson's request. They were subsequently printed in the *Fair Account* in an attempt to counterbalance the town's *Short Narrative*.

3 But as Zobel, *Boston Massacre*, portrait caption between 196-197, noted of merchant and justice of the peace James Murray (see supra), a transplanted Scot living in Boston, "the irascible Murray was not the man to allay Boston's intense anti-Scottish, anti-Jacobite feelings." The anti-Scot sentiments running beneath the surface in Wilkes's *North Briton* dispute continued on with the earl of Bute's presence at George III's court. Anti-Scottish tendencies detectable in Boston simply mirrored those still present in London.

4 "The Whisperer" no. IV and "The Address, Remonstrance, and Petition of the Lord Mayor, Aldermen, Common Council, and Livery of London" to the King were printed in adjoining columns in the *Boston Gazette*, 30 April 1770. The Londoners were protesting the removal of a judge, arguing for appointments on good behavior rather than at pleasure—an issue that would resonate with protesting colonists. Hulton would not have appreciated the "The Whisperer's" opening lines: "BRITONS, *Awake! arise! at the voice of liberty*, of truth and *nature: This voice is sounding through* ENGLAND; and must be heard. *Break the chains, which bind and disgrace you;* CHAINS, *that have been forged by tyranny, upon the anvil of* imposture."

[Henry Hulton to John   Esq.]

Dear Sir   *4 May 1770*[1]

As the people in America had been so long suffered to resist the constitutional authority of Great Britain uncorrected, You will hardly have been surprised at those events that have taken place at Boston; but I am sure you must have felt for the servants of the Crown, and have sympathized with us in the insults, persecutions, and distress, under which we have laboured.

The resolves of the several Assemblies being adopted as principles by the people, combinations were formed to defeat the operation of the Revenue Laws, prevent the Importation and Sale of British Goods, and persecute and distress all those who come not into agreements proposed to answer those ends. The few who were so hardy as to refuse submission to the terms prescribed, were marked for oppression. Their names were published in all the papers as persons to be avoided, and held in infamy and abhorrence.

The Servants of the Crown, particularly the Military, were insulted and the grossest abuses and indignities used to some of the lower officers of the Revenue, in several parts; but no Governour, no Magistrate, stood forth to stem the torrent, to protect the injured, or maintain the authority of the Laws. The infection was general, and the fanatic rage of independant Levellers bore down all order, and respect to Government. I think the disease has been universal through the British dominions. Let me except one part of its subjects. To the honour of Scotland, her sons have kept free from the general contagion. They have not joined either at home or abroad, in the defection from authority, but proved themselves good Subjects, and supporters of Government and order.

From the unrestrained licence permitted to the Mob, it became unsafe at Boston for any one who did not adopt the popular measures; the Mob assembled frequently about the houses and shops of the persons called Importers, to insult and abuse them, and their Customers, if any should dare to enter their shops. As they were in their acts of outrage at one house, a person named Richardson passed by; the word was given he was Informer. They pursued him to his dwelling and proceeded to such violence, that at length he fired on them and killed a boy. A few nights after the Mob attacked the centry at the Custom House. He was supported by a party from the Main Guard. The insults and abuse of the Mob increased, and some of the men fired, and killed three or four people. The alarm was given, the town Arms seized, and town and Country took to Arms. Notwithstanding the Officer and his men were that night committed to Goal, nothing would satisfy the people next day, but the two Regiments must withdraw from the town into the Castle; some thousands were assembled together. They expected the Country to come in, and were determined to try the Issue. The Governor in Council received such a Message from the people, and by the unanimous advice of his Council, he desired Col D[alrymple] to withdraw the two Regiments into the Castle, where they now are.

The Demagogues of the people had now carried one main point, and could exercise their power uncontrouled. The getting rid of the Military was a necessary step to getting rid of the Commissioners, and the first being done, there was little difficulty in the latter.

They had long loaded their newspapers with the most injurious and bitter invectives against us, holding us out as Enemies to their Country. They now charged us as Assassins and abettors of murder and contrivers of a plot to massacre the inhabitants, and objects of their immediate Vengance. To give these accusations the appearance of truth, and to induce a belief of them in the minds of the people, it was given out that they could prove orders were sent from the Custom house to Richardson to fire, and that several Guns were fired out of the Custom House windows the night the people were killed by the Soldiers.

A Committee of the Leaders of the people was set up evidences were sought to depose to facts that never existed. Bills of Indictment were found against three persons belonging to the Custom House, for Murder, by fireing out of the Windows. They were committed to Goal, and after several days confinement bailed out. All this raised the passions of the people in town and country against the Commissioners to a pitch of fury not to be described, and answered the intentions of the Demagogues, by making us retire for our own security. Mr. Robinson went for England, Mr. Burch and his family to my house in the Country, Mr. Paxton to a friend's house at Cambridge.

A little french Boy who was servant to Manwaring, one of the Officers of the Customs accused, was the evidence against his Master, but Manwaring produced the evidence of two persons who were in company with him at his lodging at the time, and of the Landlady of the house. He was several times had before the Justices but dismissed for want of proof. However, the Grand Jury found a bill not only against him, but against one of the persons who was in company with him at his lodgings.

The Porter of the Custom House, and the Messenger's son, on examination, are said to have given such evidence as made in favour of the Military. They were several times examined and told there was evidence to prove that Guns were fired out of the Custom House, and if they did not confess they should be committed, and hanged themselves.

The Superior Court met about the middle of March and resolved with the unanimous consent of the Bar to adjourn to June. When this got abroad, the Demagogues came into Court, and urged their proceeding to business, and they sat accordingly the 21ᵗ.

Government was then prostrate, seeing the people had got all power into their hands, and the Superior Court so far over awed, as to depart from their resolution of adjourning. Mr. Burch and myself resolved to retire out of the province for a while, till the passions of the people should subside, and something like order be restored. And we went directly to Piscataqua, in the Government of New Hampshire, leaving our families at my house.

On Friday the 20ᵗʰ April the tryal of Richardson came at Boston, and the Judges when they summed up the Evidence gave it unanimously as their opinion in their charge to the Jury that the crime could not amount to more than manslaughter, if so much; about 9 the next morning the Jury brought in their verdict guilty of Murder, to the astonishment and horror of every honest Man, thereby establishing a new doctrine, that from hence forth no man is safe, either out of or in his house. The Court gave no sentence, and it is supposed by some that they will not accept the verdict. They immediately adjourned to the 29ᵗʰ of May. When the Jury brought in their verdict guilty there was an universal clapping of hands, and signs of applause.

After the adjournment of the Superior Court at Boston, we returned to my house but found matters at Boston still more inflamed, and further measures of resistance gone into. Several ships are arrived from London loaded with goods, which the Importers have been compelled to reship for London. No partial repeal will satisfy them, and they are supported in their opposition by the Accounts and publications received from home. They hold town meetings almost daily, and a paper called the Whisperer and the Remonstrance of the Livery of London have there publickly been read.

We see no prospect of being able to hold a Board in Boston, nor is there a place of rest for the soles of our feet in America. The times are violent and distressing, and our situation truly lamentable.

Your favour of the 6ᵗʰ of June I did not receive till the 9ᵗʰ of October. I can give you no favourable account of Mr. Mitchell. We appointed Mr. Roupel[2] Collector of Charlestown, till a new one entered on the Office in consequence of a Treasury Warrant. Mr Hincks is still with us in the same situation, and desires his best respects to you. I beg my best respects to Mrs. W.

---

1 Hulton, "Letterbooks," 1:29-36.
2 George Roupell.

[Henry Hulton to Johan von Walmoden]

Mr. Le General de Walmoden   5 May 1770[1]

I was honoured a few days ago with your favour from Lausanne in Switzerland, and it gives me great concern to hear of your long indisposition, and I sincerely pray that you may find relief, and be restored to your desired state of health and usefullness.

On your return to London you will find great advances made in luxury, and licentiousness since you left it; the certain consequences of great commerce, wealth and an easy Government. It is a melancholly revelation, that those circumstances which advance a nation the most rapidly tend to destroy good morals, and by depraving the individual, undermine the foundations of Government.

The spirit of faction and licentiousness that has so long prevailed at home, has given great encouragement to the Colonies to continue in their resistance to the authority of Parliament.

From the constitution of Government in these Countrys, and the first principle of the British Nation in their foreign establishments, there is little likelihood that such measures will take place, as may secure the obedience of this Country to Great Britain.

No nation will retain remote Colonies long in subjection, the Government of which is established upon a popular plan; yet the New England Governments are the most popular that can be devised; and where commercial views are the first object, the honors of the crown, and authority of Government, will be ill[-]supported.

Indeed, at this time the situation of the servants and friends of Government in this Country is much to be lamented. There is no security for any one who does not adopt the popular clamour and join in the measures of the reigning faction. I think it may be called reigning, for it is possessed of all authority, power and there is such a general lachete,[2] that no Governor, or Magistrate, dare, or is inclined to set himself against it, or to maintain the authority of the Laws, by protecting the quiet subject who would pay obedience to them.

It has been my lot to be called out to a great deal of toil and combat in the public service. I realized no advantage by an exchange from my establishment at home to the one here, except being placed more immediately under observation, and being made more accountable, may be called such. But as things are in this Country, few people would be desirous of the distinction; no honour can be gained and everything may be lost by clamour, malice, and misrepresentation. Life, for the time, is made unhappy; for nothing is more disagreeable than a continued state of toil, combat, suspense, and anxiety. Though one can render little service, and therefore may not have much to plead on that head, yet the enduring a life of tryal, remote from one's country and friends, amongst a people adverse to us, for the Office we bear, should give one some pretentions to future favor. And I trust we shall be properly considered for what we have done and endured in the service.

On our return from the Castle, no one would rent me a house in the town, and I was obliged to purchase one in the Country a few miles from Boston, where I now live and endeavour in my retreat to forget as much as I can the disorderly town, which I seldom visit but to attend the Board. And I enjoy at least domestic happiness, which these turbulent people cannot deprive me of; we have two little boys that make the chief of our present pleasures, and I hope will be comforts to our future age.

The Assemblys of most of the Colonies, having denied the authority of the parliament of Great Britain to impose taxes on America for the purpose of raising a Revenue, and this being adopted as a principle by the people, a resistance to the operation of such laws became patriotic; and combinations were joined to prevent the importation and sale of British Goods, and either from principle, or from threats, and measures most of the people in trade in the several towns were brought to sign such agreements as the committees of the Merchants and traders thought fit to propose to answer the ends intended.

The few traders in Boston who had the hardiness to refuse to sign these agreements were voted enemies to their country, and were to be oppressed by every means; their names were published in all the papers, and every one was forbid to hold any commerce or intercourse with them.

It had been a practice for some weeks for the people to gather every Thursday about the shops of some of the persons called Importers (or who would not sign the agreement,) to insult and abuse them, and their Customers, if any should dare to enter their shops. There were two Regiments in the town, but no Magistrate would call upon them ro support the peace; and from the principle of disaffection to the British authority, and the unrestrained licence permitted to the mob, it became very unsafe for anyone who did not adopt the popular measures.

Frequent insults were offered, particularly to the Military, and in every squabble between them and the towns people, the latter took all the advantage of the Laws to harrass and distress the soldiers. As the Mob were in their acts of outrage at one house, a person named Richardson passing by, he was insulted, and called an Informer. He fled to his house, where they pursued him, threw stones, broke his windows, and proceeded to such violence that he threatened to fire on them if they did not desist; and as they persisted, he fired, and killed a boy, upon which he, and another Man with him were committed to goal. Some nights after, the Mob insulted and attacked the Centry on guard at the Custom house. The porter of the Custom house ran to the Main Guard, to acquaint them of the distress the Centry was in, and a party from the Main Guard came to his support; the insults and abuse of the Mob increased; some of the soldiers fired and three or four men were killed; the town was ready for the alarm, the town arms were seized, the bells rung, and town and Country took to Arms. The Captain of the Guard, and the Men that fired, were that night committed to Goal, yet the ferment increased the next day, and a Message was sent to the Lt. Governor in Council from the people in Arms, that nothing would satisfy them, but the immediate removal of the two Regiments to the Castle; otherwise they would try the issue. The Council unanimously advised for their removal, and to prevent consequences, the Governor agreed to it.

The Demagogues of the people having carried this material point, next laboured by every means to lay the odium of these unhappy events to the Commissioners. They charged them in their publications as accessaries to the Murders, and left nothing undone to obtain evidence that the Commissioners sent orders to Richardson to fire; and to prove that Guns were fired out of the Custom house Windows on the people, at the time the Soldiers killed the men mentioned. To enrage the people the more against the Commissioners, and point us out as the objects of their vengeance, the evidence of the servants that were in the house was disregarded, and they published representations, which themselves could not believe to be true. These people have adopted a popish doctrine, that any means are allowable to bring about a good end, and it is shocking to see and hear of their proceedings. In this state of affairs we could not pretend to do any business in Boston. Mr. R[obinson] went for England. Mr. B[urch], Mr. P[axton] and myself with our families retired from the town, and waited to take further measures as events should arise.

Since the troops are withdrawn great quiet has been kept in the town. So they give out that the Commissioners may remain, and do business there in safety; but who would be dependant on their caprice? the Lieut. Governor came down to my house on Monday evening, the 19th March. He said a Deacon had said we might be in town in safety, but on being asked if he and his council could advise us to it, and assure us of protection, he could not say any such thing, and we have kept our Board adjourned.

The Superior Court met on Tuesday the 13th of March, and with the unanimous consent of the Bar agreed to adjourn to June. As soon as it got abroad, the Demagogues, as a Committee from the town, came into Court, and urged their proceeding to business, saying the blood of their Citizens lay on the ground.

The Court met again on Wednesday the 21st March, and on the next day proceeded to business, having been so far over awed by the Committee of the people as to alter their own resolution of Adjournment.

We had been threatened with prosecutions on Account of our Memorials to the Treasury: and finding the Superior Court were sit[t]ing on Thursday the 22d March, Mr B[urch] and myself resolved to go out of the province for a while; and we set out immediately for New Hampshire Government, which has kept the quietest of any in these times of trouble.

The sons of liberty were desired by advertisement to attend the funerals of the people that were killed. Upwards of 1200 attended the funeral of the boy that was killed by Richardson; and the people on their return being displeased with something that was said by a Gentleman in the street, they fell upon him, tore his clothes off his back and pursued him with rage to a house where he took shelter, and before they could be appeased, he was obliged to appear at a Window, acknowledge his fault and ask pardon. At the funeral of the Men that were killed, a greater procession attended, amongst whom was Mr. T[emple]. And the day that the Demagogues went into the Superior Court to remonstrate with the Judges why they did not proceed to tryal of the Criminals, they had dined at Mr. T[emple's] house, from whence they proceeded to the Court.

---

1   Hulton, "Letterbooks," 1-19-28
2   cowardice.

[Henry Hulton to Robert Nicholson]   *Brooklyn near Boston   11 May 1770*[1]

Dear Sir

I wrote to you at the beginning of the year 1769 in answer &c. to a letter I received about Christmas, since which I have not been favoured with any from you.

I have lived in the Country for near twelve months past, as retired as my business would allow from the turbulent and disorderly town of Boston. My family are in good health and our situation would be agreeable enough, if these people would suffer us to live in peace. But contentions and broil seem necessary to the existence of a Bostonian, and indeed our present circumstances are very critical and alarming, as our lives and properties depend on the caprice of our Sovereign Lords the people.

The inclosed will shew you further the state of matters in this Country and I shall say nothing more thereon, for perhaps we may differ in opinion as to the conduct of the people, both at home and abroad, and as to measures which should be taken by Government. I should be glad to hear of your and your family's health and welfare. Mrs. H. And my sister desire to join with me in best regards to yourself and Mrs N. I beg you will make my best respects and Compliments to both your family [and] friends.

I am, Dear Sir, your &c.

H Hulton

---

1   Hulton, "Nicholson Letters," 47-48.

[Ann Hulton to Elizabeth Lightbody] *Near Boston 29 May 1770*[1]

Whilst I am waiting for an Opportunity to write to Dear Mrs L. by some ship for Liverpool, I received her agreeable Letter, was made happy about Xtmas by your former one dated September.

I thought your candid disposition would make favorable allowance for a delay in writing, and your late favor convinces me of it. I hoped to be able to give you a more favorable Account of Affairs in America, and our situation, than has been in my power for some-time past, and there is more risque in giving a true Account of Matters and Events, than one's friends in England can easily imagine. I believe my Brother has wrote lately to Mr N[icholson]. You will probably hear from him all the News from hence, better than I can relate and I would chuse more pleasing Subjects. It indeed gives me pleasure to hear of your happiness in your little Family, and the pleasing prospects from hence. It would be matter of great Joy to me to hear of the Addition of a Son, that the many trials of your patience and resignation may be more amply rewarded in this Life. In the future I've no doubt they will and I have only to wish in regard to futurity that I may share in your bliss. Though We are widely seperated at present, and our trials may be very different in kind, yet such as the alwise Disposer knows to be best for each of Us.

What pleasure would it be if I could but now and then see some of my old friends, and have a little converse with them. Methinks it would disscipate every care and alleviate every trouble. But this is not a State to enjoy all we wish for, if we have any Supports there is reason for thankfulness. I enjoy health and have a good Brother for whose safety indeed I am more anxious than for my own, but I trust that Kind Providence which has preserved, will still protect Us. My Brother lives on a Spot of Earth which he calls his own, and a lone House so retired that not one person in 50 in Boston ever saw it before, yet the Situation so agreeable to Mr. and Mrs. H. that they would not chuse to change it for any other Spot in New England. And we have found no want of Company, for we have been near 20 of family for some time till today. Now eight of them have left besides my Brother and Sister[,] who are just set of[f] for Rhode Island, to return in 10 Days time. When I immediately set down to write to my friend, my only Companion left being my Nephew Tom, who interrupts Me not a little with his prating and playing, I ask him what he will have to Miss L., whether he won't send Love. He says, no, but she'll not take it amiss, as She may be assured it is because he does not know her, or he would be exceeding fond of her, I'm certain. He is a fine lively boy, and a sweet disposition. Harry is very stout; walks alone. I am, Dear Madam, Your Affectionate A Hulton

---

1   *Loyalist Lady*, 20-21.

[Henry Hulton to Robert Nicholson]   *Brooklin near Boston   12 June 1770*[1]

Dear Sir

I did not receive your favour of the 5th January till the 16 May, when I had wrote the inclosed letter, but I delayed sending it till I could write in answer to the matter you desired me to make inquiry about. I have had little acquaintance in the town of Boston, as few people there are inclined to shew any of the civil offices of society to the Servants of the Crown.

I have not been in Boston these past three months past. They who put the power into the hands of the mob now feel the scourge themselves, and the town is little short of a state of anarchy.

My family are very well, but we live in a state of alarm, distress and anxious expectation.

Mrs. H. and sister join me in best respects to Mrs N. and I am with great regard Dear Sir yours &c.

---

1   Hulton, "Nicholson Letters" 48-49.

[Henry Hulton to Thomas Hutchinson]   *21 June 1770*[1]

Sir

I take the liberty of laying before your Honour, the circumstances of an outrage committed on me Tuesday night the 19th instant.

About midnight I was awaked by a gentle knocking at the House door; hearing it repeated I got out of bed, and asked who was there, a Man answered he wanted to see Mr. Hulton. What is your business with him at this time of night? answer, I want to deliver him a letter that came by the express this morning from New York. Question, Who are you I am Capt. [blank] from the Granades,[2] and have been detained at Cambridge, which has made me thus late. I'll come down. I'll stay says he. I slipt on my clothes, took my sword in my hand, and just opened the parlour window. The man beg'd I would let him have a night's lodging as it was so late. I answered I would not open my door at that time of night; but put my hand out, and said, give me the letter; he said I have a letter indeed, and moved as with intention to push the Window up, upon which I claped it down: and instantly, with a damn you, he struck several violent blows, that broke through the frames of the upper sash, but resting on the middle frame, prevented their hurting me. As soon as he gave the first blow, all the lower windows of the South and West sides of the house (being eight) were instantly broke, in like manner. I had not heard the least noise before, and had no apprehension of their being any people in company. The noise this made raised the family in a great fright and alarm; the people without soon after went away, making a loud noise and huzzaing.

---

1 Hulton, "Conduct of the Commissariat," 233-234. Ann Hulton's deposition about the incident, given to justice of the peace James Murray at Castle Wiliam on September 5th, and the deposition of Mary Mitchel, a servant, also given to Murray, are on 235-238.

2 Presumably grenadiers, though Hulton may have not heard it that way.

[Henry Hulton to Lord North]   *25 June 1770*[1]

My Lord

The situation of affairs in the town of Boston having rendered it impossible for the Commissioners to carry on the service. Mr. Burch, Mr. Paxton and myself have been obliged for some months past to give our chief attention to our own safety.

In consequences of the affair of the 5[th] of March Mr. Burch and myself retired for some time to Piscataqua, and Mr. Paxton to a friend's house at Cambridge, and after our return from Piscataqua we thought it necessary to keep out of the way, whilst the Superior Court was sit[t]ing.

We were unwilling to take refuge in the Castle, as long as there was any probability of safety for ourselves in the Country, being desirous to give the people of Boston time to recover from the violence of passion, and an opportunity of shewing towards us a behaviour becoming good subjects.

As we found no likelihood of a change of disposition in the people, Mr. Burch, who had not been in Boston since the middle of March, at length took a house in the Country, and we were in hopes to have rested in quiet in our houses some miles from Boston, until we could know the commands of Government.

Several outrages were committed on our Officers and others in the town of Boston, before the people proceeded to an actual attempt on ourselves. But after the attack on me made on the night of the 19th instant (a relation of which is contained in a letter to the Lt. Governour, a copy of which I beg leave to inclose) We found it absolutely necessary for the safety of ourselves, and families, to retire to Castle William, where we have been received with great civility and kindness by Colo. Dalrymple, and the Lt. Governour has ordered the apartment of the Governour and Lt. Governour for our accommodation.

There were some expressions made use of by the Mob when they attacked me, which were heard by my servant, but as I did not hear them myself I did not insert them in my letter to the Lt. Governour, such as dead or alive we'll have him. He'll fire. No he darn't fire, we'l come again. And I was told by a Gentleman that one of the Council (on the morning of the night I was attack'd) said to him that they were determined to drive off the Commissioners, and when the matter was considered in Council two or three of the Members suggested that the Commissioners had got themselves attacked in order to bring a reproach on the province.

It is now two years since we were obliged to make this place an asylum from the rage of the people, and on that occasion we are assured of future protection, and support, and of, the reward of Government. We were indeed afterwards enabled to resume the exercise of our Commission in Boston, and in some manner to carry on the Service. But returned to a life of distress, persecution, and painful anxiety, and ourselves and the officers of the Board, are quite wore down, and overcome with the length and severity of our dishonourable sufferings.

Yet I should still think myself happy, if by any thing I could do, or endure, I could render any service to my Country, but I fell a double pain in what I suffer, from the repeated indignities done to the authority of Government.

H. H.

---

1   Hulton, "Conduct of the Commissariat," 229-232.

[Henry Hulton to Thoms Bradshaw, Esq.]   *Castle William   29 June 1770*[1]

Sir

It has been a great aggravation of the distresses under which I have laboured, that I have not been honoured with any letter from you, or had your sentiments in any wise communicated to me.

Our situation has been the most severe, and we have undergone a life of constant anxiety for the service, and for ourselves.

After a wearisome time of outward insult, indignity and persecution; of family dread, and distress; we have at length taken shelter in this Castle; but not before I was drove from my own house at midnight, narrowly escaping assassination.

I have taken the liberty of laying before my Lord North the circumstances of this assault on my house and person.

Whatever measures may be taken by Government, for repressing the disorders and licentiousness that prevail, and for restoring and supporting its authority, the Servants of th Crown must do, and endure a great deal, and for a long time, before they will be any wise respected, or at ease. A sense of duty, inclination, and zeal for the service, will carry men a great way; but the best minds will be damped by a long endurance of persecution from their enemies, and neglect from their friends.

This is the time when good servants are most wanted, and must be cherished, if the service is to be carried on. Not a man but shrinks from the service, in the state it is. Where is the support for the Officer? Where is the protection for the Man? Reproach and insult were sufficient for a while, the most ignominious treatment of a Revenue Officer became sport, and pastime of the people; and now, we are assaulted in our houses, and it is doing public Service to destroy us.

I have been subjected to many extraordinary expences by coming to America, being separated from my family, bringing them out here, being drove off, and living in the Castle, being obliged from necessity to buy and repair a house in the Country, as no one would rent me one in town—and now again by being drove to the Castle, all these, with the extraordinary expence of living, from the circumstances of the times, have encreased my disbursements far beyond my appointment from thee Crown.

You know Sir the situation I was in before I came to America, and you know my services before that time, and I challange your experience of Men, since your engagement n public business, to produce a more faithful servant of the Crown. You are sensible Sir under what expectation I came out to this country, and I have that confidence in you, expecting something in my favour, from your representation of my services, and support of my pretentions.

---

1   Ibid., 238-241.

[Ann Hulton to Elizabeth Lightbody]

Castle Island, near Boston   25 July 1770[1]

It is about Seven weeks ago that I did myself the pleasure of writing to Dear Mrs. Lightbody. Since that, you will have heard my Brother has been driven from his own Habitation and afterwards retired with his Family to this place[2] for safety. I have often thought of what you said, that surely we did not live in a lone House. It's true we have long been in a dangerous situation, from the State of Government. The want of protection, the perversion of the Laws, and the spirit of the People inflamed by designing men. Yet our house in the Country has been a place of retreat for many from the disturbances of the Town, and though they were become very alarming, yet we did not apprehend an immediate attack on our House, or that a Mob out of Boston should come so far, before we had notice of it, and were fully persuaded there are Persons more obnoxious than my Brother, that he had no personal Enemy, and confident of the good will of our Neighbours (in the Township we live in) towards him, so that we had no suspicion of what happened the night of June the 19ᵗʰ —we have reason to believe it was not the sudden outrage of a frantic Mob, but a plot artfully contrived to decoy My Brother into the hands of assassins. At Midnight when the Family was asleep, had not a merciful Providence prevented their designs, we had been a distressd Family indeed.

Between 12 and 1 o'Clock he was wakened by a knocking at the Door. He got up, enquired the person's name and business, who said he had a letter to deliver to him, which came Express from New York. My Brother puts on his Cloaths, takes his drawn Sword in one hand, and opened the Parlor window with the other. The Man asked for a Lodging—said he, I'll not open my door, but give me the letter. The man then put his hand, attempting to push up the window, upon which my Brother hastily clapped it down. Instantly with a bludgeon several violent blows were struck which broke the Sash, Glass and frame to pieces. The first blow aimed at my Brother's Head, he Providentialy escaped, by its resting on the middle frame, being double, at same time (though before then, no noise or appearance of more Persons than one) the lower windows, all round the House (excepting two) were broke in like manner. My Brother stood in amazement for a Minute or 2, and having no doubt that a number of Men had broke in on several sides of the House, he retired Upstairs.

You will believe the whole Family was soon alarmed, but the horrible Noises from without, and the terrible shrieks within the House from Mrs. H. and Servants, which struck my Ears on awaking, I can't describe, and shall never forget.

I could imagine nothing less than that the House was beating down, after many violent blows on the Walls and windows, most hideous Shouting, dreadful imprecations, and threats ensued. Struck with terror and astonishment, what to do I knew not, but got on some Cloaths, and went to Mrs. H.'s room, where I found the Family collected, a Stone thrown in at her window narrowly missed her head. When the Ruffians were retreating with loud huzzas and one cryd he will fire—no says another, he darn't fire, we will come again says a third—Mr. and Mrs H. left their House immediately and have not lodged a night since in it.

The next day we were looking up all the Pockit Pistols in the house, some of which were put by, that nobody could find 'em and ignorant of any being charged, Kitty was very near shooting her Mistress, inadvertently lets it off. The bullets missed her within an inch and fixed in a Chest of Drawers. Here was another miraculous escape, so that we have reason to be thankful, we are all safe and well, though truly Prisoners in a Castle, the old place of refuge.

But there is no security from the virulence of Lying Tongues. Can you believe it, that a person shall suffer abuse, an attack upon his House, and attempt on his Life, and afterwards the reproach of having done it himself. This is really the case, the persons who are so vile as to be at the bottom of the Mischeif, have in order to remove the odium from themselves, and the Town, industriously spread this report, that Mr H. hired people to break his own Windows, for an excuse of his removal to the Castle, and to ruin this Country.

However ridiculous this Aspersion, yet it is believed or seemingly believed by one half of the people, as we are told. But the more sensible and moderate are ashamed of the absurdity, and freely say, that this outrage against Mr H. will hurt their Country more than anything which has been done yet. And for the honour of the Township we lived in, I must say, the principal People, have of their own accord taken up the affair very warmly, exerting their endeavors to find out the Authors, or perpetrators of the Villainy. They have produced above twenty witnesses, Men in the Neighborhood who were out a Fishing that night, that prove they met upon the Road from Boston towards my Brother's House, Parties of Men that appeared disguised, their faces blacked, with white Night caps and white Stockens on, one of 'em with Ruffles on and all, with great clubs in their hands. They did not know any of 'em, but one Fisherman spoke to 'em, to be satisfied whether they were Negroes or no, and found by their Speech they were not, and they answered him very insolently. Another person who mett them declares, that one of 'em asked him the way to Mr. H's house, and another of 'em said he knew the way very well. After all, you may judge how much any further discovery is likely to be made, or justice to be obtained in this Country, when I tell you that the persons who were thus active to bring the dark deed to light, were immediately stop'd and silenced, being given to understand (as I'm well informed) that if they made any further stir about the matter, they might expect to be treated in the same manner as Mr H. was. However, so much is proved as to clear Mr H. from the charge of doing himself the mischief, one would think.

This instance shews the State this Country is in. It is not the case of one, but of every faithful Officer and Loyal Subject here that is; to suffer abuse, persecution calumny and reproach, and if they seek redress or any personal attempts to do them Justice, it is not to be expected, but threats of greater evils.

What Government intends doing to remedy these, We are yet strangers, or whether anything effectual will be done. Here's a report that the Board is to be removed to the Jerseys. That place would be as agre[e]able as any part of America to us, but whether the Board be removed, called home, or abolished, we have reason to hope my Brother's interest will not be prejudiced.

If G[reat] Britain leaves Boston to itself, though its own honour will not be maintained thereby, it will certainly be the greatest punishment that can be inflicted on the place and people, but a cruelty to some individuals, who have shewn themselves friends to Government. The Town is now in the greatest confusion, the People quarreling violently about Importation, and Exportation.

The New Yorkers having broke through their nonimportation agreement, is a heavy Stroke, and though 90 out a 100 of the Merchants and traders here, want to do the same, yet they are terrified to submit to [the][3] Tyranny of that Power they at first set up, and are going to reship their British Goods, though it's expected there will be some broken Noses first, and that these combinations cannot hold long. However, the Trade of the Town is ruined, and the principal Branch, that of Ship Building, which supported some hundred of Families, is removed by the Glasgow Merchants to other places, because their Goods were not allowed to be [disposed][4] of here: — and in return, the Town or Leaders of the[5] resolved to banish all the Scotchmen from the [Place] and began with one McMasters, an honest industrious Tradsman, who had 3 or 4000£ Sterling in Effects, and more in outstanding debts here. Without any preten[sions but] that he was an Importer, they gave him warning [to] Quit the Town within 3 days, or he must take the consequences (which means Taring and Feathering), a most cruel violence, with which they intimidate and force everyone to submit to their demands. The poor Man not complying, they [seized] him at noon day, put him into a Cart, exhibited him through the Town, and were going to Tar and F[eather] him, but that they forced an Oath from him, that he would leave the place. And now he and his Brother [are] ruined men and forlorn Wanderers upon this Island, lost [his] property and [l]ost his [senses]

I've wrote more freely to you than I should have done; but as I have that confidence in my friend that my letter will not be exposed. I would not have my name or my Brother's mentioned in a Sea Port Town as sending any news from hence. You may not know, though I do the risque of [it], therefore I gi[ve you] the hint. My Respects to Mr L.

I (am de)[ar Madam Your Affectionate] A. H.

1　Loyalist Lady, 22-27.
2　Castle William.
3　Inserted by the editors.
4　Ditto.
5　There are breaks and insertions through to the end of the paragraph, from presumably illegible parts in the letter. See Nicolson, "A Plan," 55-102, which draws from this letter and others by Ann and Henry to help connect the experience of Scottish-born Boston merchant Patrick McMaster to the "ethnic violence" that accompanied colonial protest.

[Henry Hulton to] M Esq.　　　　　　　　　　*30 October 1770*[1]

I wrote to you of the 10th instant, since which the trial of Captain Preston came on before the Superior Court. It continued during several days, and was considered as one of the most solemn and important that has come before the Court. Every thing was conducted with the utmost order and decorum; and the prisoner on the most impartial trial, has been honorably acquited. The event of this tryal may be considered of the utmost consequence, as establishing the principle of resistance to assault by the Military, as well as civil subject.

The Lawyers on the side of the Prisoner, and the Judges in their charge to the Jury have fully supported this principle. There is now a greater appearance of our being able to carry on business quietly in Boston, than at any time since we came out; but the alteration in the temper of the people may arise from what they see has been done, and their apprehensions of what is to follow, and will probably go off, unless further regulations take place, which are generally expected.

---

1 Hulton, "Letterbooks," 1:37.

[Ann Hulton to Elizabeth Lightbody]

Brooklyne near Boston
21 December 1770[1]

Dear Mrs. Lightbody's kind favor gives me great pleasure though received three months after the date. It affords me some satisfaction to know that you and your family was well then, (for it's many months since I heard anything from Old England) it bring to remembrance former times and the agreable hours I spent with you.

I am much obliged to you for the kind concern you express for us, in this hostile Land, and our late situation in it.

I bless God I can say, that after many changes, dangers and trials in Life, I now enjoy health, and ease, peace, and plenty, and that my Brother with his Family, are quietly reinstated in his beloved Habitation, after near five Months Exile at the Castle. It's Six weeks since we returned here. We find the face of things exceedingly changed indeed. To be exposed to the rage of a frantic mob, or subject to alarms and fears, is a dreadful situation, especialy where there's no Government or Law. But upon the appearance (or some steps towards Establishing) of these supports of Society, and protecting of Individuals, the desperate Invaders, and abettors of the disturbances disapear. Peace and Order takes place, and the past Scenes of confusion and disorder, appears as a dream.

We never thought ourselves more safe from the Sons of Violence, than at present. Yet our Security and the continuance of it, under a kind Providence depends on Circumstances, Chiefly the Authority and Support of Government. From thence the Impartial Trial and honorable acquital of Captain Preston and the Soldiers has the most happy Effect. It has exposed the Conduct of the Faction, and opened the Eyes of the People in general, convinced them that they have been deceived by false opinions, and false representations of Facts. It has ascertained the right of Self defence, which they were taught to beleive was illegal without the aid of a civil Majistrate. These Trials together with that of the Custom House Officers charged with Firing out of the C[ustom]H[ouse], and the Suborning of false Witnesses against them which appeared on the Trial, and the witness since commit[t]ed for Perjury.[2]

These things have laid open a Scene of Iniquity that the greatest Advocates are now ashamed of the Cause, and most persons wish to be thought friends to that Government which appears determined to punish, and reward, according to des[s]erts.

Many persons have told us that we shall never receive any more insults or attacks here, for the man (say they) is gone that sent out the Assassins to Mr H.

There's great reason to believe their design was upon his Life. I hope he will never have occasion to defend himself or his House, yet we are provided against the worst with Fire Arms—a great Dog and a Bell at the top of the House, to give Notice to the Neighborhood in case of necessity. We have no doubt of the good disposition of People in the Country towards my Brother from the abhorrence they in general shewed at the former outrage, and their endeavors to find out the Authors, as well as the solicitude they expressed for our return home, and offers to Watch and guard our House, by nights in their turns, if we were under any Apprehensions. But that we are not at present. Far from Insu³[lt or] abuse, we have met with every civility and respect possible, both in Town and Country, from all sorts of people.

Our acquaintance increases to more than we can well keep up in a visiting way, every one seems desirous to make out Situation agre[e]able to us, and to banish the prejudices we may have received against it.

It's not a little that will destroy the partiality of Mr. and Mrs H. for their rural retreat, a short banishment serves to heighten their enjoyment [of] it, even in the depth of winter. Two fine Boys adds to their happiness, and afford constant entertainment to their Aunt by their innocent prattle. They have the Countenances of Cherubs, and Constitutions for Farmers, Strong and hearty.

My paper allows no more than to assure you your Friends here joyn in wishing you every happiness they enjoy

My best respects to Mr Lightbody and your Sisters — Miss H. and Mrs. R. L. — J. Hincks is here now, engaged at Cards well and Easy; as [usual] knows not how many Neices or nephews he has, [whether] 5 or five and twenty. I am

Dear Madam, Your Affectionate A.H.

---

1   *Loyalist Lady*, 28-30.
2   Edward Manwaring's servant, Charles Bourgatte, who was convicted of perjury, sentenced to the pillory, then flogged.
3   Original editorial insertions follow in brackets.

[Henry Hulton to Robert Nicholson]   *'Brooklyn near Boston 29 March 1771*[1]

Dear Sir

I did not receive your favour of the 15 September till the 21 December, and am obliged to you for the newspapers. You acknowledge the receipt of my Letter of the 12 June and I imagine you must have heard of the assault that was made on my house at midnight seven days after, which obliged us to take refuge once more in Castle William, where we remained 'till the 7 November. And as the passions of the people seemed then to be in a good measure subsided, we ventured to return to our dwelling, and we have passed the Winter quietly and comfortably, and if there was good Government in this Country, our situation might be supportable enough. The Winter had been remarkably fine, and though we are without publick diversions, yet we do not regret our removal from the town, or feel the time heavy on our hands. Business, books, and friends leave us no vacancy, and the Winter evenings have never been long, or dreary; indeed, there have been Concerts and Assemblies in Boston, but we have never been at them. People wonder how we could live in the Country and thought we never should be easy there; however, we feel ourselves happy, and think we enjoy more pleasure and satisfaction than they who are in town. My business gives me exercise and employment, my books and friends entertainment, my farm amusement, and my children pleasure. I have two boys and the Boston one rivals the Old England one with many people, and they who flatter us say we bear the bell for fine children. They have both the true Boston disposition for rioting, and the house is never quiet whilst they are awake. All my family enjoy health and we have every real good in our power that the place or society can afford, and if this people will let us rest in quiet I hope we shall enjoy them in comfort. Mrs H. and my sister join me in best respects to yourself and Mrs N. My best Compliments to all your family connections. I remain with great regard, Dear Sir, your &c.

Henry Hulton

---

1   Hulton, "Nicholson Letters," 49-51.

[Henry Hulton to Robert Nicholson] *Boston 3 August 1771*[1]

Dear Sir

I am obliged to you for your favour of the 8th April, with some newspapers enclosed. I had the pleasure of writing to you in May and June the last year, but do not find I have written since 'till the 29 March past. We have been very quiet since our return from the Castle, and the people will continue so long as they are allowed to disown the authority of Great Britain with impunity.

It is happy for this society that such a gentleman as Mr. Hutchinson has in these times arisen amongst them, and been appointed their Governor. Since the Stamp Act affair many gentlemen of property and liberal minds have been left out of the Council and Assembly, and more violent and less informed people brought in, and the General Court has so long refused and denied without being compel[l]ed to obey, that they now want the Governor to act without regard to the King's instructions. Even the Governor, with his superior abilities, temper and moderation, cannot lead them to do that which is right, or prevent them from doing absurd and extravagant Acts.

They tax people here for their Profession or Employment, under the term <u>Faculty</u>. By this Law they made us pay taxes for our salaries from the Crown.

The Governor received an Instruction lately whilst the Assembly were sitting, not to pass the Tax Bill unless the Commissioners of the Customs were excepted for their Salaries. The answer to the Governor on his message thereon was "we know of no Commissioners of the Customs, nor of any right the King has to establish a Revenue in this Country." The Governor prorogued them the next day without passing the Tax Bill that had been prepared before his message was sent.

In the month of May Mrs H. and I made a journey through some part of this Province and Connecticut. Nothing less than the Enthusiasm of the first Set[t]lers and their violent spirit of Independency could have made people undergo the labour of reducing these lands to a state of cultivation. After cutting down the trees, the land is very rocky and scarce any English grain is produced in these parts. Indian Corn and Hay are the chief produce. It is amazing to see the quantities of fine timber that are destroyed. They girdle the trees, which die and in time fall down, rot and perish on the ground without use. The people never can grow rich upon these Lands, but they increase wonderfully. The spirit of equality prevails throughout the Country, and they have no notion of rank or distinction in society. They are at first shy of admitting you into their houses, and will shew more respect to one another than to those who appear to be something above them. It is a favour done you, if they acco[m]modate you for your money. As they become acquainted, they ask you a thousand strange impertinent questions, sit down by you when they should wait at table, and perhaps ask if the young man (meaning your servant) is not to dine with you. Indeed, in these two Provinces are few persons settled who may be called Gentlemen, I mean men of property, education and liberal minds. The first sat down in a wood, built a shed, and lived on salt pork, and to this day they seem to have got little further. In travelling there are no fresh provisions to be had, and their liquor is sour cyder and a little New England Rum.

As the family increases, the young men go back into the woods, and do as their fathers did before them. There seems no prospect of advancement, or chance of opulence for them, and as their principles bring all on a level, they feel no oppression from anyone above them, and see nothing to excite envy, or raise admiration, but leave us without emulation, or desire of distinction. And what is human nature? If these passions are not excited, everything noble and great is damped, but from these people's original principles, education and government, and the extent of Country yet uncleared there seems no prospect but of their remaining as they are for many generations. Since the Stamp Act affair, they have attempted to manufacture homespun, but as every farmer goes through the whole process, it is awkwardly done at the best and they spend much time that might be better employed in the farm. The women do not work in the fields and the children are not employed. Great numbers of people have come from the Southward, and other parts of late years to settle on Lands in the Eastern back parts of this Province, and that of New Hampshire. They take up lands without authority, live without Law or Government, Priest, or Magistrate, and if better regulation and order than I expect does not take place, it will not be many years before other such insurrections and civil broils as have happened in N[orth] Carolina will arise in different parts of this Continent. How weak, then, are the people of property on the coast, in resisting the only power that can protect them, and establish order and good government amongst them.

We have been very happy in our rural abode since our return from the Castle. The business of the Board calls me often to town and as one Member is absent[3] it leaves me little time for other matters. When at home I am fully employed with my family and farm. My little prat[t]lers are become very agreeable companions, and my domestick comforts make up for any chagrine I may have suffered from outward circumstances. I have built a new Barn and made a large crop of hay that almost fills it. Mrs H. and my sister desire to join with me in their best wishes and regards for yourself and family, and I remain with great esteem, Dear Sir, yours &c.

H. H.

Some Specimens of the justice of a Boston jury. Mr. Otis, the Patriot, published in the newspapers the most gross abuse on the Commissioners of the Customs and spoke many reproachful speeches against them, particularly pointing at Mr. Robinson, as that he would break his head the next time he met him. Mr R. called him to account in the Coffee house for these affronts and gave him a very good drub[b]ing. The action for damages was lately tried and the jury gave Mr Otis £2000 damages. Mr. Robinson is still in England and I suppose will now remain there sometime longer. Another action of assault and broken head was tried and the jury gave £5 damages, but these parties were both Boston gentlemen.

One Owen Richards, who had been many years Tidesman in this Port, some time ago was assaulted and taken from his duty on board a ship, strip[p]ed naked, put into a cart and covered with tar and feathers, and for several hours led about the town, a shocking spectacle, hissed, beaten and abused the whole time. Actions were brought against some of the parties concerned in this outrage and the facts were proved to the satisfaction of the Court. The cause was tried by the same jury and before the same court that had tried Mr. Otis's action a few days before. The parties were acquit[t][ed, and Richards left to pay his own costs—a pretty state of society this, for the servants of the Crown.[4]

---

1 Ibid., 52-59.
2 Hutchinson's message to the House of 4 July 1771 prompted the House's rejoinder the next day, in *Speeches of the Governors*, 306 and 307, resp. See supra 72 n. 153.
3 John Robinson, who was in London. John Temple had been replaced by Benjamin Hallowell.
4 Zobel, *Boston Massacre*, discusses both incidents, on 147, 151 and 229, 231, resp.

[Ann Hulton to Elizabeth Lightbody]   *undated*[1]

I have Dear Mrs. Lightbody's agreable favor of the 28 February. It gives me real pleasure to hear you and your family are well, and that the alarming Apprehensions which you must have had for those [who][2] are dear to you were over. The Hannahs, I hope, are both perfectly [recovered].

I would gratify your Curiosity, or rather answer your obli[ging] enquires, about this Country, where your friend's Lot is cast. I am not thoroughly acquainted with the Town of Boston. It is in short like a large Seaport Town in England, and the People speak as good English as anywhere. It is built on a Peninsula and about two mile[s] Long, joynd to the Continent by a piece of Land called the Neck, which is a mile Long, and twice as broad as a great Street. This is the only way by Land out of the Town. The main Street entering the Town is a mile Long; there are a great number of By Streets and hobbling Pavements. The publick buildings are the Exchange, the Town House, and Fennil Hall, there are 2 Episcopal churches, besides the King's Chaple, but one Presbyterian (properly called) and about 12 Independant Congregationalists. Some of these Ministers are very flaming Preachers; that is, they take occasion to inflame the People, both by their Sermons and Prayers against Government and all belonging to it, particularly Dr. C[oo]per and Dr. Chancy &c. It may seem strange, but I believe it's very true, that the Sunday after my Brother was attacked in his own House, with an apparent design upon his Life, after we were gone to the Castle — Dr Ch[aun]cy preached a Sermon on that occasion and told his people plainly out of the Pulpit that the Commissioner broke his own windows, to cast odium on the Country, and the next day this Rev. Dr. went all about, impressing this opinion on the People. And however ridiculous it may seem, it was actually believed by two thirds of the People in Boston, Untill those of our Township of their own accord exerted 'emselves to bring the matter to light, [and brought] Several Evidences before a Justice of Peace, who swore to meeting the Villains disguised upon the Road and that they enquired the way to Mr H's house, nay, the Evidences went so far as naming particular persons, upon which they were Stop'd and privately threatened that if they proceeded further in Information they should suffer, so there the enquiry ended.

But since People have spoke their opinion more freely, many have declared they believed Mr T— (then a Commissioner) sent them out. He has certainly a heart capable of such an action; as diabolical a one perhaps as ever possessed a human breast. Before the Commission was established he was Surveyor General, and he imagined if he could get rid of the Commissioners, he should be reestablished in that office. And his whole study and business was to harrasse, distress, counteract, and if possible to overturn the Board at which he satt and he almost succeeded. He Stir[re]d up the People to persecute every Member of it, making 'em believe if they drove away the Commissioners, they would get rid of pay[in]g Duties. But since they find these hopes are vain, that T — is discarded by the King, and Sunk in oblivion in London, this Country has been more peaceable and the abuse of the Commissioners in a great measure ceased, not but the seeds of discord and sedition that has been sown, still remains, and there are not wanting persons who are industrious to inflame and stir up the People, encouraged by the Lenity of Government and no doubt the fruit will break forth in some future day. I wish it may not be in ours.

His Majesty's Instructions to his Government are the present Subjects of Contention, and we all in an uproar on a new occasion. You must know that the manner of Laying Taxes by the Province here are arbitrary, and partial, and though they don't allow G: Britain has any right to tax 'em here, they have extorted very exorbitant and oppressive Taxes from the Crown Officers, and the King in order to relieve 'em from this oppression, in His late Instructions [to the Governor] forbids his Assent to the Tax Bill unless the Commissioners are excepted in it from any Tax on the Saleries, as well as the Governor.

If these Instructions had arrived a day later it would have come too late for this year. This affair has made a great noise, but no further consequences. I hope the Storm is almost over, but no Tax Bill passed. We think ourselves happy in a retreat from the Town, where every cross wind or what thwarts their inclinations raises a Storm [and ferment.] The Climate agrees well with us all. We are on as healthy [a spot] as any part of No[rth] America, yet I can't but think O[ld] England a healthy Climate on the whole. The extreams of heat and cold are [severe] here, and the vicissitudes so sudden, now we are melting with heat and anon perhaps the wind may turn Easterly and we may chill with cold. However the excessive heat of Summer continues not Long, little Spring, fine Autumns, and very Long winter Season, most part keen frost, which we think as pleasant weather as any.

It was thought hardly practicable for a Gentleman's Family to live in Winter in the Country here, till my Brother made the attempt, and now it is become the taste to reside in the Country, so that there [are] no Houses to be had. My Brother's is esteemed one of the most desirable places (as I've heard several Gentlemen say) in this part of the Country, from the improvments he has made, merely in convenience and neatness. As to the situation, there's no very extensive prospect from the House, being surrounded with Hills and Woods at a good distance. This makes it more habitable and warm in Winter, but from our Ground near we have fine Views. The House built on a Rock, supplyd with good Water Springs, with a Large Lawn in front, Shrubs and flowers on the borders of it to imitate Nature in its Wildness and variety. We keep two Cows. Hay and Apples the chief produce of the Land. Have made 90 Barrels of Cyder in one Year, and at same time consumed 100 Bushils of Apples in the Family. The Children almost Live upon 'em when ripe. I have attempted to give you an idea of our place and situation[,] as you are pleased to desire, and admitting it may be possessed in peace, in quiet, Mr and Mrs H. would not I believe chuse to exchange it for any other in America.   ³the cheapness of Living, it can only be comparatively so in regard to London, for it is dearer upon the whole than any other part of England, Though Provisions as Flesh, Fish and Fowl, are about the same prices as in Chester Market, yet every other article is dear as in London, particularly Houses, and pine wood, and this is a proof of it that a Single person can't Board and Lodge in Boston under £35 Sterling a year, [nor] could my Brother have a House there for his Family for Less than £50 a year.

We can't boast of such agreable neighbors as you have, both in Town and in country, nor any very near, but those we have are inoffensive to us. The circle of our acquaintances is very large, more than we can well keep up, for it is not afternoon Visits those we seldom go without dineing too. Wednesdays and Saturdays we have always Company at home, seldom less than 10 or 12on Saturdays to dine with us. Kitty, whom I sent to Mrs H., proves a usefull Servant and very good Cook. She has a white Girl and two Negroes under her in the House, besides the Nursery maid and Farmer.

There's a little genteel Town about 4 Miles off called Cambridge, where a number of Gentlemen's Familys live upon their Estates, and there is an Assembly there in the Winter to which my Brother Subscribed. They all seemed pleased at his joyning their Society, everyone endeavoring to make it as agreable to us as possible, about 20 couple[s] generally danced once a fortnight. I went twice or thrice in the Winter.

There are a great many Meeting Houses in the Country as well as the Town, no less than Six within 3 or 4 Mile[s] of us round about, one of 'em a field's length off our house, to which we all go on Sunday when we don't go to Town. There's a new Meeting House built two M[iles off] in which Mr Whitefield preached one of his last Sermons. It was a Kind of consecration Sermon. I heard him that once; he had always a very crouded Audience at Boston whilst he remained here. This Meeting House has never been fixed with a Minister, though many have been on Trial in twelve months past. But at length a Mr. Gordon, from Stepney near

London, comes over to America, with strong recommendation. He receives an Invitation to this Congregation and is so extreamly well[-]liked, that the patron of it, is going to build a House for him and his wife for their Lives.[4] This new Meeting is opposid by its neighbors, who will not permit the Dues p[ai]d by its members to be taken from the other Meetings tow[ar]ds Supporting this; that is, to make it a distinct Congregation by Authority.

Upon which the Patron is so disgusted that he threatens to make it an Episcopal Church, if Mr Gordon will conform and go to England to recieve Orders. We went the other Sunday to hear this Gentleman. My Brother was much pleased with his Sermon and delivery; but it seems surprizing to us that so good a Preacher should quit a Place in England for America, where here's not so much want of Ministers. Perhaps you may know this Mr G. makes Me mention him. You see I write you all the news I can, though I must own none very interesting to you in peaceable times here. I took a large Sheet.

Winter Cards were sent to 40 or 50 persons in this form: A Party of Ladies and Gentlemen intending to dine at such a place on—desire the pleasure of Mr. and Mrs. — Company. Mr. and Mrs H., declining the invitation, as well as many others, are excused afterwards from sharing in these parties, which they are very glad of, and think themselves on the best terms with them all that is, that of civility and respect, visiting now and then. Indeed, for sometime after we left the Town Mrs H. did not visit Mrs B[urch,] but several persons spoke to her, saying that Mrs B. was under great concern that any distance or shyness should be between em. Mrs H. — fd, She would visit Mrs B., but She would not meet Mrs S. there. If She did, would instantly leave the House. Accordingly She went, and who should come driving in immediately to her but Mrs S. Mrs. H. got up, saying as She had other company, She would take her leave at present, and went away ere the other—to account for this breach of politeness would be too tedious to describe the Lady and all her behaviour, but she's the most singular Character I ever met with—such a mixture of the Agreeable and the Audacious, and her conduct was unaccountable till she no longer kept up appearances. Her Husband a good natured, insignificant besotted Man, he entertained his Ladies in one Part of a great House, and She her Gentlemen at the other.

I took a large Sheet, thinking it would contain all I have to say, but have exceeded its limits. Mr. and Mrs. Hulton went a Circuit of 300 Miles (to see some of the Country) at Whitsuntide.[5] I had a Journey of 260 Miles.

It is only the Vast and extensive in its Original State that engages the Curiosity of the Traveller here, and to be sure We see a great variety of Noble Prospects at the cost of much fatigue bad roads and hard fare. As to the Elegancys of Life, the improvements of Art, or fine cultivated fields of Grain, Nobody needs expect to see these in greater perfection or are they to be expected at all in the Wilds of America. All the Luxury and Elegance that is in this Province is confined to Boston, and twenty Miles round. If you travel further, it is necessary to carry your Provisions with you.

Here we follow the fashions in England and have made great strides in Luxury and Expence within these three years, Especialy in that of Dress and the young Ladies seem as smart as those we left in England. The only publick Entertainment and amusements are in an Assembly in the Winter in Boston, and Feasting and Partys going out into the Country[,] having a Dinner and a Dance, this is very Common and often not returning home till day break, but we have avoided 'em; however, we are going today on a small Fishing Party. We are entirely seperated from Mr. Burch's family since a West India Family came over, a Mr Sobers, for you must know their taste and way of Life proved upon further acquaintance quite different to ours, dis[s]ipation and pleasure, indulgence and Luxury, being the business of their Lives and every day devoted to it. Mrs. Sober suited em exactly, till her Conduct became notorious and her house avoided by all Ladies of Character, and they (Mr. and Mrs. S.) were forced to leave this Country for Barbadoes, where their Estate is. But before this arrives Commodore Gambia[6] and his Lady. She [is] young, genteel, and Lively, joins or leads the gay circle with great Vivacity (consisting of 4 or 5 Ladies and some Officers of the Army and Navy), but Mrs. G[ambier] could not bear Mrs S. and the tone being given against her, Mrs B. would have dropped her if they could, when they could not keep her up. The first Party of Pleasure after Mrs G. arrived was in the depth of Winter.

My Brother, though in the publick Office that he is, is Obliged to see and entertain a deal of Company, as well as to shew Civilities where he receives 'em, yet his recourses for pleasure is in the enjoyment of a few friends and in retired and Domestick Life. And his two fine Boys contribute not a little to it, being a constant fund of entertainment. Besides that, he anis he has too much business on his hands to allow time for Frolicks. He is, I am confident, the only Man of business in the Commission it to be observed that whatever dissentions there is between the Ladies, it does not reach to the Gentlemen at their Board. I have given you a long history publick and private. And trust you will reckon this two or three Letters, and read it accordingly at different times, that you may not be quite tired and wish me not to write again; depend on it, never so much at once. It will always give me pleasure to hear of Yours and Your happiness, and I hope you and Mr L. will enjoy it long with your Children in your new House, since Your former neighbours are removed and You have those near that are agreeable to you. I hope it was not want of health that occasioned Mr N[icholson?] to go live at the Park, that's but a Step. Hope theirs and Mr. C[ropper?] Family are all well. I wish to be remembered with Kind regards to all friends.

      Yours   A H.

---

1   *Loyalist Lady*, 38-47. The editors did not venture a guess as to when this letter was written, but it appears to have been soon after the July 1771 confrontation between Hutchinson and the House over taxing the commissioners' salaries, and well before the birth of the Hultons' third son, Edward, the following October.

2   This and other bracketed insertions were made by the editors; likewise for the blank space later in the letter.

3   Left blank by the editors.

4   This personal tie may explain why Hulton was a subscriber to Gordon's *History* (see 86 n. 206 supra).

5   The week of the Pentecost, beginning on Whitsunday, the seventh Sunday after Easter.

6   Gambier.

[Henry Hulton to Jacob Preston, Esqr.] 31 *August 1771*[1]

I had the pleasure to receive your kind letter of the 15th October from Sienna in March last, and have waited writing to you till I might expect a letter would meet you in London where I hope this will find you, safely returned, pleased with your tour, yet satisfyed to sit down in Old England, and be happy in the society of your old friends again; and I flatter myself it will be some addition to the pleasure you will receive in seeing them to hear of the health, and welfare of your friends that are most remote from you. I Bless God my family have been and are all well and enjoy every blessing this place can afford. You have been in the World of politeness, and pleasure; you have ranged through the great, the gay, the grand, and magnificent. May you have treasured up the useful, and ornamental, so as to be able to pass retirement agreeably or to appear in public with advantage and respect. I am persuaded from the sentiments of your heart and the improvements you have made, that you will appear with reputation in life; but that which in a great measure will constitute the happiness of it, is yet to be tried, and I trust your good judgment, and good stars, will direct you right.

We have been quiet in our own habitation since our return from the Castle, in November last. Though remote from my County and friends, and retired from the World, I have still enjoyed Domestic Comforts, and found resources within myself and the little circle about me: my Wife, my Children, my Books, and my farm. He that never looked through a Microscope is a stranger to a World of Entertainment; so is he who neglects the little pleasures at home, that are within his reach. They may appear trifling at first, and by many are overlooked; but cultivated, you find the fund increase. They solace in every hour and afford comfort under every disquietude from without. My little prat[t]lers are become very agreeable companions; they make our rural abode chearful to us. Tom is an amiable Child, quite mild, tender, and affectionate. Harry is a curled[-]pated, stout, and bold, black eyed rogue—talks almost as well as Tom, repeats what he says, and does what he does. They seem to have both fine constitutions, are in brave health, and the house is never free from noise. The Business of the Board calls me often to town, and when at home, I find full employment with my family, and farm.

In the month of May your Sister and I made a journey through some part of this Province and Connecticut. An Account of our tour must be the very reverse of what I expect to hear of yours. You have seen the World in its polished, we, in its rude State. You have gone over the Boasted remains of Antiquity, and observed the Conscious pride of those who demand respect from the lustre of their descent, and glory in what they have been. We have seen the face of nature as it was left at the flood; uncleared, and uncultivated and mankind in a state of equality. But though we cannot glory in heroic actions or claim the honours of an illustrious Ancestry, yet do not think that we are without an imaginary superiority, that we do not pride ourselves in the possession of advantages over others. Happy delusion!

Where are the people, or where is the mortal, that has not a little fund of this self-flattery? That cannot place himself in some point of view, where he can look down upon others? This gratification to pride is a most comfortable cordial, and makes the wretched support many evils—but what, say you, is your boast? Why, we boast a glorious Independency. We look on the rest of the World as Slaves, and despise titles, and honour. And as we cannot glory in what we have been, we pride ourselves in what we shall be. The little Island of Great Britain is a small inconsiderable spot; We shall be the Empire of the World, and give Law to the nations.

---

1   Hulton, "Letterbooks," 1:38-41. Hulton scratched out Preston's name, leaving only the "Esqr."

[Henry Hulton to Robert Nicholson]   *Boston 5 November 1771*[1]

Dear Sir

I received your kind favour of the 25 of July and the 1st of September.

Mrs H. has lately lain in of another Boy, that is to be christened Edward, so that I have a growing family of Americans. We are very happy in our domestic life and become every year more attached to our rural habitation.

My farm this year will turn out very well. I make 70 barrels of Cyder, and besides a large crop of hay, I have great plenty of fruit, and garden stuff for the Winter. And I expect the value of my produce to pay the interest of my money, and the expence of a farmer, gardener, and labourer, and I get the benefit of a great deal of health and amusement into the bargain.

I could not conceive a domestic situation in this Country wherein I could be happier than I am at present. We are indeed out of the World of business, of politics, and pleasure, but we have a World of happiness within ourselves. I have seen enough and wish rather to be ignorant of, than know more of mankind. We are upon civil terms with all we would be desirous to be acquainted with. I endeavour neither to flatter or offend; it is not the genius of this people to offer much of the former (to any servant of government at least) and I do not find a disposition in them at present to shew much of the latter, and separate from my office. I do not believe I have any personal enemies. I meet with nothing to mortify me in my intercourse abroad, and feel no wants that I have it not in my power to gratify, so that if our bounds of enjoyment are narrow, yet the absence of higher luxuries of the refined amusements and pleasures of life is fully compensated by the ease and tranquility of mind one enjoys in this sober retirement.

I congratulate you on the encrease of your family, Mrs H. and my sister desire to join in presenting their best compliments to yourself and Mrs N., and I remain with great regard, Dear Sir, &c.

---

1   Hulton, "Nicholson Letters," 59-61.

[Ann Hulton to Elizabeth Lightbody] *Boston 20 March 1772*[1]

I take the opportunity of a Ship bound immediately for Liverpool to acknowledge the receipt of Dear Mrs. Lightbody's agreable favor, of 30th November and the Packet, (which never Comes in less than three months) And to assure her that it gives me sincere pleasure, to hear of her and her Familys welfare, and of your enjoying pleasure in little rambles abroad. Here we reckon a few hundred Miles but a little way, where everything in Nature is upon a large Scale.

I am obliged to you for your intelligence in regard to persons and affairs in or about Liverpool.

Poor Ned. Hinck's case gives me great concern. I heard of it from my Aunt, and wrote to her in January. Am afraid by yours, there was but little hopes of his recovery. It must prove indeed a severe Trial, if she should Lose so good a son. J[ohn] H[incks] is well, we see him here, pretty often. I doubt he does not yield that comfort to his Mother that he might do, in writing more frequent.

I don't know that he is concerned in any business at present, besides that of his office under the Commissioners of the Customs. It is the best place in their Gift, that may not be superceded by the Treasury. Yet there are some infelicities attending it, to serve a number of Masters, who are not all disposed, as my Brother is, to make those under them happy. He receives £80 a year Salary and £20 a year from my Brother[,] which makes it £100 Sterling. This seems a pretty income for a young Man, Yet it would not do for one to settle upon in this Country, and I doubt not He would gladly remove from Boston, if anything offered else where more for his advantage. I have heard my Brother often say, that when he put him into this office, it was not that he thought it an advantageous Establishment for him; his only motive was to remove him from the dangerous situation he was in, in London, without employment, and that he thought something certain for him would be better than pursuing uncertain schemes.

You have heard perhaps of another American being born in our family, a Edward Hulton, he is now five months old, a fine lively boy, but all my three Nephews are ill at this time of the [w]hooping Cough.

A melancholy affair has happened lately here, which affects us much, and thrown several Families we are acquainted with into deep distress — Mr. and Mrs. John Apthrop [Apthorp], who lived in our Neighborhood, at Cambridge, having a handsome independent fortune, lived in a very genteel way, and made the greatest figure of any Gentleman in the Provence (he had lived some time in England and in Italy) but set down at last in his own Country, where he married his second wife, a very handsome and amiable yong lady; had two Girls by her. He seemed to have everything this world could give, excepting a Son. This was his ardent wish, which Heaven granted about 12 Months ago. (Governor Hutchinson and my Brother were Sponsors.) Something still was wanting for happiness. Mr A., to vary the Scene, and escape a Winter, resolved to vissit the Southern Provences. Mrs A., an obliging wife, attends him, though as a tender Mother, she quits her dear little family with the greatest reluctance. They both took leave of us in October last and about the middle of November they embarked from New York for North Carolina, which is a few days passage. But alas! They have never been heard of since, though it's four months ago. We have hoped the Vessil might have been drove to some of the West India Islands, but by this time, there's too much reason to fear that the vessil was lost at Sea. Violent Storms arose a few days after it sailed. Mrs. A.'s father and mother are in the utmost Affliction, three Infants are left without a Parent, and many aggravating circumstances besides.

I fancy the Spring is opening upon you in Old England, whilst we are surrounded with a deep Snow and freezing with severe cold. A long and sharp winter we shall have, and perhaps, towards May or June suddenly emmerge from the depth of it, into the height of Summer, without the pleasure of a Spring, or but a short one. Yet here are pleasures which even this frozen state and sequestered Situation affords, for there are but few days but what we might make excursions in Sleighs (carriages without wheels that travel extreanly quick, 10 or 12 Miles an hour). While nature Smiles in a bright Sky, and a white world around us, we don't in the least envy the inhabitants of the Town, finding here no want of Society as you may think, when Mrs. H. had near 50 Lades from Boston &c. to vissit her in her Lying in. We are farmers without expecting to reap any proffit, besides that of health and pleasure. I believe it's very conducive to my Brothers's Health, being obliged to ride to own frequently, and the relaxation and amusement which his little Farm affords. He has made great improvements, and built barns, Stables, and many conveniences, amongst the rest a Green house, in order to preserve Vegetables in the Winter, and raise early plants so that we may be supplied all the year round. Though this appears quite a necessary, and is general[1]y approved as a great convenience, yet it's what has not been done before in this Province. I have studied Gardening here, and by my observation, and experience, have acquired a little Skill, so that I am Director General of the Vegatible Tribe. Though our farmer is a good common Gardener, yet many things we require, which are not used to be raised here. We put in the green house last fall 500 heads of the finest Celery that ever was seen here, I mean for the table; as to fine Gardens, there's no such thing attempted by any Gentleman, for besides the Severe Frosts destroying everything, Labour hire is so dear, it would require a Nabob's fortune to keep fine Gardens in taste. But I have been told that it's only of late years that Greens or Cabbages have been raised in this Country at all, or in any plenty. All Greens and roots are called by the name of Sause here. As to fruits, Apricots and Necterans are rarities indeed, but Peaches, Strawberries, and Gooseberrries grow wild. Yet these, compared with those cultivated in gardens in Old England, are in Size as crabs to Apples, and of little value. We have these in Garden cultivated, besides, curannce and rasberries, but all scarse with us, the Birds devouring 'em when ripe.

My Brother has planted some hundreds of Fruit Trees of all sorts, so that we hope to have plenty. His Land, his 30 Acres, every field an Orchard, reckoned the greatest Apple Farm and the finest fruit in this Provence. We have plenty of standing Peach Trees, improved by Pruning. English wheat does not succeed here, but Hay and Pasture land with Indian Corn and Apples.

There's a great enemy to the Fruit, a kind of Worm that rises out of the Ground into the Trees as soon as the Frost breaks, destroys the Apples ere they Bud, and all the Leaves, so that all the Trees round us, appears with a most dreary aspect in Summer. There's only one remedy to prevent this Evil, found out, that is, Taring all the Trees for about 3 months every Evening after sunsett. This is a great piece of work for our Farmer, for if one evening be missed, it renders all ineffectual, and even the practice destroys the Trees in time, to guard against which, a girdle of cloth is bound round each Tree. By this means my Brother has preserved his Fruit, whilst many of our Neighbors, who would not be at the trouble and expense, have all been destroyed, and unless the practice be universal, these Vermin, which are a growing Evil, can't be extirpated. And this makes both good Cyder and apples very rare here at this time of Year, and the Latter very acceptable to our friends at Boston and round us, not withstanding the plenty of Apples Trees in this Country.

It's not so very cheap Living in this Country as some imagine. Though provisions are plenty, yet they grow dearer, I believe, all over the world, as it's what the Inhabitants here complain of. Some think the Navy and Army has helped to raise the price of things. However, I believe the People are so civil to us Strangers, or new comers, to make us pay more handsomely for everything than they do their own people. Fish is the cheapest thing for which he must Send to Boston. Butcher's meat passes our Door; we pay for mutton and veal 3d and 3½d Sterling a pound. Beef something Less. Pork more. Fresh butter is not to be procured in Winter, but we get fine Tub Butter at 6½ Sterling a pound.

Our wild fowl are cheifly Quails, Partridges, Pigeons and Robins — woodcocks and Snips are great variety. We never saw any Larks here; plenty of Tame Fowl in Season. Fat ducks we pay a shilling a piece for, and 6d or 7d for chickens. We have rabbits and Hares, but very different from what they are in England. What they call hares are more like Rabbits, small and white as Snow, and unsavory meat, near as white as rabbits.

Squrrils are eat here — After all, it's not the price, but the Quantities of provision, the great Feasts and increasing Luxury, that is expensive to House Keepers. Your Cooks and confectioners are imported from London, and there are few families when the[y] make a Dinner but hires professed Cooks. (These are what we have never had in our house.)

Besides there are several essential articles extreamly Dear. The price of firewood at this time is 2d Sterling a square foot each way, so that I am surprised any who pinches with cold and poverty don't run away to a warmer climate, but in the Southern Provences provisions are dearer.

Upon the whole it's very easy for a Family to expend 4 or 500 a year. Mr. J[ohn] A[pthorp] did not spend less than £1000 a year, cheifly in entertaining elegantly.

We in this retreat are never better satisfied [than] with plain Roast and boiled, yet we must keep up [some] Society with those who shew us civilities. At this time we are seperated from all the world by a [deep snow], and thankfull we are provided against this Siege [by] Store of Salt Provisions. We kill two hogs and [cure] 16 Hames besides upon Winter — are twelve in [family].

Finding myself obliged to put the first sheet under cover, am not so genteel to send it blank, but have [filled] it with Triffles, which occurs to my thoughts. I should be glad you would be so obliging to order for me 4 pair Pumps, and 4 pair Shoes, of good black Everlasting from Mr. Garnet. I shall advise again which way to send 'em, perhaps towards Autumn. Only desire he will please to get 'em ready.

The Gay party I mentioned in my last were broke up when Commodore Gambia[2] went. Admiral Montague and his Lady are more sedate rational folks go to Bed at 10 o'Clock. She [is a w]oman of strong S[ense], a gracefull person, and great Address, takes care of the education of her Children, and instructed her Sons in Latin, as I heard her say.

I proposed writing to Chester by this conveyance, but doubt if this will come in time, or whether [the ship] can sail this weather. My Brother and Sister [joyn] in respects to [Mr. And] Mrs. L. and Miss L. with

Dear Madam, your Affectionate
      A Hulton

---

1   *Loyalist Lady*, 31-38, where it is dated 1771 rather than 1772. Either Ann Hulton or the editors erred. The mention of Edward Hulton's birth five months previous—which occurred in October 1771—is one proof. Another is the mention of Henry Hulton as "sponsor" for the baptism of John Trecothick Apthorp, and that took place on 23 January 1771, as recorded in Franklin Bowditch Dexter, ed., *The Literary Diary of Ezra Stiles*, 3 vols. (New York: Charles Scribner's Sons, 1901), 1:85. Ann notes that that event took place roughly a year before the Apthorps drowned at sea, the "melancholy affair" she alluded to in this letter. Burch too had been a "sponsor."

2   Gambier.

[Henry Hulton to unknown correspondent]   *21 April 1772*[1]

I did not receive your favour of the 29th June till about four months after, and am much obliged to you for your kind remembrance and correspondence.

I observe it is the general notion at home, seeing that we are at present quiet, that we are returned to a sense of our duty as peaceable, loyal and obedient. Whereas the principle of denying the authority of Parliament is as fixed as ever, and the quiet that is, is purchased either by making concessions or not enforcing the Laws.

The conduct of Britain with regard to her Colonies seems to have been directed entirely on commercial principles. The Question has been, how shall we extend our commerce, not how shall we support our authority? And the restrictions that have been adopted, have been Ministerial, not national ones. This Minister has had one plan, the next another. No general Parliamentary and national conduct has been fixed on, to be abided by; so that Government has by a change of measures been let down, and the respect to its authority has been very much lessened.

The Constitutional Government of several of these Colonies is already independant of the Sovereign. Maryland does not know the King. His name is not used in their courts; it is my Lord Proprietor. Pensilvania is a proprietary Government. Connecticut and Rhode Island chuse their own Governours. And the Counsel of Massachusetts Bay, who are to advise the Governour in cases where the King's honour and service is concerned, are chosen by the people, whose spirit is to resist his authority. What can be expected, or rather what may not be prognosticated from such constitutions of Government, in a Country situated so remote from G. Britain, where the people increase amazingly, and may settle on fresh Lands, without end?

The authority of Government should be well established, before it is proposed to raise a Revenue from any people. Would the powers of the Crown have been thought sufficient for this purpose, in Colonies so constituted as those above mentioned, supposing they were near to the seat of Empire? Would the Stamp Act have gone down in Yorkshire, or Scotland, supposing them under the constitution of Maryland or Connecticut? How much less in places so remote?

The late Mr. Charles Townshend[2] once sent for me, and told me they proposed to lay some fresh duties on American Imports and desired me to suggest to him what Goods imported from Great Britain it might be best to lay a duty on. It struck me as an improper thing to burthen our own exports to our Colonies with duties. I answered, "it may be best, Sir, before you lay any new duties to see those well[-]collected that are already laid."

He then said, they intended to appoint a Board of Commissioners, and more Officers in America. I answered, "it may be best, Sir, to see that the Officers already there, are protected in doing their duty." After this I was no more sent for, and though my name was put the first in the Commission, I never solicited the appointment, nor was I ever spoke to by the first Lord, or Chancellor of the Exchequer on the matter.[3]

For myself, I have continued to live quietly at my Farm for these eighteen months past, and we carry on the business of the Board at Boston in the best manner we can; but smug[g]ling prevails to a great degree in most parts of America. I have now three Boys, and from any thing I can yet see it is probable that I, and my family after me, will remain in these parts. I see little prospect of compensation for all my extra Service and sufferings, but I rather think that my conduct heretofore was a bar to my advancement. I made many Enemies in Germany, by my labouring for the public; and we have had no small combat in this country to establish ourselves, which has drawn on us the resentment of many people. And at this remote distance we may be misrepresented, and injured, without knowing it. However, I have through the whole acted upon the same principles, and I am not disheartened, or sink in the least. I have the consolation of having done my duty; of having stood against many storms, to the loss of friends, and to preventing the advancement of my own fortune.

I am not solicitous about my return to England. I find myself happy with my family here, and I am only concerned for my children's education, and their Establishment. I do not think I should feel myself happy in England; that country is only fit for people of large fortune to live in, or for those who are in the way of acquiring one. My principles were a bar to my fortune. But though in this I can rejoice, yet the thought of submitting to neglect, when one is conscious of having deserved well of one's country, is too mortifying, and I do not intend putting it to the risk. We may be here rudely treated by the Mob, but we know nothing of the high looks of the proud. We have had a long and severe Winter, and from the begin[n]ing of March, to the middle of April, hardly any body from Boston could get to us, the Roads being full of snow. But though retired from the World of business, and pleasure, we have not been without employment, and pleasing amusements; the time has never been tedious, or our situation irksome. Indeed, I have never found time to do half the business I proposed. The Board, and the Farm, Books, and letter writing, company, and my children; all require some time, and I never find any of it on my hands. The spring now opens upon us, and we shall have a deal of agreeable occupation in the Garden, and field. I long, &c.

My Sister is the chief director about the Garden, and we raise sufficient for our Winter store, being obliged in our situation, and in this climate, to lay up a good deal of necessaries in the fall, and I make from my farm about seventy barrels of Cyder.

I shall be glad to hear of your success in the scheme for a Canal. I think it must prove of great benefit to the City. It seems to me that the natural advantages in the neighbourhood of Chester have not been attended to. No part would be better for a manufacturing Coun-try, than from Flint to Chester: a navigable River, plenty of Coal, cheapness of provision, vicinity of Ireland, for the raw materials of Wool, Yarn, Hides, Skins, &c.

Chester itself has a very fine situation, the best walks, market, and Society. In short, [it] is the most agreeable place for a Gentleman to put on his night cap in, of any I have seen. But it is not for young and active people to settle there.

Poor Williamson. Your letter is the only Account I have had of his death. I should be much obliged to you to write me particularly as to persons and things with you. You cannot make your letter too long. There are two young Gentlemen from Chester here, who now and then do us the favor to come over. Ensign H., a son of Admiral H., and W Griffith, a Midshipman on board the *Captain*, son of Mr. Ralph G.

---

1   Hulton, "Letterbooks," 1:42-48.
2   He died in September 1767, apparently of typhus, just as the uproar caused by his program was beginning to grow.
3   Meaning the Duke of Grafton (first lord of the Treasury) and Charles Townshend (chancellor of the exchequer).

[Henry Hulton to Mr. de Ruling] *May 1772*[1]

Mr. de Ruling at Hohenthurm
Proche de Halle, Saxe

I had the pleasure to receive your favour of the 14th July and I hope you received a letter from me which I had the honour of writing in August last.

I am concerned at the disappointment you met with in the management of your Estate, and for the distresses of the people from the scarcity of Provision. The people in this Country, I believe, are more at their ease than the peasantry in any other. They are proprietors of the soil they cultivate; they know no subjection to great Lords, and enjoy the benefits of protection from a Government whose authority they are always disputing. Independency was the principle the first settlers set out upon, when they quitted England, to cultivate the wilds of America: and the same spirit is continued in their descendants. And from the immense country that remains to be cleared, and settled, and the mildness of the British Government, it is probable they will be several ages before they are brought into that state of order, and subordination, that prevails in European nations.

We have continued in quiet in our habitations for a considerable time past, and I enjoy much satisfaction with my family in my rural retirement, taking great pleasure in the occupation of the farm: planting trees, and shrubs, clearing and improving my little Estate.

I have now three stout boys, who give us great delight. The first seven or ten years after marriage is certainly the happiest in life; a Man is then fixed, his concern about his Establishment is over. A circle of little domestic comforts take place of roving desires, and the calm pleasures of his family, the affection of his Wife and the innocent of his children, give him peace and satisfaction, which he in vain sought in crowds, in the eye of admiration, and the pleasures of novelty. After a while come the cares of the family; attention to the education, and providing for the Establishment of the Children, and anxiety as to their conduct.

This is but an indifferent part of the world either for the Education, or Establishment of children; and by many years residence in this country, one becomes lost to one's friends, one's Interest, and connections at home. However, we must accommodate ourselves to circumstances, be satisfied with doing our duty, and leave the event to providence; not repining at the loss of some comforts, nor being greatly anxious for the future.

---

1   Hulton, "Letterbooks," 1:49 51.

[Ann Hulton to Elizabeth Lightbody] *c August 1772*[1]

In my last Letter I desired to favor of you to bespeak for me of my Shoemaker Mr. Garnet, 8 pair of Black Everlasting Pumps and Shoes, and could wish to have added to them a pair of Black Silk Shoes, if you can get any Strong[-]figured or Spotted black Silks (black Satten is not servisable). If a remnant and not very dear, I should have no Objection to two pair.

Let the Shoemaker pay for it, and charge it in his Bill, which I shall desire Cousin Sukey Hincks to send Cash to you for payment of — There is another commission which I am desired to beg the favor of you. That is a small Crate of Staffordshire ware, if to be bought at Liverpool. I sent a Crate of the Yellow ware from thence which cost about £3 to my Brother and they are now almost demolished. My Sister liked them much and desires to have another Crate, if I could trouble you to buy 'em. But she Says if there's any new fashion or invention of Mr. Wedgwood of this kind of ware, that is approved. Should prefer it to the Yellow over again, but chuses the usefull and neat, rather than Ornamental, as they are for common Servise; therefore nothing Gilt, and no matter how few Tureens.[2] One is sufficient, as we have several China ones, but if they can't be had without two Tureens, it can't be helped. Chuse Sause boats rather without Spoons, as these break. But drinking cups, Jugs and[3] we could dispense with a good many in the Crate, along with the Dishes plates, &c.

Now, as to sending these things to Boston, we must wait till a Liverpool Vessil comes here, but would desire they may be sent by the first Opportunity. I doubt it's hardly to be expected this side of Xmas. For the payment of what you Lay out on this account you will likewise call on Cousin S. H. I shall mention it to her. The Shoes may be sent in a Box, each pair (tell the Shoemaker) to be lapd well in paper. I forgot to mention a pair of Cork Golo-shoes. Should wish to have a pair. Please tell him to make 'em Long enough, and the Top Leather all in a piece, and let him paste some white Sheep's Leather within the bottom of the Shoes, for they are general[l]y too wide in the Winter, though the[y] may fitt in the Summer. I used to pay him 4/6 a pair,[4] but the last he charged somthing more; perhaps it was for Carrege. I can buy here as cheap as them, but not to fit so well.

This I expect to go by an extraordinary conveyance indeed, that is by a Ship belonging to Chester.

Mr. and Mrs. Hulton desire to joyn me in respectfull Compliments to you and Mr. L: They are intending themselves a Little Tour soon of about a Thousand Miles, and will be at Least two or three Months away. I am to be left with [the] care of my three Nephews, fine hearty Boys. The Measles are at every House almost in Boston, and about us.

My Brother, who has been continualy making Improvements in his Habitation, has this Summer built a Kitchen, [a] Room over it, and a Dairy. Whilst this was doing, Our House was broke open one Night, and most of our Plate carried off, and I doubt we shall never find it again.

We have never heard anything of poor Mr. and Mrs. Apthrop [Apthorp], who I mentioned in my last as Lost in their passage from New York. Their friends are all gone into Mourning.

I have just received a letter from London, [which] gives me the pleasure to hear Mrs. Ashton was got quite well, and that your Sister was well at Mr. Collys. I am sorry, alas, for their Loss in Young Mr. Colly; it must be a severe stroke.

There are two great inconveniences for Families [in this] Country, the want of good Servants, no one [will c]all another Master. It's owing partly to there   is, no distinctions, scarsly in the So[ciety], another is the want of good Schools for Education. Here is a Colledge indeed, but the Independancy and Liberty with which the Youths are brought up, and indulged, makes too many of 'em proficients in Vice. So that my Brother would not trust a Son of his [there] on any account, and I believe, therefore, my little Nephews would be sent to England for Education. But here's lately a worthy Clergyman proposes to begin a private academy upon a new Plan, and to take a few Boys, of which numbr my nephew Tom is to be [one a] year or two hen[ce. A]t present, he is my Pupil. It will be 20 Miles off us where[5]

We was lately by invitation at a publick Dinner given at Cambridge, on one of the Youths taking his degrees, at which there was four hundred Ladies and Gentlemen Set[t dow]n at one Table [out] of Doors, under a Cover made on purpose. It was a genteel Entertainment and a pretty Scene.

I am Dear Mrs. Lightbody's Affectionate A. Hulton.

---

1   *Loyalist Lady*, 47-50, the editors noting (on 47n): "This letter is undated except in the penciled script of some former owner of the MS. The date is obviously correct." Probably so; Ann wrote that Henry and Elizabeth's planned trip to Canada would be "soon." They left on August 26th.

2   Elizabeth Hulton's interest in stylish dinnerware (see too Ann Hulton's letter to Elizabeth Lightbody of 21 November 1772, at 274-275 infra) nicely illustrates themes explored in Neil McKendrick, "Josiah Wedgwood and the Commercialization of Potteries," in McKendrick, John Brewer, and J. H. Plumb, eds., *The Birth of a Consumer Society* (London: Europa Publications, 1982), 100-145. For the impact of a growing consumer community on the American revolutionary movement see T. H. Breen, *The Marketplace of Revolution* (Oxford: Oxford University Press, 2004).

3   Left blank by the editors.

4   four shillings, six pence.

5   Left blank by the editors; likewise for other parts of the paragraph.

[Ann Hulton to Elizabeth Lightbody]   *Boston 25 August 1772*[1]

I have dear Mrs. Lightbody's kind favor of 12 March. I esteem it more so, as you did not wait for my acknowledgment of your former one, of November, though I wrote immediately on the receipt of it; I think it was in March.

The Disorder which attacked you was very alarming, yet I can imagine you composed and resigned under it, but not so your friends. They no doubt were full of anxiety and distress on your account, as your friend in America would have been had she been present.

I hope all danger of any return of those symptoms was over when you wrote, and that you have recovered Your health and strength, though probably it may be long before, after being weakened so much.

Here is a Gentleman who had a violent spitting of blood, at times, for three Years, which reduced him to such a weak and emaciated State, that he was not able to walk, and his Life was despaired of. Yet he is now in a good State of health, though very thin. It was 18 years before he perfectly regained his health. I asked him lately, what Means he found benifit by, He said that giving over all business and care, he quited the Town, the Country Air, riding a great deal in it, Dieting partly on Milk, was the method he used and which he found conducive to his Recovery and health. This Gentleman is a Scotchman, his name, Logan.

I mention him particularly as he is a very worthy character, and a great friend of my Brother's. He says his equal is not to be met with in this Country, or scarsly in any for Assiduity, faithfulness and fortitude in Serving his friends, and in times of the greatest danger and distress. And that from his understanding Skill, probity, and diligence He would be a valuable treasure to any great Man of Fortune, that could afford to allow him 3 or £400 a year—as a Steward to Manage his affairs. He is my Brother's right hand in regard to his advice about his Farm, being one of the best farmers in this Country, and he often tells him that he owes his agreable place of abode to him — for he purchased this House and Land for my Brother in his own name; at the time nobody would Lett or Sell to a Commissioner. We can't but think it fortunate that what was purchased from necessity, almost without knowing anything more than that it was a place to put his family in, should prove one of the most desirable places in this Provence, as it seems to be by what everybody we see here tells us.

This Worthy Man (as I have mentioned him I must tell you his story), Mr L., has been, alas! very unfortunate. He possessed a pretty fortune, which he employed in Trade as a Merchant in Boston, in Partnership with another person who injured him notoriously. He went off with all Mr L.'s effects, and he after a fruitless pursuit of him for about twelve Months, from one West India Island to another, is obliged to Sit down with his wife and family in a Cottage, or small house, two or three Miles of us, on a little place in the Customs of £50 a year, which he since obtained. This is but penury here. He is expecting Sir Francis Bernard will procure something better for him, and justly so, if it be in his power, from his unwearied attention to his interest and services rendered him in his absense, for which he will not receive any gratuity, otherwise than as a Gentleman. But there's no other channel scarsely to perferment than through Members of Parliament who can serve the Minister. A Life of Servises and Sufferings, even in the cause of Government, without this will avail nothing. But what is more discouraging to faithfull Servants of the Crown than to see the Vilest Characters and its greatest Enemies countenanced and advanced?

I am greatly concerned for A[un]t H[incks]'s Affliction in the Loss of her Son; did not hear of it till five Months after, from Miss Tylston. Letters are so long in coming by the Packet. J[ohn] H[incks] seemed much affected at first on hearing it. There's little prospect of his getting anything better than the place he has under this Board.

I suppose you are now fixed in an agreable House of your own, May you Long enjoy it with your family in Comfort. I doubt [not?] the things I left in your house would be in your way and give you some trouble. I should pay the Porterage of 'em.

The disagreable affairs to which they belong, and which has occasioned me so much trouble are never finished yet. I have never received anything from the West Indies, where there's about £1000 lying in debts. The Gentleman to whom I sent the Power to recover 'em is now in London, and has promised to write we soon about them, and as soon as I hear from him shall write Mr. Earle on the subject.

Whatever money I received for the Estate &c. I put into the Bank Stock, agreable to Mr Earle's advice, and there it still lies, till the affair can be adjusted between Mr. J[ames] G[ildart] and the other Creditors, which I found beyond my power to do.

---

1   *Loyalist Lady*, 50-53.

[Henry Hulton to Jacob Preston] *28 October 1772*[1]

On my return last week from Quebec, I had the pleasure to meet your letter of the 4th of August; the contents giving us great joy, and we are impatient to hear of your happiness being compleated.

I am so much hurried with publick and private business on my return that I can only write a few lines by Mr. Reeves, who intended to sail tomorrow.

We had an agreeable tour on the whole, and traversed many Woods, and mountains, unpassed by coach or chaise before. We crossed the Lakes George, Champlain, and went down the river St. Lawrence from Montreal to Quebec. We returned to Montreal by Land, and from thence to Quebec. [Canada] is a fine well settled Country; the soil luxuriant, but the people very lazy and dirty, yet very chearful, and happy. We were out 54 days, in which time by land and water we travelled 1380 miles and returned in good health, and spirits, and found all our family very well. This journey, you must know, is looked on as a great affair, and your sister is considered as a most heroic Woman, to have made such a tour, and I assure you she behaved heroically, and never was daunted or lost her spirits, under any difficulty. And we were sometimes in circumstances that put our fortitude to the tryal.

We were in an open Batteau on Lake Champlain, with a corporal and four soldiers. The second day at noon it blew a storm. There was no house or shed within 40 or 50 miles of us. All around us rocks! mountains! untrod, inhospitable Woods! The sky settled black, threatening a deluge of rain. We put ashore, made fires, raised a frame, threw the sail over it, laid our bed on some logs, eat a hearty dinner of cold beef, and slept comfortably the night. The three following nights we passed in wretched log houses, and were five nights without taking our clothes off, yet neither of us got cold, or were fatigued with the Voyage. We crossed Lake George likewise in an open Batteau. It blew hard, and rained all the time; but the wind was fair, and we thought it a fine passage in six and [a] half hours.

Such journeying by Land you cannot conceive, as some part of our travels were such Woods, such rocks, and mountains, with such trees fallen, and falling, hanging over one's head so tremendous, as made one forget the difficulties of the road beneath. However, chaise and horses held out wonderfully, and all the country were amazed at seeing our Carriage, crying such a one never was that road before and asked what we called it, what we were laden with? We had our own liquors, and our Coachman is a tolerable Cook, or we should have been miserably off.

---

1   Hulton, "Letterbooks," 1:52-54.

[Henry Hulton to Robert Nicholson]   *Boston   21 November 1772*[1]

Dear Sir

I had the pleasure to receive your Letter of the 4 of September. I give you joy of the increase of your family, eight children. You would really make a figure in North America, which is as prolific, I believe, as any part. We have only three. Two of them are now ill of the measles, which have prevailed very much in these parts of late.

This has been a great Cyder year with us. We finished our grinding this day, and I have made 87 barrels from off my farm. It has sold very cheap in town, for 5/sh a barrel, but I dispose of none. I have about 800 apple trees. We raise a great deal of garden stuff, and last year I built a green house for my Winter store, so that we have plenty during the Winter.

About a month ago Mrs H. and I returned from a tour we made to Montreal and Quebec, which to the surprize of every body here we performed in less than 8 weeks. We travelled by land and Water 1380 Miles, and went to Lake George in our own post chaise through Woods over Rocks and Mountains unbent by coach or chaise before. We were seven days on Lake Champlain in going and six in returning. In the latter we were in an open Batteau. One night we slept in the Woods without any covering but the Boat's sails, and four nights we lay on the floor in Log houses. However, we surmounted all our difficulties, and returned to our family in good health and spirits, fully satisfied with our domestic comforts, not having found any habitation more agreeable than our own, however Canada is a fine Country, very well settled from Montreal to Quebec, and rich in its produce of wheat. But the people are ignorant, indolent and dirty, yet simple in their manners, chearful and happy.

Mrs H. and my sister desire to join with me in presenting our best respects to you and Mrs. N. I remain with great regard

Dear Sir, &c.

---

1   Hulton, "Nicholson Letters," 65-67.

[Ann Hulton to Elizabeth Lightbody]

Brooklyn near Boston
21 November 1772[1]

Having a short notice of a vessil just sailing for Liverpool, I would write a few Lines.

Am anxious to hear how Dear Mrs. Lightbody does. Hope it has pleased God to recover and establish your health since that interruption of it, which your last favor informed me of; shall be very glad to hear of yours and your family's health.

We have a sick house at present. My Nephews Tom and Harry are ill of the Measles; hope they will do well, though the latter has them violently.

I wrote to you in August last, and desired the favor of you to buy, and send a small Crate of Staffordshire Ware by a vessil from Liverpool, for my Brother. I mentioned that if there is any new invention or fashion since the Cream colour, Mrs. Hulton woud chuse it rather than that, but by no means gilt cream colourd, as some are, They are wanted for daily and common use. Besides that, the plain or figured Edge we esteem genteeler. I hear there has been lately a large importation of them to Boston. However, we shall now wait till we hear from you and are in hopes of some variety in the fashion, from Liverpool. Be that as it will, we shall be obliged to you; I am sorry to give you the trouble.

I desired too some Shoes to be made by Mr. Garnet for me. If they are done, please to send them in a box at [the]same time, and call upon Cousin Sukey Hincks to pay whatever you Lay out on our accounts.

There must be a great consumption of the cream[-]coloured Staffordshire ware, for they are universaly used, I beleive, all over this Continent.

My Brother and Sister, who have traveled lately near 1400 Miles, say they found them at every house.

I think I mentioned in my last that they were setting out on a journey to Canada, they returned by the 20ᵗʰ of October. This adventure of theirs has made a great Noise here at Boston, and amased everybody, to hear where they had been, for it was before thought an impracticable thing for a wheeled Carriage to pass through the trackless Woods that lyes between this and Canada, or an idea of [the] difficulties encountered in traversing the Wilds of America. Mrs H. surmounted them all, and endured the hardships with great resolution. A kind Providence preserved them both through many dangers in the way.

By Brother writes by this opportunity to Mr Nicholson [and] probably gives him some account of his journey.

The Sons of Liberty in Boston are using all [their] endeavors to raise a Riot. The pretence is the Salaries appointed by Government for the Judges here. We are told from Gentlemen who know the people well that it will be imposible for them ever to raise a Mob that will attack us again; that the disposition of the People in general towards my Brother, and particularly in our Town is so well known, that they will not attempt to disturb him on any account.

We have been alarmed with a report of Pirates hovering about the Coast, which deters Ships from going out for sometime past. There is some foundation for it, but the Governor and Admiral can't yet fathom the bottom of it² A Sloop of War is sent out in quest of them.

My Brother and sister joyn in best Respects to you and Mr Lightbody.

I am

Your Affectionate

Friend and Humble Servant

A Hulton

J. Hincks is here at present and very well.

---

1   *Loyalist Lady*, 54-56.
2   Space left open by the editors.

[Henry Hulton] to Rev Mr.　　　　　　　　　*3 December 1772*[1]

I did not receive your favour of the 26th December till four months afterwards, and the barrenness of matter in this part of the world must be some apology to our friends for our not writing more frequently than we do. I may say our, for I believe Mrs. H. is as blameable in that respect as myself. You would hardly think it, but really in this retreat she finds means to fill up her time, pretty much with domestic business; and the Board and other matters, leave me none on my hands. The leisure I have is most agreeably spent within the compass of my farm. However, to acquire fresh ideas, and lay up some chat for old age, we found ourselves disposed this summer to make a tour through this wild country. And a great Journey we accomplished, to the wonder of all the good people in Boston. In Europe you are invited to ramble by the works of Art, the pomp of Courts, the amusements of public places; but here it is all rude nature, nature in its first state; and the progress of society and cultivation is worth observing. The daring setler sits down in the inhospitable wood, raises a log house, girdles the trees, plants a little corn and potatoes, keeps a pig or two, and by degrees gets a Cow and other Cattle. Perhaps no other setler is within some miles of him. How he gets through the dreary Winter, or the little brood with which he is surrounded, are brought into the World, and reared, is amazing. But he that providentially careth for the Raven feedeth them.[2]

In such a Journey as we made, you will imagine there were many inconveniences to be put up with, and poor accommodations in respect to diet, and lodging to be expected. All these we rubbed through very well; but such roads! such rocks and mountains! inhospitable woods! as we went through, untrod by Coach or Chaise before, how we got through them is amazing. We went in our own post chaise through Albany to Lake George and without any accident.

In the Western extremity of this province we travelled through a country for twenty miles of immense Woods, rocky, and rude, called the Green Woods. Many thousand of trees that have been girdled lye perishing on the ground; others, decayed, hang across the road, ready to fall. Many of them are from 2 to 4 feet in diameter, and from 70 to 150 feet high, so that one forgets the difficulty of the road, in the apprehension from the impending trees.

The lower town of Quebec is close to the water['s] edge on one side, and joins to a lofty hill on the other, which makes it very strait, close and confined. The way to the upper town is very disagreeable, steep, slippery, and dirty.

The Ramparts of the upper town are as high again as the tops of the houses in the lower. The Bishop's palace, the Intendant's Religious houses, and churches, make the chief part of the upper town. The streets are badly paved, and dirty; the town is mostly rebuilt since the siege. There is a fine extensive view of the River and Country from the Ramparts, which inclose a great deal more ground than is built upon. We visited the Indian Village of Loretta, and went to see the falls of Montmorenci, and Chandiere. The latter are the most striking; but the Waters were low at that season. We traversed the plains of Abraham, with great attention.

This conquest, after viewing the country, the situation, and works of the Enemy, I believe must appear very extraordinary to the military Gentleman. There does not appear to be any other place where they could have effected a landing, but just where it was made; and that was very critical, and hazardous. Another day would have prevented the success of that attempt, as a Battalion was to have taken post there, and the gaining the heights, through the narrow pass where they got up, might have been prevented by a small number of Men.

Wheat is the staple of Canada and they raise and export great quantities of this Grain. There is a great simplicity and civility amongst the people, yet without any mauvais[e] honte,[3] for they address you with all that freedom and ease so natural to the french. However they may have been oppressed formerly, no people can be more at their ease than the Canadian under their present Government. They pay no taxes, and have the free enjoyment of their Religion. Luxury has as yet made no advances amongst them; they are even ignorant of many comforts, and conveniences, which their soil would afford, and a moderate ingenuity would find out, but which a commerce with other people, must in time shew them. They are a chearful, lazy, dirty, happy people. Their Religion, and the length and severity of their Winter, allow them fewer days of labour than other Countries, yet in their working days they do not do half the work of our people. But their idle time is not so much spent in vice, as in chearful dissipation; every one has his house, and calash;[4] and their pleasure is to drive about, dance, and sing. Yet in spite of all their laziness, they must grow rich: nature amply repays for the severity of the Winter, by the clothing she gives the soil; and as soon as the snow melts, the vegetation is surprizing. They bestow no pains in manuring, or improving the Lands; yet the soil along the River side is very rich, and fertile; and great quantities of dung are left every year on the ice to be carried away; and they are so lazy as to suffer a great deal of Grass to remain uncut, and grow to waste, though their cattle are half starved in the Winter for want of fodder. Indeed, their cows are poor, small, miserable Creatures, but they have no idea of a Dairy, or of making an house clean. They never wash their floors. Their butter they make by beating it between their hands and never put salt to it; and they know nothing of cheese. The Peasantry are all dressed alike, in a rough flannel jacket, with a Hood. They eat a great deal of bread, and but little flesh meat. The oven and the pott are the chief Arts in their Cookery.

The road from Quebec to Montreal is on the side of the River St. Lawrence. The country is well settled all along the banks, and you travel in Post Calashes, with great dispatch.

We were six days on Lake Champlain in an open Batteau on our return. One night we slept in the woods and four nights in Log houses, without taking off our clothes, and it rained very hard most of the time we were on Lake George. To avoid some of the terrible bad roads we had passed, we came a round of 50 miles from Albany through Connecticut. Yet in this rout we had 15 miles of road inconceivably bad. The houses in Connecticut are pretty well built, and the people manufacture a good deal of their own clothing. There is an entire equality amongst them; they are all settled on their own Lands, and seem a comfortable set of Farmers, or Yeomanry. But they have no idea of a superior, or of a Gentleman, other than themselves. For there they are all Gentlemen, and independent. Happily, we arrived at home without any accident, and I bless God our children are all well, and we enjoy peace, and even domestic comfort.

---

1 Hulton, "Letterbooks," 1:55-61.
2 Having in mind, perhaps, Job 38:41, King James version [hereafter KJV]: "Who provideth for the raven his food? When his young ones cry unto God, they wander for lack of meat."
3 If intended literally, it is false shame; idiomatically it was closer to shyness or, if Hulton intended any irony, a disingenuous deference.
4 A small, two-wheeled carriage.

[Henry Hulton to Robert Nicholson]   *Brooklyn near Boston   10 May 1773*[1]

Dear Sir

I received your favour of the 3 of March and am much obliged to you for the newspapers.

Our journey to Quebec was thought very extraordinary. We made circuit of near fourteen hundred miles, and traversed many woods and mountains that had never been beat by wheels before. I should now think it hardly prudent for a woman to undertake such an expedition, but Mrs H. supported all her difficulties with great spirit. I had read Knox's campaigns before we went this journey, which you say you have been reading lately.[2] You will perhaps be pleased with hearing farther of this Country, and I intend to send you some extracts from my journal for your amusement, but shall hardly have time to write them out before the ship sails. You will see a good description of Canada in Emily Montague written by Mrs. Brooke.[3]

From the time we left our own house to our return we did not meet with comfortable accommodations except at the Collectors of Quebec—It is amazing how rapidly the back parts of this Country are settling, and with what little means of living people sit down in the inhospitable woods.

We have had a very short pleasant Winter of only three months and now we are in full Summer, it is very warm everything is in full blossom and the Country is delightful. Indeed, we find no inconveniences in living here the year round, and would not exchange our situation for any in the town or neighborhood. This Climate certainly improves from the back country being cleared and this part of the World is not only healthy but would be agreeable enough if we had good Government in it. But I fear we shall have much trouble before that is established.

There is a negro girl born in Affrica going from hence to England by desire of Lady Huntington. She has shewn a great genius for Poetry, and her works are to be published in London. She is certainly an extraordinary instance of natural genius. She has only been 8 or 9 years from Guinea. I have not seen her, but am told she has read most of the best English books and translations from the antients, and that she converses upon them with great propriety.[4]

There is a boy now shewing in Boston 10 or 11 years of age, tall and strong, so that he will lift the stoutest Man from the ground.

They have had a very good Assembly and Concert in Boston this Winter. They may talk of discouraging British Manufactures but there is no place where luxury advances faster. They have now a great number of elegant Chariots — the dressing of every young ladies head for the Assembly or Concert costs at least _ a dollar. We abound in hair dressers; however rigid and severe the old people may have been, the young ones are forward enough in following every thing that is fashionable and genteel.

My family are all well in health. Mrs H. and my sister desire to join me in presenting our best respects to Mrs N. and yourself. I am, Dear Sir, &c.

IIII

---

1   Hulton, "Nicholson Letters," 62-65.

2   Captain John Knox, *An Historical Journal of the Campaigns in North America for the years 1757, 1758, 1759, and 1760, etc.,* 2 vols. (London: W. Johnston and J. Dodsley, 1769).

3   Frances Brooke, *The History of Emily Montague* (London: J. Dodsley, 1769).

4   Phillis Wheatley, taken as a child from Gambia by slave traders and bought by the Wheatley family of Boston in 1761, was about to achieve wider fame with the publication of her collected poems in London during the summer of 1773. She was manumitted that fall, her skills as a self-taught writer—which included an expertise in Latin that may have rivaled Hulton's—impressing many in Boston society, but not enough to insure a comfortable life. She died impoverished and all but forgotten in 1784.

[Henry Hulton to Robert Nicholson]

Boston 7 July 1773[1]

Dear Sir

I send you inclosed the extracts from my journal to Quebec, mentioned in my last letter. The printed Letters inclosed will shew you the state we were in four or five years ago, and the proceedings of the Assembly thereon will shew you the state we are now in — There seems no more prospect of our being peace and quietness than when we first arrived in this Country. You will excuse my caution in saying no more on this subject.

I am, Dear Sir, &c.

H H

---

1   Hulton, "Nicholson Letters," 68.

[Henry Hulton to unknown correspondent in London]

Boston 1 October 1773[1]

I had the honour to receive your two very kind favours of the 12th January, and 26th of February. And it gives me great satisfaction to find you enjoy so much consolation at present, and such animating hopes for the future. Happy consequences of the review of a life well spent.

Through many toils, and many duties done,
Through many combats Virtues prize is won;
That prize is sweet reflection on the past,
And humble hope of heavenly Bliss at last.

In our tour to Canada we did not pass within 300 miles of the falls of Niagara, and that would have been too long and hazardous a journey for us to have made, merely for the curiosity of seeing them.

I enjoy real pleasure from the enlarged idea of the works and goodness of the great Creator, which you indulge in your last letter. You seem to be got on the threshold of heaven, and to anticipate the happiness enjoyed by the blessed inhabitants above. The thought is greatly animating, and should influence us to cultivate such sentiments and dispositions, as will be most likely to render us acceptable companions of such a society.

In the mean time my links and attachments to the present World are strengthening. I have now three little prattlers, and Mrs. H. is ready to lay in of a fourth. Anxiety for their establishment will soon take place, but alas! What shall we do with them in this Country?

From the principles and practises that have long prevailed here and the neglect of the Mother Country, we have a melancholly prospect before us.

Yet without correcting the disorders in the present Governments, new and interior Establishments are going on. If we cannot keep the colonies on the Sea Coast in Order— what shall we do with those a thousand or 1500 miles inland?

You will have heard of the persecution and abuse of our worthy Governour and other Gentlemen have undergone on account of some of their letters, written to the late Mr Wheatley,[2] being returned and printed here. Under this apprehension, people will be cautious of writing any account of the transactions here, and offering their opinions thereon. It beho[o]ves us to be quiet and to suffer in silence, whilst the Servants of the Crown are in this situation. I think it very happy that I have sufficient of domestic pleasures, and amusements to fill up my leisure hours. I have no roving desires, no cravings after objects beyond my reach, and feel no vacancy of enjoyment when at home. In this simplicity and retirement, if the passions are not agitated by the new, the agreeable, and surprizing, the heart is less corrupted, and the mind is more composed tranquil, and satisfied, than in the World of business and pleasure.

I cannot enough express the great sense I have of the regard you shew, and the good wishes you offer for me and mine,

O could my verse the poignant griefs assuage,
Or sooth the pains that wait on reverend age,
The Muse should all thy weary hours beguile,
And smoothe times rigid furrows to a smile.

But better comfort than the Muses have You,
A consolation in past life's review.
Faith to thy soul doth heavenly aid impart,
Sooths all thy pains, and cheers thy drooping heart.
Still may She smile with a benignant ray,
And usher thee to everlasting day.

---

1   Hulton, "Letterbooks," 1:62-65.
2   That is to say, Thomas Whately.

[Henry Hulton to the Rvrd. Mr.   ]   *8 October 1773*[1]

We continue in our old state of domestic comfort, and retirement; with little variety to animate us, yet without having desires to disturb us; and we find no vacancy of enjoyment at home. This summer has past over pretty free from outward disturbance. We were only once alarmed, on occasion of the letters from the Governour, which were returned from England and printed here. At that time the people were in a great ferment, and threatened Vengeance to us all. But the storm soon subsided; however, it is as readily raised again, on any occasion. The feebleness of this Government and the dispositions and principles of the people will always subject the Servants of the Crown to popular insults, and abuse; but it is our business to suffer anxiety, and be silent. Redress is not to be expected, and only worse treatment would follow if it was to be known that we had dared to complain. When I was assaulted in my house 3 years ago at midnight, I got no relief by my complaints, and when I was pelted by the Mob this last summer, I took it quietly, and said nothing. And I am told they now say I am such a patient[,] quiet Gentleman, they will trouble me no more.

It may relieve the mind to unburthen its cares to its distant friends, but in our remote situation the sympathy that is raised at the recital of our troubles, only gives pain to our friends, without alleviating our distress; the expressions of their feeling and regard, may arrive when the mind is at ease; when the past trouble is forgot; and when it only feels a concern for having raised a painful sensation in the minds of its friends.

Notwithstanding the general prejudices, I believe we have many friends in this Country and that we are as much esteemed as any persons can be, who are in the service of the Crown. We endeavour to live quietly, neither to flatter or offend; and by an even civil behaviour, bearing and forbearing. Whatever we may be in public character, we rub on in private life pretty well, but there is no answering for the people if any popular prejudice takes them, or if it should be thought necessary to the political plan to get rid of us at once; we must then submit to the torrent.

I have the pleasure to acquaint you that Mrs. Hulton was happily delivered of a fourth son on the 2d instant. She and the infant are both very well, and he takes to the breast very kindly. She suckles him herself. Her last words were, I wish I could know how Netty was; tell her we have got boys to match her Girls, and there is no fear of their living to be old Maids in this Country. These children are only pleasures at present, but anxiety in their Education and Establishment will soon take place. This is a bad part of the World for children to learn proper principles. The authority of the Minister and Magistrate, of the parent and Master, is lost. The glorious spirit of liberty has got the better of all restraint and subordination, and there is a great depravity amongst the young people of Boston.

There is a very ingenious young Clergyman has lately fixt himself at Salem about 20 miles from this, and takes in about a dozen Youths at once to educate, and I intend to place my Children with him. His name is Nickols; he was bred at Oxford, and came from Barbados here.

We have had a fine long summer, but some months of it have been very warm. We slept for a month together under a sheet only, with a window open. The extremes of heat and cold here are very great. We had a day lately in the morning, the Thermometer was at 76, in the afternoon at 110. Yet these New England Governments are the only liveable parts of America. All to the southward of New York is unsupportable in the summer months, and a man had much better be in any of the West India Islands, than in the Carolinas in that season.

---

1   Hulton, "Letterbooks," 1:66-69.

[Ann Hulton to Elizabeth Lightbody]   *undated*[1]

I had the pleasure to receive Dear Mrs. Lightbody's favor in May, together with the Cask of Staffordshire ware, and box with Shoes, all which gave Satisfaction, as I then acknowledgd by letter to you Hope you received it, and that you are paid [by] Cousin S[ukey] Hincks what you laid down for those Articles.

It will give sincere pleasure to your friends in America to hear that you and yours enjoy health. I hope Mr. L. is quite recovered of his disorder, which he was affected with when you wrote. Was sorry to hear of the return of your Stomack complaints, though trust it is not dangerous, Wish you long to enjoy your agreable habitations in Town and Country, and every felicity in your Family. That we may meet in a better world I need not say is my most ardent wish. — When we reflect on the goodness of Providence in Supporting and carrying us through difficulties and trials, what an encouragement is it to hope and trust That he intends to Lead us to a durable felicity.

The Events that have occurred with us since I wrote last, are the addition of another Son to my Brother (which makes four boys) and the removal of J[ohn] Hincks to New Providence at the Bahamas, as Comptroler of the Customs there. It was about three Months ago that he sailed. I have wrote Aunt Hincks twice since, first acquainting her of his Embarking, and afterwards of his arrival at the Port. He found the Island in very Sickly State, a Company of the 14th Regiment which had been on the Expedition to St Vincent's haveing brought a Malignant Fever that spread over the Island, had carryd off most of the Soldiers, and Officers, some of whom H. was particularly acquainted with, and had flattered himself to meet there.

Altogether, made it very melancholy to him. Yet we have great reason to hope he would escape the destemper, as the violence of the Contagion was pretty well over when he arrived, he said, and it was 10 or 12 days after his arrival when he wrote to my Brother. We are now preparing some Pork, Beef, Pickels &c. whatever is eatable (and proper to send him) will be acceptable by Lieut. Griffith in a King's Vessil, which is going to be Stationed there. And no small joy will it be to H. to see his old acquaintance G. He is son to Mr. Griffith, Attorney in Chester.

Boston is reckoned to be one of the healthiest Climates on this Continent, yet the great Extreams of the Seasons, and Sudden changes of the weather must be trying to Constitutions. Mrs H. says she's sure we shall lose Seven years of our Lives by living here, yet we have all had a pretty good share of health hitherto.

There are some disorders which People here am most Subject to; as Rhumatisms and Consumptions, the latter takes off many Young persons. There's another terrible disorder, called here the throat Distemper, which attacks Children cheifly. This sometimes Spreads, and sweeps away numbers in a short time.

To give you some idea of the great and sudden changes of the weather, at which times few persons escape colds, It is so hot generaly in the few hot Summer months that people will Lodge with their windows open upon them and only a Sheet to cover 'em — when suddenly the wind perhaps changes to East and pierces one through —the Pores being open by the violent heat preceding. The next day we have been obliged to have a fire in the parlour. The Thermometer was observed to be between 30 and 40 degrees different in two days together, last Summer—The hottest day in Summer, it rises to about 100 degrees, and the coldest, it is several degrees below 0. — The last Winter was the most moderate and the Summer the longest ever known here (by what they say.) It has continued near Seven Months to the Middle of this Month.

You would perhaps expect to hear an account of our political State, rather than of the Seasons and Weather. Indeed, one is not more subject to vicissitudes than the other. When it appears a calm, we never look upon it as settled. It depends very much on what Wind blows from your quarter of the World. When dark clouds and Storms threaten us across the Atlantic, then the tempest subsides here, and a profound Calm succeeds for a while. But then those impending Clouds being blown away, this Calm is followed by commotions and hurricanes. The Patriotic friends in England (particularly one who enjoys very lucrative office under Government) have wrote that *here they have nothing to hope from the justice but everything from the fears of those in Administration.* As they impute every indulgence to timidity in Government. You'l not wonder that we are still in the midst of Storms and alarms — a dreadful State of Society.

I have not heard from Chester a long time; hope friends there are well. In regard to your inquiry about J[ohn] H[incks] and his new Employment at the Bahamas, It is doubtless a promotion in point of Rank, but as to profit, it depends cheifly on Fees, and therefore it's uncertain whether it will be to his advantage in this respect, till he has made trial.

The climate of new Providence, where he is, They say is healthy, though to the Southward the Sea breezes moderating it greatly. There is another good circumstance— he writes that they had the advantage of Boston in this—that the Officers of the Revenue are there all treated with respect by the Inhabitants. Otherwise it must have been disagreable in a confined Society, as it is, to one who likes Company. It is (what they say the healthiest places often are) a Dry Barren Soil. Does not produce many necessarys of Life, as I understand, but plenty of Fish, particularly Turtle, and other Luxuries, as Pine Apples, Oranges, Limes, &c. They are supplied with provisions from North America &c.

If it does not prove so advantageous or agreable an Appointment as J. H. or my Brother could wish for him, It's probable it will only be for a time, and that something better may turn up for him, after a while. It were to be wished it could be independant of the Board of Customs in North America—At a Board which consists of a number of Persons, the majority of whose Votes determine everything relating to the Board, and each member having their private Opinions, and prejudices, their different connections, and Attachments. It can not be expected that they should be harmonious in all points. The case here is otherwise, and Hincks has his Enemies as well as friends at the Board. My Brother says he is unfortunate in a talent for ridicule, and raising Mirth, which has occasioned him to sacrifice his interest, and friends, for the diversion of Company, in unguarded hours, by talking too freely of some of the Commissioners, by which he made them his Enemies, and gave them advantage over him. I know my Brother has suffered a deal of uneasiness and vexation on his account, and I believe many contests with his Brethren. If J. H. had more prudence and less wit, he would have been in a much better situation (my Brother says) than he is, or has been in.

I have wrote you more freely on this Subject, as you make particular inquiries about him, and in confidence that you will not let anything be known which you think might add to the Afflictions of his poor Mother. It's very possible you may have heard otherways, of the prejudices of some members of the Board against Hincks for Mr. Humphreys, who was appointed to his Office Clerk of the Ministers to the Board m[ar]ried a Miss Gardner, I believe a Sister of Major Gardner, who used to live with Mr Tarleton. Another Sister of hers has been sometimes at Mrs Hinckes, at Chester. Mr. Humphreys is a Sober, industrious Young Man; he was born at Constantinople. Miss G. came over with one of her Sisters to New York, a Brother of theirs residing there. Miss G. afterwards married Mr H[umphreys] on a short acquaintance. He came to Boston 2 or 3 years ago as Agent Victualer. He was very ill used by some persons here, who misrepresented him to his principals at home, by which he lost his employment, and you may suppose then in an unhappy situation, in a strange Country, and Mrs. Humphreys very sickly. Mrs Montague, the Admiral's Lady, who was acquainted with a Brother of Mrs. Humphreys, and having, I believe, a great opinion of Mr. H[umphrey']s merits Interested herself much in his favor to procure from the Commissioners the vacant office under them. The subject led me to mention this, and you know some of the connections.

I am much obliged to you for the Pamphlet in Prose by Miss Aikin. Both this and the Poems which Dr. Percival sent my Brother at same time have afforded us great Entertainment.[2] The young Lady has a fine poetic genius indeed. My Brother has recomended and promised the reading of them to Miss M[ontagu], the Admiral's Daughter, who is a very genteel young Lady about fifteen.

I have inclosed the little poem which my Brother sends to Miss Lightbody, and another for Cousin Hannah. My best Compliments to them, to Mr Lightbody, and to Your Sister, Mrs Robert L.

I am Dear Mrs Lightbody's

Affectionate friend

A. Hulton

There were several young Ladies here desiring a Copy of the Poem, so my Brother got a few Coppies printed.

---

1   *Loyalist Lady,* 56-62. The editors did not attempt to date this letter either. It could not have been any earlier than 2 October 1773 and the birth of Preston Hulton, to which Ann refers in the third paragraph.

2   See 246 n. 2 infra, Henry Hulton to Robert Nicholson, 29 January 1774, for the books in question.

[Ann Hulton to Elizabeth Lightbody]   *Boston   25 November 1773*[1]

My Brother and Sister in their Adventure to the Northward went as far as Quebec. Theirs was the first Post Chaise that ever accomplished the journey, I believe, through Woods and Wilds, over Rocks and Mountains, that were deemed impassable for a Wheel Carriage before, and with only one and the same pair of Horses too, which performed surprisingly. The Carriage, Horses, and one Servant who road on Horseback were left on this Side when they crosd the Lakes. They returned home pleased with their Journey, very partial to Canada, and especialy to Montreal.

Their success has put many persons here on the thoughts of making the like Excursion. A Gentleman here, who has been at Antigua, says that Sir Edward Payne said to him, I hear you have roads now between Boston and Canada, for that Mr. and Mrs. H. have gone it in a Carriage.

I have not seen Knox's journal, but there are places where the Indians would receive very unfavorable impressions of Xtianity. Though without the Soldiers, to see every Vice not only dishonorable to Xtianity, but shocking to humanity, prevail, and practiced, under the Cloak of Religion. Such places there are in the World.

The Books my Brother is reading to us at present are the Voyages of Commander Byron &c. by Hawksworth, Jartin's Sermons, and Beattie on Truth — this last is said to be the best answer to the modern Sceptics that has been published.[2]

Colonel Leslie (who commands the Soldiers at Castle William) sent it us. This is an Amiable and good man, the Father of his Choir, and the Soldiers who all look up to him with respect, and affection. He's of a Noble Scotch family, but distinguished more by his humanity and affability.[3] The former Colonel was an exact contrast: proud, haughty, and voluptuous, devoted to self, and Self gratification. Hated in general by those under his command, and universaly despised. The retreat of the Regiments from Boston on the 5th of March, the military can none of 'em forgive him for.[4]

We have seen here a greater variety of Characters than perhaps we should ever have been acquainted with in England. We are Seldom without Company. This last Summer a very agreable Lady spent some time with us. She had been married about two years to Captain Williams of the *Active* Man of War, stationed at Boston. He is first cozen to Lady North.

Mrs. W. is quite a woman of fashion, bred in high Life and exceeding Lively and agreable. They are by this time arrived in England and she will have many strange Anecdotes to tell Lord N. of what she had seen in this Country the few months they were here. The reason of their quiting this Station before the time was out was Their having a great inclination to return to England and the Admiral would not refuse 'em when an opportunity offered of changing Captain Williams's command from the *Active* to the *Lively* Man of War, which was was ordered for England.

The Ships Laden with Tea from the East India House are hourly expected. The People will not suffer it to be landed at Boston, they demand the Consignes to promise to send it back. Mr. Clark resolutely refuses to comply; will submit to no other terms than to put it into warehouse till they can hear from England. They threaten to tear him to pieces if it's Landed. He says he will be tore to pieces before he will desert the Trust reposed in him by the Consigners. His Son, who is just arrived from England (he was at Liverpool last Summer), and all the family were got together the first night, rejoicing at his Arrival, when the mob surround the House, attacking it with Stones and clubs, did great damage to the House, and furniture, when young [Clark] spoke to 'em, told 'em if they did not desist [he should] certainly fire a Gun at them, which he did, and wounded a man, it's supposed, for they retreated carrying off a man, but they threatened to destroy every person in the House if anyone of their associates was killed. And a great number of Stones, each so large as to have killed any person they had hit, were thrown about the Table where the family were at Supper, but Providence directed 'em so that they did not fall on any person. All the avenues to the House at same time were guarded by armed Men to prevent Mr. Clark escaping.[5] This was beyond anything of the kind since we came here.

My Brother joyns me in best respects to you & Mr L.; likewise to Miss Lightbody, to whom he desires to [send] the inclosed Poem. I am, Dear Madam,
Your Affectionate friend A. H.

1   *Loyalist Lady*, 62-65, but also from the original, Murdock Ms. 23, Houghton Library, one of only two originals there that Harold Murdock had in hand when he and Charles Miner Thompson edited the letters for the book. The changes that Murdock and Thompson made in the text—or I should say, what appear to my eye to be changes in capitalization, spelling and punctuation—are minor, but differences there are. The second original letter is infra 316-318, from April 1775.

2   John Hawksworth, *An account of the voyages undertaken by the order of His Present Majesty for making discoveries in the southern hemisphere* (London: T. Strahan and T. Cadell, 1773); James Beattie, *An Essay on the Nature and Immutability of Truth* (London: Edward and Charles Dilly, 1770), which had been printed in a new edition that year (1773). There were over four dozen collections of sermons published in London in 1773, none of whose titles show a connection to "Jartin"; nor do any collections for earlier years, in either England or the mainland American colonies. The original of the letter, current location unknown, is not available to check against Murdock and Thompson's transcription.

3   Leslie, who would rise to general by 1776 and serve in the American theatre throughout the coming war, was the second son of the 5th earl of Leven (who also held the title 4th earl of Melville). The family had once been a powerful presence in Scottish politics.

4   She referred to Colonel William Dalrymple.

5   Drake, *Tea Leaves*, 34, 210 recounts this incident at Richard Clarke's home. Also see Labaree, *Boston Tea Party*, 104-125.

[Henry Hulton to Thomas ___ Esqr., London]

Castle William
2 December 1773[1]

On Monday the 29th Mrs. H. and myself came to this Island, on a visit to Colonel Leslie, being an engagement of a week before. The proceedings of the Town that day in respect to the Tea Consignees were very violent. Hall, with the Tea on board arrived the day before, and nothing would satisfy the people, but that the Tea should be sent back in the same bottom.[2] Before we had finished dinner, the two young Mr. Clerks, Mr. Hutchinson, and Mr. Faneuil, the Tea Consignees, came to the Island for shelter. The Town for sometime had drawn Committees from the neighbouring Towns, to meet their Committees in Faneuil Hall, where it is said they were shut up in the Evenings and concerted their plans secretly. The next day, Tuesday the 30th November, was a numerous Meeting of the people, not from Boston alone, but from that and the neighbouring towns. They were now no longer town meetings, but the people, and assembled in the old South Meeting. During their sit[t]ing, and resolving, the sheriff appeared with a Message from the Governour, directing them to disperse at their peril. This message they treated with the utmost contempt, and used very gross and rude expressions towards the Governour. And in the afternoon they met again. The Governour had already found himself unsupported by his Council, and now Government was prostrate; the ferment was very high indeed and everyone was big with apprehensions. Mr. B[urch] and Mr. P[axton], having alarming advices brought to them at Dorchester, came over to the Castle that day at noon.

On Wednesday morning the Governour came to the Castle on a visit and returned soon after. It was the opinion of us all that we could not pretend to do business in Boston, and that the Castle was the only place where we could be in security; and indeed, for the quiet of our families, and our own safety, we did not think it right to return to sleep in our houses, though we might ride into the Country in the day time. Mr. Hallowell went on Tuesday in search of intelligence, slept at a friend's house, and returned on Wednesday evening to the Castle; and that evening Mr. Clark, the father, came from Salem by Water, w[h]ere he had retired from the fury of the people.

We are received and treated with the greatest kindness and politeness by Colonel Leslie and the Gentlemen of the 64th. But I am concerned at the inconvenience and trouble we occasion. I fear we are in for the Winter campaign on this Island. This frequent family dread, and distress, is very severe; it is more than can be borne, or can be expected to be endured by any servants of Government, in civil offices. A Certain Gentleman about five years ago gave great hopes of reward to those who faithfully persevered in well doing. I suppose he meant in the Kingdom of Heaven, for I have seen no signs of it on Earth; after five long years further of toil, and warfare, of patient endurance and humble submission to our hapless fate.

The people on Tuesday broke up their meeting after taking Hall's ship into their care and custody; placing 25 men on board her, and appointing signals of alarm; and being told to lie in readiness, and prepared, it is said seven men are kept ready, to carry Expresses into the Country, on any emergency. They likewise sent an Express to New York and Philadelphia, to acquaint their friends of their doings. P. R. is gone over again to the true sons, and distinguished himself on the present occasion. J. W. was Moderator on Tuesday. The Gentlemen who has shown the most spirit in opposing these measures is G. E.[3]

The Consignees would have stored the Tea here, and have waited for orders, but that would not do, no; they must send it back at their own risk, in the same bottom. Now, the Gentlemen are not to be found; a day of Grace is given for fifteen days. If it is not then gone, something very mighty is to be done. The next attack is on the Custom House Officers—the tone is we'll make them clear it out, and the Governour to grant his Let pass, too. It must, and shall be done, say they. This morning Bruce is arrived with more tea.[4] The speaker lately received a letter from Dr. F[ranklin] with the copy of one from L[ord] D[artmouth] to him, said to be of the consoling kind, which has been shewn about, and has tended to keep up their spirits. But these consoling Epistles are cruel strokes to the more distressed servants of Government. I have left the Women and children in my family subject to dayly fears and alarms, and their greatest distress would be to see me enter my own dwelling.

---

1   Hulton, "Letterbooks," 1:70-74. Hulton scratched out the last name.
2   Captain James Hall, of the *Dartmouth*.
3   "P.R." most likely referred to Paul Revere, "J.W." to Joseph Warren, and "G.E." is most definitely Boston merchant George Erving, a onetime smuggler who, as Tyler, *Smugglers and Patriots*, 214, put it, had become a "government party man after his sour experiences with nonimportation." See Henry Hulton's letter of 19 June 1774 at 302-303 infra for Erving.
4   Captain James Bruce, of the *Eleanor*.

[Henry Hulton to Richard   Esq.]   *Castle Island 3 December 1773*[1]

I wrote yesterday to Mr. Irving with a detail of matters at Boston and intended giving you a relation of intelligence come to hand, but last night the inclosed publication came to us, and as it contains the people's own account of their proceeding, it is unnecessary to say any thing further thereon. We can only fly here for shelter from the storm, and sigh over this prostration of order and Government. Great pains are taken to draw in the people of the Country to adopt the violent measures of the capitol. Many towns have had meetings, [militia] trainings, and have sent Committees to the committees and meetings in Boston. We are verging, tending, hastening to rebellion. We feel mighty bold, having nobody to oppose, and threaten blood, slaughter, and destruction—and to be sure, they may do as they please with the few harassed and distressed servants of Government. The spirit is said to be general, and to be sure no one dare to speak, or act, against the popular opinion. Town meetings, papers, and pulpits, are filled with sedition; and the people are almost stark mad. Give up the Tea duty; will that satisfy? No. For then shall we require to be freed from all duties imposed by the Mother Country. In short, if one thing is granted, another will be required, and there is no medium between supporting authority, and giving up the country.

---

1   Hulton, "Letterbooks," 1:74-75, with the last name of the addressee scratched out.

[Henry Hulton to P   Esq. London]   *Castle William 8 December 1773*[1]

The inclosed Memorandum and News paper will explain to you the reasons of my writing from this place. My family at Brooklyn are all very well, but are under concern from the situation of affairs in this province. It is very severe on the servants of Government in civil offices to be thus subjected to the violences of the people, and obliged to seek for shelter in this Castle, particularly at this season of the year.

This is the third time of our flying here for protection. Four times have we retired into the country from our habitations. Once I was assaulted in my dwelling house at midnight, and once I was pelted in the streets of Boston by the Mob. Now it is really purchasing an employment at too dear a rate to be subject to all the distresses which we have undergone for six years past. Add to this, misrepresentation to our superiors, and neglect from home.

It is probable that some measures will be resolved on by Government on the advices that will be received by this Vessel, either to support its authority, or to give way. If the latter, there will soon be little need for Commissioners of the Revenue in America; and if the former, they will still lead (for some time to come, at least) but a very disagreeable life, and every one must wish to get out of this line of service, without some better encouragement, and support than we have hitherto had.

The great indulgence shown to Mr. Robinson is severe upon us, who must do his duty and be deprived the rotation of visiting England. I believe the fresh leave given to Mr. R. has prevented Mr. B[urch] from making use of his leave of absence, and going home this year.

I imagine the people of Boston will wait the return of their Express sent to New York before they proceed further—If the Tea is imported into the ports to the southward, the violence of opposition may subside for the present. We must conduct ourselves as circumstances shall arise; and a week's time will probably determine whether we may visit Boston again this Winter, or not.

We are happy here at present under the protection of a most amiable Gentleman, and in the society of the Gentlemen of the 64 Regiment. We put them to inconveniences, but they do every thing for our accommodation, with great politeness and kindness.

---

1   Ibid., 1:76-78, addressee's last name again deleted, but it is almost certainly Jacob Preston, Elizabeth Hulton's brother.

[Henry Hulton to addressee unknown] *8 January 1774*[1]

I received your favour of the   July on the 8ᵗʰ October. You will have heard before this arrives of the opposition made to the reception of the Tea sent here for sale by the East India Company, and of the destruction of three Cargoes of the said Tea on board the Vessels in this harbour. During the violence of this storm, the Commissioners retired to the Castle; and as it subsided after the Tea was destroyed, we returned to our families at Christmas, and held a Board again in Boston on the 30ᵗʰ December. But as all authority is in the hands of the people, our continuing either to exercise our commission, or to remain in quiet in our dwellings, depends on their pleasure. And whatever measures may be adopted by Government, there seems little prospect of peace for us. I have had a life of severe toil, and combat, in the public service, three years contest with fraudulent contractors in Germany and six years uphill labour to establish an American Revenue.

I have thrice been obliged to take shelter in the Castle and several times have gone into the Country during the rage of the people's passions. Yet after my return from one of these excursions I was assaulted in my house at midnight and this last summer I was pelted by the Mob in coming from a public Provincial Entertainment, where I had dined by the Governour's invitation. And yet, separate from my being a Commissioner, I believe the people owe me no ill will; nay, rather, that in my private character I am respected by them, but they are as mad now as they were in the time of the Witches; instead of the Devil and Witches, you only need to write Commissioners and Taxes.

In this state of society, the people, under the influence of popular leaders, are led to every extravagance. And the disorders of the multitude are not to be considered, or corrected, as in old countries, where order and Government are established, and where the authority of the Magistrate is respected. Here, before subordination is known, or admitted, disorder prevails; and before good Government is Established, Anarchy is introduced. Hence proceeds every thing narrow and illiberal in sentiment and practice; an envy at superior fortune, or talents; a disrespect toward all distinctions of rank, and authority; and a corruption of manners, without a refinement in taste.

In the present state of Government and temper of the people, there can be little consolation without doors for Officers of the Crown; and I am happy, as my chief pleasures are domestic, in having much comfort at my own fire side; but it was distressing in the height of the storm to leave my family. Children are great pleasures till trouble, or distress, arise, and then there is equal anxiety for their safety, and happiness. I bless God we are now all happy, and well, under our own roof, where we shall wait with solicitude the issue of these matters, if the people suffer us to remain in quiet.

---

1   Ibid., 1:78-81.

[Henry Hulton to Jacob Preston]   *18 January 1774*[1]

I wrote to you from the Castle with an account of our situation, and the proceedings of these people. Since Christmas we have returned home, and have remained in quiet in our dwelling, and the Board has been held as usual at Boston. And I imagine we shall continue undisturbed for two months to come; and then there will be anxious expectation of the measures from Great Britain. Whether our resolves will be considered as a declaration of War, or as the impotent rage of seditious subjects, yet I think important consequences will arise from our proceedings. Your sister and I differ in opinion as to the Measures that will be pursued; but we agree that whatever plan may be adopted, we shall in no wise be at rest. If the Colonies are to be reduced to obedience, what is to become of us till order is established? If they are to indulged in their pretentions, we cannot be suffered to remain in the exercise of our Commission. If we are removed to another part of the Continent, we shall be exposed to the like indignities we have experienced. If we are recalled, there is an end of authority. If we remain at Boston, we must stand the issue of the storm.

A little before the late violent agitations I made a present to the Boston Ladies of a little Poem—a few copies of which are inclosed in a packet to you, in a box sent from the Board to Mr. Leake. And you will be so good as to receive it and distribute the copies to the Ladies, our friends, as directed. Indeed, I am told that I have a strong party amongst the Women, and that, let what will happen, we shall remain in our habitation undisturbed; but there is no answering for the conduct of the people when their passions are inflamed, and when any object of their resentment is within their reach. The Tea consignees, who are all Gentlemen of, and largely connected with, Boston, are still the objects of great resentment, and are obliged to keep themselves sheltered at the Castle.

---

1   Ibid., 1:81-83. Another letter to Jacob Preston (given the reference to "your sister" in the first paragraph).

[Ann Hulton to Elizabeth Lightbody]   *Boston 25 January 1774*[1]

Dear Mrs. Lightbody will find the inclosed was wrote above two months ago. I understood then that there was a vessil bound for Liverpool, but after writing it, could not hear of any such opportunity. Though it is now an old Letter, and a mere Scrawl, yet I send it, at same time desiring you will destroy it, as soon as you have read it.

By Captain Marsh I had the pleasure to receive your agreable favor of October last, along with the pamphlet. Was glad to hear so good an account of you, and your family, and that you, Mr. and Miss Lightbody had made an agreable Tour, which I hope contributed both to your healths and amusement. My Brother desires his respects to you and Mr L., and advises him by all means to ride at least Ten Miles every day; it is what he does 3 or 4 days in the Week, and finds benificial. He recommends to him, likewise, instead of Malt Liquor, to drink Spruce Beer at Meals, which is esteemed very Sweetening to the Blood. However, he don't pretend to prescribe as a Doctor. No doubt you have had the best advise, but he desired me to mention it from him, and that he heartily wishes Mr. L.'s recovery.

You may see by the inclosed Letter, I did not stand upon the form of one from you. Did you know when I confine myself long to writing, how my health suffers by it, I am perswaded my friend would excuse me writing frequently such long letters as my inclination desposes to, when I sit down to communicate my thoughts to you.

Nothing but necessary business, or to keep up a communication with some valuable friends, who will indulge me in the pleasure of hearing from them, would ever prompt me to use my pen.

I must own, I am not disinterested in my correspondence, but expect a return of pleasure, and satisfaction, for what I send out, however trifling be the value of the Adventure. You will allow me to treat with you in the Mercantile Stile, who have been conversant in these matters lately. Yet be assured a kind regard to you and the hopes of hearing of your health and welfare is the first Motive.

I have been engaged several weeks past on a disagreable subject. Examining Account and papers, and preparing a Letter of several sheets, to send Mr. Earle by this opportunity, in order to Lay before him, and other Gentlemen whose interest is concerned, a State of the Affairs, and to have them brought to a conclusion. But when I attempt to settle the Affairs, I find so many difficulties and obstacles to the completion of them, that I think it necessary to write to Mr. James Gildart,[2] to be satisfied in some points, before that Letter be sent (or the whole of it). When I left England There were several Affairs depending, particularly a Law suit in Chancery with one Thomas Fearns, which I hope by this time is determined, though I am not acquainted with the decision. It was for a considerable Sum, Mr. T. G. and my late Brother were the Plaintiffs.

Mr. Francis Gildart was employed on their side, and Mr. Pickance was Attorney for the Defendants.

When I am satisfied in regard to this and other matters from Mr. G., I shall (though it's not in my power at this distance to act) propose a plan for accommodating the Affairs, and bringing them to a final Issue, so as I doubt not will meet with the Approbation of the Creditors in general. Some of the principal of them required of me, that I should do nothing further of consequence in these matters, without acquainting them, and with this view I write to Mr. Earle, Though I cannot expect or desire further from him, than to communicate the contents of my Letter (to him) to some others of the Gentlemen, who are interested, and if several of them woud joyn in endeavoring to adjust and conclude the Affairs, I doubt not it may be Effected before X'mas.

You may wonder why I trouble you with this subject, but I would desire the favor of you to acquaint Mr. Cropper with what I now write upon it. My compliments to him, and if he will please to Apply to Mr R. Earle, he will be further informed, as I have wrote him by this opportunity.

I should be glad to Know whether that Law suit be decided, and if it is in favor of the Plaintiffs, what might be the Sum recovered. Perhaps it may be publickly known, but if not, Messrs. Cropper and Carter could learn upon inquiry of Mr. Pickance, if not otherways.

And if you will please to advise me as to this, it would be of servise. I could wish to know further whether (in case the Affairs with Mr. Gildart &c. should be Settled) Mr. Lightbody's House will allow me to order the Money to be remitted into their hands, in order to take up the Bond from Mr G., provided he has not received sufficient.

As it will be proper to Lodge it with a third person who will do me that favor. At present it is in the Stocks, and it would be improper to transfer it thence, till there's a certainty my intention of concluding the Affairs will not yet meet with Obstructions.

I understand Captain Marsh intends coming out again to Boston early this Spring, when I may expect to hear from Mr. Gildart, and also hope for the favor of Your Answer.

---

1   *Loyalist Lady*, 65-68.

2   Presumably the same James Gildart who had been friends with John Hulton, whose younger brother failed to join up with Henry in Germany back in 1751.

[Henry Hulton to Robert Nicholson]

Brooklyn near Boston 29 January 1774[1]

Dear Sir

I received your favour of the 7th of October by Captain Marsh, with the newspapers and a packet from Dr. Percival, who has been so obliging as to send me two Vols. of his Works, and Miss Aikin's Poems, the latter of which I have read and have been greatly delighted with the perusal.[2]

You will have heard before this arrives of the reception the Tea sent for sale by the East India Company met with during the violence of the Storm the Commissioners retired to the Castle, but after the destruction of the Tea, the fury of the people subsided, and we returned to our families before Christmas, and held Our Board again in Boston on the 30th December. But everything depends on the good pleasure of the People, who have all authority in their hands.

You will excuse me entering on the subject of the present American disputes; by your letter I can see you are a stranger to the views and conduct of these people, and no one can have a proper idea of affairs here who has not been in this Country.

I have had a life of labour and combat in the publick service, and the prospect before us is still very unfavourable, as whatever measures may be adopted by Government, it will be a long time before the Commissioners can be any wise in quiet. However, I have the consolation of having done my duty, and amidst the gloom that is around us, I have at least a sunshine in domestic comforts. But these which are the sources of our first pleasures in prosperity are likewise what give the keenest edge to adversity; and to distress; and to be obliged to fly from one's family, to leave them exposed to the madness of the people, is very severe, and can only be felt by those who have been in the same circumstances. But however the people may be incensed, yet I do not believe they mean to do me any personal injury, nor do I apprehend I shall be an object of resentment, otherwise than as a member of the Board.

The Tea Consignees are still at the Castle, where I imagine from the temper of the people they will be obliged to pass the Winter.

I happened to be at the Castle on a visit to Colonel Leslie when those Gentlemen and my Brethren came there for shelter. We were there from November 29 to December 23—and nothing could exceed the politeness and kindness of Colonel Leslie towards us all. This gentleman is son of the Earl of Leven, and a most amiable worthy character he is. Young Mr. Clark, one of the Tea Consignees, was at Liverpool last summer. I inclose some newspapers for your perusal, and a copy of a little poem for your Daughter. I wish you and yours may enjoy all happiness. We shall be in a state of anxious incertitude for some time to come. Indeed, when shall we be at peace, after six years of allarm and distress?

I beg my best compliments to your Brother's and Mr. C[ropper's] and Mr. L[ightbody's] families. Mrs H. and my sister desire to join me in presenting their best respects to Mrs N. I remain, Dear Sir, &c.

HH

---

1   Hulton, "Nicholson Letters," 69-72.
2   Thomas Percival, *Essays Medical and Experimental*, 2 vols. (London: J. Johnson, 1772, 1773); and Anna Laetitia Aikin, *Poems* (London, 1773). Percival was a well-regarded physician; Aikin enjoyed considerable popularity as a writer, with her poems going through various editions. Percival had lived in Warrington, to the east of Liverpool, before he moved to Manchester; Aikin lived there too before her marriage. Both had Presbyterian backgrounds. There are brief entries for each in the *Oxford DNB*, 43:576-676 and 3:736-738, resp., with Aikin's under her married name, Barbauld.

[Ann Hulton to Elizabeth Lightbody] *31 January 1774*[1]

You will perhaps expect me to give you some Account of the State of B[oston] and late proceedings here, but really the times are too bad and the Scenes too shocking for me to describe. I suppose you will have heard long before this arrives of the fate of the Tea — Whilst this was in suspence, the Commissioners of the Customs and the Tea Consignees were obliged to seek refuge at the Castle. My Brother happened to be there on a visit of a long engagement to Colonel Lesley when those other Gentlemen came over. He continued there about twenty days, in the mean time visiting his own House (about 8 miles from the Castle) several times. The Colonel and the Gentlemen of his Choir rendered the retreat as agreable as possible by their polite Attention to every Refugee. After the destruction of the Tea, my Brother returned Home and the other Commissioners left the Castle, the violent fury of the People having subsided a little. One would have thought before that all the malice that Earth and Hell could raise were pointed against the Governor. Mr. Paxton (one of the Commissioners) and the Tea Consignees, two of whom are the Governor's Sons, the others are Mr. Clark, a respecta[ble] Old Gentleman, and his Sons, with two other Merchants, Mr Haliwell, another Commissioner, and likewise of this Country, was an object of their threats.

The Tea Consignees remain Still at the Castle. Six weeks since the Tea was destroyed, and there is no prospect of their ever returning and residing in Boston with Safety. This place, and all the Towns about, entered into a written agrement not to afford them any Shelter or protection, so that they are not only banished from their families and homes, but their retreat is cut off, and their interest greatly injured by ruining their Trade.

It is indeed a severe case, and can hardly be credited, I think, that the Governor's Sons should be treated as fugitives and outlaws in their own Country. One of them lately went from the Castle, and with his Wife to her Father's House, a Gentleman at Plymouth, 40 Miles from Boston. They had no sooner arrived there but the Bells tolled and, the Town Assembling, instantly went to the House, demanded that Mr. Hutchinson should depart immediately out of the Town. Colonel Watson, his father[-]in[-]law, spoke to them, saying that it was so late at Night, and the Weather so severe, that Mr H. and his wife could not without great inconvenience remove from his house that night, but promised them, they should go in the Morning by 9 o'Clock. The time came, and they were not gone, when the Town bells tolled again, and the people gathered about the house. Upon which the Young Couple Sett off in a great snow storm, and nobody knows since where they are.[2]

But the most shocking cruelty was exercised a few Nights ago upon a poor Old Man, a Tidesman, one Malcolm. He is reckoned creasy [crazy]; a quarrel was picked with him, he was afterward taken, and Tarred and feathered. There's no Law that knows a punishment for the greatest Crimes beyond what this is, of cruel torture. And this instance exceeds any other before it. He was stript Stark naked, one of the severest cold nights this Winter, his body covered all over with Tar, then with feathers, his arm dislocated in tearing off his cloaths, he was dragged in a Cart, with thousands attending, some beating him with clubs and Knocking him out of the Cart, then in again. They gave him several severe whippings at different parts of the Town. This Spectacle of horror and sportive cruelty was exhibited for about five hours.

The unhappy wretch, they say, behaved with the greatest intrepidity, and fortitude all the while. Before he was taken, defended himself a long time against Numbers, and and afterwards, when under Torture, they demanded of him to curse his Masters, the King, Govenor, &c., which they could not make him do, but he still cried, ["]Curse all, Traitors.["] They brought him to the Gallows and put a rope about his neck, saying they would hang him. He said he wished they would, but that they could not, for God was above the Devil. The Doctors say that it was impossible this poor creature can live. They say his flesh comes off his back in Slakes.[3]

It is the second time he has been Tarred and feathered, and this is looked upon more to intimidate the Judges and others than a spite to the unhappy Victim, though they owe him a Grudge for some things particularly he was with Governor Tryon in the Battle with the Regulators, and the Governor has declared he was of great servise to him in that Affair, by his undaunted Spirit encountering the greatest dangers.

Governor Tryon had sent him a gift of ten Guineas just before this inhuman treatment. He has a Wife and family, and an Aged Father and Mother, who they say saw the Spectacle, which no indifferent person can mention without horror.

These few instances, amongst many, serve to shew the abject State of Government and the licentiousness and barbarism of the times. There's no Majestrate that dare or will act to suppress the outrages. No person is secure. There are many Objects pointed at, at this time and when once marked out for Vengence, their ruin is certain.

The Judges have only a week's time allowed them to consider whether they will take the Salaries from the Crown or no. Governor Hutchinson is going to England as soon as the Season will permit.

We are under no apprehension at present on our own Account, but we can't look upon our Safety, secure for Long[4]

---

1 *Loyalist Lady*, 69-72.
2 Elisha Hutchinson and his wife, Mary. He went to England with his father in 1774, not realizing that he was going into exile. Caught in Massachusetts by the outbreak of war, Mary did not join him there until several years later.
3 For the Malcom affair see supra 59 n. 108.
4 Apparently the rest is missing; the editors did not say.

[Henry Hulton to Thomas   Esqr. London]   *15 March 1774*[1]

I have received your favour of the 28th December, and am much obliged to you for your communication: it is great satisfaction to hear from you, though you have little consolation to give us, and you in return can only expect to receive accounts of our troubles, and distresses, increasing.

The people have been incouraged in their excesses by the accounts they have received from their friend the Dr.,*[2] and the neglect, or decay, tenderness, or supineness, or call it what you please, of Government, certainly has rendered their resistance to authority more daring, and the persecution to the Officers of the Crown more outrageous, and violent; and they will, if not soon prevented, go on til they have got rid of every thing that they call a Yoke, check, or restraint, from the Mother Country—having set aside the chief Justice, and prevented the legal importation of Tea. The Courts of Admiralty, and the other branches of the Customs, will be the next objects. How they will settle the matter of power, and Government amongst themselves, is another question; at present they are in a wretched state of thraldom. Everyone is sensible of the power they have assisted to raise, they feel the oppression, yet hardly any one dares to complain, or exert themselves to be relieved.

I feel much of the prostration of Government, but our immediate concern is for ourselves and families. And though I do not think I have any personal Enemies, yet when the matter is ripe for execution, I must share in the further sufferings, and dishonor, that will be brought on our service. This season of suspence and apprehension is dreadful. Hitherto the threats of the people have been confined to Mr. P[axton] and Mr. H[allowell], and it is shocking to hear the execrations that are dealt out respecting them.

The spirit that is first stir[r]ed up in Boston spreads like wildfire through the country. They have established Committees of Correspondence with all the Towns, and the like is now carrying on from the several provinces with each other. It is supposed that a scheme is in agitation to form a General Congress, where they are to settle a bill of rights, to be demanded of Great Britain.

The temper of the people is now raised to that pitch, that there would be no security to the Board if it was removed to another part of the Continent; though had it been established at first elsewhere, it might not have met with that resistance, and those insults, it has found. If the measures of Government should be to support its authority, where must we be placed till these measures have operated? If none are to be taken, the best step will be to recall the Board, or else the Crown will certainly suffer indignity, in the treatment the Board will receive.

The worthy Lt. Governour is gone "where the wicked cease from troubling, and where the weary are at rest."[3] I believe the Governour and Lt. Governour had wrote to Mr W[hately] to explain further the matter of the letters, and we do not think that matter will end with the Dr.'s acknowledgement, which is a very extraordinary thing indeed. Pray then, who did he get them from? Every Gentleman In Office with whom he has had any communication, must certainly oblige him to answer that question. Nobody doubted that he was the sender of the Letters, but none of His Majesty's British servants have been suspected as capable of betraying his American servants and service, in the manner alledged by the Dr.

---

1   Hulton, "Letterbooks," 1:83-86. The last name of the addressee has been scratched out.

2   "*Franklyn," inserted at the bottom of the page.

3   "There the wicked cease from troubling; and there the weary be at rest." Job 3:17 (KJV) In reference to Andrew Oliver, who had died just days before.

[Henry Hulton to John ___ Esq.]

Boston 24 May 1774[1]

I have received your three favours of the 5th February, 9th March and 9th April, in the latter some Minutes of the 31st March and copies of the Blockade Act.

We are now preparing to remove to Salem, where I apprehend they will be well pleased to receive us, though the patriots of Boston have been endeavouring to prevail on the other towns in this Government, and in the several provinces, to break off all Commerce with Great Britain; and to endeavour to distress the W. India Islands. On the other hand, the well[-]disposed part of the Inhabitants have been forwarding an address to our late Governour, and as he is now going home, he will be able to give the best account of the present dispositions of the people. They do not as yet seem thoroughly awake to the evils that await them. But when the Act[2] has begun to operate, and they find other places, instead of adopting their follies, take warning by their misfortunes, I imagine they will pay the money, profess a disposition to be peaceable and obedient, and pray the General to intercede for them. And when order and good Government are once restored at Boston, I hope we shall sit down there again, and be upon a better footing than ever.

---

1   Hulton, "Letterbooks," 1:87-88. Last name eliminated.
2   Boston Port Act, to take effect on June 1st.

[Henry Hulton to Samuel ___ Esq.]

24 May 1774[1]

As you have withdrawn yourself from the busy scene, an Epistle from this American land may be some amusement to you in a leisure hour. At least, I am sure you would have a satisfaction to hear of us, if it was only a detail of our domestic matters— As to our public ones, I am weary both of thinking and writing about them. The Nation, however, now, not only seem to know both us and our practises, but to be so roused, as to be resolved to bring us to order and obedience. Our professed loyalty, which our daring resistance of Government, our roaring for liberty, yet exercising the severest tyranny, and oppression, are now all known and acknowledged; and the Constitution is to be mended; but what are we to get for undergoing this seven years' persecution? It will now be said the Commissioners have been sadly misrepresented, and ill[-]used, but where is the consolation for all our sufferings, and expences, for all our family dread, and distress, under the tyranny of a Boston Mob?

We have been happy, during the late years of disturbance, to be retired from the town, and in our Country retreat have avoided a great deal of public notice. So that except my going to the Board, or our making particular visits, we were seldom from home. As members of society we gave no offence, and except my being a Commissioner, the people were very well satisfy'd with me. Happy in our domestic turn, and little amusements about our fields, and garden, we screened ourselves at home, whilst the storm raged around; we entered into no disputes about rights, and liberties, and not being particularly obnoxious, we only shared in the general execrations against Government, taxes, and Commissioners. This was in the general, but at some time, when the liberty pulse beat high, we were all distress and dismay. The Governour, Commissioners, all were to be sacrificed; they were not worthy to live. In such times, after spending nights in terror, expecting to be attacked, and have the house pulled down, I have been obliged to fly thrice to the Castle, and three or four times to different parts of the Country. After my return from one of those excursions, four years ago, I was assaulted in my house at midnight, and narrowly escaped being assassinated.

Our family has been growing through all our distresses. We have now four stout boys, who some years hence may be a guard and protection to us. Our present concerns for their education, and establishment; the prospect here for youth is but melancholy. Added to the natural democratic spirit of these people, the late agitations about liberty, has set the common people and youth loose from all restraint—the authority of the parent, and master, of the minister, and magistrate is lost. The clergy depending on the people for support have been obliged to preach to their passions, and adopt their prejudices, and they have assisted very much to forwarding that licentiousness with regard to order, and Government, that prevails.

We are infatuated with foolish notions of Independence, with an enthusiastic spirit of liberty. The original leven of pride and obstinacy has been well fermented in this American land, and it will be difficult to bring the people to a right sense of their dependance on, and cordial affection to any power that pretends to be their superior.

Trained up in the principles of equality, and abounding in the means of subsistence, they revolt against acknowledging a superior, and view with an evil eye the possessors of those advantages which create respect and beget distinctions in society; and therefore we need not wonder if the sentiments of gratitude prevail less amongst them than people who have been bred in those degrees of subordination and dependence, which arise in states more ancient and civilized.

To acknowledge a benefit implys a consciousness of our wants, and dependence; and is a mortification of our pride; the sacrifice of which, we are hardly induced to make, till compelled by necessity.

All the youth go through the same course of Colledge education, and each continues in that seminary till he takes a degree, whether he be intended for trade, for sea, or the farm, as well as for any of the learned professions. By this course of education, many learn more than is necessary to qualify them for their future occupations in life, and all get such a smattering of law, and Government, as to enable them to be politicians, to make them factious, and litigious; whilst those who are intended for the practice of Law, and physic, have not the opportunity of acquiring a proper knowledge in those exercises, for there are no Establishments in the Colledge for instruction in the branches belonging to those professions; and in the line of Divinity, they only train Ministers for a particular sect.

By this mode of education, the youth seem to be prepared for entering upon any sort of occupation, or business, and it is very common to see persons change their employment, from one business to another, to dart suddenly into a new profession, and to be at the same time a trader, a Judge, and a General.

---

1   Hulton, "Letterbooks," 1:88-93. Again, last name excised.

[Henry Hulton to unknown addressee, in London] *19 June 1774*[1]

The hurry we have been in of late has prevented my writing to you. Besides, as I knew Mr. Stewart would communicate to you an account of all matters that occurred till he joined you, I thought I could not give you any fresh intelligence.

The late Act has not yet operated sufficiently to bring these people to their senses. Instead of endeavouring to recover the favour of Government, the obstinate and perverse disposition of the majority leads them to measure the very reverse of procuring reconcilement.

The leaders, or the committee of Correspondence, are endeavouring to bring in the country to a solemn league and Covenant, not to have any dealings with Great Britain: and you will see the proceeding of the Council and Assembly have been in no wise pleasing to the General, as the former received a pretty severe rebuke in offering their Address; and the General Court is dissolved, for going into matters foreign to the business of the Province; however, it is said they have appointed Members to a General Congress.

The General's conduct has been very sensible. He says little, but acts with spirit. And from what I have seen of him, I rejoice that the honour of the Nation at this time is put in such hands. Added to the natural disposition of these people, they seem to be held by a delusion that gets the better of what good sense they otherwise may have had. They flatter themselves with an idea of their consequence, and importance. Like a Merchant on the brink of bankruptcy, they imagine that every sail is the Vessel that is loaded for their relief. They lose sight of impending evils, to catch at clouds; nay, they think the Deity is to interpose by a Miracle, and instead of hearkening to the plain words of the Act, obey and live, they figure to themselves a thousand evils by complyance—yet by delay and disobedience are laying up for themselves a load of certain evil, sorrow, and distress. For I am fully perswaded that till the terms of the Act are complied with, the port will not be opened, and that if their obstinate spirit is not soon reduced, they will pass a miserable Winter.

The great clamour now is against the Commissioners of the Customs, for causing the fuel and provision Vessels to be duly searched at Marblehead. If they could pass easily without a thorough inspection, the intentions of the Act might be greatly evaded.

Our Board is now removed to Salem and there are no Officers of the Customs left in Boston. I come over to Brooklyn on Thursdays, and return on Monday or Tuesday morning.

The Merchants who signed the Address are about inquiring into the correspondence that has been held by the Town committee, and propose taking measures thereon. Mr. George Erving has shewn the most spirit in this business, and has great merit for his endeavours: and I hope in a little time that the well[-]disposed in the town will be able to make head against the popular leaders.

---

1 Ibid., 1:93-96.

[Henry Hulton to unknown addressee]   *6 July 1774*[1]

I received the favour of a letter from you in March. We have been for some time past a good deal harried and unsettled. In consequence of the Boston port act, our Board is removed to Salem, but my family remain at Brooklyn and I am frequently going between the two places. The act has not yet operated as could be wished; the people of Boston, instead of complying with the requisitions of it, have been urging the other Colonies to give them support, and join to counterwork the measures of Government; and they build much on the resolutions of the Assemblies and Towns to the southward; and the leaders of the faction are indefatigable in alarming the country, and stir[r]ing the yeomanry up, to a resistance of the authority of Great Britain. They are drawing them into a solemn League and Covenant, not to Import or use British Goods, and they and the Ministers have influenced the minds of the people to such a height, that when the new Acts which are daily expected arrive, and the alteration in the Government takes place, it is to be apprehended they may resist the operation of them in such a manner as may draw on more serious consequences. As for the town of Boston, it is now pretty well tied down, having four Regiments and a company of Artillery encamped on the Common, and several Men of War in the harbour; but though their commerce is at a stop, yet their spirit is not humbled. They are still very stubborn and obstinate, and prove themselves the true descendants of the race from which they sprung. I am afraid they will require yet further correction before they are brought to a sense of their duty. At present, there does not seem a disposition towards it. They look to a General Congress, and expect assistance from the other Colonies. If they are still supported by them, and should not be damped by spirit and resolution of Government, every thing may be expected that can be supposed of mad fanatics, though the consequence must be their own destruction.

Every one is intent and anxious for the issue of these affairs; they engage all conversation, and every one's thoughts. Whilst one abhors the leaders, one cannot but pity the deluded multitude, who are led to the brink of ruin. The principle adverse to the authority of Parliament is too deeply riveted to be removed, till they have felt the weight of the authority and the hand of power I fear must be exerted before we are brought to a proper respect to Government.

Many of the principal Merchants in Boston made an attempt in the Town Meeting to dissolve the Committee of Correspondence, but they were borne down by numbers; they have since protested against the proceedings of the Committee.

My family are all well at Brooklyn, but if there should be disturbances in the country, they must flee to Boston, or the Castle. I just write this from Salem, as Admiral Montagu sails tomorrow, as I thought our family friends would be anxious to hear of our situation at this critical time. I apprehend within a month or six Weeks we shall see how far the phrenzy of the people will lead them. The General behaves with great good sense, and spirit — they wanted a Fast, which he not granting, they are to have a day of prayer of their own appointing the 14th instant. The General has given some very good answers to addresses presented to him. The Council's Address he would not hear read through. I hope this will find you and your family and all our friends well and happy. There is no probability of our being otherwise than in a state of hurry, alarm and anxiety for some time to come.

---

1   Ibid., 1:96-99.

[Ann Hulton to Elizabeth Lightbody] *8 July 1774*[1]

My Dear Friend's favor of the 1st March I esteem the kinder, as she did not wait to hear from me. Hope you would receive afterwards a packet of several Letters wrote at different times and sent [by] Captain Marsh, who sailed from Boston in February last.

The concern you express for your friends in these troublesome times here, deserved an immediate acknowledgment. But indeed, I've waited some weeks for the opportunity of a Liverpool Vessil, which I heard was expected, yet none has arrived this Spring, and I can't delay it longer, though as I understand Letters by London Ship are generaly put in at Portsmouth — a long way to travel by Land.

I imagine you will be desirous to Know how the New Acts of Parliament operate here, and how your friends are affected by the Commotions and disturbances of the Publick. I am sorry to say there appears no disposition yet in the People towards complying with the Port Bill. — They carry their Melasses and other Goods easily by Land from Salem, and find little inconvenience at present from its operation. The distress it will bring on the Town will not be felt very severely before Winter, when Roads will be impassable. There's little prospect of Boston Port being Opened this Year. The Leaders of the Faction are only more unwearied, and are pursuing every measure to draw the People onto resistance, and to irritate Government more and more, and which probably will end in the total ruin of the Town and the Individuals.

It is now a very gloomy place, the Streets almost empty, many families have removed from it, and the Inhabitants are divided into several parties, at variance, and quarreling with each other; some appear desponding, others full of rage. The People of Property of best sense and Characters feel the Tyrany of the Leaders, and foresee the Consequences of their proceedings, would gladly extricate themselves from the difficulties, and distress they are involved in by makeing their peace with G. Britain, and speedily submitting to the Conditions and penalties required

These who are well disposed towards Government (more from interest than principle, it's to be feared, as there are few willing to acknowledge the Authority of Parliament) are termed Tories. They daily increase, and have made some efforts to take the power out of the hands of the Patriots, but they are intimidated and overpowered by Numbers, and the Arts, and Machinations of the Leader, who Governs absolutly, the Minds and the Passions of the People — by publishing numberless falshoods to impose on their credulity, and various artifices to influence or terrify. The Ministers from the Pulpit and the Committee of Correspondence by writing inflame the Minds of the ignorant Country People. Their endeavors to engage the Other Colonies to shut up their Ports, and the Merchants here to joyn in a Nonimportation Agrement, proving without effect. The next plan is in opposition to the Merchants, and which if it spreads must be attended with the ruin of most of 'em here 'tis a Solemn League and Covenant not to use any British Manufactures till the Port is opened, and the New Acts repealed. This is a deep and diabolical scheme, and some people are taken into the Snare, but it's to be hoped the progress of it will be stopd. General Gage, who conducts himself with great good sense and spirit, issues a Proclaimation Against it to warn 'em of its Consequences. They are startled in general; however, the little Town of Marlborough has had the Audacity to burn the General In effigy, with the Proclaimation.

There are four Regiments and a Train of Artillery now encamped on the Common at Boston, and several Men of War [in][2] ye Harbour, though as yet we are in no wise humbled. We [expect] support from the other Colonies, and build much on a general Congress to be held in September or October of Deputies from all the [Colonies]. We are told that Blocking up the Port is the best thing that can be for Americans, that it will unite the Colonies against G. B., distress their Manufactorers and raise our friends, a numerous body, as we have been informed by Dr. Frankland, viz., the Dissenters and the Commercial part of the nation, to exert themselves in our favor, and that we may expect a Rebellion there, which will answer our purpose, and we shall become intirely free and Independant. But if we now submit — Our Lands will be taxed — Popery introduced, and we shall be Slaves for ever. I mention these as Some of the Artifices and Arguments which Keep up the spirit of opposition, [by] which the People are inflamed to the highest degree.

However, I don't despair of seeing Peace and tranquility in America, though they talk very high and furious at present. They are all preparing their Arms and Amunition, and say if any of the Leaders are seized, they will make reprizals on the friends of Government. Three weeks will bring on the Crises.

Have not room to say all I would. Mr H. at Salem, his family at Home. Can't be very easy as times are, though well in health. Heard lately from Hincks he was well a month [ago]. Best respects to all yours and to Mr. Cropper's Family, [I wish] much happiness to the young married Couple. I shall note other matters [when] I write next. Your Affectionate

Friend & Servant   A H.

I hope for the pleasure soon of hearing from you. If there are no vessils bound for any Port in this Colony, it's all one if you send Letters to New York or Philadelphia, Directing for your friend the Commissioner at Salem. They will no doubt be conveyed safe here, as he informs me. I've now filled every blank space.

---

1   *Loyalist Lady*, 72-76.
2   This and the bracketed words that follow were inserted by the editors of *Loyalist Lady*.

[Henry Hulton to unknown addressee] *12 August 1774*[1]

Since the receipt of your letter of the 20th ulto little material has occured here.

The *Scarborough* arrived with the Regulating Acts the 6th instant and the General called a meeting of the Members of the new Council on Monday last. Only ten qualified that day. Four or five excused themselves, or took time to consider. Twelve were necessary to form the Board, so they adjourned to Tuesday next, without doing business. The next day, last Tuesday, a Town Meeting was held at Boston by adjournment, in the face of the Act. I am fully persuaded that everything that can be expected from the spirit and ability of a commander will be found in the general, but it is a bad presage, where Men of property who are appointed to the posts of honour and authority, shrink back, and betray a timidity of spirit. Til the resolves of Government are known on the proceedings of Congress, I have little expectation of any spirited measures being taken by the advice of Council. On the other hand, I am persuaded that everything short of open force will be done to intimidate individuals, perplex, distress, and resist the measures of Government. This Congress would seem to draw the matter near to a crisis. And it cannot be long before Great Britain must determine to support its authority effectually, or give way to the demands of the Colonists. If she is firm, we must be either subjects, or Rebels. And when it comes to the point, I think few will be mad enough to rank themselves in the latter class. There has been a Gentleman here, who has excelled even the warmest of the sons in the cause of liberty, yet a servant of the Crown and an old Englishman. He endeavoured to stir up the people of New York to violent measures, and is now said to be gone to this Congress, a self[-]chosen Delegate. Fame will no doubt have reported him to you.

---

1   Hulton, "Letterbooks," 1:100-101.

[Henry Hulton to unknown addressee]   14 & August 1774[1]

The General has been at Boston these two or three days past. I hear he sent for the Select Men, and acquainted them that if they had any business that they thought necessary to call a town meeting upon, and they would propose it to him, he would consider it. That they said they had an Adjournment of one already to be held, upon which he said that by the late Act that could not be, and that he should take care the Act should be carryed into execution. However, we are going to have country meetings to advise &c. in this alarming Crisis. This was suggested by the Boston town meeting in July, perhaps thinking to evade the Act thereby, and to make the resolves more general and formidable.

Could it be imagined that the alteration that appears in the Billeting Act would be effectual? Under that Act the troops will yet be distressed for Quarters, unless provided at an heavy expence to the Crown. The money that has been already paid for Quarters at Boston, and expended in building that strange Blockhouse at Castle William, would have built noble Barracks in the Town, and it must come to that at last.

We keep receiving budgets of letters every Packet from Scotland, and Ireland; which mode of intelligence generally arrives a month after the Vessels are arrived at their Ports. But what does it avail, though we hear of Vessels from Holland, and Hamburg, with cargoes of Tea, and could send Accounts to the ports before they arrived. Alas! These Vessels never come nigh their ports of discharge before they are cleared of all their illicit goods by small Vessels on the Coast. Smug[g]ling never was so extensively carried on as at this time. Iit is now more patriotic than ever to distress the Commerce of Great Britain. A number of small Vessels employed in cruizing on the Coast is the only means to put a stop to smug[g]ling. The Men of War may give protection to such Vessels, but never of themselves will suppress this illicit commerce.

---

1   Ibid., 1:102-103.

[Henry Hulton to unknown addressee, Esqr.] *Boston 8 September 1774*[1]

I did not receive your favour from Bath of the 1st March till the 18th ultimo. Since which I have had the pleasure to hear of your arrival at Antigua, by a letter from Mr. Merlin at the Custom House, and I rejoice to hear such agreeable Accounts of your family, and to find you enjoy health and chearfullness. The peace and tranquility I enjoyed at Brooklyn is now at an end, and we have the most gloomy prospect before us.

When the Boston Port Act took place our Board was removed to Salem and we remained pretty quiet till the regulating Act began to operate. A Town Meeting was soon after called at Salem, in defiance of the Law. The morning it was to be held, the General came to Salem and caused the people to disperse. The Committee who called the meeting was taken before a Magistrate; two of them entered into Bail, the rest refused. The Magistrate was afraid to commit them. On this, other Towns held meetings and chose Delegates to County Meetings, supposed with intention to chuse representatives to a Provincial Meeting. County Meetings were held, and it is said they are to establish a new Government at Worcester. The Courts of Justice met; no one would serve on Juries under the new Act. The Courts were shut up. Twenty-six Members had qualified as Councellors. The people set about intimidating them; some voluntarily resigned, others were surprized in their houses by large bodies of people, threatened in the severest manner, and compelled to give up. Now all the Country were preparing their Arms, and melting down all the lead they could come at into bullets. The General the 1st instant caused the powder in the Magazine at Medford, near Cambridge, to be removed to Castle William. The next day the people from many towns, to the number of three or four thousand, assembled at Cambridge and seized the persons of Mr. [Thomas] Oliver, the Lt. Governour,[2] of the High Sheriff, and some of the Counsellors, and compelled two Counsellors to resign, and the High Sheriff to sign a paper that he would not Issue the Writs under the new Act. Mr. Oliver was permitted on his parole to go to Boston, to see the Governor, and returned to the people again. He was not apprehensive of all their designs, and gave such an Account of the matter to the General as made him not to suspect any danger to the Lt. Governor. Otherwise, the General would have taken measures for his security and protection. When Mr. Oliver returned home, the people grew more violent, and outrageous; and they finally compelled him to sign a paper renouncing his seat as Counsellor.

Whilst the people were assembled at Cambridge, and were waiting the return of Mr. Oliver from Boston, the Commissioners of the Customs passed through the town, on their return from Salem. The people suffered my chaise to go quietly along, but soon pursued Mr. Hallowell, and he narrowly escaped being taken; he happened to have a brace of pistols; the cry was, stop him! he has killed a Man! and when the chase grew warm, he got out of his chaise on his servant's horse, and with a pistol in each hand, kept the people off and got safe to the Guard at Boston. In the evening I left Brooklyn, and all the Commissioners, with the Counsellors that have not signed, are now in Boston, and my family are packing up to remove into town. The General has directed a redoubt to be thrown up, and some Guns to be mounted at the neck. The Select Men have been to remonstrate against it, and we are threatened with Twenty and thirty thousand Men, being to march down and destroy all before them.

The Country is in a state of Anarchy, and distraction; and dreadful calamity I fear will be the issue of this disorder, and licentiousness.

---

1   Ibid., 1:104-107.
2   Lieutenant Governor Andrew Oliver had died in March 1774; Thomas Oliver, who was not a relative, succeeded him. Thomas Oliver would be Massachusetts's last royally-appointed lieutenant governor. He, like the Hultons, fled the province in March 1776. He too would be proscribed and banished, with property left behind sold at public auction. He lived out his days in England as an exile and died at Bristol in 1815.

[Henry Hulton to unknown addressee, Esqr.] *Boston 13 September 1774*[1]

I wrote to you a few days ago, and sent the letter by one of the Transports that were expected to sail for England. But she is now ordered to New York, and has taken the letter with her, and I suppose you will receive mine from thence.

Appearances here grow every day more hostile. The General is fortifying the Neck, seven Regiments are in the town, and Castle, and more are sent for from Quebec, and New York. The people, on their part, are all arming, melting their lead into bullets, and drag[g]ing Cannon into the Country. They have long lost all respect for Government; deluded, and inflamed by their Priests and Patriots; ignorant and insolent; and confident in their numbers, they are rushing into Rebellion, and drawing on themselves the severest Calamities. They absolutely deny the authority of Parliament; will not submit to its Laws, and have defeated the execution of them, and it is said are proposing to form a new Government to be established at Worcester.

On occasion of an alarm lately sent through the Country, that the soldiers had killed some of the people, and the Admiral had fired on the town of Boston, the people in many towns of Connecticut took to their Arms and marched towards the relief of Boston, and were reluctantly sent back on finding the Account prove false. A Justice of the peace remonstrated with them, and told 'em it was high treason to take up Arms against the King, upon which he was brought before the tribunal of the People, and obliged to sign a recantation of their own drawing up.

The remaining Counsellors, the Commissioners, all in office, and others, have taken shelter in Boston, as the only place of safety. Such numbers of new inhabitants makes it difficult to get houses. I have hired one, but shall not be able to get into it this fortnight. My family are all well, but still at Brooklyn. I wish to get them to town as soon as possible, though I have no apprehensions from our Brooklyn people.

---

1 Hulton, "Letterbooks," 1:108-109.

[Henry Hulton to Saml. Martin Junr. Esqr.]   *12 December 1774*[1]

I do not trouble you with a detail of the proceedings of these people. I suppose every newspaper will be filled with them. It were endless to relate all the instances of cruelty and oppression that have been practised within a few Months past. And now the Inquisitions appointed in consequence of the resolves of the Continental Congress are exerciseing a tyranny over the minds, bodies, and Estates of the people in the several Provinces; no one can speak or write, eat or drink, or wear, buy, or sell any thing, without undergoing the scrutiny of an Inquisitor. And many instances of torture and oppression I fear there will be, before the powers of Government operate effectually in restoring order.

---

1 Ibid., 1:110.

[Henry Hulton to unknown addressee]   *February 1775*[1]

I should sooner have acknowledged the receipt of your favor of the 25th July, which came to my hands in October last, had I not imagined from its contents I should soon receive a further letter on the matter contained therein; in the meantime, however, please to accept my best acknowledgements for the trouble you have had on our account, and I shall be very glad to hear from you, without having other subject than your own welfare, which it will always make one happy to hear of. I observe your city is again entered into the African trade, and that you are a party concerned in the Adventure, and I wish you success in your enterprize. It is a necessary business. But I have always lamented that the first branch of our commerce, should make a breach on our principles of humanity. Yet We Americans, so jealous of our own liberty, such assertors of the rights of mankind, make no scruple to exercise the severest tyranny over the unhappy natives of Affrick.

I imagine American matters are the general subject of conversation, and that you are all amazed at our violent and audacious proceedings. As you may not be thoroughly informed of affairs here, I shall endeavor in as concise a manner as I can, to give you an account of our present situation, and the causes of it. The evil has been long growing, and is now near come to a head.

You will no doubt have read the resolutions of our Provincial and Continental Congresses; and will have seen by the Accounts published by the people themselves, that they deny the authority, and refuse obedience to the Acts of the British Parliament; that we are in a state of Anarchy, the Courts of Justice, the civil and Militia Officers who were appointed by the Crown, being suspended; and new Militia Officers and Men raised by the people, are trained for action, and a new Treasurer appointed by them to receive the Provincial Taxes, in defiance of the King's Governour.

The resolves of the Continental Congress are now executing in the several provinces, and political Inquisitors are appointed in each town to pry into the Conduct of individuals, that they observe the orders prescribed respecting the Importation and Exportation of British Goods &.

The past concessions of Great Britain have given them confidence, and their forte is in her weakness; they expect to raise a clamour amongst the Manufacturers at home, that they will fight their battles, for the parade they here make of resistance is all a flash, without bottom. They are without order, and discipline, Officers and money, Military stores and places of defence.

It is well known that the southern provinces had imported a supply of Goods sufficient for two or three years, before the resolutions of the Congress took place, and that none of the Colonies can keep to the resolutions of the Congress: and if the nation is united, and shew firmness and spirit, the Americans must soon submit to the authority of Parliament.

It were endless to relate all the instances of cruelty, and oppression, that have been practised for some months past in this Country on those persons who have been deemed by the people unfriendly to American liberty. Every one who did not conform in all things to the will of the people was considered as a proper object of persecution; many, to save themselves and families from destruction, signed to any articles that were imposed upon them, and were compelled to make the most humiliating submissions. Still, this would not satisfy. And he who would not take up Arms, say all that they said, and justify all that they did, was judged to be a Tory, and an Enemy to his country, and therefore to be expelled the society.

So adverse are the deluded people to the Government and authority of Great Britain, so confident in their numbers and their cause, that they seem to brave her power, and dare her to the combat; and perhaps the only cure for their disorder is the severity of her chastisement. This I imagine they will feel, but to make good subjects of them afterwards will be a difficult task.

We have now a formidable force assembled here, waiting the Orders of Government, on the resolutions of Parliament; whilst the people of the country are levying and training their Militia, having chosen their own Officers, and keeping what they call minute Men ready for action, in case of any attack or alarm.

The Winter has passed off thus far without any material disturbances.

The temper and forbearance of the General, the good conduct of the Officers, the Order and discipline observed by the Troops, amidst repeated insults, and provocations, are highly to be commended.

Lord Percy's great condescension wins upon every one, and the people must own and admire the gentle manners and good behavior of the Military in general.

Having acquainted you with the present situation of affairs here, I am now to endeavour to point out the source of these Evils, and the causes of this depravity.

The original then from whence these Evils spring is the Constitution of these New England Governments; and the causes which have urged on their progress in depravity is a long indulgence in illicit trade, and the neglect of the Mother Country to correct the evils and disorders, which their Constitutions and Commerce must of necessity occasion.

The first British settlers in these Colonies were separated from the parent state about 150 years ago. Wild Enthusiasts and violent Republicans, they came out in a storm amidst the rage of contending Parties and settled in the Wilderness. The spirit of Enthusiasm was increased in the gloom of the forest. The hardships of their condition, the severity of their occupations, and their remoteness from civil life, increased the ferocity of their manners; whilst their ease in acquiring landed property, and the Democratical form of Government they adopted, cherished their natural independency of spirit.

Great Britain, distracted by the turbulence of factions, and glad to get rid of a troublesome set of people, let them assume what forms of government they pleased. But that which appeared eligible for infant Colonies, and in a state of Virtuous simplicity, was found incompatible for a more advanced state of society, and had a natural tendency to deprave the people.

With the increase of numbers, the improvement in Commerce, Arts, Luxury, and Civilisation; Faction and intrigue, Wants, and Necessities, Frauds and Crimes kept pace.

The Councellors and Executive Officers being elective (in some of the provinces annually) and therefore subject to frequent changes from the caprice of the people, every one was tempted to look to the people for their approbation, and the Magistrates could hardly have the virtue and fortitude to execute the Laws, and do their duty, when it thwarted with a popular prejudice. Hence the Laws lost their spirit and energy from the want of some superior power to cling to for protection, every one became timid and suspicious, and cast about before he said or did anything, to see how it would affect his popularity.

In like manner the Ministers of the people, who depended on the people for their choice, support, and continuance in the Parish, were obliged to adopt popular prejudices and to preach from the holy book, not what they judged the fittest, but what the people would have to be the right doctrine. Hence the pulpits have been made the Vehicles of sedition; from thence the people have been urged to treason, and rebellion, and to destroy a Tory, has been preached up as a justifiable act.

To have told the people their duty in the simple and pure manner of their great Master, and to have insisted on the plain precepts of Morality, as an essential part, would have been reprobated by many as placing merit in good works; and therefore highly criminal, whilst the abstruser points of Divinity were topicks inexhaustible, and inexplicable, and were good substitutes to preach upon, in the room of moral duties, and the strick observance of outward Ordinances gave a good appearance to the World, and served as a cover to deceit and guile. For from the principles of the Constitution, Art and duplicity became necessary.

The lower class, feeling their consequence, became assuming, pragmatical, and insolent. Idle, and inquisitive, they wasted their time in political meetings and Cabals, judging and determining upon every one's principles, and conduct.

Ever jealous and envious of superior talents and fortune, they endeavoured to pull down and depreciate all those who were above them; or who distinguished themselves in the state, by their Virtue and abilities. Turbulent and restless, they were forever the dupes of crafty knaves, by whom they were continually engaged in faction and sedition, and were now led into rebellion. Men of property, dreading their displeasure, were timid and fearful. Not having their due weight in the state, what must they do? They were obliged to have recourse to Art, to supply the want of power, and by coaxing and trim[m]ing, by Address and plausibility, they endeavoured to win on the passions of the intemperate Vulgar, and from habit and necessity, from timidity, and Art, the mixture of fear and cun[n]ing is wrought into the practise of society, and the intercourse of Offices.

As commerce increased, the sources of depravity increased therewith. The tillage of the soil was severe. Agriculture, which should have been the first principle in the settlement of an extensive continent, soon gave way to one more grateful to indolence, and avarice; and the neglect and indulgence of Great Britain tended to increase that depravity which Commerce introduced. They settled Colonies on Commercial principles only, encouraged them by Bounties, cherished them with care, and protected them on every occasion; but neglected to provide for the support of her Authority and Government over them. She passes Laws which she never inforced, and submitted to innovations on her prerogative, without inflicting any punishment on the offenders, till at length her authority was denied, and her Laws trampled underfoot.

The Sugar Act of the 6th Geo. II, made to gratify the West India Planters, operated to debauch the minds of the North Americans, without producing any benefit to the Revenue.

The masters of Vessels easily reconciled themselves to an Oath, on the breach of which penalties inflicted by the Law were never inforced, and the Merchants readily submitted to a Law of Revenue, which was never carried into execution; and the price of the evasion of which was only a small sum to the Officers of the Customs for conniving at the breach of an Act, which their superiors did not chuse to inforce. But when the Ministry turned their thoughts towards raising some Revenue, when they greatly reduced the duties, but insisted on the small sum that was laid to be duly paid; then it was found out, that the Law was unconstitutional, that the parliament had no right to lay any Duties in America, and therefore it was no crime to evade the payment of them. The Oath it enjoined was therefore esteemed in no wise obligatory, and they who had their own interest to serve by this kind of Casuistry, soon reconciled themselves to the Doctrine. To defraud the Revenue was deemed patriotic. Perjury became licensed, and Rebellion established on principle. Grown wanton with indulgence and prosperity, they seem to brave all authority, human and divine, and to be ripe for correction.

---

1   Ibid., 1:111-122.

[Henry Hulton to Robert Nicholson]   *Boston 21 February 1775*[1]

Dear Sir

I did not receive your favour of the 15 October till the 28 January. Though our Port is shut up, yet if you write by opportunities to any of the neighbouring Ports to the care of the Collector of such Port, it will be forwarded to me. I am much obliged to you for the concern you express on my Account. On the 2 September I quitted my habitation in the Country, and my family have been with me in Town since the middle of October, as this is the only place of security in the province for the servants or friends of Government. I imagine American matters are the general subject of conversation, and that you are all amazed at our violent and audacious proceedings.

You will no doubt have read the resolutions of our Provincial and Continental Congresses, and will have seen by the accounts published by the people themselves, that they deny the authority and refuse obedience to the Acts of the British Parliament. In consequence of which we have been for some time in a state of anarchy. The Courts of Justice being suspended, the Militia Officers superceded, and new ones appointed by the people, and a new treasurer nominated by them, to receive the Provincial taxes in defiance of the King's authority.[2]

The resolves of the Continental Congress are now executing in the several Provinces, and Political inquisitors are appointed in each town to pry into the conduct of individuals that they observe the orders prescribed, respecting the Importation of British Goods &c. The past concessions of Great Britain have given the people confidence, and their forte is in her weakness. They expect to raise a clamour amongst the manufacturers at home, that they will fight their battles for them, for the parade they here make of resistance is all a flash without bottom. They are without Officers and Money, Military Stores, and places of defence, they have no sense of Order, and will never submit to discipline.

It is well known that the Southern provinces had imported a supply of goods sufficient for two or three years, before the resolutions of the Continental Congress took place, and that none of the Colonies keep to the resolutions of the Congress; and if the Nation shews firmness and spirit, the Americans must soon submit to the authority of Parliament.

It were endless to relate all the instances of cruelty and oppression that have been practised for some months past in this Country on those persons who have been deemed by the people unfriendly to American liberty. Everyone who did not conform in all things to the will of the people was considered as a proper object of persecution; many, to save themselves and families from destruction, signed to any articles that were imposed upon them, and were compelled to make the most humiliating submissions. Still, this would not satisfy and he who would not take up arms, say all that they said, and justify all that they did, was judged to be a Tory, and an Enemy to his Country, and therefore to be expelled the Society.

We have now a formidable force assembled here, waiting the Orders of Government, on the resolutions of Parliament, whilst the People of the Country Levying and training their Militia keeping what they call minute Men ready for action, in cases of any attack or allarm.

The Winter has passed off so far without any material disturbances. The temper and forbearance of the General, the good conduct of the Officers, the Order and discipline observed by the Troops amidst repeated insults and provocations are highly to be commended. Lord Percy's great condescention wins everyone and the people must own and admire the gentle manner and good behaviour of the military in general.

A Provincial Congress has been sitting at Cambridge since the first instant, till within these few days they have published Resolves "strictly forbid[d]ing the People from furnishing the Army with any military Stores, or supplying them with necessaries to enable them to take the field." "Urging the militia in general to perfect themselves in military discipline, and the Towns and Districts to encourage the manufactory of firearms and Bayonets; and recommended to them to cause their respective proportions of the Province tax to be paid into the hands of Mr Henry Gardner of Stow, lately appointed treasurer of the Province by the former Congress." And after appointing the 16 of March to be kept as a day of fasting and prayer, they adjourn to meet at Concord on the 22nd of March.

Thus after seven years of trouble and trial, our situation is become still more critical and interesting. We are not subject to such frequent allarms for our own safety as heretofore, but we are concerned for the consequences which the madness of this deluded people will occasion, as it is hardly to be expected that anything less than the hand of correction can bring them back to order and obedience.

I condole and congratulate on the changes in your family, and I beg to present my best Compliments to all your family connections. Mrs. H. and my Sister desire to present the same to Mrs N. and yourself. They and the children have had their health very well through all our hurries and troubles.

I remain with great regard, Dear Sir, &c.

H H

1   Hulton, "Nicholson Letters," 72-78.
2   See supra 164-171. Note that parts of this letter are virtually identical to another that Hulton wrote that month, supra 310-314.

[Ann Hulton to Elizabeth Lightbody]   *April 1775*[1]

I acknowledged the receipt of My Dear Friend's kind favor of the 20th September the begining of last Month, though did not fully Answer it, purposing as I intimated to write again soon. Be assured, as your favors are always very acceptable, so nothing you say passes unnoticed, or appears unimportant to me. But at present my mind is too much agitated to attend to any subject but one, and it is that which you will be most desirous to hear particulars of, I doubt not in regard to your friends here, as to our Situation, as well as the Publick events. I will give you the best account I can, which you may rely on for truth.[2]

On the 18th instant, at 11 at Night, about 800 Grenadiers and light Infantry were ferry'd across the Bay to Cambridge, from whence they marched to Concord, about 20 Miles. The Congress had been lately assembled at that place, and it was imagined that the General had intelligence of a Magazine being formed there and that they were going to destroy it.

The People in the Country (who are all furnished with Arms and have what they call Minute Companys in every Town ready to march on any alarm), had a signal, it's supposed by a light from one of the Steeples in Town, upon the Troops embarking. The alarm spread through the Country, so that before daybreak the people in general were in Arms and on their March to Concord. About Daybreak a number of the People appeared before the Troops near Lexington. They were called to, to disperse, when they fired on the Troops and ran off, upon which the Light Infantry pursued them and brought down about fifteen of them. The Troops went on to Concord and executed the business they were sent on, and on their return found two or three of their people Lying on the Agonies of Death, scalped and their Noses and Ears cut off and Eyes bored out—which exasperated the Soldiers exceedingly. A prodigious number of People now occupying the Hills, woods, and stone walls along the road, the Light Troops drove some parties from the hills, but all the road being inclosed with stone Walls served as a cover to the Rebels, from whence they fired on the Troops, still running off whenever they had fired, but still supplied by fresh Numbers who came from many parts of the Country. In this manner were the Troops harrased in their return for seven or eight Miles. They were almost exhausted and had expended near the whole of their Ammunition [when] to their great joy they were relieved by a Brigade of Troops under the Command of Lord Percy with two pieces of Artillery. The Troops now combated with fresh Ardour, and marched in their return with undaunted Countenances, receiving Sheets of fire all the way for many Miles, yet having no visible Enemy to combat with, for they never would face 'em in an open field, but always skulked and fired from behind Walls, and trees, and out of Windows of Houses. But this cost them dear, for the Soldiers entered those dwellings and put all the Men to death. Lord Percy has gained great honor by his conduct. Through this day of severe Servise he was exposed to the hottest of the fire and animated the Troops with great coolness and spirit. Several officers are wounded and about 100 Soldiers. The killed amount to near 50, as to the Enemy we can have no exact account, but it is said there was about ten times the Number of them engaged, and that near 1000 of 'em have fallen[3]

The Troops returned to Charlestown about Sunset, after having some of 'em marched near fifty miles, and being engaged from Daybreak in Action, without respite, or refreshment, and about ten in the Evening they were brought back to Boston. The next day the Country poured down its Thousands, and at this time from the entrance of Boston Neck at Roxbury round by Cambridge to Charlestown is surrounded by at least 20,000 Men, who are raising batteries on three or four different Hills. We are now cutt from all communication with the Country and many people must soon perish with famine in this place. Some families have laid in stores of Provisions against a Siege. We are threatened that whilst the Out Lines are attacked with a rising of the Inhabitants within, and fire and sword, a dreadful prospect before us, and you know how many and how dear are the objects of our care. The Lord preserve us all and grant us an happy Issue out of these troubles.

For several nights past I have expected to be roused by the firing of Cannon. Tomorrow is Sunday, and we may hope for one day of rest. At present a Solemn dead silence reigns in the Streets, numbers have packed up their effects and quit[t]ed the Town, but the General has put a Stop to any more removing, and here remains in Town about 9000 Souls (besides the Servants of the Crown). These are the greatest security; the General declares that if a Gun is fired within the Town <u>the inhabitants</u> shall fall a Sacrifice — Amidst our distress and apprehension I am rejoyced our British Hero was preserved. My Lord Percy had a great many and miraculous escapes in the late action — This amiable Young Nobleman, with the Graces which attracts admiration, possesses the virtues of the heart, and all those qualities that form the great Soldier — vigilent, active, temperate, humane, great command of temper, fortitude in enduring hardship and fatigue, and Intrepidity in dangers. His Lordship's behavior in the day of trial has done honor to the Percys. Indeed, all the Officers and Soldiers behaved with the greatest bravery, it is said.

I hope you and yours are all well and shall be happy to hear so. I would beg of you whenever you write to mention the dates of my Letters which you have received since you wrote, specialy my last of March 2d.

I am not able at present to write our Dear friends at Chester. Would desire the favor of you to write as soon as you receive this, and present my [compliments and] respects to your and my friends there, and likewise the same to those who are near to you.

I wrote not long ago both to Miss Tylston and to my Aunt H[incks]—have not heard yet from the Bahamas.

Have never heard from Mr Gildart or Mr. Earle yet.[4]

The *Otter* Man of War is just arrived Sunday Morning.[5]

---

1   *Loyalist Lady*, 76-80. The editors put a (?) between April and 1775. This is the second letter now in the collections of the Houghton Library (Murdock Ms. 24); the first is dated 25 November 1773 (see supra 286-288).
2   Starting in the next paragraph, extending through the paragraph thereafter and most of the one following, to be picked up again midway through the fourth, Ann drew a line to the left of the text, and noted in the left margin (writing perpendicular to the text): "What is marked with these Lines, you are at Liberty to make as publick as you please. Let the merits of Lord Percy be known as far as you can."
3   The British suffered some 270 casualties, over 70 of those killed, out of a total of perhaps 2000 engaged. There were somewhere between 3000 and 4000 militiamen who fought them, with perhaps 50 killed and somewhat fewer than that wounded. Note how close Ann's account is that of Henry, at 318-319 infra, both in style and content.
4   The editors to a *Loyalist Lady* (80n) noted that "three or four lines" near the bottom of the page were missing, torn away from the rest of the letter.
5   The last sentence stands alone, on the back of another page.

[Henry Hulton to J⸺ Esqr.] *April 1775*[1]

The intelligence that will be received by this opportunity I imagine will make you a good deal anxious for our safety, and though we are hardly sufficiently informed or composed, yet I will endeavour to give you a state of our present situation.

On the 18th instant, at eleven at night, about 800 Grenadiers and Light Infantry were ferryed across the Bay to Cambridge, from whence they marched to Concord, about twenty miles. The Congress had been lately assembled at that place, and it was imagined that the General had intelligence of a Magazine being formed there, and that they were sent to destroy it.

The whole of these New England people have been long furnished with Arms, and for a considerable time past they have kept what they call Minute Companys in every town, ready to march on any alarm. It seems upon the troops embarking, the signal by a light from one of the Steeples was given to Charles town across the Water, and this was forwarded through the Country, so that before day break the people in general were in Arms and on their march to Concord. About day break a number of them appeared before the troops, near the meeting house at Lexington. They were called to disperse; when they fired on the Troops and ran off, upon which the Light Infantry pursued them and brought down about fifteen. The Troops went on to Concord, and executed the business they were sent on; and on their return found two or three of their people not yet dead, yet scalped and their Noses and Ears cut off, which exasperated them very much. Numbers of People now occupied ths hills, Woods, and stone Walls along the road. The Light troops drove some parties from the hills, but all the road being inclosed with stone Walls, served for a cover to the Rebels, from whence they fired on the Troops, still running off whenever they had fired, but still supplyed by fresh numbers, who came from many parts of the Country. In this manner were the Troops harrassed in their return for seven or eight miles. They then were almost exhausted, and had expended near the whole of their Ammunition; when to their great joy, they were relieved by a Brigade of troops under the command of Lord Percy, with two pieces of Artillery. The Troops now combated with fresh ardour, and marched on their return with the best countenance, receiving sheets of fire all the way for many miles, and yet having no visible Enemy to combat with, for they always skulked and fired from behind walls and trees. They likewise possessed themselves of the houses on the road side, and fired from the Windows on the Troops, but this cost them dear, for the Soldiers entered those dwellings, and put all the Men to death. Lord Percy has gained great honour by his conduct. Through this day of severe service he was exposed to the hottest of the fire, and animated the troops with great coolness, and spirit.[2] Several Officers are wounded and it is imagined about 150 men are killed and Wounded, but that near 1000 of the Rebels have fallen.

The Troops returned to Charlestown about sun set, after having some of them marched near fifty miles, and being engaged from day break in action without respite, or refreshment. And about ten in the Evening they were brought back to Boston.

The next day the Country poured down its thousands and at this time from the entrance of Boston neck, at Roxbury, round by Cambridge to Charlestown, is surrounded by the Rebels. There are many reports of their intentions, but none to be depended on. We are now cut off from all communication with the Country and many people must soon perish with famine in this place. But we have laid in a store of provision for some months. The Rebels threaten to attack the Lines, but I think they will hardly be mad enough to attempt it. There are 13 Battalions and four ships of the Line here, and the people of the town seem disposed to be quiet, but we are not without apprehensions, and are ardently wishing for the arrival of the forces from Europe.

---

1   Hulton, "Letterbooks," 1:123-127.
2   Hulton wrote a poem in tribute to Percy, transcribed at 399-403 infra.

[Henry Hulton to Robert Nicholson] *Boston 7 May 1775*[1]

Sir

I had the honour to write to you of the 8th October 10 and 12th of December.

You will no doubt have been particularly informed of the affair of the 19th of April from the best authority, and therefore I shall only endeavour to give you an account of our present situation, and of such matters as may be worthy of observation in this day of tryal and trouble.

Since the return of the Troops on the day above mentioned, the environs of this Town have been possessed by the Rebels, whilst every measure has been taken within to strengthen and secure the Lines, and the Common, against an attack, or surprise.

It cannot be doubted that the affair of the 19th of April was an happy event for the servants of Government, and the people called Tories in Boston. Before that day, there were many people very urgent with their friends in town to get them to remove out of it, and it was pressed upon them in such a manner, as expressed some speedy and sudden destruction being to fall on the place. And there are now very strong reasons for judging what the intended destruction was to have been.

Many of the Officers of the Army lodged in private houses in the Town. On Monday 24th April it was intended to have a public dinner of the servants of the Crown, in honour of St. George, and Lord Percy was to have given a Ball on the Wednesday following. Now from all circumstances, it is believed there was a plot laid to have sacrificed the Officers of the Crown on one of these two nights. That the Military were either to have been taken off in their Lodgings after their return home on the 24 at night, when they were to be supposed to be in liquor, or that the whole assembly were intended to have been blown up at Lord Percy's ball. There were upwards of 2000 men in Town provided with Arms, and on their rising, on one of these occasions, the people of the Country, who were all ready, were to have rushed down in thousands on the lines. Happily, the affair of the 19th hath disconcerted their plot; the People in Boston have since been disarmed, and we are now under no apprehension, except of the town being set on fire by some of the Desperadoes who remain; for most of the inhabitants have abandoned their dwellings, and are now scattered all over the Country; every house and farm is filled with these fugitives, and thousands of these raging, misled fanaticks probably in a short time will fall a prey to famine, and disease. But no distress of the people will turn their leaders from their purposes. The whole Country is now in a state of madness, and the distemper may probably run through the Continent. Perhaps the same treatment as is applied to natural Lunaticks, may be best to these political ones; and hunger, and delay, be more effectual than immediate force to reduce them to their senses.

Two Delegates have been here from the Assembly of Connecticut, to inquire into the truth of matters. Though they may be persuaded that the reports they received before they came here were untrue, yet there is hardly any probability of the people of the Country receiving for truth any thing that combats with their prejudices; they are possessed with the notion that Great Britain means to enslave them. But this may only be thrown out to justify their rebellion. There is no doubt that a plan of resistance has been long concerted, and that these people mean to try to be independant of Great Britain: and they are much instigated to the measures they take, by the letters they receive from England. We have no great opinion of the bravery of these people, yet their enthusiasm will supply the place of courage, and their Jewish obstinacy of dispoition, will make them endure severe calamities, before they will submit. The face of this Country has great advantage for defence; all along the road are woods, hills, and enclosures of stone walls, so that an Army might be much harrassed on their march, but particularly convoys of Provision, by a people who are all Enemys, and in Arms, and who will never appear in the fair field before regular Troops.

But who will apply the whole of their power, under the influence of fear, and cunning; and exercise it under every advantage they can derive from a knowledge of the Country, its defensible passes, its heights, and defiles.

As yet they have made no advances by raising any works against the Town, and they are supposed to be waiting for the resolutions of the General Congress. If that body should resolve to support Massachusetts bay in their revolt, we may expect that the united endeavours of the Continent will be exerted against Great Britain; but if the Congress should be for pacific measures, these people will probably fall off, and return to their habitations.

If this Province should be supported by the other Colonies, and it should not be thought adviseable to hazard the lives of many brave troops in the interior parts of the Country, the way of reducing the Colonies to obedience by a Naval War is more open and sure, without the loss of many brave Britons.

The superiority of the power of Great Britain on the ocean will always enable her to regulate the commerce of America on what condition she pleases: and if America should still be obstinate, she may reduce this Country to the terms of shipping all their produce, and receiving all their supplies in British bottoms. The Merchants at home may find full employment for all their Vessels, and the resistance of the Americans tend to the increase of the British naval power.

The ports of Boston, New York, and Philadelphia, may be easily secured. One ship will keep Charles town in order. Virginia and Maryland may be awed by a few ships; at least nothing can go without the Capes, if a single Frigate cruises between them, without her notice. And if Rhode Island be taken into the hands of Government, it may be a place of Arms for Army and Navy, be a seat of Commerce, of resort and refuge, for all the well[-] disposed to Government.

It will probably be a considerable time before this Province is restored to a state of order and Government, and there does not seem to be any place of shelter for the Board out of Boston on this coast. The operations of War may make it very inconvenient and distressing to us, already reduced to salt Provision; and we are cut off from all supplys by market, and from all communication by Post with other parts.

Halifax has no communication by post with other parts, is very remote from, and uncertain for correspondence with every other place, and for several months in the Winter is intirely shut up.

In the present state of affairs in America, I can see no place where we can be in any degree of safety, and be open to a communication by post with the Southern ports, but at Montreal. The post is six days on its way between Boston and New York, and it is little more between Montreal and New York. If it should be thought advisable for us to remove there, it would be necessary that immediate permission should be given, that we might act as circumstances should arise: for if we go up the River St. Lawrence, it should be before the fall of the Year.

---

1   Hulton, "Letterbooks," 1:146-153. Hulton told readers that he had placed this letter out of order, after one on July 30th, and that they ought to read this one first.

[Henry Hulton to Sam] *London 21 May 1775*[1]

I wrote to brother Preston with an account of the affair of the 19th April, which I imagine he hath communicated to you. Since that time our anxieties and distresses have been increasing, as the Rebells have occupied all the Country round the Bay, from Roxbury to Charlestown, and cut us off from all supplies and Provision by Land, or communication with the Country by post, or otherwise; and the Port is blocked up by Act of Parliament.

Consider the situation we were in after the 19th April, surrounded by all the Country in Arms, and having a more dangerous Enemy within; for all the inhabitants were armed, and ready to rise on any attack being made from without. Nay, it is not doubted but a plot was concerted for an assault, and insurrection, to have taken place after a publick entertainment, to have been given in honour of St. George, the execution of which was disconcerted by the affair of the 19th of April.

The Inhabitants have since been disarmed, and many thousands of them have abandoned their dwellings and are now either wandering in the Country, or are associated with the Rebel Troops, who fill all the neighbouring towns.

The lines at the neck, the Common, the heights in the town are all fortified and every measure has been taken to put the place in the best state of defence. We have now near 5000 men in Garrison, and are impatiently waiting the arrival of the troops from Ireland; when it is expected the Army will march into the Country. Our chief wants at present are of fresh provision, and forage, and I fear the hot weather confinement, and salt provision, will occasion a sickness amongst us in town.

There is no doubt but there had been a general concerted plan amongst the Colonies of a revolt from the authority of Great Britain, and the affair of the 19th of April only brought on the matter a little sooner than they might have chosen to have entered on the execution of it. Had the plan laid by Sir Francis Bernard been carried into execution, it is probable all would have been quiet here long ago, but by delay, and expedients, these Colonies are near lost to G. B.

The account of the affair of the 19th April was the Signal of alarm to all the Colonies to the southward, and all the reports we receive from those Quarters are of an hostile complexion. It is said the Connecticut people have taken Ticonderoga, that they have voted to raise 6000 Men to join the Massachusetts people and that Rhode Island has voted 1500, that at York and Philadelphia they are all preparing for resistance and that the Virginians have taken Lord D[unmore] prisoner, and carried him into the interior part of the country, so that it looks as if the rebellion would be general, and require more force than we shall have this summer, and very vigorous exertions of power to quell it. In the meantime, our prospect is very gloomy and the concern about our young family fills us with many anxieties.

---

1   Hulton, "Letterbooks," 1:127-130, with the last part of the first name, and the full last name, erased, though family friend Samuel Horne seems the likely recipient.

[Hulton to unknown addressee]   *12 June 1775*[1]

The alarming advice you must have received of the state of affairs in this country, I do not doubt will have made you, and all our friends, very anxious on our Account. And indeed, our situation for some time past has been critical, and disagreeable, and the prospect before us is by no means pleasant. Since the 19th of April the town has been blockaded by the people of the Country, who are all in Arms. All supplies by Land are cut off from us, and every means used to prevent Provision, forage, and fuel, from being sent from the neighbouring ports by Water.

We are threatened with attack, and assault, from the people, and they have indeed hitherto behaved very audaciously; they have drove off the Cattle, and burnt Houses, and stores, on Islands just under our Eye; however I do not apprehend they will dare to make an attack upon the town. And when the troops from Ireland arrive, it is expected the Army will occupy the Country, and chase the people from this neighbourhood. In the mean time we are much in want of forage and fresh provision. We are anxious for our future distination, as there seems no prospect of peace and comfort on this Continent for some time to come.

If the Army gives the Rebels in this neighbourhood a severe check soon, it may prevent an open revolt of the other Colonies, and reduce these people to their senses, but at present they are possessed with all the wildness of Enthusiasm, and all in obstinacy of the Jews, and nothing but a severe calamity seems likely to bring them to order and obedience.

Most of the inhabitants of Boston have abandoned their dwellings, and are now fugitives in the Country, or are joined with the people that are in Arms in the Neighbourhood; those who stay in town are threatened by the Rebels to share in the destruction of the place, if they do not come out, and we have been apprehensive lest the town be should be set on fire by some of the Desperadoes within.

Many of the friends to Government have withdrawn themselves to other places, and we are soon likely to have few left but the Military and crown officers. In this situation, you must imagine we undergo no little perturbation of Mind for the event; in the best view, much destruction and calamity must ensue; and though successful, we must expect to lose some men, some friends, and acquaintances. Amongst those who are retiring from the place is my friend Mr. Nickols, a Clergyman who will be the Bearer of this Letter to you. He was educated at Oxford, and has been engaged in the instruction of youth for some years past in this province; but from the circumstances of the time, he has been obliged to give up his Academy. He was the only one of the Establishment in this Province engaged in such an undertaking, and I thought he was deserving of every encouragement, but without support from Government I fear the scheme cannot succeed; though if Government hereafter expects to have good subjects, they must cherish the Church of England, have public Schools on Royal foundations, and a Royal University in this Country. Mr. Nickols will inform you particularly of our family circumstances. He is very well esteemed here, and I believe carries with him introductions from Lord Percy to the Duke of N[orthumberland?] and other persons of rank.

---

1   Ibid., 1:130-133.

[Henry Hulton to   Esq.] *19 June 1775*[1]

I did not receive your favour of the 25 February by Sir Henry Calder till yesterday. Perhaps we may have later letters by the Vessel in which M[r.] Coffin is come, for we have some packages on board not yet landed, and were confident to hear from our friends by that opportunity. But put[t]ing letters into boxes is a bad way of conveyance.

I take notice of the Account inclosed in your letter, but have not yet time to look into it, or to write upon business; indeed, we are in too great an agitation of spirits to attend to any thing but our immediate situation.

The reinforcement to the Army from Ireland came very timeously, for the Rebels have been strengthening themselves all around us, ever since the 19th April, and the Generals only waited the arrival of these Regiments to enter upon action. We are now very anxious for the arrival of the second Division, and there must be another to that, before the Army can operate effectually round this place, for the whole of the people are in Arms, the Country is very strong by nature, and the Rebels have possessed themselves of all the advantageous posts, and have thrown up entrenchments in many parts.

From the heights of this place we have a view of the whole town, the harbour and Country round, for a great extent, and Last Saturday I was a spectator of the most awful scene my eyes have beheld.

In the morning of the 17[th] it was observed that the Rebels had thrown up a breastwork, and were preparing to open a Battery on the heights above Charlestown, from whence they might incommode the ship[p]ing and destroy the north part of Boston. Immediately a cannonading began from a battery on the North part of the town, and the ships of War on those Works, and on the Enemy wherever they could be discovered within reach of their Guns. Soon after 11 O'Clock the Grenadiers, Light Infantry, Marines, and two Battalions marched out of their Encampment, and Embarked in Boats, and before high Water were landed on a point of Land to the Eastward of Charlestown, and they immediately took post on a little eminence. Great was our trepidation, lest they should be attacked by superior numbers, before they could be all assembled and properly prepared; but more Boats arrived and an additional number of the Troops were landed unmolested, and the whole advanced on the side round the hill, where the Battery was erected, without any attack. On that side of the hill, which was not visible from Boston, it seems very strong lines of Intrenchments were thrown up, and were now occupied by many thousands of the Rebels.[2] The Troops advanced with great order towards the intrenchments, but were much galled in the assault, both from artillery and small Arms, and many brave Officers and Men were killed and wounded. As soon as they got into the Intrenchments, the Rebels fled, and many of them were killed in the trenches, and in their flight the Marines in marching through Charlestown were fired at from houses, and there fell their brave Commander, Major Pitcairn.[3] His son was likewise wounded. Hearing his father was killed, he cry'd out, I have lost my father! Immediately, the Corps returned, We have lost a Father! Upon the firing from the houses, the town was immediately set in flames, and at four o'clock we saw the fire and the sword, all the horrors of War raging. The town was burning all the night. The Rebels sheltered themselves in the adjacent hills and the Army possessed themselves of Charlestown neck. We were exulting in seeing the flight of our Enemies, but in an hour or two we had occasion to mourn and lament—dear was the purchase of our safety. In the evening the streets were filled with the wounded, and the dying; the sight of which, with the cries and lamentations of the Women and children over their husbands and fathers, pierced one to the Soul. We were now every moment hearing of some Officer or other of our friends and acquaintances who had fallen in our defence, and in supporting the honour of his Country. General How had his Aid de Camp wounded, who is since dead. The Major and three Captains of the 52 are killed. Most of the Grenadiers and Light Infantry, and about eighty Officers are killed and wounded.[4]

Immediately after the Action on the side of Charlestown, a brisk cannonading began from the Lines on Roxbury, but without much effect. It should seem that the Troops were not thoroughly apprized of the whole of the Works that had been thrown up by the Rebels on Bunker hill before they landed, and that we were unacquainted with the face of the Country on the opposite side, and the depth of Water in Mistick River, when we made the attack; for if there had been a floating Battery, or two, to have flanked the lines of the Rebels, and have played across the neck from the Mistick side, it is apprehended we should have lost very few Men in driving them from the strong post they had here formed. Whereas it appeared that, out of 1500 Men that were engaged, upwards of 1000 were killed or wounded, about 600 more that were landed were kept as a reserve Corps.

As the Rebels fled they met a body of 2000 coming to their support, who took to their heels likewise upon a Cannon being fired amongst them, when they were advanced near to the neck. Had there been 2000 fresh troops, it is probable they might have drove the fugitives several Miles and have possessed themselves of Cambridge; but the Troops contented themselves with maintaining and securing the post they had gained by so dear a purchase.

The Rebels have occupied a hill about a mile from Charlestown neck. They are very numerous and have thrown up intrenchments and are raising a redoubt on the higher part, whilst the Ships and Troops cannonade them wherever they can reach them. In the same manner, on the other side of Boston Neck, on the high Ground above Roxbury meeting house, the Rebels are intrenching, and raising Batteries.

Such is our present situation. We have been cut off from all supplies from the Country since the 19th April and the Rebels do every thing in their power to prevent any provision coming to us from the neighbouring parts by water. However, we have salt meat, and some fresh fish, and considering how we were surprized into a blockade, I think the town has held out wonderfully, without being distressed for eatables. Many thousands of the Inhabitants indeed abandoned the place after the 19th April, under the apprehension it would be destroyed, and if we had not carryed our point on Saturday, the operations on the other side would have made us soon very uneasy in Boston.

1   Ibid., 1:134-140. Once again, the name was obliterated. Thomas Falconer of Chester wrote to his friend Charles Gray, M. P. for Colchester, on 9 August 1775, that the "best account I have seen of it [the battle of Bunker Hill] was written by a lady at Boston to another lady at this place." See HMC, *The Manuscripts of the Earl of Buckinghamshire, the Earl of Lindsey, the Earl of Onslow, Lord Emly, Theodore J. Hare, Esq., and James Round, Esq., M.P.* (London: Her Majesty's Stationery Office, 1895), 307. This certainly sounds like something from Ann Hulton to Elizabeth Lightbody, though if so it is not among the letters assembled in *Loyalist Lady*. And even if it was from Ann, it may have been the account written by Henry above or in the next letter and sent as an enclosure.

2   The "many thousands" were not even a thousand along this line of defense, the now famous stone wall and rail fence stretching down to the far shore. There may have been as many as three thousand militiamen on the peninsula at some point during the day, with perhaps half of those engaged with the enemy at any given time.

3   Pitcairn was actually killed just outside the rebel redoubt on Breed's Hill. He was among those leading the third wave in a successful assault, the first two having failed to reach the enemy lines.

4   There were roughly 2500 British troops who were engaged in the fighting and they suffered well over 1000 casualties, with just over 200 killed and the rest wounded. American casualties were under 500, with perhaps 150 killed.

[Henry Hulton to Robert Nicholson]   *Boston   20 June 1775*[1]

Dear Sir

I had the favour of a letter from you about two months ago. For these two months past our situation has been critical and allarming, the town being blockaded, and the whole Country in arms all around us. The people have not only cut us off from all supplies by land, but they do their utmost to prevent any kind of provision being sent us from the neighboring ports. And as we were surprized into these circumstances, I wonder we have held out so well as we have done. We have bread, salt meat, and fresh fish, and there appears no distress for want of subsistance. Many thousand of the inhabitants abandoned their dwellings in apprehension that a speedy destruction would fall on the place, and indeed we have been wonderfully preserved. The affair of the 19th of April prevented the execution of a diabolical plot, and had not the Troops gone out on the 17th instant, it is probable that the town at this hour would have been in ashes.

The reinforcement to the Army from Ireland came very timely, for the Generals only waited the arrival of these Regiments to enter upon action.

We are now very anxious for the arrival of the second division, and I am affraid it will be necessary to have another to that before the Army can operate effectually round this place.

The Country is very strong by Nature, and the Rebels have possessed themselves of all the advantageous posts, and have thrown up Entrenchments in many parts.

From the heights of this place we have a view of the whole town, the harbour and country round for a great extent, and last Saturday I was a spectator of a most awful scene my eyes have beheld. In the morning of the 17[th] it was observed that the Rebels had thrown up a breastwork and were preparing to open a Battery on the heights above Charlestown; from whence they might incommode the ship[p]ing, and destroy the north part of Boston. Immediately a Cannonading began from the Battery on the north part of the town and the Ships of War on those Works and on the enemy, wherever they could be discovered within reach of their guns. Soon after eleven o'clock the Grenadiers, Light Infantry, Marines, and two Battalions marched out of their Incampments and embarked in Boats, and before high water were landed on a point of land to the Eastward of Charlestown, and they immediately took post on a little eminence. Great was our trepidation lest they should be attacked by superior numbers before they could be all assembled and properly prepared, but more boats arrived and an additional number of troops were landed unmolested, and the whole advanced, some on the other side round the hill where the Battery was erected, and some through part of Charlestown. On that side of the hill which was not visible from Boston, it seems very strong lines were thrown up, and were occupied by many thousands of the Rebels. The troops advanced with great order towards the intrenchments, but were much galled in the assault, both from artillery and small arms, and many brave Officers and Men were killed and wounded. As soon as they got to the intrenchments the Rebels fled, and many of them were killed in the trenches, and in their flight.

The Marines, in marching through part of Charlestown, were fired at from the houses, and there fell their brave Commander Major Pitcairn. His son was likewise wounded. Hearing his father was killed, he cried out I have lost my Father. Immediately the Corps returned, we have lost a Father! How glorious to die with such an Epitaph. Upon the firing from the houses the town was immediately set in flames, and at four o'clock we saw the fire and the sword, all the horrors of war raging.

The town was burning all the night, the Rebels sheltered themselves in the adjacent hills and the neighbourhood of Cambridge, and the Army possessed themselves of Charlestown neck. We were exulting in seeing the flight of our Enemies, but in an hour or two we had occasion to mourn and lament. Dear was the purchse of our safety. In the evening the streets were filled with the wounded and the dying; the sight of which, with the cries and lamentations of the women and children over their husbands and fathers, peirced one to the soul. We were now every moment hearing of some officer or other of our friends and acquaintance who had fallen in our defence and in supporting the honor of our Country. General Howe had his aid de camp wounded, who is since dead. The Major and three Captains of the 52d were killed, or died of their wounds. Most of the Grenadiers and Light Infantry, and about eighty officers are killed or wounded.

The Rebels have occupied a hill about a mile from Charlestown neck. They are very numerous and have thrown up Entrenchments, and are raising a Redoubt on the higher part, whilst the ships and troops Cannonade them wherever they can reach them. In the same manner, on the other side of Boston neck, on the high ground above Roxbury Meeting, the Rebels are intrenching and raising a Battery. Such is our present situation.

In this Army are many of noble families, many very respectable, virtuous and amiable characters, and it grieves one that Gentlemen, Brave British Soldiers, should fall by the hands of such despicable Wretches as compose the banditti of the Country, amongst whom there is not one that has the least pretence to be called a gentleman. They are a most rude, depraved and degenerate race, and it is a mortification to us that they speak English and can trace themselves from that stock.

Since Adams went to Philadelphia, one Warren, a rascally Patriot and Apothecary of this town, has had the lead in the provincial Congress. He signed Commissions and acted as President. This fellow happily was killed in run[n]ing out of the trenches the other day, where he had commanded and spirited the people to defend their Lines, which he assured them were impregnable. You may judge what the herd must be when such a one is their Leader.[2]

Here it is only justice to say that there are many worthy people in this province, but that the chief of them are now in Boston and that amongst the Gentlemen of the Council particularly are many respectable and worthy characters.

I beg my best Compliments to Mrs N. and all friends with you, and remain with great regard, Dear Sir, yours &c.

---

1   Hulton, "Nicholson Letters," 78-86. The editors of *Loyalist Lady* included this letter as part of an appendix, on 97-100. They worked from the text provided them by the Reverend Jones. Jones may have had the original letter; he may also have passed along a copy—just as the version in the "Nicholson Letters" is a copy, not the original.

2   Dr. Joseph Warren. Hulton's raw emotions spill forth here.

[Henry Hulton to Robert Nicholson] 30 *July 1775*[1]

I wrote to you by the *Cerberus* Man of War, with an account of the action of the 17th June. Mr. Coffin tells me that his son John, who is bred to the sea, is going Mate of a Vessel to Liverpool. He is a very clever young fellow, and will give you an Account of the state of Affairs here, which it would be too long to relate fully in the compass of a letter. Neither should I chuse to make a detail of all the matters, relative to our present situation.

The Rebels have thrown up strong lines of intrenchments all round the Bay and have been very audacious in their attempts upon the Islands in the harbour, and their attacks upon our outposts. They lately burnt the Lighthouse, and two nights ago attempted to surprise and carry off the out Guard at Bunker hill.

We are much in want of fresh provision and forage, and the town is very sickly. And it is said the Rebels have several disorders reigning amongst them.

The remaining inhabitants of the Town that are adverse to Government are removing out of it, and indeed most of the Families of our friends that can get away are Embarking for Britain, and other parts, to escape from the impending calamities. We trust that we shall yet have a considerable reinforcement to the Army this fall and have large supplies of Provision, fuel &c. from Europe, otherwise our prospect for the Winter will be very gloomy. For we are cut off from all communication with the Country, and every day are subject to alarms, never going to bed without expectation of an attack, and frequently are awaked with Cannonadings in the night.

My family, thank God, continue pretty well, but I have many anxieties on their subject, and wish I could persuade Mrs. H. to take herself and children to England. But she will not quit the place without me, so we must wait the event; and I trust that the Almighty will grant us a happy issue out of all these troubles. But what private person can think much of enduring these evils, when Earl Percy goes through all toils and dangers with the greatest chearfulness, and alacrity, and gives life and spirit to the service, by his being the foremost in all the fatigues and hazards of his profession.

Early in July the Generals Washington and Lee arrived at Cambridge, being appointed by the Continental Congress to the command of their Army, which is now to be called the Army of the Confederated Provinces.

The Rebels on the side of Roxbury threw up entrenchments near our advanced post, and frequently fired at the Lines with some pieces of Cannon, and almost daily attacked and fired upon the Centries, which sometimes drew on a cannonading on our part. But in general the Lines and Centries received their fire without returning it. Brown's house on the Neck, where the troops had a post, was at different times set on fire, and at length consumed. The Rebels had the audacity to go over to Long Island, four miles down the harbour, where about a dozen men were employed in mowing, and carried them off, with all the stock on the Island, and the next day returned and set fire to the house in the sight of several Men of War who fired at, and pursued them, but with no effect. About the middle of July several transports arrived with our Regiments of foot from Ireland, which had been at New York, but had Orders sent to them from the General to proceed to Boston, without landing there. At this time about 2000 Connecticut people have possessed themselves of New York, and all who will not join against Great Britain are to be expelled the Country, and at Philadelphia they are disciplining several Regiments to join the general cause.

July 31st. At 1 o'clock this morning we were waked with a furious cannonade of great Guns, and an heavy fire from small Arms in several Quarters, and apprehended the Enemy were making a general attack on the town in all parts. We have been long threatened that the town should be set on fire in different places, by the people within, whilst the Rebels, under favour of their numbers without, would attempt a general assault. They have been provided with several hundred Whale boats from Nantucket for some time past, which row with prodigious swiftness, and in these they venture to go upon Islands in sight of the Men of War, whose Boats cannot reach them. And they are so light as to be easily carried upon Men's shoulders from place to place. In the midst of so much noise, under these apprehensions, consider the distress of a family of Women and Children, not knowing which way to flee for shelter. However, this affair has proved to be a feinte from our side in different parts, at the same time the Enemy made a second descent at the Light house, and killed the Officer and some of the troops that had lately been stationed there, and made prisoners of the rest of the party that was not destroyed.

---

1 Hulton, "Letterbooks," 1:141-145; also included, by a different hand, with variations in spelling and punctuation, in Hulton, "Nicholson Letters," 86-90.

[Henry Hulton to unknown addressee] *10 August 1775*[1]

I had the pleasure to write to you in February last, since which we have undergone a great deal of anxiety and distress. The chief occurrances are of such notoriety, I shall not repeat them. Since the affair of the 19th April, this place has been blockaded by the Rebels, who are strongly intrenched all round the Bay, and we have been cut off from all communication with the Country since that time, and they have prevented, all in their power, any supplys of provision or fuel coming to us from other parts; but as there appears a general disposition of revolt from the authority of Great Britain through out the Continent, so no other Colonies except Halifax, and Quebec, will send any thing for our support. The attack of Bunker's Hill on the 17th June does great honour to the valor of our Troops, but cost us dear, and must be a caution to us how we attack the Enemy in their strong holds. However, that assault was absolutely necessary to the maintaining ourselves in this place.

Most of the inhabitants of Boston are removed, or are going out of it to other parts to avoid the impending calamities. The Town has already been very sickly, both amongst the Army and the people, and it is very lamentable to be witness to so much distress which you cannot relieve, and to see your Children and friends languishing for fresh provision, and the comfortable accommodations they have been accustomed to. But the present evils appear light in comparison to what must be apprehended in the course of Winter, if we are not powerfully supported and relieved from home. However, we live in hopes that Great Britain will exert itself, and that we shall have a large reinforcement of troops and supplys of provision and fuel from Europe before the Winter.

The Rebels have provided themselves with some hundreds of Whale Boats from the Island of Nantucket, which row with prodigious swiftness; in these they make descents on the Islands in the harbour, in sight of the Men of War; and they have been very audacious in these attempts. A little while ago they burnt the Light House, and some nights after landed there again, burnt the dwelling house, killed an Officer of Marines that was stationed there, and made his party prisoners.

We are exposed to frequent alarms, and are sometimes awaked at Midnight with furious cannonadings, and scarce a day passes without an exchange of musketry from some of the advanced posts.

The several Towns have sent Representatives to a Provincial Assembly, and those Representatives have chosen a Council, who have taken upon them the Government of the Province, but they have not appointed a Governour.

The proceedings of the Continental Congress appear as the effusions of wild fanatics. Their schemes will involve the Continent in ruin, but can never be carryed into effect. They talk of forming the United Colonies into a Mighty Empire, of establishing a Continental Revenue, maintaining a standing Army of 27,000, disciplining the whole people, raising a naval power, providing for an extensive Commerce, opening their Ports to all Nations. Surely they have forgot that they reckon without their Host, and will be made to feel the chastisement, due to their insolence. I am sorry that England should have given birth to one of their chief Generals.

---

1   Hulton, "Letterbooks," 1:153-156.

[Henry Hulton to unknown addressee]   *Boston 11 October 1775*[1]

I wrote to you between the 20th September and this day, and gave my letter to Mr. Fluker, under cover to Mr. Samuel Horne. Mr. F. went along with General Gage, and Mr. Burch's family sailed the same time, in another ship for London. Just as they embarked, Col. D[alrymple] landed from England. That day an express arrived from Quebec with very alarming accounts of the invasion of Canada by the Rebels under General Schyler.

October 13

I attended yesterday as Bearer to L[ady] P[epperell]. Never was a young person more generally or deservedly lamented. Poor Sir William; he is quite inconsolable! And we all grieve and lament. Oh! It is a great breach on our society. But alas! We are so much roused to attend to our present support, and safety, that we cannot have leisure to reflect on other calamities. Our supplies of provision are scanty and uncertain, and we dread the approach of Winter. No one is provided with fuel or victual. Yet in the midst of our distresses, some of the young and gay are preparing for the Winter's amusement. And it is said a Tragedy is in rehearsal.

October 18th. Last night at 9 o'clock we were amused with a cannonading for about an hour. We thought it had been from the Charles town side, but it proved to be the Rebels exercising their armed Gondaloes, which came down from Cambridge river and fired at the tents in the Common. Happily, they did no mischief but to themselves, for one of their Guns burst, overset, or blew up the Boat and several of them were said to be killed or wounded Mr. L. is come back from Halifax, and is going to Newport to look after his family.

October 23d. Yesterday we received Accounts that the Rebels at St. Johns in Canada had met with a severe check from the Regulars and Indians, that 1000 of them were killed and wounded.

October 25th. For two nights past the Troops have been under Arms in expectation of an attack from the Rebels. It is said that Dr. F[ranklin] and a Deputy from the Congress are come to Cambridge, to urge on the Rebels to an immediate attempt upon Boston.

We have had a great deal of rain, and it is very severe on the soldiers to be still in camp, but the Rebels feel the hardship of the season more severely; they are without proper clothing, and it is thought they will not long be kept together. Several Deserters are come in, and many are got in of late who have been amongst the Rebels, and we have various Accounts of the cruel treatment that the Tories in the Country have met with. Mr. Edward Brinley's Wife at Roxbury, whilst laying in, had a guard of the Rebels always in her room, who treated her with great rudeness, and indecency, exposing her to the view of all their crew, as a sight to see, a tory Woman! and stripped her and her children of all their Linen and clothes. Mr. B. is in Chief Justice Oliver's house at Middlebro, but his Daughter in law, who lived in it, was turned out, and all his cattle and stock have been sold. Mrs. Thomas at Marshfield has people living in her house on her substance, who never suffer her to speak to any one, or go abroad without them.

Captain Wallace has commenced hostilities on the Rhode Island side. We sent our schooner there to get provision. Unluckily, she arrived in the midst of the fray. About 1000 people from the Continent had got over, and were possessed of the heights about Newport, in order to prevent all supplies being sent them. Poor Mr. Dudley fled from his house.[2] Captain Wallace sent them word [that] if they entered the Town he would lay it in Ashes. He had before fired upon Bristol, and all the coast are terrified, knowing what a Man he is. We hear the Rebels have a great number of large Boats ready at Cambridge and Watertown, that a few nights ago they had 7000 Men drawn out to embark in them for an attack on Boston, that General Lee commanded them, but that they could not settle who should go first, and so it passed off.

October 29th. About three weeks ago Captain Mourt and Lieutenant Dawson went down with some troops on an expedition to the Eastward. This day we hear that they have burn Falmouth in Casco bay.

By advice this day from Kennebeck we hear that the Committee there had sentenced a Man to be buried alive for wishing success to the King's troops, and that the sentence has been executed upon him. By a Deserter come in this morning it is said notice is brought that the Town is to be attacked this night in three places.

November 3. The General, by Proclamation, recommended an association of the inhabitants for maintainance of order within the Town, and between 4 and 500 have subscribed. What measures will be taken with those who don't subscribe, we do not yet know.

Poor Sir W. P. spent an hour or two with us the other Morning; he has a great attachment to us and our family, and seems fond to unbosom himself to us. Grief preys much upon him, and I fear he will hardly overcome his affliction; indeed, he seems rather desirous of dying, nor can be roused to wish for life, though the interest of his children so much depend upon it. "The ways of heaven are Dark and intricate"[3] that such heavy afflictions should befall so virtuous a character; for I never met with a man of a fairer mind, less corrupted by the World, or possessed of a more benevolent heart.

Notwithstanding all the threats and allarms of the Rebels, they have as yet made no attack on the town. But the Troops undergo a great deal of watching, and fatigue; several Redoubts are casting up about the Common, and we expect soon to have some large sea Mortars mounted that will reach to Cambridge. The Rebels have built many large Barracks round the Bay, and some are building on Bunker's hill for the Army. All the Houses near the water side round the town will be occupied by the Troops, and many old houses are now pulling down by the soldiers for fuel. Great is the want of that article, and of forage. What think you of ten Dollars for a cord of Wood, four Dollars a hundred for Hay, and two Dollars for a Goose? But the light horse Gentlemen give any price.

It is said that Doctor [Benjamin] Church is under confinement by the Rebels on suspicion of having corresponded with General Gage, and that parties run high among them whether he shall be hanged, or not.[4]

November 10th. Some Vessels are now got in with Troops and Stores from England, and Ireland. Last night it blew very violently at NE with rain. Many ships were seen in the bay in the afternoon; they prove to be a fleet of transports from the Eastward, loaded with wood.

Yesterday a party of Light Infantry landed on Phips's Farm and brought off a number of Cattle, without the loss of a man. A great number of the Rebels came down as they reimbarked, but were dispersed, and many of them supposed to be killed by the fire from the Man of War and Batteries at Charlestown.

November 13th. Blows hard at NW, which keeps out the ships from Europe, many of which must now be on the Coast, and for whose arrival we are very anxious, as every one is in want of fuel and provision. We have been deluged with rain, and now it is a frost and very cold, yet the poor Soldiers are still in their tents without straw. Surely there will be subscriptions at home and donations sent out of many comforts and necessaries for them. What will become of the inhabitants, the Women and Children through this dreary Winter, I know not, but the prospect is gloomy. General Lee has wrote to an Officer, adviseing him to come over to them, for that they have got the Army in a net, and shall soon drive them into the sea, or put them to the sword. But he is considered as a wicked madman, and the Troops are in such spirits that when the reinforcements arrive, they hope to drive the Rebels from this neighbourhood.

November 16th. Yesterday we were greatly distressed with a report that the *Minerva* was lost on Scilly Island and all the people but 11 had perished, but it now appears there was no authority for the report.

November 25th. Several Vessels are got in from Nova Scotia with Hay, and the *Phenix* Man of War has been arrived from England for a Week past, but most of her Convoy are still out, and we are very anxious for the arrival of a Brig that came out with her, with Ordnance stores of great consequence, as several Vessels have lately been taken in the Bay.

The Rebels have thrown up some new Works near to Charlestown, where the Light Infantry landed, which occasions the troops' fresh labour to erect a battery to oppose them.

November 26th. Several ships got in yesterday evening, but the weather is very tempestuous. Between 4 and 500 of the town people were sent off two days ago, and landed at Point Shirley. The Country people, it is said, will not receive them till they have been thoroughly smoaked, dreading the small pox.[5] About 4000 Inhabitants and refugees now remain in the town.

Mr. Hallowell went down to the Light house to assist in putting up a new Light. An Armed Transport went down to protect the workmen and it is now lighted again, and 40 or 50 Soldiers are shut up in it. A Rebel schooner took a Brig near to the Light house two days ago. The Transport cut her cable and chased them, when the Rebels left the prize and escaped, but first set her on fire, which was extinguished by a boy of the crew that had hid himself on board. Several Men of War have been sent in search of the Ordnance Brig. They have spoke with her off the Capes, but been seperated from her by the violent winds, and are returned with loss of sails &c., and she is still out.

November 29th. Having read this letter to Mrs. H., she would by no means have me send it, as she hates to write any thing that only serves to make others unhappy. And says there is nothing in it to give you pleasure, and that I make the worst of our situation. So pray, be not over[-]anxious and distressed about us, for we hope to rub through the Winter tolerably well. We want only a few Chaldron of Coals, a few tidbits [of] Beef, pork, pease and potatoes, which I hope we shall be supply'd with by arrivals within a Week or ten days. Mr. Nicholson has sent me a fine Cheshire cheese. I wish I had ordered some potatoes from Liverpool, but have got a few bushels out of one of the Liverpool Vessels, at 8/sterling per bushel.

---

1   Ibid., 1:156-166.

2   Charles Dudley, who for years bore the brunt of local resentment when he tried to enforce the navigation acts in Rhode Island. He had succeeded John Robinson as the collector in Newport when Robinson was appointed to the customs commission. Like so many of the English-born customs officials who came to the colonies in the Revolutionary era, he returned to England—in his case, after the British evacuation of Boston. Like the Hultons, he went to Halifax first before re-crossing the Atlantic.

3   From lines spoken by Portius, a son of the Roman hero Cato, in Joseph Addison's 1713 play "Cato" (Act 1, scene 1), most accessible now in Christine Dunn Henderson and Mark E. Yellin, eds., *Cato: A Tragedy and Selected Essays* (Indianapolis: Liberty Fund, 2004), 9:
    Remember what our father oft has told us:
    The ways of heaven are dark and intricate,
    Puzzled in mazes, and perplexed with errors:

4   Church, an intimate of John Hancock, Samuel Adams, and other Patriot leaders, started feeding information to Gage in 1774, when he had at the same time begun sitting in the Massachusetts Provincial Congress. Not found out for nearly a year, he was later imprisoned and put on a ship in 1778, which went down at sea—with Church presumably still aboard. If there had been no Benedict Arnold, perhaps he would be better remembered today for his treachery. Still, the essay on him for *Sibley's Harvard Graduates,* 13:380-398, opens, "Benjamin Church, the traitor..." He and Benjamin Thompson, the future Count Rumford, are the primary subjects/suspects in Allen French's *General Gage's Informers* (Ann Arbor: University of Michigan Press, 1932). Also see David James Kiracoffe, "Dr. Benjamin Church and the Dilemma of Treason in Revolutionary Massachusetts," *New England Quarterly* 70 (1997): 443-462.

5   For Boston's smallpox outbreak, set in the context of a wartime epidemic, see Elizabeth A. Fenn, *Pox Americana* (New York: Hill and Wang, 2001), 46-55, and passim.

[Henry Hulton to unknown addressee] *November 1775*[1]

I am much obliged to you for your favour of[2]　　and am much concerned you should have so much trouble in our affairs.

I had the pleasure to write you in August by my sister, who fled in a ship for Bristol, with many other passengers from the impending calamities. And I hope you will hear from her on the subject of the matters in your Letter.

We are still in the situation we have been in for several months past, environed by the Rebels, and under difficulties in regard to our subsistance. The troops have undergone great fatigue and hardships; and many of them are still encamped on Bunker's hill, though the weather has been and continues very severe. We have been deluged with rain and it is now a hard frost, and every kind of provision, forage and fuel is very scarce and dear. However, we hope for supplies of all kinds from Europe, and that we shall yet have considerable reinforcements of troops this fall. And I trust the operations in the spring will be so extensive, powerful, and vigorous, as to bring the War to a speedy issue.

In the mean time, we undergo many difficulties, but we have rub[b]ed on pretty well through all our alarms and troubles, and I thank God all my family are in pretty good health and spirits. Mine has been a life of toil and persecution in this service, and I have been subjected to many heavy expences, and considerable loss of property, yet no one is more desirous of repose, or would cultivate peace more than myself. But it has been my lot to combat, and suffer, and though I hope in the course of another year that these people will be reduced to obedience, yet the comforts of tranquility and social intercourse, cannot be expected. The temper and disposition of the Americans will hardly be reconciled to the authority they may with reluctance be brought to acknowledge; and it must be very unpleasing to a humane mind to see the necessary exertions of power that must be employed, to reduce the refractory to obedience, and to dwell in a country suffering under the calamities of War. But we must submit to our fate, and make the best of circumstances that befall us; and if we cannot reproach ourselves that the evils we suffer arise from any misconduct of our own, we can bear them with greater fortitude, and draw consolation from right principles.

1　Hulton, "Letterbooks," 1:167-169.
2　Left blank.

[Henry Hulton to Mrs.   ] *30 November 1775*[1]

Dear Madam

I had the pleasure to receive your letter to my sister of the 1ˢᵗ August, a few days ago, under cover of one from Miss T. You will no doubt have heard from my sister from Bristol, for which place she Embarked with many other passengers in August, who fled from our impending calamities. I had the pleasure of a letter from you by Mr. Totty and should sooner have written in return, could I have communicated any thing agreeable in regard to the circumstances of Cozin J.[2] or our own. His situation is in a small Island and in a confined society, but whatever inconvenience may attend it, his lot at this time is better than that of any Officer on the Continent. You will have been sufficiently informed of the events that have befallen us; we have still greater evils to apprehend, for it is impossible in our situation not to anticipate all the calamities of War. When I consider the hardships and fatigues the soldiers endure, the miseries of many people, and the general distress of every family, I almost forget my own misfortunes, and have great reason to be thankful that all my family yet enjoy so much health and so many comforts. Indeed, I am happy in a companion who possesses uncommon fortitude, and who never repines, or sinks under any difficulties that we are to encounter. And my four boys enjoy good health and contribute greatly to our amusement and pleasure. Your favorite name, Edward, is given in my family to my third son, who is a fine sprightly boy. They are all now under inoculation. But these connections, the sources of our comforts, are likewise the cause of a great deal of anxiety, especially under every alarm and difficulty, many of which we have undergone, and must still expect to experience.

These times call forth many characters into action, and they of distinguished abilities make their Virtues, or crimes, conspicuous—Here are two Gentlemen of our Country, the one the object of admiration, the other of abhorrence; the one does honour to his rank, to his country, to human nature; and is truly an illustrious character; the other from pride, disappointed ambition, and a corrupt heart, is involved in the guilt of rebellion, and is prostituting distinguished talents, by leading on a deluded people to their destruction. Such are Lord P[ercy] and Mr. [Charles]Lee.

We are very happy in the society of Mr.[3]   when he is ashore, which is but seldom. He is now a Lieutenant and much respected as a sensible, well[-]behaved Man.

---

1   Hulton, "Letterbooks," 1:169-171. The name is missing.
2   John Hincks.
3   Blank space.

[Ann Hulton to Elizabeth Lightbody]   *Chester 17 January 1776*[1]

I have Dear Mrs Lightbody's agreable favor of Yesterday's date, and the pleasure to hear that you and your family enjoy health. Pray, accept my sincere good wishes for the continuance of your domestic happiness, and my best thanks for your Kind invitation, Be assured, it would make me happy to Meet you, my Dear friend, anywhere, and to talk over past scenes and events, provided the present gloomy scene was dispelled. I suppose you have heard that Mr. Tylston talks of going up to London with Miss Lem towards the end of next Month. They have almost perswaded your Sister and I to be of the party, This is not determined on, but if I don't accompany them I am engaged to go to Mrs Hignet's, when Mrs T. leaves Chester.

The uncertain and anxious state I am in on account of my Dear friends and Connections in America admits not of spirits to think of Journeys of pleasure, or to write long letters, though I have much to say; indeed, the constant daily engagements we have here allows me not leisure hardly to write to my Brother. By the latest Accounts from Boston, the Town was still invironed by the Enemy, who were urged to make a general attack upon it (by a deputation from the Congress). They had often threatened it and made some efforts. They had a great number of large boats, and one night the latter end of October, 7000 men were drawn out to embark in them. General Lee had harangued them, but they could not agree who should go first on the desperate attempt.

The greatest Mischief they did was to themselves, for one of their Guns burst overset or blew up the boat, with all the people in it. They are numerous but in a wretched condition, In Rags, dirt, and vermin, with consequent distempers, which were spread through all the Towns and it's said 1200 of the fugitives out of Boston were dead since the Siege.

The King's Troops endured great fatigues yet were in good spirits, and hoped to drive the Rebels.

Provisions and fuel were scarce and very dear, supplies uncertain. Heavy rains, Tempestuous weather, and the Winter set in very severe. Some vessils with Troops and Stores arrived; more seen off in the Bay, but kept out by contrary winds and it was to be feared some Provision Ships had been taken by the Provincials.

In this dreary situation are my Dear friends in Boston. Judge, then, what I feel. And there are other aggravating circumstances. Whilst they are looking out for present support for themselves and their little ones, they grieve and lament for the Loss of a most amiable woman, Lady Pepperril. A great breach it is in their Society, and proves an almost unsupportable Affliction to Sir William, left with four small Children. My Brother says, "the ways of Heaven are dark and intricate." That such heavy affliction should befall so virtuous a Character! For he never met a man of a fairer mind, more uncorrupted by the world, or possessed of a more benevolent heart. They had been greatly distressed, too, with a report that the Vessil in which I and fifty passengers sailed for England was lost on one of the Scilly

Islands, and that all the crew but eleven perished. They had no way of being satisfied to the contrary, but on Enquiry there appeared no Authority for the report. It was supposed to have arisen from some wicked people, to distress those who had friends on board the Ship.

Amidst all these alarms, dangers, and distresses, the Small pox spread Universaly, which Obliged them to innoculate the Children. Dear little creatures, God preserve them; support their Parents in this day of trial, grant relief to their anxious cares, and deliverance from the impending calamities.

My Brother says that Ships to Boston laden with Provision might make a prodigious Voyage of it. The articles they want are Beef, Pork, pease, and Potatoes, Coals, and Oates &c. He bought a few bushels of Potatoes out of a Liverpool Ship at 8/Sterling a Bushil. Beef sold at 16d and 18d a pound, and a Goose at 10/Sterling. I mention this, desiring you will please to make it known, probably some Merchants may send out Cargos from Liverpool the sooner this Spring the better. Insurance will be but the same as in Time of War.

I wish to hear when any Vessil goes. I would send out several Articles on freight, if I could.

I wrote to Mr R. Nicholson on this matter, and he was so obliging to answer me immediately, promising to let me know further. Please to acquaint him and other gentlemen what things are wanted at Boston, and they promote the sending of 'em out to the great Advantage of the Owners.

My Brother received your favor to me, wrote at Warrington, August 23, for which I can only return my thanks, being a stranger to the contents of it, but I doubt not it gave him some pleasure. Pray, did you ever receive My Letters wrote in March and in April last?

I am sorry to hear you have so much trouble with my Shoe maker. I shall be glad to have the shoes when they are done, but not to give you trouble about 'em. Please let me Know how to direct to him.

Mr G: Colquit's being driven back is a disagreeable circumstance. So many of your friends will be writing to you, that I shall not pretend to send you any news from hence at present, but beg my best respects to Mr. and Miss Lightbody, and to Mr. & and Mrs. R. Nicholson, and an interest in your prayers for our friends at a distance, and your Affectionate friend and Humble Servant,

Ann Hulton[2]

---

1 *Loyalist Lady*, 80-84.
2 The editors rendered the signature as "Anne." I suspect she signed with a flourish, making a swirl that could look like an "e."

[Henry Hulton to Robert Nicholson]

Boston 22 January 1776[1]

Dear Sir

I received your favour of the 5th September on the 27 November, and am much obliged to you for your kind present of a Cheshire Cheese, which was very acceptable, for every kind of provision and fuel has been very scarce and dear. Though we have had reports that a number of Ships were coming out with supplies for this place, yet few have arrived and the Army has been obliged to pull down a great many houses for fuel, Hay has been sold at a Guinea the hundred, Beef at 16 and 18 Sterling by the Quarter, and turkies for 3 and 4 dollars each; however, we have rubbed on thus far pretty tolerably, and as a considerable quantity of Coals are lately arrived for the Army, and we are in expectation of great quantities of necessaries of all sorts arriving soon, we keep up our spirits and do not fear being starved; and, as to the Rebels, we are under little apprehension from them — We have certainly undergone a good deal of anxiety and to be sure our situation is far from being agreeable, but we must submit to our lot and bear up as well as we can under unavoidable circumstances. And I am happy in a partner that possesses great fortitude under all our difficulties and distresses; indeed, it would be a strange thing for us to live in a state of peace and quietness, free from apprehensions and allarms. However, we have peace within ourselves and under our own roof, while all around us is hostile filled with the din of Arms and dreadful note of preparation.

I did not receive your two favours of the 26 September and 2nd October till the 16 instant. I am much obliged to you for the little book of moral tales by Dr. Percival,[2] which I have begun to read to the Children. The Doctor sent me his books of Medical Essays, which I lent to an able Physician of my acquaintance, who speaks much in their favour and holds the Doctor in high consideration, and I have great respect for Dr. Percival's Character.

I made application in behalf of the Ship commanded by Captain Robinson, agreeably to your request; so did Mr. Coffin and I believe there will be no difficulty in getting her employed in the King's service.

I am obliged to you in paying respect to my recommendation of Mr. John Coffin, and his Father is sensible to the notice you have taken of him.

I imagine every one is now convinced of the intentions of the Americans, of which we on this side the Water had long been persuaded and could not but lament to see a man in the confidence and service of the Government, deceiving Administration, working himself into the favor of Men of Science by his Philosophy and deluding well disposed people at home, whilst he was fomenting the flames of rebellion in America.

This arch-traitor! This most atrocious of Men is Dr. Franklin! The only question now seems to be, whether it is more advisable to transport the Scepter of Empire to the Delaware, than to retain it on the Thames? And I hope there is no old Briton can hesitate at the question.

The intentions of these people are no less than to establish one or more independent Republicks.

This town is now deserted by most of its inhabitants, friends as well as Rebels; however, we have plays acted by the Officers, and Assemblies and Concerts are just set a going—but I imagine our Winter Quarter amusements will not be of long continuance; for we expect an early, vigorous, extensive, and decisive Campaign. The Winter began very boisterously, but it seems to soften away, and is likely to go off soon without a severe frost.

The only cheap thing here is house-rent and the dwellers therein are frequently changing. Many people are glad to get a family into their house with the furniture standing whilst they flee from fear or to join the Rebels.

I am going to remove to my friend's Sir William Pepperill's house, that has a large garden and pasture adjoining, so that we hope to have all kinds of vegetables, and food for our Cow within ourselves during the Summer, which are great objects in our situation.

I was much concerned to see the account you sent me of my friend Mr C[ropper], pray how is my old friend Mr Bassnett? My best respects await all your family friends.

I imagine you will have heard of my Sister, who went from hence in August last. I had a letter from her of 25 September at Bristol, which is the only one yet come to hand. Mrs. H. desires her best respects to Mrs N. and Mrs B., with congratulations to the latter on the birth of her Son.

I am with great regard, Dear Sir, your most obedient Servant.

H H

---

1   Hulton, "Nicholson Letters," 91-95.

2   Thomas Percival, *A Father's Instructions to His Children* (London: J. Johnston, 1775), which Percival issued in three installments into 1776. It was reprinted many times over the next decade.

[Henry Hulton to   Esqr.]   *24 January 1776*[1]

When we lived at Brooklyn we were happy in our neighbourhood to Sir William. And Lady Pepperrill, and their society contributed very much to render our situation agreeable to us. The circumstances of the times at length drove both our families for shelter to Boston, and in our common sufferings we were greatly comforted and solaced by each others society and friendship. Indeed, the continuance of such connections would have rendered any circumstances supportable, for never were two persons better formed for all the Offices of social affection and intercourse, but alass! We were deprived of one of these amiable friends by death a few months ago, and the other has hitherto only brooded over his sorrow, and wasted his hours in unavailing grief. His friends wished him to change the scene and to divert his melancholy by new objects, remote from the din of Arms. But dreading the severity of a Winter's passage, they were desirous he should stay till the spring, before he undertook the Voyage. However, as he remains still without consolation, and his health is greatly impaired, we are now anxious he should go home,[2] as soon as possible, and he embarks by this opportunity for London, with four little children.

There is no person whose society we should more wish to retain than Sir William Pepperrill, and therefore nothing could make us submit to the loss of it, but the consideration of his health and interest. When you know him, I am sure you will esteem him as a Gentleman possessed of the fairest mind and most uncorrupted heart. To alleviate the sorrows of so worthy a character, I am sure will give you great satisfaction, and I have assured him of your kind offices of friendship, adapted to his feelings and situation; and may we beg that the Ladies of your family will assist him with their advice, in the best manner of placing his daughters in a train of education.

---

1   Hulton, "Letterbooks," 1:171-173. Name again excised.

2   It is interesting that Hulton should characterize Pepperrell's leaving for England as going "home." The first William Pepperrell in Massachusetts was indeed an Englishman, born in Devon, but he arrived in the 1670s. The Sir William of Hulton's acquaintance was actually born in Massachusetts as a Sparhawk, the son of Nathaniel Sparhawk and the first William's grandaughter Elizabeth. He took on the Pepperrell name, inherited the baronetcy awarded to the second William Pepperrell to honor his service at the siege of Louisbourg, and the family lands near Kittery. He lived in grand style, with a townhouse in Boston and a country estate outside Roxbury that he leased from Francis Bernard, which is what made him a "neighbor" to the Hultons. He attended Harvard and had made only one visit to England before he went into exile, so it was "home" to him in only an idealized sense, as he, like so many of his loyalist colleagues, effectively became a man without a country after the coming of war. There is a brief sketch of Pepperrell in *Sibley's Harvard Graduates*, 16:397-403.

[Ann Hulton to Elizabeth Lightbody]   *Chester 22 February 1776*[1]

I have wanted to hear good news from Boston to write to Dear Mrs Lightbody in better spirits, and not so gloomy a Letter as I wrote you before.

Last Sunday I received one from my Brother, but have been so much engaged since, that had not an opportunity of writing till now. The Arrival of several Transports with provision and forage, and a new Admiral[2] to the command of the fleet at Boston, was a very seasonable relief, and my Brother seems to write in good spirits, though, at the best, their situation to us must appear very disagreable and even terrible, yet I rejoice that his children are all recovered from the Small pox, and that they had rubbed so far through this dreadful Winter.

He writes by way of Journal, the last Letter beginning the 2d December and concluding the 15th January, so that it contains a good deal of what we have heard by newspapers before. The poor Soldiers endured great hardships and fatigues, deluged with rain, then chilled with frost whilst they were in their Tents without Straw. Surely (says he) there will be subscriptions at home and donations sent out of many comforts and necessaries for them.

When they were at the greatest extremities for want of supplies, General Lee wrote to an Officer, advising him to come over to them, for that they had got the Army in a net, and should soon drive them into the Sea or put them to ye Sword.

This wicked Madman (for he is looked upon in that light by those who know him in Chester, as well as in Boston) went with 1200 Men to Rhode Island and carried away all the Officers of the Crown that would not take the shocking Oath he imposes.

The Rebels made a demand on the Collector at Rhode Island of the King's Money, upon which he had fled on board the *Rose*, Man of War. They then seized on his house and effects, and turned his Wife out of doors. It is said (since this) that General Lee is gone to Canada. The cruelties which are exercised on all those who are in their power is shocking. By advice frm Kennebec, the Committee there had sentenced a Man to be buried alive for wishing success to the King's Troops, and that the sentence had been executed upon him. At Roxbury Mr Edward Brinley's wife, whilst laying in, had a guard of Rebels always in her room, who treated her with great rudeness and indecency, exposing her to the view of their banditti, as a sight "See a tory woman," and stripd her and her Children of all their Linnen and Cloths.

On the 18th December the Rebels exercised their Artillery upon Boston; a 24 pound shot fell into the Garden of the House occupied by Lord Percy. During that Night and the next day there was a great discharge of Shells from Mortars against the Rebels in the opposite works, which silenced them.

When the Letter concluded, they seemed to be under little apprehension from the Enemy, if they could but get fuel and Victuals. What had been imported sold at an extravagant price. All the old houses and a number of wharves were pulling down to consume. The Rebel privateers were laid up; several of them had been taken, and it is to be hoped there will hereafter be better protection afforded the King's Ships to those of his Subjects. Admiral Shuldam is arrived at Boston.

I wrote to Mr R. Nicholson by the Carrier on Monday and sent two parcels, to be forwarded in a Cask with other things to my Brother by the Ship for Boston. He desired particularly some Cobled Coals, if they could be sent, and I doubt not Mr. N. will if he can — I shall have Money to remit him (Mr N.) and I will desire him to pay you what you have paid for my Shoes, &c. I desired Miss Lem to mention My recieving 'em some time ago.

We have just been drinking tea at your Sister's She's well, desires her love, as does Mrs. Tylston.

This day poor Miss Griffith's remains was brought to Chester from Bristol to be interred here.

This Morning Dr. Weaver and Mrs. Richardson were married —a wedding much the Subject of conversation — With best Compliments to Mr. and Miss L.

I am, Dear Mrs Lightbody's Affectionate friend, &c.

A. Hulton

---

1 *Loyalist Lady*, 84-87.

2 Admiral Molyneux Shuldham, who had been dispatched to replace Admiral Samuel Graves. For context see John A. Tilley, *The British Navy and the American Revolution* (Columbia: University of South Carolina Press, 1987), 51-66

[Henry Hulton to Samuel   Esqr.]   *Boston 9 March 1776*[1]

The distress and anxiety of mind we have been under for a week past are not to be expressed, and we are still surrounded with difficulties and dangers. This place is now going to be evacuated by the Army, and every one is urgent and anxious to get on board the Transport assigned him. The Commissioners and their Officers are to embark on the *Hellespont*, Captain Leicester, and we expect the fleet will proceed to Halifax and, if it pleases God that arrive safe there, I shall write more particularly by the first opportunity. In the mean time you may be informed in what circumstances we shall have been left by some of the passengers who are going from hence in the Packet, and who will probably be heard of at the New England Coffee house.

March 17th. On board the *Hellespont*, Nantasket Road, Boston Harbour.

We embarked the 10th in a great hurry, and fell down here the 12th, greatly crowded and in want of seamen, and many accommodations; but we are to have some seamen from the Admiral, and the Carpenters are fitting up berths for the passengers, and I trust in God we shall be preserved and get safe to Halifax, where it is said we are to proceed. From thence I imagine we shall take the first good opportunity to embark for England. You will therefore please not to send anything for me to this Country, if not already sent, till you hear further from me. My family are as well as can be expected in our situation.

---

1   Hulton, "Letterbooks," 1:173-175.

Journal at Boston. Saturday December 2nd 1775[1]

This Evening the Tragedy of "Zara" was performed at Faneiul Hall by young Gentlemen of the Army and Ladies, to a numerous audience, with great applause.

December 3. Very alarming advices of the 8th November are received from Quebec that St. Johns is taken by the Rebels, and revolted Canadians, that General Carleton had abandoned Montreal and was going down the River from thence to Quebec, that 1500 Rebels under Arnold were advanced to point Levy by the way of Kennebec, and the Rebels from St. Johns were coming on. At the same time, only a few hundred of British and Canadian subjects were at Quebec in Arms to defend the place, which it was apprehended would fall into the hands of the Rebels, though the *Lizard* Man of War was arrived from England a few days before. General Carleton applied to General Gage for a reinforcement of troops by express, which arrived at Boston October 8, the day General Gage embarked for England. It was at first proposed to send a Battalion of Marines, but afterwards, on account of the advanced season—fearing the ships could not get up to Quebec, it was laid aside. Had the Troops gone at that time, they most probably would have arrived in time to have defeated Arnold's party, and have saved the place.

By Accounts this day from Rhode Island, every thing there was in the utmost confusion. The Rebels had a number of troops on the Island, and had made a demand on the Collector of the King's money in his hands, upon which the Collector fled on board the *Rose* Man of War; they then seized on his house and effects, and turned his Wife and family out of doors. A squadron of three ships of 36, 24 and 20 Guns are said to be fiting out at Philadephia, with the intention to attack Captain Wallace in the *Rose* Man of War at Newport.

The Assembly of Rhode Island have passed an act to punish with death any one who shall supply or correspond with his Majesty's fleet or Army. And the Rebel Council of Massachusetts have passed an act to encourage the fitting out of Vessels of War, and to establish Courts of Admiralty within the province.

The Brig with Ordnance stores which has been in the Bay for some time past, but kept out by contrary winds, has been twice spoke with by Men of War, and brought in company with them, in sight of the Light house, and yet drove out again, and separated from the King's ship, and is now said to be taken by the Rebels. There are a Mortar, shells, fire Arms

&c. on board, which we are now to apprehend will be used against us. And the Rebels keep continually advancing their works nearer to us.

There was a report last night that a large fleet was in the Bay, but nothing appears of them, and what with all this bad news, and hard[-]hearted Winds, we are much alarmed and distressed. If the ships with troops, fuel and Stores should be drove off the Coast, we shall be in a sad situation. Starved and Bombarded. What great events depend on little causes. The want of a Regiment at Quebec may lose that province, and the Ordnance brig falling into the hands of the Rebels may distress us greatly, cause the loss of a great number of Men, and be the means of lengthening out the Rebellion.

December 5th. The *Boyne* Man of War sailed for England, with General Burgoine on board. The 65 Regiment are to go to Halifax to secure that place against an attack from the Rebels, and the *Somersett* Man of War, now there, and the *Asia*, at New York, both of the Line, which were to have gone home, are now detained to remain in America.

Several ships have been lately taken in this Bay by the Rebels, in small sloops, and schooners, which watch for single Vessels in Creeks and harbours, and come upon them suddenly. It is now found that Cape Cod is a good and safe harbour, where a ship of War is to be stationed to receive inward bound Vessels under her protection, and small schooners are to cruize for and Convoy Vessels coming in to that Harbour.

December 7. A Rebel Brig Privateer was sent in taken by the *Fowey*, Captain Montagu. She had 10 Guns and 75 Men on board, and many of the crew are European subjects. Her Colours were a pine tree on a white ground, and the Captain's Commission was signed by John Hancock, President of the Provincial Congress.

December 16. The *Tartar* Man of War, Captain Meadows, sailed for England with the crew of the Rebel brig on board, and the 65 Regiment sailed for Halifax.

A number of Wharfs and houses are now taking down by the soldiers, by the General's order, for fire wood; it is said 500 houses are to be pulled down.

Several Vessels from Halifax got in this evening with forage &c.—Advice is received from Halifax that the 2nd Regiment is got in there from Europe, and that two Regiments are gone from Ireland for Quebec.

December 17. The ships that sailed yesterday morning are come to at Nantasket, the wind being contrary, and it is said the 65 Regiment is countermanded.

Accounts are received from Rhode Island that Captain Wallace has landed some Marines and Sailors on Conohassett, his boats having been insulted by the people on shore, who fired on them, and killed one of his men; that he had burnt thirty houses, and killed some of the Country people.

December 19. The Rebels are extending their works on Phips's Farm, near the Water side, opposite to Barton's point. On Sunday they fired a shot that entered the *Scarborough* Man of War, lying off Barton's point, and she is removed lower down.

Yesterday one of their 24 pound shot fell into the Garden near the house of Mr. William Vassals, now occupied by Lord Percy. During the night and this day, there has been a great discharge of shells from Mortars erected at Barton's point, against the Rebels in the opposite works.

December 30. Admiral Shuldam in the *Chatham* and the *Niger*, Captain Talbot, arrived at Nantasket. Two store ships, two Transports with 12 Companys of the 17 and 55 Regiments, and an ordnance brig came in from Europe after long passages.

1776. January 5. The *Scarborough*, Captain Barclay, with several armed ships and 2 or 300 Marines, saild on an Expedition.

January 8th. This Evening after the Play, the farce called "The Blockade of Boston" was to have been acted, but at ½ past 8 o'clock, just as the farce was to begin, the Alarm Guns were fired, and all the Officers run out of the house to their posts. Immediately the remaining houses at Charlestown were in flames, and a brisk platoon firing, with the discharge of Cannon, was heard from the Redoubt on the heights above Charlestown: so that we imagined the Rebels were attacking the Redoubt. But the whole proved to be a party of the Rebels, that had come over the Mill dam, where they surprised 3 or 4 People in one of the Houses below, having had notice by a deserter the night before how these houses were occupied. The Rebels carried away the people, set fire to the houses and ran off, upon which some of the Soldiers began firing and occasioned the continuance of it for some time, before they found they had no Enemy to fire at, which occasioned a great shouting throughout the Rebel Army, and they have certainly in this affair got the laugh against us.

By advises received from Virginia, Lord Dunmore has published a Proclamation, requiring all his Majesty's subjects able to bear Arms to repair to his standard, and has liberated all the slaves and white servants belonging to Rebels.

General Clinton is going to Embark to take the command of an Army to the southward, supposed to be for Virginia—Mr. Reeve is going his secretary. It is imagined that a number of foreign troops are on the sea for the southern part of this continent.

Several Vessels have arrived lately with fresh Meat and other victuals, which have sold at an extravagant rate. Some Coals have carried, but they are confined to the use of the Army. However, as we have rubbed on thus far we hope to get through the Winter without being starved, or burnt down. There has been no cannonading of late, and if we can get fuel and Victual, we seem to be under little apprehension from the Enemy. The weather has been very changeable, and we have had a great deal of high winds and rain, some severe cold and frost, but frequent thaws.

General Lee with 1200 Men from the Rebel Army has been at Rhode Island and carried off the Deputy Collector and Searcher, they not taking a shocking Oath which he would have imposed upon them. The Comptroller was frightened and compelled to take it. Several of the Meetings[2] are now occupied as Barracks &c. for the use of the Army.

Two Privateers have been at the Island of St. Johns and carried off Mr. Calleck and some other inhabitants with their effects, and sent them to Cambridge, but General W[ashington] released and suffered them to home again.

February 13. Admiral Graves sailed from Boston in the *Preston*. Several Companys of Grenadiers and Lt. Infantry under the Command of Major Musgrave went over the Ice to Dorchester neck at four in the Morning; at the same time, Colonel Leslie, with a party from the Castle, landed at the other end of the Neck, and the troops burnt all the houses, and returned without any loss, bringing off about 10 prisoners. A Captain's Guard with about 60 men made their escape.

February 29. The Rebels have been very busy for several days past in their works at Phips's Farm, and a new battery is preparing against them under Mount Whoredom. They are daily expected to begin to play on the town from their Cannon and Mortars.

March 2. At ½ past 11 o'clock at night the Rebels began to play on the town with Cannon and Shells from Phips's Farm and Roxbury. Their shot were much elevated, and struck houses in many parts, but did little damage; the firing continued til day break.

March 3d. At night the Cannonading repeated. Brought down our beds from the upper rooms, and laid them on the parlour floors.

March 4th. At ½ past 7 in the evening a most heavy Cannonading began from all sides on the Rebels, and continued without intermission till day break. The 5th. in the Morning, the Rebels were found to have possessed themselves of the heights on Dorchester neck that commanded the town, and many thousands of them were seen very busily employed in throwing up a breast work. All the Country are said to have been called in, and that 30,000 Men are now actually in the works round the Town.

At noon, about 3000 troops were embarked, supposed to attack the new Lines forming on Dorchester Neck. Great is our anxiety for the success of this expedition, which may probably determine our fate. In the afternoon it blows very hard; the troops cannot land; the Rebels are strengthening themselves all the while; whilst the ships with the Soldiers are obliged to come to anchor, and some of them get on shore in the Gale of Wind. Our anxiety and distress increases. At night the Rebels keep us alarmed with firing on the town, and wounded some of the soldiers in the Barracks. The 6th. in the Morning, it is said that the General has given orders to desist from the attempt on Dorchester neck, and that the Troops are to come back, and the Town is to be evacuated. The orders are soon confirmed and a new scene of General distress and confusion begins. Now every one is to look out for a transport to embark in, for fly we must from the town immediately. Houses are left and furniture neglected; where shall we go? All rush to be accommodated, yet there are not half ships enough to carry away the people and stores that are to be shipt off. It is said that the want of Provision is the cause of the Army abandoning the Town. Lamentable is the sight of distress, and confusion! At night we are under fresh apprehension of a cannonading from the Rebels, who are supposed to be erecting batteries to play on the ships to prevent their going out of the harbour.

March 7 and 8. All hurry and bustle in the town, every one packing up and shipping off their Effects. The Commissioners have a loaded Victulour appointed by the Admiral to carry them, their families and Officers. The ship cannot take in their Goods, or be fit to receive them till unladen. Ship some of our effects in the Custom House schooner, and on board a sloop.

When it was known abroad that the General intended to evacuate the Town, some of the principal inhabitants wrote a letter to the General of the Rebel Army, intreating him to desist from Cannonading on the town, or incommoding the Troops in their Embarkation and departure, if he would wish to preserve the town from destruction, which they apprehended would be the consequence of a contrary conduct. The answer to this letter was that as it came from no authority, he should pay no regard to it.

March 9th. Soon after dark the Rebels began a furious cannonading from several parts, which continued the whole of the night. At 11 o'clock went to bed. At Midnight was awaked by a speedy message from Mr. Dudley, acquainting me that Mr. H[allowell]'s family had been greatly alarmed by the Cannonading in their Neighbourhood, and that they were immediately embarking on board ship. Went to bed again.

March 10. At 3 in the morning a violent rapping at the door. Mr. W. called to acquaint us that the General had just given orders for all the transport ships to fall down at 12 at noon to Kingroad, and that we must lose no time in embarking. What accumulation of distress! A severe season! A pressing foe! Hundreds of people to be crammed on board each Vessel, without seamen to navigate them, or provision to support the passengers on the Voyage. Oh! the heart[-]racking pangs of every parent; the ruin of fortune; the shipwreck of property are not attended: go we must, and fly from the wrath of Man, unprovided against the rude elements, trusting only in an almighty protection for our deliverance. At five o'clock, before daylight, left our dwelling, carrying with us only our bed[d]ing and necessary linen, and leading our little ones in our hands, a mile through the town to Hutchinson's Wharf. Thus like Aeneas from the Flames of Troy, bearing not my Sire, but an Infant in my Arms, and fled! And where. Alas! The Wharf was soon covered with fugitives, and their Effects, no boats were to be had, no seamen were in the ship. With the assistance of a Captain of Marines I got my family on board a lumbered Vessell, unprovided, unaccommodated for any Voyage.

The rest of the morning I employed in forwarding the papers of the Board, but was obliged to embark without them, though they were sent off the next day. Taking a last farewell of my dwelling, and shipwrecked substance, which I was obliged to abandon. I cast a look on my old faithful dog Argus; he seemed to know, and sympathize in my distress, and drew tears from my Eyes.

At 12 o'clock embarked on board the *Hellespont*, saw a number of my packages, with books, Looking Glasses, China, and other valuable furniture on the Wharf, which could not be taken off.

With difficulty we got under way, incommoded by a number of Vessels, crouded with people as anxious to depart as ourselves. For want of sailors, 12 Marines are lent to us, to get the Vessel down; we have only three Tidesmen, half seamen to assist us, and now are full of passengers without any accommodation for their Lodging &c. Come to Anchor abreast of the Town, the wind freshens, and we drive, get up the Anchor, and go near the Man of War.

We see the Rebels very busy at Dorchester neck, and suppose they are erecting a battery, to incommode the ships going out. Lye down on the Cabbin floor. 36 Men, Women and Children in the Cabin, and state room.

March 11th. The marines are got to our liquors, and are most of them drunk, and very riotous. What distress! Hail a ship, the Captain a Lieutenant in the Navy, comes on board, takes off the drunken Marines with great difficulty, tumbles them pell mell into the boat. A horrid scene of noise, swearing, and blasting. Captain Collins in the *Nautilus* lends us four hands, to help us down. Get down to King road, come to Anchor.

March 12. The *Chatham*, with the Admiral on board, is near to us. Write to the Admiral. We are to go down to Nantasket, and then we are to be accommodated. Many ships are coming down as crouded and unprovided as ourselves—one of them runs foul of the Admiral's Stern, and carrys away his poop Lanthorns, and Stern Galleys. Blows hard.

March 13th. Get down to Nantasket, and the Admiral sends a letter to Commodore Banks to assist us.

March 14th. Commodore Banks comes on board us in a small boat, not belonging to his ship *Renown*, says he has no seamen or boats on board, that they are all in town to assist the troops, can give us no assistance. Only lends us a Carpenter to make up Cabbins.

Mr. P[axton] goes on board the Admiral, sends a line at Night that when the Admiral comes down, we shall be accommodated. Blows hard.

March 15th. The *Nautilus* went out on a cruize, and has taken away the four seamen lent us. Many things necessary to be done for our accommodation, and fitting the ship for sea, which cannot be till we get seamen, and the ship is further discharged. rains hard.

March 16th. One Mr. Taylor, a Merchant of Boston and now a passenger on board one of the Transports outwards, went up the shrouds of the ship, and threw himself into the Sea and was lost; shocking instance of distress and despair! At Midnight a heavy Cannonading is heard between Dorchester neck and the Town, which continues till day light.

Sunday March 17. St. Patrick's day. Fine Weather. The fireing last night was all from our side, to cover the embarkation of the Troops, who all got on board, before day, without any attempt from the Rebels to molest them, nor did they attempt to enter the town, till the evening after the retreat was compleated. This Morning the General went on board the Admiral's ship at King road and Nantasket. There are about 700 of the Inhabitants of Boston, Refugees and civil officers in the fleet.

March 18. Fine Weather.

March 19. Blows fresh. The *Savage* Sloop and eight Transports arrive from Halifax.

March 20. Fine day. Cannonading at the Castle in the afternoon. At 9 at night the buildings at Castle William all in Flames. The Rebels had begun to fire from a battery at Dorchester neck this afternoon and a Cannon from the Castle that was fired against it burst on the second discharge, and killed three and wounded dangerously four others.

March 21. The Admiral in the *Chatham* came down to Nantasket with the General Officers on board, and several ships fell down with Troops from Kingroad. The *Fowey* Man of

War, with about twenty sail get under way, being the first division of ships to proceed to Halifax, but the Wind being contrary, they came to Anchor again.

The *Fowey* is passing through the Fleet run foul of our ship, and distressed us for some time.

Still in want of seamen, and greatly incommoded with the lumber and discharge of our ship, which being a victualler, a number of orders are continually served upon her for a few Casks of provision for each Vessel. One family from on board of us is accommodated with a passage on board one of the Transports that came in two days ago.

March 22. Snow. fair.

March 23. Snow storm blows hard, very cold. Cabin Crowded, smokey and dirty.

March 24. Gale at NW. Continues very cold. Two ships drove ashore last night. Our Long-boat drifted from us and lost.

March 25. Blows hard. Frost. *Fowey* sails with about 50 Vessels under Convoy. Moderate weather.

March 26. Snow storm. Very cold. Very busy discharging Provision, and taking in ballast, which the Admiral sends on board in flat[-]bottomed boats. The fleet to sail tomorrow.

March 27. All hurry and bustle on board, discharging provision. The Fleet to sail this afternoon. The Admiral sends more flat bottom boats on board with ballast for us. Get seamen from the *Lively*. Most of our baggage on board the Custom House schooner. The General sends to beg we will leave her to assist in discharging the Transport ship that is now aground. At 4 o'clock the fleet got under way. Order the Custom house schooner along-side us. All our baggage tossed upon Deck, and tumbled into the hold, whilst the Anchor is getting up. At 5 o'clock set sail. Between 60 and 70 ships under convoy of the *Chatham*, *Centurion*, and *Lively* Men of War. The Cabin and State room crammed with Women and Children, the Steerage filled with Gentlemen, and Women Servants passengers. Between Decks crouded with Men servants, and Negros, and the Quarter Deck loaded with Sheep, Pigs, and Poultry. Upwards of 70 People on board, and the fire place, and conveniences for cooking will not dress Victuals for more than thirty. Fair Wind, moderate Weather for two days, contrary winds for two days. very sick, dirty, and uncomfortable.

March 30th and April 1st. Rainy and tempestuous. Mrs. H. wet in her Cabin.

April 2d. Wind fair at noon. See Land in the afternoon, arrive at Halifax at 8 in the Evening.

April 3. Go on shore, the town crouded, no houses or Victuals to be got. Every one distressed and embarrassed. Luckily the Collector procures one small appartment, at his sister's. Lay down ourselves and Children on the floor. No accommodations to be got for Mr. Hallowell's family. They remain on board.

April 10th. Mr. H[allowell']s family at length got into Quarters. Lodgings most extrava-gantly dear. And provision scarce. Many people who lived at their ease in Boston are now here without shelter or the means of subsistance. We still sleep on the floor. Most of the troops still on ship board.[3]

1   Inserted at this point in ibid., 1:176-221, and with that an end to the first volume.

2   Local congregational chuches.

3   This marks page 197 in the first volume of the "Letterbooks." 198 was left blank, and 199-214 contained "A Journal of a siege at Quebec, in a Letter dated Quebec May 12ᵗʰ 1776," author unidentified. Hulton had it transcribed (or possibly transcribed it himself) and inserted it here. I did not, in turn, transcribe it for this volume. Hulton stopped numbering pages after this "Journal," left two pages blank, then offered his closing thoughts, which follow.

*   *   *   *   *

I am persuaded that the present war on the part of Great Britain was unavoidable (without relinquishing her authority), and to any one who lived in America, it was very apparent, that anarchy, and ruin, must be the consequence of the general principles and practises. It was obvious that the great grievance the people laboured under was the popular constitution of their Charter Governments; and it had long been a reproach to Great Britain that she neglected to reform them.

In the progress of Societies, Nations have generally risen to opulence, made advances in arts, refinements and Luxury, before they have sunk in corruption. But in America they have become depraved before they have been refined, and I can only account for it from the licentious Constitution of their Governments, and the neglect of Great Britain, which enacted Laws of Revenue at the same time that She winked at the open violation of them, so that illicit trade was a general practise; and a corruption of morals was accelerated by an avowed connivance of Smugling, and a flagrant prostitution of Custom house oaths.

When smug[g]ling became established and principle corrupted, the people of course revolted from the laws and authority of Great Britain, and became enemies to order and Government.

In a commercial light, it was high time to break with the Americans and to put the trade on a new footing; for they not only traded with You, on Your own Stock, but the credit they obtained at home was used to carry on a circuitous commerce with several foreign parts.

The produce of the British Merchants' goods was employed to purchase teas in Holland, and to procure cargoes of Molasses from the foreign Islands, which were run into North America. All this while they were living in luxury, and increasing their substance, on the British Capital.

When I first arrived at Boston, I was struck with two things, which convinced me they were in the high road to destruction.

There were five printing Offices in the town, each of which published a Weekly News paper. And there were five vendue Warehouses.[1] The people were all politicians, and all selling off their goods at any rate to raise money, and at the latter end, the goods were immediately sent, as they arrived from England, to the vendue warehouse, to be sold for what they would fetch.

In respect to their Governments, for want of some Superior power to cling to for protection, every man was affraid of his Neighbour, and cast about him before he said or did any thing, to see how it would affect his popularity, and they all stood in awe of the creature that was erected into the popular Demagogue. It appears fine at a distance, and in idea, to contemplate their free Constitutions; but in practise they are big with every evil, as every one who has lived under them and has possessed either property or talents superior to the vulgar has felt, and must own. And if ever America is recovered from its State of depravity, and its inhabitants are brought to be a free, and happy people, the first reformation must be in the Constitution of their Governments.

When I was at Rhode Island I waited on the Governor, and he afterwards caused it to be signified to me that he hoped I would excuse his not making me a visit in return; and I understood the reason, that it would affect his influence with the people, if he visited one of the King's Officers.

At the time I was there, one of the late Governors was a Clerk to the inferior Court, and I was told that the man who had beat the Drum about the town for publick Sales was made a Judge. In short, in that most licentious State of Society, the Multitude elevated, or depressed annually, according to their caprice, to the prostitution and disgrace of all Order and Government.

---

1   Where goods could be sold or auctioned to the public.

[Henry Hulton to Robert Nicholson] *Halifax, Nova Scotia 8 May 1776*[1]

Dear Sir

Yesterday I received your favour of the 7th of March. And am much obliged to you and Mr L[ightbody] for the stores you have been so kind to send us, and for the trouble you have taken with those sent from my Sister, and for the newspapers now received. All these are very acceptable, for every kind of provision is very scarce and dear, and I imagine the Industry's Cargoe will come to a very good Market. Capt M has called upon me, and if I can render him any service I shall be glad of it.

You will have heard of the evacuation of Boston. The circumstances attending our retreat have been somewhat severe upon the people in the Civil Departments, and our situation in this place is not such as to make us desirous of continuing in it. Most of those who can get away are removing from hence, and I hope we shall be able to embark in a short time for England.

Mrs H. joins with me in presenting best respects to yourself and Mrs N. I beg you will make my compliments to all friends with you. I remain with great regard, Dear Sir, your most obedient, humble Servant.

H H

---

1   Hulton, "Nicholson Letters," 96-97.

[Ann Hulton to Elizabeth Lightbody]   *Wem 14 June 14 1776*[1]

Dear Mrs. Lightbody's kind favour of the 30th May, I had the pleasure to receive here, was glad to hear you were taking pleasure in your Visit to Matlock, hope you will all reap benefit by it, particularly that Miss L's health will be confirmed, and may you long enjoy health and peace and every domestick blessing.

Though you had not desired it, I fully intended to write you, my Dear friend, when I should hear from my Brother, as I am perswaded your benevolent heart would participate in the Sufferings of your friends, and in what gives pleasure too, therefore this I should most readily communicate. Two or three days ago I received a Letter from my Brother dated Halifax, April 19th 1776. He says "after all our Perils and troubles we are thank God got safe to this place, and my family are in health.

It is wonderful how we have been preserved through all our alarms, Dangers, and distresses. We suffer in Loss of property with many worthy persons, here alas! are many families who lived in ease and plenty at Boston, that now have scarce a shelter, or any means of subsistence. However, the fugitives in general seem to bear thier Adversity with great fortitude." He says nothing of coming to England, but that they wait for the next advices from London.

I desired my Aunt Hincks to acquaint Mr R. Nicholson. I would have sent you a more particular account of their departure from Boston, and their Voyage to Halifax, which I have from my Brother's Journal, that a Gentleman in London has sent me, but that I am Straitened for time, having many Letters to write at once, to my friends. It is the Most Affecting Narrative to me I ever read; perhaps I may trouble you with some extracts from it sometime hence.

Not being certain whether you continue still at Matlock, I intend to send this in a packet to Chester, and am afraid of being too Late for the Newsman. I am at Mrs. Swanwick's at present, think to return to Chester by the beginning of July. Am glad to hear your Sister is got so well; I thought the Country Air would be of servise to [her.] [2] She was very poorly when I was at Chester Mrs Tylston and she talked of taking a jaunt to Wem, whilst I am here, but don't hear whether they will or not. Mrs T. is, I believe, at Mrs. Hall's still. Mrs.

Swanwick desires her Love to you. At H. and Mrs. Whitworth's. Staid here about 10 days, and Mrs. W. Brett and Miss were here. All friends this way are well.

My best respects to Mr & Mrs L.

I am, Dear Madam,

Your Affectionate

Friend and Humble Servant

A Hulton

---

1   *Loyalist Lady*, 87-88.
2   Editors' insertion.

[Henry Hulton to Ann Hulton] *Halifax 18 June 1776*[1]

Sister:

This place is now pretty quiet, for the fleet, with the Army, sailed on an expedition nine days ago, yet all kinds of Provision are still very scarce and dear, except fish. But in short, there is no Country round Us to raise any supplies and it has been a strange waste of publick monies to attempt an establishment, in spite of Nature. For as to Soil and Climate, it is wretched indeed. We are now near Midsummer, without the comforts of that Season, or hardly the signs of vegitation. Most of the Boston people here have been sick and feel uncomfortably in this foggy chilling air, that obliges Us to keep fires, and yet at intervals We relax, and get colds, with the moist heat. A few days ago we hired a one horse Chaise to take a ride to Fort Sackville, which is ten miles, for which We were to pay three Dollars. We set out, expecting to see some thing of a Country, but all the road was along side the Bason on our right, with rocks and burnt Woods on our left, and there is nothing better to be seen for forty miles to Windsor, where they tell Us it is open into a fine Country. The horse failed Us on our return, and I had to drag and beat him most of the way home. However, for our comfort We have a better prospect before Us. After many difficulties and delays, We have at last brought matters to a conclusion, have engaged the Ship *Aston Hall*, Captain Parker, to carry Us to our Officers to London.

---

1   Hulton, "Letterbooks," 2:5-6, the first entry in this second volume.

[Ann Hulton to Elizabeth Lightbody]

Stanstay near Wrexham
19 August 1776[1]

I have long waited for good news, which I can now communicate to my Dear friend, of my Brother's safe arrival in his Native Country, with his family all well. They sailed from Halifax the 18th July. The next day were seperated from thier Convoy in a heavy gale of wind, off the Isle of Sables, and with great difficulty they kept from driving to the Shore. Through the rest of the Voyage had mostly stormy weather. Mrs H. was sick the whole time. Upwards of 50 passengers on board. My Brother and Sister and their four boys Landed at Dover the 15th instant. Leaving the rest of the Passengers and thier Servants all on board the Ship (except the Child's maid). The Wind still blew high.

What great dangers they have escaped, How long and painful the suspence I have been in, agitated between hope and fear. It has indeed been a time of severe trial to me.

Thanks be to God for his goodness in preserving them, and delivering me from the distressing apprehensions I have been under, particularly of late, which I could not avoid, as I supposed them to embark the beginning of July.

I doubt not you will joyn me in acknowledgments to Heaven, and let it encourage your and my trust in future.

My Brother writes me from Kensington, the 18 instant, when they had just arrived at the Reverend Mr. Heald's, who married a Sister of Mrs. Hulton's. Mrs. Heald had lain in about a fortnight, but had lost her little one, a boy. She has four girls, and the eight cozens were all gone to Walk in Kensington Gardens.

My Brother says he can't answer for Edward, that he won't beat some of his new relations before he returned—he is a Lively arch boy and was a favorite with the Military Gentlemen, particularly Lord Percy.

My Brother seems desirous to get down into the Country, but must continue in London a while to wait on his Superiors. There is a good house open for him and his family at Mr Preston's in Charles Street, Berkley Square.

I hope this will find you, your family, and Cozin H. T. all. I beg to be kindly remembered to 'em all.

> I am, Dear Madam,
>> Your Affectionate
>>> A Hulton

I've been here 3 Weeks for Country Air, but the Weather has been so bad, for the most part wet and windy, that have had little benefit of it. Here is good Company in the house Mrs. Cooper and Mrs. Wilbraham.

I think to go to Parkgate, again to Bathe, when our friend Mrs. T. returns. Hope we shall have Cosin H. T.'s company there too.

---

1 *Loyalist Lady*, 89-90.

[Henry Hulton to Robert Nicholson]

Charles Street Berkeley Square
22 August 1776[1]

Dear Sir

We sailed from Halifax the 18 of July and had rather a rough passage, but thank God I landed with my family safe at Dover the 13 instant and we feel ourselves very happy in being once more in our native land; of which blessing no one can be sufficiently sensible who has not lived out of it, and I would wish all murmurers to make the experiment, especially if they are sons of liberty: that they may enjoy the sweets of it for a while under the Boston Demagogues. I am perswaded that in no Country in no period of time there ever was a state of society in which the people were so improved, so generally comfortable and happy, as in the present state of Great Britain. In other Countrys, where you see the magnficence and splendor of the great, they are counterballanced by the poverty and misery of the Peasantry; they are oppressed, whilst the other live in luxury. But in England, there is an air of ease, an appearance of general opulence, and every one seems to enjoy their property in security, and to speak and act with freedom. Such a view must strike every stranger and make him wish to enjoy the life in this blessed land, where he can live without dread of oppression from the Great without fear of offending a popular Demagogue and having his house pulled down by the Rabble. I met a Letter from my sister a few days after my arrival, the contents of which damped the pleasure I received on my first coming to town. She informed me of the death of two of my old friends Mr. C[ropper] and Mrs. Rogers]; I sympathize with you and Mr C.'s family in your loss.

The many severe circumstances we have of late experienced, the frequent scenes of mortality and distress that have been around us, made us in a manner almost resigned to any events and little anxious about life, but when we came to see the happiness of this land, we were almost tempted to say "it is good for us to be here." Indeed, several of the Americans I have conversed with in town say they had no idea of the opulence and grandure of this place, that it is not a City, but an Empire of itself, and is alone a match for ten America's. We are at present at Mr. P[reston]'s house, and propose going to make him a visit in Norfolk, as soon as I can conveniently leave the town.

I shall be happy to hear of your family's welfare; you will please to present our best Compliments to Mrs N. and Mrs B., and I remain with great regard, Dear Sir, your most obedient, humble Servant.

H H

---

1 Hulton, "Nicholson Letters," 98-100.

[Henry Hulton to Ann Hulton]

Beeston Hall near Norwich
November 1776[1]

Sister

We left London the 24th September and lay that night at Newmarket. The next day we came to Mr. Burch's, where we passed two Nights. They live at the house his Uncle left him at Cressingham, within 5 miles of Swaffham. It was then the races at Swaffham, and we went with them to the Assembly where was a fine shew of Ladies and Gentlemen.

We arrived at Norwich on Saturday, the 28th September. Mr. and Mrs. Preston were waiting for Us and received Us with the greatest affection and kindness, and conducted Us immediately in their Coach to Beeston. The House is in a park, situated rather low, with a piece of Water at the bottom. The front has the appearance of a Monestery, and one is surprized after passing through a large hall on entrance and leaving the appartments on the right, with a suite of three large lofty rooms to the left, fronting the Water.

Mr. P. had one of the Gentlemen Improvers here to modernize his grounds, and is busy in levelling his Lawns, removing Gardens, Walls and trees, and laying down a new kitchen Garden more remote from the house. It would grieve You if You were here to have such a fine kitchen garden cut up, as the present one is to be laid in a lawn. But so it must be; our ideas are more extensive than were those of our Ancestors. They were cribbed up in small appartments, and sat on little Cane Chairs, admiring the pretty inclosed garden edged with box and yew trees. We now indulge in elbow Chairs, in appartments 20 by 30, fifteen feet high, and must extend our new, over[-]improved grounds as far as the eye can see, without a disagreeable object intervening. But yet the main business of Art is to conceal art, for all would be spoiled if You were not made to think it was all Nature. We have every thing here to make in and out doors agreeable. A warm reception, an excellent table, a large library, a good garden—fine rides, horses and Carriages. Mr. P is no sportsman, but nevertheless finds employment, and fills up his time very rationally. He attends to his affairs, repairs the house and barns on his Estates, has greatly improved the roads in the Neighbourhood, and is now busy with the improvements about his house and garden, and is really a very virtuous good Character and a Christian, which for a Man of taste, fortune and education that has made the grand tour, is saying a great deal in this luxurious Age. He pays a Schoolmaster for instructing the Children in the Neighbourhood, and advises the Minister to hear them their Chatechism, and last Sunday Tommy and Harry were Chatechized at Church in the afternoon Service, along with the other Children. Mrs P. is a very sensible, polite amiable Woman; her behavior is very affectionate towards the Children, and we are made very happy in the cordiality of our treatment, in the cheerfulness, ease and kindness of our Hosts.

I have only been twice at Norwich. The City is very large but the Streets are many of them narrow. We went to the Sessions Assembly, which is the first Week in October and one of the most brilliant in the Year. The rooms are very spacious and there was a great shew of Nobility and Gentry.

I wished much for You on a visit to Mr. Petres, a Gentleman in this Neighbourhood. You would there have been amazed and delighted with a kitchen and fruit garden, such an one I have not seen: four Acres of ground inclosed, each Acre divided by a Wall. Such quantities of all kinds of fruit! And a new hot house building sixty feet deep, with such abundance of Pines, that all the Servants may live upon them. Then such extensive frames of Glass as high as the Walls, that will remove and cover a whole side of Wall to bring fruit forward. Add to this a vast melon ground. In short, the whole seems calculated to furnish fruit and garden stuff for a whole town rather than for a private family. But it is his hobby horse, and people may exceed in the most innocent amusements.

We took a ride the other morning to see a house about six miles off, lately built by a Mr. Norris, and it is really a curiosity. It is entirely on a Plan of his own, and differs from all others I have seen. The Stairs are in the Center and the landing place opens into a Gallery. The many odd ways and contrivances, from the ground floor to the top, makes it really worth seeing. This Country is rather low, is much inclosed, well[-]cultivated, and abounds in Churches.

What a sad reverse of fortune for Miss W—. The next person you mention, Mr. K—, has had as strange a reverse, on the other hand. The good things of life are desireable, but many pay too dear a purchase for them. Yet from the respect that is paid to Wealth, however acquired, and the neglect that is shewn to Virtue, however generally acknowledged, it requires the force of the best principles, and a constant realizing of futurity, for the mind to support itself amidst the frowns and the Scorns of the World. And it is truly lamentable, if whilst the mind labours under the evils of life, a gloominess is cast over its future prospects by erroneous Principles of religion. I was concerned to hear of the State of despondency in which You mention Mrs. B. to have died, and I fear her depression might in some part arise from her mind being early impressed with the gloomy doctrines of Calvin.

---

1   Hulton, "Letterbooks," 2:7-12.

[Ann Hulton to Elizabeth Lightbody]   *Chester 10 November 1776*[1]

I had the pleasure lately to hear of My Dear friend, that you were well.

Intended to write you by this Opportunity, and would not omit it, though indeed I have not had time to transcribe from the journal of the Retreat from Boston.

I am perswaded you will be pleased to hear that I am got into agreable Lodgings. It is at Mr. Sproston's, in Watergate Street Row, where Mrs Wrench's used to keep the Card Assembly. I have a good Comfortable Lodging room, besides a parlour to myself (though it's to the Row and consequently Dark), and I board likewise in the house. The situation, you know, is not far from my friends. I wish you was in reach of this circle, but we are not to expect everything we wish. A number of Ladies have been so obliging to call on me in my new Apartments, and I have been engaged every Afternoon, except twice, since I came here a fortnight ago. However, It is a falling off to be sure from the last house I was at, where I had the pleasure of your Company. That was transient and the parting added to the mortifications I have met with in changing Scenes. The impressions of the past, pleasing or otherwise, cannot be effaced, and when a Solitary hour allows room for reflection, it still appears a wonder to Me that I am here in my Native Country, escaped from the dangers and free from dreadful alarms. That I can go to be without Apprehensions of Cannonadings, by which I used to be roused, and rise up without anxious thoughts, for supplies, and safety by day, and walk out and see plentiful markets and easy countenances, Instead of deserted Streets, empty market-places, or to meet discontents looks, and anxious distress.

How wonderful are the ways of Providence, and by what severe discipline we may be taught the value of the common blessings of Life. Thanks to a Kind Providence that it was temporary, that the scene is changed, both with myself and my friends, for whose safety I have felt more than when I was amidst the alarms and horrors of War. I received a letter from my Brother a few days ago, when he was near setting out to return from Norfolk to London. He seems greatly pleased with the journey, their reception and entertainment there, and charmed with Mr. and Mrs. Preston, thier characters, and thier Kind and affectionate treatment. I doubt not they enjoyd with peculiar pleasure the soothing kindness of thier friends, after the roughs and storms they have passd through. By this time my Brother is at Sir George Baker's near Kensington Square — to reside the Winter, or till June next, if all be well.

Tomorrow I am to visit your Sister and meet Mrs. Potts's there. Beg my best Compliments to Mr. and Miss L:

I am, Dear Madam, your Affectionate

A Hulton

---

1   *Loyalist Lady*, 91-92.

[Henry Hulton to Ann Hulton] *Kensington 25 August 1777*[1]

Sister

I can now acquaint You of our being fixed in an habitation. It is Mr. Taylor's house at Burcot, near Wells, Somersetshire. Our baggage is gone down, and we are just set[t]ing off for Bath. I hope We shall find all circumstances agreeable to Us in our new settlement, and I do not fear when We are once set down in the Country but we shall be very happy; and that is more than we could expect to be in the neighbourhood of London. Men of my Principles and dispositions are not much sought for; and it is in retirement only that I can preserve respect to myself—but it comports more with my temper, and fortune, to withdraw from the bustle of Society than to combat with the worthless and vain, and see the arts and intrigues of designing Men. From the experience I have had, I am the more reconciled to retirement. The Commerce of the World does not heighten our opinion of human Nature; and if we maintain right principles, through the intercourses of active life we shall find that We must sacrifice many gratifications to support them, and be subjected to many mortifications, by the preference we have made of Principle, to worldly interest. And therefore, there should seem to be some thing more necessary than the meer consciousness of Virtue to enable Us to support our integrity through all circumstances: and the older I grow, the more I am fixed in my first Principles, and persuaded of the folly of abandoning them for any earthly good. It is of small consequence whether we are great or little for the short time we are here; but it is of high importance whether We act a Virtuous or a dishonorable part; whether We maintain our integrity, or submit to guilt and depravity. The Sentiments We cultivate, and the conduct We support at present, will be the source of our honor and comfort hereafter, or of our future shame, remorse, and punishment.

---

1   Hulton, "Letterbooks," 2:13-15.

[Henry Hulton to Ann Hulton] *Burcot near Wells 19 September 1777*[1]

Sister

We left Kensington with Tom and Harry the 25 August and came to Wells by Andover and Frome. The Maids, with Edward and Preston, set out on Tuesday, and went by the way of Bath, and we all met together on Thursday evening. And the next day the Maids and Children removed to their new habitation at Burcot, and Dan got there at Night. The situation is very pleasant, within a Mile and half of Wells, and there is a fine prospect all the way to town.

I found a School at Wells which was very well recommended to me. The Master is a Clergyman and has about twenty boys for education in his own house. I was well pleased with his Character, and have placed the three oldest there at School; the rates are 20 Guineas boarding, and Schoolings.

After giving Orders to the Workmen and set[t]ling the Children, We made a little tour till the house should be ready for Us.

At Bath We ordered some furniture, and went on to Bristol; from thence We crossed the Channel to Chepstow, and after seeing Pensfield, We passed on to Nieuport, Cardiff, Cowbridge, Neath, and Swansea. Nothing certainly can be more charming than the prospects in this tour. Tthe Country is in high cultivation, and the hills are inclosed and improved to the Summit, and You are forever opening from one luxuriant Scene of smiling hill and cultured Vale to another; with views of the Channel and the distant hills in England, frequently breaking upon You. All the houses are Whitewashed on the outside, which gives a very clean, chearful appearance to the Villages. The roads, the entertainment, and accommodations are all very good, and the Weather was delightful all the time we were out. We returned to Chepstow and went round by Gloucester to Bristol, and in short, all the way to this place is through a Country rich in its soil, and cultivation, and beautifully diversified, with frequent prospects of land and Water intermixed.

---

1   Ibid., 2:16-18.

[Henry Hulton to Robert Nicholson]   *Burcot 27 September 1777*[1]

Mr. R. Nicholson

Since I last had the pleasure of writing to You I made a tour to Dorsetshire and Somersetshire, with a view to fix my family, as the places I had visited in the North did not answer my expectations on the whole.

The Neighbourhood of Wells appeared to me for several reasons an eligible part to settle in, and finding a house near that town to be let, I entered into treaty for it, and have now removed my family to it.

I am now more set[t]led, retired, and at my ease, than I have been for some years past. It is a calm after a Storm. I look back on perils and dangers that have been escaped; on troubles and difficulties that have been encountered, and surmounted.

If We can review the efforts We have made, without a consciousness of guilt, We may enjoy satisfaction, though our endeavours have been unsuccessful. I can truly say that I have been more intent to do my duty, and serve the publick in the Offices I have held, than to advance my interest; and if I have not been very fortunate, at least I am not now unhappy. It is often from our ignorance that things are heightened in our opinion, and from our knowledge of Men we may become better reconciled to retirement. After all the combat for honors, Wealth, and Power, for which so many sacrifices are made, the chief of outward good is comprized in Simplicity and Sympathy—happy is he who knows how to value them. Whilst I enjoy these I shall think little of the want of many of those things, which are the objects of general pursuit, and estimation.

---

1   Ibid., 2:19-20.

[Henry Hulton to Ann Hulton]   *Burcot 14 October 1777*[1]

Sister

I received Your favor of the 24 instant and am very much concerned at Your ill state of health, and wish You may find benefit from the Waters in Leicestershire, where You propose going.

We have experienced many circumstances to shew Us how precarious and uncertain is health, and all sublumary good; at the same time, We have to acknowledge the enjoyment of many mercies and relief in many distresses; and I am thankful that I am now in such circumstances of health, peace, and comfort.

I can look back on the trials and difficulties in my past life with satisfaction, and gratitude. I can leave the busy Scene without regret, for it was to me a life of thankless toil and combat for the publick.

My disposition leads me to enjoy and improve retirement; and it is a great blessing to have leisure to cultivate our understandings, and to detach ourselves from the World.

I enjoy the most substantial blessings in life, and pine not for things out of my reach, or envy others their enjoyments. My domestic comforts are great, and the little boys give Us every hope that We can desire from them; and they are placed much to our satisfaction. Edward asked Tom what he must do to be good, and now behaves very well. Little Preston is my Companion in my walks, and we are very happy together—See, Papa, the baa Lambs; then he is frightened at the Cows, and cries, there's a Bull. But the joy is to see the meeting of the Brothers, when the Boys come home.

We walk to meet them over two fields. Preston kisses them all, over and over, then he runs off with Edward and tells him all about Kitty and Polly; whilst Tom and Harry are both at once telling their stories about their Schooling to their Mama and me.

---

1   Ibid., 2:21-22.

[Henry Hulton to Ann Hulton]

Burcot 10 December 1777[1]

Sister

I received Your favor of the 10th Ulto. The sameness of our daily occupation and the few occcurences that We meet with in our new mode of living, prevent my writing more frequently. However, We had one event here which You must have heard of at the time, that surprized Us a good deal. Mr. Taylor, our Landlord, came down to Wells Last month. You may remember that Mr. Cuthbert and I had a good deal of altercation with him in Germany, and it was a little odd my receiving his visit for the first time, in his own house. I had called to see him at Wells, when he was not within. The next day he came over and spent some hours with Us, and invited Us to dinner for the day following. Accordingly We went, and I thought he shewed a desire of being upon good terms, and nothing would satisfy him but he must have the Children to dinner likewise. The Carriage was sent for them, and he seemed very well pleased with them, and at going away he gave each of them something. Edward kept it in his hand till he came to the light at home. He thought it had been a half-penny, but seeing it was a Shilling, he cried out, I am a Shilling Man. In the course of conver-sation, Mr. Taylor said that no Man had found more friends than himself, had enjoyed more health, or had been more prosperous. Yet, says he, "I would not wish to live life over again." I am afraid it had its stings. I happened to say something of Virtue—he stopt me short. "What have you lived so long in the World, and talk of Virtue." He was in perfect health and good spirits when we parted, and the next evening he returned from Dinner quite hearty, but suddenly expired at nine o'clock. He was a Man, bold, rude, and uncultured, but of very strong natural parts: and had the talent to make himself useful to great Men. To the World, he sacrificed, took advantage of extraordinary opportunities, and amassed a prodigious fortune, but with all his affluence was wretched. He built a pallace, of which he had no enjoyment, for he lived without domestic consolation, the sure consequence of unprin-cipled attachment.

The consideration of such a Character, and his sudden exit, may be a lesson of instruc-tion to all, and shew to those who are bent on acquiring this World's good, by every means the insufficiency of it when acquired, the uncertain tenure by which it is held, and the vanity of their pursuits.

In this retreat We have great pleasure in our domestic comforts, and though we have contracted the circle of our amusements, we have not reduced the means of our happiness. Retirement opens fresh sources of entertainment to the virtuous and rational mind: and that peace and tranquility which arises from moderated passions, the culture of the mind, and innocent employments, is beyond any thing that the World can give. I feel no lassitude or wearyness, or ever have an hour on my hand, though I follow no Country diversions.

When I look back coolly on the life of persecution we led, and the dangers We have escaped, I shudder, and am greatly thankful for our deliverance, and that we are all alive in such comfortable circumstances. In the hurry of action, our spirits were wonderfully supported; and we did not seem impressed with sufficient apprehensions from the impending evils. Now they are over, we can trace back many instances of extraordinary protection and deliverance, and I hope they will never be forgotten by me or mine.

Nothing now gives me so much concern as Your circumstances and state of health.

I hope Providence will support You under Your trials, and that You will find Your health mastered by the means You propose useing, and that We shall meet in comfort in the Summer. It may be happy for Us that the mind is sometimes damped to the enjoyment of the surrounding objects of pleasure, and that it does not find consolation in the things without it. Happy, if the pain of body leads Us to seek tranquility of mind, where only it can be found, and happy, if from the loss of worldly good we are led in search of treasures more durable, that cannot be taken from Us.

---

1   Ibid., 2:23-27.

[Henry Hulton to Ann Hulton]   *Burcot   March 1778* [1]

Sister

I have the pleasure of Your favour of the 5th instant, which relieved me from some anxiety, as I began to be fearful that You were prevented writing by sickness. I am very sensible how much You are interested in my happiness, and indeed there is nothing at present that gives me so much concern, as a regard for your health and comfortable settlement. I dread Your having any further matters to distress or affect You, and wish You to bring Your affairs into a narrow compass, to secure what property You have, and attend only to make Your life comfortable and easy to You. When You have set[t]led Your affairs, I suppose You will pursue Your intention of going to Leicestershire, and when You have tried those Waters awhile, we shall hope to see You here, where You will find simplicity and sympathy. We are here in peace and retirement, and know little of what passes in the World. And happy is it for Us in these distracted times that We are somewhat removed from the fury of the Storm. Alas! The prospect is gloomy, and I fear the issue of these publick calamities. Who could have imagined the progress of this rebellion and present state of affairs? Rapid are the advances of Commercial Nations towards their summit of Glory, but short the duration of their Splendour. The internal corruption that great commerce produces would soon urge a Nation to its decline, without the ingratitude of its Colonies. But there is an hand unseen that directs the whole; and it is no wonder that he should make wicked nations the instruments of each other's punishments. However, individually We may learn to submit, and adore, and lament to see the World that is passing away, distracted by the violence of human passions. And if We are in some measure disturbed thereby, yet it should render the prospect before Us more pleasing and delightful. For my own part, I could very much forego any further pursuits of ambition, or interest—the peaceable enjoyment of retirement in national Studies, and little intercourses of Society, would give me the greatest Pleasure; and if it was not for my Children's sakes, I should not wish to engage again in the business and bustle of life. I have had my share of them; and from experience, I would not desire to renew a commerce with the interested and unprincipled World.

I should dread to be in a Society, exposed to constant Cards and dissipation. It is a fine expression of Hotspur's in Harry the 4th "Our time is short, to spread that shortness basely 'twere too long."[2] We have some Society within our reach, enough for to amuse Us. We go once a week to town, to a Card Assembly. Our Play is very moderate; and in short, to People of our turn, whose chief pleasures are domestic, our situation is pleasing, and having the Children so nigh is a great comfort.

---

1 Ibid., 2:29-32; 28 is blank.
2 From Henry IV, Part 1, Act 5, scene II, Hotspur before he challenges Prince Hal and is slain:
O gentlemen, the time of life is short!
To spend that shortness basely were too long
If life did ride upon a dial's point,
Still ending at the arrival of an hour.
And if we live, we live to tread on kings,
If die, brave death, when princes die with us!

[Henry Hulton to Robert Nicholson] *Burcot 12 March 12 1778*[1]

Mr. R. Nicholson. Liverpool.

I had proposed myself the Pleasure of writing to You for some time past, but deferred it from time to time, as I had little worth mentioning to my friends in my present situation.

I cannot now amuse You with the relation of perilous adventures; but I can say that I am thankful in having this retreat from the Storm; that I enjoy peace and tranquility, and many domestic comforts.

I can look back at leisure on the various events in my past life, and with gratitude acknowledge many surprizing escapes and deliverances. I almost shudder to think on the many circumstances of danger and distress from which I have been delivered. And when I view, after all, ourselves and the little brood around Us, in health comfort and safety, it really greatly affects me; and many of the sentiments of David[2] rise in my mind, and I hope and trust that he who has hitherto preserved Us, will continue to guide and direct Us.

I know very little of what is passing abroad, except what my Newspaper shews me; and the account in Your last letter was matter of great surprize to me, both the rise and fall of our old friend. He seems to have been a very bold Adventurer—That he should have risqued so much in America, in these times, is surprizing, and that afterwards he should have had credit to carry on such extensive concerns is no less so.

His original business I imagine was very profitable to him. Success therein led him on to further enterprize. Aiming at too much has undone many. When intemperate passions of any kind get the dominion, People lose sight of Principle and Prudence in pursuit of the favorite object. It is difficult to hold the reins upon appetite, to keep in the right path when tempted by Pleasure, or gain, or to maintain right Principles when the support of them exposes one to mortification and neglect. And yet I am persuaded that, sooner or later, every bad Man is sensible of the emptiness and insufficiency of every earthly good that has been purchased by the sacrifice of his integrity; and that no good Man ever repented that he had made passion and interest yield to truth and Virtue.

It gave me great Pleasure to hear that Mr. Lightbody's family were coming to Bath. I wish You had been of the Party. It is a long time since We met. I flatter myself with much satisfaction in talking over matters with my old friends. There is great consolation in a relation of past adventures to those who sympathize with Us, and feel for Us, &c.

---

1   Hulton, "Letterbooks," 2:33-35.
2   Presumably King David of Israel, in his role as the psalmist.

[Henry Hulton to Charles Dudley]   *Burcot 25 March 1778*[1]

Charles Dudley Esq.

I am obliged to You for two of your favors, the former on the 10th October and one of the 19th instant.

I have been affected in like manner with Yourself by the untoward events that have happened, and the gloomy prospect of affairs, so that I have had no heart to write to any of my friends. And amongst all my fellow sufferers, in this day of our calamity, there is no one I have sympathized with more heartily than Yourself, who endure the pain of seperation, added to losses, and other distress. But it gives Us much satisfaction to hear You have such good accounts from Mrs. Dudley, that She supports herself with so much fortitude. May You and She still keep up Your Spirits, and amidst the gloom that surrounds you, may You trust in an Almighty friend for guidance and direction; and may he be Your comfort and support.

Alas! who could have imagined that We should be reduced to so humiliating a State! Which ever way we cast our eye, we see nothing to give Us consolation. Publick and private distress are before Us. May they have the effect that is intended by the Almighty in his chastisements. Vain wish, You'l say, —Alas! I fear so. — Bid me, look around, see the torrent of fashion overwhelming every Principle of truth and duty. Ask me, what Nation can stand when the bulk of its individuals are profligate? I fear the description and apprehension are too just.

I think it happy that I removed my family from the Neighbourhood of the Capital. Considering our dispositions and all circumstances, I do not think We could have set down any where more to our satisfaction, as events have turned out. We have avoided a great deal of mortification and uneasiness by retreating from the bustle of the World. We are content with the enjoyment of domestic peace, and tranquility, though we have some Society within our reach. And it is great satisfaction to Us to have the Children so nigh to Us as Wells, which is within two miles. The Boys come on very well; their tempers and dispositions are very good and we flatter ourselves that they will be comforts to Us. If We are deprived of some enjoyments, We should endeavour to make the most of those that remain, and not pine after things that are out of our reach. But We often overlook what would afford real happiness, in the pursuit of imaginary pleasure. The little circle about Us may afford sufficient for our support and comfort, if properly cultivated; and if We cannot figure in Courts, or command the applause of popular Assemblies, we find resources within the compass of our own fire side, our books, or our garden.

There is a luxury enjoyed by the contemplative mind, greater than any the Epicurean can partake, and procured without toil, expence, or guilt. His Sentiment harmonizing with Nature: when the heart, softened and tranquilized by the view of creation, joins in the morning gratulations of the peaceful creatures around, and exults in the opening splendour of the day, the verdant face of the earth, and the happiness partaken by so many rational and animated beings. For my own part, I have more joy in seeing the progress of vegitation than in the splendour of a Court, and much greater pleasure in the singing of the birds, the lowing of the Cattle, and the bleating of the Sheep, than in the finest Concert. Stupid Creature, some will say—but I say, Nature is beyond Art in every thing. And he who has not brought himself to a thorough relish for the beauties of the former, I do not allow to be a proper judge. Alas! The depraved taste of Man, the vanity of his pursuits, and the inordinancy of his Passions! We all live to appear happy in the eyes of others, not to be really so in ourselves. We court applause, and depend on the voice of the multitude. We accumulate wealth by crimes and perish without enjoying it. A little while ago I had the opportunity of seeing one of the favorites of fortune, who had amassed great Wealth, but withal was wretched. It was Peter Taylor. He died here suddenly in November last. The day before he died I dined with him. He was then very hearty and well, in the course of conversation he observed, that no Man had found more friends, had enjoyed more health, or been more fortunate than himself; yet, says he, I would not wish to live life over again. Alas! People often pay a dear purchase for this World's good, and are afterwards disap[p]ointed. The consciousness of guilt damps the enjoyment.

I am obliged to You for the communication in Your letters, for I hear nothing relative to our American friends from any one.

The same restless and vacant mind continues with one, and the same intriguing Spirit with another.

The epithet gentle is well applied, for the poor Man will for ever be a Prey to violent Passions.

I congratulate the Congress on the choice of their Ambassador. But I apprehend the Services of his Embassy will never answer the expence of his Wardrobe. With regard to Mr. Fisher, I am a little at a loss to comprehend his fishing plan.

There is a satisfaction in having seen the World, and it is necessary to know something of it, to be able to get through life, with any tolerable degree of safety and success. But I do not think they are to be envied, whose Commerce in Society leads them much amongst the artful, and unprincipled, and who are engaged in a continual round of competition for interest, or honors. And I would rather remain in ignorance, than acquire knowledge at the expence of my happiness; for to detect the foibles and depravity of the human heart, through its wiles and intrigues, and the turbulence of its passions; what is it, but to make Us disgusted with our fellow Creatures?

When we say of any one that he knows the World well, it supposes him to have had a deal of evil communication; and therefore if he has preserved good morals, he is a wonderful creature. For alas! In general the heart soon becomes corrupted by interest, and seared and hardened by the Commerce of the World, like a beaten path. You will say, how this Man moralizes, turns Cynic, and shews a disap[p]ointed and discontented mind.

It is good to draw resources from necessity. Perhaps had I gone before the wind with a prosperous gale, I might have thought the Voyage pleasant, and have shared in the pleasures that were going forward. But I might then have been less attentive to the making a safe port at the end of the Voyage than now, after being ruffled with Storms, and sometimes becalmed—in which Latter state I now am—and I cast an eye back on the Storms and distresses in my past Voyage, with wonder and gratitude for my deliverance; and I look forward with calmness, seriousness and attention. I could sit down in tranquility, without wishing to know or be known, without desiring any more intercourse with the busy world, if a sense of duty and regard to my family did not call me into it.

Our enjoyments are in a small compass, but our little Companions make them sweet and pretious. We are not much exposed to rude intruders, but are blessed with the two most comfortable fire side Companions, Simplicity and Sympathy. Now and then apprehension will cast a gloom, and care and anxiety intrude; but there is a still voice within that says peace be still, look to the experience of past mercies, and trust that He who hath delivered, will still deliver. In this retreat I have one great blessing, in having my time at my own disposal, and if I do not employ it in cultivating the understanding, and amending the heart, then are reflection, experience, and leisure, bestowed in vain.

Indeed, I find great consolation in an old book that is much neglected by the gay and prosperous; but however it yields solid comfort in the hours of solitude, in the time of Sickness and distress. The Author of it says, in the World Ye shall have tribulation, but he bids Us be of good cheer, and tells us that he has overcome the World, and that he is gone to prepare a place for Us. Happy tidings! To all who are weary with their journey, and grieved in their present miserable habitations.[2]

1 Hulton, "Letterbooks," 2:39-46.
2 Hulton referred, of course, to the Bible and the good news—the "happy tidings"—of the resurrected Christ. Thus the preceding paragraph, and "peace, be still," as Christ calmed the waves on a stormy Galilee and reassured his frightened disciples, whose faith had faltered in the tempest.

[Henry Hulton to William Pepperrell]　　　*Burcot　28 March 1778*[1]

Sir Wiliam Pepperril London

I received Your favour of the 10th November but have been so much affected with the lamentable state of affairs, that I have had no heart to write to any of my friends, and I can now only say that I droop and mourn. Alas! Who could have imagined our being reduced to so humiliating a state. As events have turned out, I think it very fortunate that I removed my family from the neighbourhood of the Capital.

We are here in a quiet retirement; and though We see little of the World, our situation is no wise irksome to Us, and it is a great comfort to have the Children at School so near Us as Wells, where we have some Society. Indeed, for People of our disposition, I do not think We could have found a more agreeable retreat. I can look back on my past deliverances with gratitude, and I trust in the same gracious protection and guidance of me and mine that I have hitherto experienced.

The reviving of Nature in the opening Season, the melody of Birds, and the gratulations of all the Animals around Us, all tend to soften the mind; to make it sympathetic in the general peace, tranquility, and joy of nature. But alas! Man's cursed passions lead him astray and make him incapable of relishing the blessings prepared for him. Or if he is disposed to enjoy the simplicity of Nature, he is soon disturbed by some evil or distress, and called to lament and grieve. Now, War, horrid War, sounds in our ears, and instead of a quiet enjoyment of the Season, and retirement, We shall brood over calamity and anticipate distress.

I know the anxieties You must have, by what I feel myself, and I hope Your Young family enjoy health and make every improvement You can desire, and if you should alter Your condition, may it be in every respect for Your, and their, advantage.

We are really much concerned for all our friends, and sympathize with You in particular in these dreadful calamities, in which We all suffer.

The future prospect is very gloomy. But let Us not despair; a ray of comfort may dart through the darkest cloud, and some events may arise that may chear and comfort Us. And let us trust in him who hath delivered, and can still deliver.

In any success that attends Your wishes, we shall rejoice. If You meet with disap[p]oint-ment, or are weary of the gay and the Great, You know where to find simplicity and sympa-thy. We will endeavour to share with You, to sooth and comfort You in any distress. &c.

---

1   Hulton, "Letterbooks," 2:36-38.

[Henry Hulton to Thomas Percival] *Burcot* *March 1778* [1]

Dr. Percival Manchester

I was greatly obliged to You for Your kind favor in October, and received much comfort and satisfaction in the perusal. There is no such earthly cordial to the drooping Spirits as the expressions of sympathy from an affectionate friend—nor can any thing animate Us more to persevere in an arduous course of duty, than the approbation and countenance of good Men.

For some time past I have been so much affected by the gloom on publick and private affairs, that I have had no heart to write to any of my friends, and the prospect before Us does not afford any thing to chear and comfort Us.

There is some satisfaction in not being exposed to many trifling and noisy intruders, in being remote from many Scenes of vanity that could corrupt, or misery that would disturb Us, in having our time at our own disposal, and Leisure to attend to the still voice of truth and Nature. I have gone through many Storms, but am now becalmed. In this retreat I have leisure to look back on a life of toil and combat; and though it has been passed to little proffit to myself and family, and I have undergone many losses and distresses; yet I have reason to acknowledge many escapes and deliverances; many instances of divine favor and protection; and I cannot see myself with all my family about me, in health, peace, and tranquility without wonder and gratitude.

The Boys come over once a fortnight, and it is great delight to hear their little tales, to see the big Joy sparkling in their Countenances, and to share in the ardour and vivacity of their minds. Their age is all novelty, and extacy. These Young ones, the joy of our hearts and the hopes of our lives, are likewise the objects of much anxiety, and their education, the inculcating right Principles into their minds, and forming them to a love of truth and virtue, must ever be matter to engage our thoughts, care, and attention. From the Parents' example, they take the first impressions, and his eye is their strictest guard. Indeed, as to some parents, it may be best their Children should be remote from them; but to any one who has a love of letters, and virtue, I think an attention to his Children's education must be his great delight.

I am highly obliged to You for the great regard and kind wishes You express for me.

I own myself somewhat wounded by my experience of the World, though I hope it does not lessen my benevolence to Mankind; and the depravity of Character I have seen in some, and the imperfections and foibles of others, tend to heighten my respect for those who have distinguished themselves by their talents and virtues. The examples of the latter animate Us to maintain the same noble course; they raise our respect for our own nature, and their is a pride and delight, mingled with affection, when we view our amiable friends and companions, supporting themselves with integrity and fortitude, through the toilsome combat of a tempting and troublesome world. And I have great pleasure in reflecting on some Characters of my deceased friends, whom I greatly respected, and by whom I was cherished, and I have still some living ones in my eye, who I think are ornaments of human Nature, and the consideration of whose virtues ought to put one in good humour with our fellow Creatures.

How I could take my book of patulae recabons sub tegmini fagi,[2] [and] forget the noise and bustle of the World. But I am soon roused from my repose and disturbed in the enjoyment of the tranquil Simplicity of Nature—every post brings a fresh allarm and now bella, horrida bella[3] sounds in our Years. Oh! The cursed passions of Man! How they deform this fair Creation. Now We shall brood over calamity and anticipate distress. May heaven avert the terrors of its wrath from this guilty land.

In letter to Dr. Percival from Page 50 [insertion follows][4]

Amidst the impurity and profligacy of the West Indies, the Character of Colonel Martin shone with distinguished lustre. He was my friend, and in his Society I was cheared, animated and improved. The Scholar and Gentleman shewed themselves at all times in his conversation and behavior, ever animated with a virtuous Patriotism. The Island of Antigua owes to him many of its best laws.

Courteous to all, humane to his Negroes, he lived in a regular performance of the divine, social, and personal duties.

So many polite accomplishments, and liberal endowments, so much publick Spirit and manly exertion of his talents, so much strictness in moral conduct, so virtuous, and christian behavior, are seldom united in one man.#

Amidst the confusion, publick spoil, and peculation in Germany, I had a friend whose integrity was unshaken, whose Spirit and fortitude were unequalled. This was Mr. Cuthbert. And there is a Military Gentleman now in America, who I have the honor to call my friend, who united with all the qualifications of the Soldier and the Gentleman all the virtues that adorn the Man and the Christian. It is the Honorable General Leslie. My heart glows when I think of these Characters. Two of them, alas! are no more, and for the third, the tear starts in my eye when I think with anxiety to what perils his life is exposed. #Addition to Colonel Martin's Character, from the other side.

At Seventy Years of Age his conversation had charms for Youth and beauty; and the Ladies would sit with eager Ears, delighted with his discourse. He had lived very much at the Court of the late Prince of Wales, and it did honor to his Royal Patron that he distinguished him, for he was withal a Person of strict Morals and a religious Man. He joined to great abilities the warmest zeal for the Publick, and was unwearied in its Service. And he was ever doing friendly kind offices to particular Persons, so that he was at once an ornament and a blessing to Society. His Table was always served with great hospitality, but till the latter part of his life he himself only drank Water.

1   Ibid., 2:47-50.
2   To lie in ease under a beech tree. These lines are from the opening of Virgil's *Eclogue*, which would have been familiar to the Edinburgh-trained Dr. Percival.
3   "Wars, horrid wars," from Virgil's *Aeneid*, 6:86, a common phrase for this generation—as shown in Hulton's 28 March 1778 letter to William Pepperrell, at 371 supra.
4   This was inserted in the "Letterbooks" at 2:55-56, five pages beyond the rest of the text. Initially Hulton had decided to excise these paragraphs, and then he changed his mind, but only after having moved on in his copying—or in the copying being done for him. This insertion is one example—another is provided in his draft of a letter to Elizabeth Lightbody on 13 January 1779 at 383 infra—of Hulton's including only letters, and possibly even parts of those letters, that he felt it was important for his sons to read.

[Henry Hulton to Ann Hulton]   *Burcot 7 April 1778* [1]

Dear Sister

I received Your favor of the 31st Ulto. Alas! You will have heard the melancholy tidings respecting our friends at Bath long before this reaches you. I had written to Mr. Lightbody and I flattered myself with the pleasure of seeing them here, when suddenly on Thursday morning I received a letter from Mr. C, with whom they lodged, acquainting me of Mr. Lightbody's death.

I thought Mrs. Lightbody might be without a female friend, and we immediately set off for Bath and got there at 7 in the evening. Mr. William Lightbody, with his daughter and Mrs. R. Lightbody, were arrived a day or two before. It was a melancholy meeting with friends after so long an absence, on such an occasion, but I am very glad we went. I am sure they took it kind, and I believe it was some comfort to them.

I did not see Mr. William Lightbody that evening. The next morning, when I went in to the parlour, I saw a Gentleman there, but had no idea that it was him, and went out again.

They shewed me in again. When he spoke to me, I really should not have known him, he was so much altered, and depressed.

That morning I assisted at the funeral, and we stayed with the family that day, and returned home on Saturday.

It is trying and extraordinary circumstances that call forth the proofs of the affection and attachment of friends. We were really much concerned for these Ladies, when we heard of their distress, and our attachment has been increased by an acquaintance with them, and we should esteem it a happiness to have them nearer our Society.

---

1   Hulton, "Letterbooks," 2:83-84.

[Henry Hulton to Mrs. Hincks]   *Burcot 15 April 1778*[1]

Mrs. Hincks

I have long wished to be able to give You consolation, having shared very heartily with You in Your afflictions, but alas! My ability to comfort is not equal to my wishes and desires for Your relief. I know indeed that You draw resources from a fountain that will never fail; and that You have better comfort at hand, than any the World can give. However, there is a cordial in the expressions of sympathy from an affectionate friend that is very chearing to the Spirits, and I am persuaded You will at least be pleased in hearing from one who was dear to You from infant Years, from one who has an affectionate feeling in Your distresses, and would wish to mitigate Your sorrows and make the remainder of the road of life in some measure more sweet and pleasant to You. Alas! We have each of Us had our trials, and difficulties, and throughout the changing circumstances and events of Life, We have experienced many things to wean us from it. Many instances of divine favor and protection, under severe trials; and are now in the enjoyment of many mercies, and comforts that should excite our gratitude and thankfulness.

In this retreat I have leisure to look back on the past and consider the future: and from past experience I ought to have my heart amended and my affections weaned from an unjust attachment to earthly good. Indeed, I have learned to be very moderate in my desires and expectations from the World. I have seen many sacrifices made to obtain the great things of life, and have often thought them purchased at too dear a rate. I have seen others who were in the same line with myself advanced to great prosperity, whilst I have been tried with severe circumstances, have met with many disap[p]ointments, and may think myself neglected: and my fortitude would have often sunk, and my Spirits have been depressed, if I had not looked beyond the present Scene of things.

Amidst pain and sorrow, affliction and distress, one glance into futurity is consolation. There is a promise to the patient continuer in well doing that may support the drooping Spirits; and We may look to him, in all our troubles, who was made perfect through sufferings.

A Christian, then, may be unfortunate, but he can hardly be unhappy. A bad Man may be prosperous, but he will ever be wretched.

> Retirement opens &c.
>
> The checking of the ardour &c.
>
> Virtue hath often &c.

I know I can say nothing on these Subjects that has not again and again occurred to You.

You have a supply of the best consolation in a mind reconciled to the will of heaven; meditating on its work and its ways, and relying on its promises and may they ever be sweet and pretious to You. &c. &c.

I had indulged myself lately in the hopes of seeing my old friends Mr. Lightbody's family at Burcot, but alas! I was called to attend his funeral at Bath, and sympathize with his family in their distress. In vain we image to ourselves in the time of absence, the pleasure we shall have in meeting our friends again, and telling over all our adventures to those who have interested themselves for Us. Alas! On our return, we find every object New, strange, and unfeeling towards Us. The eye that longed to see Us and the heart that glowed with affection for Us, are sunk and cold. This has been my fate again and again. And on my return to London this last time, if it had not been for my connections by Marriage, I should have been a solitary Being.

---

1 Ibid., 2:51-54.

[Henry Hulton to Thomas Cotgreave] *Burcot 15 April 1778*[1]

Mr. Cotgreave Chester

From the experience I have had of the World I am sufficiently satisfied with the busy scene and reconciled to retirement: not from an indolent disposition, for I would wish to be active as long as I can be useful. But the Scene I would wish to avoid is that where one sees much of the intrigues and corruptions of the human heart in the combat for interest and honors.

I do not think they are to be envied who advance themselves by the sacrifice of Principle—They have their good in possession and many stings therewith. The Just have theirs in reversion, and the anticipation of it is sweet, not in reversion only, but really there is a present satisfaction, a serenity and peace which the virtuous mind enjoys in all circumstances, that far surpasses all the tinseled and varnish glory of the vain and profligate.

In retirement We try what resources We can draw from our own minds. We look down upon the World, as from an eminence. And We correct a great deal of the false notions we had contracted, and find that the real good of life is more in our own Power than We had imagined.

Alas! To what a sad state are we not reduced? But our Constitution, a constant Prey to faction, wants energy for the government of remote territories. Whilst we are disputing, the time for action is lost.

I wish we may learn to make the most of the resources within ourselves, but I fear We have not the Virtue to contract our desires and reform our manners.

Commerce and Colonization have urged Us rapidly forward, but in their progress have spread the Seeds of Moral and Political destruction, and the prospect before Us is truly lamentable.

1   Ibid., 2:56-57. The Cotgreaves were a prominent Chester family. Notes about the family are included among the Bennett papers collected in the Cheshire Record Office (see supra 26 n. 4).

[Henry Hulton to Robert Nicholson]   *Burcot 25 April 1778*[1]

Mr R. Nicholson Liverpool

I received Your favor of the 24 Ultimo and was then happy in the prospect of meeting our friends. But alas! A few days brought Us melancholy tidings, and instead of the Pleasure I had indulged myself in, I was called to assist at the funeral of our friend.

In vain, in the hours of absence, do we image to ourselves the satisfaction We shall have in meeting again with those who are dear to Us; in telling over our tale, and relating the many wonderful incidents in our past life to those who are interested for Us.

Time wears out the traces of remembrance of Us from some, chills the ardor of affection in others, and bears many many of our friends to the state of oblivion. We return and find the houses, and the Churches, the publick paths the same. But where are the people who enlivened the Scene; with whom we spent the social hour; the eye that cheared at our sight, the heart that glowed with ardor at our approach? Alas! They are no more. New Persons are sprung up; they find other objects to engage and entertain them.

We become Strangers where we once were familiar and find ourselves in solitude in the midst of a Crowd. And it is well, that it is so ordered—the lesson is severe, but the duty it teaches is necessary to our happiness. It was not meant that we should find any sure rest or support in earthly comforts.

They drop from Us, or We become incapable of enjoying them: and when We are told where real happiness only is to be found, if We neglect to secure it, we can only reproach our own folly for our disap[p]ointment and loss.

I shed a tear at the remembrance of my old friend, Mr. Bassnet. He was an Israelite indeed. It pleased heaven to try him with afflictions, which he bore with great resignation, and is now gone to his reward.

In the late interview with our friends, I felt myself advanced to the middle age, seeing Young Ladies whose Mothers I had remembered very young.

---

1 Ibid., 2:58-59.

[Henry Hulton to Mrs. Tylston]   *Burcot 24 August 1778*[1]

Mrs. Tylston Chester

I had always a very high sense of Your friendship, and the experience I lately had of Your great kindness to my Sister has strengthened my sentiments of esteem and regard, and [I] could not leave Chester without a grateful sense of Your goodness.

As I was persuaded from the interest you were pleased to take in our happiness, that you would be desirous of hearing from us, so I was long in hopes that my Sister would be able to have the pleasure of communicating to You some favorable accounts with respect to herself. In these lingering and uncertain disorders, we are ready to flatter ourselves they may take some favorable turn, and we are unwilling to add to the concern of our friends by giving them unpleasing advices; and sensible of the Sympathy of Your feelings, I even now am averse from writing, as I would much rather conceal my own troubles than communicate what I am persuaded must give pain to others. But your friendship requires I should make you acquainted with the state of my Sister's health, though I know it will occasion you concern.

The foundation of her disorder seems to lye in her stomach, which will not bear or digest properly any food. She continues weak and low, is not able to take exercise, nor is She relieved by that She uses, and seems to despair of being better. She is not able to read or write, but moves about, and sits in company. And though She is reduced in her looks, yet She does not appear so bad as would be expected in one who takes so little sustenance, and is so much oppressed as She is by her disorder.

Thank God, the rest of my family are well in health, and Mrs. H. is dayly expecting to lye in. She has always kept up good Spirits and been a support and comfort to me in all my troubles. Many we have undergone together—those of a publick nature were turbulent and allarming; but we were in some degree carried through them by the bustle of action, and having many companions in adversity.

The domestic afflictions and the silent griefs that are felt unseen and retired from the world, can only be supported by the influence of right Principles, and happy it is for us that they afford us consolation under every trouble and distress.

In this retreat, though we have little variety to amuse us, yet we do not find our time hang on our hands. As I have no engagements in publick or private business, I bestow my leisure in reading and writing what I think may tend to the instruction of my children—they are objects of constant care and anxiety, and if I cannot greatly advance their fortune, I will endeavour to fix them in such principles, and train them in such habits, that they may become virtuous and useful members of Society.

I think there is no place has more of the general advantages for the comfortable accommodation of life than Chester, and had I thoughts only of sit[t]ing down in retirement, I should have cast my view that way. But my disposition is active, and the object I have fixed for my employment is a quantity of unimproved land, if I can meet with it.

The pleasures of social intercourse, and the sympathy of affection in a small Society, far over ballance, in my opinion, all the pomp and vain shew of the Capital. In the extensive and dissipated intercourse of the metropolis, the heart can find no resting place, and it must contract the circle of its engagements if it would receive satisfaction itself, or communicate pleasures to others.

I am very sensible we have many friends in your Society, and indeed I think I could feel myself happy almost in any place where I could enjoy an intercourse with so many affectionate friends and well wishers, as I believe I have in your neighbourhood. It is your happiness to be a blessing to the circle around you, to contribute greatly to the pleasure and comfort of your friends, and to chear many a drooping heart. And may you long enjoy your health, and the heart felt satisfaction that arises from the exertion of warm benevolence, and generous friendship.

My Sister desires me to express her particular and grateful sense of all your kindnesses to her. She shed tears at the account I have given of her, saying, She has distressed at the concern it would give her friends. Mrs. H. joins me in every sentiment of respect and regard.

---

1   Ibid., 2:85-89.

[Henry Hulton to Mrs. Michell]

Burcot 7 September 1778[1]

Mrs. Michell

In our retired situation we have little to communicate that can yield entertainment to our friends. Our employments and amusements for the last year have been in a narrow circle; and the greatest pleasure we have had has been in walking across the fields and meeting our boys when they came from school—happy age of health and innocence—the Spirits all alive, the heart uncorrupted. It is [a] great delight to see their disinterested affection, to share in their joys. Thank God they come on as well as can be expected and I trust will be comforts to Us. Having no engagements of publick or private business, I endeavour to employ my time in the best manner I can, with an eye to their improvement. I am no sportsmen, have neither dog, nor Gun. Indeed, I cannot see to shoot. However, I have great delight in roving over the fields, with my book in my hand, and we have many pleasant walks, and fine prospects about us, and we pick up a good deal of comfort in our retreat, and our little companions make our enjoyments sweet and pretious to us. We are not exposed to many rude intruders, but are blessed with the two most comfortable fireside companions, Simplicity and Sympathy.

---

1   Ibid., 2:93-94.

[Henry Hulton to Elizabeth Lightbody]

Mrs. Lightbody   Liverpool   *Burcot 8 September 1778*[1]

I was much obliged to You for the favor of two letters I received from You at Chester, and I should esteem myself very happy to be in the neighbourhood of such desirable friends as those of your family. The sympathy of communication with those who feel for us is great consolation, and alas! We each of us have those trials, as make us acquire comfort and support from affectionate friends.

Your kind letter to my Sister of the 15th August was duely received, and she is much penetrated with Your goodness and affection to her, but her state of health will not admit of her writing. And indeed, I have not found that she has received relief in her disorders from the change of air, and new objects, and she herself seems to despair of being better; and it is matter of great trouble to see the pain that one cannot aswage, the distress that one cannot relieve. During this time I have been in constant anxiety for Mrs H., who has wonderfully supported her spirits and borne up to the time of her relief with great fortitude. She was happily delivered of another fine boy on Sunday morning, the 6th instant, and thank God both the Parent and child are in the way to do well.

With a family of five boys, I cannot but have many anxieties for their future welfare, and as I have no engagements at present in publick or private business, I bestow my leisure in the way I think may best answer to their improvement.

I should wish to be more actively employed, to be more useful to them, and the publick, but as providence has cast my lot in this situation, I endeavour not to pass my time altogether unproffitably. I have a desire that my Children should reap some advantage from my having lived; that they should be distinguished by liberal endowments, and virtuous improvements; and would flatter myself that if in future life they find advantages from the benefits of a right cultivation, they may reflect with pleasure that they owed something to the example and precepts of their father.

I am much concerned to hear that Miss Lightbody has been so poorly, and hope she will find benefit by the Waters, and& that all your young family will be comforts to you. We are deprived of some blessings to teach us not to trust in any earthly good others are spared to us to chear and solace us in our journey, and happy for as amidst the evils of life, that there is a sure rock on which we may stand unmoved.

---

1   Ibid., 2:90-92.

[Henry Hulton to Thomas Cotgreave]   *Burcot   13 January 1779*[1]

Mr. Cotgreave Chester

I received Your kind favor of the [blank] and am much obliged to You for the great regard You shew me, and very sensible of the nature of your friendship. From the experience of the world we are taught to prize those connections which are founded in truth and sincerity; and it is great comfort to be esteemed and cherished in more advanced life by those who have known us from our early years. I have long lived remote from youthful connections, and those of that day are continually dropping off.

From the unpromising accounts you had received of my Sister's state of health, You will not doubt have been expecting to hear of her dissolution. She endured a great deal for many months, and it pleased God to release her a few days ago from the pains and miseries of mortality, and from the hopes we may entertain of her we may consider the exchange as happy to her, though awful and affecting to Us. But indeed, to those who can look forward with the hope of the Christian, there is great consolation under every evil of life, and the death of friends, though depriving us of much comfort in our welfare, yet may be supported by faith, which assures us that it is only a dark passage to a glorious state—that it frees us from pain and sorrow to transport us to happiness eternal. May this be our consolation under the severest trials; and may we look forward with joy, and persevere with truth and faithfulness to the end.

---

1 Ibid., 2:60-61.

[Henry Hulton to Mrs. Hincks] *Burcot 13 January 1779*[1]

Mrs. F. Hincks Chester

The long duration of my Sister's illness, and the little hopes that could be entertained of her recovery, made us only pray that her latter end might be made easy to her. She endured a great deal for many months, but for some weeks past had been gradually declining, and seemed freer from pain than heretofore. For several days She appeared composed and resigned, and, on Saturday evening, quietly exchanged this world for a better—happy exchange—from the dogs of mortality—from the pains and distresses of human Nature, to the felicity of heaven. "To the faithful there ariseth up light in the darkness."[2] And amidst the present gloom and distress, I can cheer myself with the glorious prospect of a blessed immortality, where all tears shall be wiped from the eyes; where there shall be no more sickness or pain; no more Sin, or Sorrow—Blessed State—where we may once again hope to meet our dear and worthy relatives; and where the smiles of the Redeemer shall chear the faithful to eternity.

Let us not then mourn as they without hope—Let us consider the day of the departure of our virtuous friends out of this World as the day of their admission to light, to life, and glory—Let us plume our wings and look forward with joy, and follow with persevering steps, they who through faith and patience are inheriting the promises.

---

1 Ibid., 2:62-63.
2 "Unto the upright there ariseth up light in the darkness: he is gracious, and full of compassion, and righteous." Psalms 112:4 (KJV)

[Henry Hulton to Elizabeth Lightbody]   *Burcot, near Wells, Somersetshire*
13 January 1779[1]

Dear Madam

From the unpromising accounts which You will have received from time to time of my Sister's state of health, I doubt not You will have been expecting to hear the melancholy tidings I have now to communicate. She is released from the pains and sorrows of mortality; and considering the long duration of her sufferings, the event, though mournful to us, may be esteemed happy to her; and we may mitigate our sorrow from the hopes we may entertain of her having made an happy exchange.

It is these circumstances that call forth the trial of our faith. It is in these circumstances that we reap the fruit of it. There is great consolation in considering our dear and worthy friends as being gone a little while before Us to a state of happiness, to which we are every day nearer approaching. There is great comfort in looking forwards with steadfast hope through the gloom that is around Us to a future state of felicity, where we hope to meet again with those who were dear to Us, and enjoy an happiness uninterrupted by Sin, by pain, or Sorrow.

I often think on the last words of my late worthy friend, Colonel Martin of Antigua, when I took leave of him in that Island. "You leave me (says he) like a "Mercury on the house top, with my wings expanded towards heaven, and only one foot on the earth." Happy state of the mind, to be so disposed; may we in like manner endeavour to have our affections so engaged, and hold ourselves so prepared.

Mrs. Hulton desires to join m[e in] best respects to Yourself and the Young Ladies, and I remain with great esteem and regard,

Dear Madam
Your most obedient
and most humble Servant
Henry Hulton

---

1   *Loyalist Lady*, 93-94. A draft of the letter is in Hulton, "Letterbooks," 2:64-65.

[Henry Hulton to Mrs. Hincks] *Burcot 10 April 1779*[1]

Mrs. F. Hincks Chester

I received Your favor of the 27th Ultimo, and am only sorry that You were obliged to make it so short from increasing infirmities, as it always gives me pleasure to hear from you, and to be informed of Your and our other friends' welfare. I am, however, very glad to know that You are much better than you have been, and to hear that All is so well and comfortably fixed. You are both of You happy in enjoying good Spirits. May they still chear you through the growing infirmities of mortality, and may you be supported by the sweet foretaste of future happiness—my idea of which is that it will be a progressive State; that it will depend very much on our present correction of the heart, and culture of the mind; and that he who brings his will most in conformity to the will of heaven, who receives corrections as mercies, and uses blessings as trusts to be accounted for, will be in the happiest state hereafter.

In this view I see the hand of heaven with gratitude in directing my lot. Through what perils of body and Soul have I not been led? And thank God, I am now enjoying a quiet repose, free from noisy intruders, with many sweet domestic comforts and Leisure for improvement. Though I have no business to engage me, I feel no lassitude or weariness, or even have an hour on my hands.

The mind that is rightly disposed can never want for proffitable occupation; and it is only from feeling its own weakness and barrenness, or, what is worse, seeking to fly from its own reflections, that it is so frequently on the wing of dissipation.

I have now finished what I proposed writing for my Children and have bound up three Volumes of what I call sketches on various Subjects.

As we advance in life, old connections drop off, and new cares, new anxieties arise, and but for these I should be very content to withdraw from the tumultuous world: but having these young plants to rear, I think my first business now is to assist in forming their minds, to endeavour to fit them for usefulness in life, and to forward their future establishment; and these duties may call me out to further activity.

---

1   Hulton, "Letterbooks," 2:66-68.

[Henry Hulton to Thomas Cotgreave]

Burcot 9 October 1779[1]

Thos. Cotgreave Esq. Chester

It would be great comfort to us to be near the Society of so valuable a friend. I have really a great sense of all the kindness and attachment You have shewn to me.

In the course of my wanderings in the world I have had a very large acquaintance with persons of different countries, professions, and characters. I had some valuable German friends who are dead, or remote. Some others that I respected are dead; and now I have few friends remaining, and except my connexions by marriage, I should almost be alone in the midst of London. Many who set out with me in life have got the start of me, but I am persuaded that none of them are more happy than myself. The world may be made to contribute greatly to our pleasure and comfort in our passage through life, but the World can never make our happiness, if it is only sought there.

We live in retirement, with much domestic comfort, and thank God all my family enjoy health, and the young folks are docile and promise to be blessings to us, and my chief amusement is in writing what I hope will hereafter be read by them with pleasure and improvement. What they may pass through often gives me great anxiety. I know from experience somewhat of the combat, the troubles, and temptations of the world; and I would wish to form their minds and guard their hearts in some measure against the day of trial, and must console myself in commenting, and trusting them to him, whose grace alone can be sufficient for them.

---

1 Ibid., 2:95-96.

[Henry Hulton to Sukey Hincks]

Burcot November 1779[1]

Miss Sukey Hincks Chester

By a letter from Mrs. J. Hincks I am acquainted with the loss You have sustained; and I sincerely sympathize with You under Your affliction, and wish it was in my power to alleviate Your grief, to comfort and relieve.

The sympathy of friends that are present may sooth[e] the heart under its affliction. The communication with those that are remote will renew, but does not assuage our grief: however, in the tribute we pay to the memory of our deceased friends, we gratify the noblest sentiments of the heart. It is a sorrow mingled with delight to contemplate their Characters.

The Parent You have lost gave an example of the Power of the Principles She professed, by the chearfulness of temper and resignation of will with which She supported afflictions and trials. And now that You are called out to experience some of the like troubles and difficulties, may you be supported under them—may you be animated to tread in her steps. And may you put your confidence in him who is alone able to save; and may he be Your Shield and consolation.

Poor A. W. has seen most of her relatives go before her. She may almost be ready to cry out, "why do his Chariot wheels delay their coming,"[2] "yet a little while, and he that shall come will come."[3] And under pressing infirmities, though we cannot glorfiy our maker by action, yet we may by resignation. "Thy will be done," is always an acceptable testimony of our obedience, be it for life, or death.[4]

I apprehend by Your late loss that You must be straitened in Your circumstances. I wish it was in my power to make them easy to You. If five pounds per Annum can be of any Service, I shall feel happy in Your accepting it. And when I draw some small rents at Chester, shall remit that Sum for You.

---

1 Ibid., 2:69-71.
2 "The mother of Sisera looked out a window, and cried through the lattice, 'Why is his chariot so long in coming? Why tarry the wheels of his chariots?'" Judges 5:28 (KJV) Sisera, a Canaanite warrior, had been slain fighting the Israelites. His mother waited in vain for him to return a conquering hero.
3 "For ye have need of patience, that, after ye have done the will of God, ye might receive the promise. For yet a little while, and he that shall come will come, and will not tarry." Hebrews 10:36-37 (KJV)
4 Here Hulton turns, not surprisingly, to the Lord's prayer, from Matthew 6:10, "Thy kingdom come. Thy will be done in earth, as it is in heaven." (KJV)

[Henry Hulton to Elizabeth Lightbody]   *Burcot 11 November 1779*[1]

Mrs. A. Lightbody Liverpool

The very kind favor of Your Letter in answer to mine, acquainting You of the death of my Sister deserved an earlier acknowledgment. And the account of your then late indisposition required my more early congratulations on your recovery. Indeed, I take an interest in Your and your family's welfare, and should be happy we were so situated as to have a frequent communication with You. But having little to write from this State of retirement, and being (as every one else must be) depressed with the unpromising appearance of affairs, I was lo[a]th to send a copy of my mind in such circumstances. However, there is a consolation even in the communication of our Sorrows to those who feel for us; and he who can vent his griefs to a sympathizing heart is half relieved.

Every Year takes from Us some of the props that we leaned on.

I had lately a letter from Chester acquainting me with the death of Aunt Hincks. She is removed from the trials and difficulties with which She was exercised here, and which She supported with so much Christian cheerfulness and fortitude, to the reward that is promised to the patient continuer in well[-]doing. I am much concerned for poor Cozin Sukey, and have written to her.

In the present state of our family we are as well in this situation as we could desire. We have some Society in Wells, though we know little of what passes elsewhere. But though all around us is gloomy and hostile, we have a Sunshine about our dwelling, and peace and comfort at our fire side. Our five boys are fine docile children—the youngest is named George. This is their day of innocence and joy. They know nothing of the corruptions of the heart. They are not aware what they are to struggle with in a troublesome and crafty world, but all these trials and difficulties arise to the imagination of the Parent: and the tear starts in the eye, when it is considered what such as yet amiable creatures may fall into from the temptations of the world, and the corruptions of their Nature. But I recollect that I have myself been a brand snatched out of the fire; and I trust that the same good providence that has so wonderfully preserved and favored me, will bless and direct these little ones.

After losses and disap[p]ointments, and unoccupied with business I should have been a prey to chagrin, and melancholy ideas in this retirement form the world if I had not engaged my mind in some rational Study.

My disposition leads me to be active, and in publick business I laboured much; in my solitude I never dropt my pen   indeed, I think time so valuable that every hour ought to be put to some use for ourselves, or others.

With this disposition, I have written and put together some Volumes of Sketches for my Children; and of late I have made extracts from the Scriptures, and am writing reflections thereon for their use, and my own.

Man engaged in the business, or pleasures of the World, neglects the most important of all concerns; he lives and dies a Stranger to himself.

There is no subject that opens such wonderful scenes to our contemplation as the consideration of our Nature and end. There is no book that can inform and satisfy us thereon but the Bible. The improvement I derive from the Study thereof and the satisfaction I feel in these exercises are great. Such employments call forth the faculties of the mind [and] the affections of the heart—they bring a man to a more intimate acquaintance with his Maker and himself. And as according to my ideas, the dispositions of mind and the habits we contract here will be the qualifications for our happiness, or the causes of our misery hereafter, so I think the entering into the invisible world as much as we can on earth is a main consolation under the troubles of this life, and a great means of fit[t]ing us for future felicity.

I would endeavour to please the imagination, and animate the passions; to shew that there is more of novelty and entertainment; more improvement to the understanding, and consolation to the heart, in such contemplations than in any other.

It gives me pleasure to hear of Your domestic comfort; may Your amiable daughters ever be blessings to You.

I am obliged to You for the general intelligence You write me, since which I have hardly heard any thing from Your part. I shall be obliged to You to suffer the box of papers to remain in Your garret, and to let any other things be sold.

---

1   Hulton, "Letterbooks," 2:72-78.

[Henry Hulton to Robert Nicholson]   *Burcot 11 November 1779*[1]

Mr. Robt. Nicholson Liverpool

The sameness of life in which my time passes in this retirement gives me little occasion to write to my friends, and the sad state of publick affairs casts such a gloom on one's mind, that we can receive no pleasure in a communication of our ideas.

However, I would wish now and then to hear of my friends; and every year makes the remainder of old connections more pretious, as it takes away some or other of those who were dear to us in our youth.

I have just been acquainted with the death of my Aunt Hincks, who was a very valuable Woman. She supported severe trials with great chearfulness and resignation, and proved the force of the Principles She professed. We are all of us exercised in some measure or other; and no doubt these things are necessary to discipline, prove and train us, that we may be weaned from this World and fitted for a better Society before our departure out of it.

We who have many young folks to bring forward into the World have a great weight on our Spirits. What a World it is in which they are to enter? How difficult to unite the great concerns! to guard their morals, and advance their interests—to procure the present good, and promote their future happiness. Alas! The future is seldom made an object, if the present can be obtained.

---

1   Ibid., 2:79-80.

[Henry Hulton to Thomas Cotgreave]   *Burcot 3 February 1780*[1]

Thos. Cotgreave Esq. Chester

I have been a considerable time looking out for an improvable Estate, which I might occupy with a prospect of advantage to my family, and I have at length met with one much to my mind in Wiltshire, bordering on Hampshire. It is a leasehold farm of upwards 800 Acres in a ring fence, and has been reducing in its value through the mismanagement of needy Tenants. I have agreed for the purchase, and am looking out for a house in the neighbourhood, as there is only a farm house on the Estate.

This business will new cast our lot, and give me full employment for some years to come; but it is in my opinion the most healthy, pleasant, and rational of any I could pursue; and I do not doubt it will be proffitable.

The mind must be employed; and when we see agreeable objects rising and improving dayly in our view, the appearance of which has been greatly assisted by our own industry, it is a source of great satisfaction to the mind. Making the barren field to smile with cultivation, seeing the increase of flocks and herds, and the giving employment to many industrious poor, are all grateful sensations; and in doing these the mind will have more pleasing reflections, than from any pursuits in the paths of ambition, or glory.

---

1   Ibid., 2:81-82.

[Henry Hulton to Thomas Cotgreave]   *Burcot 18 March 1780*[1]

Mr. Cotgreave

It was with great concern that I received the account of the melancholy event communicated in Your letter of the 11th instant.

I sympathise sincerely with You in Your affliction, and can image the severity of Your distress to be seperated from one with whom You had been united by the tenderest affection from infant years.

We are all of us ready to offer arguments to compose the mind labouring under affliction; but it is difficult to be reconciled to the severe stroke when it affects ourselves, though it is the unavoidable lot of humanity to undergo it. And in vain do we seek for consolation under it, if we are not supported by the principles of Christianity. They carry us beyond the present scene, and enable us to realize futurity. They reconcile us to the loss of every present good, and to our own departure out of life. Under their influence the time of separation from our friends appears only a short interval; and we anticipate the joyful union again—the glorious morn of the resurrection, and behold ourselves and them rising free from the incumberances of mortality to life, to light, and glory.

The best consolation under the loss of our friends is to have this hope in their death; and the best encouragement to resignation under present trials and afflictions is to keep this prospect in view for ourselves; and I am confident you enjoy both these sources of comfort.

---

1   Ibid., 2:97-98.t

[Henry Hulton to Elizabeth Lightbody]   *Blissmore Hall near Andover*
13 July 1780[1]

Mrs. E. Lightbody Liverpool

The receipt of Your favour of the 9th Ultimo gave me great pleasure. It came to hand a little before I left my late habitation, and we have been so much harried with packing and unpacking and the business of our farms that I have scarce had an hour of leisure since.

I feel very much for the family of my late worthy friend, Mr. R. Nicholson, and wish it was in my power to yield better consolation than words.[2]

From the calamities of war, added to the ordinary troubles of life, we have been called out to a deal of suffering in ourselves and friends; and I heartily sympathize with all those who feel the rod of affliction; but we have it from the best authority that it is good for us, and I wish we may all of us improve the evils of life to our spiritual advantage. I hope in your family You are to experience an increase of happiness. May every branch of it in the connections they form be united with persons worthy of them, and be blessings to You and to the world.

These young ones are sources of pleasure, are objects of constant care and anxiety. In their welfare we are so much interested, that we can hardly form an idea of happiness to ourselves seperate from it. Yet on how many delicate circumstances does their success or misfortune in life depend. The management of their bodies, the right culture and disposition of their minds, their early habits, and intimate connections, all influence their future well or ill being.

I wish You were nigher to Us, and should think myself happy in a frequent communication with you. We have each our cares and our troubles. They would be lighten[ed] by communication; for next to the consolation of heaven, is the commerce of liberal, honest, and sympathizing minds.

Thank God, I am blessed with a worthy partner in my cares, and with as yet promising and dutiful children.

---

1   Ibid., 2:99-100.
2   Nicholson had died on 19 August 1779 in Liverpool, where he was also buried.

[Henry Hulton to Thomas Percival]   *Blissmore Hall 1 September 1780*[1]

Dr. Percival Manchester

Though I have not have the pleasure of hearing from You of a long time, yet I have had some tokens of your remembrance, and am obliged to You for your communications.

My intercourse with Your part is lessening every year. I lament the loss of several valuable friends since I was last favored with a letter from you, and would wish to cherish those that remain, and to have now and then the satisfaction of hearing of their welfare. I condole with you in your particular losses, and hope the remaining branches of your family will be spared to be comforts to You.

I had for a considerable time been looking out to purchase a large tract of improvable land, and at length met with a farm, to my mind containing near 1000 Acres, which I bought, and have removed my family from Wells to this place, in the neighbourhood of my farm.

It was matter of concern to me to be so long unemployed, and as we are still in a State of uncertainty as to our publick Service, I thought engaging in my present Scheme was the best use I could make of my time.

From the change of circumstances in life, we are called out at different periods, to the exertion of different virtues, and it is good for us to be so disciplined, and trained.

The pursuits of Science are pleasing, but activity is a duty, and Spirit is necessary to carry us through the toil and combat of the world. For myself, I would give up all views of worldly advantages for the pleasures of reading and writing; but I have many others to be interested for, and therefore I must not give way to chagrin from past discouragements and disap[p]ointments, but still exert myself in some way to be useful. How wise is the order of providence! To rouse us from indolence to duty by necessity.

---

1   Hulton, "Letterbooks," 2:101-102.

Miscellaneous Pieces

Written on traversing the Plains of Abraham[1]

On Fame's fair list the Soldier seeks to rise
By arduous acts, a dang'rous enterprise
Thro' Death's wide field intrepidly proceeds,
With mind resolv'd, & fixt on valient deeds.
Thus up to Fame, the Kentish Hero rose
And reap'd fresh laurels midst Canadian snows.
Britain laments his fate, reveres his name
And Wolf is graven on the lists of fame,
That Name whenever youthful soldier reads
His Soul shall glow to emulate his deeds
And Age with tears of gratitude shall tell
Wolf bravely fought & crownd with glory fell.

---

1   Hulton, "Observations," 226-227; also in *Loyalist Lady*, Appendix, 106-107. For Wolfe as hero, with a nice color reproduction of Benjamin West's commemorative painting of the scene, see Simon Schama, "The Many Deaths of General Wolfe," in *Dead Uncertainties* (New York: Alfred A. Knopf, 1991), 3-70, a "fictional history" account that raised academic eyebrows, not least those of Gordon S. Wood. See Wood's 27 June 1991 *New York Review of Books* piece, as reissued, with an afterword, in Wood's *The Purpose of the Past* (New York: Penguin Press, 2008), 94-109.

Written in America. 1773[1]

Without entering into the dispute as to the right of the British Parliament to impose Taxes on America, I would beg leave to submit some thoughts to consideration, which good policy, and a regard to our own interest, might allow to have weight in influencing our judgments in this matter.

Before we make an alteration in any circumstance in life, we should consider the value of the good we put to hazard, and the risque we run of being sufferers by the exchange.

In the present political case we should place the benefits arising from obedience against the burthens we are compelled to submit to.

To induce us to submit with chearfulness, we should consider that the Government to which we pay obedience has the power to protect us; and that from the genius of the British Constitution, from the commercial interest, and good policy of that nation, we have every desirable security; that its authority over us will be exercised with justice, and gentleness; and for our own real advantage, as that must be the best means of promoting its own welfare. And to make us prize the blessings we enjoy under this Government, we should consider the circumstances to which we should be reduced, were we withdrawn from the protection of Great Britain.

In the wide spread Colonies of America, where the Country is continually increasing in inhabitants and improving in cultivation, there will be frequent occasion for alterations and amendments in their Governments, Laws, and provincial regulations. And where can those inhabitants find such a model of Government, as in the British Constitution? Where can they be directed so well as by the wisdom of a British Senate? How could the frequent jarring interests of different provinces be adjusted without bloodshed, but by the interposition of the authority of that Government? And how could the power of the whole Continent be collected, and applied on any emergency, without its supreme command.

When we consider the many encouragements given by Great Britain for the cultivation of this Country, and the production of articles of commerce; when we compare the duties paid by the Subject in America, with the Duties and Taxes paid by the Subjects in Great Britain, for that protection which is common to both, we shall see great cause to admire the tenderness and indulgence of Government towards us.

In the infancy of Societies, as in the early stage of life, there is an impatience under the restraints of authority; the violent passions of youth often plunge it into the greatest distresses, and Societies have often been thrown into confusion and disorder by the turbulence of factions, demagogues who have abused the licence of the press, and credulity of the people, to serve their own interested, or ambitions purposes.

If there should be any persons who endeavour to persuade us into a confidence of our sufficiency to our own Government, defence, and protection; let us look well into the Characters of such men and the motives for their conduct before we suffer ourselves to be influenced by their patriotic pretensions.

It may answer the purposes of a present interest to flatter the passions of the multitude; but he who would secure a solid reputation to himself by promoting the real good and happiness of his country must not expect a present approbation; he will have to combat with the views of particular persons, and many popular prejudices that will expose him to the reproaches of interested minds, and the general censure of his contemporaries.

Let us consider our present state; our wide spread Continent; the different religions, Constitutions, and Interests, of the Colonies; their capacity for offence, and defence; seperately, and collectively, dependent, and Independent of Great Britain. Let us then ask ourselves, by what means the present welfare of America can be best secured, and its future interest promoted? Can we say at this time that we of ourselves are sufficient to these things? Or shall not we be compelled to own that our present security and future happiness depend on maintaining the power and supreme authority of Great Britain. That under her auspices we must establish that Order and Government which must be the basis of every thing that shall make us great hereafter. Let it be sufficient to our ambition, to lay the firm foundation; and let posterity wait for those materials that may be furnished by the hand of time for erecting the goodly and lasting fabrick. But if ever we shall be led by designing Men to a vain relyance on our own ability, and dare to combat the only power that can protect us at present, and open the paths to our future greatness, we shall by sad experience be taught that though we may for a while distress her, yet that we have ruined ourselves. For supposing Great Britain should require no allegiance from Us, and in return withdraw its protection; or that we by an opposition to its authority would compel that Nation to acknowledge our independence, in either case we should find ourselves a prey to every foreign invader; our extension would be our weakness; and the several provinces would in their turn become subject to the tyranny of Demagogues, the disorders of Anarchy, and all the calamities of Civil War.

Let us then see that we can only rise to greatness by a reflection of glory from Great Britain. That every assistance we lend her in support of her power is repaid by the protection she yields us against outward enemies, and by the establishment she makes for the maintaining of Order and Government within, and that our present peace and welfare, and future happiness and glory, depend upon securing that protection and support, by our duty and affection.

*Ne, pueri, ne tanta animis assuescite bella: Neu patriae validas in viscera vertite vires.

Virg.[2]

---

1   Henry Hulton, "Sketches," 97-110, William L. Clements Library mss, University of Michigan.
2   In effect: do not, my sons, become enthralled by war; neither should you turn the violence of war upon your homeland. Virgil's *Aeneid*, 6:832.

Written in America. 1775[1]

GIVE EAR, O YE PEOPLE!
ERE IT IS TOO LATE BE WISE![2]

When Countries are occupied by contending Armies, few fall by the sword, in comparison with those who perish by famine, and disease. For when Agriculture is at a stand, Commerce interrupted, and supplies cut off, those evils necessarily follow. The produce of the Country is consumed by the military or destroyed in hostile depredations: and the wretched inhabitants perish with hunger, or fall a prey to disease.

The sword may be sheathed at the command of a General, but who can stay the rage of the destroying Angel that walketh in darkness?

In vain do ye boast of your numbers; they will only hasten the progress of famine, and serve for food to the pestilence. When they enter the dwelling, they are not to be satisfied but by destruction; and every circumstance attendant on war, is fuel to these destroyers.

The Infant and the Aged, the weak and the infirm, fall immediate victims. Even the strong man must faint in a lack of bread,and not long be able to support want, poverty, and wretchedness.

Ye! who have introduced Anarchy, and disorder; who have led the people into treason, and rebellion, and are now plunging them into all the horrors of War, consider!

But why call on You, You cool destroyers of Man's happiness! who seek to make this goodly theatre of earth a hell! No, let me call on You, Ye People! to consider, and know, from facts.

In the last war in Germany, several of the Bishoprics became occupied Countries, the scene of action between the Armies of Great Britain and France. They were not enemies or rebels; but it was their misfortune, in the course of the war, to be occupied by both parties.

After the first crop and stock were consumed, the lands in many parts remained long uncultivated. The peasants were harrassed, the Country exhausted, and its nobles in want of bread. In April 1761 the City of Warburg had every appearance of calamity. The streets were unpaved, the windows all broken, no furniture was in the houses, not a bed, sheet, or blanket was to be got in the town, nor a morsel of bread to be purchased with money. The wretched inhabitants on the Dymel followed the Army, imploring bread from the Soldiers. They refused money; it would avail them nothing. They cried out, bread! bread!

There were large Villages in the neighbourhood of Warburg, where the crow of the Cock, the barking of the Dog, and the low of the Cattle were not heard; where no smoke ascended from the late social hearth, or wretched inhabitant remained to mourn over the fate of his companions. But all was silence, and desolation. Yet did this reduced country groan under the miseries of war for near two years longer.

---

1 Hulton, "Sketches," 111-117.
2 The first line being offered, perhaps, as a variation on Psalm 49:1 (KJV): "Hear this, all ye people; give ear, all ye inhabitants of the world..."

An Ode
Humbly Inscribed
To
Earl Percy
at Boston
On St. George's Day
1775 [1]

AN ODE.

Genius of Britain! hear my pray'r!
Make thou our sons thy choicest care,
 And as our Fathers brave:
 To valour and the pow'rs of Art.
 With warm benevolence of Heart,
 That still delights to save.

2.

Let virtue crown—request no more,
 In vain for blessings you implore,
 The Genius straight-reply'd;
 Not mine to give—I point the way,
That leads the youth to virtue's day,
 By toils, & dangers tryed.

3.

Up you step 'Till he must ascend,
Unwearied still with Foes contend,
 Nor cast a look behind
 Nor at the Syren's soothing voice,
 Delay the purpose of his choice,
 And vigour of his mind.

4.

But few with steady Eye proceed,
Intent, by ev'ry arduous deed,
To gain th' ascent on high.
There in the velvet lap of ease,
Wasting in sloth their golden days,
See some supinely lie.

5.

Can heav'nly spirits then descend,
And prone to Earth ignobly bend,
Nor' pant for virtuous Fame?
Can Laurel Wreaths, fair valour's prize,
The Bays that ornament the Wise,
Present their Charms in vain?

6.

Virtue attending all the while,
Answer'd the Genius with a smile,
Complacent, full of grace;
Lo here! whom love of Virtue fires,
One that is worthy of his Sires,
An honour of his Race.

7.

Behold a Youth! illustrious born
Ardent in life's first opening morn,
Forsakes his native shore,
Whatever Wealth or Fortune brings,
Whate'er from Royal Favour springs,
These he possess'd before.

8.

But not content with these alone,
He seeks for honours all his own,
With unabating zeal.
Fir'd with the love of virtuous deeds,
Through toils and dangers he proceeds,
And braves the adverse Gale.

9.

Look where across th' Atlantic main,
Faction & Discord, Furies reign,
Inflaming civil Broil,
Where the mad people without cause,
Spurning at Britain, & her Laws,
To their own ruin toil.

10.

Led by a wanton savage Child,
Boastful and rude, fierce & wild,
Uncultur'd, unrefin'd;
Stranger to ev'ry softer Art,
That aids the Genius, warms the heart,
And liberates the Mind.

11.

Lo! Where amidst that wayward Race,
He shines with most distinguish'd grace,
And admiration draws;
Averse to own superior worth.
To honour Genius, Manners, Birth,
They yield a mute applause.

12.

Soft'ning their Duty with his smiles,
The Troops, thro' all their martial toils,
Undaunted persevere:
With chearful ardour each one serves,
While Percy o'er himself preserves,
A discipline severe.

13.

The Dragon by St. George subdued,
Was Emblem of a factious brood,
A Monster, fierce and wild,
My Percy! such thy Foe to day;
O! might he bow beneath thy sway!
Subdued by Actions mild.

14.

For if Example could avail,
Thy gentle Manners would prevail,
And bend the rudest mind,
Exerting each persuasive Art;
With all the virtues of the heart,
To civilize Mankind.

15.

But as with mad tumultuous rage,
The Dragon dares the battle wage,
And braves thy utmost ire,
While indignation's in thine Eye,
Beneath thy arm, the Fiend shall lie,
Shall tremble, and expire.

16.

So virtue spake—and let me join,
One ardent wish, one pray's of mine,
On this auspicious Day,
May all who Royal George oppose,
Of Britain, & her King the Foes,
Be humbled and obey.

Non usitata non tenni ferar Penna, biformis per liquidam aethera Vates.[2]

Te vidit insons Cerberus aureo Cornu decorum, leniter atterent Caudam; et recedentis trilingui ore pedes, tetigitque crura.

Hor.[3]

---

1   Hulton, "Sketches," 151-162. Hulton and Percy grew close during the Boston siege. Like Hulton, Percy believed that London had been far too lenient for far too long, and that a state of rebellion existed well before Lexington and Concord. Even so, initially he had thought that the people would not be "mad" enough to resist a show of force. Their tenacity on 19 April 1775 earned his grudging respect. Though he served honorably in the war until he returned to England in 1777, he had sat in the House of Commons for Westminster before his posting to Massachusetts and had never been a true enthusiast for using the military as a solution to a political problem. He went where his duty took him, despite his reservations. He later succeeded his father as Duke of Northumberland and inherited the family seat at Alnwick Castle. See Charles Knowles Bolton ed., *Letters of Hugh Earl Percy* (Boston: Charles E. Goodspeed, 1902).

2   The effusive, less-than-literal sort of translation that Hulton would have been raised on—which in turn probably shaped his own poetic notions—is nicely captured in Thomas Creech, *The Odes, Satires, and Epistles of Horace*, 4th ed. (London: W. Taylor, 1715), 67, who rendered this passage from Horace's *Odes*, II:xx, 1 as: "No weak, no common Wing shall bear, My rising Body thro' the Air."

3   Ibid., also from the *Odes*, II:xix, 30, which Creech translated as: "Thee Cerberus saw, and show'd the Way; He wag'd his tail, grew wond'rous kind; He licked thy feet, he fawn'd and whin'd."

On Masonry[1]

1. We sing, the mysteries divine!
   That Masons can conceal;
   Nor yet betray the secret sign,
   Or lift the sacred veil.

2. When first the great Almighty, Sire,
   Commanded from his throne,
   Chaos, and night, he bid retire,
   Be light___ and Glory shone.

3. Then Wisdom unto Man was given,
   The Gloom withdrew its shade;
   He saw the mighty host of Heav'n,
   And glorious light display'd.

4. When Nature's Temple he surveys,
   New scenes of wonder rise,
   What Art could such a structure raise?
   From Earth, unto the skies!

5. Tis here he every duty learns,
   And treasures in his heart,
   Next, he the secret signs discerns,
   And myst'ries of his Art.

6. Fair Truth, Benevolence, and Love,
   With all the social train,
   In Wisdom, Strength, and Beauty move,
   While Friendship links the chain.

7. We boast alliance with the Great,
   The Hero, Sage, and King;
   But yet more honours in our State,
   Than Wealth, or Titles bring.

8. For we indulge no sordid view,
   Nor Gold for entrance crave;
   The Man that's just, sincere, & true,
   Tho' naked, we receive.

9. Chearful in labour we appear,
   And all harmonious join;
   For why? the Graces still are near,
   And present are the Nine.

10. Whene'er oppress'd with rugged toil,
    They aid the drooping cause;
    On all our labour still they smile,
    And crown us with applause.

11. Our actions bear the strictest test,
    Of Compass, rule, and Square.
    We take our Brother to our breast,
    And truths pure emblems wear.

12. Expos'd on Earth to toil and woe,
    Yet sure there's pow'r to save,
    Resign'd we feel the fatal blow,
    Nor dread the gloomy Grave.

---

1   Hulton, "Sketches," 169-174. Hulton had joined a Masonic lodge when he lived on Antigua. He appears to have been fairly active in the Order while there, but less so when he lived in Massachusetts. Hulton helped out St. John's Lodge (in Boston)once when it needed a meeting place, but there is no other record of his involvement in *Proceedings in Masonry* (Boston: Grand Lodge of Massachusetts, 1895). For the difficulty of linking political allegiance with membership in the Brotherhood, see my "Freemasonry and the American Revolution," *The Historian* 55 (1993):315-330.

A Rhapsody
written on crossing Lake George[1]

The trees have now changed their hue, and the huge lofty mountains stretch their broad sides over Lake George, in russet sadness; frightful perpendiculars! Eager the ear attends, the eye explores; no chearful sound of bell, no faithful barking dog is heard; no heart reviving smoke from rural lot is seen; no smiling spot, blest by the toil of man, or trace of human footstep! A chilling horrour seizes on the mind. All around is silence; vast rocks and mountains! Upon whose brows hang lowering clouds; stern as the eye-brow in a giant's front: and underneath, is all untrod, inhospitable Woods.

Wretched the State of him that's exiled from the social face of man, doomed to a double share of woe; he who can vent his Griefs to sympathizing hearts, is half relieved. *Dreadful enough in such a night as this to have been drove for shelter to these woods.

God be praised that we are safe on shore.— Ye dreary wilds! Ye horrour-brooding Hills! Ye gloomy shades! Ye haunts of savage beasts! Farewell! Welcome the cultured soil, the social hearth, and all the joys of blessing, and being blessed.

*It rains incessant whilst the small skiff impetuous drives, before the boisterous gale. The soldier mariner, with either hand employed; conducts the sail, and guides the helm— for seven long hours with steady eye attentive. Nor through the whole dares lift his hand to taste his fav'rite dram.

The storm encreases, night approaches, big with growing horrors.

---

1   Hulton, "Sketches," 127-130.

Contrast in Canada and London[1]

On a Journey made to Canada, I could not help remarking the Contrast of appearances between Canada, and London; and if happiness is to be estimated by the chearful enjoyment of Life, the preference is much in favour of the former.

In Canada—

A clear blue sky chearful Countenances—hearts at ease—open houses—a simple city of manners—an ignorance of Luxury—a contentment with their lot—innocent amusements seasoning their homely fare with hearty communication—and their simple enjoyments, with enlivening vivacity.

Happy Canadian, who lives sans souci—feels no want—knows no anxiety—but in his flannel Jacket, drives about in his Cariole—with appetite keen—with spirits light as the air he breathes with heart all chearfulness—laughs, sings, and dances life away.

This is surely the Country, where the plant called heart's ease, so rare elsewhere, grows like a weed, and is found at every Cottage.

Weep Grandeur, Wealth, and Pride; be mortified vain man! acknowledge the hand of the God of nature blessing simplicity. Own the folly of thy pursuits, and that to be happy is to control, not pamper, thy luxurious appetites.

In London.

An heavy gloomy sky suspicious Countenances—anxious hearts—barred doors—a display of wealth—a refinement of taste—self gratification encreased—the heart contracted the passions inflamed—principles corrupted—Greatness satiated with Pleasure, and pining under the weight of enjoyment—Wealth mortified—men in Office soured and discontented—Thousands living beyond their means, to vie in appearance with those above them, and of course wretched.

---

1   Ibid. 123-126

On *Climates*[1]

The curious enquirers into the rise of the Arts and Sciences have endeavoured to account for the progress of them in the different countrys where they have flourished, according as the temperature of their situations, or forms of Gvernment,were favourable for the cultivation of them. Thus it was natural that the clear sky, and serene climate of Egypt, should favour improvements in Astronomy; and that the power of eloquence should be carried to their greatest height, in the Grecian and Roman states.

In those happy regions, where nature under the agreable influence of the superior bodies, appeared lovely through all the seasons and forever lavish of her unexhausted stores, enlivened the genius, and exhilarated the spirits with luxuriant variety in that period of time, when the powers of human understanding had every incentive to improvement, being animated by all the noble sentiments attendant on a virtuous Patriotism; we may well imagine that genius would make its strongest efforts; that the powers of harmony should be attuned to the softest compositions; and the imitative arts carried to their highest degree of perfection.

After the destructive rage of Gothic barbarity, ignorance and superstition triumphed for many ages over Europe; Science long drooped and Art seemed to have expired. But at length the Muses, long frightened from earth, seemed to be willing to revisit their former dwellings; they loved their antient haunts and frequented the banks of the Tyber, but alas! they found not their wonted Asylum. Science was discouraged from attempting to establish in the now gloomy habitations. There was no invitation for truth: error and ignorance had riveted themselves in the seats of power; and Genius was either cramped by horrid prejudices, and gloomy superstition; or deterred from appearing by the dread of punishment.

In tracing the progress of the Arts to the present period, it has been observed that in their advances to the northward, they have sunk from that enlivened expression of them which glows in the animated originals; that under the influence of a rigid sky, where nature is not lavish in furnishing luxuriant scenes, the chilled imagination teems with but barren images and that the passions, unharmonized to soft composition, are often cold and languid in their expression.

Though Genius in the works of Art is greatly assisted in its improvements by the advantage of favourable climates, yet the advances in Science, depending more on a long stretch of thought in the investigation of truths, on a clearness of conception, a strength of judgment, and retentiveness of memory, the improvements herein may be assisted by a cooler region, that braces the nerves, give spirits to the animal frame and fits it to support the mind through studies that require unwearied application, and therefore in such a country, where the genius of its Government encourages a freedom of enquiry, it may be expected that there will be found the strongest efforts of the human mind, towards discoveries in philosophy, and advances in Science; and to this it may be greatly owing that Britain boasts of having produced some of the noblest ornaments of mankind: those who by the arduous exertion of the capacities of the human Soul, have carried its powers to the most amazing heights: her Bacon and Boyle; her Newton and Locke.

I believe few persons have lived for any time in places remote from each other. Without experiencing an alteration in their animal constitution, and mental abilities; and thus we may in some measure account for the characteristics of different nations.

By being braced in the severe climate of the North of Germany, the mind is enabled to support an intense application to laborious enquiries. And does not the cloudy sky, and uncomfortable season of November, in England, much encourage that chagrin and gloomy disposition so observable among the Britons? Whilst the serenity of Seasons, and smiling face of nature in the south of France, inspire the mind with chearfulness and gaiety.

It would carry us beyond the bounds of a short essay, and be too nice and physical an enquiry, to trace the various degrees of effect which different climates may have on the human constitution, and passions. I would only endeavour to shew, that we must allow them to have a good deal of influence: which I believe will be granted by those who have made efforts to enlarge their genius and improve their mental powers in different places. Their operations on others will be hardly distinguished; for the soils of every climate would have much the same rude and barren appearance if we suffered them to remain uncultivated; it is only by due preparation and labour, that we know the one to be more luxuriant in its produce than the other.

As the far greater part of the Globe to the Southward of the antient seats of the Arts and Sciences continues in the rude uncultured state of savage barbarity, we have it not in our power to judge how far the genius of the native inhabitants of the hotter climates might be influenced by their several situations; perhaps by the advantage of a right cultivation they might make improvement in many Arts, and a rapid progress in several Sciences, that have as yet been little known or cultivated amongst Europeans; but it is impossible to know the lustre of the Diamond that is yet overcrusted with earth.

We can only judge what progress we might expect in the Arts and Sciences in the hotter climates from observing the effects they have on the mental abilities, passions, and constitutions of Europeans.

To make advances in Science requires a mind long trained in an arduous employment of its rational powers, in tracing and comprehending all the intermediate ideas that carry us on to the discoveries of truth. Together with the clearly conceiving, distinguishing and retaining our ideas, it is necessary that we enjoy a strong animal constitution that will support us through the severity of perplexed enquiries.

If the mind does not retain a continued, even possession of its powers, its progress will be desultory and vain; if its imagination is overheated, its conceptions will not be agreeable to the nature of things: they will be confused and irregular, inconsistant with truth; if its passions are inflamed, its judgment will be weakened; it will view things through a false medium, and its determinations will be rash and unjust. Whilst under the power of imagination and passion, a confused train of ideas will make strong, quick, and transient impressions on the mind; and if it be frequently agitated with such violence, it will be unwilling to attend to the tedious tracing of its ideas, to the recollecting of those passed through the mind, and consequently the memory will be weakened. Add to the whole, if the animal spirits are irregular, if sometimes they are greatly elevated, at others sink into a languid state, we are then as incapable of a due attention to the investigation of truth.

But these are said by most Europeans to be the unhappy influences of the hot climates on their minds and constitutions. They are formed for applications to Science, and attention to discoveries of truth in the northern regions; but they experience a debility of the faculties both of body and mind by a long continuance near the Equator, and in such a state it is impossible to attend to laborious enquiries with steadiness and vigour.

Under the oppressive influence of the Sun in the torrid Zone, the genius of Europeans can make but feeble and transient efforts; the animal spirits are too much exhausted, the passions too variously and violently agitated, to give sufficient life to an extensive performance. If an animated one is produced there, it will not be labored or long; it will be quickly conceived and suddenly finished; for the mind being incapable of a long attention its determinations will be speedy and decicive.

But besides the effect of different climates on the human race, there are those arising from various forms of Government, dyet, customs, religions, education, and the different orders of subordination in the Society; the influence of each should be distinguished, if we would characterize any particular place, or people. And though we have hitherto confined ourselves to the operations of the climate on the human frame in the cultivation of its powers, yet we would endeavour to shew that some other circumstances may have concurred to retard genius in its progress to the Southward.

A Government established on principles of liberty, in a well ordered Society, will animate us with noble and generous sentiments for the good of the whole and greatly assist the improvement of genius; but if the Society is composed of different orders, wherein the one is in a state of slavish subjection to the other, the influence which that Government will have on the subordinate order will be discovered in their ignorance, meaness, and timidity; whilst the superior one will be tinctured with a severity of disposition and unfeelingness of heart to the calamities of others; and in proportion as the commerce between the two orders is encreased, the higher one will sink from its elevatedness of mind and dignity of sentiment; for, by insensible degrees we fall off from our noblest endowments; and it requires assiduous care and application to support our virtuous and generous improvements, and preserve our nature from sinking into a base and corrupted state.

But the most fatal effects of a commerce with the inferior order will appear in the impressions it will make on young and tender minds, which should be early formed to sentiments of humanity and decency. But from the influence of the brutal manners and mean sentiments of the ignorant vulgar, will be much in danger of contracting low dispositions; all [of] which are prejudicial to the advances of genius.

To the former unhappy circumstances which attend Europeans in their establishments to the Southward there is a further retardment to the progress of Genius, by being far removed from the best opportunities of instruction.

By the advantage of an early cultivation, the mind contracts an attention to improvement; it enlarges its capacities and is urged to the exertion of its abilities. But if no pains have been taken to establish right principles in morals, if the mind hath had no opportunity of expansion by the advantage of a liberal education, what can we expect from such a character, but that it should take a wrong bias, be excited to actions by the impulse of its passions, and prove an injurious member of the Society.

There is nothing more happy to young minds than being placed under the care of a skilful Master, who discovering the first dawnings of Genius, can smooth those paths of Science to which the natural inclination of his pupil leads him; and by rendering the road to knowledge pleasant and easy, greatly facilitate the advances of youthful genius.

But how difficult is the gaining such an Assistant? How few are capable of forming the minds of Youths? How rare to meet such a skilful instructor far remote from Europe? Besides, in those distant parts there is not that spur to quicken the industry of young minds; they are not animated by that applause which attends proficients in Science in our large seminaries of learning; and where there is little prospect of acquiring distinction, or advancement, we shall hardly be excited to an arduous exertion of our abilities.

By observing the respect paid to great characters, we are animated with emulation; and this passion, when rightly influenced, is a noble incitement to young minds.

Indeed, to the honour of the subjects of Britain established in the West Indies, they whose fortunes allow it are not sparing in giving all the advantage of a liberal education to their offspring. They place them for instruction in the best seminaries of Europe, and are grateful and generous to their instructors: and indeed, the progress of these Youths in languages and Science is generally rapid. But being far removed from those who must have the greatest interest in their happiness, they are in danger of not being so well established in those principles which form the moral character as others. Having no interested inspectors of their conduct, they experience not those admonitions and reproofs which are the wholsome discipline to young minds; they have not before their eyes the animating examples of those who are dearest to them; nor their repeated precepts, to pursue the amiable paths of truth, and virtue. But having generally the means of acquiring every desireable accomplishment, they are much exposed to the violence of passion; and it is no wonder, under such circumstances, that but few laboriously exert their genius in rational and improving Studies, or that the conduct of many in future life should be often at variance with the pure dictates of virtue.

My Son, fear thou the Lord and the King, and meddle not with them that are given to change.

H. S.[2]

—Ecce per orbem.
Mitis turba Deum, terras exosa furentes Deserit: atque hominum damnatum avertitur agmen.

Petron. Art.[3]

---

1   Ibid., 61-96.
2   Initials for holy scriptures, in this case Proverbs 24:21:"My son, fear thou the Lord and the king: and meddle not with them that are given to change." (KJV).
3   From Petronius's *Satyricon*, 124, loosely translated: the gentle gods flee the troubled earth, and in disgust leave mankind to furiously drive itself to destruction.

The Voluptuary[1]

Let us suppose the Voluptuary enjoying the highest scenes of delight that can be painted by the votaries to pleasure.

Where the charms of novelty are added to the embellishments of Art, and refinements of taste. Where there is all that fancy can write, with the magnificent and grand, to delight the eye; all the powers of harmony to please the ear; to soften, sooth and subdue the heart: and either Indies explored, and all the powers of the culinary art employed, to please the palate; to gratify the high pampered and luxurious appetite.

Intent only on present gratification; forgetful that abstinence and oil are necessary to give a relish to pleasure; he consumes his fortune in a course of licentious indulgence; and wastes life in a round of animal enjoyments, and profligate attachments; a Stranger to the sweets of domestic consolation, the endearments of a virtuous connection.

The eye of his understanding darkened by the corruption of his heart, long bent down to earth, and fixed on gross, and sensual pursuits, at length laments that the indulgence of appetite has weakened the powers of enjoyment. But it is over the imbecility, not the depravity, of his nature that he mourns. Still is his heart swollen with pride, and unmindful of its Creator. Unable to find consolation from within, or to receive comfort from without; tortured at present, yet dreading the future; he is ever restless, and unsatisfied; eager to pursue, yet incapable to enjoy. Now, palled with the creature; impotent and weak; languid, yet craving; desire must be stimulated by refinement in luxurious indulgence; whilst the body, debilitated, becomes more alive to the feelings of its own imbecilities, and urges the mind to rapacious means of gratifying appetite, and supporting luxurious dissipation; and the heart selfish and contracted in its affections, is insensible to the wants and miseries of others. Rapacious to acquire, what with profusion he may waste; he lays wait for the wealthy, and unguarded Heir, and coolly meditates his ruin. Artful, smiling, and insinuating, he wins on his unsuspecting innocence. With an air of frankness and generosity in his manner, and the hospitality of his table, he gains on his confidence; and by a semblance of honesty, takes advantage of the openness of his youthful heart. Fatal lures! But too frequently and successfully employed, by artful rapacity, to seduce the innocent and spoil the opulent.

Unhappy Youth! Little didst thou dream in the hour of festivity and mirth, in the midst of convivial joys, that thou wast then doomed, the prey of the destroyer. That when the fatal dice were introduced, the cast was to be for thy fortune; and that he should purchase his present affluence, at the expence of thy undoing. For, see the rapacious Spoiler now triumphing at thy credulity. Bold, assuming, and prophane! Nor will he leave thee, till thou art rendered as licentious as himself; totally stript of thy property; unprincipled and wretched.

But ere long the miseries which the unfeeling Voluptuary has brought upon others, await himself. Though void of Principle, and thoughtless of futurity, in the hour of profligate success; yet distress, sickness, and pain awaken the pangs of reflection and the horrors of guilt. The immortal Soul, conscious of its divine origin, reproaches itself for its own baseness and depravity; in submitting to the weakness and corruption of its gross companion, and the consideration of the meanness of the objects it stooped to pursue; the sacrifices it made to obtain them; and their incapacity, to satisfy its desires, is a fresh source of torment.

Now! He shudders at the wrath of the Almighty, and anticipates the punishments of the damned. Now! He blasphemes, and despairs. And now! Amidst the torture of disease, and the agonies of his mind, with impious hand he commits the most atrocious of crimes, finishing life by an accumulation of guilt, and rushing unsummoned into the presence of his Maker.

Mr. H. has more than once beheld the character in real life which he has here painted.

The Soul of Jonathan was knit with the Soul of David and Jonathan loved him as his own soul.

H. S.[2]

Plerumque gratae divitibus vices Mundaeque parvo sub lare, pauperum Cenae, sine aulaeis et ostro, sollicitam explicuere frontem.

Hor.[3]

Illud enim honestum (quod saepe dicimus) etiam si in alio cernimus tamen nos movet, atque illi, in quo id inesse videtur, amicos facit.

Cicero[4]

---

1   Hulton, "Sketches," 29-40.

2   Initials, again, for holy scriptures. The full passage of 1 Samuel 18:1 (KJV), reads: "And it came to pass, when he had made an end of speaking unto Saul, that the soul of Jonathan was knit with the soul of David, and Jonathan loved him as his own soul."

3   I turn again to Creech, *Horace*, 110, who rendered this passage from the *Odes*, III:xxix, 13, as: "From thy disgusting Plenty fly, Thy Palace leave, that mount on high." More modern translations can be decidedly different—but even if more accurate linguistically, Hulton's understanding of what the passage was meant to say may have come closer to that of Creech than later editors.

4   From Cicero, *De Officiis*," Book 1, line 55, in effect: for truly, if we find another who possesses that moral goodness that I have stressed, we are drawn to that person and want to become friends.

Simplicity and Sympathy[1]

Hail! all hail! my most belov'd Companions!
Cheared by your smiles, with satisfaction
I enjoy retirements sweets. hail! divine
Simplicity! Thou, to the moral sense
Yet undepravd, whether in publick, or
Domestic life, endear'd associate.
Oft in my pensive, solitary walks,
By meditation led; thou strewest with
Delight my path; and o'er all that's good, o'er
All that's fair around, sheddest a thousand
Graces, new, and various. Mild Nature's
Sweetest child; on all her works attendant:
Except where Man deforms. And Man alone
Deforms, or in the natural, or the
Moral world; else all we see, or hear is
Order, harmony, and love. Solaced
By thee, e'en solitude is pleasing. Thou,
And heart-soothing Sympathy, Sisters dear.
Give me, to my homely fare, high relish:
Make my domestic hearth most grateful; and
Fit my Soul for converse sweet with heaven.
For there ye dwell, and knit and chear the blest
Society, of just men, perfect made.
Hail! Soul-consoling, balmy Sympathy!
Without thee all is joyless; and with thee,
There is a sun-shine still o'er fortune's frown.
O! ne'er cease, twin Sisters, to rejoice my
Heart; and tho' ye shun the lofty domes of
Luxury, let my low roof receive you.
Here deign to dwell, and let me ever know
You highest luxury to the mind! heart
Intercourse, of friends most dear! thro' cares, and
Toil, thro' sickness, grief, and pain, endear'd the
More by you! The minds still poor without you.
And midst the gorgeous pomp of state, and the
High pampering of the sumptuous board, unchear'd
Unsatisfied—still pants for you.

From the general pursuits of mankind, one would be led to think, that the stream of happiness flowed but in one channel; but it is the depravity of our passions that misleads our judgment, and yields the heart captive to the corruption of our nature.

We pursue things as our chief good, which from the constitution of our Being, it is impossible they should afford us real happiness. We neglect the cultivation of those dispositions which would tend to our comfort and peace; and we slight the possession of those objects which alone can satisfy the desires of the Soul and form its true felicity. But we all live to appear happy in the eyes of others, not to be really so in ourselves. We forego domestic comfort for foreign amusement; inward peace for outward glare. He who never looked through a microscope is a stranger to a world of entertainment; so is he who neglects the little pleasures at home that are within his reach. They may appear trifling at first and by many are overlooked, but cultivated, you find the fund increase; they solace in every hour, and afford consolation under every disquietude from without.

It is wonderful what new scenes of delight open to the mind disposed to relish the beauties of Nature, and a state of domestic tranquility. Free from anxious cares, from many trifling and noisy intruders; from many scenes of vanity that would corrupt, or of misery that would disturb. it is at leisure to attend to the finger of the Almighty, ever pointing out new entertainment. All is then peace, harmony, and enjoyment; and it wonders how it could be so long misled by a vain shew, and disquieted in vain; when there was so much of satisfaction to be enjoyed, under its own roof, and in the contemplation of truth, and nature.

In this disposition of mind we correct, in a great measure, the false notions we had contracted; and we find that the real good of life is more in our own power than we had imagined. He who has the fewest wants is in the way of enjoying the most real pleasure; and he who can find resources in books and nature need not regret his being remote from the bustle of business, and scenes of dissipation.

It is pleasing to see the works of nature, and of Art, in other countries; and to notice the manners of people in different parts of the world. The mind becomes enlarged by such observations and acquires many new ideas. But after having passed over all these objects it remains unsatisfied; there is still a void, and a craving. The ostentatious display of wealth and magnificence, the courtly civilities of the Great, and the used, and unmeaning expressions of esteem from the gay and the vain do not fill the heart; it sighs for the pleasures of social communication, and domestic comforts, under an humble roof, after having seen all the parade and glory of life.

It is very material to our peace, whether the persons with whom we are associated are people of chearful or gloomy dispositions. The matters of great consequence to our happiness do not frequently arise: but there are constant domestic occurrances, there are daily circumstances that appear bright, or are cast in the shade, according to the temper we are in; and the most common events may be occasion of pleasure or pain to ourselves, and those about us, from the disposition with which they are received.

Some persons, disquieted and unhappy, are forever sowing cares at their threshold. Uneasy at present and anxious for the future, they cast a gloom on every countenance. They require their troubles to be ever soothed; and yet contribute nothing to the joy of others. But the fountain of sympathy will soon be dried up, if it is not mutually replenished, and he who is forever exhausting the common stock, without contributing any thing to its supply, will pass many of his days uncheared by the offices of benevolence.

Sympathy is the electric fire, the animating flame, that darts from the collision of congenial minds: each glowing with the like ardour; but the dark, and gloomy mind, neither receives nor returns the vivid either.

We may do a great deal of good without much expence, and it is a necessary duty, for well disposed minds, to appear frequently in the intercources and offices of life.

They can hardly go abroad, but their hand may raise the head bowed down with misfortune. Their smiles may smooth the brow wrinkled with care, or their sympathy chear the heart oppressed with sorrow. Nor will they ever want occasion of shewing the sweetness of their disposition under their own roof, by endeavouring to make the stations of their domestics easy to them by their mildness and affection, enabling them to go through their offices with chearfulness, and diligence.

Endeavour to make the most of what comforts fall in your way. Do not prevent the enjoyment of the present hour by dwelling on misfortunes that are passed, or anticipating evils that may never happen. Cherish a disposition to be happy yourself, and to communicate pleasure to others. Let thine eye sparkle at another's enjoyment, and thy heart share in the felicity he receives. Then will every door be opened to thee with gladness and all thy neighbours will count thee in the number of their friends.

And God said Let there be light in the firmament of heaven to divide the day from the night: and both be for signs and for Seasons and for days, and years.

H. S.[2]

Non varios obitus norunt variosque recursus, certa sed in propias oriuntur sidera luces, natalesque suos,occsdumque ordine servant.

Manil[3]

---

1   Hulton, "Sketches," 41-60.

2   Holy scripture: "And God said, Let there be lights in the firmament of the heaven to divide the day from the night; and let them be for signs, and for seasons, and for days, and years." Genesis 1:14 (KJV).

3   Manilius, *Astronomica*, Book 1, lines 475-477, in effect: the constellations are constant and know their proper place, and each displays its stars regularly, at the proper time.

My dear Children:[1]

I propose from time to time to write short Essays, with intention to establish You in right principles, and to regular Your future conduct; and having no view but to Your happiness, I hope you will suffer them to have due weight; yet not to be followed meerly from respect to authority, but from choice and approbation.

May You be led to admire the amiableness of truth and virtue, and to find that "wisdom's ways are ways of pleasantness, and that all her paths are paths of peace."[2]

In every worthy and noble enterprize there are some difficulties to be encountered; but the mind that is resolved to excell will suffer no discouragements to damp its endeavours, but with a persevering ardour overcomes every obstacle and finds its strength and Spirits encrease from surmounting difficulties.

Whilst the slothful and the timid waste their lives in inglorious ease, and submit to neglect and contempt; the well[-]cultured Youth with virtuous endowments sees respect and honour attend his laudable pursuits, and the manly exertions of his abilities; and has the satisfaction of being able to give a good account to his Maker of the talent commited to his trust.[3]

It should be the first business of a rational Being to establish the mind in right principles and acquire useful knowledge. To bring that knowledge into action, by an industrious application of its abilities in some useful profession, and to discharge its duties to Society by a regular and prudent conduct In life, should be the objects of its constant attention.

Remember that all improvements of the understanding should lead Us to the amendment of our hearts, and the correction of our practice; that doctrines are revealed, not as matters of speculation, but for the sake of the duties they require; and that to advance in knowledge, whilst we neglect to correct the temper and improve in virtuous dispositions, will only increase our condemnation.

May You, my dear Children, find Your greatest pleasure in rational Studies, in a wise and virtuous employment of your time and talents. If these once engage your affections, You will never be under the necessity of going abroad for amusement. You will not seek relief from langour in the company of the dissipated and vain; or be obliged to submit to mortifications by finding yourselves intruders into the Society of the wealthy, or Great. If You rise to any distinction in your professions, You will find the industrious application of your Youthful honors in acquiring knowledge and improving Your virtuous endowments will prove an ornament to Your Age, and draw respect and reverence to your characters. If You meet with disap[p]ointments and misfortunes, You will find your Youthful acquirements will be the best solace in Your retirement, and obscurity. Though neglected by the Great and the Gay, You can converse with the Wise and the Learned of antiquity; and above all, can have the consolation of looking up to Your Maker for his favor and blessing; and entertain Yourselves with the hopes and prospect of soon joining the blessed society above, of just Men made perfect.

Labour, therefore, my dear Children, to establish Yourselves in right principles, to acquire useful knowledge; to rectify Your judgments, to govern your passions, to improve your good dispositions, and to direct Your behaviour with prudence and discretion. That being raised above every vicious and mean thought, sentiment, and action, You may be led to think and act suitably to the dignity of Your rational nature, and the noble ends of Christianity.

---

1   [Henry Hulton], "With a view to fix right Principles in the minds of Children, and lead them to just Sentiments and a virtuous Conduct," 9-48, Norfolk County Record Office, MC 36/139, 481X1.

2   On wisdom: "Her ways are ways of pleasantness, and all her paths are peace." Proverbs 3:17 (KJV)

3   Here Hulton alludes to the parable of the talents in Matthew 25:14-30, with its variation in Luke 18:11-27 (KJV).

Sloth is the Parent of Poverty,
And Vice the Mother of Disease;
Infamy and ruin are their attendants here,
And Misery their portion hereafter.
Industry is the Child of Virtue,
And Truth the Daughter of Heaven;
The Almighty smiles on their union,
And Wealth and Respect are their offspring.
Know, my Son!
That thou art formed for Action.
That thou art a Being,
rational! accountable! immortal!
That thy happiness depends
On the favour of thy Maker,
Which can only be obtained,
By living in obedience to his Commands,
And relying on the promises of his Gospel.
Let Sincerity dwell in thy heart,
And Virtue be the object of thy choice;
Walk in the path of Integrity,
And keep futurity ever in thine Eye.
For tho' Wealth shou'd be poured into thy lap,
And the King shou'd raise thee to honours,
Tho' Nature shou'd give thee Talents to please,
And thy Manners be polished by Art;
Yet if Truth be not the guide of thy life,
And obedience to the will of thy Maker,
Thy first, and fixt principle of duty,
Thou wilt be but a miserable Creature;
Wretched in thyself!
Without consolation for the present,
Or hope in futurity!
Exiled from the presence of thy Maker!
And the Society of the blessed!
Keep therefore thine integrity,
Do the thing that is right,
For that shall bring thee peace at the last.

What am I?

What is my Being, aim, and end?

I think, I act, approve or condemn those actions. I feel pleasure or pain of body, or mind: they are distinct, yet connected parts of me. I see thousands of other such beings as myself. The earth produces fruits and grain; and the immense bodies of heaven perform stated regular motions; enlightening, chearing, and vivifying the earth, animals, and men.

All this speaks the work of a wise contriver. I am told that this state of the earth and heavens has been continued for several thousand years, in constant Order, during a succession of many races of inhabitants on this Globe.

The infinite number of heavenly bodies of immense magnitude, which perform the courses assigned them; and the diversity of Animals, even of the minutest kind, which are constantly supported on the earth, shew the attention of infinite wisdom to the smallest, as well as greatest, of its works. And when I consider the hand of an all-wise Being, ever acting by creation and providence, from an unnumbered series of Ages past, through an immensity of space, I am lost in wonder and admiration at the greatness of the wisdom, the power, and goodness that are displayed in the works of Nature; and I again ask, what am I amidst the wonderful Volume? In what page of the Book of Nature is my name written?

I find myself classed in the rank of beings as one of the race of Man. What then, is Man? Here opens a new Scene of wonder to the mind: The History of our Race. This, which would otherwise have been a subject of doubt and uncertainty, of fable, and absurdity, is clearly made known to Us by revelation. For "life and immortality are brought to light by the Gospel."[1]

There we are acquainted with the formation of Man in a State of Innocence, his yielding to the temptation of the Devil, and his fall; his subjection to the curse of labour and sorrow in this life, and of death at the close of it. "In Adam all die."[2] Here the Scene would seem to end, with a tremendous gloom on the wretched race. But behold! A new scene appears, wonderful beyond the imagination of the most enraptured Poet to conceive. Though fallen, not lost. The contemplation of the works of Nature excite our highest admiration; the consideration of those of Grace overcome and overwhelm Us in wonder, gratitude, and praise.

The Almighty with his curse included a promise—"The Seed of the Woman should bruise the Serpents head."[3] From amongst the fallen race of Adam he reserved to himself a peculiar people, to record his Name, be the dispensers of his Laws, the Instruments of his Judgments, and from amongst whom a Savior in due time should be born.

The History of this People, their idolatry, and stubbornness; their confidence in the favour of heaven, whilst their hearts were depraved and disobedient to its commands; their being the instruments of divine vengeance on guilty nations, and themselves frequently the objects of its just correction, are strong proofs of the forlorn State we are in by Nature—and should warm our hearts with the most lively gratitude for the blessings of the Gospel, and the grace of God through Jesus Christ our Lord. For behold! The promise of God is accomplished.

"A Virgin shall conceive and bring forth a Son," was prophesied by Isaiah[4]—and in due

time the Savior of the World, Jesus Christ, the Son of God, as born, became Man, submit[t]
ed to take our nature upon him, lived a life of the most exemplary piety and Virtue, in the
most humiliating State; performed many miracles as testimonies of his Mission—published
the most simple yet sublimest system of religion, to amend our hearts, inform our understandings, and regulate our practise. And assured Us of immortal happiness after this life,
as the reward of our obedience. And finally, to purge away the guilt of human Nature, to
obtain our pardon, and the remission of our Sins, and as a Seal to his Mission, he submit[t]
ed to persecution, torture, and death, from the hands of the obstinate Jews, his implacable
Enemies, and to establish our faith, rose again form the dead, and ascended into heaven.

We now see the end of our Being—Immortal happiness. We are told how it is to be
obtained. "To him who endureth to the end, the same shall be saved."[5] Human life is a
warfare, a state of trial, and discipline—many difficulties are to be surmounted, and many
temptations overcome in our course; but if we look to the object before Us, with a ste[a]
dfast eye, and under the influence of right principles, and just affections, we implore the
divine assistance, we shall not be turned from our pursuit. And Our Savior hath promised
that his grace shall be sufficient to him who faithfully endeavours.

---

1   "But is now made manifest by the appearing of our Saviour Jesus Christ, who hath abolished death, and hath
     brought life and immortality to light through the gospel." 2 Timothy 1:10 (KJV)

2   "For as in Adam all die, even so in Christ shall all be made alive." 1 Corinthians 15:22 (KJV)

3   "And I will put enmity between thee and the woman, and between thy seed and her seed; it shall bruise thy
     head, and thou shalt bruise his heel." Genesis 3:15 (KJV)

4   "Therefore the Lord himself shall give you a sign; Behold, a virgin shall conceive, and bear a son, and shall
     call his name Immanuel." Isaiah 7:14 (KJV)

5   "And ye shall be hated of all men for my name's sake: but he that endureth to the end shall be saved." Mat-
     thew 10:22 (KJV)

What is Religion?

Religion is that homage and worship which rational Creatures give to their Almighty Creator.

To order it aright, we should acquaint ourselves with the Nature and Condition of Man; and raise our ideas, as far as we are able to comprehend that Supreme Being, who giveth unto all ife, and breath, and all things: The Author of Nature, and Sole Governor of the Universe; who upholdeth all Worlds, was before all, existeth through all, and endureth the same for evermore. A God, perfect in holiness, infinite in power, wisdom, and goodness; independently happy, unchangable in truth, and faithfulness; and abundant in mercy and loving kindness, towards the Children of Men.

Man was at first created after the image of God, with a rectitude of mind and will; with inclinations adapted to his true happiness and Subject to the influence and direction of reason. But by disobedience his understanding was darkened, his will corrupted, his inclinations depraved; he became subject to Sin, liable to sickness and pain, misery and death.

This was the life of the world at the coming of Christ. And to destroy this man of Sin and reinstate mankind in a capacity of favor with their Maker, Christ came into the World. He brought life and immortality to light. He opened the Gates of heaven for the admission of fallen Man to eternal day; and procured for the sinful race a fresh title to immortal happiness.

How amazing is the work of creation and providence? How astonishing the mercy and grace of redemption? The mind is overwhelmed in contemplating the wonderful love and goodness of its Creator and Saviour. Filled with the vast ideas, it bows with the profoundest awe, reverence, and gratitude; and with the most humble and heart felt devotion, offers up its ardent acknowledgments of praise and thanksgiving. It laments whilst it adores. It mourns over the depravity of its nature and grieves at the precious purchase of its happiness. It elevates its views towards heavenly objects, it strengthens its affections to its Redeemer, and fixes its principles of duty towards its Creator; resolving on a life of obedience to his commands, submit[t]ing with humble resignation to his Will, and trusting to his Promises for Salvation, and happiness.

It is not the bigotry of a Sect, a zeal for forms, or modes, dry opinions, or a fruitless faith, that constitute Religion. No! Religion is a far nobler thing: It lieth in the image of God on the Soul, in a likeness to God, and Jesus Christ; in heavenly dispositions; in a rectitude of Spirit and purity of heart that elevate the Soul above the dross and corruption of mortality; that engage the affections in an ardent love of goodness, virtue, and Truth; and influence the Man to actions of Justice, kindness, and charity.

The religious Man is not a follower of a Sect or Party; but the Disciple of Jesus Christ and of him only. He learns his duty from his gospel and makes him, and him only, his great example. He relies on the goodness and providence of his Almighty Creator, and pays a ready and exact obedience to all his Commands, never resting in externals, in opinions, forms, or sets of words, but attending to the correction of his heart, training it to virtuous dispositions, and elevating it to eternal things. Impressed with the Principles of truth and righteousness, and influenced by benevolence, candour, mildness and peace, the religious Man becomes established in a solid and rational piety, and leads a life of steady and active Virtue; which by preparing him for the happiness of the world to come, makes him enjoy at the same time the greatest happiness this state is capable of affording.

Which is the way to happiness?

The first business of a rational Creature is to consider his own nature and the end of his Being; and to know the relation in which he stands to the objects around him.

When he considers the works of creation and providence, he says, Surely there must have been an infinitely wise, powerful, and good Being that made me and all the world; that supports the whole in existence. He is my Creator, and constant benefactor. I was formed by his power, and live upon his bounty. I am sensible of my dependence upon him. What is then the duty he requires of me? I look into his holy word; I there find that myself and all of the human race are Creatures of time, yet formed for eternity. That on our present conduct, our future happiness depends. The mind is filled with the vast idea—looks forward to its final doom with awful dread and is lost in the contemplation—yet receives consolation from the promises of its Maker. It finds him declaring himself a God of love—delighting in the happiness of his Creatures and requiring from Man, as his first duty, "to love the Lord his God with all his heart."[1] This is such an affection of mind towards God, as includes a prevailing desire and endeavour to please him, and delight in his favour; and he finds it declared in the Gospel. "This is the love of God, that we keep his Commandments"[2] He becomes anxious to know what are these Commandments that are to be the lines of his duty; on the observance of which, the divine favour and his own happiness depend. He looks further and with joy and delight he finds the Sum of the divine will, and his duty, comprehended in few words, and to the justness of which commands his own right reason and uncorrupt affections, entirely acquiesce. "He hath shewed thee O Man! what is good, and what doth the Lord thy God require of thee, but to do justice, to love mercy, and to walk humbly with thy God."[3] From affections influenced, and actions guided, by this line of duty, happiness will result; and every deviation from it, in sentiment or conduct, will be the source of disquietness, pain, and misery. For as the main object of the pursuit of a rational and immortal Being should be its final happiness, so whenever it departs from the path that leads to that end, it will always be unhappy. Ever restless and discontented, it will find a vacancy in itself, a deficiency in the things without it, and desires not to be satisfied, amidst the pomp, the wealth, and the pleasures of life.

By fixing these truths as principles in the mind, and regulating the desires of the heart thereby, we shall be growing more and more in those Graces and Virtues which will render Us the objects of our Maker's favor and love. We shall be dayly advancing in happiness here and preparing for the felicity of heaven hereafter.

The line of duty is simple and plain, and directs a life of active obedience to the will of our Maker. "To walk humbly with God," we must be impressed with just sentiments of his infinite wisdom, and of our own blindness, and ignorance, of his almighty power and our weakness and impotence, of his all-sufficiency and of our indigence, wants, and necessities, of his purity and holiness and of our guilt and depravity, of his loving kindness, tender mercy, and forgiveness and of the selfishness of our corrupt affections, and our proneness to envy, malice, and uncharitableness,

If with sincerity we thus contemplate the infinite perfections of the Almighty, and our own poverty, guilt, and wretchedness, though we may lament our low condition by Nature, yet we adore and rejoice in the happy estate that we are placed by Grace, that we are made "heirs of God, and joint heirs with Christ."[4]

We may rejoice that though we are weak, yet that We have an all sufficient support and protection at hand; and under all circumstances, may chearfully acquiesce in his disposal of Us, and relye in his dispensations towards Us; persuaded, that his providence will order all events for our best interest. "There is no want to them that fear him."[5] That is, to them who live under an humble and reverent Sense of his Being and Providence, and make the obedience of his commands the rule of their duty and the main business of their lives. But that business includes a second part, from the relation in which we stand to the Society around Us. And to our fellow Creatures we owe a variety of duty and obligations, according to the relation in which we stand to the community in general and the individuals that compose it. We owe fidelity to the King and obedience to the Laws of the State, and truth and Justice to all Men.

There is no merit in our performing these parts of duty. We should be highly blamable if we in any wise deviated from them. But the shewing Mercy, enjoined Us in the command of the Almighty, is part of that duty, in which we may most display the impression we have of respect to the Lawgiver and the superiority of the divine virtues over our own selfish and corrupt affections. If we are duly impressed with a sense of our own wants, weakness, and dependence, We shall be desirous of cherishing benevolent dispositions, and puting them into practise, by relieving, or mitigating, the distresses of others. Such sentiments and conduct will not only procure Us a present satisfaction, and conciliate the affections of others towards Us, but will provide Us a fund of consolation and support in case of future distress, and secure Us the favour of the Almighty, and an happiness in reserve, when all earthly good shall fail Us.

---

1   "And thou shalt love the Lord thy God with all thine heart, and with all thy soul, and with all thy might."
    Deuteronomy 6:5 (KJV)

2   "Whosoever believeth that Jesus is the Christ is born of God: and every one that loveth him that begat loveth him also that is begotten of him.
    By this we know that we love the children of God, when we love God, and keep his commandments." 1 John 5:1-2 (KJV). Or, from John 14:15 (KJV): "If ye love me, keep my commandments."
3   "He hath shewed thee, O man, what is good; and what doth the Lord require of thee, but to do justly, and love mercy, and to walk humbly with thy God?" Micah 6:8 (KJV)
4   "The Spirit itself beareth witness with our spirit, that we are the children of God.
    And if children, then heirs; heirs of God, and joint-heirs with Christ; if so be that we suffer with him, that we may be also glorified together." Romans 8:16-17 (KJV)
5   "O fear the Lord, ye his saints: for there is no want to them that fear him." Psalm 34:9 (KJV)

What is my business here?

As a Social Being, and connected with other Creatures of the same nature with myself, I find I have been born weak and helpless; that my support through the feeble state of infancy has been owing (under the blessing of heaven) to the care and attention of others, that from them I have received shelter, food, and clothing; and to their affection I owe my being relieved under many wants, and diseases; protected from many dangers, and instructed in the principles of religion and virtue; and that I am now in a situation of supporting myself with reputation and credit in Society. I see everyone around me active and busy, in some office or employment, that tends to make them useful Members of the Community. And from the general industry I find a supply ready for all my wants, so that I need not toil in the field for my daily bread; or labour at the anvil or loom, for the necessaries of furniture or clothing. Yet they who are exempted from the more laborious Offices, I see employed in other duties, in defending, or serving the State, or in carrying on the trade and commerce of the Nation, or they contribute by their Superior knowledge in different professions to the health and interest, the present or future happiness of others.

If every one else is busied to contribute in some manner to the general good, shall I alone be an indolent Spectator of the manly exertions of others? Some duty certainly belongs to me. Some office or profession is open, wherein I may be useful to others and may act a Character that may be approved by my Maker, and be honorable to myself.

Let me then endeavour to make the best use of the faculties God has given me. Let me exert them in some particular profession or employment with assiduity and integrity; and trust to the blessing of heaven for success.

Such should be the resolution of the wise and virtuous Man, sensible of his relation to Society; and whatever may be his circumstances or situation, he must be sensible that he cannot want a line of proper duties that require the exertion of his talents.

In himself he will find the latent seeds of corruption, of pride and selfishness; a proneness to crimes, and an unwillingness to perform those duties he owes to his Maker, and his fellow Creature. He will find many violent passions to be subdued and unjust affections to be mortified before he will see clearly and resolve steadily to walk in the path of truth and duty. And after all, will be sensible of an aptness to fall into error and contract guilt, without the assistance of divine grace and keeping futurity ever in his eye. For it is the influence of that faith that can alone keep the mind steady in its course, amidst the numerous temptations with which it is surrounded, and the many corruptions of its own nature.

The wonderful endowments of body and mind, with which our nature is furnished, all shew us formed for action; and the surprizing improvements that have been made in Arts and Sciences, by the ingenuity and application of human talents, shew that Man is capable of continual advances; and that there is no set[t]ing limits to the exertions of human genius. This should stimulate Us to the utmost exertion of our abilities in some laudable pursuit for the advancement of our reputation, the publick utility, and the service of our Maker.

Who will shew Us any good?[1]

This is the language of the Men of the world; ever in the pursuit, never in the possession, of happiness. They seek it in the Creature and are disap[p]ointed; they seek it not in the Creator, where it is only to be found.

To make a just estimate of happiness, we should consider our nature, and end.

We find ourselves composed of a body and Soul; the former of which is earthly, gross, and Sensual; the latter spiritual, and immortal.

Whenever, therefore, we are urged to pursuits that tend to the gratification of the animal part by a breach of the spiritual, we offend against our own real happiness; and till our moral sentiments are greatly depraved, we shall find every deviation from truth attended with a compunction of mind and a degree of misery, in proportion to the consciousness of the guilt of the offence.

If the criminal gratification be only a transient pleasure, it will be followed by remorse. If it be an acquisition of fortune or honour at the expence of a virtuous principle, the mind will revolt from its subjugation to the mean complyance. Conscience will damp the ardour of enjoyment, and cast a gloom over all the glare of guilty greatness; and the Soul will feel itself oppressed by any earthly good, that is purchased by the sacrifice of virtue.

Let then your pursuits for the benefit or pleasure of the body be regulated by those principles which further the happiness of the rational part. By subduing intemperate desires, you will be freed from most of the evils that distress human nature, and You will find yourself more disposed to those pursuits which improve and adorn it.

Be assured, that to rational Beings the cultivation of their moral powers, the Study of Truth, and the practise of Virtue, are the only sure sources of happiness, that these are in thy own power and depend not on the things without thee.

Cherish then the Stock that is given thee, and the fund will increase; employ thy times usefully, and rationally now, and thou wilt have a never failing stream of pleasure from within thyself. Thou wilt have no occasion to look abroad and say, "Who will shew me any good"? but from thine own storehouse, may be able to supply others, and be the means of enriching them, without exhausting thyself; and thus enjoy an encrease of satisfaction, by the communication of virtue, and knowledge.

---

1   "There be many that say, Who will shew us any good? Lord, lift thou up the light of thy countenance upon us." Psalm 4:6 (KJV)

Written on walking over Chester Walls, after many Years' absence[1]

Thro' many scenes, thro' many Lands I've stray'd,
Since last mine Eyes these ancient Walls survey'd,
And God be prais'd I live, again to see,
Thy gentle current; ever hallow'd Dee,
Smooth and serene thy Waters ever glide,
Borne on rude Waves, I've stem'd a troubled tide,
Have many toils, have many dangers past;
Since from thy verdant banks I parted last,
Full many foreign streams since thine I've known,
From northern Elb, unto the rapid Rhone.
     When War in fury on the Dymel reign'd,
What Christian Blood, its peaceful waters stain'd!
What dire distress oppress'd Westphalian Swains,
When Famine & Disease, stalk'd o'er their plains!
In silence numb'ring more than slaughter'd dead,
For Nobles perish'd from the Lack of Bread.
May Cestria's Daghters ne'er such horrors know,
Nor with thy Stream e'er mix the tear of Woe.
War's rage I saw beneath the burning Sun,
And Lands by British Valour dearly won,
Spent years of youthful Life in Caribb_Isles,
Where the tame Slave for pamper'd luxury toils;
Oh! grief, to toil beneath oppression's rod,
And live, and die, unknowing of his God!

In vain we seek repose, in vain retreat,
When Storms and Tempests on our footsteps wait;
Doom'd to fresh toils beyond th' Atlantic Main,
I cross'd the mighty Ocean once again.
Thro' pathless Woods of lofty pines I stray'd,
And Nature's rude, uncultur'd form survey'd;
Pass'd the drear Mountain, the extended Lake,
And saw the Falls that o'er St. Lawrence break;
Explor'd the Pass, & traversed o'er the Plain,
Where Wolfe immortaliz'd the British Name.
Hail! blest Canadians, on whose snowy Plains,
Simplicity, mild Nature's darling reigns,
There rosy health, and temperance reside;
And heart-ease grows at ev'ry Cottage side.
With heart dispos'd to social gen'rous views,
To seek fair peace, and court the sylvan Muse,
My fate severe now doom'd me to engage,
The brunt of Faction, and the peoples rage;
Intemp'rate Men! who daringly intrude,
Lawless, audacious, insolent and rude.
For years I droop'd, while Peace & Order fled,
And stern Rebellion rais'd his horrid head,
Oh! be the painful hours, the Cares forgot,
That in this part of life were doom'd my Lot.
May Britons still be open, bold, and free,
But never know licentious liberty.
Thanks to my God, I view my native place,
And tread o'er youthful walks, in health & peace,
But where's the partners in my boyish plays,
Who shar'd the pleasures of my sportive days?
Many I miss who chear'd the social hour,
Many who shone in pride of beauty's pow'r;
Where's he, with mind enlarg'd by Science's Lore,
With lib'ral heart, enrich'd from virtue's Store,
Whose sympathetic Soul could balm impart,
And sooth the sorrows of an aching heart:
Whose ways from early Youth my mind approv'd,
Seeing in him those virtues that it lov'd,
O'er many Friends I shed a tender tear,
And still the heart laments o'er Tylston's bier.

Clos'd were their lives, e'er their meridian day,
But thine preserv'd beneath the searching ray;
Preserv'd, and trust for some wise end design'd,
For keep this Maxim graven on thy mind;
In wisdom God ordains, let man obey,
And act with truth, where'er he points the way.
Whether he chears thee with a gracious smile,
Or dooms thy future Life to care, and toil,
With steady Faith on his firm arm rely,
Truth, at thy heart, and heav'n in thine Eye,
Then if his Summons come, or soon, or late,
Bless'd be thy present hour, & bless'd thy future fate.

---

1   Hulton, "Sketches," 199-206.

UNDERNEATH THIS STONE

ARE DEPOSITED THE REMAINS OF

HENRY HULTON ESQ.

WHO DIED FEB. 12TH. 1790

AGED 59

HE MARRIED ELIZABETH

THE ELDEST DAUGHTER OF

ISAAC PRESTON ESQ.

WHO TOGETHER WITH THEIR SONS

SURVIVED TO LAMENT THE LOSS

OF A KIND PARENT

AND AFFECTIONATE HUSBAND

AND ALSO

ARE DEPOSITED THE REMAINS OF

ELIZABETH

WIDOW OF HENRY HULTON ESQ.

WHO DIED APRIL 16, 1805 AGED 66

AND OF CHARLES SAMUEL

THEIR GRANDSON

SON OF HENRY AND SOPHIA HULTON

HE DIED OCT. 10.1805. AGED 5 WEEKS[1]

---

1   Inscription on a vault cover, placed in what is now the floor to the crypt of St. Mary's Church, Andover. Though the stone is worn and cracked, the inscription was cut deep and is legible still.

Index

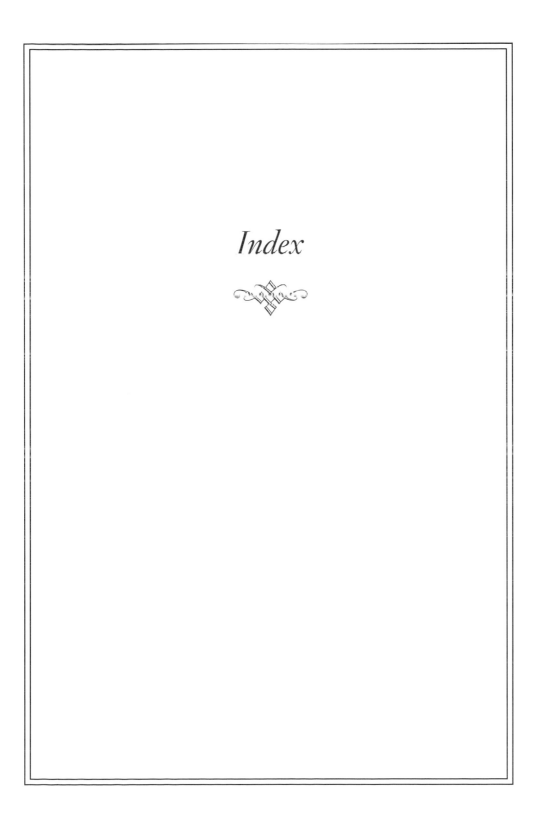

Index